PLANTS OF
SOUTHERN
INTERIOR
BRITISH COLUMBIA
and the
INLAND NORTHWEST

PLANTS OF SOUTHERN INTERIOR BRITISH COLUMBIA and the INLAND NORTHWEST

Edited by
Roberta Parish, Ray Coupé and Dennis Lloyd

Written by

Joe Antos

Ray Coupé

George Douglas

Rich Evans

Trevor Goward

Marianne Ignace

Dennis Lloyd

Roberta Parish

Rosamund Pojar

Anna Roberts

First printed in 1996   10 9 8 7 6 5 4 3
Printed in Canada

The Publisher: Lone Pine Publishing

202A, 1110 Seymour Street	206, 10426 – 81 Avenue	1901 Raymond Ave. SW, Suite C
Vancouver, BC V6B 3N3	Edmonton, AB T6E 1X5	Renton, WA 98055

Canadian Cataloguing in Publication Data

Main entry under title:
Plants of southern interior British Columbia and the inland northwest

    Previously published as: Plants of southern interior British Columbia.
    (ISBN 1-55105-057-9)
    Includes bibliographical references and index.
    ISBN 1-55105-219-9

    1. Botany—British Columbia—Handbooks, manuals, etc.
2. Botany—British Columbia—Handbooks, manuals, etc.
3. Botany—Idaho—Handbooks, manuals, etc.
4. Plants—Identification—Handbooks, manuals, etc.
I. Parish, Roberta, 1948– II. Coupé, R., 1952– III. Lloyd, Dennis, 1950–
IV. Antos, Joe, 1950–
QK203.B7P56 1999   581.9711   C99-910468-3

Editorial Director: Nancy Foulds
Project Editor: Roland Lines
Botany Editor: Linda Kershaw
Text preparation: Jennifer Keane, Roland Lines, Linda Kershaw, Nancy Foulds
Layout and Production: Gregory Brown, Bruce Timothy Keith, Carol S. Dragich
Cover design: Carol S. Dragich
Cover photos: Ian Mackenzie, Alex Inselberg
Separations and Film: Elite Lithographers Co. Ltd.

We acknowledge the financial support of the Government of Canada through the Book Publishing Industry Development Program (BPIDP) for our publishing activities.

PC: P3

Table of Contents

LIST OF KEYS AND ILLUSTRATIONS

Keys

Illustrations

ACKNOWLEDGEMENTS

The editors would like to thank the authors who wrote or co-wrote the sections of the book—Ray Coupé, George Douglas, Rich Evans, Trevor Goward, Marianne Ignace, Dennis Lloyd, Roberta Parish, Rosamund Pojar, Anna Roberts and Wilf Schofield. Joe Antos wrote many of the keys and reviewed the vascular plants.

We are especially grateful to Andy MacKinnon and Jim Pojar, the editors of *Plants of Coastal British Columbia* (Pojar and MacKinnon 1994) and (with Ray Coupé) *Plants of Northern British Columbia* (MacKinnon et al. 1992), for their cooperation and willingness to share their material, some of which has been integrated into this guide.

We also appreciate Chris Marchant's insightful review of the vascular plants. Bruce McCuen and Roger Rosentreter completed a thorough review of the lichen section, and Trevor Goward reviewed the mosses. Nancy Turner kindly reviewed the ethnobotanical information. Rich Evans edited the entire text for consistency and terminology. Fraser Russell, Rick Tucker, Phil Youwe, Val Miller, Ted Lea, Tom Braumandl and Maureen Ketcheson provided a detailed review of the distribution and habitat of each species. Arnold Baptiste and Leona Fletcher assisted Marianne Ignace with extracting ethnobotanical information from the literature and files and compiling a data base.

Many people contributed their beautiful photographs to this guide. We would like to acknowledge the talents of Blain Andrusek, Gerry Allen, Joe Antos, Frank Boas, Robin Bovey, Joan Burbridge, Adolf Ceska, Ray Coupé, Blake Dickens, Mathis Duerst, Katherine Enns, Dave Fraser, Trevor Goward, Leslie Hill, Marianne Ignace, Alex Inselberg, Derek Johnson, Linda Kershaw, Ted Lea, Dennis Lloyd, Ron Long, Robin Love, Bill Merilees, Robert Norton, Jim Pojar, George Powell, Dave Ralph, Rick Riewe, Anna Roberts, Hans Roemer, Martin Ross, Rob Scagel, Bela Sivak, Carol Thompson, Nancy and Robert Turner, Ted Underhill, Dale Vitt, L.K. Wade, Ron Walker, Cliff Wallace, Cleve Wershler, Michael Wheatley, George Whitehead, Brian Wikeem, Dave Williams, J.M. Woollett and John Worrall. We are grateful to the Penticton Museum, the Nelson Kootenay Museum Association, B.C. Parks, the B.C. Forest Service and the Ministry of Environment for allowing us access to their photographic materials for this guide. Jean Heineman and Shelley Church assisted Dennis Lloyd in locating and coordinating the collection of these photographs.

Trevor Goward drew the lichen illustrations—some are original drawings for this publication and the remaining were originally published in *The Lichens of British Columbia: Illustrated Keys* (Goward et al. 1994). Patricia Drukker-Brammall's bryophyte illustrations from *Some Common Mosses of British Columbia* (Schofield 1992) are reprinted with the kind permission of W. Schofield. John Maywood also prepared some original bryophyte drawings. The B.C. Forest Service made available the beautiful illustrations of Shirley Salkeld, Peggy Frank, Sherry Mitchell and Kristi Iverson. We are especially grateful to University of Washington Press for permission to use the illustrations of Jeanne R. Janish and John H. Ramely from *Vascular Plants of the Pacific Northwest* (Hitchcock et al. 1955–69) and to the Royal British Columbia Museum for permission to use illustrations by Christopher Brayshaw (Brayshaw 1976, 1985, 1989), Mary Bryant (Taylor 1963), Betty Newton and Ann Hassen (Szczawinski 1962), Elizabeth J. Stephen (Douglas 1982, 1995; Taylor 1974c; and unpublished), and R.A. With (Taylor 1973, 1974b). Kristi Iverson assisted Ray Coupé in locating and acquiring the illustrative material.

Thanks are due to the following staff at Lone Pine Publishing for their assistance in putting this guide together: Shane Kennedy, Nancy Foulds, Bruce Keith, Roland Lines, Greg Brown, Linda Kershaw, Jennifer Keane and Volker Bodegom. Our thanks also go to Glenn Rollans, formerly of Lone Pine Publishing, who helped with the early stages of the project.

Financial assistance for the preparation of this guide has been provided by the B.C. Forest Service Research and Silviculture programs and the Canada-British Columbia Partnership Agreement on Forest Resource Development: FRDA II.

Roberta Parish, Ray Coupé and Dennis Lloyd

ACKNOWLEDGEMENTS

Photograph Credits

All photographs are printed by permission. The numbers refer to pages; the letters indicate the photograph's relative position on the page.

Joe Antos and **Gerry Allen**: 68e, 112c, 171c, 185a, 186c, 211d, 241b, 258b, 267a, 303b

Frank Boas: 52a, 54b, 54c, 54d, 55d, 58c, 64a, 64c, 69c, 71d, 75b, 77b, 78b, 80c, 81d, 82a, 82d, 83a, 83b, 84b, 84c, 86c, 86d, 92a, 92d, 93b, 94a, 94c, 95a, 96a, 111b, 117a, 153b, 158a, 160, 161b, 161c, 168a, 170a, 170c, 172c, 173b, 174a, 175a, 178a, 178b, 179a, 179b, 180a, 180b, 182a, 191a, 191c, 194b, 195b, 195c, 196c, 199b, 205c, 207b, 208a, 208b, 211a, 214a, 215c, 219a, 223a, 237b, 238b, 240b, 242a, 244c, 245b, 247a, 247b, 252c, 253b, 254a, 259c, 261a, 263a, 271a, 273b, 277a, 282a, 283b, 285a, 287b, 288c, 290b, 294a, 300a, 301c, 301d, 302a, 302c, 306a, 306b, 307b, 318a, 318b, 330b, 346c, 346d, 355c, 362a, 362b, 363a, 363b, 363d, 364c, 384a, 385a, 386a, 387b, 387c, 388a, 388b, 389a, 391b, 394a, 395b, 396a, 396b, 396c, 397a, 397c, 398b, 399a, 400a, 402a, 403a, 403b, 408a, 408b, 418a, 420a, 434a, 435a

Robin Bovey: 366b, 373a, 377b, 385b, 387a, 389b, 390a, 391a, 392a, 392b, 393b, 394b, 395a, 400b, 401a, 401b, 402b, 404b, 406a, 406b, 409a, 411b, 414b, 415a, 415b, 416a, 416b, 417a, 417b, 419a, 419b, 420b, 421a, 421b, 422a, 423a, 423b, 424b, 425b, 426a, 426b, 427a, 428a, 430b, 431a, 431b, 432a, 432b, 433a, 433b, 433c, 435b, 436a, 437b, 438a

B.C. Ministry of Forests, Research Branch: 30b, 32b, 39a, 39b, 40d, 41a, 41b, 42d, 44b, 45a, 45b, 45c, 45d, 46d, 47b, 57b, 68b, 76b

Ray Coupé: 13, 15a, 16a, 16c, 17d, 18a, 54a, 56a, 58b, 61c, 72a, 73a, 74a, 78a, 79a, 80a, 85a, 87d, 96c, 98b, 99c, 117b, 133a, 151d, 162b, 174b, 187c, 189c, 217c, 226a, 260a, 260b, 269c, 274a, 276b, 285c, 285d, 298a, 300e, 303c, 303d, 367c, 368b

R. Blake Dickens: 32a, 40c, 43c, 55a, 70c, 79c, 98a, 170d, 171a, 176a, 286d, 306c

Leslie Hill: 34c, 109d, 116b, 149c, 151a, 152b, 181b, 192b, 193c, 216a, 216c, 221a, 267c, 267d, 268b, 296c, 304c

Alex Inselberg: 14b, 15b, 53b, 66c , 67c, 70b, 84a, 205b, 213c, 294b, 297d

Kamloops Forest Region: 60a, 110a, 110c, 118c, 120b, 127a, 138a, 139a, 153a, 171d, 198b, 200b, 201a, 204a, 210c, 218, 284a, 286c, 300c, 305c, 313c, 331a

Linda Kershaw: 97b, 148b, 149b, 186b, 215b, 219b, 223d, 270a, 354d, 369a, 376a, 384b

Dennis Lloyd: 12, 17a, 18c, 28a, 29d, 33a, 34a, 34d, 36a, 38a, 38d, 44d, 47a, 47c, 47d, 48a, 48d, 56b, 56c, 66b, 67a, 73c, 97a, 111a, 115b, 121c, 127b, 127c, 130b, 143a, 159a, 174c, 175b, 188b, 196b, 225a, 250d, 266a, 275a, 287d, 289c, 296a, 304b, 313a, 336a, 336b, 363c, 365a, 365b, 367b, 371a, 376b

Bill Merilees: 30a, 41c, 41e, 61a, 62b, 68c, 93a, 96d, 98c, 112b, 115c, 116c, 125a, 157d, 172a, 184a, 190b, 191d, 200a, 217d, 228a, 241c, 241d, 253c, 258c, 259a, 266c, 278a, 289a

Nelson Forest Region: 57a, 57c, 65a, 72b, 81b, 81c, 83c, 83d, 140b, 153c, 171b, 173a, 188a, 189a, 193d, 194a, 195a, 205a, 209b, 210a, 210b, 213b, 222a, 222b, 253a, 264c, 268a, 287a, 287c, 307a, 359c

Robert Norton: 51, 60c, 74b, 74c, 87a, 95d, 116d, 144b, 168b, 172b, 172d, 173c, 179c, 184b, 191b, 192c, 192d, 194c, 196a, 197d, 204c, 211b, 215d, 225b, 244a, 254b, 261b, 273a, 274b, 286b, 290c, 296b, 317c, 319b, 322b, 323b, 327b, 342b, 344b, 346a, 350b, 359a, 359b, 375a

Jim Pojar: 28d, 31b, 48c, 52b, 52c, 55c, 58d, 60b, 66a, 68d, 72d, 73d, 80b, 82c, 87b, 87c, 94b, 95c, 99b, 109a, 109b, 110b, 111c, 121b, 124a, 126b, 128b, 131a, 131b, 133b, 134c, 147b, 150c, 157a, 161a, 170b, 181a, 182a, 187a, 187b, 190a, 190c, 197a, 197c, 199a, 204b, 209a, 210d, 213d, 215a, 220b, 225c, 227c, 228b, 232b, 240a, 241a, 244b, 245a, 250a, 250e, 252b, 256a, 262a, 270c, 277c, 288a, 288b, 301a, 302d, 303a, 318c, 342c, 350a, 353b, 354a, 356b, 362c, 364a, 365c, 366a, 367a, 369b, 371c, 372a, 372c, 377a

Anna Roberts: 17c, 18b, 55b, 61d, 62a, 67d, 69a, 71a, 71e, 72c, 75a, 75c, 75d, 76a, 76c, 92b, 92c, 113a, 114a, 118a, 119a, 119b, 122a, 122b, 123a, 123b, 126a, 132c, 136b, 138b, 140a, 143c, 144a, 146a, 146c, 163b, 163c, 164a, 169b, 175c, 185d, 186a, 198a, 217a, 220a, 232d, 233a, 233b, 234b, 235a, 235b, 236b, 236c, 237c, 238a, 239a, 239b, 254c, 262b, 264b, 275b, 306d, 313b, 313d, 314a, 314b, 314c, 315b, 315c, 316a, 316b, 317a, 317b, 318d, 319c, 320a, 320b, 321a, 321b, 321c, 322a, 322c, 323a, 323c, 324a, 324b, 324c, 324d, 325a, 325b, 326a, 326b, 326c, 327a, 327c, 328a, 328c, 329a, 329b, 330a, 332a, 332b, 333a, 333b, 334a, 334b, 335a, 335b, 336c, 337a, 337b, 338a, 338b, 341a, 341b, 341c, 341d, 342a, 344a, 344c, 344s, 345b, 345c, 346b, 347a, 347b, 347c, 347d, 348a, 348b, 348c, 349a, 349b, 350c, 350d, 351a, 351b, 351c, 352a, 352b, 353a, 353c, 354b, 354c, 355a, 355b, 355d, 356a, 356c, 357a, 357b, 358a, 358b, 425a, 427a, 429a, 439b

Carol Thompson: 36b, 37c, 70a, 71c, 81a, 81e, 145c, 185c, 214c, 227a, 252a, 262c

Dale Vitt: 390b, 393a, 397b, 398a, 399c, 404a, 405a, 405b, 407, 409b, 410a, 410b, 411a, 412a, 412b

Ron Walker: 33b, 69b, 71b, 93c, 95b, 96b, 113c, 115a, 120a, 129a, 135a, 137b, 143d, 151c, 156b, 162c, 164b, 169a, 176c, 183c, 183d, 188c, 194d, 212, 214d, 217b, 232c, 235c, 236a, 236d, 246a, 246b, 247c, 251, 261c, 263b, 267b, 270b, 294c, 301b, 364b, 368a

Mike Wheatley: 53c, 66d, 67b, 70d, 82b, 109c, 128a, 129b, 132a, 134b, 135b, 139b, 141b, 145a, 151b, 156a, 157b, 158b, 168c, 187d, 197b, 216d, 223b, 234a, 256b, 264a, 271b, 276a, 278b, 289b, 300d, 302b, 304d

George Whitehead (Selkirk College Collection): 53d, 53e, 65b, 65c, 65d, 86a, 86b, 112a, 118b, 121a, 132b, 142c, 147c, 152a, 162a, 163a, 193b, 200c, 207a, 213a, 216b, 219c, 221b, 232e, 249a, 255b, 257a, 283c, 284c, 285b, 286a, 290a, 294d, 295a, 297b, 297c, 300b, 304a, 305b

Dave Williams: 28c, 29c, 30d, 34b, 35a, 42b, 42c, 43b, 44a, 44c, 46a, 46b, 49, 62c, 79b, 80d, 99a, 113b, 116a, 134a, 141a, 150b, 153d, 165a, 185b, 189b, 214b, 221c, 221d, 223c, 250b, 250c, 266b, 269a, 269b, 278c, 284b, 284d, 295b, 295c, 298b, 298c, 315a, 319d, 328b, 359d, 371b, 372b, 378, 418b, 422b, 424a, 429b, 430a, 434b, 436b, 437a, 438b, 439a

John Worrall: 30c, 31a, 31c, 32c, 32d, 33c, 35b, 35c, 37a, 37b, 38c, 39c, 39d, 43d, 48b

Additional Photographers: Blain Andrusek: 117c, 147a; **B.C. Forest Service**: 149a, 211c, 258a; **B.C. Ministry of the Environment**: 242b, 242c; **B.C. Ministry of Forests**: 14a, 16b, 17b; **B.C. Parks Service**: 29a, 29b, 36c, 41d, 43a, 46c, 68a; **Joan Burbridge**: 125b, 143b, 150a, 157c, 159b, 255a, 257b; **Adolf Ceska**: 77a, 142a, 148a, 264d, 342d, 386b, 375b; **Mathis Duerst**: 28b; **Katherine Enns**: 53a, 226b, 248b, 299a, 299b, 336d, 399b; **Dave Fraser**: 42a; **Trevor Goward**: 414a,428b; **Marianne Ignace**: 21, 22, 23; **Derek Johnson**: 114b, 223e, 245c; **Ted Lea**: 38b, 40a; **Ron Long**: 63d, 130a, 137a, 139c, 227b, 249b, 249c, 271c, 299d; **Robin Love**: 124b, 299c; **George Powell**: 136a, 136d, 145b, 182c; **Dave Ralph**: 141c, 141d, 146b, 182d, 183b; **Rick Riewe**: 289d; **Hans Roemer**: 61b, 266d; **Martin Ross**: 85b; **Rob Scagel**: 138c, 142b, 165b, 193a, 201b, 283a, 305a, 319a; **Bela Sivak**: 331b; **Robert and Nancy Turner**: 64d, 248a; **Ted Underhill**: 40b, 73b, 277b; **L.K. Wade**: 259b, 305d; **Cliff Wallace**: 58a; **Cleve Wershler**: 64b; **Brian Wikeem**: 136c, 182e, 183a, 192a, 232a, 297a; **Jim M. Woollett**: 79d

8

Illustration Credits

All previously published drawings are reprinted by permission of their respective publishers. The individual illustrators have been identified where possible. The numbers refer to the pages on which the illustrations appear in this book; letters indicate whether an illustration appears with the top entry (a) or bottom entry (b) on a page.

T. Christopher Brayshaw: From *Catkin Bearing Plants (Amentiferae) of British Columbia*, by T.C. Brayshaw. 1976. Occasional Papers of the British Columbia Provincial Museum, no. 18. Victoria: 30, 31, 74a, 74b, 75a, 75b, 76a, 76b, 77a, 77b, 78a, 78b, 79a, 79b
From *Pondweeds and Bur-reeds, and Their Relatives: Aquatic Families of Monocotyledons in British Columbia*, by T.C. Brayshaw. 1985. Occasional Papers of the British Columbia Provincial Museum, no. 26. Victoria: 307a, 307b
From *Buttercups, Waterlilies and Their Relatives in British Columbia*, by T.C. Brayshaw. 1989. Royal British Columbia Museum Memoir No. 1. Victoria: 72a, 203, 204a, 204b, 205a, 205b, 206, 207a, 207b, 208a, 208b, 209a, 209b, 210a, 210b, 211a, 211b, 212b, 213a, 213b, 214a, 214b, 215a, 216a

Mary Bryant: From *The Ferns and Fern-allies of British Columbia*, by T.M.C. Taylor. 1963. 2nd. ed. British Columbia Provincial Museum Handbook No. 12. Victoria: 361, 362b, 363b, 364a, 364b, 365b, 366a, 366b, 367b, 368b, 369a, 369b, 370, 371b, 372a, 372b, 374, 375a, 375b, 376a, 376b

Patricia Drukker-Brammall: From *Some Common Mosses of British Columbia*, by W.B. Schofield. 1992 . 2nd. ed. Royal British Columbia Museum Handbook. Victoria. Reprinted by permission of W.B. Schofield: 384b, 385a, 385b, 386a, 386b, 387b, 388a, 388b, 389b, 390a, 391a, 392a, 392b, 393a, 393b, 394a, 394b, 396a, 397a, 398a, 398b, 399a, 400a, 400b, 401a, 401b, 402a, 402b, 403a, 403b, 404a, 405a, 406a, 406b, 407a
Original line drawings. Printed by permission of W.B. Schofield: 408a, 408b, 410a, 410b, 411a, 412a

Peggy Frank: Original line drawings: 97b, 182a, 299b

Trevor Goward: Original line drawings: 413, 414b, 416a, 416b, 417a, 417b, 418a, 418b, 419a, 419b, 420a, 421a, 421b, 422a, 422b, 423a, 424a, 424b, 425a, 425b, 426a, 426b, 427a, 428a, 428b, 429a, 429b, 430a, 430b, 431a, 432a, 432b, 433a, 434a, 434b, 435a, 436a, 436b, 437a, 437b, 438a, 438b, 439a, 439b

Kristi Iverson: Original line drawings: 53a, 56b, 67a, 88, 90, 92a, 93b, 94a, 298a

Jeanne R. Janish: From *Vascular Plants of the Pacific Northwest. Part 1: Vascular Cryptogams, Gymnosperms, and Monocotyledons*, by C.L. Hitchcock, A. Cronquist and M. Ownbey. 1969. University of Washington Publications in Biology, vol. 17. University of Washington Press, Seattle: 28, 29, 32, 33, 34, 35, 36, 37, 38, 39, 41, 42, 43, 44, 45, 48, 281, 282b, 283a, 283b, 285b, 286a, 287a, 287b, 288a, 288b, 289a, 289b, 290a, 292, 293, 294a, 294b, 295a, 295b, 296a, 296b, 297a, 297b, 298b, 299a, 300a, 300b, 301a, 301b, 301b, 301b, 303a, 304a, 304b, 305a, 305b, 306a, 306b, 311, 313a, 314b, 315b, 316a, 317a, 317b, 318a, 318b, 319b, 320a, 321a, 321b, 322a, 322b, 323b, 325a, 327a, 327b, 328a, 328b, 330a, 330b, 332b, 333b, 336b, 337a, 337a, 337b, 338a, 338a, 338b, 342b, 353a, 362a, 365a, 367a, 370, 373a, 374, 377a, 378a
From *Vascular Plants of the Pacific Northwest. Part 2: Salicaceae to Saxifragaceae*, by C.L. Hitchcock and A. Cronquist. 1964. University of Washington Publications in Biology, vol. 17. University of Washington Press, Seattle: 49, 72a, 146b, 147a, 147b, 151a, 198a, 198b, 199a, 199b, 200a, 200b, 201a, 201b, 215b, 251b, 252a, 252b, 253a, 253b, 254a, 254b, 255a, 255b, 256a, 256b, 257a, 257b, 258a, 258b, 259a, 259b, 260b, 261a, 261b, 277a
From *Vascular Plants of the Pacific Northwest. Part 3: Saxifragaceae to Ericaceae*, by C.L. Hitchcock and A. Cronquist. 1961. University of Washington Publications in Biology, vol. 17. University of Washington Press, Seattle: 52a, 52b, 53b, 58a, 61a, 65b, 68a, 68b, 69a, 70a, 70b, 71a, 80b, 145b, 148a, 178a, 178b, 179a, 179b, 180b, 216b, 217a, 240a, 240b, 241b, 242a, 242b, 243, 244a, 244b, 245a, 245b, 246a, 246b, 247b, 248a, 248b, 249a, 262a, 263a, 263b, 264a, 264b, 265, 266a, 266b, 267a, 267b, 268a, 268a, 268b, 269a, 269b, 270a, 270b, 271b, 278a, 278b
From *Vascular Plants of the Pacific Northwest. Part 4: Ericaceae through Campanulaceae*, by C.L. Hitchcock, A. Cronquist and M. Ownbey. 1959. University of Washington Publications in Biology, vol. 17. University of Washington Press, Seattle: 82a, 82a, 83b, 150a, 152a, 152b, 153a, 153b, 166, 170b, 175b, 181b, 183a, 183b, 184a, 185a, 186a, 186b, 187a, 187b, 188a, 189a, 189b, 190b, 191a, 191b, 192b, 193a, 193b, 194a, 194b, 195a, 195b, 197a, 197b

John Maywood: Original line drawings. Printed by his permission: 384a, 387a, 395a, 395b, 396b, 397b, 398a, 399b, 404b, 405b, 409a, 409b, 411b, 412b

Sherry L. Mitchell: Original line drawings: 67a, 185b, 190a, 310, 321b, 322a, 330a, 377b

Betty Newton and Ann Hassen: From *The Heather Family (Ericaceae) of British Columbia*, by A.F. Szczawinski. 1962. British Columbia Provincial Museum Handbook No. 19. Victoria: 89, 91, 93a, 94b, 95b, 96a, 97a, 98a, 272, 273a, 273b, 274a, 274b, 275b, 276a, 276b

John H. Rumley: From *Vascular Plants of the Pacific Northwest. Part 5: Compositae*, by A. Cronquist. 1955. University of Washington Publications in Biology, vol. 17. University of Washington Press, Seattle: 67b, 110b, 111a, 111b, 112a, 112b, 113b, 114a, 114b, 115a, 115b, 116a, 116b, 130b, 133b, 134b, 135a, 135b, 136a, 136b, 142b, 143a, 143b, 144a

Shirley D. Salkeld: Original line drawings: 50, 73a, 95a, 117b, 123b, 131b, 146a, 148b, 149a, 149b, 166, 172a, 256a, 261a, 309, 310, 311, 312, 313a, 313b, 314a, 314b, 315a, 315b, 316a, 316b, 317a, 317b, 318a, 318b, 319a, 319b, 320a, 320b, 321a, 322b, 323a, 323b, 324a, 324b, 325b, 326a, 326b, 327a, 327b, 328a, 328b, 329a, 329b, 330a, 330b, 331a, 331b, 332a, 332b, 333b, 334a, 334b, 335b, 336a, 336b, 337b, 338a, 338b, 339, 339a, 341a, 341b, 342a, 343, 344a, 344b, 345a, 345b, 346a, 346b, 347a, 347b, 348a, 348b, 349a, 349b, 350a, 350b, 351a, 351b, 352a, 352b, 353b, 354a, 354b, 355a, 355b, 356a, 356b, 357a, 357b, 358a, 358b, 359a, 360, 361, 370, 371a, 371a, 371b

Elizabeth J. Stephen: From *The Figwort Family (Scrophulariaceae) of British Columbia*, by T.M.C. Taylor. 1974. British Columbia Provincial Museum Handbook No. 33. Victoria: 69b, 166, 167, 168a, 168b, 169a, 169b, 170a, 171b, 172b, 173a, 173b, 174a, 174b, 175a, 176a, 176b
From *The Sunflower Family (Asteraceae) of British Columbia. Volume 2: Astereae, Anthemideae, Eupatorieae and Inuleae*, by G.W. Douglas. 1995. Royal British Columbia Museum, Victoria: 118a, 118b, 119a, 119b, 120a, 120b, 121a, 121b, 122a, 122b, 123a, 124a, 131a, 132a, 132b, 134a, 137a, 137b, 138a, 138b, 139a, 139b, 140a, 140b, 144b, 145a
Original line drawings. Printed by permission of the Royal British Columbia Museum: 230, 231, 232a, 232b, 233a, 233b, 234a, 234b, 235a, 235b, 236a, 236b, 237a, 237b, 238a, 238b, 239a, 239b

Dagny Tande-Lid: From *Flora of Alaska and Neighboring Territories*, by E. Hultén. 1968. Stanford University Press, Stanford: 82a, 110a

R.A. With: From *The Rose Family (Rosaceae) of British Columbia*, by T.M.C. Taylor. 1973. British Columbia Provincial Museum Handbook No. 30. Victoria: 55b, 56a, 57a, 57b, 58b, 60a, 60b, 61b, 62b, 63, 64a, 64b, 65a, 66a, 66b, 218b, 219a, 219b, 220a, 220b, 221b, 222b, 223a, 223b, 225a, 225b, 226a, 226b, 227a, 227b, 228a, 228b
From The *Pea Family (Leguminosae) of British Columbia*, by T.M.C. Taylor. 1974. British Columbia Provincial Museum Handbook No. 32. Victoria: 155, 156a, 156b, 157a, 157b, 158a, 158b, 159a, 159b, 160b, 161a, 161b, 162a, 162b, 163a, 163b, 164a, 164b, 165a, 165b

Miscellaneous: Original line drawings. Courtesy of the British Columbia Ministry of Forests, Research Branch: 26, 35, 36, 38, 39, 40, 41, 42, 44, 45, 47, 48, 50, 51a, 51b, 54a, 54b, 59, 62b, 67b, 84a, 84b, 86b, 150b, 180a, 181a, 196a, 196b, 221a, 243, 247a, 250a, 250b, 277a, 277b, 281, 285a, 293, 302b, 333a, 363a, 368a, 379
From *Hepaticae of North America*, by T.C. Frye and L. Clark. 1937. University of Washington Publications in Biology, vol. 6. University of Washington Press, Seattle: 411b, 412b
From *The Lily Family (Lilaceae) of British Columbia*, by T.M.C. Taylor. 1974. 2nd. ed. British Columbia Provincial Museum Handbook No. 25. Victoria: 296b, 298a
From *The Sunflower Family (Asteraceae) of British Columbia. Vol. 1: Senecioneae*, by G.W. Douglas. 1982. Occasional Papers of the British Columbia Provincial Museum, no. 23. Victoria: 117a, 117a, 124b, 125a, 125b, 126a, 126b, 127a, 127b, 128a, 128b, 129a, 129b, 130a

About This Guide

For many, plants are simply appreciated for their appearance and often pleasing fragrance, but an increasing number of people wish to be able to name plants and know more about them. This guide is designed for anyone interested in learning about the plants of southern Interior British Columbia. It presents a simple yet thorough account of all the major land-plant groups, and a few of the aquatics, that occur in our region. It has been written for a wide range of potential users, including residents of the southern Interior who have an interest in their natural surroundings, travellers who want a simple and easy-to-use plant guide, high school and post-secondary students studying the flora of British Columbia, and natural resource specialists requiring an up-to-date reference to the plants of this region.

Plants of Southern Interior British Columbia is the third in a series of guides to the flora of British Columbia. It has been preceded by *Plants of Northern British Columbia* (MacKinnon et al. 1992) and *Plants of Coastal British Columbia* (Pojar and MacKinnon 1994). This guide covers the flora of part of the province not specifically covered in those two previous guides—a region that offers abundant opportunities, in settings of splendid natural beauty, for studying, photographing or simply admiring plants.

This guide describes the common native plants of our region, as well as some introduced species that have become naturalized. Most species descriptions include a colour photograph and line drawings to illustrate the general habit (what the whole plant looks like) or specific details. Less common or localized species are described in the 'Similar Species' sections.

Simple keys and other identification aids are given for larger and more difficult groups. The use of specialized terms is minimized, but some are unavoidable, and these are defined in the glossary or explained and illustrated in the introductions to the different plant groups.

The flora of our region is as large and diverse as the vast geographic area it occupies. We have tried to balance the representation of plants from all parts of the region and from both forested and non-forested habitats. Although the guide is quite comprehensive, technical manuals will have to be consulted for definitive identifications of some species. For large, complex groups, such as the sedges (*Carex* spp.), we have described the species that are most common and most widely distributed.

This guide also includes information on human uses of plants, plant systematics, ecological descriptions and other interesting information. We have compiled the information on aboriginal uses from both published and unpublished accounts.

How to Use This Guide

The plants in this guide have been organized into life-form groupings—trees, shrubs, wildflowers, grasses and grass-likes, ferns and their relatives, mosses and liverworts, and lichens. Within these broad groupings we have organized the plants by large families and by groups of smaller families. In some cases we have placed plants that are often confused with each other on the same page so that a direct comparison can be made. Browsing through the illustrations in the guide to find those species or groups of species that a plant specimen most closely resembles may be the quickest way to identifying some plants.

For other readers, the quickest way to identify an unfamiliar plant is to start with the key to major family groups on page 25. Once you have determined your plant's family group, turn to the appropriate section in the guide and proceed through any keys or other identification aids provided. Then carefully compare your specimen to the illustrations and written plant descriptions to determine the species or group to which the specimen belongs. Keep in mind, however, that the keys and other identification aids are only for those species described in this guide. Sometimes it may not be clear which characteristics provide the most consistent distinctions between closely related species. In such cases, several characteristics should be used for the most accurate identification. For easy reference, field characteristics that are most important for species identification are printed in bold type.

For the most difficult groups, especially those with very similar species, a technical key is needed for positive identification. We have provided keys, with specialized terms kept to a minimum, for most of the major plant groups in this guide. These are simple keys that rely on vegetative and floral characteristics. Flowers are often necessary to distinguish among species or genera, but when all that remains on the specimen is the fruit or withered flowers, a bit of imagination and reconstruction may be necessary to determine the path to follow in the key. When confusion arises at a branch in the key, examine both options, then determine which looks more plausible for your specimen.

Plant Names

Both the common and scientific names are given for the plants in this guide. The common and scientific names of the vascular plants largely follow Douglas et al. (1989–94). The scientific names of the mosses largely follow Anderson et al. (1990), while the liverworts follow Stotler and Crandall-Stotler (1977) and the lichens follow Egan (1987).

Scientific names are generally more widely accepted and more stable than common names. For example, the scientific name *Vaccinium membranaceum* always refers to the same species, even though different people in different places might refer to it as a blueberry, a huckleberry or a bilberry, and more specifically as the 'big,' 'big-leaved' or 'black' version of the plant. However, scientific names are not always stable or universal. The bog-orchids and rein-orchids, for example, are placed in the genus *Platanthera* in this book, but some other works put them in the genus *Habenaria*. Where alternative scientific or common names are used in our region, we have included the synonyms in the text and the index.

Our Region

For the purpose of this guide, southern Interior British Columbia is defined roughly as the southern third of the province excluding the coastal areas (see the map on the inside front cover). It is bounded on the west by the crest of the Coast and Cascade mountains and on the east by the crest of the Rocky Mountains. The northern boundary of our region is loosely defined by the northern limit of Douglas-fir (*Psuedotsuga menziesii*), western redcedar (*Thuja plicata*) and western hemlock (*Tsuga heterophylla*) forests as the principal forest types south of Prince George. North of here the flora changes rapidly and contains many plants that are typical of the boreal conditions that extend across northern Canada. The southern boundary of our region has been arbitrarily set as the Canada/USA border, however we recognize that this boundary is artificial and there is a great overlap in the flora of our region with that of northern Washington, Idaho and Montana.

This area we refer to as 'our region' is vast. It encompasses three degrees of latitude and nine degrees of longitude, and it is a land of contrasts—in climate, physical geography and vegetation. It includes some of the most arid and some of the wettest continental climates in Canada; some of the most diverse landscapes in North America, from high, rugged mountains to deep, broad valleys, gently rolling plateaus and eroded badlands; and an equally impressive array of ecosystems, including verdant coniferous forests, broad-leaved deciduous forests, lush subalpine meadows, alpine tundra, wetlands, grasslands and shrub-steppes.

Climate

The climate of southern Interior British Columbia varies with latitude, elevation, distance from the Pacific Ocean and orientation of the mountains to the prevailing westerly winds.

The Pacific Ocean is a source of heat and moisture, and as frontal systems from the North Pacific move onto the Coast and eastward across our region, they encounter successive mountain barriers that are roughly perpendicular to their direction of travel.

As moisture-laden air masses rise over the Coast Mountains and cool, they drop large amounts of precipitation on the Coastal slopes west of our region. These now-drier air masses continue to move eastward and descend over the eastern slopes and adjacent plateaus. Their ability to hold moisture increases as they are warmed by compression, and as a result there is much less precipitation here than on the Coast. For example, the mean annual precipitation at Vancouver is 120 cm, while that at Summerland in the south Okanagan is only 30 cm. This pronounced rain shadow in the lee of the Coast Mountains is most strongly expressed in the valley bottoms of the southern Interior, which have the driest climates in British Columbia.

The air masses pick up moisture as they continue eastward over the plateaus, until they are forced to rise once again, this time over the Columbia Mountains. They deposit their moisture on its western slopes, creating a zone of relatively high precipitation known locally as the 'interior wet belt.' Precipitation levels here approach Coastal values, and there are lush, green forests of western redcedar, western hemlock and, in the wettest areas, mountain hemlock (*Tsuga mertensiana*). Unlike at the low elevations on the Coast, however, about half of the annual precipitation here occurs as snow, and snowmelt in late spring and early summer provides much of the moisture required for plant growth. The eastern slopes in the lee of the Columbia Mountains are again considerably drier than the western slopes.

Finally, the air masses reach the western slopes of the Rocky Mountains, where they again rise, cool and release much of their remaining moisture before leaving the province.

The mountains also restrict the westward flow of cold, continental, arctic air masses from east of the Rockies. Except for the occasional intensive surge of very cold arctic air in winter, our region has a more moderate winter climate than the northern parts of British Columbia or the plains of central Canada. The northernmost parts of our region are subject to more frequent and more severe incursions of cold arctic air, while the southernmost parts of our region, especially in the south Okanagan, are more strongly influenced by the dry, hot air masses of the Great Basin. This area of the southern Interior is often described as the northern limit of desert, and it has many plants in common with the dry areas to the south.

Vegetation Zones

The vegetation of our region ranges from lush, green coniferous forests to dry shrub-steppes to mountain tops void of all but the hardiest plants. To simplify the description of plant distributions, we have divided the region into five broad vegetation zones (see the map on the inside back cover) that are loosely based on *Forest Regions of Canada* (Rowe 1959), *Physiographic Subdivisions of British Columbia* (Holland 1976) and the authors' collective understanding of broad vegetation patterns in the region. Areas within each of these zones share similar climates, physical geographies and plant assemblages.

Coast/Interior Transition

As its name implies, the Coast/Interior Transition contains elements of both mild maritime habitats and more severe continental conditions. It occurs in the rain shadow on the eastern slopes of the Coast and Cascade mountains, where the moderating influences of mild Pacific air masses reduce the influence of winter outbreaks of cold arctic air that are familiar to most of our region. This is largely a mountainous area of moderate relief and narrow, steep-sided valleys. In it, one can find many typically Coastal species, such as mountain hemlock, Pacific silver fir (*Abies amabilis*) and salmonberry (*Rubus spectabilis*). Many typically Interior species also prevail in the predominantly montane forest vegetation.

Dry Southern Interior Plateaus

The dry southern Interior plateaus also lie in the rain shadow of the Coast and Cascade mountains. The Fraser Plateau, situated north of Clinton, is largely a flat and gently rolling landscape, with large areas of unbroken upland underlain by massive volcanic basalt flows.

The Thompson and Okanagan plateaus, located south of Clinton, are more dissected, with rolling uplands of low relief and broad valley basins.

The southern Interior plateaus also include many areas of high relief, especially along their western and eastern flanks. These parts of the plateaus have a great diversity of rock types and include granitic, sedimentary and volcanic formations.

Glaciation and subsequent erosion and deposition by meltwaters are the dominant processes to shape these plateau landscapes. As the glacial ice retreated from the plateaus it deposited outwash materials, terraces and deltas, and its meltwater eroded channels. Small lakes, low-gradient streams and shallow, wet depressions are common throughout this area.

Forests of Douglas-fir are typical of low to mid elevations on the plateaus. The undergrowth is generally open, often park-like and made up of grasses and other plants that can tolerate extensive periods of summer drought. Pinegrass (*Calamagrostis rubescens*) is the most abundant grass on the plateaus. The many grasses and other palatable native forage plants make the plateaus the centre of British Columbia's cattle industry.

At higher elevations on the plateaus, where the annual precipitation is higher and the temperatures are cooler, the Douglas-fir gives way to lodgepole pine (*Pinus contorta* var. *latifolia*) and spruce (*Picea* spp.) with a nearly continuous undergrowth of feather mosses. These forests contain many plants typical of the wet Columbia Mountains to the east.

The highest elevations on the plateaus are cold and snowy, and they have subalpine forests of spruce and subalpine fir (*Abies lasiocarpa*) and occasionally small alpine areas.

Arid Basins

The arid basins occur in broad valleys that are deeply cut into the southern Interior plateaus by the Fraser, Thompson and Okanagan drainage systems. Large glacial lakes once occupied much of these basins and extensive lakebottom deposits dominate the Thompson and Okanagan basins.

Erosion from rivers cutting into the plateaus and the deposition of terraces by glacial water dominated the formation of the basins. These processes have created spectacular landscapes, especially along the Fraser River north of Lillooet, where the river has cut down 300 m into the plateau, leaving steep valley walls, and many terraces, cliffs and gullies. In addition, wind and other erosional forces created sand dunes and hoodoos for British Columbia's very own badlands.

Low elevations, an intense rain shadow in the lee of the most massive Coast Mountains and hot dry air masses that push up from the south all combine to give the basins the hottest and most arid climates in British Columbia. The basins are home to prickly-pear cactus (*Opuntia* sp.), big sagebrush (*Artemisia tridentata*), mariposa lily (*Calochortus* sp.) and many dryland grasses, as well as western rattlesnakes, burrowing owls, California bighorn sheep, spotted bats and many other plants and animals, many of which occur nowhere else in the province. Our arid basins are the northern limit of distribution for many species that have a centre of distribution in the Great Basin of the western United States.

Much of the arid basins are dominated by grasslands and dry, open forests. Bluebunch wheatgrass (*Agropyron spicatum*) is typically a dominant species of the grasslands. Big sagebrush and a well-developed surface crust of lichens and bluegreen algae are characteristic of low-elevation grasslands. Other common grassland plants include needlegrasses (*Stipa* spp.), fescues (*Festuca* spp.), low pussytoes (*Antennaria dimorpha*) and large-fruited desert-parsley (*Lomatium macrocarpum*). The southern part of the Okanagan Basin is the northern limit for many grassland and shrub-steppe plants, such as antelope-brush (*Purshia tridentata*), threetip sagebrush (*Artemisia tripartita*), red three-awn (*Aristida longiseta*) and narrow-leaved desert-parsley (*Lomatium triternatum*).

Forests in the arid basins often consist of very open, park-like stands of ponderosa pine (*Pinus ponderosa*) and Douglas-fir and many of the same shrubs, forbs and grasses that are common in the grasslands. Other common species in these dry forests are saskatoon (*Amelanchier alnifolia*), arrow-leaved balsamroot (*Balsamorhiza sagittata*), yarrow (*Achillea millefolium*) and rosy pussytoes (*Antennaria microphylla*).

Wet Columbia Mountains

East of the southern Interior plateaus is the wet Columbia Mountains vegetation zone, which includes the Columbia Mountains and the Rocky Mountains north of Golden. This zone is largely drained by the Fraser, North Thompson, Columbia and Kootenay rivers and

their tributaries. These river valleys further divide the Columbia Mountains into a series of four mountain ranges—the Cariboo, Monashee, Selkirk and Purcell.

The Columbia Mountains are characterized by steep, rugged slopes and relatively narrow valleys, several of which contain long, narrow lakes and hydroelectric reservoirs. These mountains include a variety of rock types, with sedimentary and metamorphic rocks predominating.

Coniferous montane forests, subalpine forests and alpine communities predominate. The forest undergrowth is generally lush and dominated by ferns, leafy forbs, ericaceous shrubs and deep, continuous carpets of moss. The diversity of plants generally increases from north to south in this zone. In the southern part of the Columbia Mountains, climates at mid to low elevations are both moist and mild because of the eastward penetration of maritime air. In fact it is so similar to a Coastal climate that cascara (*Rhamnus purshiana*) and other typically Coastal species are common here. This area also has the greatest diversity of conifers in the province, with 17 out of a possible 22 conifer species represented.

East Kootenays

The dry, eastern slopes of the Columbia Mountains, the Rocky Mountain Trench south of Golden and the western slopes of the southern Rockies form the East Kootenays vegetation zone.

The Rocky Mountain Trench, which separates the southern Rockies from the Columbia Mountains, is a broad intermontane plain often several kilometres across and running the full length of the southern Interior. It contains several large lakes and the Kootenay and upper Columbia rivers. The extreme southern part of the trench contains several plants that occur nowhere else in the province, as well as several dryland species common to the shrub-steppes of the arid basins to the west.

The eastern slopes of the Rocky Mountains form the boundary between cordilleran flora of western North America and the flora of the Great Plains to the east. The Rockies are steep-sloped mountains with narrow valleys, bold, castellated peaks, sheer-walled cirques and impressive cliffs and rock faces. The rocks are largely sedimentary and metamorphic, with limestone predominating. Areas underlain by limestone or marble are often associated with distinctive plant communities that contain many rare and unusual plants. Dry forests with grassy undergrowth dominate mid-slopes, while cool, snowy subalpine forests prevail at higher elevations. Forests of cedar and hemlock, more reminiscent of the wet Columbia Mountains, occur locally near Fernie.

Fire and Ecosystem Dynamics

Disturbances have a major influence on vegetation patterns in the southern Interior. Fire, insect outbreaks and windthrow are the main natural disturbances. Disturbance is not a simple factor, but a variety of phenomena that can destroy or damage plants, often releasing space and nutrients and altering growing conditions. In different parts of our region, disturbances have different spatial scales, intensities of destruction and frequencies of occurrence.

Before Euroamerican settlement on the dry plateaus, frequent low-intensity surface fires removed the small trees and shrubs from the forests and left the mature, more fire-resistant trees, such as Douglas-fir, ponderosa pine and western larch (*Larix occidentalis*), largely intact. Frequent low-intensity fires also encourage the spread of some plants, such as many of the grasses, that quickly resprout following the removal of the above-ground foliage. Lodgepole pine, which maintains its seed in fire-resistant cones for several years, is often abundant on sites with moderately frequent, often stand-destroying fires. Red raspberry (*Rubus ideaus*) and golden corydalis (*Corydalis aurea*), the seeds of which can be stored in the forest floor for decades or longer, are also common following moderate fires. Large fires, many of which destroyed a thousand hectares or more of forest, also occurred from time to time.

In the wet climates of our region, the cool, humid summers inhibit frequent fires but encourage the build-up of large quantities of fuels. Fires only occurred every two or more centuries, but when they did occur they were intense and killed most of the trees. Such fires tended to happen during prolonged hot, dry spells, often in conjunction with strong winds that pushed the fire over several hundred or thousand hectares.

Humans have also introduced many disturbances to our region. Before Euroamerican settlement, many of the aboriginal peoples burned areas to improve the habitat for hoofed mammals. Many of the activities we undertake today continue to create disturbances that alter the natural pattern of vegetation. These practices include agricultural activities, livestock grazing, the development of transportation corridors, timber harvesting, mining and urbanization. Many non-native plants have also been introduced—some intentionally, others accidentally—and some of these are so aggressive that they are replacing some of our native species.

Habitats

Forested Habitats

Forests dominate most of our region. The variety of our forests is a reflection of the broad ranges of climate, geology, topography and soil present here. But these physical factors alone do not determine the variety of forest communities—the stages of forest succession (from recently established to old-growth) further add to a diverse mosaic of forest cover.

Broadleaf Deciduous Forests

Within our region, broadleaf deciduous forests are largely made up of trembling aspen (*Populus tremuloides*), paper birch (*Betula papyrifera*) and black cottonwood (*P. balsamifera* ssp. *trichocarpa*), of which trembling aspen occurs on the widest range of sites, generally at low to mid elevations, on moist sites in dry climates and on mesic to slightly dry sites (often in association with paper birch) in moist and wet climates. Grasses and a great variety of wildflowers form the undergrowth of aspen forests. Aspens, which produce root suckers, regenerate quickly after major disturbances, such as fires. Cottonwood forests are most prevalent along streams or on other moist to wet soils. Tall shrubs, such as red-osier dogwood (*Cornus stolonifera*) and black twinberry (*Lonicera involucrata*), dominate their undergrowth.

Broadleaf deciduous forests play an important role in maintaining the overall biodiversity of our region. Many of our songbirds and other wildlife are closely associated with these forests. Upland deciduous forests are pleasant places with their lightly filtered light, vibrant contrast of colours and good prospects for viewing wildlife. The brilliant yellows and oranges of their fall foliage adds to scenic values of many parts of our region.

Dry Forests

Dry forests of drought-tolerant trees, such as ponderosa pine, lodgepole pine and Douglas-fir, prevail in warm valley bottoms, on valley slopes and on dry plateaus in the central part of our region.

These forests often have open canopies that allow grasses, such as pinegrass, Idaho fescue (*Festuca idahoensis*) and bluebunch wheatgrass, to dominate the undergrowth. At low elevations these forests are often interspersed with grasslands, creating a picturesque parkland setting. Many of these dry forests provide critical winter habitat for large hoofed mammals, such as mule deer, elk and bighorn sheep. In wet climates, dry forests are restricted to sites with thin or rapidly drained, sandy soils.

Wet Montane Forests

Wet mid-montane forests are the most productive forests in the southern Interior, and they include the widest variety of native trees in the province. These forests occur in the 'wet belt' where the climate is sufficiently wet and mild that western redcedar and western hemlock are common, and majestic forests of several-hundred-year-old trees occur. Douglas-fir

is also found throughout wet montane forests, and western white pine (*Pinus monticola*), western larch, hybrid white spruce (*Picea glauca* x *engelmannii*) and lodgepole pine are common in the southern half of the region. In the cold, wet, montane climates of the northern part of our region, hybrid white spruce, lodgepole pine and often subalpine fir predominate, replacing the cedar/hemlock forests. Similar forests also occur on wet sites on the plateaus. The undergrowth of wet montane forests is typically lush, with many ferns, wildflowers and shrubs growing above a verdant carpet of mosses.

Subalpine Forests

High-elevation forests occur throughout our region in mountainous terrain and at upper elevations on the plateaus. The climate is severe, with cool, short growing seasons and long, cold winters.

In our wettest subalpine climates wildfires are uncommon and many forests are old, with trees of widely ranging sizes and ages. Subalpine fir and Engelmann spruce (*Picea engelmanii*) are the most characteristic tree species, and the forest canopy is often open and patchy. Subalpine forests of the 'wet belt' have a luxuriant undergrowth with many of the same species typical of wet montane forests, in addition to many characteristically subalpine species, including white-flowered rhododendron (*Rhododendron albiflorum*), Sitka valerian (*Valeriana sitchensis*), bracted lousewort (*Pedicularis bracteosa*) and Merten's sedge (*Carex mertensii*).

In rainshadow climates, subalpine forests are often dominated by lodgepole pine, alpine larch (*Larix lyallii*) and whitebark pine (*Pinus albicaulis*), with an undergrowth of dwarf ericaceous shrubs, grasses and dryland mosses and lichens. Near the upper limits of tree growth, subalpine forests are often intermixed with treeless communities. These subalpine parklands provide some of the most spectacular scenery and wildflower communities in the region.

Non-forested Habitats

Non-forested habitats often form only a small component of the landscape, but their contribution to the overall biological diversity is disproportionately large. Non-forested habitats often contain rare and unusual plants, are frequently critical habitats for many species and have high aesthetic values. These habitats generally occur where it is too dry, too wet, too saline or too cold for trees to survive. In some areas, such as avalanche tracts, forests are absent because disturbances are too frequent for trees to become established.

Grasslands

Southern Interior grasslands, such as the big sage shrub-steppe communities of the arid basins of our region, usually occur where it is too dry to support trees.

Both the grasslands and the dry, warm forests of our region are northern extensions of widespread ecosystems that occur south of our area. Native grasslands occur primarily in broad, arid, low-elevation basins, such as those of the Okanagan, Thompson and Fraser rivers. Smaller areas of valley-bottom grasslands occur in the southern Rocky Mountain Trench.

16

Grasslands also occur on plateaus in the northern part of the region near Riske Creek and Alkali Lake, and in the Merrit area, where they often occur as parklands with small areas of interspersed dry coniferous or aspen forests. Throughout the southern Interior plateaus, small areas of grassland occur as isolated 'balds' at mid to high elevations on warm, steep southern slopes. These often contain a mixture of grassland and dry forest species.

Bluebunch wheatgrass is the most abundant plant species in our grasslands. Other grasses, such as fescues, needlegrasses and bluegrasses, are also common, as are many showy wildflowers that bloom in spring and early summer. Most grasslands in our region are grazed by domestic livestock, and on severely overgrazed areas, there are many weedy, often introduced plants.

Wetlands

Southern Interior wetlands are common at low to high elevations. They provide important habitat for many species of wildlife, and many of our more unusual and interesting plants, such as sundews (*Drosera* spp.), are found in wetlands.

Wetlands are classified according to substrate type, water sources and nutrient levels. In our region, fens and marshes are most common and bogs are less common. Meadows and shrub-carrs occur more commonly on the Fraser Plateau in the northern parts of the region.

Fens are peatlands with nutrient-rich waters derived at least in part from groundwater and runoff from adjacent mineral uplands. They commonly occur in shallow basins on the plateaus, along slow-flowing watercourses and along lake edges. Sedges, grasses, reeds and mosses are common fen plants. Many of the fens in the northern portions of our region also have an abundant cover of shrubs, such as willows (*Salix* spp.) and scrub birch (*Betula glandulosa* var. *glandulosa*).

Marshes are wetlands that are permanently or seasonally inundated and support an extensive cover of emergent, non-woody vegetation rooted in a mineral-rich substrate. Marshes characteristically have a mosaic pattern of pools and channels of shallow, open water interspersed with stands of sedges, grasses, rushes and reeds. Where open water occurs a variety of floating and submerged aquatic plants flourish. Marshes occur around the edges of many lakes in our region. Creston Marsh and the Columbia River marshes south of Golden are important examples of large marsh complexes. Marshes are crucial to the continued survival of many species of waterfowl and other wildlife in the province.

Bogs are acid peatlands with stagnant, low-nutrient waters derived largely from precipitation. Bog surfaces are elevated above the groundwater table, largely because of the accumulation of sphagnum-derived peats. The vegetation is dominated by peat mosses (*Sphagnum* spp.), with scrub birch, Labrador tea (*Ledum groenlandicum*), trapper's tea (*L. glandulosum*), cottongrass (*Eriophorum* sp.) and lichens also present. Bogs are relatively uncommon in our region and usually occur in shallow, closed basins at mid to subalpine elevations. They are more common to the north in poorly drained areas with a boreal climate and in areas with a maritime climate along the Coast.

Meadows and shrub-carrs develop on mineral soils that are periodically saturated but rarely inundated. They receive most of their moisture from runoff and seepage from surrounding areas. They often occur in depressions in grassland areas and between forests and fens and marshes on the dry plateaus. They are often associated with areas of high alkalinity and low-lying frosty areas in dry climates. Meadows are herbaceous communities dominated by grasses and grass-like plants, and they therefore resemble grasslands. Some of the common plants of meadows are foxtail barley (*Hordeum jubatum*), Baltic rush (*Juncus balticus*), Nuttall's alkaligrass (*Puccinellia nuttalliana*) and silverweed (*Potentilla anserina*). Shrub-carrs are shrub-dominated communities with a hummocky soil surface that results in a mix of wet and dry microsites with corresponding wet and dry plant species, including scrub birch, short-fruited willow (*Salix brachycarpa*), kinnikinnick (*Arctostaphylos uva-ursi*), mat muhly (*Muhlenbergia richardsonis*), Baltic rush and star-flowered false Solomon's-seal (*Smilacina stellata*).

High-elevation Habitats

Alpine communities occupy high elevations throughout the southern Interior. The long, cold winters and cool, short growing seasons create conditions too severe for the growth of most woody plants except in dwarf (ground-hugging) forms. Alpine flora is highly specialized to cope with the harsh conditions of these environments, and the great diversity of alpine ecosystems and landscapes, with their complex mosaics of habitats, are of special interest.

Heaths are dominated by dwarf, evergreen shrubs of the heather family. Other common species include crowberry (*Empetrum nigrum*), partridgefoot (*Luetkea pectinata*) and mountain sagewort (*Artemisia norvegica* ssp. *saxitilis*). The ground cover forms a thick springy carpet often so dense that it obscures the ground below. In our region heaths are most common in areas of deep snow accumulation.

Alpine meadows are common where prolonged snowmelt keeps the soil moist all summer, and they are dominated by herbaceous plants, such as arrow-leaved groundsel (*Senecio triangularis*), Sitka valerian, arctic lupine (*Lupinus arcticus*), globeflower (*Trollius laxus*), western meadowrue (*Thalictrum occidentale*), common horsetail (*Equisetum arvense*) and many species of sedge and grass. Alpine meadows share many species in common with subalpine parklands, which they often border, and they provide a spectacular floral display in mid summer.

Alpine rocklands and steeplands include rock outcrops, cliffs, boulder fields, tallus and scree slopes, wet runnels and gullies and avalanche tracts. In many of these habitats soils can be thin or nearly absent, and the plant cover is sparse and discontinuous. Common plants include dwarf willows, moss campion (*Silene acaulis*), drabas (*Draba* spp.), cinquefoils (*Potentilla* spp.), grasses, sedges and many species of lichens and mosses. These habitats have some of the most distinctive and often the rarest plants of our region.

Disturbed Habitats

These include rights-of-way (trails, roads, railways and power lines), recently logged areas, agricultural areas and clearings, settled areas and other sites frequently or severely disturbed by human activity. These habitats are often dominated by introduced Eurasian weeds, such as lamb's-quarters (*Chenopodium album*) and great mullein (*Verbascum thapsus*), and by horticultural species of legumes, such as sweet-clover (*Melilotus* sp.), and grasses, such as cheatgrass (*Bromus tectorum*) and smooth brome (*B. inermis* ssp. *inermis*). Native species, such as fireweed (*Epilobium angustifolium*) and Sitka alder (*Alnus crispa* ssp. *sinuata*), also occur on disturbed habitats.

Aboriginal Peoples' Plant Use and Knowledge

Southern Interior Aboriginal Cultures

Archaeologists are able to trace the southern Interior aboriginal peoples to about 10,000 years ago, when the glaciers of the last great ice age retreated and created the current watersheds, including the Fraser and Thompson river system and the Columbia watershed.

The Interior aboriginal peoples' own sense of origin refers to the doings of the 'Old One' or creator, who brought order to the country and nature's work and created the people, animals and plants inhabiting it. He then sent Coyote, the trickster-transformer, to finish his work. Coyote's often foolish and selfish actions left landmarks throughout the southern Interior, and changed the characteristics of plant and animal species to what they are now.

The Plateau culture is the largest group of aboriginal peoples in the southern Interior. Their homelands stretch from the eastern slopes of the Coast Mountains to the Rockies. In the United States, the Plateau culture area stretches into east-central Washington, Idaho and Montana. Except for the Tsilhqot'in (Chilcotin), whose language is of the Athapaskan family, the Plateau peoples in our region speak languages of the Interior Salish language family.

The Interior Salish Plateau peoples comprise the Secwepemc (Shuswap), St'at'imc (Lillooet), Nlaka'pmx (Thompson) and Okanagan. In the past, they were semi-nomadic hunting-gathering peoples who spent the coldest months in underground pit houses near the valley bottoms. For the rest of the year they lived in temporary shelters as they pursued the abundant salmon resources in the streams and creeks of their territories, fished for trout in highland lakes, hunted deer, elk, caribou, mountain goats, sheep and many small animals in the mountains, and gathered a variety of plants as a significant part of their diet.

The Stuwix (Nicola) were an Athapaskan-speaking people of the Nicola-Similkameen Valley, but they were absorbed into the Okanagan and Nlaka'pmx during the early 19th century.

To the east of the Interior plateaus live the Ktunaxa (Kootenay), whose language is a linguistic isolate, and whose culture is similar in some ways to that of the Plains peoples.

First Nations of Southern Interior British Columbia

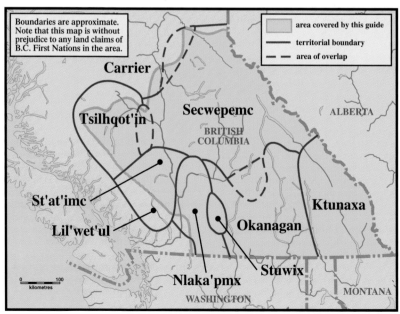

While the aboriginal peoples of the Interior plateau probably numbered more than 40,000 before the arrival of Europeans, they were reduced to less than a quarter of their original population during the 19th century. This population decline was mainly due to diseases, such as smallpox, measles, tuberculosis, influenza and diphtheria. Today, there are about 20,000 aboriginal people living in the southern Interior.

First Nation's self-designation	Name used by Europeans
Tsilhqot'in	Chilcotin
Stuwix	Nicola
Secwepemc	Shuswap
(Upper) St'at'imc/Stl'atl'imx	Upper Lillooet/Fraser River Lillooet
Lil'wet'ul, L'il'wet7ul	Lower Lillooet (Pemberton/Mt. Currie)
Nlaka'pmx, Nle7kepmx, Nlha7kápmx	Thompson
Okanagan	Okanagan
Ktunaxa	Kootenay/Kutenai

Plant Use

Next to fishing and hunting, the aboriginal peoples of the southern Interior relied heavily on plants for food, for medicines for their physical and spiritual well-being, and for many of their tools and implements. Moreover, plant knowledge was an essential part of overall cultural knowledge and meanings, and it was related through stories, place names, beliefs and values. The ecologically diverse homelands of the southern Interior peoples contain a great range and variety of plants available to them at different locations, elevations and seasons throughout the year. Surplus plant foods, or essential plant materials occurring only in certain locations, were traded among communities or nations.

Plants as Food

Southern Interior aboriginal people ate a great variety of plants, including fleshy fruits, seeds and nuts, root vegetables, green vegetables, a few mushroom species, tree lichen, tree cambium and other tree products.

Many species of berries, including several kinds of blueberries and huckleberries (*Vaccinium* spp.), saskatoon berries (*Amelanchier alnifolia*), strawberries (*Fragaria* spp.), raspberries (*Rubus* spp.), currants and gooseberries (*Ribes* spp.) and wild cherries (*Prunus* spp.) were harvested in great quantities and provided carbohydrates, vitamins and other nutrients. Soopolallie berries (*Sheperdia canadensis*), which are very bitter to the Euroamerican palate, were an important food and trade item. They were whipped into a froth (often called Indian ice-cream), or were used to make a thirst-quenching beverage. Hazelnuts (*Corylus cornuta*) and the seeds of whitebark pine (*Pinus albicaulis*) were welcome sources of protein, carbohydrates, fats and vitamins.

Bulbs were harvested from several species of the lily family, such as yellow glacier lily (*Erythronium grandiflorum*), mariposa lilies (*Calochortus* spp.), chocolate lily (*Fritillaria lanceolata*), tiger lily (*Lilium columbianum*) and nodding onion (*Allium cernuum*), and roots from western spring beauty (*Claytonia lanceolata*), called wild potatoes, bitterroot (*Lewisia rediviva*), balsamroots (*Balsamorhiza* spp.), silverweed (*Potentilla anserina*) and some others. Certain roots had to be sun-dried or slow-cooked in pit ovens to convert the indigestible carbohydrate inulin into digestible fructose (Kuhnlein and Turner 1992).

Some of the green vegetables and fresh shoots that were eaten included cow-parsnip (*Heracleum lanatum*), barestem desert-parsley (*Lomatium nudicaule*), called Indian celery, and the new shoots of balsamroots and fireweed (*Epilobium angustifolium*). These plants provided welcome nutrients in early to mid spring after people had subsisted on stored foods for several months.

Edible horsehair (*Bryoria fremontii*) was another food staple. Once this lichen was made edible and palatable by long slow-cooking, which gave it a slightly licorice-flavoured but bland taste, it was preserved in cakes. It also served as an ever-present famine food.

The Interior peoples ate and valued many parts and products of trees. These included the sweet inner cambium of lodgepole pine (*Pinus contorta*), which they harvested in late spring when the sap was rising. Since the cambium has a laxative effect, they also valued it for 'spring cleansing' the body at this time of year. A sweet delicacy was fir sugar, a crystalline sugar that formed on the branches of fir trees only in certain years during hot weather in late spring.

Finally, various plants, including field mint (*Mentha arvensis*), Labrador tea (*Ledum groenlandicum*) and trapper's tea (*L. glandulosum*), provided beverages and tonics (Turner 1974, Turner et al. 1980, Turner et al. 1990, Turner and Ignace 1990–94).

While Interior aboriginal peoples still harvest some food plants in large quantities today, especially the berries, the use of root plants, wild greens, tree products and lichen has declined since the 19th century with the increasing availability of commercial carbohydrates (flour, rice, sugar, etc.) and gardening produce (potatoes, turnips, carrots, beans, etc.). However, many contemporary elders gathered these plants during their youth, and occasionally they continue to do so today.

Plants as Medicines

The concept of 'medicine' among North American aboriginal peoples comprises ingredients or acts involved in the healing of—or causing harm to—the physical, spiritual or emotional well-being of a person. Plants and plant knowledge to promote both physical and spiritual well-being were an important and integral part of the concept of medicine. Hundreds of plants were known to aboriginal peoples for their medicinal value.

Among the medicinal plants the Interior peoples know and use or used were tonics or purgatives consumed to prevent illness, medicines for many specific illnesses or conditions affecting the respiratory tract and internal organs, and medicines for cuts, sprains, sores, aches and skin conditions. Herbal medicines were taken internally or applied externally—usually as infusions (plants steeped in boiled water) or concoctions (boiled plants or plant parts)—either for a prescribed period of time or until the condition improved. Some plants had 'partners,' and the recipes for some medications called for the healing ingredients of two or more plants that complemented one another.

One important medicine was the pitch or resin of coniferous trees, especially firs (*Abies* spp.), which was mixed with grease and applied to infected cuts and to remove slivers imbedded in the skin. In fact, the term for 'fir' in the Interior Salish languages means 'healing tree.' Its bark was also considered an important cough and cold medicine.

Some plants were know as 'good luck medicines' or charms, and collecting and preserving them in a private place was said to promote good luck in gambling, or it would make a person fall in love with you.

A number of plants were commonly known and used medicines, while many others, especially those that were known to be toxic and had to be administered carefully, were handled by specialists only. The traditional concept of healing among the aboriginal peoples of the Interior was holistic—the treatment of conditions and diseases revolved not only around the treatment of symptoms, but around the general improvement of the person's well-being or the prevention of physical and emotional sickness. The use of tonics, purgatives, and the combinations of foods and medicines and sweat-bathing promoted good health in this way.

Interior aboriginal peoples used a number of plants as scents or cleansing agents, including juniper (*Juniperus* sp.), fir boughs and rose bushes (*Rosa* sp.). The idea of cleansing involved both physical and spiritual cleansing, and these plants played an important role in the handling of the dead and diseased (see Turner et al. 1990, Turner and Ignace 1990–94).

Other plants, such as tobacco (*Nicotiana* sp.) and big sagebrush (*Artemisia tridentata*), were medicines in the sense that they were burned to communicate with other worlds and to ensure spiritual community among people gathered for a purpose. It was also a custom to repay nature with a gift of tobacco when harvesting plants for food, medicine or technology.

Through the forced cultural change and colonization of the past 150 years, along with the availability of Euroamerican medical care and pharmaceutica, knowledge about plants as medicine has greatly diminished. Some aboriginal elders, however, still know about and use medicinal plants, and young people are becoming increasingly interested in the preservation and application of such knowledge. Certain plants and plant products, such as pitch, balsam bark, juniper and soopolallie sticks, are still used in many aboriginal households.

Plants in Technology

Before the availability of commercially made implements, plants were the source of a vast range of tools, household implements, building materials and fuels.

Underground houses were constructed with lodgepole pine poles, and temporary lodges were made by covering a framework of wooden poles with woven reed mats. Canoes were made from the bark of paper birch (*Betula payrifera*) until metal tools became available and dugout canoes made from the trunks of cottonwood (*Populus balsamifera* ssp. *trichocarpa*) tended to replace birch bark canoes. Bows, fishing spears and digging sticks were all made of hard woods, such as yew (*Taxus* sp.) or juniper, and arrows were made from saskatoon or rose wood.

Interior peoples used plant fibres to make much of their clothing. For example, they wove cloaks, skirts and even socks from the bark of sagebrush (*Artemisia* sp.). Even clothes made of animal hides were tied to the use of plants, because the hide-scraping poles, tanning sticks and frames were made of cottonwood. After being tanned, the hides were smoked using rotten fir wood, 'punky wood' or pine cones to preserve and colour them.

Baskets made from birch bark or woven cedar roots were important storage and carrying containers. Basket-makers used other plant fibres or plant dyes to weave or imbricate various designs into their baskets. An important plant fibre in the lives of the Interior peoples was hemp dogbane (*Apocynum cannabinum*), also called Indian hemp. After its bark was peeled off, the dried stems were pounded to yield a fibre that was then spun into a strong rope or twine, which was used for fishing nets, fishing line, bowstrings and many other purposes. Hemp dogbane occurred in few locations, and it was a much-desired trade item throughout the southern Interior.

As with food and medicinal plants, the knowledge and use of plants in aboriginal technology has declined during the past century.

Plant Harvesting

The aboriginal peoples of the Interior often harvested the plants they used for food, medicine or technology while they were travelling in pursuit of game and fish. They had a very detailed knowledge of which plants were ready at what elevation and in which area during what part of the year. Certain prolific food plants, such as berries and roots, were collected in well-known and well-tended locations, and whole communities often stayed near these gathering locations for days or weeks to process them. All food-gathering locations were regarded as communal property, and the chiefs would ensure that resources were equally distributed among the people (Teit 1909).

Food harvesting and propagation involved certain resource management techniques, such as landscape burning, selected harvesting of crops, pruning of berry bushes, loosening the soil and replanting immature bulbs while harvesting mature ones (Turner and Ignace 1990–94).

Plants in the Knowledge System

Plants in general provided a way of classifying and speaking about the world for Interior aboriginal peoples. In the aboriginal world view, plants were an integral part of all living things, and of the entire universe, rather than being considered separate from them. Accordingly, the Interior Salish languages have no separate word for the life form 'plant,' although some suffixes exist that make an item or object recognizable as a plant or plant part.

There are a number of generic plant terms—'tree,' 'flower,' 'berry,' etc.—and hundreds of plant species are named by one or more terms in each aboriginal language. Some of these cannot be broken down into component meanings, while others are complex descriptive terms that refer to the colour, shape, use (by humans or animals) or consistency of a plant. Thus, in the Interior Salish languages, the term for yarrow (*Achillea millefolium*) translates as 'chipmunk's tail,' and brown-eyed Susans (*Gaillardia aristata*) are called 'little salmon eyes' in Secwepemc.

Many plants that are not harvested or directly usable function as ecological indicators—their occurrence in a particular location indicates the occurrence of other harvestable plants or animal habitats, the vicinity of water, the elevation or the cardinal direction. The blooming of certain plants in the valley indicates the spawning of trout in highland lakes or other animal movements in the mountains.

Some of this information was poetically expressed and transmitted through the stories or mythology of the Interior peoples. Likewise, some months in the calendars of the Interior peoples are based on the ripening of plants and plant-gathering activities. Thus, the Eastern Secwepemc called April *Pellscwicwem*, 'the month when yellow glacier lilies show growth,' and July was called '[berries]-getting-ripe month.' Place names also often reflected the occurrence of important food or medicinal plants, and a large number of indigenous place names are named after plant species occurring in the area.

Current Aboriginal Plant Knowledge

With the introduction of commercial produce and processed foods, many aboriginal foods are rarely used today. Similarly, many traditional crafts that rely on plant fibres are a dying art, and knowledge about medicines and the place of plants in the natural environment has been lost.

In recent years, however, many young aboriginal people have become interested in knowing about plants and harvesting them. Among many of the First Nations of the Interior and elsewhere, elders, interested community members and researchers have tried to archive plant knowledge, hoping not only to preserve it, but also to reintroduce the use and knowledge of plants to younger people. Much of the aboriginal plant research with the peoples of the Interior has been carried out by ethnobotanist Dr. Nancy Turner, in collaboration with other scientists and with native elders and their communities.

However, even where ethnobotanical knowledge remains, the continued practice of aboriginal plant harvesting faces obstacles—increasing urban development and resource extraction (clearcut logging, strip mining, etc.) has altered the landscape. In many parts of the southern Interior, housing subdivisions have taken over once-prolific berry patches, and mining has destroyed access to and the use of pharmaceutical repositories at many high elevations. Logging at least temporarily alters the flora, and it changes the availability of berries and medicines for decades. Overgrazing by horses and cattle has destroyed many areas where important food plants, such as spring beauties or yellow glacier lily, once grew. Finally, introduced weeds compete with the indigenous-use species for habitat. To prevent further damage, or perhaps to reverse existing damage and endangerment, indigenous plant species must be treated with the same respect the aboriginal peoples of long ago were taught to show them.

Note

In the information on aboriginal plant use, we have included only the information that the aboriginal peoples of the Interior would deem fit to share with the general public. It is our understanding that the aboriginal peoples of the Interior also reserve for themselves the intellectual property rights on their knowledge about these plants.

While the published and unpublished sources for the above information, and the specific information on aboriginal uses of plants given in this guide are cited in the list of references at the end of this book, the true authors of this information are the elders of the Interior First Nations, who provided this information in collaboration with anthropologists, botanists and linguists. They are too numerous to acknowledge here, but their names and biographical information about them can be found in the respective publications. Their invaluable contribution to ethnobotanical knowledge is hereby acknowledged.

While this guide records the aboriginal medicinal uses of many plants, it is not intended as a 'how to' guide for their use and preparation, nor does it advocate such use or experimentation by readers. Indeed, many of the plants used for medicinal purposes are poisonous and require careful handling by specialists, as noted above.

Notes on Collecting and Growing Native Plants

Some of the first expeditions to explore the Pacific Northwest included naturalists who collected specimens and seeds to take back to the Old World. Early botanical publications described the region's flora from these specimens, which whetted the appetites of many European gardeners. This interest resulted in the arrival in the Pacific Northwest of the young plant explorer David Douglas in 1824. His mission was to collect specimens and seeds of the region's flora for the London Horticultural Society. His collections and notes were immense, and they greatly added to the knowledge of the flora. The scientific and common names of many of our native plants commemorate him, such as 'Douglas-fir,' 'Douglas maple' and *Crataegus douglasii*. Many of our native species are still used in the horticultural trade of Europe.

Throughout this book we have included notes on the propagation of native plants. However, as a general rule **wild plants should not be dug up**. In the past it was common to transplant wild plants to the garden, and some of our rarest and most beautiful wildflowers are threatened with extinction because of past collecting practices. One might think that digging up a few plants from the wild is harmless, but this is not the case, and the uncontrolled collection of native plants has caused significant harm. In addition, the chances of successfully transplanting well-established native plants from the wild are very low. The best way to propagate native plants is to start them vegetatively (from cuttings or layering) or from seeds.

Many of our native plants are now becoming available in nurseries. It would be wise, however, to check that these plants have been propagated and not collected from the wild.

Many of our native plants grow under conditions that are very different from those of most home gardens. By paying close attention to these conditions the success of establishing a 'naturalized' garden that requires less care and maintenance is greatly improved. Growing native plants can be very satisfying, but in all cases this should be tempered by a strong conservation ethic so that others who follow can have the same pleasures of viewing plants in their native setting.

INTRODUCTION

The Species Descriptions

The plants in this guide have been organized into life-form groupings—trees, shrubs, wildflowers, graminoids (grasses and grass-likes), ferns and their relatives, bryophytes (mosses and liverworts) and lichens. Within these broad groupings we have organized the plants by large families and by groups of smaller families. In some cases we have placed plants that are often confused with each other on the same page so that a direct comparison can be made. Browsing through the illustrations in the guide to find those species or groups of species that a plant specimen most closely resembles may be the quickest way to identifying some plants.

For other readers, the quickest way to identify an unfamiliar plant is to start with the following key to major family groups. Once you have determined your plant's family group, turn to the appropriate section in the guide and proceed through any keys or other identification aids provided there. Then carefully compare your specimen to the illustrations and written plant descriptions to determine the species or group to which the specimen belongs. It should again be noted, however, that these keys and other identification aids include, for the most part, only the species described in this guide.

Key to the major plant family groups

1a. Plants small, without vascular tissue; leaves absent
or very small, with at most a single vein (non-vascular plants) 2

  2a. Plants without spore-bearing capsules;
  leaves absent; plants of various colours .... **lichens** (p. 413)

  2b. Plants with spore-bearing capsules; leaves
  often present; plants generally green to yellowish green .... **bryophytes** (p. 379)

1b. Plants small to very large, with vascular tissue,
producing either spores or seeds; leaves generally
present and many-veined (vascular plants) 3

  3a. Plants without flowers or seeds,
  but producing spores on the leaves,
  in leaf axils or in small cone-like structures; herbaceous 4

    4a. Leaves divided into segments,
    often large (5 to more than 100 cm long);
    spores produced on the leaf surfaces .... **ferns** (p. 360)

    4b. Leaves small (usually less than
    1 cm long) or lacking, not divided
    into segments, spores produced
    in cone-like structures or at the
    base of the leaves .... **horsetails, clubmosses and spikemosses** (pp. 370, 373)

  3b. Plants producing seeds; flowers
  often present; herbaceous or woody 5

    5a. Plants woody (low, trailing shrubs to trees) 6

      6a. Plants generally with a single main stem
      and usually over 5 m tall when mature .... **trees** (p. 26)

      6b. Plants generally with multiple stems,
      usually less than 5 m tall at maturity .... **shrubs** (p. 49)

    5b. Plants herbaceous (wildflowers and grass-like plants) 7

      7a. Petals usually number 4 or 5
      (or multiples of 4 or 5); leaves generally
      with branched veins, variable in shape .... **dicotyledons** (p. 104)

      7b. Petals usually number 3 (or a multiple of 3);
      leaves with parallel veins, often long and narrow;
      includes orchids, lilies and many plants with non-showy
      flowers, such as grasses, sedges and rushes .... **monocotyledons** (p. 279)

TREES

Trees are woody, single-stemmed plants over 10 m tall at maturity. Their large size makes them the most conspicuous plants in the landscape. Some of our willows (such as Bebb's and Scouler's willows), small trees (such as black hawthorn, Rocky Mountain juniper, western yew, cherries and others) occasionally reach 10 m in height but are typically shorter. These species are described in the 'Shrubs' section.

Included here are both coniferous and broadleaf species. In our area, all the conifers (except the larches) are evergreen and retain their needle- or scale-like leaves for more than one season. The larches have deciduous, needle-like leaves that turn bright yellow or orange in the autumn and fall from the tree. All the broadleaf trees in our area are deciduous. Many provide brilliant autumn contrasts of yellow and orange against the background of dark green conifers.

Except where the climate is too severe (such as arid grasslands or cold alpine areas), trees dominate the vegetation of our area. Many of our trees are restricted to a narrow range of climatic conditions in our area. For example, hemlocks and redcedars occur only in our mild, wet climates, black spruce, a typically boreal species, grows in wetlands in the northern parts of the region, and ponderosa pine occupies warm arid sites. Other species, such as lodgepole pine and trembling aspen, occur over a wide range of climates.

Trees, whether alive, dead or decaying, provide habitats for many different organisms. They were also important for aboriginal people and provided sources of food, medicines, tools and shelter. The harvesting of trees and their conversion to lumber and other products supports the economies of many communities in our region. Forests are becoming increasingly more valued for recreation, as sources of new medicines and foods, and as sources of clean water and air.

Key to the trees

1a. Trees with broad leaves; flowers and fruits in catkins 2

  2a. Male and female catkins on separate trees; leaves finely toothed or with rounded teeth 3

    3a. Leaves triangular to heart-shaped with round stalks ... ***Populus balsamifera* ssp. *trichocarpa***

    3b. Leaves round with pointed tips and flat stalks .... ***Populus tremuloides***

  2b. Male and female catkins on same tree; leaves with double-toothed edges 4

    4a. Leaves triangular-shaped; bark peels readily .... ***Betula papyrifera***

    4b. Leaves oval-shaped; bark shiny and dark .... ***Betula occidentalis***

1b. Trees with needles or scale-like leaves 5

  5a. Trees with scale-like leaves, concealing the twigs 6

    6a. Leaf-covered twigs flattened; cones egg-shaped .... ***Thuja plicata***

    6b. Leaf-covered twigs round or squarish; cones round .... ***Chamaecyparis nootkatensis***

  5b. Trees with needles 7

    7a. Needles in clusters of 15 or more on short shoots; deciduous 8

      8a. Needles 3-angled, in clusters of 15–30 .... ***Larix occidentalis***

      8b. Needles 4-angled, in clusters of 30–40 .... ***Larix lyallii***

    7b. Needles single or in bundles of 2, 3 or 5; evergreen 9

      9a. Needles in bundles of 2, 3, or 5 10

        10a. Needles in bundles of 3, 10–20 cm long .... ***Pinus ponderosa***

        10b. Needles in bundles of 2 or 5 11

          11a. Needles in bundles of 2, stiff, pointed, 2–7 cm long .... ***Pinus contorta***

          11b. Needles usually in bundles of 5 12

            12a. Seed cones egg-shaped and almost stalkless, scales thick; needles with smooth edges 13

              13a. Cones 5–8 cm long, disintegrating to release seeds .... ***Pinus albicaulis***

              13b. Cones 7–22 cm long, opening while attached to tree .... ***Pinus flexilis***

*Pinus
monticola* *Pinus
contorta* *Pinus
albicaulis* *Abies
lasiocarpa* *Abies
amabilis* *Abies
grandis*

*Tsuga
heterophylla* *Picea
engelmannii* *Picea
glauca* *Pseudotsuga
menziesii* *Thuja
plicata*

BLACK COTTONWOOD • *Populus balsamifera* ssp. *trichocarpa* *P. trichocarpa*

GENERAL: Deciduous tree, to 40 m tall; trunk straight, to 1 m in diameter; crown narrow and columnar when young, becoming open, irregular and flattened with age; twigs with large, distinctive, **long, slender, reddish-brown buds** (2 cm long) covered with **sticky**, fragrant, yellowish gum.

BARK: Smooth, greenish to grey when young, becoming deeply furrowed and grey with age.

LEAVES: Triangular to heart-shaped, with **pointed tips** and finely toothed edges; dark green above, silvery green **often stained with rusty resin blotches below**, turning yellow in autumn; stalk round in cross-section.

FLOWERS: In male or female **catkins** borne on separate trees; hanging (female catkins 8–10 cm long); appearing before leaves.

FRUITS: Smooth, green, **bead-like capsules**; **split into 3 parts, releasing seeds with fluffy white hairs** that fill the air and resemble cotton or snowflakes.

ECOLOGY: Widespread and common on moist to wet lowlands, riverbanks, gravel bars, streambanks, lakeshores, swamps, seepage sites and disturbed uplands, mostly at low to mid elevations, but also in moist subalpine sites; withstands periodic flooding; shade intolerant; very frost resistant.

SIMILAR SPECIES: Balsam poplar (*P. balsamifera* ssp. *balsamifera*) is another subspecies of *P. balsamifera*. It has a more northern distribution and its fruit capsules split in two instead of three parts. • Trembling aspen (*P. tremuloides*, p. 29) is smaller than black cottonwood, and it has shorter leaves (to 7 cm long) with flattened leaf stalks and chalky-white bark.

NOTES: Black cottonwood cambium was occasionally used as food in many parts of our region, but it was only eaten when fresh in spring. The Secwepemc and Nlaka'pmx used the cottony seed fluff as a stuffing for pillows. The inner bark was used to make soap and a medicinal tea. The sticky resin on the buds has a pungent odour in spring and is used as an ointment for small cuts or as a makeshift glue. The Secwepemc used large trees to make dugout canoes. • Black cottonwood is an important stabilizer of riverbanks, and it maintains river islands and enhances fish habitat. Along streams, it provides shade, which keeps water temperatures low, and its decaying leaves provide a rich source of nutrients for caddis flies, mayflies and other insects—the food of young salmon and trout. Its twigs and buds also provide food for deer, moose and elk. Beavers prefer eating the inner bark and use the stems to construct dams. Woodpeckers nest in cavities in the trunks of old and decaying or dead trees. • **Black cottonwood rarely exceeds 200 years in age. It is our largest broadleaf tree and probably our fastest growing tree (to 2 m per year).** It is cultivated commercially for short-rotation fibre production. Its pulp is used in high grade paper for books and magazines. The wood is light coloured and straight grained, with a fine, even texture. It is used for making furniture, boxes and veneer. The high water content of black cottonwood makes it a poor source of firewood—it gives off little heat and generates lots of ash and soot. • The name *trichocarpa* is from the Greek *thrix*, 'hairy,' and *karpos*, 'a fruit.' The fluffy mass of seeds produced each spring gives rise to the common name 'cottonwood.'

TREMBLING ASPEN • *Populus tremuloides*

GENERAL: Small- to medium-sized **deciduous tree**, to 30 m tall; trunk 50–75 cm in diameter; **short, rounded crown**; extensive male or female clones formed by root suckers; lacks resinous buds.

BARK: Smooth, with a waxy appearance; **greenish grey to white**, with black scars where branches previously grew; becoming furrowed at base and grey to blackish with age; **does not peel** and lacks the dark, horizontal slits (lenticels) typically found on birch species.

LEAVES: Nearly circular, with abruptly pointed tips and **irregularly round-toothed edges**; deep green above, paler below, turning bright yellow to occasionally orange in autumn; **stalk flattened in cross-section**.

FLOWERS: In male and female **catkins** on separate trees; hanging (4–7 cm long); appearing before leaves.

FRUITS: Slender, **cone-shaped capsules** containing many tiny, light brown seeds with white fluffy hairs.

ECOLOGY: Widespread at low to subalpine elevations; most common in northern part of our region; occurs on a wide variety of sites, ranging from moist, open forests to the edges of dry grasslands; unable to tolerate saturated soils for prolonged periods; very shade intolerant.

NOTES: Trembling aspen reproduces mainly from root suckers following disturbances, such as cutting or fire. Reproduction from seed is rare in our area because the short period of seed viability seldom coincides with environmental conditions suitable for germination and early survival. Trembling aspens can occur in huge, long-lived clones that may be thousands of years old and cover several hectares. Individual clones are best distinguished in autumn or spring, when all trees of a clone leaf out or drop their leaves simultaneously. • The Carrier used rotten aspen wood as a diaper material and as a lining for baby cradles. The Nlaka'pmx sometimes made dugout canoes from this tree, and the Secwepemc used aspen to make tent poles and drying racks. There are records of early settlers extracting a quinine-like drug from the intensely bitter-tasting inner bark. • Trembling aspen provides important habitat for a number of wildlife species. Beavers feed on the bark and shoots, and cut down trees to construct dams and lodges. Many bird species nest in cavities of old or dead aspen. • Wood products made from aspen include pulp, flakeboard, lumber, studs, veneer, plywood, matches, chopsticks and novelty items. Aspen makes particularly good sauna benches and playground structures because the wood does not splinter. • The white bark and autumn colours of aspen are an

aesthetically pleasing contrast to dark conifers. Although trembling aspen is fast growing, it is not used as an ornamental because of its susceptibility to rot, insects and diseases, and because its roots tend to invade and plug sewer and drain pipes. • The common name refers to the leaves, which flutter in the slightest breeze. It is also known as quaking aspen, golden aspen, mountain aspen, popple, poplar and trembling poplar. An aboriginal name for trembling aspen translates as 'women's tongue' or 'noisy leaf.' French Canadian trappers reportedly believed that this tree supplied wood for the 'True Cross,' and since then it never ceased trembling.

PAPER BIRCH • *Betula papyrifera*

GENERAL: Deciduous tree, to 30–40 m tall; trunk to 75 cm in diameter, often **multi-stemmed**; crown loosely pyramidal when young, develops into a relatively short, round, open crown with upward-angled branches with nodding tips.

BARK: Reddish to coppery-brown when young, maturing to **white or cream**, with conspicuous **dark, horizontally elongated lines** (lenticels); **readily peels in sheets** exposing a reddish-orange inner bark that turns black with age; deeply fissured and black at the base of old trees.

LEAVES: Oval with pointed tips, and **coarse, irregular, double-toothed edges**, 15–20 teeth per side; 5–9 cm long; pale green, turning yellow in autumn.

FLOWERS: In male or female **catkins** borne **on the same tree**, appearing before leaves; female catkins shorter and thinner than male catkins.

FRUITS: Small, **winged nutlets** in erect female catkins that fall apart upon ripening.

ECOLOGY: Widespread and common at low to mid elevations on moist parts of southern Interior plateaus, Coast/Interior Transition and wet Columbia Mountains, in moist forests, seepage sites and on floodplains; also on disturbed moist uplands; restricted to seepage sites and floodplains in our hot dry climates; unable to withstand long periods of drought or saturated soils; shade intolerant and extremely frost tolerant.

NOTES: Paper birch is fast growing but rarely lives more than 140 years. The paper birch found in our region represents one of six varieties distributed across Canada. It hybridizes extensively with other birch species including water birch (*B. occidentalis*). Paper birch favourably influences site productivity through its ability to cycle nutrients and contribute organic matter from falling leaves to the soil surface. It readily sprouts from cut stumps and re-sprouts following wildfires. Paper birch provides valuable browse for wildlife such as deer and moose. The seeds attract many birds in autumn. • The aboriginal peoples of our region used the bark widely to make baskets, canoes and baby cradles. They stripped it from the tree in rectangular sheets in late spring, and sewed it with split cedar or spruce roots. The Carrier also used the bark to make toboggans. The Secwepemc made soap and shampoo from birch leaves, and the Nlaka'pmx used birch sap as a tonic. • Paper birch with its showy bark and delicate foliage makes an attractive ornamental for landscaping. **Do not peel bark from live trees, as this causes permanent, unsightly black scars and can kill the tree.** • Paper birch wood has a fine, even texture and uniform grain and can be easily worked on a lathe. It is used for veneers, pulpwood and many specialty items, such as ice cream sticks, toothpicks, spools and toys. It makes excellent firewood, because it splits easily and burns cleanly. • Recent research indicates that betulinic acid, which makes birch bark white, shows promise in treating skin cancer and may one day be an ingredient of sun screens and tanning lotions. • Other names for paper birch are 'white birch,' 'canoe birch' and 'silver birch.' The species name *papyrifera* means 'paper-bearing,' and it refers to the papery bark.

WATER BIRCH • *Betula occidentalis*

GENERAL: Coarse shrub or small deciduous tree, to 10 m tall; downy surface on young twigs becoming covered with **wart-like crystalline glands** that look like octopus suckers (under 10x magnification).

BARK: Usually smooth, thin and **shiny, dark reddish brown**, with long, horizontal whitish lenticels; **does not readily peel off.**

LEAVES: Egg-shaped, broadest below middle, **with double-toothed edges**, tapering gradually to a blunt or sharp tip; 3–5 cm long; shiny, **yellowish green above,** pale and dotted with fine glands below, turning yellowish brown in autumn.

FLOWERS: In separate male or female catkins on the same tree; **developing at same time as leaves**; male catkins drooping, **female catkins erect**, not woody or cone-like.

FRUITS: Tiny, hairy **nutlets** with wings broader than the seed.

ECOLOGY: Widespread and locally common at low to mid elevations on our dry plateaus and in East Kootenays, on moist to wet, nutrient-rich soils, streambanks, seepage sites and forest openings.

NOTES: Hybrids of water birch and paper birch (*B. papyrifera*) occur in our area. The two species form offspring of tremendously variable but intermediate characteristics. The bark of hybrids tends to peel readily with age. • Birches reproduce from seed and from sprouts after cutting. • Water birch provides important habitat for many species of birds and mammals that live near streams, lakes and marshes. • The Okanagan recognized water birch as the birch whose bark does not peel off. They used it mainly for firewood. The Flathead harvested sap from hollowed-out cavities and drank it as a sweet beverage. • Water birch is too small to be used commercially but has been used locally for fence posts and fuel. • The genus name *Betula* means 'pitch,' and it refers to the bituminous content of the bark, which is responsible for its high flammability. The common name refers to this birch's affinity for water— it grows predominantly along watercourses and lakeshores.

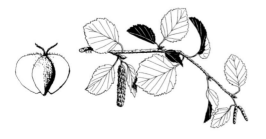

WESTERN LARCH • *Larix occidentalis*

GENERAL: Large, **deciduous conifer**, to 55 m tall; long, clear trunk, to 1–1.3 m in diameter; open, pyramidal crown; short branches.

BARK: Thin and scaly when young, becoming thick (to 15 cm), plated, deeply furrowed, **reddish brown** and resembling ponderosa pine from a distance when older.

LEAVES: Deciduous needles, soft, pale yellow-green, turning **bright yellow in autumn**, triangular in cross-section; **in circular clusters of 15–30** on spur twigs, and singly along current year's growth.

CONES: Oval when closed, egg-shaped when open (2–4 cm long), on short stalk; scales wider than long; **long, slender bract tips extend beyond scales.**

ECOLOGY: Widespread and common in mixed upland stands; often associated with our drier cedar/hemlock forests at low to mid elevations in wet Columbia Mountains south of Shuswap Lake and mid-elevation Douglas-fir/lodgepole pine forests east of Okanagan Lake; most common on north aspects at 900–1,500 m; very shade intolerant; grows in even-aged stands or as large individuals that have survived wildfires.

SIMILAR SPECIES: Alpine larch (*L. lyallii*, p. 33) has hairy young twigs, 4-sided needles and occurs at high elevations. Alpine larch is known to hybridize with western larch where their populations overlap.

NOTES: Western larch is the largest of the larches. It is well known for its changing crown, which is lustrous green in summer, bright yellow in autumn and bare in winter. Its autumn colours enhance the beauty of many landscapes. • Western larch grows in ecosystems with frequent forest fires. The thick bark and early self-pruning of mature trees provides some fire protection, although older trees are frequently fire-scarred at the base. Larch seeds germinate readily and grow rapidly on fire-blackened soils. Fire prevention and selective logging, coupled with its shade intolerance, have contributed to a reduction in the abundance of larch in many areas. The larch casebearer (*Coleophora laricella*), accidentally imported from Europe, is a major pest that feeds on young foliage. • The native peoples of our region used the bark and foliage of western larch medicinally. It produces a sweet-tasting gum that hardens when exposed. At any time of year, the Secwepemc, Nlaka'pmx, Okanagan and Ktunaxa broke off this gum and chewed it. Galactan, a natural sugar in the gum, resembles a slightly bitter honey and can be used for medicine or baking powder. Trees can be tapped for a sap from which moisture is evaporated to produce a syrup that is mixed with sweeteners. • Western larch yields exceptionally high quality construction materials and is often used in heavy construction. It also makes good firewood. The bark contains Arabino galactan, a water soluble gum used for offset lithography and in pharmaceuticals, paint and ink products. • Western larch is also known as western tamarack, tamarack, hackmatack or mountain larch. It was described in 1806 by the Lewis and Clark expedition but was not recognized as a new species until 1849, when it was named by Thomas Nuttall.

ALPINE LARCH • *Larix lyallii*

GENERAL: Deciduous conifer, to 10–25 m tall; short, straight, sturdy trunk, to 30–60 cm in diameter, tapering into a broad, **irregularly shaped crown**; gnarled, irregularly spaced branches; twigs densely hairy.

BARK: Thin, smooth and yellowish grey when young, developing dark reddish-brown, fissured and scaly surface with age.

LEAVES: Deciduous needles, pointed, light green, turning golden-yellow in early autumn, square in cross-section, 0.5–3 cm long; in **bunches of 30–40** on twig spurs or singly on current year's growth.

CONES: Elliptic, upright, purplish when young, turning brown at maturity, 3–5 cm long; scales rounded, lower surface with matted hairs at maturity, with **slender-tipped bracts extending beyond scales**.

ECOLOGY: Locally common and widespread in Selkirk, Purcell and Rocky mountains, and in Cathedral and Manning parks, on high, cool, exposed slopes often with rocky, coarse-textured soils; favoured on north aspects where snow falls early and stays late; extremely shade intolerant and hardy.

SIMILAR SPECIES: Alpine larch can be distinguished from its low-elevation relative western larch (*L. occidentalis*, p. 32) by the **woolly hairs that cover its buds, young twigs and lower cone scales**. Its needles are square in cross-section rather than triangular as in western larch. The two species sometimes hybridize where their distributions overlap.

NOTES: Alpine larch ekes out an existence on sites that are too cold for most other trees. Its deciduous nature helps it resist snow and avalanche damage. For most of the year branches are bare, except for the blackened, dead cones. Unlike the thick-barked, fire-resistant western larch, alpine larch has thin bark and a low resistance to surface fires. • Mountain goats, bighorn sheep and black and grizzly bears all feed in alpine larch stands. Blue grouse apparently feed on larch needles. A survival soup can be made from the young twigs of alpine larch. • Although its wood is heavy and hard, alpine larch is not used commercially because of its small size, poor form and inaccessibility. Its unusual hardiness makes it ideal for reclamation work at high elevations. It greatest value, however, is aesthetic. The soft green of newly opened needles delights springtime hikers, and the autumn sight of golden trees against a background of fresh snowfall and blue skies is breathtaking. • Alpine larch is also called woolly larch, tamarack, Lyall larch and subalpine larch. The species name *lyallii* honours a Scottish surgeon and naturalist, David Lyall, who first described this species in 1858.

 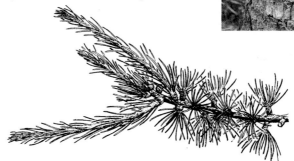

PONDEROSA PINE • *Pinus ponderosa*

GENERAL: Large **conifer**, to 15–30 m tall; straight trunk, to 1–1.5 m in diameter, with a slight taper; symmetrical, broad, open crown (very old trees have flattened tops); many stout branches.

BARK: Light **orange-brown to cinnamon**, with deeply incised, black fissures and large, **puzzle-shaped plates** that easily flake off; dark brown to black and scaly when young; 8–10 cm thick on older trees.

LEAVES: Evergreen needles, in **bundles of 3**, yellow- to grey-green, flexible and slender, 10–20 cm long (**longer than those of any other conifer in B.C.**).

CONES: Oval to broadly conical, 8–14 cm long, borne in groups of 1–3, reddish purple when young and brown at maturity; with thick scales **armed with a firm sharp prickle**; seed quite small (6–8 mm long) with a large wing (2.5 cm).

ECOLOGY: Forms open forests in our hot, dry valleys at low elevations (to about 900 m), and to 1,500 m on dry, southern exposures; ranges north to about Clinton and Little Fort; very tolerant of high temperatures and drought.

NOTES: Ponderosa pine rarely exceeds 400–600 years in age. Natural fires frequently burn through ponderosa pine forests. Mature trees are protected from ground fires by their thick bark and self-pruning, which reduce the risk of fire reaching the canopy. Seedlings, however, are readily killed by fire. Successful fire control and selective logging during the past 40–50 years has led to the replacement of ponderosa pine by more shade-tolerant Douglas-fir (*Pseudotsuga menziesii*). • Ponderosa pine forests provide important spring and autumn range for cattle, and winter range for many wildlife species including deer, elk and bighorn sheep. The seeds attract many birds and small mammals. Ponderosa pines also have tremendous aesthetic appeal. Stands of the widely spaced, stately trees with warm and beautiful cinnamon-coloured bark are park-like. • In spring, the Nlaka'pmx, Okanagan, Secwepemc and Ktunaxa collected and ate the cambium from young trees. The Okanagan used the reddish pitch as chewing gum. Many Interior native people gathered the seeds in autumn and used the wood to produce quick, hot, smokeless fires. Fissures in older bark give off a vanilla-like aroma. • Ponderosa pine produces a light softwood that is used in construction, sashes, frames, mouldings, cabinets and crates. • Ponderosa pine is also known as yellow pine, western yellow pine, bull pine and rock pine. It was first described by Lewis and Clark in 1804. The name 'ponderosa' was given to it by David Douglas, in recognition of the great size of the trees.

LODGEPOLE PINE • *Pinus contorta* var. *latifolia*

GENERAL: Medium-sized **conifer**, to 20–25 m tall (rarely to 40 m); straight, slender trunk, 30 cm in diameter (rarely to 90 cm); short, open, pyramidal crown.

BARK: Thin, orange-brown to grey, covered by small, loose scales.

LEAVES: Evergreen needles in **bundles of 2**, yellow-green, pointed, stiff and often twisted, somewhat square in cross-section, 2–7 cm long; seedlings have an initial cluster of 3–6 needles.

CONES: Short cylindrical to **asymmetrical and lop-sided**, 2–5 cm long, tawny, **armed with prickles**; **often remain closed and hanging unopened in clusters** when mature.

ECOLOGY: Widespread and common from low elevations to treeline on a wide variety of soils and drainage conditions, from rock outcrops to deep, rich soils to saturated organic deposits.

NOTES: Lodgepole pine is **distinguished from all other pines** in our region by its needles, which are borne in **bundles of two**. • Lodgepole pine rarely lives for more than 300 years. It is abundant where forest fires have been common. Unlike ponderosa pine (*P. ponderosa*) and western larch (*Larix occidentalis*), mature lodgepole pine has thin bark and is easily killed by fire. However, many lodgepole pine cones are sealed shut by a resin that must be melted before the seeds are released. A tremendous amount of seed is stockpiled between fires to re-populate burned areas. Initial densities of lodgepole pine as high as 100,000 trees per hectare are not unusual. When they reach about 100–140 years of age, extensive, even-aged stands of lodgepole pine are susceptible to mountain pine beetle attacks. In turn, large areas of beetle-killed trees provide a hazardous fuel complex that contributes to highly destructive fires. • Interior native peoples used the trees to make fishing spears and poles for constructing their dwellings. The sweet, succulent inner bark of lodgepole pine was an important food of the native peoples of the Interior. It can be harvested in late May or June when the sap is running. It was usually eaten fresh, although the Secwepemc also dried it for later use. The Secwepemc also used lodgepole pine bark in a remedy for coughs and tuberculosis. • Lodgepole pine wood is light-coloured

and straight-grained, and it has a soft, even texture. It makes high quality lumber that is easily worked with power or hand tools. These qualities make it useful for constructing windows, doors, mouldings and furniture and for framing residential buildings. • Lodgepole pine is also known as black pine, scrub pine and mountain pine. It is often incorrectly called jackpine, which more properly refers to *P. banksiana*. The name 'lodgepole pine' was given to this plant by Lewis and Clark, who observed the narrow, straight stems being used as poles to support tipis and lodges.

WHITEBARK PINE • *Pinus albicaulis*

GENERAL: High-elevation conifer, seldom more than 15 m tall; often with several **twisted stems** (to 60 cm in diameter); **sprawling crown** resulting from snow breakage.

BARK: Brown scaly plates with narrow fissures; thin, smooth, greyish white to chalky white when young.

LEAVES: Evergreen needles, in **bundles of 5**, stiff, slightly curved, dull to bluish green, 3–8 cm long; clustered toward branch tips.

CONES: Conical to egg-shaped, 5–8 cm long, purplish turning brown, often very pitchy; thick scales with blunt triangular tips that lack prickles; solitary or in pairs, **almost stalkless, disintegrating to disperse seeds** and **seldom falling from trees intact**; seeds large (8–12 mm), elliptic, dark brown and wingless.

ECOLOGY: Infrequent and locally common in Monashee, Selkirk, Purcell, Coast and Rocky mountains above 1,500 m to treeline; scattered elsewhere at high elevations; frequently on dry, southern exposures and exposed windswept ridges, often on very thin soils; drought resistant, shade intolerant and frost hardy.

SIMILAR SPECIES: Whitebark pine closely resembles limber pine (*P. flexilis*, p. 37), which grows on the western slopes of the Rocky Mountains in the southeast Kootenays. Limber pine cones are 2–3 times longer, and they remain intact when mature. • Whitebark pine is distinguished from western white pine (*P. monticola*, p. 38) by its stout, stiff, shorter needles and much shorter cones.

NOTES: Whitebark pine is unique among native pines in that its cones do not open until they disintegrate at maturity. Whitebark pine seeds are heavy and wingless, falling near the base of the tree. Seed dispersal depends on Clark's nutcrackers, which in turn depend on the seeds for food. Many mammals, including grizzly bears and red squirrels, also eat the seeds. • Whitebark pine is not used commercially for lumber but is valued for wildlife habitat, watershed protection and aesthetics. It has potential for stabilizing snow and soil on steep terrain in high-elevation reclamation projects. Whitebark pine grows slowly and lives long, but is highly susceptible to blister rust when young. • Interior Salish, including the Nlaka'pmx, Okanagan, Secwepemc and St'at'imc and Ktunaxa, harvested whitebark pine seed in early autumn. They crushed the nuts and mixed them with saskatoon berries for eating or pounded them to make a fine flour. They roasted cones in pits overnight before removing the seeds. The Secwepemc and Flathead Salish sometimes scraped off the cambium and ate it. The fibrous roots were used to sew bark together and to weave watertight containers and canoes. • The species name *albicaulis* is from the Latin *albi*, 'white,' and *caulis,* 'a stem.'

LIMBER PINE • *Pinus flexilis*

GENERAL: Small- to medium-sized conifer, to 9–15 m tall; **short, stout, tapered stem**, to 35–60 cm in diameter; often **crooked, broadly rounded crown** (deformed and shrub-like on windswept ridges); large plume-like, often hanging branches nearly reach the ground.

BARK: Light grey and smooth, becoming dark brown and furrowed into scaly ridges or rectangular plates; 2–5 cm thick on old trees.

LEAVES: Evergreen needles, in **bundles of 5,** dark green, slightly curved, rigid, 3–8 cm long; triangular in cross-section; densely crowded on ends of branchlets.

CONES: Cylindrical, 7–22 cm long, lustrous yellow maturing to light brown, **short-stalked and unarmed**; scales thick, rounded and blunt; opening while attached to the tree; seeds **large, thick, wingless,** reddish brown and darkly mottled.

ECOLOGY: Locally common on western slopes of Rocky Mountains in southeastern part of our area, at 1,500–2,000 m; mainly as scattered individuals on a wide variety of substrates, but most frequently found on rocky ridges and steep rocky slopes with a southern exposure; shade intolerant, frost hardy and drought resistant.

SIMILAR SPECIES: This species is sometimes confused with whitebark pine (*P. albicaulis,* p. 36) particularly where their ranges overlap in the Rockies. Both have similar form, foliage and nut-like wingless seeds, but **limber pine cones are 2–3 times longer than those of whitebark pine and remain intact upon maturity**.

NOTES: Limber pine has a restricted distribution in our region. Its slow growth rate, drought resistance and ability to withstand harsh climatic conditions make it suitable for regenerating high-elevation windswept slopes. It is an extremely long-lived tree; the oldest known individual is more than 1,000 years old. • The large seeds of limber pine are a nutritious food source to birds and small mammals and were important to early pioneers and native people. Clark's nutcracker plays a significant role in dispersing the heavy seeds. They cache seeds on windswept ridges and south aspects where snow does not accumulate. The location of both limber and whitebark pines probably reflects the dispersal activities of Clark's nutcracker rather than any site preference of the pine. • Limber pine has potential as an ornamental tree or shrub. Several cultivars, including a dwarf form, are available commercially. • Limber pine is also known as white pine or Rocky Mountain white pine. It was first described by Dr. Edwin James, an army surgeon, in 1820. The species name is from the Latin *flexi,* meaning 'bent' or 'pliant,' and it refers to the flexible, rope-like branches that bend to release snow in winter.

WESTERN WHITE PINE • *Pinus monticola*

GENERAL: Beautiful, large **conifer**, to 30–50 m tall; straight trunk, often over 1 m in diameter, with little taper; symmetrical, open, conical crown of horizontal, conspicuously whorled branches with ascending tips.

BARK: Very **thin, silvery grey and smooth**, often with resin blisters when young, develops into thick, dark purplish-grey, **square plates on mature** trunks.

LEAVES: Evergreen needles, in **bundles of 5**, thin, soft, bluish green, 5–12 cm long, with a whitish waxy coating.

CONES: Long (**12–25 cm**), slender, cylindrical and slightly curved, resinous, greenish when young to reddish brown at maturity; scales flattened and lack prickles; **hanging** from high branch tips.

ECOLOGY: Widespread and common in Columbia Mountains near Shuswap, Kootenay and Arrow lakes, also scattered along leeward slopes of Coast Mountains where wet coastal influence is felt; at low to subalpine elevations on a wide range of sites from bogs to well-drained sandy soils; intermediate in shade tolerance, frost hardiness and drought resistance.

SIMILAR SPECIES: Our other 5-needle pines, whitebark pine (*P. albicaulis*, p. 36) and limber pine (*P. flexilis*, p. 37), are restricted to high elevations, and their needles are usually less than 5 cm long.

NOTES: Western white pine is commonly infected by blister rust, a fungus that was accidentally introduced on the Coast in the early 1900s and spread to the Interior about 1930. It infects all the 5-needle pines in North America. The rust generally erupts as cankers on the branches within 2.5 m of the ground. As the canker spreads to girdle the branch, the part beyond the canker dies. Pruning branches before the rust spreads to the main stem has proven successful in saving young white pines. Attempts to eradicate currants and gooseberries (*Ribes* spp.), which serve as an alternate host in the life cycle of the rust, have been unsuccessful. • The Eastern Secwepemc used white pine bark to make canoes. Interior native people occasionally ate the seeds and the Secwepemc and Nlaka'pmx used the pitch medicinally. • The non-resinous, straight-grained wood has good dimensional stability, which makes it suitable for mouldings, sashes, frames, doors, interior panelling and furniture. The wood is ideal for carving because of its fine grain and uniform texture. It is also highly prized for pattern making. • Western white pine is named for its light-coloured wood. It is also known as mountain white pine and silver pine. It was described and named by David Douglas in 1825. The species name *monticola* is from the Latin *monti*, 'a mountain,' and *cola*, 'to dwell.'

SUBALPINE FIR • *Abies lasiocarpa*

GENERAL: Large **conifer**, to 25–30 m tall (sometimes to 35 m), prostrate shrub at timberline; tapered trunk, to 30–60 cm in diameter (sometimes to 1 m); dense, **long, narrow, cone-shaped crown** terminates in a conspicuous spire; horizontal to downward sweeping, distinctly whorled branches that reach the ground when open grown.

BARK: Smooth, ash-grey, with **raised resin blisters** when young; becoming patterned in **blocky scales** with dark grey fissures with age.

LEAVES: Evergreen needles, flat, dark green, with **blunt, often notched tips**; crowded and tending to curve upward, **whitish lines (stomata) on both surfaces**.

CONES: Cylindrical, purplish grey, 6–10 cm long, often covered with pitch; sitting **upright**, mostly near top of tree, **disintegrating on tree** when mature, leaving a central spike.

ECOLOGY: Widespread and common in cool, moist, snowy, subalpine forests; also common at low to mid elevations on a wide range of sites in our moister climates; extremely shade tolerant and frost hardy, intolerant of drought and high temperatures.

NOTES: Subalpine fir is the most widespread true fir in western North America and the smallest of our true firs. Its dense, A-shaped crown readily sheds snow and ice. The lower branches sometimes take root, resulting in vegetative reproduction called 'layering.' Layering contributes to the development of clusters of trees at timberline. Subalpine fir rarely exceeds 400 years in age. It is prone to Indian paint fungus (*Echinodontium tinctorum*) and bark beetle attack with age. • The Secwepemc, Okanagan and St'at'imc called subalpine fir the 'medicine tree.' Like the pitch of grand fir, its pitch, extracted from blisters, was taken internally to cure tuberculosis. A tea made from the bark was used as a cough remedy. Interior native people used the sweet-smelling boughs for bedding and as a wash. • The wood of subalpine fir is light, generally straight and even grained and ranges from whitish to yellowish brown in colour. Commercially, it produces construction materials, plywood, boxes, crates and pulp. Subalpine fir has a poor reputation because of its low wood density and high moisture content and because much of the wood being used is from old trees with centre rot. • Subalpine fir is often erroneously called balsam. It is also known as white balsam, alpine fir and Rocky Mountain fir. The species name *lasiocarpa* is from the Greek *lasio*, 'shaggy' or 'hairy,' and *carpos*, 'a fruit,' and it refers to the cones, which fall apart upon maturity.

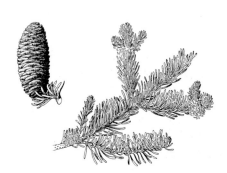

PACIFIC SILVER FIR • *Abies amabilis*

GENERAL: Large **conifer**, to 25–40 m tall; trunk to 60–80 cm in diameter; rigid, dense, cylindrical to cone-shaped crown (broadly rounded on older slow-growing trees); branches perpendicular to trunk and distinctly whorled.

BARK: Thin, smooth, ash-grey, with large irregular chalk-coloured blotches and **resin blisters** on young stems, becoming ridged and scaly with age.

LEAVES: Evergreen needles, lustrous dark green, white-banded below, flat, with a central groove above, **notched at tip; lying flat along both sides of twigs, needles along top of branch point forward**.

CONES: Cylindrical to **barrel-shaped**, green turning deep purple when ripe, 8–15 cm long; sitting **stiffly erect** in upper canopy, **disintegrating on tree** when mature, leaving a central spike.

ECOLOGY: Scattered and locally common in cool, moist forests at mid to subalpine elevations in valleys on leeward slopes of Coast Mountains in southwest part of our region; very shade tolerant.

NOTES: Pacific silver fir grows best in a wet climate, but it tolerates summer drought if there is adequate moisture early in the growing season. Its most serious threat is the balsam woolly aphid, a defoliating insect introduced from Europe. Because of fires, insects, rot, avalanches and windthrow, individuals rarely live beyond 500 years. • The Lil'wet'ul probably used this tree like grand and subalpine firs, and used the branches to cover berries in their baskets when packing them home. • The wood of Pacific silver fir is odourless, light in weight and colour, and has a clean appearance. It is used commercially for doors, windows, furniture parts, mouldings and food containers. The wood properties are very similar to those of western hemlock and the two are often marketed together. • A sticky pitch from this and other true firs, known as Canadian balsam, is used as a mounting material for microscope slides. • Pacific silver fir is sometimes planted as an ornamental. • The common name refers to the silvery lower surface of the foliage. Another common name, 'balsam fir,' refers to the pitch contained in blisters on the trunk. Pacific silver fir is also known as amabilis fir. The species name *amabilis* is from the Latin *amabili*, 'lovely.'

GRAND FIR • *Abies grandis*
A. aromatica

GENERAL: Large **conifer**, to 25–40 m tall; straight trunk, to 50–85 cm in diameter; conically symmetrical crown; branches sweeping downward and turning upward.

BARK: Relatively smooth, ash-grey, with white blotches when young, deeply furrowed with reddish-brown scaly ridges on old trunks; **blisters** contain sticky, **balsam-odoured resins**.

LEAVES: Evergreen needles, flat, flexible, deeply grooved, very dark green and glossy above, 2 white lines (stomata) below, **blunt and notched at tip**; spreading horizontally at right angles to twig, in flat, **comb-like rows**; crushed needles give off a **pleasant citrus smell**.

CONES: Cylindrical to barrel-shaped, bright green to dark purplish at maturity, 5–10 cm long; **sitting upright** on highest branches, **disintegrating on tree** when mature and releasing large-winged seeds, leaving a central spike.

ECOLOGY: Confined to southern valleys of Kootenay and Arrow lake regions, southern Selkirk and Purcell mountains, at low to mid elevations; shade tolerant.

SIMILAR SPECIES: Grand fir can be distinguished from Pacific silver fir (*A. amabilis*, p. 40) by the flat, spreading arrangement of its needles. Some Pacific silver fir needles point forward along the tops of the twigs.

NOTES: Grand fir is moderately fast growing and fairly short-lived, averaging 250–300 years. It is very susceptible to Indian paint fungus (*Echinodontium tinctorum*), lacks decay-inhibiting properties, and does not exude pitch to cover wounds. • Grand fir bark bears blisters that contain a fragrant, transparent, resin that has been used on insect bites and small cuts to prevent infection, to clean teeth and as a glue. Native people used grand fir in the same way as subalpine fir (*A. lasiocarpa*). • The soft, light, odourless, relatively weak wood is primarily used for pulp. All firs make attractive Christmas trees because of their wonderful aroma and naturally dense symmetrical crowns. • Grand fir was first described by David Douglas, and it was first cultivated in 1830 from seeds he took back to Great Britain. • The common name refers to the large size of the mature trees. Other common names are white fir, balsam fir, yellow fir and lowland fir. The species was originally given the botanical name *A. aromatica* because of the odour of its crushed needles.

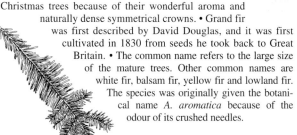

WESTERN HEMLOCK • *Tsuga heterophylla*

GENERAL: Large **conifer**, to 35 m tall; clear trunk, to 75 cm in diameter; short, open, pyramidal crown with a **flexible drooping leader**; slender drooping branches with **delicate, feathery foliage**.

BARK: Scaly, russet brown to dark greyish brown when young, developing furrows separated by flat ridges with age; thin, even on older trees; inner bark **dark orange, streaked with purple**.

LEAVES: Evergreen needles, flat, blunt, yellowish green; short and **unequal in length**; arranged in **flat, feathery sprays**.

CONES: Elliptic, purplish green turning light brown when mature, 1–3 cm long; scales thin with wavy edges; **hanging on short stalks**, falling **intact** when mature.

ECOLOGY: Widespread and common on a wide variety of sites at low to mid elevations in Columbia Mountains and wet parts of East Kootenays; also scattered throughout leeward slopes of Coast Mountains where Coastal climatic conditions prevail; prefers acidic soils with thick humus; seedlings commonly found on decaying logs and stumps; very shade tolerant but not frost or drought resistant.

SIMILAR SPECIES: Western hemlock cones are half to one-third the length of cones of mountain hemlock (*T. mertensiana*, p. 43). These two species can also be distinguished by their **needles, which are arranged radially around the twig in mountain hemlock** and in flat sprays in western hemlock.

NOTES: Western hemlock usually achieves a maximum age of about 500 years in the Interior. Old Interior hemlock stands are generally heavily infected by Indian paint fungus (*Echinodontium tinctorum*), a stem rot that commonly forms conks (shelf-like growths) on the trunk. • Some Interior native peoples used hemlock boughs as a disinfectant and deodorizer. The boughs are excellent bedding material, and they were sometimes used medicinally. • Western hemlock wood is fairly hard and strong, and it has an even grain and uniform colour. It resists scraping and is easy to machine, so it is widely used for doors, windows, staircases and mouldings, louvred cupboards and decorative doors, and general construction. It provides an alternative to oak, maple and birch for flooring. It also treats well for use as pilings, poles and railway ties. It is one of the best pulpwoods and is a source of alpha cellulose for making cellophane, rayon and plastic. • The soft, feathery foliage of western hemlock makes it an attractive garden ornamental. Several cultivars, including a dwarf form, are available commercially. • Western hemlock is also known as Pacific hemlock and West Coast hemlock. The needles, when crushed, have an odour similar to herbaceous hemlock, hence the common name. The species name *heterophylla* means 'variable leaves.'

MOUNTAIN HEMLOCK • *Tsuga mertensiana*

GENERAL: Medium-sized **conifer**, to 10–25 m tall (low sprawling shrub on windswept ridges); strongly tapered trunk, to 60–100 cm in diameter, but often smaller; narrow, pyramidal crown with a **slightly drooping leader**; slender drooping branches irregularly spaced on trunk.

BARK: Thin and rough when young, becoming thick, hard, grey to dark brown with deep, narrow furrows with age.

LEAVES: Evergreen needles, stout, blunt, bluish green, with a semi-circular cross-section; **radially arranged**, in all directions around branch and in star-like clusters.

CONES: Oblong to cylindrical, purplish, turning brown, 2–8 cm long; scales thin with rough edges; **stalkless** and **hanging, falling intact** when mature.

ECOLOGY: Locally common at subalpine to treeline in Coast/Interior Transition and central portions of Columbia Mountains near Revelstoke, in cool moist forests on north aspects with acidic soils and deep organic deposits; does best in sheltered mountainous locations with heavy snowfall; very shade tolerant.

SIMILAR SPECIES: Mountain hemlock has cones that are 2–3 times longer than those of western hemlock (*T. heterophylla*, p. 42). These two species can also be distinguished by their needles, which are arranged radially around the twig in mountain hemlock and lay flat in western hemlock.

NOTES: Mountain hemlock reaches 800 years in age. It is slow growing and occurs in areas that have a deep, insulating snow pack that accumulates early in autumn. The crown architecture of mountain hemlock sheds snow readily and avoids breakage.
• The species is considered important for watershed protection and aesthetics. The wood is considered inferior for construction materials. The bark contains large quantities of tannin.
• Mountain hemlock is sometimes called black hemlock. The species name *mertensiana* honours Karl Mertens, a German naturalist and physician who first described the species in Sitka, Alaska. The genus name *Tsuga* is from the Japanese *tsu-ga,* 'tree-mother.' The spruce-like cones prompted early taxonomists to consider mountain hemlock a species of spruce. John Muir also referred to it as hemlock spruce.

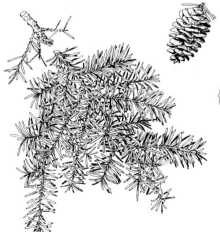

ENGELMANN SPRUCE • *Picea engelmannii*

GENERAL: Large **conifer**, to 25–40 m tall, or prostrate shrub at treeline; cylindrical trunk, to 30–90 in cm diameter; symmetrical, narrowly pyramidal crown; **twigs finely hairy** (when viewed with a hand lens) with **residual peg-like structures when needles are removed**.

BARK: Very thin, purplish grey, broken into large, thin, **loosely attached scales**; silvery-white inner bark.

LEAVES: Stiff, evergreen needles, pointed and somewhat sharp to the touch, bluish green, squarish in cross-section; **spreading on all sides of twig**, but tending to curve and point upward and toward branch tips; with an unpleasant odour when crushed.

CONES: Oblong-cylindrical, light chestnut-brown, 2–8 cm long; **scale tips are narrowed, papery, thin and jagged**; hanging on short stalks; opening in autumn and falling intact later in winter.

ECOLOGY: Widespread and common on a variety of sites at subalpine to treeline; also extending to low elevations on seepage sites, floodplains and lakeshores; moderately shade tolerant and frost hardy.

SIMILAR SPECIES: The distributions of Engelmann spruce and white spruce (*P. glauca*, p. 45) overlap throughout our region. At low and mid elevations, they often form hybrids with characteristics intermediate between the two spruces. This hybrid white spruce (*P. glauca* x *engelmannii*) is often called interior spruce. **The cone scales of Engelmann spruce are flexible, narrowed toward the tip and ragged, and those of white spruce are stiff, smooth and rounded at the tip.** Hybrid white spruce has cone scales that are intermediate between them.

NOTES: Engelmann spruce is long-lived—to 1,000 years old. It is one of the most cold-tolerant species in the world, able to survive temperatures down to -60° C. When mature, it can also tolerate considerable summer frost. • The Nlaka'pmx and Secwepemc made canoes from the bark, used the split roots for sewing baskets and bark canoes. The pitch was widely used as a poultice for sores and slivers. The Nlaka'pmx also boiled the tips of branches and used them as a wash for purification. The Carrier chewed the emerging needles as a treatment for coughs. • Engelmann spruce is one of the most important commercial species in the Interior. The wood is quite uniform and strong. It is used to produce construction lumber, plywood, mine timbers, poles and ties. Its long fibres, light colour and low resin content make it an excellent source of pulp. Because the wood has very little pitch it is also used for food containers including barrels. Its resonance qualities make it valuable for piano sounding boards and violins. The bark is sometimes used in tanning leather. • Engelmann spruce is named after George Engelmann (1809–84), a German botanist, physician and meteorologist who moved to the U.S. in 1835. Other common names include Columbia spruce, mountain spruce and silver spruce. The genus name *Picea* is from the Latin *pix* or *picis,* meaning 'pitch-pine.'

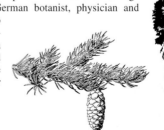

WHITE SPRUCE • *Picea glauca*

GENERAL: Medium-size **conifer**, to 20–35 m tall; slightly tapered, slender, cylindrical trunk, to 40–75 cm in diameter; narrow to broadly pyramidal crown often extending to the ground; branches drooping slightly; twigs hairless with **residual peg-like structures when needles are removed**.

BARK: Thin, irregularly shaped, **flaky scales**; light greyish brown.

LEAVES: Stiff, sharply pointed, blue-green, **evergreen needles**, square in cross-section; tending to be crowded on upper side of twig; with a **skunk-like odour** when crushed.

CONES: Oblong-cylindrical, light brown, 3–8 cm long; scales are thin and rounded, with **smooth, thumbnail-like edges**; nearly stalkless, hanging; opening in autumn and falling intact later in winter.

ECOLOGY: Widespread and common on western half of Fraser Plateau at low to mid elevations, in wet draws, depressions, swamps, floodplains and seepage sites; shade tolerant.

SIMILAR SPECIES: Hybrid white spruce (*P. glauca* x *engelmannii*) is the most common, widespread spruce at low to mid elevations in our area. Individual trees share characteristics common to both white spruce and Engelmann spruce (*P. engelmannii*, p. 44) , and most trees have intermediate leaf, twig and cone characteristics. Pure white spruce forests are most common north of our region and east of the Rockies. • Black spruce (*P. mariana*, p. 46), another low-elevation spruce, has cone scales that are rounded and shorter than those of either white or Engelmann spruce. The cones of black spruce are also persistent, and they remain on the tree for several years.

NOTES: White spruce and its hybrids reach 250–400 years of age. They are often shallow rooted, and they are susceptible to windthrow, especially on shallow or wet soils. Large-scale blowdowns are prime breeding areas for spruce beetle, which can spread into mature timber and kill thousands of hectares of old-growth spruce. • Historically, white spruce provided shelter and fuel for settlers and native people. The Tsilhqot'in ate the cambium, and the Secwepemc, Nlaka'pmx and Tsilhqot'in chewed the hard resinous pitch. The roots were widely used for sewing and lashing objects together. Spruce pitch and extracts from boiled needles were used for medicinal purposes. The boughs were used for bedding. • White spruce is one of the most widely distributed conifers in Canada. Its resilient, straight-grained wood makes it one of the most important commercial species in Canada, widely used for construction materials and pulp. Less well-known uses include musical instruments, paddles, containers and log homes. • A dwarf (3 m tall), perfectly conical ornamental variety of white spruce with a dense foliage is called *Picea glauca* var. *albertiana* 'Conica.' • White spruce is also known as Canadian spruce, western white spruce, Alberta spruce, skunk spruce or cat spruce. The last two names refer to the pungent odour produced when the needles are crushed. The species name *glauca* is from the Greek for 'grey,' and it refers to the colour of the foliage.

BLACK SPRUCE • *Picea mariana*

GENERAL: Small **conifer**, to 10–15 m tall; short, slender, tapered trunk, to 15–40 cm in diameter; narrow, **irregular crown**; **top compact and somewhat club-like**; drooping branches, the lower of which often reach the ground; **twigs blackish and hairy** with residual peg-like structures when needles are removed.

BARK: Thin, dark grey, **flaky scales** covering olive-green inner bark.

LEAVES: Short **evergreen needles, stiff and sharply pointed**, dark blue-green, squarish in cross-section; spread radially around twigs.

CONES: Egg-shaped but broadly rounded at tip, dull grey-brown, 1–3 cm long, in **dense clusters that remain on tree for 20–30 years**; **scale edges have small, irregular teeth**, are stiff and open only slightly when mature.

ECOLOGY: Widespread and common at low to mid elevations on northern Fraser Plateau; scattered in northern parts of Columbia Mountains; in cold wet forests of valley bottoms subject to cold-air drainage with a short frost-free period; also on bogs and coarse soils; shade tolerant, very frost hardy.

NOTES: Black spruce grows slowly and may reach 250 years of age. The lower branches of black spruce commonly rest on the ground and often take root (layer), which results in dense patches of young trees surrounding a parent tree. • Native people used the needles for making spruce beer, and the pitch for chewing gum, caulking and holding false teeth in place. • The wood's long fibres make it ideal for making facial tissue and other paper products. • Other common names are bog spruce, swamp spruce, short-leaf spruce and eastern spruce. The species name *mariana* refers to Maryland, but although black spruce's wide geographic range extends to the eastern U.S., it is not actually found in Maryland.

INTERIOR DOUGLAS-FIR • *Pseudotsuga menziesii* var. *glauca*

GENERAL: Large **conifer**, to 25–35 m tall (rarely exceeding 40 m); clear, long cylindrical trunk, to 1 m in diameter; compact, pyramidal crown with irregular branching (older trees often have flat tops); **buds pointed, shiny, reddish brown.**

BARK: Grey-brown, smooth, with resin blisters when young, becoming **thick** (8–20 cm) and **corky**, with tawny-brown ridges separated by dark, **vertical fissures** with age.

LEAVES: Spirally arranged **evergreen needles**, yellow-green or blue-green, flattish, with pointed tips but **not sharp to the touch**, 2–3 cm long; smell of camphor when crushed.

CONES: Narrowly oval-egg-shaped, green, turning light brown when mature, 5–11 cm long; with **prominent, 3-pronged bracts that extend beyond scales**; hanging; falling intact after seed dispersal.

ECOLOGY: Widespread and common on a wide variety of sites at low to mid elevations; restricted to dry, warm aspects at subalpine elevations; generally absent from saturated soils; relatively drought resistant, moderately shade tolerant and not frost hardy.

SIMILAR SPECIES: There is also a Coastal variety of Douglas-fir (*P. menziesii* var. *menziesii*) that occurs mostly west of the Cascade and Coast mountains. The Interior variety is distinguished by its bluish-green needles and its shorter cones, which are less than 8 cm long, while the Coastal variety's cones are more than 10 cm long.

NOTES: Douglas-fir is readily separated from all other conifers in our region by its cones, which bear prominent, 3-pronged bracts that extend beyond the scales. • In the dry parts of our region, Douglas-fir's thick bark and tall, clear bole help protect it from fires. • The abundant seeds of Douglas-fir support large populations of small mammals and birds. Many mule deer in our region rely on mature Douglas-fir forests for winter survival, both for shelter and for food. • Many Interior native peoples ate Douglas-fir seeds. The Nlaka'pmx and Secwepemc made a tea from young twigs and needles. The Ktunaxa chewed dried sap, which was said to be good for treating colds. Douglas-fir boughs played a role in many ceremonial functions, including mourning, sweat-baths and the washing of twins. They were widely used as bedding in camps and pit houses. Rotten wood is used to smoke buckskin, thus preserving and dyeing it. Occasionally, the Interior native peoples were able to harvest fir sugar—a crystalline sugar that appears on the branches in early summer under rare climatic condi-

tions. The Interior Salish people called this sugar 'tree-breastmilk.' • Douglas-fir is one of the world's best-known commercial tree species. The wood is strong and durable, and it produces excellent construction materials, window and door frames, cabinets, flooring, siding, veneers, plywood, railway ties and poles. Its fragrant branches make it a popular Christmas tree. Douglas-fir has been successfully introduced to forests in the temperate climates of Europe, Australia and New Zealand. Douglas-fir bark has been used in tanning leather. • The name 'Douglas-fir' honours botanist David Douglas. It also distinguishes Douglas-fir from the true firs, the genus *Abies*, with which it was originally classified in 18th-century botanical literature. The genus name *Pseudotsuga* is derived from the Greek *pseudes*, 'false,' and *Tsuga*, the genus name for hemlock.

WESTERN REDCEDAR • *Thuja plicata*

GENERAL: Large **conifer**, to 40 m tall; clear tapered trunk, to 3 m in diameter, **buttressed at base**; crown conical when young, becoming irregular, often with a dead or broken top with age; drooping branches with upturned ends.

BARK: Thin, reddish brown, **fibrous**, pulls off in long strips.

LEAVES: Evergreen, short, **blunt, scale-like leaves**, shiny yellowish green; **in pairs and of 2 types**—1 pair folded and the other flat; in **flattened, fan-like sprays of small branches**; very aromatic when crushed.

CONES: Many, **small**, elliptic, brown, 12 mm long, each composed of a few scales; in **clusters** on branch ends.

ECOLOGY: Widespread and common in Columbia Mountains, Coast/ Interior Transition and wettest parts of East Kootenays, on moist and wet sites at low to mid elevations and occasionally at lower subalpine elevations; also scattered and infrequent on low-elevation floodplains and seepage sites on Thompson and Okanagan plateaus; tolerates saturated soils with a stagnant water table, prefers rich, moist sites; shade tolerant; low resistance to drought and frost.

SIMILAR SPECIES: Yellow cedar (*Chamaecyparis nootkatensis*) in our region is restricted to a few locations in the Kootenays and on the leeward slopes of the Coast Mountains. Its scale-like leaves resemble those of western redcedar, but they are **all alike**, so that the leaf-covered **twigs appear 4-sided** rather than flat. Yellow cedar has **rounded cones** unlike the elliptic cones of western redcedar.

NOTES: Western redcedar's distribution on upland sites in our region closely parallels the distribution of western hemlock and western white pine, and it defines the boundaries of the 'wet belt.' • Western redcedar reaches ages of 1,000 years in the wettest parts of the Columbia Mountains (e.g., the headwaters of the Adams, Shuswap and Seymour rivers). • Coastal native people used long strips of the fibrous bark for making baskets, blankets, cloaks, ropes and mats; the wood was used for dugout canoes, roofing and siding materials. Interior native people living where redcedar occurs used its roots to sew baskets, and used its wood to make dip-net hoops and handles, drying frames and other implements. • The wood resists decay, splits easily into planks, is relatively light and free of pitch or resin. Redcedar wood is important for making siding, panelling, patio furniture, clothes closets, chests and caskets. The wood weathers to a beautiful silvery grey. Leaf oil extracts are used to make perfumes, insecticides, medicinal preparations, shoe polish and deodorants. Because of its decay resistance, the wood makes excellent utility poles, fenceposts, pilings and siding. Fallen trees remain sound for hundreds of years. Ironically, most old Interior redcedars have substantial centre rot, and mechanical and life-sustaining processes are supported by a relatively thin, solid outer shell. • A dwarf form (1 m tall) with bronze-gold foliage, *T. plicata* 'Cuprea,' is used as an ornamental. Another rarity, 'Excelsa,' makes an excellent dark-green hedging material. • Western redcedar is also known as Pacific redcedar, giant cedar, arbor vitae and shinglewood. The name 'arbor vitae' is a Latin phrase meaning 'tree of life,' and there are various different accounts of its derivation. The species name *plicata* comes from a Greek word meaning 'folded in plates,' and it refers to the arrangement of the leaves.

48

SHRUBS AND SMALL TREES

Shrubs are woody, usually multi-stemmed plants that are less than 10 m tall when mature. In this section we have also included dwarf shrubs, which are less than 30 cm tall at maturity. Many dwarf shrubs live in alpine habitats where small size is advantageous for survival and growth. Also included are woody vines, such as honeysuckle (*Lonicera* sp.) and twinflower (*Linnaea borealis*), which seldom attain substantial height but often exceed 1–2 m in length.

The shrubs of our region represent a wide variety of families and genera. For the most part we have organized this section into major plant families and genera, and by similar species within those groupings.

Our region's wide range of habitats is reflected in the diversity of our shrubs. In the moist, cool climates that are dominated by closed coniferous forests, where soils are more acidic and decomposing woody material abounds, shrubs of the heather family (Ericaceae) are common. The arid shrub-steppes of our region are at the other extreme—moisture deficits occur over much of the year and temperatures in the summer reach beyond 40°C. In these habitats shrubs such as big sagebrush (*Artemisia tridentata*) and antelope-brush (*Purshia tridentata*), typical of the Great Basin in the U.S., are common.

Many of the shrubs of our region have fleshy edible fruits, which were an important part of the diets of all Interior native peoples. Many of these fruits, such as the berries of saskatoons (*Amelanchier alnifolia*), raspberries (*Rubus* spp.), blueberries (*Vaccinium* spp.) and currants (*Ribes* spp.), were gathered in great quantities and dried for later use. They were important sources of carbohydrates, vitamins and other nutrients for people during the long winter. The leaves, bark and other plant parts were also used as medicines and for making a variety of tools and implements. Many of our shrubs are also important food sources for the wildlife in our region. For example, willows (*Salix* spp.), red-osier dogwood (*Cornus stolonifera*) and saskatoon form a major part of the winter diet of moose and mule deer. Also, birds, bears and small rodents feed heavily on many of the shrub fruits.

WESTERN DWARF MISTLETOE • *Arceuthobium americanum*

GENERAL: Fleshy shrub, parasitic on branches of pines; clusters of yellowish or greenish-brown, **segmented stems**, 2–6 cm long, **emerging from host branches** when plant flowers, but otherwise growing inside host.

LEAVES: Reduced to tiny, **paired scales**.

FLOWERS: Inconspicuous, small, **greenish yellow**; separate male and female flowers on short stalks, 2 to several in **whorls at each stem joint**.

FRUITS: Greenish or bluish, sticky, **egg-shaped berries** that explosively eject a single, sticky seed.

ECOLOGY: Widespread and common at low to mid elevations on our plateaus and in East Kootenays; most commonly parasitic on lodgepole pine (*Pinus contorta* var. *latifolia*), but also reported on ponderosa pine (*P. ponderosa*).

SIMILAR SPECIES: Other species of dwarf mistletoe are found primarily on Douglas-fir (*Pseudotsuga menziesii*), western hemlock (*Tsuga heterophylla*) and western larch (*Larix occidentalis*), and occasionally on other pines (*Pinus* spp.), true firs (*Abies* spp.) and spruces (*Picea* spp.).

NOTES: Western dwarf mistletoe causes stem swelling and a disorganized growth of branches called 'witches'-broom.' Mistletoe infections can cause significant reductions in the growth of lodgepole pine. • The common name appears to be derived from the Old English word *mistletan. Tan* means 'twig,' and some sources say *mistl* means 'different,' hence *mistletan* means 'different-twig.' Others say *mistl* comes from Old German *mist,* 'dung,' in that after a bird eats the berries, the seeds are deposited on trees in sticky bird droppings.

Ribes: the currants and gooseberries

In our region the currant family is represented by a single genus, *Ribes*. Our species are usually called gooseberries if they are spiny or currants if they are not. The fruits of several of these native species, like those of their cultivated relatives, are widely used for making jams and jellies.

Our *Ribes* species are all deciduous shrubs, and many are armed with thorns and prickles. Their leaves are lobed, often in a 'maple-leaf' shape. The leaves, flowers and fruits are often hairy and may bear sticky glands. A key recognition feature for the group is its clusters of red, blue or black berries, which usually bear the remains of the flowers at their tips. You can also recognize *Ribes* species by their flowers, which are distinctive in that the **sepals are usually showier than the petals**. The sepals are fused into a calyx that varies in shape from flattened and saucer-like to bell-shaped or tubular. The calyx divides at the top into five lobes, which alternate with the five inconspicuous petals.

Most species of *Ribes* are easily propagated from seed sown in autumn, from hardwood cuttings taken in autumn or by layering.

The blister rust fungus that kills western white pine (*Pinus monticola*) and other 5-needle pines (such as whitebark pine, *P. albicaulis*) requires *Ribes* as an alternate host for part of its life cycle. Because of its relationship to this severe pathogen, the introduction of *Ribes* to the home garden should be done with caution, and only disease-free stock should be used.

Hearne (1801) wrote that currant berries 'have a very great effect on some people if eaten in any considerable quantities, by acting as a very powerful purgative, and in some cases as an emetic of the same tissue; but if mixed with cranberries, they never have that effect.'

The genus name *Ribes* is from a Persian word meaning 'acid-tasting.' The word 'currant' means 'dried grape,' and it is a contraction of *corinthiaca*, as in *Uva corinthiaca*, a small grape from Corinth. The name 'gooseberry' appears to be derived from the Flemish *kroes* or *kruys bezie* or the Swedish *krusbar*, a word that has two meanings—either 'cross-berry' or 'frizzle-berry.' The cross refers to the three spines at the leaf node of *Ribes grossularia*, which resemble a cross. 'Fizzle-berry' became translated into 'crisp berry' or *uva-crispa*, hence *R. grossularia* may also be *R. uva-crispa* in old books.

Key to the currants and gooseberries

1a. Stems armed with spines or prickles (gooseberries) 2

　2a. Several flowers, in spreading or drooping clusters, saucer-shaped; berries black, bristly-glandular; leaves notched at base .... *R. lacustre*

　2b. 3 or fewer flowers, tubular bell-shaped; berries bluish purple, smooth; leaves squared off at base to only slightly notched .... *R. oxyacanthoides*

1b. Stems without spines or bristles (currants) 3

　3a. Leaf lobes conspicuously rounded 4

　　4a. Berries bluish to black; floral tube (hypanthium) twice as long as sepals; leaves generally greater than 3 cm broad .... *R. viscosissimum*

　　4b. Berries red; floral tube about equalling sepals; leaves generally less than 3 cm broad .... *R. cereum*

　3b. Leaf lobes not conspicuously rounded, more or less sharply pointed 5

　　5a. Lower surface of leaves (and usually base of flower and fruit) sprinkled with yellow crystalline glands (resin dots); berries black with a whitish bloom when mature 6

6a. Flowers greenish with purple tinge, 15–50 in 15–30-cm-long, erect to ascending clusters with conspicuous leafy bracts; leaves mostly deeply 5-lobed .... ***R. bracteosum***

6b. Flowers white, 6–15 in spreading, 4–15-cm-long clusters lacking leafy bracts; leaves mostly more shallowly 3–5-lobed .... ***R. hudsonianum***

5b. Leaves without resin dots; berries red (or purplish black in *R. laxiflorum*) 7

7a. Base of flower and fruit smooth (without bristly glands); flower clusters dropping; leaves mostly 3-lobed with lobes somewhat rounded .... ***R. triste***

7b. Base of flower (ovary) and fruit bristly with stalked glands; flower clusters erect to ascending; leaves 5–7-lobed and lobes sharply pointed 8

8a. Berries purplish black; flowers red to purplish; stalked glands on flower base (ovary) less than 0.5 mm long .... ***R. laxiflorum***

8b. Berries dark red; flowers greenish white to pinkish; stalked glands on flower base up to 1.2 mm long .... ***R. glandulosum***

SKUNK CURRANT • *Ribes glandulosum*

GENERAL: Low, deciduous shrub, to 1 m tall, **without thorns; branches reclining or often trailing.**

LEAVES: Maple-leaf-shaped, with **5–7 sharply pointed lobes and toothed edges,** fresh green turning bright red in autumn; veins smooth and sparsely glandular; **strong skunky odour** emitted when crushed.

FLOWERS: Greenish-white to pink, glandular-hairy, saucer-shaped calyx; in **erect to ascending clusters** of 6–15.

FRUITS: Dark red berries, covered in **stalked glandular hairs** (lollipop-like); disagreeable odour and flavour.

ECOLOGY: Widespread and common at low to subalpine elevations in wet Columbia Mountains, East Kootenays and eastern Fraser Plateau, in moist forests and clearings.

SIMILAR SPECIES: Trailing black currant (*R. laxiflorum*) has reddish-purple flowers, longer, hairy calyx lobes and purplish-black berries. It is uncommon in our region but locally common in moist and wet climates in the Rockies. • Red swamp currant (*R. triste*) has 3-lobed leaves and red, smooth (non-glandular) berries. It is also common in the northern part of our region at low to mid elevations.

NOTES: Skunk currant is named for the skunky smell emitted when it is bruised. It is also called fetid currant, for the same reason. The species name *glandulosum* refers to the characteristic glandular hairs on the fruit.

NORTHERN BLACK CURRANT • *Ribes hudsonianum*

GENERAL: Erect, **deciduous** shrub, 0.5–2 m tall, **without thorns**; **yellow, crystalline glands (resin dots)**; smooth bark.

LEAVES: Maple-leaf-shaped, 5–9 cm across; **3–5 rounded lobes**; **toothed edges**; many **resin dots** below.

FLOWERS: White, saucer-shaped calyx, with **resin dots** but not glandular-hairy; borne in spreading to erect, 4–10-cm-long clusters of 6–15 flowers.

FRUITS: Black berries, with a waxy bloom, **usually speckled with a few resin dots**; disagreeable, bitter flavour.

ECOLOGY: Widespread and common at low and mid elevations in moist and wet forests, seepage areas and wet openings; absent from our warm, arid climates.

SIMILAR SPECIES: Stink currant (*R. bracteosum*) and northern black currant both have distinctive yellow crystalline glands (resin dots), but stink currant has longer flower clusters (15–30 cm) and it has greenish flowers. Stink currant is typically a Coastal species, and it is rare along the western edge of our region.

NOTES: Northern black currant has a sweet 'tomcat' odour that is unpleasant to some people. • Several Interior native groups, including the Carrier and Secwepemc, ate the berries, although the Carrier called them 'toadberries' and did not eat them very often.

BLACK GOOSEBERRY • *Ribes lacustre*

GENERAL: Erect to spreading, **deciduous** shrub, 0.5–2 m tall, covered with **many small, sharp prickles**, with **larger, thick thorns** at leaf and branch bases; bark on **older stems is cinnamon-coloured**.

LEAVES: Somewhat **maple-leaf-shaped**, mostly with **5 deeply indented lobes** and **toothed edges**, bases notched at intersection with stalk; not glandular or hairy.

FLOWERS: Reddish, saucer-shaped, glandular-hairy calyx with small pink to purple petals; in hanging clusters of 7–15 flowers.

FRUITS: Dark purple berries covered with **gland-tipped hairs**; palatable but insipid.

ECOLOGY: Widespread and very common at low to subalpine elevations in moist and wet forests, open seepage areas and clearings; on dry forested slopes of subalpine ridges; often on rotting wood.

SIMILAR SPECIES: Northern gooseberry (*R. oxyacanthoides*) also has bristles and spines at the leaf bases. Its leaves have a straight base (not notched), and its fruit is smooth (not glandular-hairy). Northern gooseberry flowers are greenish yellow, bell-shaped and in small clusters of 2–3.

NOTES: Black gooseberries were eaten fresh or cooked by all Interior native groups. The Lil'wet'ul boiled the berries to make a tea that was said to be good for colds. The Okanagan made a menthol-flavoured tea from the leaves, and it was said to be good for colds and diarrhea. Today the berries are made into jam. • The spines of black gooseberry, like those of devil's club (*Oplopanax horridus*), cause allergic reactions in some people. Also like devil's club, the prickly qualities of black gooseberry were believed to have special protective powers for warding off evil influences, such as malevolent snakes.

SQUAW CURRANT • *Ribes cereum*

GENERAL: Spreading to erect, **deciduous** shrub, 0.5–1.5 m tall, **without thorns; young branches have fine sticky hairs** and mature greyish to reddish brown.

LEAVES: Small, **kidney-shaped** to somewhat broadly fan-shaped, with **3–5 shallow lobes** or coarse round teeth; sparsely hairy and often glandular on both surfaces.

FLOWERS: Greenish white to slightly pinkish, urn-shaped, borne singly or in small clusters on a drooping stalk; finely hairy and often sticky glandular.

FRUITS: Small red berries (currants); bitter and not palatable.

ECOLOGY: Scattered and locally common at low to mid elevations on Okanagan and Thompson plateaus and basins and in dry East Kootenays, in open ponderosa pine and Douglas-fir forests and open warm, dry, rocky slopes.

NOTES: The St'at'imc, Nlaka'pmx, Secwepemc and Okan-

agan ate squaw currants but considered them tasteless. The Nlaka'pmx and Secwepemc also considered them a tonic, and they ate them to relieve diarrhea. The flowers are an important food source for early humming-birds. • The species name *cereum* means 'waxy' and refers to the glands on the leaves, which give them a waxy appearance.

STICKY CURRANT • *Ribes viscosissimum*

GENERAL: Erect to spreading, straggly, **deciduous** shrub, 1–2 m tall, **without thorns**, covered with **soft, sticky hairs**; bark is reddish brown and shreds with age.

LEAVES: With 3–5 somewhat rounded lobes and toothed edges, covered with **soft sticky hairs** on both surfaces.

FLOWERS: Greenish-white to pinkish, tubular bell-shaped calyx covered with **soft, sticky hairs**; borne in rounded clusters of 6–12 flowers.

FRUITS: Blue-black, very sticky berries; not edible.

ECOLOGY: Scattered and locally common at mid to subalpine elevations, up to timberline on Okanagan and Thompson plateaus and dry East Kootenays, in dry to moist forests and openings.

NOTES: The blue-black berries are, according to David Douglas, 'musty and very disagreeable,' and they may cause vomiting, but the Nlaka'pmx, Okanagan and Ktunaxa occasionally ate them. • As its common name suggests, this species is certainly the stickiest of the currants. The species name is derived from the Latin *viscosus,* meaning 'sticky' or 'viscid,' and it refers to the glandular hairs that secrete a sticky gum and are found over the entire plant, including the berries.

WESTERN MOUNTAIN-ASH • *Sorbus scopulina*

GENERAL: Several-stemmed deciduous shrub, 1–5 m tall; winter buds and young growth white-hairy and **sticky.**

LEAVES: Divided into **9–13 narrowly oblong leaflets,** with **sharp-pointed tips** and sharply toothed edges along most of the length.

FLOWERS: Small and **white,** up to 200 in showy, **flat-topped to rounded clusters.**

FRUITS: Orange to scarlet and **berry-like**, without any whitish bloom.

ECOLOGY: Widespread and common at low to subalpine elevations in moist forests, openings and clearings; generally absent from warm, arid parts of our plateaus and southern Rocky Mountain Trench.

SIMILAR SPECIES: Sitka mountain-ash (*S. sitchensis*, below) has broader leaflets with rounded tips and more finely toothed edges, more rounded flower clusters, rusty hairs and non-sticky winter buds.

NOTES: The Lower Nlaka'pmx ate the fruits of western mountain-ash. Birds eat the berries of both mountain-ash species, especially after they have fermented. Deer, moose and other ungulates eat the twigs. • Mountain-ash are most easily started from seeds sown in late autumn. They are very difficult to propagate from cuttings. • The name 'mountain-ash' is a misnomer, as this is not an ash at all; however, it may have acquired the name because its divided leaves resembled those of the ash (*Fraxinus* sp.). • *Sorbus* was either the Latin name for the mountain-ash, or the Greek name for the oak, depending on whom you believe. The species name *scopulina* means 'of the rocks or cliffs.'

SITKA MOUNTAIN-ASH • *Sorbus sitchensis*

GENERAL: Several-stemmed deciduous shrub, 1–4 m tall; winter buds and young growth with rusty hairs, **not sticky**.

LEAVES: Divided into **7–11 oblong leaflets** with **rounded tips; edges are finely toothed mostly above middle.**

FLOWERS: Small and **white**, not more than 80, in **round-topped clusters.**

FRUITS: Red, berry-like, with whitish bloom; edible but extremely tart and bitter.

ECOLOGY: Scattered and locally common at mid to subalpine elevations in open coniferous forest, along streambanks and in clearings; generally absent from warm, arid climates of our plateaus.

SIMILAR SPECIES: Western mountain-ash (*S. scopulina*, above) has narrow, sharp-pointed leaflets with sharply toothed edges along almost their entire length.

NOTES: Some southern Interior native people occasionally ate mountain-ash berries, and the St'at'imc picked the small shoots in the spring and ate them raw. The bark was used in medicinal mixtures for coughs and fever. The Nlaka'pmx elder Annie York added a cluster of mountain-ash fruits to the top of a jar of blueberries when canning them (Turner et al. 1990). • The European mountain-ash (*S. aucuparia*), also called rowan or service tree, is widely planted as an ornamental in the south and central Interior. 'Rowan,' or 'roan,' is from either the Swedish *runn* (a secret) or the Old Norse *runa* (a charm), from the old belief that the mountain-ash has the power to avert the evil eye. It was traditionally the tree from which ladder staves were cut, and because of the tree's magical powers, they were called *run-stafas* (mysterious staves), which appears to have given rise to 'rungs' of a ladder.

SASKATOON • *Amelanchier alnifolia*

GENERAL: Deciduous shrub to small tree, 1–5 m tall; stems smooth; bark dark grey to reddish; often spreads by underground or creeping stems and forms dense colonies.

LEAVES: Thin and **round to oval**, with **regularly toothed edges mostly on upper half**; appearing smooth but finely hairy below, **leaf blade notched or straight at base**.

FLOWERS: White and showy with **linear to oblong petals, narrowed at base**; in short, leafy clusters of 3–20 at branch tips.

FRUITS: Purple to nearly black, berry-like pomes (apple-like), with white bloom; edible, sweet.

ECOLOGY: Widespread and common at low to mid elevations in dry to moist forests, on open, dry, warm slopes, in moist gullies in grasslands and on disturbed sites; occasionally in dry open forests on warm aspects at subalpine elevations.

NOTES: Saskatoon provides winter browse for many hoofed mammals, and many bird species eat the berries in August. • Saskatoons were the most popular and widely used berry for central and southern native peoples. In the Secwepemc language, saskatoons are called 'real' or 'ordinary' berries. Dried saskatoons were a common trading item, especially between the Interior and the Coast. Native people recognized up to eight different varieties based on differences in flowering time and size, texture and sweetness of the fruit. Berries were eaten fresh or dried in cakes or like raisins for storage. Maple and saskatoon sticks were boiled together to make a medicinal drink for women following childbirth. • Horticulturists have developed several varieties for commercial and garden use. Saskatoons are easily propagated from wild seedlings or from root cuttings. • The name 'saskatoon' appears to be a shortened version of the Blackfoot name for this bush, *mis-ask-a-tomina*. Another common name is 'serviceberry.' Early reports referred to the fruit as a 'poire,' 'wild pear' or 'service berry,' with pear-like leaves and fruits.

BIRCH-LEAVED SPIREA • *Spiraea betulifolia*

GENERAL: Deciduous shrub, mostly 25–60 cm tall, spreading vigorously from rhizomes; **not hairy**.

LEAVES: Oval to oval-oblong, but wider towards tip and **leaf base tapering to stalk**, usually **coarsely double-toothed above middle**; dark green above, pale green below.

FLOWERS: Tiny and **dull white**, often with pale pinkish or lavender tinge; in **dense, nearly flat-topped clusters**.

FRUITS: 5 **pod-like, beaked capsules**, joined at base.

ECOLOGY: Widespread and common at low to subalpine elevations in open, dry to moist forests, open, dry, rocky slopes and clearings.

SIMILAR SPECIES: Subalpine spirea (*S. densiflora*) has a similar flat-topped cluster of flowers, but its flowers are rosy-pink. It occurs infrequently at mid to subalpine elevations in the southern part of our area. • Birch-leaved spirea is sometimes confused with saskatoon (*Amelanchier alnifolia*, above), but the leaves of birch-leaved spirea are more oblong and coarsely toothed, and their bases taper to the stem, while saskatoon leaves are more rounded and regularly toothed, and they have notched bases.

NOTES: The St'at'imc used this plant to make a medicine for stomach ailments and diarrhea. • All of our native spireas are easily propagated from seeds, cuttings or offshoots from the rhizomes, however, once they are established they often spread extensively and may be difficult to contain. • The species name *betulifolia* (birch-leaved) echoes the common name. This species is also called flat-top spirea.

PYRAMID SPIREA • *Spiraea pyramidata*

GENERAL: Spreading to erect, **deciduous** shrub, mostly 0.5–1 m tall, usually with extensive rhizomes; **finely hairy throughout**, but especially among flowers.

LEAVES: Oval-oblong to lance-shaped, smooth and **coarsely toothed above middle**.

FLOWERS: Tiny and **rose-pink**, but varying from off-white to pink; in open, **pyramid-shaped clusters** approximately twice as long as broad.

FRUITS: 5 finely hairy, pod-like capsules, joined at base.

ECOLOGY: Widely scattered and locally abundant at low to mid elevations in our moist and wet climates, in moist to wet spruce forests, wetland edges and clearings.

SIMILAR SPECIES: Pyramid spirea is suspected of being a hybrid between birch-leaved spirea (*S. betulifolia*, p. 55) and pink spirea (*S. douglasii* ssp. *menziesii*, below), and you sometimes encounter mixed populations of all three species, with a variety of intermediate individuals.

NOTES: The Nlaka'pmx made a tea by boiling the stems, leaves and flowers to use as a tonic and beverage (Turner 1990). • The genus name *Spiraea* is from the Greek *speiraira*, the name of a plant used in wreaths, and some garden varieties of spirea are called 'bridal-wreath.' The species name *pyramidata* refers to the pyramidal inflorescence.

PINK SPIREA • *Spiraea douglasii* ssp. *menziesii*

GENERAL: Much-branched, deciduous shrub, to 1.5 m tall, from rhizomes and with **woolly young growth**.

LEAVES: Oblong to oval, **smooth, with toothed edges above middle**; dark green above and pale below.

FLOWERS: Numerous, tiny, **pink to deep rose**, in **dense, elongate clusters** that are several times longer than broad.

FRUITS: 5 pod-like capsules, joined at base, persisting after leaves fall.

ECOLOGY: Scattered and locally abundant at low to mid elevations in wet Columbia Mountains and Coast/Interior Transition, in mesic to wet open forests, wetlands and clearings; often very abundant in wet frost-prone depressions.

SIMILAR SPECIES: The Coastal subspecies (*S. douglasii* ssp. *douglasii*) has matted grey hairs on the lower surface of the leaf. It may occur in the extreme west of the Coast/Interior Transition.

NOTES: Interior native groups did not use pink spirea much. The Nlaka'pmx elder Annie York noted that her mother made brooms from the branches (Turner et al. 1990). • Pink spirea is an attractive garden ornamental, and it is easily propagated from its plentiful offshoots. The creeping underground stems are invasive, however, and they often overtake large portions of the garden. Pink spirea readily takes over wet land if it is not kept down. • Pink spirea is also called hardhack, a name that may be derived from the difficulty encountered by early settlers and pioneers in hacking their way through dense masses of this bush.

BLACK HAWTHORN • *Crataegus douglasii*

GENERAL: Large **deciduous** shrub to small tree, to 8 m tall; bark grey, rough and scaly; with **stout, straight thorns** 1–3 cm long.

LEAVES: Oval, thick and leathery, dark green above, paler below, with **5–9 small lobes at top**.

FLOWERS: White, showy, saucer-shaped, with 5 rounded petals; in flat-topped clusters at branch tips.

FRUITS: Clusters of small, **blackish-purple pomes** (apple-like) with a large, hard seed; edible but not very juicy; wither soon after ripening.

ECOLOGY: Widely scattered and locally common at low to mid elevations along streambanks and lakes, on warm, open slopes and in open deciduous forests; generally absent from dry, cold climates of south Chilcotins.

SIMILAR SPECIES: Columbian hawthorn (*C. columbiana*), also called red hawthorn, is smaller and has long, slender, curved thorns and red fruits. It also grows along watercourses and on dry hillsides in our region.

NOTES: The spines of black hawthorn had many purposes including probing skin blisters and boils, piercing ears, and as fish hooks and game pieces. Black hawthorn wood is very hard and fine grained, and it made durable tool handles and weapons. • Interior peoples sometimes used the dry, seedy fruits medicinally. The Nlaka'pmx considered the fruits to be good against diarrhea. The bark was used to treat diarrhea, dysentery and stomach pains. • The name *Crataegus* is from the Greek *kratos*, 'strength,' because of the great strength of the wood. The common name 'hawthorn,' from the Anglo-Saxon *haguthorn*, 'a fence with thorns,' comes from its early use as a hedge.

MALLOW NINEBARK • *Physocarpus malvaceus*

GENERAL: Deciduous shrub, to 2 m tall; with arching branches and **brown, papery, shredding bark**.

LEAVES: Divided into **3–5 lobes** with **toothed edges and deep veins**, shiny dark green above, lighter below, **hairy on both surfaces**.

FLOWERS: White, with 5 **rounded petals**, in half-rounded clusters at branch tips.

FRUITS: Pairs of **inflated, hairy, reddish capsules, joined on lower half**, each with a shiny yellowish seed inside.

ECOLOGY: Scattered and locally common at low to mid elevations in southeastern part of our region, east from Okanagan Lake, on dry open, rocky slopes and in open ponderosa pine and Douglas-fir forests.

SIMILAR SPECIES: Pacific ninebark (*P. capitatus*) occurs in our area in the 'wet belt' south of Shuswap Lake. It is generally larger, grows in wetter habitats than mallow ninebark and has fruits with 3–5 essentially hairless capsules.

NOTES: The hairs on the leaf surfaces, calyx lobes and young branches are star-shaped when viewed under 10x magnification. • The Okanagan used this plant as a good luck charm to protect their hunting equipment. • Mallow ninebark is easily propagated from cuttings but is slow to establish from seeds sown in autumn. • This species is apparently called ninebark because it is believed that there are nine layers of fibrous bark on the stems.

CHOKE CHERRY • *Prunus virginiana*

GENERAL: Deciduous, often straggly shrub or occasionally small tree, 1–4 m tall; trunks twisted or crooked; bark smooth, dark reddish to greyish brown, **without prominent horizontal slits** (lenticels).

LEAVES: Thin, **broadly oval** and **tapering at both ends**, with fine, **sharply toothed edges** and short pointed tip; dull green above, greenish below.

FLOWERS: Small and white, saucer-shaped with 5 rounded petals; in **long clusters** at branch tips that resemble bottle-brushes; faintly scented.

FRUITS: Shiny, red to purple or black cherries; edible but with a very astringent aftertaste.

ECOLOGY: Scattered and locally abundant at low to mid elevations in open forests, grasslands and clearings on warm aspects; often on dry, exposed warm aspects and among rocky outcrops.

NOTES: The name 'choke cherry' is very apt because the fruits produce a choking sensation when eaten. Interior native peoples enjoyed choke cherries, in spite of their astringency and large stones, and they ate them fresh as a snack or dried for winter use. The cherries make excellent jelly. The Secwepemc consumed choke cherry juice to gain strength after sickness. Jellies and syrups are also favoured by all Interior native peoples. Many species of birds also eat choke cherries. • Choke cherry wood was used for handles, especially on root-diggers, and the bark was shredded and used for decorating basket rims. A decoction of the bark was used as a tonic as well. • Many North American plants bear species names like *pensylvanica* or *virginiana* because the earliest North American botanists began collecting in the eastern U.S.

PIN CHERRY • *Prunus pensylvanica*

GENERAL: Deciduous shrub to small tree, usually 1–5 m tall but up to 12 m; bark dark reddish brown with large, widely spaced, **orange, horizontal slits** (lenticels), peeling in horizontal strips.

LEAVES: Thin and **lance-shaped**, with **round-toothed edges**, gradually tapering to **long pointed tip**.

FLOWERS: Small and white, saucer-shaped with 5 rounded petals, in flat-topped clusters of 5–7.

FRUITS: Small, **bright red cherries**, 4–7 mm long; thin, acid flesh.

ECOLOGY: Scattered and locally common at low to mid eleva-tions in moist warm climates of our region, in dry to moist forests and open places; often abundant after fire.

SIMILAR SPECIES: Bitter cherry (*P. emarginata*) is a more Coastal species that occurs infrequently in the southern half of our area. It also has a flat-topped flower cluster, but the cherries are larger and the leaves are much less pointy-tipped than those of pin cherry. Pin cherry probably hybridizes with bitter cherry where their ranges overlap.

NOTES: Warning: Pin cherry stones and leaves, like those of other *Prunus* species, contain toxic **cyanide**. The flesh is not harmful, but poisoning and death have occurred in children who consumed large quantities of berries without removing the seeds. • The Carrier, Nlaka'pmx, Secwepemc and St'at'imc reportedly ate the fruit of bitter cherry, but pin cherry appears to be more abundant in their territory and probably both were used. There were never enough cherries to preserve for winter and they were unsuitable for drying. Cherry bark has waterproof properties and it was used to wrap implements and decorate baskets. The Carrier used an infusion of the bark as a remedy against blood spitting. • Pin cherry is also called bird cherry, as birds like them so much it is often hard to find any ripe fruit on the trees.

Rubus: the raspberries

The raspberries are a huge group of interbreeding, poorly defined species complexes. Fortunately, our common species are reasonably well behaved botanically, and they are not too difficult to identify. The key feature of the group is the familiar red or black raspberry-like fruit. The *Rubus* species include well-known cultivated and wild varieties of raspberries, blackberries, boysenberries and marionberries.

Rubus species can be erect shrubs, trailing dwarf plants or aggressive climbing vines. Many have stems armed with prickles or thorns. The leaves are usually lobed or divided into leaflets, and they usually have toothed edges. The flowers are usually showy and white to red and have five broad petals surrounding a large cluster of stamens. The familiar raspberry-like fruits are actually clusters of small, single-seeded drupelets.

Key to the raspberries

1a. Plants armed with bristle-like prickles 2

  2a. Petals pink to red, usually well over 1.5 cm long; fruit salmon-coloured to red; stems often armed, chiefly near base; leaves not prickly .... *R. spectabilis*

  2b. Petals white, usually less than 1.5 cm long; fruit red, occasionally yellowish; leaves frequently prickly above .... *R. idaeus*

1b. Plants unarmed 3

  3a. Stems erect, woody, rarely less than 50 cm tall 4

    4a. Petals red; leaves compound, with 3 leaflets .... *R. spectabilis*

    4b. Petals white; leaves palmately lobed and maple-leaf-shaped .... *R. parviflorus*

  3b. Stems mostly trailing, essentially herbaceous, seldom if ever as much as 50 cm tall 5

    5a. Petals more or less reddish, 10–16 mm long; plants without runners .... *R. arcticus*

    5b. Petals white, mostly less than 8 mm long; plants usually with runners 6

      6a. Leaves with 5 leaflets, sometimes only 3, but lower pair divided nearly to base .... *R. pedatus*

      6b. Leaves with 3 leaflets .... *R. pubescens*

R. spectabilis   *R. idaeus*   *R. parviflorus*

R. arcticus   *R. pedatus*   *R. pubescens*

DWARF NAGOONBERRY • *Rubus arcticus*
R. acaulis

GENERAL: Low, trailing, unarmed dwarf shrub, to 10 cm tall, from **creeping rhizomes**; flowering stems erect, annual, non-woody, finely hairy but without prickles.

LEAVES: Divided into 3 leaflets with coarsely toothed edges; round or heart-shaped in outline.

FLOWERS: Pink to reddish pink, with nearly erect petals; **usually solitary**.

FRUITS: Raspberry-like clusters of red drupelets.

ECOLOGY: Scattered and locally common at low to high elevations in wetlands, cold, wet seepage forests and peaty seepage areas in mountain meadows and alpine tundra; absent from our hot, arid climates.

NOTES: The berries have an excellent flavour and can be eaten raw or made into jams, jellies or for flavouring liquor. The Secwepemc called them 'false wild strawberries' and probably ate them. • The origin of the common name 'nagoonberry' remains a mystery. *Rubus* is Latin for 'red,' and it refers to the colour of the fruits of many species of this genus.

TRAILING RASPBERRY • *Rubus pubescens*

GENERAL: Low, trailing, dwarf shrub, to 30 cm tall; **slender runners** and erect flowering stems have long, soft hairs but **no prickles**.

LEAVES: Divided into **3 oval to diamond-shaped leaflets** with **pointed tips** and **toothed edges**.

FLOWERS: White or rarely pink, petals are nearly erect to spreading; 1–3 flowers on short branches covered with stalked glands.

FRUITS: Raspberry-like clusters of dark red drupelets; edible.

ECOLOGY: Widespread and common at low to mid elevations in moist to wet forests, wetlands and clearings.

SIMILAR SPECIES: The leaves of trailing raspberry resemble those of red raspberry (*R. idaeus*, p. 61), which is an erect shrub. The leaflets of red raspberry are toothed to the base, while those of trailing raspberry rarely are.

NOTES: The berries were eaten fresh by the Carrier and probably by other Athapaskan groups. They sometimes refer to it as salmonberry, a name that more properly refers to *R. spectabilis*. Carrier women with 'sickness in their womb' drank an infusion of boiled raspberry stems (Carrier Linguistic Committee 1973). • Trailing raspberry is easily propagated from rooted runners. • In the 16th century, raspberries were called *rasps*, *raspis* or *raspises*. The exact origin of these names is not clear, but they may have come from the 15th-century word *raspis* (a fruit from which a drink could be made); from *vinum raspatum* (a sweet red French wine) or a wine made from *raspes* (grapes with the seeds removed); or from *resp* which means 'shoot' or 'sucker.'

FIVE-LEAVED BRAMBLE • *Rubus pedatus*

GENERAL: Low, trailing, unarmed dwarf shrub, less than 2 cm tall, with long **creeping stems** (runners) that root at their nodes and short, erect flowering stems with 1–3 leaves.

LEAVES: Usually divided into **5 glossy leaflets** or oval-shaped lobes, with **coarsely toothed edges** and prominent veins.

FLOWERS: White, with the petals spreading or bent backward; solitary on **very slender stalks.**

FRUITS: Small, **raspberry-like clusters of a few bright red drupelets**; juicy and flavourful.

ECOLOGY: Widespread and common at low elevations to subalpine parkland in moist, mossy, usually coniferous forest, wetlands and clearings; common in areas of late snowmelt; most abundant in our wet, snowy climates and absent from our dry plateaus and arid basins.

NOTES: The berries, although very small, are tasty, and they were casually eaten by Interior native people when they were hunting and travelling.
• Five-leaved bramble makes an excellent ground cover in cool, shady, preferably mossy locations and is easily propagated from rooted 'runners.' • The name 'bramble' is from the Old English *braembel*, which derived from *brom,* meaning 'a wiry or thorny shrub and originally referred to the blackberry (*R. fruticosus*). Although called a 'bramble,' five-leaved bramble has neither thorns nor prickles. The species name *pedatus* means 'a foot,' and it may refer to the five leaflets as 5-toed prints in the moss.

RED RASPBERRY • *Rubus idaeus*
R. strigosus

GENERAL: Erect, deciduous shrub, to 1.5 m tall, with **prickly, bristly to almost unarmed stems** and shredding **yellow to cinnamon-brown bark**; similar to cultivated raspberry.

LEAVES: Divided into **3 saw-toothed and sharply pointed leaflets** on flowering canes (3–5 leaflets on first-year canes), with end leaflet longest.

FLOWERS: White, drooping; borne singly or in small grape-like clusters.

FRUITS: Raspberry-like cluster of red drupelets; falling intact from plant, smaller and tastier than domestic raspberries.

ECOLOGY: Scattered and often abundant at low to subalpine elevations, mostly in Coast/Interior Transition, wet Columbia Mountains and East Kootenays, in clearings and other disturbed habitats; less common in mature, dry to wet, open forests.

SIMILAR SPECIES: Black raspberry (*R. leucodermis*), also called blackcap, has flattened, hooked prickles and dark reddish to black fruit. It is common in open forests in the southern third of our region. • Salmonberry (*R. spectabilis*), another prickly-stemmed raspberry, is particularly common on the Coast, and it occasionally enters our area along the Coast/Interior Transition. It occurs along streams and logged-over areas. Salmonberry has pink flowers and salmon-coloured fruit.

NOTES: Wild raspberries were eaten by all central and southern Interior native peoples, who continue to make jam and jelly from the fruit. The St'at'imc made a cough medicine from the dried petals. The Secwepemc and Nlaka'pmx made a decoction from the roots as a stomach remedy. The Carrier made a tea from the leaves, used either as a beverage or for amenorrhea. An infusion of boiled stem was given to women for 'sickness in their womb' (Carrier Linguistic Committee 1973).
• The species name *idaeus* means 'from Mt. Ida,' which is on the Mediterranean island of Crete.

THIMBLEBERRY • *Rubus parviflorus*

GENERAL: Erect, **deciduous, unarmed shrub**, 0.5–2 m tall, with shredding bark; often forms dense thickets through an extensive network of rhizomes.

LEAVES: Large, **soft and maple-leaf-shaped**, with 3–7 toothed lobes; **finely fuzzy on both sides**; on long glandular stalks.

FLOWERS: Large, white, with 5 broad petals, **crinkled** like tissue paper; in long-stemmed clusters of 3–7 flowers at branch tips.

FRUITS: Shallowly domed, dull, hairy, raspberry-like clusters of scarlet red drupelets; juicy, with an insipid to sweet taste depending on growing site.

ECOLOGY: Widespread and common at low to subalpine elevations in open forest, openings, clearings, roadsides and seepage areas; largely absent from warm arid climates of our plateaus and southern Rocky Mountain Trench.

NOTES: All native groups in the central and southern Interior ate thimbleberries, usually fresh with other berries such as red raspberries (*R. idaeus*) or black raspberries (*R. leucodermis*). However, these berries are difficult to pick and they were seldom gathered in large enough quantities to be dried for winter storage. As well, they do not dry readily or keep well in grease. The young shoots were peeled and eaten raw or cooked with meat in a stew. The large, maple-like leaves were widely used as temporary containers, to line baskets, to separate berries in the same basket or as a surface on which to dry the berries. The large soft leaves make a good, biodegradable toilet tissue substitute for hikers and backpackers when the need arises. • The species name *parviflorus*, meaning 'few- or small-flowered,' is misleading, as this species has large blossoms.

OCEAN SPRAY • *Holodiscus discolor*

GENERAL: Deciduous shrub, to 4 m tall, with clusters of **arching stems**; young stems are ridged and slightly angled at each leaf, older ones have brownish, peeling bark.

LEAVES: Broadly triangular, with **lobed or coarsely toothed edges**, hairy on both sides and especially **woolly beneath**; dull green, reddish-tinged in autumn.

FLOWERS: Tiny, **white to cream-coloured**, in **dense pyramidal clusters** at branch tips; flower clusters turn brown and remain on plants over winter as clusters of seeds.

FRUITS: Tiny, **light brown, hairy achenes**.

ECOLOGY: Scattered and locally common, primarily at low elevations throughout southern half of our region, in dry, open forests and clearings, often on sandy or gravelly soils; absent from arid basins.

NOTES: The name 'ocean spray' aptly describes the distinctive creamy-white inflorescences of this shrub. • Ocean spray is also called creambush or ironwood, this latter name reflecting its hardness and strength. It was used by virtually all groups in our region to make bows, digging sticks and arrow, spear, and harpoon shafts. The Okanagan used the wood to make tipi pins, gambling sticks, prongs, fish clubs and drum hoops. The St'at'imc used it to make the upper section of harpoon shafts and gaff hook handles. • The species name comes from the Greek *holo* (whole) and *diskos* (a disk), in reference to the unlobed or 'whole' disk surrounding the ovary.

Rosa: the roses

Our native roses, like their cultivated relatives, are spiny, deciduous shrubs with showy flowers. The combination of prickly or thorny stems and pinnately compound leaves is usually enough to identify a rose even without the unmistakable flowers or fruits. Some species have two types of prickles. One type is found at the **nodes** (the points where the leaves join the stem). These are often larger than the prickles on the rest of the stem (along the **internodes**). The compound leaves usually have 5–11 oblong leaflets with toothed edges. The showy, pink to rose-coloured flowers have five broad petals surrounding a cluster of yellow stamens. They produce many seeds that are borne in the red, fleshy fruits, which are called 'hips.'

The Tsilhqot'in ate the fresh petals and made the hips into a tea. The Carrier scraped the cambium from the roots, soaked and then boiled it, and applied the ointment to sore eyes.

Conspectus of the roses

species	*R. acicularis*	*R. nutkana*	*R. woodsii*	*R. gymnocarpa*
thorns	more or less densely covered with various-sized straight prickles	large pair of straight to somewhat curved thorns at each branch node; rarely with smaller, inter-nodal prickles	pair of straight prickles at each branch node; often many smaller, weak internodal prickles, especially on young shoots	many slender, soft prickles, mostly all the same size
leaves	coarsely double-toothed; teeth often gland-tipped	both single and double-toothed; teeth often gland-tipped	coarsely single-toothed; teeth not gland-tipped	double-toothed; teeth often gland-tipped
flowers	usually solitary; petals, 2–3 cm long	usually solitary, occasionally in groups of 2–3; petals 2.5–4 cm long	usually in clusters of 3 or more; petals about 1–2 cm long	usually single; petals 1–1.5 cm long
fruits	pear-shaped, purplish, 1-2 cm diameter, with constricted neck and persistant calyx	round, purplish red 1-2 cm in diameter with persistant calyx	round, red, 6-12 mm in diameter, with persistant calyx	round to pear-shaped, about 6 mm in diameter, calyx absent from mature hips

PRICKLY ROSE • *Rosa acicularis*

GENERAL: Deciduous shrub, to 1.5 m tall, stems usually densely covered with many **straight, bristly prickles.**

LEAVES: Divided into **5–7 oblong leaflets,** each **doubly toothed,** usually **somewhat hairy on underside.**

FLOWERS: Large and **pink,** with 5 broad petals; **borne singly** on short side branches.

FRUITS: Scarlet, round to pear-shaped fleshy hips, with sepals remaining at top.

ECOLOGY: Widespread and common at low to mid elevations in open forest and on open slopes, floodplains, clearings and other disturbed areas.

NOTES: Prickly rose is the floral emblem of Alberta. • Rose hips are high in vitamin C, and they are one of the best natural sources of this vitamin, with 10–100 times more of it than other foods, as well as providing calcium, vitamin A and phosphorus. They are used to make herbal teas, jams and jellies, and were also eaten by native people on a casual basis or in times of scarcity. The seeds were discarded and only the outside rind was eaten. Rose hips are eaten through autumn and early winter by coyotes, bears and other wildlife. • *Rosa* is the classical Latin name for the rose, and *acicularis* means 'prickly.'

BALDHIP ROSE • *Rosa gymnocarpa*

GENERAL: Spindly, deciduous shrub, to 1.5 m tall, usually with **many soft, straight prickles,** occasionally unarmed (especially on younger stems, which are usually covered with **stalked glands**).

LEAVES: Compound with **5–9 toothed leaflets,** smooth on both sides.

FLOWERS: Pale pink to rose, small (1–2 cm across) with 5 broad petals; borne singly at end of branches on glandular stalks.

FRUITS: Orange to scarlet, pear-shaped, fleshy hips; without attached sepals.

ECOLOGY: Widespread and common at low to mid elevations throughout southern half of our region, in dry to moist, open forests and openings; absent from arid basins.

SIMILAR SPECIES: Several introduced rose species are occasionally found in disturbed sites in our region. They can usually be separated from our native species by their curved prickles. • Baldhip rose occasionally hybridizes with prickly rose (*R. acicularis*, above) and perhaps with Nootka rose (*R. nutkana*, p. 65).

NOTES: All Interior Salish people widely used baldhip rose for medicinal and spiritual purposes. The St'at'imc used it to cure many sicknesses, and it has spiritual connotations and was used for protection for new dance initiates, young people at puberty, or relatives of the deceased. The Nlaka'pmx thought of baldhip rose as the 'little relative' of Nootka rose. A pleasant tonic can be made from the young leaves and twigs. A decoction was also used as an eyewash for sore eyes. The leaves and bark were dried, toasted and the resulting powder was smoked. The spines of baldhip rose were considered poisonous, causing swelling and irritation if touched. The hips were not usually eaten, except as a famine food, and if ingested they were said to give the person an 'itchy bottom.' • In baldhip rose, the sepals fall away from the hip early, leaving the end of it 'bald.' Baldhip rose is also called dwarf rose. The species name is Greek for 'naked fruit,' and it also refers to the 'bald' hips.

NOOTKA ROSE • *Rosa nutkana*

GENERAL: Spindly to stout, **deciduous** shrub, to 3 m tall, with a **pair of large thorns at base of each leaf**, usually without internodal prickles.

LEAVES: Compound, with **5–7 toothed leaflets** with more or less **round tips**; slightly hairy beneath.

FLOWERS: Pink and large (4–8 cm across), with 5 broad petals, borne singly at end of side branches.

FRUITS: Purplish-red, round hips, with sepals remaining at top.

ECOLOGY: Scattered and locally common at low to mid elevations in generally open, often disturbed habitats, seepage areas, floodplains and lakeshores.

NOTES: The foliage and young stems of wild roses are browsed by wild ungulates and domestic livestock. • The medicinal and spiritual uses of Nootka rose were similar to those of baldhip rose (*R. gymnocarpa*, p. 64). The Interior Salish believe this plant offers protection from any bad influences and cleanses people after contact with the dead. The Secwepemc made arrows from rose wood, and rose leaves were chewed and put on insect bites to alleviate pain and swelling.

PRAIRIE ROSE • *Rosa woodsii*

GENERAL: Deciduous shrub, to 2 m tall, with **freely branched stems**, armed with **a pair of straight prickles at base of each leaf**; young shoots bristly.

LEAVES: Divided into **5–7 oblong, single-toothed leaflets**, usually somewhat **hairy below**.

FLOWERS: Pink, rather small, with 5 broad petals; usually **in few-flowered clusters** on short side branches.

FRUITS: Dark red, round to oval, fleshy hips, with sepals remaining at top.

ECOLOGY: Widespread and locally common at low to mid elevations on our dry plateaus and in dry East Kootenays and their arid basins, in grasslands, dry open forests, rocky slopes and clearings.

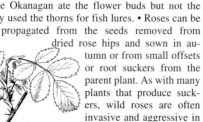

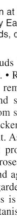

NOTES: The Okanagan ate the flower buds but not the hips, and they used the thorns for fish lures. • Roses can be propagated from the seeds removed from dried rose hips and sown in autumn or from small offsets or root suckers from the parent plant. As with many plants that produce suckers, wild roses are often invasive and aggressive in the home garden. • Prairie rose is also called Woods's rose. The species is named for Joseph Woods (1776–1864), an English botanist who studied the genus *Rosa*.

SHRUBBY CINQUEFOIL • *Potentilla fruticosa*

GENERAL: Low deciduous shrub, 30–130 cm tall; **silky-hairy** young branches and brown, shredding bark.

LEAVES: Divided into **3–7 greyish-green leaflets**; often with **curled edges**; lightly hairy.

FLOWERS: Golden yellow, saucer-shaped (small and pale at low elevations to larger and brighter at high elevations); solitary or few, in clusters near branch tips.

FRUITS: Clusters of seeds with **long, straight hairs**.

ECOLOGY: Scattered and locally common at mid to subalpine elevations in open, often moist habitats, such as peat bogs, tundra and high-elevation meadows; also in dry meadows, cliffs, rocky slopes and gravelly river flats in areas with calcium-rich soils; generally absent from Fraser Plateau, arid basins and wet Columbia Mountains.

NOTES: Our only truly shrubby *Potentilla* species, shrubby cinquefoil is a popular garden ornamental, with many cultivars. It is easily propagated from soft-wood cuttings taken early in summer. • 'Cinquefoil' is from the Latin *quinque*, meaning 'five,' and *folium*, meaning 'leaf,' and refers to the fact that many *Potentilla* species have five leaflets and their flower parts are in fives. *Potentilla* is from the Latin *potens*, referring to the medicinal properties of some cinquefoils. The species name *fruticosa* means 'shrubby.'

ANTELOPE-BUSH • *Purshia tridentata*

GENERAL: Rigidly branched, deciduous shrub, 1–2 m tall; grey or brown bark and **twigs covered with dense woolly hairs**.

LEAVES: Wedge-shaped with 3-toothed tips; hairy to woolly and **silvery greenish on upper surfaces, greyish woolly below**, edges usually rolled under.

FLOWERS: Bright yellow, numerous, **funnel-shaped**, with 5 deciduous petals on a **hairy and glandular calyx**; **solitary** on very short, leafy branches.

FRUITS: Spindle-shaped seeds, velvety and glandular.

ECOLOGY: Widespread and common at low elevations mainly in very arid southernmost parts of Okanagan Basin and southern Rocky Mountain Trench; in dry sagebrush grasslands and dry open ponderosa pine forests; favours sandy soils.

SIMILAR SPECIES: The wedge-shaped, 3-toothed leaves of antelope-bush closely resemble those of big sagebrush (*Artemisia tridentata*, p. 67) with which it is often found. Big sagebrush has many composite flowers in a loose terminal cluster and blooms in late summer and autumn.

NOTES: Antelope-bush is an important browse plant for deer and other hoofed mammals. The seeds are often taken by chipmunks, ground squirrels and deer mice, and clusters of seedlings can often be seen sprouting from old seed caches. • This plant is useful for covering dry slopes and sandy sites. Although it can be propagated by layering, antelope-bush grows best from seed with winter stratification. Direct seeding on rangelands in late autumn has been successful.

COMMON RABBIT-BRUSH • *Chrysothamnus nauseosus*

GENERAL: Compact shrub to 1 m tall; **flexible** stem branches, covered with **dense felt-like hairs**.

LEAVES: Long and narrow-linear, with **dense greyish, velvety hairs** on both surfaces.

FLOWERS: Small and yellow, borne in small, **composite heads** of usually 5 disk flowers in dense inflorescences at branch tips; blooms in late summer.

FRUITS: Linear hairy seeds.

ECOLOGY: Widespread and common at low to mid elevations throughout Fraser, Thompson and Okanagan basins and adjacent low-elevation plateaus, as well as dry East Kootenays, in grasslands, dry, open ponderosa pine and Douglas-fir forests and disturbed areas.

SIMILAR SPECIES: Green rabbit-brush (*C. viscidiflorus*) is restricted to the extreme southern Okanagan Basin in our region. It **lacks the dense felt-like hairiness on the twigs**, and it has **very brittle twigs**. Its leaves are often spirally twisted.

NOTES: After childbirth, Okanagan women used the leaves as sanitary napkins and Northern Secwepemc women drank a tea made from its leaves to ease cramps. The St'at'imc drank an infusion from the leaves to cure sore throats. The branches were used for smoking hides. • The genus name *Chrysothamus* means 'golden-crowned,' in reference to the flowers, and the species name refers to the smell of the plant, which is sweet and cloying, but not nauseating. The common name arose because this plant is heavily browsed by jack rabbits, as well as deer and mountain sheep.

BIG SAGEBRUSH • *Artemisia tridentata*

GENERAL: More or less erect, branching, **greyish, evergreen, aromatic shrub**, to 2 m tall; greyish, shredding bark on older branches and densely hairy young twigs.

LEAVES: Wedge-shaped, 1–3 cm long, mostly **3-toothed at tip** (some upper leaves without teeth); both surfaces with **dense, greyish hairs**; often persistent throughout winter.

FLOWERS: Small and yellow, borne in **composite heads** of 3–5 disk flowers in elongated, loose inflorescences; blooms in late summer.

FRUITS: Sparsely hairy seeds.

ECOLOGY: Widespread and common at low to mid elevations in Fraser, Thompson and Okanagan basins and southern Rocky Mountain Trench, in arid grasslands; intolerant of alkaline soils.

SIMILAR SPECIES: Threetip sagebrush (*A. tripartita*) is generally smaller, has leaves that are deeply cleft into three narrow, linear divisions and has 5–8 disk flowers in its composite heads. It occurs in similar to slightly moister habitats than big sagebrush in the most southerly parts of our region. • Vasey's big sagebrush (*A. tridentata* var. *vaseyana*) is a higher-elevation variety of big sagebrush that occurs at mid to moderately high elevations (over 1,150 m) in the southern half of our region.

NOTES: Southern Interior native peoples used the sagebrush leaves and branches to make teas for colds, and they used the leaves widely as a fumigant and dried as a smudge. The Secwepemc also used the tea to soak sore feet. The Nlaka'pmx wove the bark into mats, bags and clothing, especially cloaks and ponchos. • Overgrazing by domestic livestock has led to a dramatic increase in the abundance of big sagebrush from its levels before Euroamerican settlement.

CASCARA • *Rhamnus purshiana*

GENERAL: Tall deciduous shrub with groups of erect stems, or small tree to 10 m tall; very **bitter silver-grey bark.**

LEAVES: Alternate (may appear almost opposite on new growth), **egg-shaped to oblong**, dark green, finely toothed, 6–12 cm long; with **10–15 pairs of prominent, parallel veins,** with short hairs below.

FLOWERS: Small (3–4 mm long), **greenish yellow**, with 5 petals; in umbrella-shaped clusters of 8–40 from leaf axils.

FRUITS: Blue-black to purplish-black berries, 5–8 mm across; edible but not flavourful.

ECOLOGY: Scattered and infrequent at low to mid elevations in wet Columbia Mountains south of Shuswap Lake and in Coast/Interior Transition, in dry to wet, often shady forests, most commonly in mixed woods.

SIMILAR SPECIES: Alder-leaved buckthorn (*R. alnifolia*) is a small shrub (0.5–1.5 m tall) that grows in swamps and wet meadows and along streambanks in the most southern Columbia Mountains. It has eight or fewer pairs of non-hairy leaf veins, and its flowers lack petals and occur in small clusters of 2–5.

NOTES: Cascara is the only deciduous tree in B.C. whose buds are not covered by scales in winter. The bright yellow inner bark turns dark brown on exposure to air and light. • Cascara bark was peeled and steeped in water to make a laxative tea (or syrup). Originally, only the fresh bark was collected, but soon it was realized that the wood contained 50% of the active compound. Overharvesting was prevented by legislation, which was rescinded after a synthetic source was developed. • Spanish priests in California named the tree *Cascara sagrada* (sacred bark), in reference to the medicinal properties of the bark or to its resemblance to the wood used for the Ark of the Covenant. The genus name *Rhamnus* is from the ancient Greek name for a similar plant.

REDSTEM CEANOTHUS • *Ceanothus sanguineus*

GENERAL: Erect, **deciduous** shrub, 1–3 m tall; smooth, **reddish or purplish bark**; new twigs have spicy flavour.

LEAVES: Alternate, **oval**, thin; 3 main veins branching from leaf base and a pair of stipules at base of each leaf stalk.

FLOWERS: Tiny and white, in **dense, fluffy, clusters** on **reddish stalks** at branch ends; fragrant.

FRUITS: Hardened explosive **3-lobed capsules**, containing shiny brown seeds.

ECOLOGY: Scattered and locally common, mostly at low to mid elevations in warm moist climates in southern half of our region, in dry to moist, open forests, openings, clearings and other disturbed habitats; infrequent on Fraser Plateau north to Quesnel; common following fire.

SIMILAR SPECIES: Snowbrush (*C. velutinus*, p. 69) is found in similar habitats, but it is usually shorter and evergreen, and it has thick, shiny leaves that are often sticky above and velvety below. It lacks the red flower stalks that characterize redstem ceanothus.

NOTES: Both *Ceanothus* species are important browse for deer—they are often called buckbrush—and they often show signs of heavy use. • The Okanagan dried the bark and made a poultice from the powder to heal burns. They also used the wood as fuel when smoking deer meat. The plant contains the toxic compound saponin, and if the flowering twigs are beaten in water they produce a soapy foam that early settlers used to call soapbloom.

SNOWBRUSH • *Ceanothus velutinus*

GENERAL: Sprawling, evergreen, spicy-scented shrub, usually 0.5–2 m tall (sometimes to 3 m); green bark.

LEAVES: Alternate, broadly oval with toothed edges and **3 main veins** branching from base of leaf; **shiny and often sticky above, velvety below**; paired stipules on leaf stalk where it joins stem.

FLOWERS: Tiny and white, borne in **dense, pyramidal clusters along side branches** near end of twigs; fragrant.

FRUITS: Hardened, explosive, **3-lobed capsules**, containing 3 shiny seeds.

ECOLOGY: Widespread and common at low to subalpine elevations in dry Thompson and Okanagan plateaus, Okanagan Basin and East Kootenays, in dry to moist forests, openings and dry rocky slopes; locally common in warm dry valleys of southwest Chilcotin; often increasing following fire.

NOTES: *Ceanothus* produce abundant, heat-resistant seeds that appear able to remain dormant in the soil for at least 200 years. Their germination is stimulated by fire, which also opens up areas where the plants can grow vigorously. • These shrubs are also 'nitrogen fixers.' Bacteria in nodules on their roots absorb nitrogen from the air and convert it into a form useful to plants, which can give these shrubs a real advantage over their associates, but they are eventually over topped by young trees. • The Ktunaxa made the leaves into a tea that was said to be good for tuberculosis. The

Okanagan used a decoction for eczema, dandruff and skin sores. The Nlaka'pmx used a decoction of the branches for arthritis and rheumatism. • In the dry Interior, the lower surfaces of the leaves are covered with a dense silky or velvety covering of hairs—the species name *velutinus* means 'velvety'—that prevents excessive water loss. This hairiness is less conspicuous in more humid Coastal areas. • The name 'snowbush' presumably refers to the dense covering of flowers, although they are usually more greenish than white. This plant is also known as greasewood and snowbush ceanothus.

SHRUBBY PENSTEMON • *Penstemon fruticosus*

GENERAL: Somewhat evergreen shrub or semi-shrub, to 40 cm tall; stems often reddish and brittle; hairless to finely hairy on new growth and glandular hairy in inflorescence.

LEAVES: Mostly **opposite** linear to broadly lance-shaped, with smooth to toothed edges; dark green and hairless above.

FLOWERS: Blue-lavender to purple, with 2-lipped corollas; lower lip white hairy within; in pairs in a short, leafy-bracted cluster at ends of stems.

FRUITS: Small capsules.

ECOLOGY: Scattered and locally common at low to subalpine elevations, on dry, rocky hillsides, cliffs, roadsides and dry open forests; mostly on warm aspects at low elevations.

NOTES: The Nlaka'pmx had many uses for this spectacular plant. They made a dye from it to colour basket materials, and they used it in pit-cooking to flavour root vegetables. A decoction of the branches was taken as a purgative, to treat ulcers and to bathe sores, eye injuries and aches from rheumatism and arthritis. The Secwepemc also used it to wash sore or injured eyes. • Shrubby penstemon is one of our showiest shrubs. It is quite hardy throughout most of our region, and it is easily propagated from cuttings or by layering. To keep the plants attractive and flowering abundantly, plant it in a gritty soil in a sunny exposure. • The species name *fruticosus* means 'shrub-like.'

SMOOTH SUMAC • *Rhus glabra*

GENERAL: Deciduous shrub, 1–3 m tall, **widely spreading from elongated shallow roots**; smooth to sparsely hairy branches with smooth bark.

LEAVES: Compound, with 7–29 **lance-shaped to elliptic leaflets**, shallowly toothed; turning deep red in autumn.

FLOWERS: Small and **yellowish**, aggregated into large **pyramid-shaped clusters**.

FRUITS: Berry-like, reddish and hairy, in clusters that persist for a long time.

ECOLOGY: Scattered and locally common, primarily at low elevations in Okanagan Basin, but scattered north along Thompson and Fraser rivers to Williams Lake, on dry open slopes, forest edges, dry cutbanks along roadsides, rocky ridges and along watercourses.

NOTES: The Northern Secwepemc smoked dry sumac like tobacco, and the Nlaka'pmx used it as a medication for ulcers and other ailments. • Despite its habit of spreading rapidly, this species is valued as a garden ornamental because of its showy fruits and fine autumn colours. • The name 'sumac' (sometimes spelled 'sumach') comes from the Syrian word *summaq*, meaning 'red.' This name was given to a small tree native to the Mediterranean region, *Rhus coriaria*, because it yielded a red dye that was used to tan morocco leathers. The genus name *Rhus* is believed to be derived from *rhous*, meaning 'reddish.' *Glabra* refers to the smooth bark of this species.

POISON-IVY • *Rhus radicans*
Toxicodendron rydbergii

GENERAL: Sprawling to erect deciduous shrub, to 0.5–2 m tall, from creeping rootstock; forms open colonies; somewhat hairy.

LEAVES: Compound with **3 pointed, more or less equal leaflets**, with prominent veins and smooth to shallowly toothed to lobed edges; **shiny green**, turning bright scarlet in autumn.

FLOWERS: Whitish yellow and inconspicuous, in dense clusters at leaf bases.

FRUITS: Berry-like, white with a greenish or yellowish cast, smooth.

ECOLOGY: Scattered and locally abundant at low elevations, mostly in dry Okanagan Basin, but also in widely scattered locations north to Williams Lake; in dry to mesic, open Douglas-fir and ponderosa pine forests, moist draws and often along trails and roadsides.

NOTES: **Caution: this is a poisonous plant.** Poison-ivy contains a volatile oil (urushiol) that can cause an itching, burning rash upon contact with the skin. It is common enough to be a major problem for people who are highly allergic to it. Pollen and even smoke from burning poison-ivy can cause the response. The shiny, compound leaves with three leaflets are the key to recognizing poison-ivy— 'leaflets three, let it be.' • Poison-ivy is sometimes mistakenly called poison-oak, but that name properly refers to *R. diversiloba*, a very similar shrub from west of the Cascades. • The Secwepemc bathed affected skin with the boiled tops of balsamroot (*Balsamorhiza sagittata*) and also drank large quantities of Labrador tea (*Ledum groenlandicum*). The Southern Okanagan rubbed the affected area with the milky latex from the stems of a related species, smooth sumac (*R. glabra*).

WOLF-WILLOW • *Elaeagnus commutata*

GENERAL: Deciduous shrub (sometimes tree-like), 1–4 m tall, from **spreading rhizomes**; twigs densely covered with rusty brown scales.

LEAVES: Alternate, oval to oblong-elliptic, densely **silvery scaly** on both surfaces, paler below.

FLOWERS: Silvery, **funnel-shaped** corollas with 4 **yellowish lobes**, borne in clusters of 1–3 at leaf bases; **very fragrant**.

FRUITS: Silvery mealy berries, about 1 cm long, each with a single large nutlet.

ECOLOGY: Scattered and infrequent at low to mid elevations on our plateaus and in East Kootenays, on sandbars, silty cutbanks, gullies, wetland edges and in disturbed areas; spreads rapidly in disturbed areas.

SIMILAR SPECIES: The hardy ornamental, Russian olive (*E. angustifolia*) has been planted extensively around homes throughout our region. It has also been used extensively on the prairies to provide windbreaks. The Russian olive has spines on its branches and narrow linear leaves.

NOTES: The tough, fibrous bark provided the Nlaka'pmx, Okanagan, St'at'imc and Secwepemc with an important material for making bags, baskets, rope and other woven materials. The Okanagan traders considered that three 13-cm-thick bundles of prepared bark were worth one blanket. The silvery fruits were strung as beads for necklaces. • Wolf-willow is also called silverberry.

SOOPOLALLIE • *Shepherdia canadensis*

GENERAL: Spreading, **deciduous** shrub, 1–2 m tall; brownish **branches covered with small, bran-like scabs**; young branches covered with many rusty spots.

LEAVES: Opposite, oval; with dark greenish upper surfaces, and a **silvery-whitish felt of hairs and rusty brown spots** (scales) below.

FLOWERS: Inconspicuous and yellowish brown, borne in clusters of 1 to several on stems, before leaves open; male and female flowers on separate plants.

FRUITS: Bright red, translucent, oval berries; juicy but extremely bitter and soapy to the touch.

ECOLOGY: Widespread and very common at low to subalpine elevations in dry to moist open forests, openings and clearings.

NOTES: Soopolallie has bacterial nodules in its roots that capture nitrogen from the air, eventually releasing this important nutrient to the soil. • All Interior native groups whip up the berries with a little water into a light froth, called Indian ice-cream. The berries are rich in iron and were either eaten fresh, dried for later use or boiled into a syrup for use as a beverage. They were an important trade item and are still valued as gifts. Native people used the berries, juice, twigs or leaves medicinally for everything from heart attacks to indigestion. Most importantly, the sticks were valued as a purgative. • The name 'soopolallie' is Chinook for 'soap' (*soop*) 'berry' (*olallie*). This plant is so-named because the berry pulp is soapy to the touch, and 'soapberry' is another common English name for it. The berries contain glucoside-saponin, which is responsible for the soapy, bitter foam produced when they are whipped. The Interior Salish name for this plant is their word for 'foam.' Other common names are 'buffalo berry,' 'hooshum berry' and 'bearberry.' The genus *Shepherdia* is named after the English botanist John Shepherd (1764–1836).

TALL OREGON-GRAPE • *Mahonia aquifolium*
Berberis aquifolium

GENERAL: Erect, **evergreen**, stiff-branched shrub, 20–100 cm tall; **yellowish bark and wood**.

LEAVES: Pinnately compound with 5–9 **leathery**, oblong to egg-shaped leaflets, **glossy green above**, with prominent **spiny teeth along edges** (resembles leaves of English holly).

FLOWERS: Bright yellow in many-flowered erect clusters; flower parts in 6s.

FRUITS: Blue berries with several large seeds and a whitish bloom, in elongated clusters; edible but sour.

ECOLOGY: Widespread and common at low to mid elevations on our dry plateaus and in dry East Kootenays, in dry to moist forests, openings and clearings; also scattered in dry open forests on warm aspects, clearings and warm rocky hillsides at low to mid elevations in remainder of our region.

SIMILAR SPECIES: The smaller dull Oregon-grape (*M. nervosa*) has 9–19 leaflets per leaf and is a Coastal species found sporadically in dry to moist, semi-shaded forest on the eastern slopes of the Cascades.

NOTES: Southern Interior native people extracted from the inner bark of the stems and roots a bright yellow pigment they used to dye basket materials or porcupine quills. Although the berries are tart, the Secwepemc, Nlaka'pmx, Okanagan and St'at'imc ate them and made a jelly from them for meats. • This species was first introduced to horticulture in 1823. The large clusters of sweet-smelling golden-yellow flowers set on the background of shiny green foliage, and the blue-grey berries, make a fine addition to in the home garden.

FALSEBOX • *Pachistima myrsinites*

GENERAL: Erect or prostrate, **dense**, **evergreen** shrub, to 60 cm tall; reddish-brown, 4-ridged branches.

LEAVES: Opposite (or nearly so), oval to elliptic, 1–3 cm long, **shiny, thick and leathery** with **toothed edges**, slightly rolled under.

FLOWERS: Numerous, **very small, maroon flowers** in small clusters along branches; fragrant; blooms in spring.

FRUITS: Small, oval capsules, mostly with a white, fleshy covering and 1–2 dark brown seeds.

ECOLOGY: Widespread and common at low to mid elevations in coniferous forest, rocky openings and clearings; generally absent from our dry plateaus, East Kootenays and arid basins.

SIMILAR SPECIES: This shrub resembles kinnikinnick (*Arctostaphylos uva-ursi*, p. 85), which has bright red berries and alternate, toothless leaves.

NOTES: Falsebox is particularly susceptible to *armillaria* root disease and often provides the first clue to the disease's presence in an area. • It provides good browse for deer. • The Okanagan-Colville people boiled the branches to make a tea for colds, tuberculosis and kidney troubles. The Nlaka'pmx used it to heal broken bones and swellings, and to heal internal ailments. • The branches provide decorative greenery in floral arrangements, and, in recent times, many people have earned a living by harvesting the branches for florists, often depleting areas near urban centres. • The genus name is from the Greek *pachys* (thick) and refers to the thick stigma. The species name *myrsinites* is from the Greek word for myrrh—smell the flowers! The common name comes from Old English *box* or Latin *buxus*. A 'box' was originally a receptacle made from the boxwood tree (*Buxus sempervirens*), whose form and foliage is reminiscent of *Pachistima* species. Falsebox is also known as mountain boxwood and Oregon boxwood.

DOUGLAS MAPLE • *Acer glabrum*

GENERAL: Deciduous shrub to small tree, 1–7 m tall; **opposite branches**, reddish twigs and **grey bark**.

LEAVES: Opposite and divided into **3–5 coarsely toothed lobes**, in typical **maple-leaf shape**, dark green above and greyish green below, turning bright red-orange in autumn.

FLOWERS: In clusters of about 10 at ends of branches, appearing with leaves; **yellow-green**; **4 petals and 4 sepals**; male and female flowers usually on separate plants, some plants (and flowers) may have both sexes; blooms in spring.

FRUITS: Pairs of winged seeds, joined at base at a sharp angle in a **V-shape**, strongly wrinkled and indented.

ECOLOGY: Widespread and common at low to subalpine elevations on moist eastern flanks of our plateaus, Coast/Interior Transition and wet Columbia Mountains, in dry to moist open forests, openings and clearings; particularly on warm southerly aspects; also in warm, dry portions of our plateaus on seepage sites and in moist gullies.

NOTES: Interior native people used the tough, pliable wood of Douglas maple to make a wide variety of goods, especially snowshoe frames. The green wood was soaked and heated before being moulded into the desired shape. Other items included throwing sticks, bows, rattles, masks and headdresses. The Nlaka'pmx and Secwepemc wove the fibrous inner bark into twine and rope. • Interior native people often mistakenly called this shrub 'vine maple,' a name that more properly refers to *A. circinatum*, which grows in coastal southwestern B.C. • Douglas maple is also called Rocky Mountain maple. The name 'maple' appears to be derived from the old Welsh *mapwl*, and refers to the knotty burls on the trunk of the European maple tree, *A. campestre*.

DEVIL'S CLUB • *Oplopanax horridus*

GENERAL: Erect to **sprawling deciduous** shrub, 1–3 m tall; stems **thick, crooked**, almost unbranched but often entangled, **armed with many large yellowish spines**; wood has distinct sweetish odour.

LEAVES: Broadly **maple-leaf shaped** (to 35 cm across), with 7–9 sharply pointed and heavily toothed lobes, on long stalks; many spines on underside; clustered at ends of stems.

FLOWERS: Small and **whitish**, with 5 sepals and petals; in dense **pyramidal clusters** at ends of stems.

FRUITS: Bright red, flattened, shiny berries in **large, showy pyramidal clusters**; not edible.

ECOLOGY: Widespread and common at low to subalpine elevations in moist shady forests, especially in wet but well-drained seepage sites and along streams, in all but the dry parts of our plateaus and East Kootenays; in wettest climates of our region it forms a major component of undergrowth on a wide range of sites.

NOTES: This fearsome plant's spines readily break off, and a wound soon festers if the spine stays embedded in the skin. This member of the ginseng family is very handsome, however, and it is gaining acceptance as a garden ornamental. Propagation is slow, whether from seeds, cuttings or layering. • Devil's club is still widely used by Interior native people for many ailments, such as stomach ulcers, thyroid conditions, syphilis and diabetes, and as an emetic, cough syrup and laxative. Various parts of the plant were ground into powders for external poultices for arthritis and rheumatism, or fresh pieces were laid on open wounds. • The genus name *Oplopanax* is from the Greek *hoplon* (weapon) and *Panax*, the name of a related, large-leaved genus.

Salix: the willows

There are about 24 native willows in our region, ranging from prostrate, dwarf shrubs to small trees. Individual species can be highly variable, and hybridization is common. Their leaves are typically long and narrow with smooth edges, but they can be nearly round, sometimes with finely toothed edges, and they vary from hairless to densely silky hairy, and sometimes have a whitish cast or bloom (glaucous). Willows have tiny flowers borne in catkins, with the male and female catkins on separate plants. The flowers develop pointed capsules that split open to release the many tiny seeds, each with a tuft of cottony hairs.

ARCTIC WILLOW • *Salix arctica*

GENERAL: Deciduous, prostrate or trailing to semi-erect **dwarf shrub**, sometimes up to 50 cm tall; stout, brown branches and **hairless** or sparsely hairy twigs.

LEAVES: Alternate, narrowly to broadly oval with **pointed tip** and smooth edges, **grey-green, with whitish cast and sparsely hairy beneath, usually with a tuft of hairs at tip.**

FLOWERS: In male or female catkins, with a **dark to black bract at base**, appearing with leaves, on prominent leafy side branches; male catkins to 5 cm long, female to 9 cm long; female flowers have hairy pistils with red styles (0.6–2.2 cm long).

FRUITS: Sparsely hairy capsules on short (0.6 mm or less) stalks.

ECOLOGY: Widespread and common in alpine tundra to open subalpine ridges.

SIMILAR SPECIES: Two other dwarf willows are often found growing with arctic willow in our region. Cascade willow (*S. cascadensis*) occurs south of Lillooet in the western part of our region. It has smaller, lance-shaped leaves that are 3–5 times as long as wide. Dwarf snow willow (*S. reticulata* ssp. *nivalis*, also known as *S. nivalis*) has strongly veined, dark green leaves that are nearly round, sometimes with long, silky hairs beneath. • Arctic willow can also be difficult to distinguish from grey–leaved willow (*S. glauca*, p. 75) and short-fruited willow (*S. brachycarpa*, p. 75).

BARCLAY'S WILLOW • *Salix barclayi*

GENERAL: Deciduous shrub, usually 1–3 m tall; dark reddish-brown branches; **yellow-green twigs, glossy, densely to sparsely hairy.**

LEAVES: Elliptic to reverse egg-shaped, with pointed tips, rounded to somewhat heart-shaped bases and **toothed edges**; young leaves are greenish and sparsely hairy, older leaves are usually hairless, sometimes sparsely hairy, with whitish cast below.

FLOWERS: In male or female catkins with a **dark bract at base**, on **short, leafy shoots**; female flowers with hairless pistils and long styles (0.5–2.5 mm).

FRUITS: Hairless capsules, on 0.5–1.5 mm stalks.

ECOLOGY: Widespread and common at mid to high elevations on lakeshores and riverbanks, and in fens, open forests, clearings and alpine and subalpine thickets.

SIMILAR SPECIES: Farr's willow (*S. hastata* var. *farrae*) is a related species of similar high-elevation habitats. It is uncommon but locally abundant in the East Kootenays. It has hairless or slightly hairy young leaves with more or less smooth edges, and shorter styles (0.2–0.4 mm long).

NOTES: Barclay's willow is a common and variable species that hybridizes with Barratt's willow (*S. barrattiana*, p. 77).

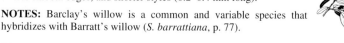

SHORT-FRUITED WILLOW • *Salix brachycarpa*
ssp. *brachycarpa*

GENERAL: Low, erect, deciduous shrub, **usually less than 1 m tall**, but sometimes to 2 m; twigs slender, densely and coarsely white- to grey-hairy.

LEAVES: Narrowly elliptic to strap-shaped, with blunt tips and **smooth edges; densely hairy on both sides, and with whitish cast beneath**; on short (0.5–4 mm) stalks.

FLOWERS: In **short and almost round to cylindrical**, male or female catkins with a pale bract at base, on short leafy shoots; female flowers have densely white woolly pistils with long styles (0.5–1.2 mm).

FRUITS: Densely woolly capsules, stalkless or on very short stalks.

ECOLOGY: Scattered and locally common at mid to high elevations in open forests, shrub-carrs, sedge fens, gravelly floodplains and lakeshores; generally absent from wet Columbia Mountains and Okanagan Plateau.

SIMILAR SPECIES: Grey-leaved willow (*S. glauca*) is another willow with catkins that arise from short leafy shoots. It is generally taller (to 3 m) than short-fruited willow. Grey-leaved willow capsules have distinct stalks. The catkins are long and remain on the plant well into winter. Grey-leaved willow is common and widespread in our region from valley bottoms to the alpine in many of the habitats of short-fruited willow.

NOTES*: Brachycarpa* means the same thing as the common name, 'short-fruited.'

PACIFIC WILLOW • *Salix lucida* ssp. *lasiandra*
S. lasiandra

GENERAL: Medium shrub or small tree, 1–9 m tall; glossy reddish-brown to yellow twigs; yellow, **duckbill-shaped buds, brittle at their base**; bark on older plants fissured.

LEAVES: Lance-shaped, tapering to a long tip; 5–15 cm long, with **toothed edges** and blades with mostly rounded base; older leaves not hairy and with whitish bloom below; **stalks with glands at base of leaf blade**; stipules prominent and glandular.

FLOWERS: Catkins appearing as leaves emerge, terminating leafy branchlets; hairy floral bracts pale yellow and falling after flowering.

FRUITS: Smooth capsules, 4–8 mm long, on short stalks (to 1 mm).

ECOLOGY: Widespread and common at low to mid elevations on wet, open sites, mostly river and stream banks and freshwater swamps; often in quiet, shallow river backwaters.

SIMILAR SPECIES: Coyote willow (*S. exigua*) is another widespread willow commonly found along rivers, but mostly on open **gravelly or sandy floodplains**. It is seldom tree-like (it grows to 3 m tall), and it spreads to **form colonies** by sprouting from widespread shallow root systems. It has linear leaves with few small, widely scattered teeth.

NOTES: Pacific willow is one of our largest native willows. It is an important component of

the winter diet of moose in parts of our region. • The St'at'imc called it 'match plant,' and they made fire drills from it. They also made a twine from the bark and rope by twisting bark and twigs together. • The species name *lucida* means 'shiny,' probably in reference to the twigs, and this species is also called shining willow.

TEA-LEAVED WILLOW • *Salix planifolia* ssp. *planifolia*
S. phylicifolia

GENERAL: Deciduous shrub, 0.5–4 m tall; hairless, dark brown to reddish-brown branches, sometimes with whitish cast; hairless to sparsely hairy and shiny twigs.

LEAVES: Elliptic to narrowly so, mostly with smooth to remotely toothed edges; young leaves sparsely hairy with short silky, sometimes rust-coloured hairs, **older leaves hairless and shiny above, sparsely silky and with whitish cast below.**

FLOWERS: In **stalkless** male or female catkins with **a hairy, dark brown to black bract at base**, appearing before leaves on previous year's growth; female flowers with densely silky pistils with long styles (0.6–0.8 mm).

FRUITS: Sparsely silky capsules on short (0.5–0.6 mm) stalks.

ECOLOGY: Scattered and locally common at low to mid elevations in fens, swamps, moist forest openings, clearings, lakeshores and streambanks.

NOTES: Native peoples used willow wood for drying meat and fish, smoking hides and making barbecue sticks, berry-drying racks, packboards, fishing weirs and snowshoes. • The leaves of many willows contain a compound related to acetyl- salicylic acid, the main ingredient in Aspirin.

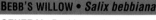

BEBB'S WILLOW • *Salix bebbiana*

GENERAL: Deciduous shrub or small tree, 0.5–5 m tall; reddish-brown branches; densely to straggly hairy twigs.

LEAVES: Elliptic to reverse egg-shaped, widest above middle, with smooth to coarsely toothed edges; **sparsely hairy on both sides**, dull green above, **grey below, with a white cast, and prominent veins.**

FLOWERS: In male or female catkins with a **pale bract at base**, **appearing just before or with leaves**, on leafy shoots or sometimes nearly stalkless; female flowers in loose catkins, with finely silky pistils, and short styles.

FRUITS: Sparsely hairy capsules on long (2–5 mm) stalks.

ECOLOGY: Widespread and common at low to mid elevations in upland forests, openings, seepage areas and wetlands and on disturbed sites.

NOTES: Bebb's willow is probably the most frequent source in our region of a wood called diamond willow, because of the striking, diamond-shaped markings beneath the bark. Fungal lesions are suspected of causing these markings. Diamond willow is often used to make decorative canes, lamps and other items of the cottage industry. • The native uses of this willow were widespread and similar to those of Scouler's willow (*S. scouleriana*, p. 77). For more information on native use of willows, see Turner (1979).

SCOULER'S WILLOW • *Salix scouleriana*

GENERAL: Tall, spindly, deciduous shrub or small, multi-stemmed tree, 2–12 m tall; branches dark brown to yellowish brown, often velvety; twigs densely velvety; bark on older stems grey and lightly fissured.

LEAVES: Reverse egg-shaped to narrowly elliptic, with tapering bases and smooth to weakly toothed edges; young leaves densely velvety; older leaves dark green above, **sparsely hairy below** with short appressed hairs (**some rust-coloured**), or densely hairy with woolly hairs, with **white cast below**.

FLOWERS: In stalkless male or female catkins with a **dark brown to black bract at base, appearing well before leaves**, on previous year's branches; female flowers with densely silky pistils, and short (0.2–0.6 mm) styles, with stigmas often twice as long as styles.

FRUITS: Silky capsules, on **stalks 0.8–2 mm long.**

ECOLOGY: Widespread and common at low to mid elevations in upland forests, seepage areas, clearings and wetlands; often occurring on drier sites than most other willow species.

SIMILAR SPECIES: When lacking catkins, or mature leaves, Scouler's willow and Bebb's willow (*S. bebbiana*, p. 76) can be difficult to differentiate. • Sitka willow (*S. sitchensis*, below) closely resembles Scouler's willow, but it has brittle twigs and dense satiny hairs on the lower leaf surface.

NOTES: The Interior Salish and Carrier peeled inner willow bark in the spring and twisted it into a twine that was strong when wet but brittle when dry. It was used for tying a variety of objects and for making fishing nets, which had to be folded wet and then soaked before using again so they would not break. Shredded bark was used as diapers, wound dressings and sanitary napkins. The bark was used medicinally as a poultice for bleeding wounds and cuts. • This common species is named for Dr. John Scouler, an associate of David Douglas.

SITKA WILLOW • *Salix sitchensis*

GENERAL: Deciduous shrub or small tree, 1–8 m tall; branches dark brown to red, grey with age, sparsely hairy with **densely velvety twigs, brittle at the base**.

LEAVES: Narrowly reverse **egg-shaped** to elliptic, with smooth or gland-dotted edges that are slightly rolled under; bright green and sparsely silky above, **satiny with short appressed hairs below**; on yellow, velvety stalks.

FLOWERS: In male or female catkins with a **brown bract at base, on short leafy shoots**; male flowers with **1 stamen**; female flowers with densely silky pistils and short styles (0.4–0.8 mm).

FRUITS: Silky capsules on short (0.5–1.4 mm) stalks.

ECOLOGY: Widespread and common at low to subalpine elevations in open moist forests, wet openings, clearings, avalanche tracks, lakeshores and wetland edges; most common in wet Columbia Mountains and Coast/Interior Transition.

SIMILAR SPECIES: Barratt's willow (*S. barrattiana*), another widespread, hairy-leaved willow, occurs sporadically in our region at high subalpine and alpine elevations of calcareous mountains, such as the Rockies and Marble Range. It is usually less than 1 m tall, and it has gnarled, stout, black, oily or sticky twigs and greyish leaves with long hairs on both surfaces. • Flowerless specimens of Sitka willow are distinguished from Scouler's willow (*S. scouleriana*, above) by their brittle twigs and the satiny lustre on the lower leaf surfaces.

NOTES: The Okanagan used a decoction of Sitka willow against stomach ailments. • This species is heavily browsed by moose in the northern parts of our region.

SCRUB BIRCH • *Betula glandulosa* var. *glandulosa*

GENERAL: Low and spreading to erect, **deciduous** shrub, 30–200 cm tall; **resinous twigs** covered with **wart-like crystalline glands** that look like octopus suckers (under 10x magnification); indistinctly fine-hairy.

LEAVES: Nearly **circular, with round-toothed edges**, somewhat **thick and leathery; glandular on both surfaces**, bright green and usually hairless above, paler and often hairy below.

FLOWERS: Small and inconspicuous, in separate male or female catkins **developing with leaves**; male catkins drooping; **female catkins erect**, about 2 cm long, neither woody nor cone-like.

FRUITS: Slightly winged **nutlets**.

ECOLOGY: Widespread and common at low to high elevations in wetlands, seepage areas and moist, cold spruce forests and along wetland fringes; generally absent from arid basins.

SIMILAR SPECIES: This variety is often difficult to distinguish from swamp birch (*B. glandulosa* var. *glandulifera*, also known as *B. pumila*), sometimes called dwarf birch, which is also found throughout our region. The **leaves of scrub birch are circular, with three or fewer lateral veins** and 10 or fewer teeth on each side. The **leaves of swamp birch are more oval, with four or more lateral veins** and more than 10 teeth on each side. Swamp birch is generally less glandular and more hairy and its nutlets have broader wings than do those of scrub birch.

NOTES: The leaves of scrub birch turn a deep orange to russet in autumn, providing seasonal colour to many of our wetlands. Scrub birch is best propagated from seed sown in autumn. • The species name *glandulosa* means 'with glands,' in reference to the twigs. Scrub birch is also called bog birch.

SITKA ALDER • *Alnus crispa* ssp. *sinuata*
A. sinuata, A. viridis ssp. *sinuata, A. sitchensis*

GENERAL: Coarse, **deciduous** shrub or small tree, 1–5 m tall; **pointed, stalkless buds** and yellowish brown, scaly bark.

LEAVES: Thin and **broadly oval** with rounded bases, pointed tips and **wavy-lobed (sinuate), double-toothed edges**; slightly sticky below.

FLOWERS: Tiny and inconspicuous, in separate male or female catkins **developing with leaves**; male catkins long and drooping; **female catkins short, woody, cone-like**.

FRUITS: Broadly winged nutlets in **egg-shaped cones, on stalks longer than cones**.

ECOLOGY: Widespread and common at low elevations to timberline in well-drained upland forests and clearings and seepage areas on northerly aspects; often forms thickets along roads or in avalanche tracks; mostly absent from our arid basins.

NOTES: Sitka alder grows in disturbed areas, often where few other shrubs can establish. • Native people widely used Sitka alder to make a reddish dye, and for fuel, smoking salmon and meat, carving and basket making. • Alders are important in improving soil fertility by fixing atmospheric nitrogen in nodules on their roots. All of our alders are easily propagated from freshly collected seed (released in autumn). • The subspecies name *sinuata* refers to the wavy or sinuous leaf edge that distinguishes this subspecies from green alder (*A. crispa* ssp. *crispa*), the northern subspecies.

MOUNTAIN ALDER • *Alnus incana* ssp. *tenuifolia*

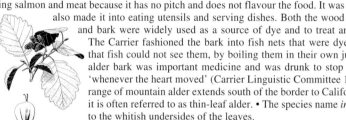

GENERAL: Coarse shrub or small **deciduous** tree, 2–10 m tall, often grows in clumps; woolly hairy to hairless twigs, **club-shaped buds on short stalks**; yellow-brown bark with distinct horizontal slits (lenticels).

LEAVES: Thin and **oval**, with rounded to somewhat heart-shaped bases, rounded to blunt tips and **shallowly lobed, double-toothed edges**; green above, **pale and hairy** below.

FLOWERS: Small and inconspicuous, in separate male or female catkins **developing before leaves**; male catkins long and drooping; **female catkins short, woody, cone-like.**

FRUITS: Narrowly winged nutlets in **egg-shaped cones** on **very short stalks.**

ECOLOGY: Widespread and locally abundant at low to subalpine elevations along streams, at edges of ponds, lakes and swamps and in other poorly drained sites.

NOTES: As in other alders, the leaves of mountain alder remain green through much of autumn. • Mountain alder was considered the best for smoking and drying salmon and meat because it has no pitch and does not flavour the food. It was also made it into eating utensils and serving dishes. Both the wood and bark were widely used as a source of dye and to treat animal hides. The Carrier fashioned the bark into fish nets that were dyed black, so that fish could not see them, by boiling them in their own juice. Boiled alder bark was important medicine and was drunk to stop bleeding or 'whenever the heart moved' (Carrier Linguistic Committee 1973). • The range of mountain alder extends south of the border to California, where it is often referred to as thin-leaf alder. • The species name *incana* refers to the whitish undersides of the leaves.

BEAKED HAZELNUT • *Corylus cornuta*

GENERAL: Deciduous shrub with many stems, 1–4 m tall; twigs, leaves and **bud scales covered in long, white hairs**, at least when young, hairless after first season; densely clumped or spreading widely by suckers.

LEAVES: Elliptic to oval, commonly with a **heart-shaped base** and sharply pointed tip; doubly **saw-toothed edges**; turning yellow in autumn.

FLOWERS: Tiny, inconspicuous, in separate male or female clusters that **develop before the leaves**; male flowers in drooping catkins, **2–3 female flowers in tiny clusters** at branch tips, erect, with protruding red stigmas.

FRUITS: Clusters of 2–3 **spherical, edible nuts**, enclosed in tubular, light green husks covered in stiff prickly hairs and projecting beyond nut into a beak.

ECOLOGY: Scattered and locally abundant at low to mid elevations, mostly in southern two-thirds of wet Columbia Mountains and along Fraser and Quesnel rivers in northern part of our region, on moist but well-drained sites in open forests, shady openings, thickets, clearings and rocky slopes.

NOTES: Many southern Interior native peoples enjoyed hazelnuts and traded them with groups who were unable to harvest sufficient quantities. An easy way to collect hazelnuts was to raid squirrel and chipmunk caches and take a quantity from each cache. It was important to ensure that some nuts were left for the animal to survive the winter. The wood of beaked hazelnut was sometimes made into arrow shafts. • The genus name *Corylus* is from the Greek word for the hazelnut (*korylos*, literally 'a helmet'). The species name *cornuta* means 'beaked.' Both names refer to the husk around the nut.

RED-OSIER DOGWOOD • *Cornus stolonifera C. sericea*

GENERAL: Many stemmed, **deciduous** shrub, 1–4 m tall, freely spreading from stems that become prostrate; **branches opposite**, with lower branches often lying on ground and rooting (layering) freely; **young stems usually bright red, especially after frost.**

LEAVES: Opposite, oval and mostly sharp-pointed with **5–7 prominent parallel veins** that converge at leaf tip; turning reddish in autumn.

FLOWERS: Small, **white to greenish**, in **dense flat-topped clusters** at ends of stems.

FRUITS: Clusters of **small, white** (often blue-tinged), **berry-like fruits**, each with a large, somewhat flattened stone; bitter.

ECOLOGY: Widespread and often abundant at low to mid elevations in swamps, moist to wet upland forests, openings and clearings.

NOTES: This species is an extremely important moose winter browse. • The Ktunaxa made a sweet-and-sour dish of dogwood berries, saskatoons and sugar. The Secwepemc used the berries as a mouthwash. The boiled inner bark was used for any kind of sickness or applied as a poultice to sores and swellings to kill pain. The branches were used for fish traps, poles and salmon stretchers. The Secwepemc made their sweathouses out of the bent branches. • Red-osier dogwood is one of our most valuable native shrubs for environmental plantings on moist soils. It is most easily propogated from cuttings, by layering or from suckers. • 'Osier' appears to be from the Old French *osiere,* meaning 'that which grows in an osier-bed.' An 'osier-bed' is a river bed. 'Dogwood' probably comes from *dag,* meaning 'skewer,' since dogwoods were once a favourite source of wooden skewers. *Cornus,* 'a horn,' may refer to the hardness of the wood. It is also the name of decorative knobs, resembling dogwood flowers, found on the ends of ancient cylinders.

MOCK-ORANGE • *Philadelphus lewisii*

GENERAL: Erect, loosely branched **deciduous** shrub, to 3 m tall; brown bark checks in strips and eventually flakes off.

LEAVES: Opposite, oval to egg-shaped, with essentially smooth edges (or some teeth on young leaves), and **3 major veins** from leaf base; slightly **sandpapery to the touch.**

FLOWERS: Usually **4 oblong, white petals**, large and showy; borne in clusters of 3–15 flowers at branch ends; fragrant.

FRUITS: Oval, woody capsules, splitting into 4 parts; contain many rod-shaped seeds.

ECOLOGY: Scattered and locally common at low elevations in warm, dry to moist climates of southern half of our region, in moist but well-drained, open forests and forests edges to open, rocky sites.

NOTES: This species is extremely variable and appears to be particularly responsive to local ecological conditions. • Its wood is strong and hard, and it never cracks or warps when it is prepared properly. The Secwepemc used it for arrows, digging sticks and breast-bone decorations. When they are bruised and rubbed with the hands, the leaves and flowers foam into a lather that was used as a soap. • The species name *lewisii* honours Captain Meriwether Lewis of the Lewis and Clark expeditions. 'Mock-orange' comes from the similarity of the sweet-scented flowers to orange blossoms. It is also known as syringa, from a previous genus name now given to lilacs.

Caprifoliaceae: Honeysuckle Family

The honeysuckle family is a diverse group of shrubs and vines with few reliable distinguishing features. Plants of this family are **woody** and their leaves are **opposite** (or occasionally whorled), but vary in shape from simple to compound or lobed. Flowers have a 5-lobed corolla that varies from saucer- to trumpet-shaped and may be slightly irregular. Like the leaves, the flowers are sometimes borne in pairs.

The family name 'Caprifoliaceae' comes from the same source as the zodiac sign Capricorn, 'the goat.' The connection is between the twisting horns of some goats and the twisting stems of the climbing vines in the Caprifoliaceae.

BLUE ELDERBERRY • *Sambucus caerulea*

GENERAL: Deciduous shrub to small tree, 2–4 m tall; **soft, pithy, whitish twigs** often with suckers from base.

LEAVES: Opposite, pinnately divided into 5–9 leaflets; leaflets lance–shaped, pointed, sharply toothed and **usually smooth and hairless**.

FLOWERS: Small and **white to creamy**, in **flat-topped clusters**.

FRUITS: Clusters of juicy, round, **powder-blue, berry-like fruits**; edible.

ECOLOGY: Scattered and locally abundant in southern part of our region (south of 50˚N), on moist to mesic sites in valley bottoms, open mountain slopes and along watercourses.

NOTES: Blue elderberry fruits have a waxy, powdery-blue bloom. Black bears often gorge on them. • The Nlaka'pmx, Secwepemc, Okanagan and Ktunaxa ate large quantities of fresh and dried fruits. The Okanagan harvested the berries in late autumn, buried them under pine needles, and then dug them up in small amounts during winter (Turner 1974). The St'at'imc would waterproof cedar-root baskets by rubbing berries inside them. • This species is also called blue elder. The name 'elder' is probably from the Anglo-Saxon *aeld*, 'to kindle,' because the hollow stems were used to blow glowing tinder into a flame.

RED ELDERBERRY • *Sambucus racemosa*
ssp. *pubens* var. *leucocarpa*

GENERAL: Deciduous shrub to small tree, 1–5 m tall; soft **pithy twigs**; crushed leaves have **strong, characteristic odour**.

LEAVES: Opposite, pinnately divided into 5–7 leaflets; leaflets lance-shaped, pointed, sharply toothed and often **somewhat hairy below**.

FLOWERS: Small and **white to creamy**, with a strong, unpleasant odour; in **dense, rounded or pyramidal clusters**.

FRUITS: Bright red and berry-like; not palatable, can cause nausea when eaten raw.

ECOLOGY: Widespread and common at low to subalpine elevations along streambanks, swampy thickets, moist clearings, and shaded forests; generally absent from our dry plateaus, arid basins and southern Rocky Mountain Trench.

SIMILAR SPECIES: Black elderberry (*S. racemosa* ssp. *pubens* var. *melanocarpa*) has black or purplish-black fruits. It occurs at mid to subalpine elevations in southern parts of our region.

NOTES: The Nlaka'pmx and St'at'imc steamed or boiled the berries into a jam. The bark and roots were boiled and the infusion was drunk as an emetic or purgative. The stems can be hollowed out to make whistles, drinking straws, blowguns and pipe-stems. This should be done with caution because **the stems, roots and foliage are poisonous or toxic.**

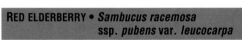

COMMON SNOWBERRY • *Symphoricarpos albus*

GENERAL: Erect, **deciduous** shrub, 0.5–1.5 m tall, spreading by a few underground rhizomes; **branches into very fine, hairless twigs.**

LEAVES: Opposite, elliptic to oval with **smooth to wavy-toothed edges, sometimes irregularly lobed on young stems.**

FLOWERS: Pink to white, bell-shaped; in clusters of a few flowers, mostly near the ends of the twigs.

FRUITS: Conspicuous clusters of spongy, **white, berry-like fruits** that **persist through winter**; considered **poisonous.**

ECOLOGY: Widespread and common at low to mid elevations in open forests, thickets, dry rocky slopes and grassy openings, in all but wet Columbia Mountains, where it is infrequent in dry to moist habitats, especially well-drained floodplains.

SIMILAR SPECIES: Western snowberry (*S. occidentalis*), also called wolfberry, commonly grows in grasslands and along dry forest/grassland fringes. It has clustered, stalkless flowers with long styles that are hairy near the middle and stick out from the floral tube. By contrast, common snowberry has short-stalked, sparsely clustered flowers with hairless styles that do not stick out from the floral tube.

NOTES: Common snowberry is one of the most widespread shrubs in North America. • The berries were not eaten by any native peoples and many considered them poisonous or toxic. In several Interior languages the name for this plant means 'corpse berries' or 'ghost berries.' The Secwepemc hollowed out the twigs to make pipe-stems, the St'at'imc squeezed ripe berries into sore eyes before going to sleep, and the Nlaka'pmx used them as a cure for diarrhea. • The berries can remain on the plants through winter, providing an important winter food source for birds. • The species is also known as waxberry.

S. albus

S. occidentalis

HIGH-BUSH CRANBERRY • *Viburnum edule*

GENERAL: Straggling to erect, **deciduous** shrub, 0.5–2.5 m tall; smooth, **reddish bark.**

LEAVES: Opposite, with **3 shallow lobes and sharply toothed edges,** hairy beneath; turning crimson in autumn.

FLOWERS: Clusters of **small white flowers** borne on short stems from between a pair of leaves.

FRUITS: Clusters of **red or orange, berry-like fruits** with **large, flattened stones**; edible, but acid and tart.

ECOLOGY: Widespread and common at low to mid elevations in moist to wet forests, seepage areas, swamps and clearings; generally absent from arid basins.

SIMILAR SPECIES: American bush-cranberry (*V. opulus*) is typically a large shrub of streambanks in the northern and southeastern parts of our region. Its leaves are very deeply 3-lobed, not much toothed, and they are nearly hairless. It has larger, showier flower clusters than high-bush cranberry, with enlarged, sterile flowers around the edge.

NOTES: The over-ripe berries and decaying leaves impart a musty-sour odour to the woods in autumn. • All Interior native peoples used high-bush cranberries where they were available. They collected them in autumn after the frost had sweetened them and ate them fresh or boiled with apples to make jam or jelly. The Carrier drank an infusion of the bark and twigs for coughs and 'blood spitting' and the St'at'imc inhaled steam from the bark to cure sore throats. The Carrier also apparently smoked the bark and the Ktunaxa made pipe-stems from hollowed-out stalks. • High-bush cranberry is also called squashberry.

BLACK TWINBERRY • *Lonicera involucrata*

GENERAL: Erect to straggly, **deciduous** shrub, 0.5–2 m tall; **young twigs 4-angled** in cross-section and greenish.

LEAVES: Opposite, elliptic to **broadly lance-shaped, with pointed tips**; often hairy below.

FLOWERS: Yellow, trumpet-shaped corollas, with a short spur at base; borne opposite, on stalks from leaf bases, each pair **cupped by a pair of large, green to purplish thickened bracts**.

FRUITS: Shiny, black 'twin' berries, cupped by 2 deep purplish maroon bracts; not considered palatable.

ECOLOGY: Widespread and often abundant at low to subalpine elevations in areas of moist or wet soil, including moist to wet forest, seepage areas, clearings, edges of wetlands and valley-bottom thickets.

NOTES: Some Interior native groups believed black twinberries were poisonous and would make one crazy. They are bitter, but they are eaten by birds and other animals in large quantities. Many Interior people called them 'bear berries' or 'grizzly berries.' • The St'at'imc made a tea from the twigs. The Nlaka'pmx used a tea made from the sticks and leaves to cure sore throats and externally to heal broken bones and sores. The Secwepemc mixed black twinberry with other plants as an arthritis medicine. Carrier boiled the leaves and used the liquid to bathe sore eyes, or applied crushed leaves as a poultice to open sores. • The honeysuckle genus, *Lonicera*, is named for Adam Lonitzer (1528–86), a German herbalist and naturalist. The species name *involucrata* means 'with an involucre,' and it refers to the twin bracts that surround the flowers and fruit.

UTAH HONEYSUCKLE • *Lonicera utahensis*

GENERAL: Erect, **deciduous** shrub, 0.5–2 m tall; greyish bark.

LEAVES: Opposite, elliptic to oblong with smooth edges and blunt tip; hairless above and smooth to often hairy below.

FLOWERS: Light yellow to creamy, trumpet-shaped corollas with short spur at base; borne **in pairs, on stalks from leaf bases.**

FRUITS: Paired, bright red juicy berries, joined at base (often of unequal sizes); edible.

ECOLOGY: Widespread and locally common at low to subalpine elevations in southern two-thirds of our region; in moist to wet forests openings and clearings; generally absent from Thompson and Okanagan basins.

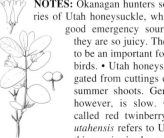

NOTES: Okanagan hunters sometimes ate the berries of Utah honeysuckle, which were said to be a good emergency source of water because they are so juicy. The flowers are reported to be an important food to early humming-birds. • Utah honeysuckle is easily propagated from cuttings of either hardwood or summer shoots. Germination from seed, however, is slow. • This plant is also called red twinberry. The species name *utahensis* refers to Utah (the state), where this species is also common.

ORANGE HONEYSUCKLE • *Lonicera ciliosa*

GENERAL: Deciduous, climbing vine, sometimes reaching 6 m high; hollow stems.

LEAVES: Opposite, with end-pair on each twig joined to form a disk; oval with hairy edges and whitish bloom below.

FLOWERS: Orange-yellow, occasionally becoming purplish on drying, with **narrowly trumpet-shaped,** 5-lobed corollas; in **clusters of 8–12 flowers at branch tips,** above disk-leaf.

FRUITS: Clusters of small, **orange-red, translucent berries** with several seeds.

ECOLOGY: Scattered and locally common at low to mid elevations on Thompson and Okanagan plateaus, in Coast/Interior Transition and in southern Columbia Mountains, in dry to mesic forests and thickets.

SIMILAR SPECIES: Red honeysuckle (*L. dioica*) occurs infrequently in the extreme southeastern part of our region. It has yellowish to purplish or reddish flowers and hairless leaf edges.

NOTES: Interior native peoples used the woody vines of orange honeysuckle for weaving, binding and lashing and for reinforcing suspension bridges over the Fraser, Thompson and other rivers. Children of the Lil'wet'ul liked to suck the sugar-filled nectaries at the base of this flower. The red to orange berries are considered inedible and may be poisonous. • Orange honeysuckle is easily propagated from cuttings and makes an attractive addition to the home garden, providing a source of nectar for hummingbirds and butterflies. • This species is also known as western trumpet honeysuckle, after its trumpet-shaped flowers with abundant nectar. The hairy edges of the leaves are responsible for the species name *ciliosa*.

TWINFLOWER • *Linnaea borealis*

GENERAL: Trailing, semi-woody **evergreen shrub;** erect, leafy stems, less than 10 cm tall; from long, more or less hairy runners.

LEAVES: Opposite, firm, shiny, broadly elliptic with a few **shallow teeth along upper half.**

FLOWERS: Pink, trumpet-like and nodding; borne **opposite on a thin Y-shaped stalk;** fragrant.

FRUITS: Dry nutlets with hooked bristles that readily catch on fur of mammals or feathers of birds.

ECOLOGY: Widespread and very common at low elevations to timberline in open to closed, mossy forests, openings, clearings and wetlands; generally absent from our hot, dry climates.

NOTES: Twinflower is easily propagated through layering. Its preference is for partially shaded sites, and it tends to spread rapidly but not aggressively. • The beautiful twin flowers of *Linnaea* produce a fragrant perfume. This species was supposedly the favourite flower of Linnaeus and was named after him by his benefactor Gronovius. The species name *borealis* means 'northern.'

KINNIKINNICK • *Arctostaphylos uva-ursi*

GENERAL: Trailing evergreen shrub, usually not over 20 cm tall; brownish-red bark; long, flexible, rooting branches **often form large mats**.

LEAVES: Alternate, oval to spoon-shaped (up to 3 cm long) with smooth edges; leathery, dark green and somewhat shiny above, paler below, hairless.

FLOWERS: Small, urn-shaped and pinkish white; drooping in few-flowered clusters at branch tips.

FRUITS: Bright red berries like miniature apples, with large, very hard seeds; edible with white mealy and tasteless pulp.

ECOLOGY: Widespread and common at low to alpine elevations on sandy and well-drained exposed sites, dry rocky slopes, dry forest clearings and hummocks in shrub-carrs; restricted to dry rock outcrops and steep southerly exposures in wet Columbia Mountains.

SIMILAR SPECIES: Lingonberry (*Vaccinium vitis-idaea*) has smaller leaves (usually not much more than 1 cm long) with rolled edges and black dots below. It is very common in the boreal forest to the north and occasionally occurs in the most northern parts of our region.

NOTES: Kinnikinnick is an alternate host for spruce broom rust. • Before Euroamerican contact, most southern Interior native groups smoked kinnikinnick, except the Carrier and other northern Athabascan peoples. The Nlaka'pmx boiled the leaves to make a tea, used a decoction of the stems and leaves as a diuretic, and fried the berries in salmon or bear fat, or boiled them in soups. • The berries ripen late and remain on plants into winter, providing forage for birds, bears and other wildlife. • 'Kinnikinnick' is from an eastern aboriginal word meaning 'mixture,' and it was originally applied to any smoking mixture. The name was brought west by fur company employees. The genus name *Arctostaphylos*, from the Greek *arktos* (bear) and *staphylos* (a bunch of grapes), and the species name *uva-ursi*, from the Latin *uva* (grape) and *ursus* (bear), both echo kinnikinnick's other name 'common bearberry.'

WESTERN BOG-LAUREL • *Kalmia microphylla* ssp. *microphylla* K. polifolia

GENERAL: Small evergreen shrub, to 50 cm tall; slender branches; spreads by layering and short rhizomes.

LEAVES: Opposite, narrowly lance-shaped, to 2 cm long, with edges rolled under; **leathery, dark green above**, conspicuously **whitish fine-hairy below**.

FLOWERS: Saucer-shaped, with **rose-pink, 5-lobed corollas** and 10 stamens; borne in a loose cluster at top of stem.

FRUITS: Nearly spherical capsules, opening by 5 slits (valves).

ECOLOGY: Scattered and infrequent in bogs and wet mountain meadows; on peaty soils; throughout much of our region, but absent from our hot, dry climates.

SIMILAR SPECIES: Bog-laurel (*K. microphylla* ssp. *occidentalis*) is a Coastal subspecies that occasionally occurs along the western edge of our region. It usually has longer leaves (more than 2.5 cm). • Western bog-laurel grows with and resembles Labrador tea (*Ledum groenlandicum*, p. 86) and bog-rosemary (*Andromeda polifolia*). Bog-rosemary has hairless, **alternate leaves** and **pink, urn-shaped flowers**.

NOTES: Caution: Western bog-laurel and bog-rosemary contain **poisonous** alkaloids. Be careful not to confuse *Kalmia* or *Andromeda* species with Labrador tea, whose leaves have brown fuzz on their undersides and tend to hang downwards. When in flower, all three species are easy to tell apart. • In western bog-laurel flowers, the 10 anthers are neatly tucked into 10 dimpled pockets on the petals, with arched filaments holding the flower open under tension. Touch a flower and watch the pollen fly! At the slightest touch by an insect probing for nectar, the stamens pop out and dust the insect with pollen. • Western bog-laurel is also called swamp laurel.

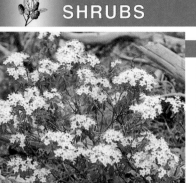

TRAPPER'S TEA • *Ledum glandulosum*

GENERAL: Stout **evergreen** shrub, 40–80 cm tall; minutely hairy and glandular twigs.

LEAVES: Alternate, **narrow, oblong to lance-shaped with edges rolled under**, often drooping; **leathery**, green and rough above, with **greenish-white hairs** (not rusty brown) and resin glands below.

FLOWERS: White, with 5 spreading petals and **8–12 protruding stamens**; in clusters at branch tips.

FRUITS: Drooping clusters of rounded, **dry capsules**.

ECOLOGY: Widespread and locally common at mid elevations in southern two-thirds of our region; otherwise widely scattered north to about Quesnel; in moist coniferous forest on acidic soils, moist seepage sites, bogs and wet depressions.

NOTES: Trapper's tea, Labrador tea (*L. groenlandicum*, below), bog-laurel (*Kalmia microphylla*, p. 85) and bog-rosemary (*Andromeda polifolia*, p. 85) contain a poisonous alkaloid, andromedotoxin, that is toxic to livestock, especially sheep. • Trapper's tea, like Labrador tea, was used as a beverage and tonic among Interior native peoples. Unlike other teas, it had to be boiled for some time, which apparently destroys the poisonous alkaloids. • The species name *glandulosum* refers to the resin glands on the underside of the leaf.

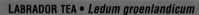

LABRADOR TEA • *Ledum groenlandicum*

GENERAL: Evergreen, much branched shrub, 30–80 cm tall; densely rusty-hairy twigs; spicy fragrance.

LEAVES: Alternate, narrow, oblong to lance-shaped with edges rolled under, often drooping; **leathery**, deep green above, with **dense rusty hairs below** (hairs on young leaves may not be rusty).

FLOWERS: White, with 5–10 protruding stamens; numerous, in short, umbrella-like clusters at ends of branches.

FRUITS: Drooping clusters of 5-parted, dry, hairy capsules.

ECOLOGY: Widespread and common at low to subalpine elevations, in peaty wetlands and moist coniferous forests with acidic soils; an indicator of wet, usually very acid and nutrient poor organic soils; often dominating bogs and cold wetland fringes; absent in our hot arid climates.

SIMILAR SPECIES: Do not confuse Labrador tea with trapper's tea (*L. glandulosum*, above), bog-laurel (*Kalmia microphylla*, p. 85) or bog-rosemary (*Andromeda polifolia*, p. 85), which all contain alkaloids, andromedotoxins, that are **toxic** to livestock, especially sheep. All three of these other species lack the brown fuzz on the underside of the mature leaves. Bog-laurel and bog-rosemary have pink flowers.

NOTES: The leaves, used fresh or dried, can be boiled to make an aromatic tea that is a favourite beverage among Interior native peoples Be careful to boil it well before drinking it (see trapper's tea, above), and it should be consumed in moderation to avoid drowsiness. Excessive doses are reported to act as a strong diuretic and cathartic and to cause intestinal disturbances. • The Secwepemc call it *secwsqe'qxe'ten*, 'bathing-dog-stuff,' because a long time ago hunters washed the noses and mouths of their tracking dogs with this fragrant tea so that their prey could not smell them. The aromatic leaves were used in corn barns to drive away mice and in homes to keep fleas away. • The genus name *Ledum* is from the Greek *ledon*, their name for a different plant. This species also grows in Greenland, hence the species name g*roenlandicum*.

FALSE AZALEA • *Menziesia ferruginea*

GENERAL: Erect to straggly, spreading, **deciduous** shrub, to 2 m tall; young twigs covered with fine, rust-coloured hairs that are somewhat glandular and sticky, and emit **skunky odour** when crushed; bark scaly-shredding on older branches.

LEAVES: Thin, oblong to elliptic with wavy, toothed edges; **light green to blue-green** and **hairy-glandular**, with **end of midvein protruding at leaf tip**; **in clusters along branches**, but especially at branch tips.

FLOWERS: Urn-shaped, with **salmon to greenish-orange corollas**; in drooping clusters at tip of previous year's growth.

FRUITS: 4-parted, dry, oval capsules.

ECOLOGY: Widespread and common at low to mid elevations in southern two-thirds of wet Columbia Mountains and Coast/Interior Transition and at subalpine elevations in East Kootenays, in shady coniferous forests with acid humus, moist openings, and clearings; scattered and infrequent in moist and wet climates elsewhere in our region.

NOTES: The St'at'imc made a tea from the sticks and leaves, which were gathered whenever convenient and dried for later use. • False azalea is very attractive in autumn when the leaves turn a brilliant crimson-orange. It can be propagated easily from seed or cuttings. Like all ericaceous plants, the seeds are small and the seedlings need two or three transplantings before setting out. Small plants make good bonsai or planter subjects. • The common names 'false azalea' and 'false huckleberry' come from its resemblance of both those plants. It is also called fool's huckleberry because the flower looks like that of a huckleberry but the fruit is a dry, inedible capsule. The genus *Menziesia* is named for Archibald Menzies, a physician and naturalist with Captain George Vancouver. The species name *ferruginea* means 'rusty,' and it refers to the rusty hairs covering the branches and leaves.

WHITE-FLOWERED RHODODENDRON • *Rhododendron albiflorum*

GENERAL: Erect to spreading, slender, **deciduous** shrub, to 2 m tall; young twigs covered with coarse reddish hairs.

LEAVES: Oblong to lance-shaped, with **fine rusty hairs** above, **end of midvein not protruding at leaf tip**; **in clusters along branches, but especially at branch tips; yellowish green**, turning beautiful shades of bronze, crimson and orange in autumn.

FLOWERS: Large, showy and **cup-shaped**, with 5 **white to creamy petals** joined at base; borne in several clusters of 2–3 flowers, around stem of previous year's growth.

FRUITS: Dry, oval capsules.

ECOLOGY: Widespread and common at mostly subalpine elevations in dry to moist coniferous forest, openings and clearings; occurs with false azalea (*Menziesia ferruginea*) at subalpine elevations in eastern parts of our region.

NOTES: White-flowered rhododendron is often called mountain misery because it grows in very thick masses on shady, moist mountain slopes near timberline. The branches tend to trail downhill, making it exceedingly difficult for bushwackers to move up through it. • The Nlaka'pmx used this plant as a scent. **All parts of the plant are reputed to be poisonous**, containing the same toxic compounds found in bog-laurel (*Kalmia microphylla*). • White-flowered rhododendron is very difficult to propagate and maintain in low-elevation gardens. It is best left in its natural environment. • The genus name *Rhododendron* is from the Greek *rhodon* (rose) and *dendron* (tree). The species name *albiflorum* simply means 'white-flowered.'

Conspectus of the blueberries and huckleberries

species	habit	twigs	leaves
V. alakaense	erect shrub; 0.5–1.5 m tall (mostly more than 60 cm tall)	somewhat angled; yellow-green; smooth or slightly hairy; older bark greyish	deciduous; 2.5–6 cm long; entire or with fine teeth on lower half; lower surface usually glaucous, with scattered hairs on midvein
V. ovalifolium	upright spreading shrub; 40–200 cm tall (often less than 60 cm tall)	strongly angled and grooved; brown, yellow or reddish; smooth; older bark greyish	deciduous; 2–4 cm long; entire or with a few fine teeth; lower surface glaucous, without hairs or midvein
V. membranaceum	upright spreading shrub; 0.5–1.5 m tall	somewhat angled; yellow-green; smooth or slightly hairy; older bark greyish, shredding	deciduous; 2–4 cm long; finely toothed along whole leaf edge; lower surface paler
V. globulare	upright spreading shrub; 0.5–1.5 m tall	slightly angled, greenish yellow	deciduous, 2–4 cm long, rounded or abruptly acute at tip; edges finely toothed along whole length
V. parvifolium	erect shrub; 1–3 m tall	strongly angled; green; usually smooth	deciduous (but a few persistent); 1–3 cm long; smooth or slightly hairy; entire (some teeth present on young leaves)
V. myrtilloides	spreading, upright; 10–40 cm tall; often growing in dense colonies	not angled; greenish; velvety hairy	thin; to 4 cm long; elliptic to lance-shaped, sharply pointed; edges smooth; softly hairy

	flowers	fruits	habitat
	bronze to pinkish green; about 7 mm long; wider than long; single in axils	bluish black to purplish black; usually without bluish bloom; 7–10 mm across	moist coniferous forests; low to subalpine elevations
	pinkish; about 7 mm long, longer than wide; single in leaf axils	blue-black; usually with bluish blooms; 6–9 mm across	moist coniferous forests, openings and bogs; low to subalpine elevations
	creamy pink to yellow-pink; 5–6 mm long, a bit longer than broad, single in leaf axils	purple or reddish black; not glaucous; 6–8 mm across	dry to moist coniferous forests; medium to alpine elevations
	pale pink to yellowish white, globe-shaped, single in leaf axils	dark purple without a bloom, 6–8 mm across	coniferous forests; low to subalpine elevations
	greenish yellow or pinkish; a bit longer than broad, 4–5 mm long; single in leaf axils	bright red; 6–10 mm across	coniferous forests; low to medium elevations; often on rotting wood or in soils rich in rotting wood
	greenish; bell-shaped; single or in small clusters at ends of branches	blue with a heavy pale blue bloom; 5–10 mm across	coniferous forests and acidic wetlands; low to mid elevations

Conspectus of the blueberries and huckleberries (continued)

species	habit	twigs	leaves
V. caespitosum	tufted, mat-forming shrub; 15–30 cm tall	round; yellow-green to reddish bark; usually finely hairy	deciduous; 1–3 cm long; light green above, paler below; toothed from tip to midpoint or below; prominently veined below
V. deliciosum	low, mat-forming shrub; 15–30 cm tall (occasionally larger)	slightly angled; greenish brown; smooth or slightly hairy	deciduous; 1.5–5 cm long, pale green; glaucous below; toothed on upper half of leaf
V. uliginosum	erect, much-branched shrub; 10–30 cm tall	not angled; branches yellowish green; finely hairy; old bark greyish red	deciduous; 1–3 cm long; strongly veined beneath
V. scoparium	low, broom-like shrub; to 25 cm tall	many, fine, erect; strongly angled; without hairs	small; deciduous; thin, pointed at top; egg-shaped; hairless, light green; edges finely toothed
V. myrtillus	low, more open, broom-like shrub; to 40 cm tall	erect, strongly angled, greenish, short hairy in grooves	deciduous, 1.5–3 cm long, egg- to lance-shaped, light green and strongly veiny on lower surface; edges finely toothed
Oxycoccus oxycoccos	creeping stems to 15 cm long	thin; creeping; smooth to slightly hairy	evergreen; 6–10 mm long; deep green above, greyish below; edges rolled under

flowers	fruits	habitat
white to pink; 5–6 mm long; twice as long as wide; single in leaf axils	blue with a whitish waxy covering; 5–8 mm across	open forests, clearings and alpine tundra; low to high elevations
pink; 6–7 mm long, about as long as wide; single in leaf axils	blue with whitish bloom; 6–8 mm across	subalpine meadows and open forest, alpine tundra
pink; 5–6 mm long, longer than wide; 1–4 from leaf axils	blue with whitish bloom; 6–8 mm across	open subalpine forests; rocky alpine tundra
pale pink, urn-shaped, single in leaf axils	bright red, 5 mm across	mid- to high-elevation coniferous forests
pinkish; urn-shaped; single in leaf axils	purple to dark red without a bloom; 4–8 mm across	mid- to high-elevation coniferous forests
pink; petals distinct and strongly bent back; 1–3 in terminal or lateral cluster	pale pink to dark red; 5–8 mm across	bogs and subalpine meadows

Vaccinium: the blueberries and huckleberries

The blueberries and huckleberries include some of our most common and best known shrubs. *Vaccinium* species have simple leaves, often with toothed edges. The flowers vary from pink to red and are usually urn-shaped. Most *Vaccinium* species can be identified from their berries, which vary in colour from red to blue or black. Lacking berries, species identification relies on subtle differences in leaf and branch shape and general habit.

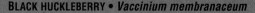

BLACK HUCKLEBERRY • *Vaccinium membranaceum*

GENERAL: Erect, coarse, densely branched **deciduous** shrub, to 1.5 m tall; young branches yellowish green and somewhat angled; bark on old branches greyish, shredding.

LEAVES: Thin, **lance-shaped to elliptic**, 2–4 cm long, with **finely toothed edges** and pointed tips; smooth, paler below, **turning red or purple in autumn**.

FLOWERS: Urn-shaped, with creamy-pink to yellow-pink corollas; borne singly in leaf axils; **appearing with or after leaves**.

FRUITS: Purplish or reddish-black berries, **without bloom**; large, round, edible; excellent flavour.

ECOLOGY: Widespread and common at mid to high elevations in dry to moist coniferous forests, openings and clearings; absent from dry parts of our plateaus, arid basins and southern Rocky Mountain Trench.

SIMILAR SPECIES: Blue huckleberry (*V. globulare*) is confined to the extreme southeast of our region. It has **leaves that are more rounded at the tip** and bluish-purple berries. • Oval-leaved blueberry (*V. ovalifolium*, below) has more blunt-tipped leaves without teeth along their edges. It has bluish-black berries with a conspicuous bluish bloom.

NOTES: The berries of black huckleberry are among the most delicious of our *Vaccinium* species. They are produced in great abundance on some sites, especially old burns at subalpine elevations.

OVAL-LEAVED BLUEBERRY • *Vaccinium ovalifolium*

GENERAL: Erect, **deciduous** shrub, to 2 m tall; young twigs brownish to yellowish or **often reddish, angled and grooved**; old branches greyish.

LEAVES: Oval, blunt-rounded at both ends, usually **lacking teeth** on edges; green above, lighter below; to 4 cm long.

FLOWERS: Globular, urn-shaped, with pinkish corollas; borne singly, at leaf bases; **appearing generally before (sometimes with) leaves.**

FRUITS: Blue-black berries with **bluish bloom**; large and edible.

ECOLOGY: Widespread and common at low to subalpine elevations in wet Columbia Mountains in moist to wet coniferous forests, openings, clearings and bogs; also scattered in Coast/Interior Transition and East Kootenays.

SIMILAR SPECIES: Alaskan blueberry (*V. alaskaense*), a common Coastal species, has whisker-like hairs along its leaf midribs and is generally less branched than oval-leaved blueberry. It is rare in our area and is restricted to the Coast/Interior Transition. • Bog blueberry (*V. uliginosum*) also has oval leaves without teeth along the edges. It has relatively thick, firm leaves, and its **blue** berries are often in small clusters of 2–4. Bog blueberry is restricted to subalpine elevations in the Coast/Interior Transition.

RED HUCKLEBERRY • *Vaccinium parvifolium*

GENERAL: Erect **deciduous** shrub, to 2 m tall; **bright green, very strongly angled branches**, smooth or slightly hairy when young.

LEAVES: Oval, to 3 cm long, **without toothed edges** (except occasionally on young leaves).

FLOWERS: Urn-shaped, with greenish-yellow or pinkish corollas; borne singly, in leaf axils.

FRUITS: Bright red, round berries; edible, a little sour for some tastes, but 'refreshing' for others.

ECOLOGY: Scattered and infrequent at low to mid elevations in moist coniferous forests; often at forest edges or under canopy openings, in soils rich in decaying wood, or often on stumps or logs; common along Coast, and locally common in our region in wet Columbia Mountains around Shuswap Lake, along Seymour River and in Kootenay Valley.

NOTES: The Lil'wet'ul and Lower Nlaka'pmx ate these berries. • The name 'huckleberry' comes from 'whortleberry' or 'hurtleberry,' both of which were from the Anglo-Saxon *wyrtil* (small shrub), a diminutive of *wyrt* or *wort* (plant). The genus name *Vaccinium* is from the Latin name for another shrub with berries. The species name *parvifolium* refers to the small leaves of this shrub.

VELVET-LEAVED BLUEBERRY • *Vaccinium myrtilloides*

GENERAL: Low, **deciduous** shrub, 10–40 cm tall; grows in dense colonies; **velvety hairy branches** especially when young.

LEAVES: Thin, elliptic to oblong or lance-shaped, to 4 cm long, with sharply pointed tips and **smooth edges**; green and **softly hairy**.

FLOWERS: Cylindrically bell-shaped, with **greenish-white** or pink-tinged corollas; borne singly or in **clusters** on short stalks **at branch tips**.

FRUITS: Small, blue berries with **heavy, pale-blue bloom**; edible and sweet.

ECOLOGY: Scattered and locally common at low to mid elevations in Fraser Plateau, northern parts of wet Columbia Mountains and East Kootenays, and widely scattered in West Kootenays, on gravelly or sandy soils, open forests, clearings and bog hummocks.

NOTES: Blueberries and huckleberries were extremely popular with all Interior native people and they were commonly traded. The juicy, flavourful berries of the more prolific species were gathered from midsummer to autumn and eaten fresh or cooked, mashed and dried into cakes. When gathered in quantity, they were either dried singly like raisins, mashed and dried into cakes for winter use, or stored soaked in grease or oil. • These are perhaps the sweetest and most flavourful of the blueberries. • In our region, fruits of *Vaccinium* species tend to be called blueberries if they are blue, and huckleberries if they are any other colour. • 'Blueberry' comes from *blaeberry*, from the 15th-century word *blae*, meaning 'blue-black.' The species name *myrtilloides* refers to the leaves, which are like those of myrtles (*Myrtus* spp.).

DWARF BLUEBERRY • *Vaccinium caespitosum*

GENERAL: Matted, **dwarf deciduous** shrub, to 30 cm tall; **rounded**, yellowish-green to reddish and often hairy twigs.

LEAVES: Oblong to lance-shaped, less than 3 cm long, **widest above middle**, with **distinctly toothed edges**; bright green on both sides, with a **pronounced network of veins** below.

FLOWERS: Small, drooping, whitish to pink, narrowly urn-shaped, 5-lobed corollas; borne singly, in axils of leaf.

FRUITS: Small, round, **blue berries** with a **pale grey bloom**; edible and sweet.

ECOLOGY: Widespread and common at low to alpine elevations in dry to moist, forests, clearings, wet meadows, moist rocky ridges and alpine tundra; generally absent from arid basins and wettest parts of Columbia Mountains.

SIMILAR SPECIES: Blue-leaved huckleberry (*V. deliciosum*), also called Cascade huckleberry, occurs in subalpine and alpine areas along the Coast/Interior Transition. It has **leaves with a whitish bloom beneath** (bright green in dwarf blueberry), and nearly round flowers (versus more elongate in dwarf blueberry). It is often abundant in subalpine meadows in the Cascade Mountains and produces a berry crop worthy of the species name.

NOTES: The berries, although small, are often plentiful and are highly prized by rodents, birds, and bears. • Native people harvested the berries by clubbing the branches onto the hand and letting the berries fall into a basket, or by using a comb-like implement, often made of yew wood or a salmon backbone. Occasionally they were cooked and partially dried right at the picking site. The juice could be collected as the berries were being cooked and slowly added to the berries as they were being dried or drunk as a beverage. • The species name *caespitosum* means 'tufted' and refers to the growth habit of the species.

GROUSEBERRY • *Vaccinium scoparium*

GENERAL: Matted, broom-like, **dwarf deciduous** shrub, 10–25 cm tall; branches numerous, greenish to yellowish green, slender, strongly angled.

LEAVES: Lance-shaped to oval, less than 12 mm long, **widest at or near middle**, with finely **toothed edges and a sharp-pointed tip; thin and light green**.

FLOWERS: Urn-shaped, with **pearly pink corollas**; nodding, borne singly in leaf axil.

FRUITS: Bright red (occasionally purplish) sweet berries.

ECOLOGY: Widespread and locally common at mid to high elevations in the southern half of our region and western part of Fraser Plateau; in dry to moist, open coniferous (most often lodgepole pine) forests and openings, often forming a dense ground cover near timberline.

SIMILAR SPECIES: Low bilberry (*V. myrtillus*), also called dwarf bilberry, a very closely related species, is distinguished from grouseberry by its coarser and not broom-like branching, larger leaves (to 3 cm long), and dark red to bluish berries. Low bilberry occurs in dry to mesic forests at mid to high elevations in the Kootenays and Rockies.

NOTES: 'Grouseberry' is a good common name for this species, as grouse eat all parts of the plant. Apparently some hunters locate good grouse habitat by searching out this shrub! • Southern Interior native people, including the Secwepemc, Okanagan and Ktunaxa, gathered the berries with a comb, because the berries are so small. The Ktunaxa name for them actually means 'comb.' They were usually eaten fresh. • The species name *scoparium* means 'broom' and refers to the often broom-like clustering of stems.

BOG CRANBERRY • *Oxycoccus oxycoccos*
Vaccinium oxycoccos, V. microcarpum, O. microcarpus, O. quadripetalus

GENERAL: Creeping, vine-like, dwarf evergreen shrub, to 40 cm long; stems very slender, wiry, finely hairy to smooth, brown to black.

LEAVES: Small, **leathery and sharp-pointed**, with **edges rolled under**; **grey-waxy below**, dark green above.

FLOWERS: Deep pink, with the **4 petals sharply bent backwards** and stamens protruding; often solitary or 2–3, each **nodding on a long, slender stem**.

FRUITS: Pale pink to dark red, juicy berries; small (8–12 mm), but appearing oversized on the plant.

ECOLOGY: Widely scattered at low to subalpine elevations in peat bogs, usually on sphagnum moss hummocks.

SIMILAR SPECIES: Creeping-snowberry (*Gaultheria hispidula*, below) is also a trailing vine-like shrub with small leathery leaves. It has short stiff hairs on the leaves and white berries with hairs.

NOTES: The tart berries of bog cranberry are closely related to our commercial cranberries. All native peoples in the Interior gathered them and ate them raw, boiled them with meat or dried them for winter use. The

Ktunaxa name for them is 'grouse-berry' because grouse like to eat them. • The name 'cranberry' may be a corruption of 'craneberry,' possibly because the flower stalk resembles the neck and head of a crane. Or it may be because the plant grows in wet places where cranes (or herons) were to be found. *Oxycoccos* is from the Greek *oxys* (bitter) and *kokkos* (berry), though the berries are more tart than bitter.

CREEPING-SNOWBERRY • *Gaultheria hispidula*

GENERAL: Delicate dwarf, creeping, matted, evergreen shrub, 10–40 cm long; slender stems covered with **brownish, flattened hairs**.

LEAVES: Small (less than 1 cm long), **closely spaced, leathery and elliptic** with edges rolled under; closely pressed, **brown scale-like hairs** below.

FLOWERS: Very small, **bell-shaped** with white or **pinkish,** 4-lobed corollas; **borne singly**, nodding on short stalks from leaf bases.

FRUITS: White, juicy edible berries with hairs and a mild wintergreen odour and flavour.

ECOLOGY: Scattered and locally common at low to mid elevations in cool, moist forests and bogs, often over sphagnum or on rotting logs; absent from warm, arid climates.

NOTES: Creeping-snowberry is closely related to the eastern North American tea-berry (*G. procumbens*), from which oil of wintergreen was originally obtained. The chemical that gives *Gaultheria* its distinctive fla-

vour is methyl salicylate, which is closely related to the main ingredient in Aspirin. It can be toxic in high doses. • Pregnant Secwepemc women bathed in a solution of the boiled leaves, stems and berries of creeping-snowberry. • The genus *Gaultheria* is named for Dr. Hugues Jean Gaultier (1708–56), a French-Canadian naturalist. The species name *hispidula* refers to the stiff little hairs on the stems and leaves.

WESTERN TEA-BERRY • *Gaultheria ovatifolia*

GENERAL: Dwarf, spreading, evergreen shrub, seldom over 20 cm long; branches slender with abundant, long brown hairs.

LEAVES: Alternate, **leathery, shiny, egg-shaped to almost heart-shaped** with finely toothed edges, 2–4 cm long.

FLOWERS: Bell-shaped, with **white or pinkish, 5-lobed corolla**, and brown, hairy calyx; **borne singly** at leaf bases.

FRUITS: Bright red, berry-like; edible and spicy flavoured.

ECOLOGY: Scattered and locally common at low to subalpine elevations in coniferous forests and subalpine bogs, mostly in southern half of wet Columbia Mountains; sporadic in northern half of wet Columbia Mountains and Coast/Interior Transition.

SIMILAR SPECIES: Alpine wintergreen (*G. humifusa*) is a small uncommon plant (up to 5 cm tall), that is scattered throughout our region. It is found on wet sites (meadows, streambanks and some wetlands) at subalpine and alpine elevations. The best differentiating character is in the flowers. The calyx of western tea-berry is hairy, that of alpine wintergreen is not. Alpine wintergreen has smaller leaves (1–2 cm long) that lack toothed edges, and it does not have long, brown hair on the branches. Hybridization between the two species produces plants with intermediate characters.

NOTES: Western tea-berry is also called Oregon wintergreen. The species name *ovatifolia* refers to the oval leaves.

WHITE MOUNTAIN-HEATHER • *Cassiope mertensiana*

GENERAL: Tufted evergreen shrub, to 30 cm tall, **forms widespread mats**; stems prostrate with erect branches, 4-angled in cross-section but nearly hidden by leaves.

LEAVES: Small and scale-like, egg- to lance-shaped, **pressed flat against stem in 4 rows**; rounded on back and grooved at base.

FLOWERS: Bell-shaped, with white corollas and reddish sepals; nodding on slender stalks near branch tips.

FRUITS: Erect capsules.

ECOLOGY: Widespread and common in alpine heath and subalpine parkland; common in snowbed habitats and on north aspects where snow lies deeper and longer.

SIMILAR SPECIES: Four-angled mountain-heather (*C. tetragona*) has a deep groove on the back of its leaves. It is less common than white mountain-heather but occurs over much the same range.

NOTES: White mountain-heather is easily propagated by layering or from cuttings. It is difficult to grow in low-elevation gardens, where it requires special care. Individual plants of mountain-heather may live 20 years or more in nature, and they are very slow growing. Admire them in their natural setting, but leave them there. • White mountain-heather branches reputedly produce a golden brown dye. • White mountain-heather resembles and is related to the true Scottish heather (*Calluna vulgaris*). The genus is named for Cassiope, the mother of Andromeda in Greek mythology. The species name *mertensiana* honours F.C. Mertens (1764–1831), a German botanist.

PINK MOUNTAIN-HEATHER • *Phyllodoce empetriformis*

GENERAL: Low evergreen shrub, 10–40 cm tall, much branched and matted; young stems glandular-hairy, becoming hairless with age.

LEAVES: Linear and needle-like, 0.5–1 cm long, **grooved on lower surface**.

FLOWERS: Showy, bell-shaped with **pink to deep rose corollas** with rolled lobes; erect to nodding in clusters at top of stems.

FRUITS: Erect capsules.

ECOLOGY: Widespread and common in subalpine and alpine heath communities, sometimes descending into cold coniferous forest on rocky sites or seepage areas; often abundant and co-dominant with white mountain-heather (*Cassiope mertensiana,* p. 96).

SIMILAR SPECIES: Yellow mountain-heather (*P. glanduliflora*) has yellowish-green, urn-shaped flowers and very sticky-glandular hairs on the flowers and flower stalks. Both mountain-heathers share the same high-elevation habitats and frequently hybridize.

NOTES: 'These cheerful bells ring an invitation to high places above the timber line, to those serene and lofty slopes where peace and quiet enter our souls' (Clark 1975a). • The genus *Phyllodoce* is named for a sea-nymph in Greek mythology. The species name *empetriformis* refers to the resemblance of this plant to crowberry (*Empetrum nigrum*), which has shorter leaves and less showy flowers. *Phyllodoce* (and *Cassiope*) species are called heathers because they superficially resemble the true heather (*Calluna vulgaris*) of Europe.

CROWBERRY • *Empetrum nigrum*

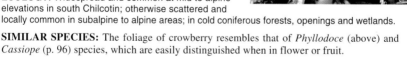

GENERAL: Creeping, matted, **evergreen** shrub, to 15 cm tall; long, freely branching horizontal stems and erect, woolly-hairy branches.

LEAVES: Linear or needle-like, with edges rolled under, minutely glandular-hairy; **usually in whorls of 4**.

FLOWERS: Inconspicuous and purplish crimson, borne singly along stem; appearing in very early spring; male and female flowers sometimes on separate plants.

FRUITS: Juicy, **black, berry-like fruits**, with large white seeds.

ECOLOGY: Widespread and common at mid to alpine elevations in south Chilcotin; otherwise scattered and locally common in subalpine to alpine areas; in cold coniferous forests, openings and wetlands.

SIMILAR SPECIES: The foliage of crowberry resembles that of *Phyllodoce* (above) and *Cassiope* (p. 96) species, which are easily distinguished when in flower or fruit.

NOTES: The Carrier and other Athapaskan groups ate the berries fresh, mixed with bear grease or boiled, mashed and dried in cakes for winter use. The berries are somewhat acid tasting and are better with sugar. They make excellent pies and jellies. Beer and sparkling wine can be made from the juice. • Crowberry is a favourite food of bears. • Crowberry is easily propagated from cuttings, and it forms a heather-like ground cover that can withstand extreme winter conditions. • Other common names are 'curlew berry' and 'crakeberry' (*crake* is Old Norse for 'crow'). The genus name *Empetrum* is from the Greek *en petros*, meaning 'on rock,' and it refers to the common alpine and rocky-slope habitat of this species. The species name *nigrum* means 'black.'

PRINCE'S-PINE • *Chimaphila umbellata*

GENERAL: Stout, slightly woody, **dwarf evergreen** shrub, to 35 cm tall, from a creeping rhizome; stems simple or branched, greenish.

LEAVES: In whorls; narrowly oblong with sharply toothed edges (mostly above middle), bright green and shiny above.

FLOWERS: Saucer-shaped, with **5 whitish-pink, waxy petals** surrounding a plump green ovary and 10 reddish stamens; several (3–10) flowers nodding in a **small cluster at top of stem**; fragrant.

FRUITS: Erect, spherical capsules.

ECOLOGY: Widespread and common at low to subalpine elevations on mossy, well-drained sites, in open to dense coniferous forests and in clearings; most common in dry forests with moist climates; absent from arid basins.

SIMILAR SPECIES: Menzies' pipsissewa (*C. menziesii*) is a smaller, more delicate version of prince's-pine found rarely in the southeast of our region. It has fewer (1–3) creamy white flowers.

NOTES: Some southern Interior native peoples boiled the leaves, stems and roots to make a tea for a beverage, or for colds and sore throats. • Attempts to cultivate prince's-pine most likely fail. It is suspected to be a root parasite and requires its host to survive. It is best left in its wild setting. • Prince's-pine is also known as pipsissewa, from the Cree name *pipisisikweu*, which means 'it-breaks-into-small-pieces,' because the leaves contain a substance that was supposed to dissolve kidney stones. The genus name *Chimaphila* comes from Greek *cheima* (winter) and *philos* (loving) and refers to its evergreen habit.

WESTERN YEW • *Taxus brevifolia*

GENERAL: Low spreading evergreen shrub to small tree, 2–15 m tall; trunks twisted and fluted; branches spread horizontally; bark thin with **dark reddish or purplish scales** that slough off and expose a **rose-coloured underbark**.

LEAVES: Flat needles with pointed tips, glossy dark green above, dark yellowish green below, arranged spirally on twigs but **twisted to appear 2-ranked**.

FRUITS: Coral-red, fleshy cups surrounding a bony seed, open at 1 end.

ECOLOGY: Scattered and locally common at low to mid elevations in wet Columbia Mountains and wet parts of East Kootenays, in moist, mature, shady coniferous forests, moist depressions and ravines, often with red cedar or hemlock.

NOTES: You can recognize yew by its distinctive bark, pointed-tipped leaves in flat sprays and distinctive fruit. Western yew lacks the typical seed cone of most other native conifers; instead it bears fleshy berry-like cups enveloping a single seed. • Bark of this species is the source of the drug taxol, used to treat ovarian and breast cancers. • **The seeds are definitely poisonous** and the fleshy **'berries' should generally be avoided**, although a wide variety of birds consume them and are responsible for seed dispersal. The foliage is reported to be poisonous to horses and cattle especially if left to rot, but it is also a preferred winter moose browse. • The heavy, close-grained wood was prized by native people. Implements such as bows, wedges, clubs, paddles, digging sticks, adze handles and harpoons were made from it. The St'at'imc considered the berries edible, but only in small amounts. The Nlaka'pmx used the bark for 'any illness' (Turner et al. 1990). • Western yew is also called Pacific yew. The name 'yew' comes from the Anglo-Saxon *iw*, but its exact meaning is not clear. The genus name *Taxus* is from the Greek name for yews, perhaps derived from *taxon*, 'a bow,' a common use for yew wood.

SHRUBS

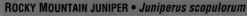

COMMON JUNIPER • *Juniperus communis*

GENERAL: Evergreen, prostrate, trailing-branched shrub, usually less than 1 m tall; forms mats or clumps to 3 m in diameter; bark very thin, **reddish brown, scaly and shredding.**

LEAVES: Needle-like to narrowly lance-shaped, usually stiff and very prickly, whitish above, dark green below; mostly **in groups of 3.**

FRUITS: Berry-like, bluish-black, very fleshy pea-sized cones; maturing in second season.

ECOLOGY: Widespread and common at low to alpine elevations in dry open forests, grassland fringes, rocky outcrops and openings; occasionally in cold, moist plateau forests and wet Columbia Mountains, where it is restricted to very dry rocky sites and southern exposures.

NOTES: Seed and pollen cones of junipers are found on separate trees. The seed cones are quite unlike the cones of most conifers. • Southern Interior native peoples seldom ate the berries, although the St'at'imc chewed them when travelling. The most common use of junipers was as a fumigant, deodorizer or cleanser, especially in connection with sickness. Boughs were burned or boiled and the strong pungent odour emitted was thought to purify the house and protect the inhabitants from infection and harmful spirits. They also boiled branches and berries to make a tea, which was taken as a medicine for many ailments, including colds, heart trouble and kidney problems. Juniper is a known diuretic. • Berries from certain species of juniper are used to flavour gin, which was first made in Holland in the 17th century as an elixir and tonic. Juniper fruit is also used as a culinary spice. • Common juniper has many growth forms and is found in diverse habitats throughout North America and Europe. • The species name *communis* means 'common,' which aptly describes this species, the only circumpolar conifer of the northern hemisphere.

ROCKY MOUNTAIN JUNIPER • *Juniperus scopulorum*

GENERAL: Shrubby evergreen tree to sprawling shrub, to 10 m tall; wide, irregularly rounded crown and **knotty, twisted trunk**; reddish-brown bark divided into narrow, flat ridges breaking into thin, **shredded, fibrous strips.**

LEAVES: Mature branches have small, **greyish-green, scale-like leaves,** opposite, barely overlapping, but covering branch in **4 rows**; young vigorously growing branches may have longer and more needle-like leaves, scattered in 2s or whorls of 3.

FRUITS: Bright to dark blue, fleshy, berry-like cones with **greyish tinge.**

ECOLOGY: Widespread and common at low to mid elevations on our plateaus, in their basins and in southern Rocky Mountain Trench, on dry rocky or sandy soils, grassy slopes, dry open forests, most commonly on warm, dry south-facing slopes.

SIMILAR SPECIES: Common juniper (*J. communis*, above) has needle-like leaves and always grows as a shrub. Its fruits lack the heavy bloom that is found on the fruits of Rocky Mountain juniper. • Creeping juniper (*J. horizontalis*), a low prostrate shrub with scale-like leaves, is distinguished from Rocky Mountain juniper by its creeping habit. Creeping juniper occurs sporadically and is locally common on warm aspects in the Fraser Basin. It often hybridizes with Rocky Mountain juniper where they occur together.

NOTES: Cones of Rocky Mountain juniper ripen in their second season, so two generations of cones may occur on the same tree. The fleshy covering of the cones must be dissolved away before the seeds can germinate. In nature, this is usually accomplished as the cones pass through the digestive tract of birds or animals. • The extremely tough wood has been used for making bows, clubs and spoons. The boughs or leaves were used for medicinal purposes in the same way as common juniper. • The berries were eaten fresh in small quantities, or drunk as a tea for many stomach ailments.

WILDFLOWERS

Flowering plants are generally divided into two subclasses—Dicotyledoneae (the 'dicots') and Monocotyledoneae (the 'monocots'). Dicots have two cotyledons (seed leaves), usually have net-veined leaves and have 4- or 5-parted flowers (or multiples of four or five). Monocots have only one cotyledon, usually have relatively long, narrow, parallel-veined leaves and have 3-parted flowers (or a multiple of three parts).

This section is organized by family, and each family by genus, so that similar species can be compared easily.

Photo sample of the wildflowers

There are illustrated keys to both the dicots (p. 104) and monocots (p. 279), but as an easy first step in identifying a wildflower, consult the following photo sample, which is organized by flower colour. Only a limited selection of our wildflowers is shown, but representatives of the major groups are included to guide you to the section of the book where flowers of each type are found.

p. 267	p. 215	p. 283	p. 225	p. 151
p. 168	p. 260	p. 192	p. 205	p. 110
p. 130	p. 216	p. 133	p. 127	p. 114
p. 131	p. 234	p. 207	p. 226	p. 261

p. 297   p. 284   p. 307   p. 151   p. 174

p. 176   p. 236   p. 249   p. 162   p. 217

p. 195   p. 143   p. 219   p. 145   p. 287

p. 146   p. 144   p. 303   p. 300   p. 250

p. 210   p. 247   p. 183   p. 150   p. 199

p. 190   p. 157   p. 302   p. 305   p. 289

p. 171   p. 238   p. 198   p. 116   p. 250

p. 141   p. 111   p. 307   p. 214   p. 221

p. 256   p. 120   p. 268   p. 285   p. 136

p. 274   p. 179   p. 270   p. 264   p. 253

p. 295   p. 197   p. 276   p. 266   p. 249

p. 117   p. 150   p. 138   p. 187   p. 189

p. 278	*p. 285*	*p. 193*	*p. 232*	*p. 254*
p. 157	*p. 135*	*p. 152*	*p. 194*	*p. 241*
p. 278	*p. 174*	*p. 170*	*p. 257*	*p. 263*
p. 116	*p. 213*	*p. 182*	*p. 205*	*p. 296*
p. 158	*p. 181*	*p. 187*	*p. 153*	*p. 264*
p. 172	*p. 306*	*p. 121*	*p. 197*	*p. 184*

Key to the herbaceous dicotyledon families

1a. Flowers in dense heads that look like a single flower (daisy-like flowers) .... **Group 1**

1b. Flowers single or in various types of inflorescences, but generally not
in dense heads that look like a single flower 2

    2a. Flowers inconspicuous, generally small and greenish,
    often infrequently produced .... **Group 2**

    2b. Flowers generally conspicuous, usually contrasting in
    colour with the rest of the plant, commonly produced on mature plants 3

        3a. Flowers irregularly shaped but symmetrical
        around a central plane (bilaterally symmetrical) .... **Group 3**

        3b. Flowers symmetrical in all directions (radially symmetrical) 4

            4a. Petals fused, at least at the base .... **Group 4**

            4b. Petals separate 5

                5a. More than 10 stamens per flower .... **Group 5**

                5b. No more than twice as many stamens as petals (10 or less) 6

                    6a. 4 petals per flower .... **Group 6**

                    6b. 5–10 petals per flower 7

                          7a. Inflorescence an umbel .... **Group 7**

                          7b. Inflorescence not an umbel .... **Group 8**

Group 1 (pp. 109–45): Flowers in dense
heads that look like a single flower.

    Asteraceae (Sunflower Family)

Group 2 (pp. 145–50): Flowers inconspicuous, small, generally similar in
colour to other parts of the plant.

    Chenopodiaceae (Goosefoot Family)
    Euphorbiaceae (Spurge Family)
    Haloragaceae (Water-milfoil Family)
    Hippuridaceae (Mare's-tail Family)
    Lemnaceae (Duckweed Family), a monocotyledon family
    Plantaginaceae (Plantain Family)
    Polygonaceae (Buckwheat Family), p. 199
    Urticaceae (Nettle Family)

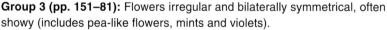

Group 3 (pp. 151–81): Flowers irregular and bilaterally symmetrical, often
showy (includes pea-like flowers, mints and violets).

    Fumariaceae (Fumitory Family)
    Lamiaceae (Mint Family)
    Fabaceae (Pea Family)
    Lentibulariaceae (Bladderwort Family)
    Orobanchaceae (Broomrape Family)
    Ranunculaceae (Buttercup Family), p. 202
    Scrophulariaceae (Figwort Family)
    Violaceae (Violet Family)

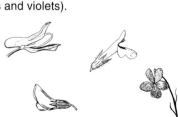

Group 4 (pp. 182–201): Flowers radially symmetrical; petals fused at least at base.

Apocynaceae (Dogbane Family)
Boraginaceae (Borage Family)
Campanulaceae (Harebell Family)
Ericaceae (Heath Family), p. 272
Gentianaceae (Gentian Family)
Hydrophyllaceae (Waterleaf Family)
Menyanthaceae (Buckbean Family)
Polemoniaceae (Phlox Family)
Polygonaceae (Buckwheat Family)
Primulaceae (Primrose Family)
Rubiaceae (Madder Family)
Santalaceae (Sandalwood Family)
Valerianaceae (Valerian Family)

Group 5 (pp. 202–28): Flowers radially symmetrical; petals separate; more than 10 stamens.

Aristolochiaceae (Birthwort Family)
Cactaceae (Cactus Family)
Hypericaceae (St. John's-wort Family)
Loasaceae (Blazing-star Family)
Nymphaceae (Waterlily Family)
Ranunculaceae (Buttercup Family)
Rosaceae (Rose Family)

Group 6 (pp. 229–42): Flowers radially symmetrical; 4 separate petals; 8 or fewer stamens.

Brassicaceae (Mustard Family)
Polygonaceae (Buckwheat Family), *Oxyria* species (p. 199)
Onagraceae (Evening-primrose Family)

Group 7 (pp. 243–50): Flowers radially symmetrical; 5 or more separate petals; 10 or fewer stamens; inflorescence an umbel.

Araliaceae (Ginseng Family)
Asclepiadaceae (Milkweed Family)
Cornaceae (Dogwood Family)
Apiaceae (Carrot Family)

Group 8 (pp. 251–78): Flowers radially symmetrical; 5 or more separate petals; 10 or fewer stamens; inflorescence not an umbel.

Caryophyllaceae (Pink Family)
Crassulaceae (Stonecrop Family)
Droseraceae (Sundew Family)
Ericaceae (Heath Family)
Geraniaceae (Geranium Family)
Linaceae (Flax Family)
Lythraceae (Loosestrife Family)
Malvaceae (Mallow Family)
Parnassiaceae (Parnassus Family)
Portulacaceae (Purslane Family)
Saxifragaceae (Saxifrage Family)

Asteraceae: Sunflower Family

The sunflower family (also called Compositae) includes many vegetables, herbs and garden flowers, as well as such well-known plants as aster, dandelion, daisy, dahlia, thistle, sunflower, zinnia and goldenrod. Worldwide this is one of the largest families of plants, with over 20,000 species occurring in most habitats on all continents except Antarctica. Several hundred species are found in southern British Columbia.

Members of the sunflower family are easily identified by their inflorescences, which are often mistaken for a single large flower, but are actually made up of many individual flowers on the broadened top of the stem. Only a few plants in a few other families have this 'composite' type of flower. The flowers are of two types, referred to as **ray flowers** and **disk flowers**. The corolla of ray flowers is strap-like, while that of disk flowers is tubular. The heads may be composed of either or both ray and disk flowers.

Attached to the rim of the head is a series of scale-like or somewhat leaf-like bracts, called the **involucre**. The **involucral bracts** are sometimes hooked, as in burdock (*Arctium* sp.). The hooks assist in dispersal by becoming attached to animals (or to clothing). Sunflower fruits are single seeds called **achenes**, which usually have a **pappus**. The pappus consists of hairs, bristles or scales attached to the top of the achene, and it often assists in wind-dispersal. The dandelion, with its downy parachute, is a familiar example.

Species of the sunflower family can be difficult to identify, especially those of some of the large groups, such as asters. Some key characters to note are the types of flowers comprising the head (disk, ray or both), the type of pappus on the seeds (or the lack of a pappus) and the presence of milky juice in the stems. Other distinguishing characters include the flower colour, leaf shape and distribution, the type of involucral bracts (including whether the bracts overlap to form more than one row) and the general hairiness of the plant.

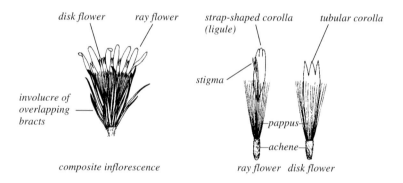

disk flower   ray flower   strap-shaped corolla (ligule)   tubular corolla

stigma

involucre of overlapping bracts

pappus

achene

composite inflorescence

ray flower   disk flower

Key to the sunflower family genera

1a. All flowers in a head are ray flowers
(with a strap-like corolla); most plants have milky juice .... **Group 1**

1b. Not all flowers in a head are ray flowers (strap-like);
central disk flowers, or all flowers, are tubular; most plants lack milky juice 2

    2a. Ray flowers present 3

        3a. Ray flowers white, pink, purple, red or blue, but not yellow or orange .... **Group 2**

        3b. Ray flowers yellow or orange, except sometimes at the base .... **Group 3**

    2b. Ray flowers absent 4

        4a. Pappus of hair- or feather-like bristles .... **Group 4**

        4b. Pappus of scales or awns, or sometimes almost absent .... **Group 5**

Group 1: All flowers in a head are ray flowers (with a strap-like corolla); most plants have milky juice.

1a. All leaves in a basal rosette (no stem leaves) 2

  2a. Achenes rough, with tiny spines and projections .... ***Taraxacum***

  2b. Achenes smooth or ribbed 3

    3a. Plants with taproots .... ***Agoseris***

    3b. Plants with short rhizomes and many fibrous roots .... ***Hieracium***

1b. Stem leaves present 4

  4a. Pappus of feathery bristles or very small scales 5

    5a. Pappus of feathery bristles; flowers yellow or purple .... ***Tragopogon***

    5b. Pappus of very small scales; flowers blue .... ***Cichorium***

  4b. Pappus of simple bristles that are sometimes barbed 6

    6a. Stem leaves generally less than 1 cm wide and
reduced in size up the stem; basal leaves usually well developed 7

      7a. Plants perennial, with short rhizomes; pappus generally
tan to light brown (occasionally white) .... ***Hieracium***

      7b. Plants annual, biennial or perennial with taproots or
fibrous roots; pappus generally white .... ***Crepis***

    6b. Stem leaves greater than 1 cm wide; basal leaves similar
in size to stem leaves or smaller (sometimes absent) 8

      8a. Pappus stalked; leaves without clasping lobes at base .... ***Lactuca***

      8b. Pappus not stalked; leaves with clasping lobes at base .... ***Sonchus***

Group 2: Heads have both ray and disk flowers; ray flowers white, pink, purple, red or blue.

1a. Leaves divided into many fine segments; rays few (usually 3–5); heads small .... ***Achillea***

1b. Leaves entire, toothed, lobed or divided into a few segments 2

  2a. Bristles occur among flowers within a head; true ray flowers absent,
but outer disk flowers sometimes appear to have rays .... ***Centaurea***

  2b. Bristles absent among flowers within a head; true ray flowers present 3

    3a. Pappus a short crown or absent .... ***Leucanthemum***

    3b. Pappus of slender, hair-like bristles 4

      4a. Basal leaves arising after (or separate from)
flowering stem, arrowhead-shaped to palmately lobed,
long-stalked; stem leaves much smaller .... ***Petasites***

      4b. Basal leaves arising before flowering stem;
stem leaves often well developed 5

        5a. Involucral bracts generally in 1 row, often similar
in colour throughout (not green at tip nor papery at base) .... ***Erigeron***

        5b. Involucral bracts in 3 or more rows, overlapping like shingles,
generally green at tip and papery at base .... ***Aster***

Group 3: Heads have both ray and disk flowers; ray flowers yellow or orange.

1a. Pappus hair- or feather-like 2

  2a. Leaves opposite, except for reduced upper leaf .... ***Arnica***

  2b. Leaves alternate or basal 3

    3a. Involucral bracts in 1 prominent row .... ***Senecio***

3b. Involucral bracts in 2 or more rows 4

    4a. Pappus double, bristles of inner row much longer than those of outer row 5

        5a. Leaves linear; stem leaves reduced upwards .... *Erigeron*

        5b. Leaves oblong; stem leaves similar in size to basal leaves .... *Heterotheca*

    4b. Pappus single, bristles in 1 row 6

        6a. Usually several flower heads .... *Solidago*

        6b. Flower heads solitary .... *Haplopappus*

1b. Pappus of bracts, scales or firm awns, or pappus sometimes absent 7

    7a. Leaves mostly basal, very large; stem leaves absent or much reduced .... *Balsamorhiza*

    7b. Basal leaves few or absent; usually many stem leaves 8

        8a. Strap of ray flowers 3-lobed at tip; heads not sticky .... *Gaillardia*

        8b. Strap of ray flowers not lobed at tip; heads sticky .... *Grindelia*

Group 4: Ray flowers absent; pappus of hair- or feather-like bristles.

1a. Leaves spiny; thistles .... *Cirsium*

1b. Leaves not spiny and thistle-like 2

    2a. Bristles common among flowers within a head;
true ray flowers absent, but some disk flowers appear to have rays .... *Centaurea*

    2b. Bristles absent among flowers within a head; ray flowers clearly absent 3

        3a. Main stem leaves opposite .... *Arnica parryi*

        3b. Main stem leaves alternate or basal 4

            4a. Basal leaves heart- or arrowhead-shaped .... *Petasites*

            4b. Basal leaves, if present, not heart- or arrowhead-shaped 5

                5a. At least some leaves lobed or deeply toothed .... *Senecio*

                5b. Leaves mostly entire 6

                      6a. Basal leaves prominent and persistent,
tufted; stem leaves often few and small .... *Antennaria*

                      6b. Basal leaves soon withering; stem leaves
numerous, well developed .... *Anaphalis*

Group 5: Ray flowers absent; pappus of scales or sometimes absent.

1a. Involucral bracts with small, hooked bristles .... *Arctium*

1b. Involucral bracts without hooked bristles 2

    2a. Lower leaves approximately triangular,
white-woolly beneath; 5 or fewer involucral bracts .... *Adenocaulon*

    2b. Lower leaves not as above; usually more than 5 involucral bracts 3

        3a. Bristles common among flowers within
a head; true ray flowers absent, but some
disk flowers appear to have rays .... *Centaurea*

        3b. Bristles absent among flowers within a head;
ray flowers clearly absent 4

            4a. Pappus of small but distinct, translucent, linear scales .... *Chaenactis*

            4b. Pappus a very small crown, or absent 5

                5a. Heads in elongate clusters, small and usually numerous .... *Artemisia*

                5b. Heads in round or flat-topped clusters, small to large
and few to many 6

                      6a. Receptacles round to conical .... *Matricaria*

                      6b. Receptacles flat to somewhat convex .... *Tanacetum*

ORANGE AGOSERIS • *Agoseris aurantiaca*

GENERAL: Taprooted perennial, 10–60 cm tall, with simple or branching stem base and **milky stem juice** (latex).

LEAVES: All basal, linear to narrowly lance-shaped, sometimes toothed or lobed.

FLOWERS: Composite heads, with **burnt orange** (rarely yellow) **ray flowers** and **no disk flowers**; ray flowers often become pink or purple with age or drying; involucre of several rows of **overlapping bracts** of various lengths, often purple-spotted.

FRUITS: Smooth achenes, with a **white pappus on a slender stalk** that is half to fully as long as body of achene.

ECOLOGY: Widespread and scattered at mid to alpine elevations in moist to dry openings, alpine meadows and dry open forests.

NOTES: The genus *Agoseris* is a group of **yellow- to orange-flowered** perennials with **milky stem juice**. The large flower heads are **solitary on a leafless stalk** and are composed entirely of **ray flowers**. Mature achenes have a pappus of many soft hairs in a cluster borne on the tip of a slender stalk. • Some southern Interior native groups chewed the leaves and especially the latex of some *Agoseris* and *Hieracium* species, for pleasure. • *Agoseris* species are quite similar to dandelions (*Taraxacum* spp.) in appearance and are sometimes called false dandelions. Orange agoseris is also called orange mountain dandelion.

SHORT-BEAKED AGOSERIS • *Agoseris glauca* var. *dasycephala*

GENERAL: Taprooted perennial, 10–70 cm tall, with a simple or branching stem base and **milky stem juice** (latex).

LEAVES: All basal, linear to broadly lance-shaped, sometimes toothed or lobed.

FLOWERS: Composite heads, with **yellow ray flowers** and **no disk flowers**; ray flowers often become pink with age or drying; involucral bracts slightly to densely hairy, fringed, sometimes purple-spotted.

FRUITS: Smooth achenes, with a **white pappus** that is nearly stalkless, or is on a slender stalk up to half as long as body of achene.

ECOLOGY: Widespread and common at low to high elevations in dry forests, openings and mesic to dry meadows.

SIMILAR SPECIES: The yellow ray flowers of short-beaked agoseris distinguish it from orange agoseris (*A. aurantiaca*, above). Also, the achenes of short-beaked agoseris are tapered at the top, while those of orange agoseris are abruptly constricted at the top. • Recently, a new pink-flowered species, *A. lackswitzii*, has been found in the alpine zone of the southern Rocky Mountains of B.C.

NOTES: The Okanagan-Colville dried this plant's latex and used it as a chewing gum. They made an infusion of the plant to wash sores and rashes, and rubbed the stem latex into sores. The roots were steeped and used as a laxative.

ORANGE HAWKWEED • *Hieracium aurantiacum*

GENERAL: **Rhizomatous** perennial, 20–60 cm tall, usually also with **short runners**; stems are usually solitary, exude **milky juice** when broken, and are **bristly-hairy** and glandular above.

LEAVES: **In a basal rosette**, narrowly elliptic to lance-shaped, without lobes, covered with **long, bristly hairs on both surfaces**.

FLOWERS: Several **composite heads** crowded in a flat- to round-topped cluster, with **red-orange ray flowers** and **no disk flowers**; involucral bracts with **long, bristly hairs and blackish glands**.

FRUITS: Ribbed achenes, with a **pappus of tawny, hair-like bristles**.

ECOLOGY: Scattered and locally abundant at low to mid elevations; very conspicuous in disturbed sites and pastures.

NOTES: The **brilliant, red-orange heads** of this introduced, weedy species have made it a garden favourite in Europe for many years, but it can spread rapidly and become a nuisance. • The species name *aurantiacum* means 'orange-coloured.'

SLENDER HAWKWEED • *Hieracium gracile*

GENERAL: Perennial, to 35 cm tall, from a short rhizome; 1 to several stems, which exude **milky juice** when broken.

LEAVES: **In a basal rosette**, broadly lance- to spoon-shaped, hairless or sometimes inconspicuously hairy and glandular on both surfaces.

FLOWERS: 1 to several **composite heads** in a small cluster, with **yellow ray flowers** and **no disk flowers**; involucral bracts with fine, blackish hairs and black glands.

FRUITS: Ribbed achenes, with a pappus of tawny, or sometimes white, hair-like bristles.

ECOLOGY: Widespread and common in moist to wet subalpine and alpine meadows; especially abundant in snowbed sites.

NOTES: Hawkweeds are a large and widely distributed group of perennial herbs. They are part of a subgroup of composites that are distinguished by having milky juice in their stems, and flower heads made up entirely of ray flowers. • The species name *gracile* means 'slender.'

NARROW-LEAVED HAWKWEED • *Hieracium umbellatum*

GENERAL: Perennial, 40–120 cm tall, with a **short, woody rhizome**; 1 to few stems, exude **milky juice** when broken, hairless (or nearly so) below, commonly with **star-shaped hairs above**.

LEAVES: A **few basal leaves**, soon withering; lower stem leaves strongly reduced; **middle leaves lance-shaped**, stalkless, unlobed or somewhat toothed with short, stiff, **star-shaped hairs**.

FLOWERS: Few to many **composite heads** in a **flat-topped cluster**, with **yellow ray flowers** and **no disk flowers**; involucral bracts **overlapping**, hairless (or nearly so), smoky green to blackish.

FRUITS: Ribbed achenes, with a pappus of hair-like bristles.

ECOLOGY: Widespread and common at low to mid elevations in dry to moist, open forests, meadows and clearings.

NOTES: Canada hawkweed (*H. canadense*) is now included in *H. umbellatum*.

WHITE HAWKWEED • *Hieracium albiflorum*

GENERAL: Perennial, 30–120 cm tall, from a woody, fibrous-rooted stem base; stems usually solitary, exude **milky juice** when broken, and **bristly-hairy (at least at the base)** and hairless above.

LEAVES: Oblong to broadly lance-shaped, often with wavy-toothed edges, and **bristly-hairy** upper surfaces.

FLOWERS: Several to many **composite heads** in an open inflorescence, with **white ray flowers** and **no disk flowers**; involucral bracts **greenish or blackish**, **often glandular** with pale or black hairs.

FRUITS: Several-ribbed achenes, with a **pappus of white or tawny, hair-like bristles**.

ECOLOGY: Widespread and common at low to mid elevations in moist to dry, open forests, openings and clearings.

NOTES: The name 'hawkweed' comes from a belief of the ancient Greeks that hawks would tear apart a plant called *hieracion* (from the Greek *hierax*, meaning 'hawk') and wet their eyes with the juice to clear their eyesight. The common name of this species reflects that it is the only white-flowered hawkweed in our region.

SCOULER'S HAWKWEED • *Hieracium scouleri*

GENERAL: Perennial, 20–130 cm tall, from a short, sometimes stout rootstock; stems exude **milky juice** when broken, usually solitary, unbranched and sparsely to abundantly **hairy**.

LEAVES: Lance-shaped and narrowed to a stalk; lower leaves larger and with **bristly hairs**.

FLOWERS: Few to many **composite heads** in a flat- to round-topped inflorescence, with **yellow ray flowers** and **no disk flowers**; involucral bracts with black, glandular, **bristly hairs and some glandless, yellow hairs**.

FRUITS: Ribbed achenes, with a pappus of whitish to tawny, hair-like bristles.

ECOLOGY: Scattered and locally common at low to mid elevations throughout Thompson and Okanagan plateaus and basins, in sagebrush grasslands, open Douglas-fir and ponderosa pine forests and openings.

NOTES: The Nlaka'pmx chewed the leaves and coagulated latex of some species of *Hieracium* (probably Scouler's hawkweed and *H. albertinum*), and at least one species of *Agoseris* (short-beaked agoseris, *A. glauca*). They broke the leaves and stems of these plants to drain the milky latex. When the latex had hardened, it was collected in a little ball and chewed for pleasure and to cleanse the mouth. • The roots of Scouler's hawkweed were steeped in hot water and the resulting tea was used as a tonic. • This species was named to honour John Scouler (1804–71), a Scottish botanist who collected in western North America.

COMMON DANDELION • *Taraxacum officinale*

GENERAL: Perennial, 5–60 cm tall (rarely to 1 m), from a simple or branched stem base and a thick, often blackish **taproot; stems solitary, hollow, leafless**, exude **milky juice** when broken.

LEAVES: All basal, oblong to spoon-shaped, **toothed or deeply lobed or divided**, tapering to more or less winged stalks, hairless except on midrib.

FLOWERS: Solitary composite heads, with **bright yellow ray flowers** and no disk flowers; involucre of **2 rows of overlapping bracts**, with the outer 1 bent backwards.

FRUITS: Greyish to greenish-brown or straw-coloured achenes, with ribs and spines on upper part; **pappus of many white, hair-like bristles**, on a stalk 2–4 times as long as body of achene.

ECOLOGY: Widespread European weed of low to mid elevations and often into subalpine; aggressive species of clearings, disturbed soils and cultivated sites.

SIMILAR SPECIES: In addition to the familiar, weedy dandelion, the genus *Taraxacum* includes a number of non-weedy members. Horned dandelion (*T. ceratophorum*) is one that occurs in our area. This native, alpine species is quite similar to common dandelion, but it has less deeply lobed leaves and its involucral bracts are not bent backwards (or are less strongly so).

NOTES: The young leaves make excellent cooked greens, and the roots can be roasted or dried and ground as a coffee substitute. The flowers are used to make dandelion wine and the whole plant can be brewed to make beer. Try coating the flower heads in flour and frying them in butter—they taste like morels. • The genus name *Taraxacum* (from the Greek *tarassein*, 'to stir up') and the species name *officinale* (medicinal) refer to this plant's use in medicine.

SLENDER HAWKSBEARD • *Crepis atrabarba*

GENERAL: **Taprooted perennial**, 15–70 cm tall; stems exude **milky juice** when broken and are usually hairy.

LEAVES: Basal leaves **deeply lobed with linear segments**; stem leaves becoming linear above.

FLOWERS: Composite heads, with 10–40 **bright yellow ray flowers** and **no disk flowers**; involucre of several rows of **overlapping bracts**, usually greyish-hairy, **often with black bristles**; inflorescence is flat- to round-topped cluster of several to many heads.

FRUITS: Greenish, slender achenes, with a **pappus of white, hair-like bristles**.

ECOLOGY: Widespread and locally common at low to mid elevations in dry, open, sandy or gravelly habitats.

SIMILAR SPECIES: Another hawksbeard common in dry, open places is western hawksbeard (*C. occidentalis*). Its **deeply lobed leaves with broad, pointed segments** and yellowish to brownish achenes distinguish it from slender hawksbeard.

NOTES: The Okanagan pounded the green tops, steeped them in hot water and used the solution as a foot bath. • The lines of black bristles on the involucral bracts give rise to the species name *atrabarba*, which is Latin for 'black-bearded.'

DWARF HAWKSBEARD • *Crepis nana*

GENERAL: **Low-growing perennial**, 2–20 cm tall, from a long **taproot**; many, branched stems, exuding **milky juice** when broken.

LEAVES: **Rounded to spoon-shaped**, unlobed, with a greyish bloom.

FLOWERS: Composite heads, with 6–12 **yellow ray flowers** and **no disk flowers**, generally borne among leaves; involucre of several rows of **overlapping bracts**, with the outer ones less than half as long as inner ones.

FRUITS: Golden brown, columnar-shaped achenes, with ribs; short pappus of fine, white, hair-like bristles that soon fall off.

ECOLOGY: Scattered and locally common at sub-alpine or alpine elevations in open, moist to moderately dry, gravelly sites.

SIMILAR SPECIES: This hawksbeard might be confused with elegant hawksbeard (*C. elegans*). Elegant hawksbeard, however, is usually found on low-elevation sand and gravel bars, and it has taller stems (20–30 cm) and roughened or short-hairy, delicately beaked achenes.

ANNUAL HAWKSBEARD • *Crepis tectorum*

GENERAL: Taprooted annual, 30–100 cm tall; stems solitary, exuding **milky juice** when broken, branched at top.

LEAVES: Basal leaves usually withering; stem leaves linear (or nearly so), **with a pair of lobes at their junction with stem.**

FLOWERS: Composite heads, with **yellow ray flowers** and **no disk flowers**; involucre of several rows of **overlapping bracts**, hairy and sometimes glandular, with the **outer ones about one-third as long as inner ones.**

FRUITS: Dark purplish-brown, ribbed achenes, with a pappus of fine, white, hair-like bristles (often deciduous).

ECOLOGY: European weed of open, disturbed sites and along roadsides, at low to mid elevations.

NOTES: The name 'hawksbeard' was given to the genus *Crepis* by the botanist Asa Grey, and it may refer to the pappus's resemblance to the bristly feathers protruding around a hawk's beak.

PRICKLY LETTUCE • *Lactuca serriola*
L. scariola

GENERAL: Biennial or winter annual, 30–100 cm tall (rarely to 2 m); stems pale green to straw-coloured, exude **milky juice** when broken, hairless throughout or prickly and short-hairy below.

LEAVES: Once- or twice-lobed and irregularly toothed, prickly on edges and especially lower midrib; leaf bases clasp stem.

FLOWERS: Composite heads, with **yellow ray flowers (often drying blue) and no disk flowers**; many heads in a large, **highly branched inflorescence**; involucre of about 4 rows of **overlapping**, irregularly graduated bracts.

FRUITS: Whitish achenes, with several ribs; pappus of **white, hair-like bristles, on a slender stalk** (beak) as long as or longer than body of achene.

ECOLOGY: Scattered and locally common at low to mid elevations on disturbed soils, including cultivated fields and clearings.

SIMILAR SPECIES: Blue lettuce (*L. tatarica* ssp. *pulchella*, **photo**) is a widespread native species in our region. It grows in moist to moderately dry meadows and shrubby communities at low to mid elevations. It is distinguished by blue or sometimes violet flowers and hairless leaves that are lobed below but simple above.

NOTES: Prickly lettuce is an introduced European weed. • The young leaves of most of our *Lactuca* species are edible. In fact, garden lettuce (*L. sativa*) is a member of this genus. • The name 'lettuce' is a direct translation of the Latin *lactuca*, which derives from the Latin *lac* (milk), and refers to the milky sap of lettuce species. Both species names—*serriola* and the alternative spelling *scariola*—mean 'of salads.' This species is called prickly lettuce because of the long, prickly hairs on its stems and leaves.

PERENNIAL SOW-THISTLE • *Sonchus arvensis*

GENERAL: Perennial, 40–150 cm tall, from deep, spreading **rhizome-like roots**; stems are unbranched and hollow, exuding **milky juice** when broken, usually yellow glandular-bristly above.

LEAVES: Broadly lance-shaped in outline, **deeply hook-lobed, with prickly edges**; leaf bases clasp stem.

FLOWERS: Composite heads, with **yellow ray flowers and no disk flowers**; involucre of **several series of overlapping bracts** with gland-tipped hairs.

FRUITS: Flattened, ribbed and cross-wrinkled achenes, with a **pappus of white, hair-like bristles.**

ECOLOGY: Widespread European weed, common at low to mid elevations in pastures, roadsides and other disturbed areas.

SIMILAR SPECIES: Sow-thistles can be distinguished from true thistles (*Cirsium* spp., pp. 134–35) by breaking their stems; **sow-thistles exude a milky latex, true thistles do not.**

NOTES: The young leaves of sow-thistle can be eaten raw in salads or cooked as a vegetable. • Perennial sow-thistle is a difficult weed to control through cultivation due to its wide-spreading roots. • The genus name *Sonchus* is from the Greek word for 'spongy,' in reference to the stems; the species name *arvensis* means 'of the fields,' where this weedy species grows. Apparently, pigs like to eat sow thistles, hence the common name.

YELLOW SALSIFY • *Tragopogon dubius*

GENERAL: Taprooted biennial or occasionally annual, 30–100 cm tall; stems leafy, often branched, exude **milky juice** when broken, noticeably **enlarged beneath flower heads.**

LEAVES: Narrow and grass-like, greyish green; **leaf bases clasp stem**; cottony-hairy when young, becoming hairless with age.

FLOWERS: Solitary composite heads, with **pale yellow ray flowers and no disk flowers**; involucre **a single row of bracts, distinctly longer than the ray flowers.**

FRUITS: Long, slender achenes that gradually taper to a stout stalk; **pappus a single series of large feathery bristles.**

ECOLOGY: Scattered and often abundant at low to mid elevations throughout our dry plateaus and southern Rocky Mountain Trench, in grasslands, roadsides, fields and other disturbed sites.

SIMILAR SPECIES: Common salsify (*T. porrifolius*), also called oyster plant, is almost identical and occurs in the southern half of our region. It has **purple ray flowers** and prefers moister habitats. • Meadow salsify (*T. pratensis*) also favours moist ground. It is distinguished by the **absence of swollen stems** beneath the flower heads and by the involucral bracts, which are generally shorter than the ray flowers. It also frequently has leaf ends that are slender, curved back and twisted.

NOTES: 'Salsify' is from the French *salsifis* and Latin *solsequium*, derived in turn from *sol* (sun) and *sequium* (follower)—a plant that follows the sun. The flowers tend to close up at midday or in cloudy weather. According to Theophrastus (372–287 BC), a Greek philosopher and scientist, the tuft of hairy pappus that extends from the tip of the closed flower resembles the beard of a goat and is the reason that this genus is commonly called goat's beard.

CHICORY • *Cichorium intybus*

GENERAL: **Taprooted perennial**, 30–175 cm tall; flowering stems branched, with small leaves, exude a bitter-tasting, **milky juice** when broken.

LEAVES: **Basal leaves deeply toothed to lobed, lance-shaped**; a few small, unlobed stem leaves.

FLOWERS: **Composite heads**, with **sky-blue ray flowers** (rarely white) and **no disk flowers**; open only in daylight; involucral bracts in 2 rows, with the outer ones fewer, shorter and loose; inflorescence of small clusters of 1–4 widely spaced heads on long branches from bases of stem leaves.

FRUITS: 5-angled, hairless achenes; pappus reduced to a **minute, fringed crown of scales**.

ECOLOGY: Scattered and locally common, mostly at low elevations on our dry plateaus, drier parts of southern Columbia Mountains and dry East Kootenays, in fields, roadsides and waste areas.

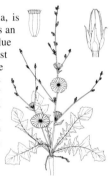

NOTES: This introduced weed, a native of Eurasia, is now established in many parts of the world. It makes an excellent garden subject with its brilliant, sky-blue flowers that close at night and on heavily overcast days. • This plant is called Belgium endive in the commercial vegetable trade. The leaves are eaten as a salad green, a practice dating back to the early Egyptians. The taproots are roasted, ground and used as a coffee substitute. They are also sold as a bitter, tangy seasoning for soups. • 'Chicory' and the genus name *Cichorium* are from the original Arabic name for wild chicory; *intybus* is Latin for 'endive.' Chicory is also called blue sailors.

YARROW • *Achillea millefolium*

GENERAL: Aromatic **perennial**, 10–75 cm tall, usually with **rhizomes**.

LEAVES: **Fern-like, pinnately dissected**, with the divisions again dissected.

FLOWERS: **Composite heads**, usually with 5 **white to pink or rose ray flowers** and 10–30 **cream-coloured disk flowers**; involucre of several rows of **overlapping bracts**; inflorescence of many heads in a **hemispheric or flat-topped cluster**.

FRUITS: Flattened **achenes, without a pappus**.

ECOLOGY: Widespread and common at low to subalpine elevations in moist to very dry, open sites and open forests; often weedy on disturbed sites.

SIMILAR SPECIES: Yarrow forms one of our most variable species complexes, and two varieties are known in our region. The subalpine and alpine form, *A. millefolium* var. *alpicola*, has a short stature, grey leaves and darker involucral edges. A lower-elevation form, *A. millefolium* var. *lanulosa*, occurs in montane and grassland areas. It is distinguished by its usually green, lightly hairy leaves.

NOTES: Yarrow was, and still is, widely used in a variety of herbal remedies. High-elevation yarrow is considered more potent than the low-elevation form. The Secwepemc placed the leaves on fires to discourage mosquitoes. They and other native people put washed and crushed roots in their teeth to stop toothaches, bathed in infusions of leaves and stems for rheumatism and used decoctions as a tonic or astringent. Yarrow contains the alkaloid achilleine, which is sometimes used nowadays to suppress menstruation. • The name 'yarrow' comes from the Anglo-Saxon *gearwe*, which may be derived from *gierwan*, meaning 'to prepare,' as in the preparation of a healing herb. The species name *millefolium* is French for 'thousand leaves,' referring to the highly divided leaves.

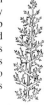

PALMATE COLTSFOOT • *Petasites frigidus* var. *palmatus* P. palmatus

GENERAL: Perennial, 5–50 cm tall, from a thick, creeping **rhizome**; flowering stems more or less white-hairy, **appear before leaves**.

LEAVES: Basal leaves kidney-shaped to nearly round in outline, **palmately lobed into 5–7 sharply toothed segments**, long stalked, green and thinly hairy above, white-woolly below; **stem leaves reduced to reddish bracts**.

FLOWERS: Terminal cluster of composite heads, with glandular and often woolly-hairy bases, **pink to purplish disk flowers and whitish or pink to purplish ray flowers** (many heads with disk flowers only); involucre a **single row of bracts** with translucent edges and tipped with tufts of hair.

FRUITS: Achenes, with a **pappus of many white bristles**.

ECOLOGY: Widespread and common at low to subalpine elevations in wet and moist forests, wetlands, seepage areas, streambanks and lakeshores.

SIMILAR SPECIES: Sweet coltsfoot (*P. frigidus* var. *nivalis,* inset photo) has shallowly cleft leaves and is common at subalpine and alpine elevations. • *P. frigidus* var. *frigidus* occurs in similar habitats but is rare in our region. Its leaves are not cleft but have broad, blunt teeth. Separating these varieties is often difficult because there are plants with intermediate leaf characteristics.

NOTES: The **flowering stems of coltsfoot species do not arise from the same points on the rhizome as do the leaves**. Because the two are separated in time as well as in space, the association between them may not at first be obvious. • The young leaves and flowers of coltsfoot make a good potherb and burning the leaves produces ashes that may be used as salt. • The genus name *Petasites* is from the Greek *petasos* (a broad-brimmed hat), referring to the large basal leaves characteristic of this genus.

var. *palmatus*   var. *nivalis*

ARROW-LEAVED COLTSFOOT • *Petasites sagittatus*

GENERAL: Perennial, 10–50 cm tall, from a creeping **rhizome**; many white, woolly-hairy flowering stems, **appear before leaves**.

LEAVES: Basal leaves large, **triangular to heart-shaped**, with **toothed edges** and long stalks, green and thinly hairy above, **densely white-woolly below, appear after flowering stems**; stem leaves reduced to a few bracts.

FLOWERS: Composite heads, with glandular and often woolly-hairy bases, **whitish disk flowers and a few whitish ray flowers** (many heads with disk flowers only); involucre a **single row of bracts** with glandular hairs at their bases.

FRUITS: Ribbed achenes, with a **pappus of many white bristles**.

ECOLOGY: Scattered and locally common at low to subalpine elevations in wetlands and wet ditches, often in standing water.

SIMILAR SPECIES: The leaves of arrow-leaved coltsfoot could be confused with those of *P. frigidus* var. *frigidus* (above), but the leaves of arrow-leaved coltsfoot are more arrowhead-shaped and have more teeth (usually more than 20 per side).

NOTES: The flower heads of coltsfoot species are predominantly male or female. The female heads usually have a few ray flowers, while the male heads have all disk flowers. • The leaves, when combined with alum as a mordant, yield a yellowish-green dye for wool.

Erigeron: the daisies

A general description of the daisies (also called fleabanes) also describes their close relatives, the asters (*Aster* spp., p. 122). Although daisies generally flower earlier in the year than asters, there is considerable overlap. The daisies also tend to have more ray flowers, with narrower rays, but again there is considerable overlap. A more reliable distinction between the two groups requires a close look at the involucral bracts. **In daisies, the bracts are arranged in a single main row. In asters, they are usually in several rows, with the individual bracts overlapping like shingles**.

CUT-LEAVED DAISY • *Erigeron compositus* var. *glabratus*

GENERAL: Taprooted perennial, 3–25 cm tall, **densely glandular** with spreading hairs.

LEAVES: Mostly basal, on long stalks, roundish in outline, **highly divided into fairly linear segments**; a few small leaves on stem.

FLOWERS: Solitary composite heads, with **20–60 white, pink or blue ray flowers** and yellow disk flowers; involucre a single row of bracts with **spreading, glandular hairs**, purplish at least towards tip; blooms in spring.

FRUITS: Hairy, 2-ribbed achenes, with a pappus of 12–20 **simple, white bristles**.

ECOLOGY: Widespread and common at low to mid elevations in arid basins and on our dry plateaus, in grasslands and on gravelly river banks; also common on exposed subalpine and alpine ridges throughout dry mountains of our region.

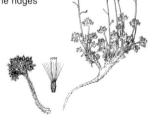

NOTES: The highly dissected leaves of cut-leaved daisy are distinctive and allow this species to be easily distinguished from other daisies in our region. • According to Steedman (1930), the Nlaka'pmx used the dried and powdered plants as a medicine against sores.

LONG-LEAVED DAISY • *Erigeron corymbosus*

GENERAL: Taprooted perennial, 10–50 cm tall; stems with dense **spreading hairs**, usually **purplish at base**.

LEAVES: Mostly basal, long and narrow, tapering gradually to the stalk, with 3 prominent veins and dense, spreading hairs.

FLOWERS: Composite heads, with **35–65 deep blue** (or occasionally pink) **ray flowers** and yellow disk flowers; involucre a **single row of bracts**, whitish- to greyish-hairy and glandular; blooms in spring.

FRUITS: Hairy, 2-nerved achenes, with a **double pappus** of 20–30 firm, white bristles and some outer scales.

ECOLOGY: Widespread and common at low elevations in Thompson and Okanagan basins and southern Rocky Mountain Trench, in open sagebrush grasslands and open forests.

NOTES: The purplish stem bases and long, pointed leaves separate this daisy from others in our region.

TRAILING DAISY • *Erigeron flagellaris* var. *flagellaris*

GENERAL: Taprooted biennial or short-lived perennial, 5–40 cm tall, **with trailing, sparsely leafy runners**; stems slightly to moderately **appressed-hairy**.

LEAVES: Mostly basal, broadly lance-shaped.

FLOWERS: Mostly **solitary composite heads**, with **50–100 white (rarely pink or blue) ray flowers** and yellow disk flowers; involucre a **single row of bracts**, finely glandular and appressed-hairy.

FRUITS: 2-ribbed **achenes**, with a **double pappus** of 10–15 white hairs and an outer ring of fine scales.

ECOLOGY: Scattered and locally common at low elevations in Fraser and Thompson basins, in dry grasslands.

NOTES: Trailing daisy has an unexplained separate northern range. The population in our region is about 1,200 km north-west of the main range, which extends from South Dakota to Texas, Arizona and Mexico. Another separate population occurs in southwestern Alberta. • The species (and variety) name *flagellaris* refers to the thread-like runners that this daisy produces.

FINE-LEAVED DAISY • *Erigeron linearis*

GENERAL: Perennial, 5–30 cm tall, with a stout root and branched stem-base; upper stems and foliage with **appressed hairs**.

LEAVES: Linear; leaf bases enlarged, hardened, or papery and sometimes sheathing stem.

FLOWERS: Solitary composite heads, with **20–45 bright yellow ray flowers** and yellow disk flowers; in volucre a **single row of bracts**, appressed-hairy and often finely glandular.

FRUITS: Achenes, with a **double pappus** of 10–20 firm, white bristles and a few short scales.

ECOLOGY: Widespread and common at low elevations in Fraser, Thompson and Okanagan basins and in southern Rocky Mountain Trench, in dry grasslands.

SIMILAR SPECIES: Golden daisy (*E. aureus*) is a yellow, alpine daisy that has considerably broader leaves than fine-leaved daisy.

NOTES: The Okanagan made a tea from this plant as a cure for tuberculosis.

THREAD-LEAVED DAISY • *Erigeron filifolius* var. *filifolius*

GENERAL: Taprooted perennial, 10–50 cm tall, with a branched, woody stem base; upper stems with **appressed hairs**.

LEAVES: Linear and thread-like, with finely appressed hairs.

FLOWERS: Solitary or several **composite heads**, with **15–50 blue (sometimes pink or white) ray flowers** and yellow disk flowers; involucre a **single row of bracts**, with appressed hairs or fine glands, or both; blooms in spring.

FRUITS: 2-ribbed achenes, with a **pappus of 20–30 slender, firm, white bristles** (rarely with a few inconspicuous outer scales).

ECOLOGY: Scattered and locally common in Thompson and Okanagan basins and southern Rocky Mountain Trench, in dry grasslands, shrub grasslands and dry open forest.

NOTES: The Nlaka'pmx used a powder made from this plant for sores (see cut-leaved daisy [*E. compositus*], p. 118).

SHAGGY DAISY • *Erigeron pumilus* var. *intermedius*

GENERAL: Taprooted perennial, 5–30 cm tall, with a branched stem base; stems usually freely branched at top, with **spreading, stiff hairs**.

LEAVES: Narrowly lance-shaped, with **copious, long, stiff hairs**.

FLOWERS: Composite heads, with **50–100 or more white** (sometimes pale pink or blue) **ray flowers** and yellow disk flowers; involucre a **single row of bracts**, with **spreading, stiff hairs** and fine glands; blooms in spring.

FRUITS: Achenes, with a **double pappus** of 15–27 slender white, obscurely barbed hairs and an outer ring of well-developed scales.

ECOLOGY: Scattered and locally common in Okanagan and Thompson basins and southern Rocky Mountain Trench, in grasslands, sagebrush and dry open forests.

SIMILAR SPECIES: Another daisy frequent in similar habitats is spreading daisy (*E. divergens*). It is distinguished by its many narrow, blue, pink or white ray flowers and broadly lance- or spoon-shaped leaves with spreading hairs.

NOTES: The Okanagan made an eye tonic from the roots of shaggy daisy. • The Latin *pumilus* means 'low' or 'dwarf.'

SHOWY DAISY • *Erigeron speciosus* var. *speciosus*

GENERAL: Perennial, 15–80 cm tall, from a branched stem base; stems **usually hairless**, but glandular in the inflorescence.

LEAVES: Narrowly **lance- to spoon-shaped**, hairless except for a fringe on leaf edges.

FLOWERS: Composite heads, with **75–150 blue or rarely white ray flowers** and yellow disk flowers; involucre a **single row of narrow and glandular bracts**.

FRUITS: Hairy, 2–4 ribbed achenes, with a **double pappus** of 20–30 white inner bristles, and short outer bristles.

ECOLOGY: Scattered and locally common at low to mid elevations in open forests, openings and clearings; generally absent from wet Columbia Mountains and parts of East Kootenays.

SIMILAR SPECIES: Showy daisy is closely related to and easily confused with triple-nerved daisy (*E. subtrinervis*), another common species of low to mid elevations. Triple-nerved daisy is distinguished by its hairier stems, leaves and involucres.

NOTES: Several horticultural forms of showy daisy have been derived from this attractive plant. Showy daisy is easily established from seed; once established, it readily maintains itself through self-seeding.

SUBALPINE DAISY • *Erigeron peregrinus* ssp. *callianthemus*

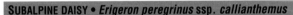

GENERAL: Rhizomatous perennial, 10–60 cm tall, with solitary stems.

LEAVES: Narrowly or broadly **lance- to spoon-shaped**, tapering to the stalk, essentially **hairless**.

FLOWERS: Mostly solitary **composite heads**, with 30–80 **pink, lavender or reddish-purple** (sometimes whitish) **ray flowers** and yellow disk flowers; involucre a **single row of narrow bracts** with pointed tips and **glandular hairs**.

FRUITS: Hairy achenes, with a **pappus of white to tan hairs**.

ECOLOGY: Widespread and common at subalpine to alpine elevations in moist to wet meadows and open forests; one of our most common daisies in subalpine meadows.

NOTES: Subalpine daisy is more aster-like than most of our daisies. • This species shows a reduction in size with increasing elevation. Smaller (usually less than 20 cm tall) subalpine or alpine plants have been treated as varieties or even separate species in this complex, but this recognition appears unwarranted. • The Nlaka'pmx called this plant 'star-flower' and used the flower heads as a pattern in basketry.

Aster: the asters

Identifying aster species requires a close examination of the colour and number of ray flowers, the **involucral bracts**, and whether the species grows from a taproot, fibrous roots or rhizomes. In many species the stems have only a few much-reduced leaves. The hairiness of the leaves, stems, and involucres and the presence of sticky glands are other useful characters. In some species the hairs are appressed (held close to the stem), in others they are spreading.

Asters closely resemble the daisies (*Erigeron* spp., pp. 118–21). In daisies, the involucral bracts are arranged in a single main row. **In asters, they are usually in several rows, with the individual bracts overlapping like shingles**. Asters also generally flower later in the year than daisies.

LINDLEY'S ASTER • *Aster ciliolatus*

GENERAL: Perennial, 20–100 cm tall, with 1 or several flowering stems growing from long, creeping rhizomes.

LEAVES: Basal and lower stem leaves have long stalks, **heart-shaped bases and sharply toothed edges**; middle and upper stem leaves are egg-shaped, with fewer teeth, on **broadly winged stalks**.

FLOWERS: Several to many **composite heads** in an open inflorescence, with **12–25 pale blue ray flowers and yellow disk flowers**; involucre of several rows of **overlapping bracts** with green tips and whitish bases; blooms into autumn.

FRUITS: Achenes, with a **pappus of whitish hairs**.

ECOLOGY: Widespread and common at low to mid elevations in moist to dry forests, openings, seepage areas and clearings.

NOTES: The heart-shaped basal leaves often wither before the flowers appear. Similar leaves may be produced on separate non-flowering shoots. • Lindley's aster is named for John Lindley, a British botanist (1799–1865) who first described this species in Sir W.J. Hooker's monumental work, *Flora Boreali-americana*. It is also called fringed aster.

SHOWY ASTER • *Aster conspicuus*

GENERAL: Perennial, 30–100 cm tall, with single, unbranched stems growing from creeping rhizomes; **glandular**, especially in the inflorescence.

LEAVES: Basal and lower leaves small and soon withering; **stem leaves egg-shaped to elliptic**, with **sharp toothed edges**, usually stalkless with **clasping bases**; leaf surfaces are **rough when mature**.

FLOWERS: Few to many **composite heads** on glandular stalks, with **12–35 blue to violet ray flowers** and **yellow disk flowers**; involucre of several rows of **overlapping**, **densely glandular bracts** with green tips and whitish bases.

FRUITS: Achenes, with a **pappus of whitish hairs**.

ECOLOGY: Widespread and common at low to mid elevations in moist to dry, open forests, openings, clearings and meadows; absent from wetter parts of Columbia Mountains.

NOTES: Being aware of this plant's excellent medicinal properties, the Okanagan and Secwepemc soaked the roots in water to wash sores, boils and infections, and the St'at'imc made an eye medicine from the flowers. • The leaves make a rattling noise in autumn, and the plant's Okanagan name means 'rattling noise' or 'shuffling noise.'

LEAFY ASTER • *Aster foliaceus*

GENERAL: Perennial, with a **creeping rhizome** or short stem base with fibrous roots; 10–25 cm tall at high elevations, 25–60 cm tall at low elevations.

LEAVES: Lance-shaped, without teeth, **often strongly clasping and lobed at their base.**

FLOWERS: 1 to many **composite heads**, with **15–60 rose-purple to blue or violet ray flowers** and **yellow disk flowers**; involucre of several rows of **overlapping, oblong bracts** with pointed tips, often some of them **long and leafy** with fringed edges and **white below**; blooms into autumn.

FRUITS: Faintly ribbed achenes, with a **pappus of white or tawny bristles** (rarely reddish).

ECOLOGY: Scattered at low to alpine elevations in dry to moist, cool forests; especially common in moist subalpine and alpine meadows.

SIMILAR SPECIES: Smooth aster (*A. laevis*) has much narrower involucres and whitish leaves, Douglas's aster (*A. subspicatus*) has involucral bracts that are yellowish or brownish near the base, and western aster (*A. occidentalis*) has much narrower leaves. • Subalpine daisy (*Erigeron peregrinus*, p. 121) closely resembles leafy aster and often grows with it, but the involucral bracts of subalpine daisy (as with all *Erigeron* spp.) are of equal size.

NOTES: Leafy aster is extremely variable and has received varying treatment from taxonomists. • The Okanagan boiled the whole plant and used it to wash sores on horses' backs. The Nlaka'pmx used it as stomach remedy.

TUFTED WHITE PRAIRIE ASTER • *Aster ericoides* ssp. *pansus* A. *pansus*

GENERAL: Perennial, 30–80 cm tall, from a **short rhizome**; **stems rough-hairy**, clustered, and branched above.

LEAVES: Basal leaves soon fall off; stem leaves **linear, with rough edges**, often spine-tipped.

FLOWERS: Many small composite heads in a large branched cluster, with **12–30 white ray flowers and yellow disk flowers**; involucre of 3 rows of **overlapping bracts**, the outer ones with **green, spiny tips**; blooms into autumn.

FRUITS: Short-hairy achenes, with a **pappus of white to straw-coloured hairs**.

ECOLOGY: Scattered and locally common at low to mid elevations in Fraser, Thompson and Okanagan basins, especially on alkaline soils, in moderately dry to dry, open forests, meadows, rocky slopes and in grasslands.

SIMILAR SPECIES: Little grey aster (*A. falcatus*) is also white-rayed, narrow-leaved and grows in dry sites in the southern half of our region. It has longer, creeping rhizomes and fewer heads than tufted white prairie aster, and its heads are borne at the branch ends.

NOTES: Most asters are easily propagated from seeds or pieces of root crown, but many of those with creeping rhizomes are somewhat invasive, and tend to overtake garden beds. These are better suited to more natural gardens. • The species name *ericoides* refers to the leaves, which resemble those of heath plants (*Erica* spp.).

OXEYE DAISY • *Leucanthemum vulgare*
Chrysanthemum leucanthemum

GENERAL: Perennial, 20–80 cm tall, from a well-developed **rhizome**, with simple or once-branched stems; typically smells strongly of sage.

LEAVES: Basal leaves broadly lance-shaped or narrowly spoon-shaped, with **coarse, rounded teeth on their edges**; stem leaves oblong, smaller and stalkless upwards.

FLOWERS: Solitary composite heads at ends of branches, with **white ray flowers** (1–2 cm long) **and yellow disk flowers**; involucre of several rows of **overlapping bracts**.

FRUITS: Round, black achenes, with about **10 white ribs** and **no pappus**.

ECOLOGY: Frequent at low to mid elevations on moist to moderately dry sites, roadsides, pastures and disturbed areas.

NOTES: Oxeye daisy is an aggressive, albeit attractive, Eurasian species. It readily invades fields and meadows (particularly where horses have grazed) and it replaces grasses. • The young leaves of this introduced plant are edible, and very sweet tasting. The flower heads can be used to make a wine similar to dandelion wine.

HEART-LEAVED ARNICA • *Arnica cordifolia*

GENERAL: Perennial, 10–60 cm tall, from a long **rhizome**, sparsely white hairy.

LEAVES: 2–3 **pairs** of **opposite** stem leaves with **heart-shaped** blades and **long stalks**; uppermost pair becoming lance-shaped and stalkless.

FLOWERS: Yellow composite heads, with **both ray and disk flowers** (usually 9–16 ray flowers); involucre of 2 rows of usually **densely hairy and glandular bracts** with pointed, fringed tips.

FRUITS: Achenes, with stiff hairs and a **pappus of white**, minutely barbed hairs.

ECOLOGY: Widespread and common in open woods in almost every montane forest type throughout our region; less frequent in subalpine and alpine, especially northwards.

NOTES: This species occasionally hybridizes with mountain arnica (*A. latifolia*, p. 126), and the intermediate forms are sometimes difficult to identify. • Arnicas are a generally montane group of perennial herbs with yellow or orange flower heads that are usually large and showy. The stems of these plants are solitary or sometimes a few in a cluster, and the leaves are opposite (in pairs), an unusual characteristic in the family. Arnica seeds have a pappus of many hair-like bristles. The **combination of yellow composite flowers, opposite leaves and a bristly pappus best distinguishes an arnica**. Individual species can often be identified on the basis of leaf shape or the number of leaf pairs. A count of the number of ray flowers can also be helpful. • Along with mountain arnica, this plant was used by the Nlaka'pmx as a plaster for swellings, cuts and bruises. The Okanagan used it as a 'love charm.'

PARRY'S ARNICA • *Arnica parryi*

GENERAL: Perennial, 15–60 cm tall, with a freely rooted **rhizome**; stems sparsely to moderately **long-hairy or woolly** and often **glandular**.

LEAVES: 2–4 pairs of **opposite**, lance-shaped stem leaves, with the lower ones long-stalked.

FLOWERS: Clusters of 1–4 (sometimes up to 12) **yellow composite heads, usually without ray flowers**; involucre of 2 rows of **bracts** with pointed tips.

FRUITS: Achenes, with a **pappus of tawny to brownish hairs**.

ECOLOGY: Scattered and often common in open, montane forests and subalpine meadows.

NOTES: The absence of ray flowers distinguishes Parry's arnica from other *Arnica* species. • The plant is named after Charles Christopher Parry, an early American botanist with the Mexican Boundary Survey, who collected the first specimen in Colorado in 1861.

MEADOW ARNICA • *Arnica chamissonis*

GENERAL: Perennial, 20–100 cm tall, from a long **rhizome**; sparsely to densely **long-hairy**.

LEAVES: 5–10 pairs of **opposite**, lance-shaped stem leaves, often with toothed edges.

FLOWERS: Yellow composite heads, with **both ray and disk flowers** (usually 10–16 ray flowers); involucre of **2 rows of rounded to abruptly pointed bracts**, tipped with a conspicuous tuft of whitish hairs.

FRUITS: Achenes, with short hairs and a **pappus of tawny or whitish hairs**.

ECOLOGY: Scattered and locally common in montane and subalpine areas, in moderately moist to wet meadows.

SIMILAR SPECIES: The only other arnica in our region with 5–12 pairs of leaves is streambank arnica (*A. amplexicaulis*). The leaves of this species are more sharply toothed and its involucral bracts are more sharply pointed and lack a tuft of whitish hairs. • Three subspecies of meadow arnica, with overlapping ranges, occur in southern B.C. These include *A. chamissonis* ssp. *chamissonis*, with toothed and stalkless leaves, *A. chamissonis* ssp. *incana*, with stalked, silvery-haired, toothless leaves and *A. chamissonis* ssp. *foliosa*, with stalked, less densely hairy, toothless leaves.

NOTES: The species name *chamissonis* honours Adalbert Ludwig von Chamisso de Boncourt (1781–1832), a German poet-naturalist and botanist on the ship *Rurik*, which visited Alaska in 1816 and 1817.

ORANGE ARNICA • *Arnica fulgens*

GENERAL: Perennial, 20–60 cm tall, with a freely rooted, densely scaly **rhizome** and persistent leaf bases with tufts of long, brown or white wool in the axils; stems robust, glandular and often hairy.

LEAVES: Mainly stalked basal leaves; 2–4 pairs of **opposite**, short-stalked or stalkless stem leaves, with distinctly **3–5-nerved, reverse lance-shaped to elliptic** blades, **entire** and more or less hairy.

FLOWERS: Usually single yellow composite heads (can be up to 3), with **both ray and disk flowers** (10–23 ray flowers); involucre of 2 rows of **blunt, hairy bracts**.

FRUITS: Densely hairy achenes, with a **pappus of white to tawny,** minutely barbed hairs.

ECOLOGY: Scattered and locally common at low to mid elevations throughout dry climates of our region, in dry forests and grasslands.

NOTES: The species name *fulgens* means 'brightly coloured.'

MOUNTAIN ARNICA • *Arnica latifolia*

GENERAL: Rhizomatous perennial, 10–60 cm tall, sparsely hairy.

LEAVES: 2–4 pairs of **opposite**, short-stalked or stalkless stem leaves with **lance-shaped to elliptic** blades and **coarsely toothed edges**; long-stalked basal leaves.

FLOWERS: 1–3 **yellow composite heads**, with **both ray and disk flowers** (8–12 ray flowers); involucre of 2 rows of **bracts** with fringed tips.

FRUITS: Hairless achenes, with a **pappus of white**, minutely barbed hairs.

ECOLOGY: Scattered and locally common, mostly at mid to high elevations, in moist to moderately dry forests, openings, clearings, along streams and in subalpine and alpine meadows.

SIMILAR SPECIES: High mountain arnica (*A. gracilis*) is relatively frequent in subalpine and alpine areas. It is distinguished by its shorter stature (10–30 cm tall), its more numerous heads (3–9) and smaller involucres.

NOTES: Some Nlaka'pmx used mountain arnica as a plaster for swellings, bruises, and cuts. The Okanagan also considered it a kind of 'love medicine.' • Most arnicas are easily propagated from seed and do best in moist, sunny, 'wild' gardens. Because they can spread quickly from underground rhizomes, they are less suited to more traditional garden beds.

ARROW-LEAVED GROUNDSEL • *Senecio triangularis*

GENERAL: Perennial, 30–150 cm tall, with several clustered stems from a fibrous-rooted stem base or rhizome.

LEAVES: Triangular to heart-shaped, with **squared-off bases** and **strongly toothed edges**, hairless except on veins of underside.

FLOWERS: Short, flat-topped, open clusters of about 8 **composite heads**, with **yellow ray and disk flowers**; involucre **a single row** of greenish bracts with black, tufted-hairy tips.

FRUITS: Faintly ribbed achenes, with a **pappus of white hairs**.

ECOLOGY: Widespread and often common at all elevations throughout our moist and wet climates, but especially common in subalpine and lower alpine elevations in moist to wet, well-drained meadows, streambanks, avalanche tracks and open forests.

NOTES: The strikingly triangular leaves, which give this species both its common name (arrow-leaved) and its species name (*triangularis*) make arrow-leaved groundsel immediately identifiable. • The groundsels are a large and diverse group. In our area, they include annual or (mostly) perennial herbs. In the southern hemisphere, groundsels include species that grow as shrubs and trees.

STREAMBANK BUTTERWEED • *Senecio pseudaureus* ssp. *pseudaureus*

GENERAL: Fibrous-rooted perennial, 20–70 cm tall; stems solitary, essentially hairless except when young.

LEAVES: Basal leaves heart-shaped to rounded, with toothed edges and **long stalks**; stem leaves few, broadly lance-shaped, toothed and **lobed at the base**, stalkless.

FLOWERS: Compact cluster of **composite heads**, with **yellow ray and disk flowers**; involucre **a single row of bracts**, tinged with purple and tufted at the tip.

FRUITS: Achenes, with a **pappus of white hairs**.

ECOLOGY: Widespread and often common at low to subalpine elevations along streams and in moist forests and meadows.

SIMILAR SPECIES: This species is often confused with Rocky Mountain butterweed (*S. streptanthifolius*, p. 128) and Canadian butterweed (*S. pauperculus*). Rocky Mountain butterweed's leaves are toothed only above the middle, and Canadian butterweed never has rounded or heart-shaped leaves.

NOTES: The flower heads of the groundsels are usually yellow, small and numerous, with both ray and disk flowers (some species lack ray flowers). The involucral bracts are green and leafy, and are arranged in a single series. The mature achenes have a pappus of white, bristle-like hairs that are sometimes barbed. The leaves are highly variable, usually at least toothed, but sometimes lobed as well.

ROCKY MOUNTAIN BUTTERWEED • *Senecio streptanthifolius*

GENERAL: Perennial, 10–60 cm tall, from a fibrous-rooted stem base or short rhizome, with solitary stems.

LEAVES: Broadly elliptic to rounded, with **toothed edges, mostly above the middle**; basal leaves long-stalked; upper leaves have winged stalks.

FLOWERS: Compact clusters of **composite heads** with **yellow ray and disk flowers**; involucre **a single row of bracts**, sometimes tinged with purple and always tufted at tip.

FRUITS: Faintly ribbed achenes, with a **pappus of white hairs**.

ECOLOGY: Widespread and often common at low to subalpine elevations along streams and in dry to moist forests and meadows.

NOTES: This species is often confused with streambank butterweed (*S. pseudaureus*) and Canadian butterweed (*S. pauperculus*). See 'Similar Species' notes under streambank butterweed (p. 127) for distinguishing features.

WESTERN GROUNDSEL • *Senecio integerrimus*

GENERAL: Perennial, 20–70 cm tall, from a short, fibrous-rooted crown; stems solitary, sparsely to densely hairy.

LEAVES: Basal leaves somewhat succulent, lance-shaped to elliptic, stalked, shallowly and irregularly toothed; stem leaves reduced upwards.

FLOWERS: Several to many clustered **composite heads**, with hairy bases, **yellow disk flowers and yellow ray flowers** (rarely white or creamy, or sometimes absent); involucre **a single row of bracts**, gradually tapering to **black tips**, hairless to moderately long-hairy.

FRUITS: Ribbed achenes, with a **pappus of white hairs**.

ECOLOGY: Widespread and common at low to subalpine elevations in moist to moderately dry, open forests and meadows.

SIMILAR SPECIES: In our region, where their ranges overlap, western groundsel could be confused with black-tipped groundsel (*S. lugens*). The latter has regularly toothed basal leaves, more prominent black tips on the involucre and is mainly an alpine species. • Another somewhat similar species with toothed leaves and purplish or blackish involucral bract tips is Elmer's butterweed (*S. elmeri*). In our region, it is found only on moist talus slopes and gravelly sites in the subalpine and lower alpine zones of the southern Coast Mountains and Cascade Mountains. Elmer's butterweed is distinguished by its

more or less sprawling habit, and leafy stems with winged leaf stalks. • A third species of alpine talus and rocky slopes is Fremont's ragwort (*S. fremontii*), a short-stemmed, few-flowered plant with small, oval to spoon-shaped, toothed leaves that clothe the stems.

NOTES: The species name *integerrimus* means 'undivided' and refers to the leaves.

WOOLLY GROUNDSEL • *Senecio canus*

GENERAL: Perennial, 10–40 cm tall, from a branched stem base, often with a short **taproot**; with several branched, **more or less white-woolly** stems.

LEAVES: Mostly basal, lance-shaped to elliptic, stalked, **strongly white-woolly**, usually without teeth or lobes.

FLOWERS: Few to many **composite heads**, with **moderately to densely woolly bases, yellow ray flowers** (rarely absent) **and yellow disk flowers**; involucre **a single row of unequal bracts**, moderately to densely long-hairy, with a terminal tuft of hairs.

FRUITS: Ribbed achenes, with a **pappus of white hairs**.

ECOLOGY: Widespread and often common at low to mid elevations in Fraser, Thompson and Okanagan basins and in driest portions of our plateaus, in open Douglas-fir and ponderosa pine forests and sagebrush grasslands; also rarely in alpine on dry, gravelly slopes along eastern slopes of southern Coast Mountains.

SIMILAR SPECIES: In the Cariboo-Chilcotin, plains butterweed (*S. plattensis*), another species with woolly stems and leaves, could be confused with woolly groundsel. Plains butterweed is an infrequent species with regular teeth along the edges of at least some basal leaves and it is seldom as densely woolly.

COMMON GROUNDSEL • *Senecio vulgaris*

GENERAL: **Taprooted annual or biennial**, 10–55 cm tall, with highly branched stems.

LEAVES: Lance-shaped to elliptic, with **deeply lobed and coarsely toothed edges**.

FLOWERS: Composite heads, with **yellow disk flowers and no ray flowers**; involucre **a single row of bracts with black tips and a tuft of hairs**.

FRUITS: Hairy, faintly ribbed achenes, with a **pappus of white hairs**.

ECOLOGY: European introduction frequent on roadsides, in waste areas and on cultivated ground.

NOTES: The black-tipped bracts and inconspicuous flowers heads distinguish this species from other groundsels. • Common groundsel often flowers late into the season and is a persistent weed in the home garden. • The name 'groundsel' appears to be derived from the Old English *grundeswylige*, meaning 'ground-swallower'—an apt name for such a rampant weed. The genus name *Senecio*, from the Latin *senex*, 'an old man,' refers to the fluffy, white seed heads.

RAYLESS MOUNTAIN BUTTERWEED • *Senecio indecorus*

GENERAL: Fibrous-rooted perennial, 10–100 cm tall, with a woody stem base, and solitary, branched stems.

LEAVES: Basal leaves are elliptic to rounded, hairless and stalked, with toothed edges; stem leaves sharply and irregularly lobed, smaller and stalkless upwards.

FLOWERS: Many **composite heads**, with **yellow disk flowers and no ray flowers** (rarely with a few short, yellow rays); involucre **a single row of bracts**, gradually tapered and **purplish-tipped**, with a tuft of hairs at the end.

FRUITS: Faintly ribbed achenes, with a **pappus of white hairs**.

ECOLOGY: Scattered and locally common, primarily at mid elevations in moist forests, bogs, fens and streambanks.

SIMILAR SPECIES: Rayless alpine butterweed (*S. pauciflorus*) is another rayless species found throughout our region, although not as often as rayless mountain butterweed. Rayless alpine butterweed has fewer heads (1–6), more reduced and succulent stem leaves, purple involucral bracts and orange disk flowers.

NOTES: The lack of ray flowers gives rise to the common name of this species. The species name *indecorus* actually means 'unbecoming' or 'unsightly,' presumably in reference to the rayless flowers.

CANADA GOLDENROD • *Solidago canadensis*

GENERAL: Rhizomatous perennial, 30–175 cm tall, with solitary stems, short-hairy at least above.

LEAVES: Mostly on stem, numerous, crowded, and only gradually reduced upwards, lance-shaped to narrowly elliptic, with **saw-toothed** or smooth edges.

FLOWERS: Many small **composite heads in dense, pyramidal clusters**, with 10–17 **yellow ray flowers and yellow disk flowers**; involucre of several rows of overlapping bracts, sometimes sticky-glandular; blooms into fall.

FRUITS: Short-hairy achenes, with a pappus of **white, hair-like bristles**.

ECOLOGY: Scattered and often abundant at low to mid elevations in many habitats, ranging from roadsides and disturbed sites to gravelly riversides and forest openings.

NOTES: The Nlaka'pmx and Okanagan used the stems and flower heads to make a tea against diarrhea, especially for babies. The tea was also used externally, to bathe colicky babies. • Goldenrod was reputedly carried into battle during the Crusades. It was commonly used as a substitute for the highly taxed English tea during the American Revolution. The leaves can be eaten as greens and the flowering heads were added to potpourris or used as a mordant for golden dyes. The dried seed heads make nice additions to dried flower arrangements. • The genus name is derived from the Latin *solidus* (whole) and *ago* (to make), in other words to 'make whole' or 'cure.'

NORTHERN GOLDENROD • *Solidago multiradiata*

GENERAL: Perennial, 5–50 cm tall, from a short **rhizome** or branching stem base; stems usually solitary and hairy, at least above.

LEAVES: Broadly lance- to spoon-shaped; edges toothed and conspicuously **hairy-fringed** (at least along stalks).

FLOWERS: Composite heads in a **rounded cluster**, with **yellow ray and disk flowers**; involucre of several rows of more or less fringed bracts, not obviously overlapping.

FRUITS: Short-hairy achenes, with a pappus of many **white, hair-like bristles**.

ECOLOGY: Widespread and common, especially at subalpine and alpine elevations, in open, dry forests, open, rocky habitats and gravelly areas.

SIMILAR SPECIES: Northern goldenrod differs from spikelike goldenrod (*S. spathulata*, below) in that the latter has an elongate inflorescence and lacks the hairy-fringed leaf edges.

NOTES: All goldenrods contain small quantities of natural rubber in their latex.

SPIKELIKE GOLDENROD • *Solidago spathulata*

GENERAL: Aromatic **perennial**, 10–80 cm tall, from a short **rhizome** or stem base; stems usually solitary, often sticky above.

LEAVES: Broadly lance- to spoon-shaped or rounded, hairless, usually with toothed edges (but **not hairy-fringed**) and long-stalked at the base.

FLOWERS: Many **composite heads** in a **long, narrow cluster**, with **5–10 yellow ray flowers and 10–16 yellow disk flowers**; involucre of several rows of **overlapping bracts**, usually blunt-tipped.

FRUITS: Densely hairy achenes, with a pappus of many **white, hair-like bristles**.

ECOLOGY: Widespread and common at low to alpine elevations in dry climates of our region, in open, dry forests, openings, clearings, gravelly riversides and terraces, streambanks and meadows.

SIMILAR SPECIES: Goldenrods may be confused with yellow-flowered species of *Hieracium* (pp. 110–12) or *Senecio* (pp. 127–29), but goldenrods can be distinguished by their many small flower heads (usually less than 1 cm wide).

NOTES: The St'at'imc boiled the plant and placed it on infected wounds, which were then wrapped in cloth over steam. Spikelike goldenrod was also used for treating hemorrhoids, and the Nlaka'pmx made a tea of it, as a tonic against loss of appetite.

 S. spathulata

 S. multiradiata

GOLDEN-ASTER • *Heterotheca villosa* *Chrysopsis villosa*

GENERAL: Taprooted perennial, 10–50 cm tall, with a woody base and several sparsely to moderately branched stems.

LEAVES: Oblong, more or less hairy or glandular, or both; basal leaves soon fall off.

FLOWERS: Several **composite heads**, with 10–25 **yellow ray flowers** and **yellow disk flowers**; involucre of several rows of overlapping bracts, with the inner ones the longest, spreading-to appressed-hairy; blooms into fall.

FRUITS: Densely **long-hairy achenes**, with a **double pappus**, with inner, white, hair-like bristles, and outer, shorter, slender scales.

ECOLOGY: Scattered and locally common at low to mid elevations in dry plateaus and arid basins, in open, often sandy habitats, sagebrush grasslands and open ponderosa pine forests.

NOTES: The genus name *Heterotheca* means 'varied, differing box or chamber.' The species names *villosa* means 'soft-haired' and refers to the hairiness of the plant.

LYALL'S GOLDENWEED • *Haplopappus lyallii*

GENERAL: Taprooted perennial, 3–15 cm tall, with a branched stem base, sometimes rhizomatous, and with several **densely glandular stems**.

LEAVES: Lance- to spoon-shaped or oblong, **glandular**.

FLOWERS: Solitary composite heads, with 13–35 **yellow ray flowers** and **yellow disk flowers**; involucre of several rows of overlapping bracts.

FRUITS: Achenes, with a **pappus of tawny bristles**.

ECOLOGY: Scattered and locally common, mainly at subalpine and alpine elevations in many mountain ranges, in meadows, on scree slopes and on gravelly ridges.

SIMILAR SPECIES: From a short distance, Lyall's goldenweed is easily mistaken for golden daisy (*Erigeron aureus*, p. 119), another brilliant-yellow alpine plant. However, golden daisy lacks the abundant glands that give the leaves and heads of Lyall's goldenweed a sticky feel, and golden daisy has mainly basal leaves.

NOTES: Lyall's goldenweed, with its low stature and brilliant golden flowers, makes a good specimen for a sunny rock garden and is easily grown from seeds. • This species was named in honour of Scottish botanist David Lyall (1817–95), an early collector of North American plants. The genus name *Haplopappus* means 'single-down' and refers to the very simple seed down or pappus.

ARROW-LEAVED BALSAMROOT • *Balsamorhiza sagittata*

GENERAL: Perennial, 20–80 cm tall, with an **aromatic, woody taproot** and a branched stem base, **softly hairy throughout**.

LEAVES: Mostly basal, **arrowhead-shaped, large (up to 30 cm long)**, long stalked, **silvery coloured** with **dense, felt-like hairs**; the few stem leaves are much smaller and narrow.

FLOWERS: Solitary composite heads, with **bright yellow ray flowers and yellow disk flowers**; involucre of several rows of overlapping bracts, **densely hairy**, especially at the base; blooms in spring.

FRUITS: Faintly ribbed achenes, **without a pappus**.

ECOLOGY: Widespread and frequently abundant at low to mid elevations throughout hot, arid climates of our region, on dry, often stony slopes, in grasslands and in open forests; also scattered at mid to subalpine elevations on plateaus and in Chilcotin Range, on dry, steep, warm slopes.

NOTES: Arrow-leaved balsamroot provides a showy, early-spring splash of colour on warm, dry hillsides. • All parts of this plant are edible and provided a very important food for Interior native people. The young leaves can be eaten raw or steamed. The Okanagan smoked the leaves like tobacco. The taproots were roasted or steamed, hung to dry and then soaked overnight. The seeds are like small sunflower seeds and native peoples dried and pounded them to use as a flour. • Deer and elk commonly graze arrow-leaf balsamroot throughout the year. Grazing by domestic sheep has apparently led to its decreased abundance in some areas. • The common name is a backwards translation of the scientific name and describes the leaf shape and the balsam pitch aroma of the woody taproot.

BROWN-EYED SUSAN • *Gaillardia aristata*

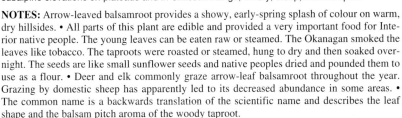

GENERAL: Perennial, 20–70 cm tall, from a **slender taproot**, with several hairy, unbranched stems.

LEAVES: Broadly lance-shaped and hairy; **basal leaves unlobed**; **stem leaves coarsely toothed** to deeply lobed.

FLOWERS: Solitary or few composite heads on long stems; 6–16 **yellow ray flowers**, with purple bases and broad, 3-lobed tips; **purple or brownish-purple** (rarely yellow) **disk flowers**, woolly-hairy toward the top; involucre of several rows of overlapping, tapered bracts, loose and spreading.

FRUITS: Densely hairy achenes, with a pappus of 6–10 **white, pointed scales**.

ECOLOGY: Scattered and locally common at low to mid elevations throughout dry climates of our region, on dry sites in grasslands and open coniferous forest.

NOTES: The Okanagan made a solution from this plant which they drank to alleviate kidney problems and bathed in to cure venereal disease. A poultice was also made to relieve backache. The Secwepemc used a solution made from this plant as a dandruff shampoo. • Brown-eyed Susan has been a favourite garden subject for many years. It is the principal parent of the more modern cultivars and is easily grown from seed. • The plant is also commonly known as gaillardia, after M. Gaillard de Marentonneau, a French botanist. The Secwepemc name for this plant means 'little salmon eyes.' The species name *aristata*, Latin for 'bearded,' refers to the many bristles on mature seeds.

CURLY-CUP GUMWEED • *Grindelia squarrosa*

GENERAL: Aromatic, taprooted biennial or short-lived perennial, 10–100 cm tall, usually with branched, hairless stems.

LEAVES: Broadly linear, hairless with regularly and coarsely toothed edges; upper leaves clasp the stem and are often sticky-resinous.

FLOWERS: Several **composite heads,** with 25–40 **yellow ray flowers** and **yellow disk flowers;** involucre of several rows of overlapping bracts, **strongly sticky-resinous** and with **green, reflexed tips;** blooms into fall.

FRUITS: Achenes, with a pappus of **several slender awns.**

ECOLOGY: Scattered and infrequent in Fraser, Thompson and Okanagan basins, in dry roadsides, overgrazed rangelands and waste places.

NOTES: The dried flower heads and leaves of this plant provide an extract used in some modern medicines to treat asthma and bronchitis. • The name 'gumweed' is apt, as the flowers are surrounded by a white, extremely sticky latex or gum. The genus is named after David Grindel (1776–1836), a Russian botanist. The species name *squarrosa* refers to the widely spreading, often downward-curving bracts.

CANADA THISTLE • *Cirsium arvense*

GENERAL: Perennial, 30–120 cm tall, with deep, wide-spreading roots and hairless, branched stems.

LEAVES: Basal leaves soon fall off; stem leaves lance-shaped, **spiny-toothed,** with irregular lobes.

FLOWERS: Many small composite heads in an open, branched inflorescence, with **pink-purple disk flowers** and **no ray flowers;** involucre of several rows of overlapping **bracts, tipped with weak prickles.**

FRUITS: Oblong, flattened achenes, with a **pappus of feathery, white bristles.**

ECOLOGY: Common and noxious Eurasian weed of low to mid elevations, primarily in settled or agricultural parts of our region, in roadsides, pastures, clearings and meadows; prefers rich, moist soils.

NOTES: Canada thistle is our **only thistle with male and female flowers on separate plants.** The heads of the male plants tend to be showier. Canada thistle is distinguished from other introduced thistles by the lack of spiny wings on its stems and by its small, almost spineless heads. • This serious weed is not easily eradicated through cultivation, which only cuts the rhizome and further spreads the plant. • Although thistles are distinguished by their spiny foliage, they are a large group whose species include non-weedy native plants and some agricultural species, such as artichoke (*Cynara scolymus*). • The name 'thistle' is from the Anglo-Saxon *thistel* or *pistel,* derived from an Indo-European word meaning 'to prick.' *Cirsium* is the ancient Greek name for thistles, and comes from *kirsos,* meaning 'a swollen vein,' for which thistles were a reputed remedy.

134

EDIBLE THISTLE • *Cirsium edule*

GENERAL: Stout **biennial or perennial**, 50–150 cm tall, with a **taproot** and sparsely to moderately hairy, ribbed stems.

LEAVES: Broadly lance-shaped, **irregularly lobed or coarsely toothed, with long** (2–5 mm), **yellow spines on the edges**; hairless or sparsely hairy above and below.

FLOWERS: Large composite heads, with **pinkish-purple disk flowers** (with their styles projecting beyond the tube) and **no ray flowers**; involucre of several rows of **slender, cottony-hairy bracts**, the **outer ones with prominent spines**; inflorescence of small clusters of heads at the ends of branches, nodding when young.

FRUITS: Purplish-black achenes, with a pappus of feathery, buff or whitish bristles.

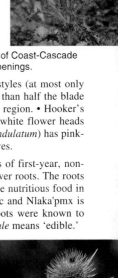

ECOLOGY: Scattered at low to subalpine elevations along eastern slopes of Coast-Cascade Mountains; frequent in wet meadows, avalanche tracks and moist forest openings.

SIMILAR SPECIES: Short-styled thistle (*C. brevistylum*) has shorter styles (at most only 1.5 mm longer than the tubular disk flowers), and its leaf lobes are less than half the blade width. It is common at low to mid elevations in the northern part of our region. • Hooker's thistle (*C. hookerianum*) is easily distinguished by its white or creamy-white flower heads and narrower, shallowly lobed, spiny leaves. • Wavy-leaved thistle (*C. undulatum*) has pinkish-purple flower heads and whitish-hairy to grey-hairy, lobed, spiny leaves.

NOTES: The Secwepemc and Nlaka'pmx ate the roots of first-year, non-flowering plants, which they report to taste like sunflower roots. The roots of most thistles are edible when cooked and can provide nutritious food in an emergency. • The name for this plant in Secwepemc and Nlaka'pmx is derived from their word for 'flatulate,' because the roots were known to cause gas if too many were eaten. The species name *edule* means 'edible.'

BULL THISTLE • *Cirsium vulgare*

GENERAL: Fibrous-rooted biennial, 30–200 cm tall, with branched, woody stems, **conspicuously spiny-winged at base of leaves**; first-year plants exist as low-growing rosettes of prickly leaves.

LEAVES: Basal and stem leaves broadly lance-shaped, deeply lobed, with **stout spines at lobe tips and on upper surface**; **leaf bases clasp stem**, forming **spiny wings descending down stems**.

FLOWERS: Large **composite heads**, with **purple disk flowers** and **no ray flowers**; involucre of several rows of overlapping, **spine-tipped bracts**.

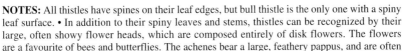

FRUITS: Glossy, light brown **achenes**, with a **pappus of whitish, feathery bristles**.

ECOLOGY: Widespread Eurasian weed; common at low to mid elevations in pastures, waste places, clearings and roadsides.

NOTES: All thistles have spines on their leaf edges, but bull thistle is the only one with a spiny leaf surface. • In addition to their spiny leaves and stems, thistles can be recognized by their large, often showy flower heads, which are composed entirely of disk flowers. The flowers are a favourite of bees and butterflies. The achenes bear a large, feathery pappus, and are often dispersed in large, airy clumps of 'thistledown.' • The thistle (probably not one of our species) is the national flower of Scotland, adopted as far back as the eighth century. Legend has it that an invading Danish army was creeping, barefoot, towards a Scottish encampment when a soldier stepped on a thistle. He yelled so loudly that the Scots awoke and defeated the Danes. The thistle was thereafter considered to be the guardian of Scotland and acquired the motto *nemo me impune lacessit* (no one shall provoke me with impunity).

135

DIFFUSE KNAPWEED • *Centaurea diffusa*

GENERAL: Annual, biennial or short-lived perennial, 10–90 cm tall, with sparsely hairy, branched stems, rough to the touch.

LEAVES: Pinnately divided into linear segments, broadly lance-shaped in outline, grey-green with a thin layer of **felted hairs**.

FLOWERS: Composite heads, with **cream-coloured disk flowers** (sometimes purplish or pinkish) interspersed with bristles, and **no ray flowers**; involucre of several rows of overlapping **bracts, with weak spines along edges, and longer spines at tips**; inflorescence of **many solitary heads** at the ends of diffuse branches.

FRUITS: Achenes, with the **pappus absent** or of minute bristles.

ECOLOGY: Widespread, aggressive weed of low to mid elevations, especially common in our dry climates, in roadsides, disturbed earth, pastures, fields, grasslands and dry, open forests.

SIMILAR SPECIES: Spotted knapweed (*C. maculosa*, below) is easily distinguished by its involucral bracts, which lack spines and have darkened, comb-like tips.

NOTES: Diffuse knapweed, which is native to the eastern Mediterranean area, has become well established in disturbed grasslands, where it is a serious weed. Animals avoid eating it because of its bitter taste and it spreads freely without any natural pests to keep it in check. A biological control program has introduced insects that attack its seed and roots. • The name 'knapweed' is a corruption of the old name *knop-* or *knob-weed*, so called because of the knob-like flower heads. The genus name *Centaurea* is from the Greek *kentaurion*, the plant of the Centaurs. It honours the centaur Chiron, who is said to have used a similar plant to heal wounds in his foot caused by an arrow that Hercules had poisoned with the blood of the Hydra.

SPOTTED KNAPWEED • *Centaurea maculosa*

GENERAL: Taprooted biennial to short-lived perennial, 20–150 cm tall, with highly branched, rough stems.

LEAVES: Pinnately divided into linear segments, broadly lance-shaped in outline, **grey with felted hairs** and glandular.

FLOWERS: Composite heads, with **purple or pinkish-purple disk flowers** interspersed with bristles, and **no ray flowers**; involucre of several rows of overlapping bracts, with **darkened, comb-like tips** and no spines; inflorescence of **many solitary heads** at the ends of lax branches.

FRUITS: Achenes, with a **pappus of white bristles** (rarely absent).

ECOLOGY: Widespread at low and mid elevations in dry climates of our region, in roadsides, disturbed earth, pastures, fields, grasslands and dry open forests; native of Eurasia, now a well-established weed in our region.

SIMILAR SPECIES: Russian knapweed (*C. repens*) is distinguished from other knapweeds by its spineless, somewhat ragged-edged involucral bracts and blackish, scaly, creeping roots.

NOTES: The outermost disk flowers are enlarged and could be mistaken for ray flowers. • Spotted knapweed is a noxious weed. Its only virtue is its abundant nectar production, much favoured by honey bees and apiarists.

Antennaria: the pussytoes

Pussytoes are **white-woolly** perennial herbs with dense clusters of small heads on top of tall, unbranched flowering stems. The flower heads are small, individually inconspicuous, and composed entirely of **disk flowers**. The achenes have a pappus of many fine, white hairs. Most species have a **large cluster of basal leaves** and a few smaller leaves on the flowering stalks. Although pussytoes as a group are easily recognized, many of the individual species are quite similar in their general appearance and can be difficult to distinguish. **The shape of the basal leaves** should be noted, along with whether or not the plants are mat-forming. **Close examination of the involucral bracts is usually helpful, as they are often more distinctive than the actual flowers.**

ALPINE PUSSYTOES • *Antennaria alpina* var. *media*

GENERAL: Mat-forming perennial, with many leafy runners; flowering stems are 1–14 cm tall.

LEAVES: Mostly basal, lance-shaped or sometimes spoon-shaped, **densely white- or grey-woolly on both sides**.

FLOWERS: Several whitish **composite heads, entirely of disk flowers**, in a tight, rounded inflorescence; involucre of several rows of overlapping bracts, generally sharp pointed, woolly below and **dark brownish or blackish green to black above**.

FRUITS: Smooth achenes, sometimes with small bumps; pappus of many fine, white hairs.

ECOLOGY: Widespread and common at **high subalpine** and **alpine** elevations throughout mountains; often in well-drained but moist snowbed sites and on dry ridges.

SIMILAR SPECIES: There is often much confusion in distinguishing alpine pussytoes from rosy pussytoes (*A. microphylla*, p. 138) and umber pussytoes (*A. umbrinella*, below). They are separated mainly by the colour of the top portion of the involucral bracts, which is dark or brownish green in alpine pussytoes, white to pink or rosy red in rosy pussytoes and brownish in umber pussytoes. The latter two species have blunt-tipped involucral bracts.

UMBER PUSSYTOES • *Antennaria umbrinella*

GENERAL: Mat-forming perennial, 5–20 cm tall, with leafy runners.

LEAVES: Mostly basal, wedge- or spoon-shaped, **white- or grey-woolly on both sides**.

FLOWERS: Several to many **composite heads, entirely of disk flowers**, in a tight, rounded inflorescence; involucre of several rows of overlapping, blunt-tipped bracts, **woolly below, white or sometimes pink to rose above**; outer bracts discoloured and brownish or dirty green.

FRUITS: Smooth achenes, with a pappus of many fine, white hairs.

ECOLOGY: Scattered and locally common at low to mid elevations in mesic to dry, open forests, openings and disturbed soils, especially common in dry grasslands; also in open ponderosa pine forests and in subalpine and alpine areas in meadows and on ridges.

SIMILAR SPECIES: Umber pussytoes is distinguished from alpine pussytoes (*A. alpina*, above) and rosy pussytoes (*A. microphylla*, p. 138) mainly by the colour of the top portion of the involucral bracts. See 'Similar Species' for alpine pussytoes.

ROSY PUSSYTOES • *Antennaria microphylla*
A. rosea

GENERAL: Mat-forming perennial, with many leafy runners; flowering stems are 5–40 cm tall.

LEAVES: Mostly basal, lance- or spoon-shaped, **white- or grey-woolly on both sides**.

FLOWERS: Several to many **composite heads, entirely of disk flowers**, in a tight, rounded inflorescence; involucre of several rows of overlapping bracts, **pink to rose, sometimes white above**, woolly below.

FRUITS: Smooth achenes, with a pappus of many fine, white hairs.

ECOLOGY: Widespread and common at low to alpine elevations in a variety of sites, including grasslands, dry meadows, mesic to dry open forests and moist to dry subalpine and alpine meadows and ridges.

SIMILAR SPECIES: Rosy pussytoes is distinguished from both alpine pussytoes (*A. alpina*, p. 137) and umber pussytoes (*A. umbrinella*, p. 137) mainly by the colour of the top portion of the involucral bracts. See 'Similar Species' for alpine pussytoes.

NOTES: The Okanagan used the roots of rosy pussytoes in their winter dance ceremony. The Nlaka'pmx chewed the stems and leaves as a cough and cold medicine.

LOW PUSSYTOES • *Antennaria dimorpha*

GENERAL: Mat-forming, dwarf perennial, with a compact, much-branched stem base; flowering stems very short and leafy, 1–10 cm tall.

LEAVES: Basal and stem leaves similar, linear to lance-shaped and **densely silky-hairy** on both sides.

FLOWERS: Solitary, whitish **composite heads** on short stalks, **entirely of disk flowers**; involucre of several rows of overlapping bracts, narrow and slenderly pointed, tinged at least in part with **brown or reddish brown**, thinly woolly below.

FRUITS: Finely hairy achenes, with a pappus of many fine, white hairs.

ECOLOGY: Scattered and locally common at low to mid elevations throughout warm, dry climates in our region, on rocky slopes, and in dry, open Douglas-fir and ponderosa pine forests, openings and grasslands.

NOTES: Low pussytoes differs from other species of *Antennaria* in having short flowering stems and solitary heads. • The stems and leaves of various species of pussytoes, including low, field and rosy pussytoes, were chewed by the Nlaka'pmx as a cold and cough remedy. • Extensive growths of low pussytoes in our grasslands often indicate overgrazing. • The genus name *Antennaria*, from the Latin *antenna*, refers to the pappus hair tips of male flowers, which apparently resemble insect antennae. *Antennaria* species are called pussytoes because the flowering heads, especially in fruit, resemble a cat's furry paws.

FIELD PUSSYTOES • *Antennaria neglecta*

GENERAL: Mat-forming perennial, with well-developed runners; flowering stems are 5–40 cm tall.

LEAVES: Mostly basal, spoon-shaped to broadly lance-shaped or elliptic, **white-woolly below, green and distinctly less woolly** to hairless above; stem leaves narrow and reduced in size upwards.

FLOWERS: Several greenish-white to dingy white **composite heads, entirely of disk flowers** in a compact, crowded cluster; involucre of several rows of overlapping bracts, narrow and pointed, with long, whitish tips.

FRUITS: Roughened achenes, with a pappus of many fine, white hairs.

ECOLOGY: Widespread and common at low to mid elevations in open, dry to moist, well-drained forests, openings and clearings; scattered and infrequent in wet Columbia Mountains.

SIMILAR SPECIES: Racemose pussytoes (*A. racemosa*, below) has a similar habit but its leaves are rounder than those of field pussytoes, and it has glandular upper stems, colourless, clear to pale brownish involucral bracts and heads arranged in a long, open cluster.

NOTES: Many species of *Antennaria* have distinct male and female plants, and males may be rare or even absent from some areas. In these species, seed is often produced without fertilization, producing offspring genetically identical to their mother.

RACEMOSE PUSSYTOES • *Antennaria racemosa*

GENERAL: Mat-forming perennial, 10–40 cm tall, with creeping, leafy runners; stems are thinly hairy below, becoming strongly glandular above.

LEAVES: Mostly basal, elliptic to rounded, **white-woolly beneath, green and less hairy above**.

FLOWERS: Several greenish-white to pale brown **composite heads, entirely of disk flowers**, in an **open, elongate cluster**; involucre of several rows of overlapping bracts, pale greenish below and colourless or pale brownish to reddish above.

FRUITS: Smooth achenes, with a **pappus of many fine, white hairs**.

ECOLOGY: Widespread and common at low to mid elevations in dry to moist forest, openings, rock slides, gravelly ridges and roadsides; scattered and infrequent in wet Columbia Mountains.

NOTES: Racemose pussytoes is the most shade-tolerant of our pussytoes and is capable of thriving on cool slopes in our Douglas-fir forests. • Pussytoes flowers, picked and dried soon after blooming, will provide lovely bouquets throughout the winter. The blossoms are often dyed. • The species name *racemosa* refers to the elongate form of the flower cluster (a raceme).

SHOWY PUSSYTOES • *Antennaria pulcherrima* var. *pulcherrima*

GENERAL: Perennial, 10–55 cm tall, with multiple stems from a short, branched or rhizomatous base.

LEAVES: Mostly basal, tufted and narrowly lance-shaped, **white-woolly above and below**.

FLOWERS: Several to many greenish-black **composite heads, entirely of disk flowers,** in a dense, crowded cluster; involucre of several rows of overlapping bracts, **brown to blackish** (sometimes white-tipped), densely hairy at their base.

FRUITS: Smooth achenes, with a pappus of many fine, white hairs.

ECOLOGY: Scattered and locally common at low to mid elevations in moist to dry, open forests and meadows; generally absent from our wet climates.

SIMILAR SPECIES: A second variety of showy pussytoes, *A. pulcherrima* var. *anaphaloides*, differs only slightly from var. *pulcherrima* in its involucral bracts, which are whitish rather than blackish. It is quite common in open forests and openings at low to mid elevations throughout the dry, central part of our region. Some taxonomists treat these as separate species.

NOTES: The species name *pulcherrima* (beautiful) echoes the common name 'showy pussytoes' in emphasizing the beauty of this plant.

WOOLLY PUSSYTOES • *Antennaria lanata*

GENERAL: Tufted perennial, from a branched stem-base; flowering stems are 10–20 cm tall.

LEAVES: Mostly basal, clustered, erect, lance-shaped, with 3 or more evident to obscure veins, **densely white- or grey-woolly on both sides**; stem leaves similar, but narrower and decreasing in size.

FLOWERS: Several greenish-white **composite heads, entirely of disk flowers,** in a compact cluster; involucre of several rows of overlapping bracts, **greenish and hairy at base, brown or greenish black higher up,** often white at tip.

FRUITS: Smooth achenes, with a **pappus of many fine, white hairs**.

ECOLOGY: Scattered and locally common in subalpine and alpine, in meadows, heath and snowbed sites.

SIMILAR SPECIES: Showy pussytoes (*A. pulcherrima*, above) also has narrow, erect, lance-shaped leaves, but is taller (to 50 cm tall) than woolly pussytoes. Also, showy pussytoes is a species of low to mid elevations.

NOTES: Woolly leaves, common on many alpine plants, may help retain heat and water in this often cold, windy environment. The white wool also reflects direct sunlight, which may prevent damage from ultraviolet radiation at high elevations where the air can be very clear and the sun intense when the clouds clear from the mountain tops. • The species name *lanata* means 'woolly.'

PEARLY EVERLASTING • *Anaphalis margaritacea*

GENERAL: Rhizomatous **perennial**, 20–90 cm tall, with **white-woolly, leafy, usually unbranched flowering stems.**

LEAVES: Mostly on stem, narrowly lance-shaped with a conspicuous mid-vein, **greenish above** and **white-woolly below**; leaf edges are often rolled under.

FLOWERS: Small **composite heads**, with **yellowish disk flowers** and **no ray flowers**, in dense, flat-topped clusters; involucre of several rows of overlapping, **papery, pearly white** bracts, with dark triangular bases, giving flower clusters an overall white appearance.

FRUITS: Very small, roughened achenes, with a pappus of many short hairs.

ECOLOGY: Widespread and locally common at low to subalpine elevations in rocky slopes, open forests, clearings, meadows, fields, pastures and roadsides; often weedy.

SIMILAR SPECIES: Pearly everlasting is related to the pussytoes (*Antennaria* spp., pp. 137–140), but it is easily distinguished from them by its **small basal leaves, which wither early, and its stem leaves, which are not much reduced in size upwards on the stem.** Pussytoes have prominent tufts of basal leaves and few, if any, stem leaves.

NOTES: The white involucral bracts are more prominent than the tiny, yellow disk flowers and give the flower heads an overall white appearance. • The Nlaka'pmx used pearly everlasting to treat rheumatic fever and coughs. The Okanagan made the roots and shoots into a tea for upset stomachs. Both groups used stalks of flowers to provide a pleasant fragrance. • Both the common name and species name *margaritacea* (Greek for 'pearly') refer to the pearly white involucral bracts, which retain their colour and shape when dried, making attractive dry bouquets. The plants usually do not bloom until midsummer, but the flowers can last until the first snows of winter.

GREAT BURDOCK • *Arctium lappa*

GENERAL: Large, **coarse biennial**, 0.5–3 m tall, with leafy stems.

LEAVES: Basal leaves large (up to 50 cm long and 30 cm wide), **egg- to heart-shaped**, green and nearly hairless above, **thinly white-woolly below**; stem leaves progressively reduced upwards.

FLOWERS: Many **composite heads**, with **purple disk flowers** and **no ray flowers**, in a branched, relatively scattered inflorescence; involucres **round and bur-like**, composed of several rows of narrow, spreading bracts with inwardly **hooked tips.**

FRUITS: Oblong, 3-angled achenes, with several ribs; **pappus of many short bristles**.

ECOLOGY: Scattered and locally common weed of low to mid elevations in settled areas of our region, in roadsides, pastures and other disturbed sites, especially in areas of high soil moisture.

SIMILAR SPECIES: Common burdock (*A. minus*) has smaller flower heads (1.5–2.5 cm wide, or rarely to 3 cm) in a narrower cluster, and its involucral bracts are angled rather than flattened.

NOTES: Great burdock is an introduced Eurasian weed. The bristly involucres form a persistent, extremely tenacious bur, which can be carried in the fur of cattle and wild animals for many weeks. The seeds are shed as the burs dry out. • In its first year, great burdock forms a rosette of large leaves which look somewhat like rhubarb leaves except for their whitish undersides. • First-year roots are eaten as a vegetable (*gobo*) in Japan. The Secwepemc used the roots of the plant as a blood purifier. • Both 'bur' (from the French *bourre*) and 'dock' (from the German) mean the same thing something that gets entangled in wool, flax or hemp fibre. The genus name *Arctium*, meaning 'a bear,' refers to the shaggy, hairy appearance of the plant.

PATHFINDER • *Adenocaulon bicolor*

GENERAL: Fibrous-rooted **perennial**, 30–100 cm tall; stems solitary, slender, **white-woolly** on lower part, with stalked glands on upper part.

LEAVES: Mostly basal, **broadly triangular to heart-shaped**, green and essentially hairless above, **white-woolly below**.

FLOWERS: Several small **composite heads**, with **whitish disk flowers** and **no ray flowers**, in a leafless, branched, glandular inflorescence; involucre of green bracts, pointing down when mature and eventually falling off.

FRUITS: Club-shaped achenes, with glandular hairs and **no pappus**.

ECOLOGY: Widespread and locally common at low to mid elevations in wet Columbia Mountains in moist, shady coniferous forests; scattered in wet plateau areas and Coast/Interior Transition.

SIMILAR SPECIES: When not in flower, pathfinder can be confused with the weedy, coarse species common burdock (*Arctium minus*, p. 141). Common burdock has somewhat similar leaves but its stems are stout, distinctly leafy and without woolly hairs, and it usually grows in open, disturbed habitats.

NOTES: Pathfinder differs from most members of the sunflower family in that it **lacks both ray flowers and a pappus**. • The name 'pathfinder' (and its species name *bicolor*) refers to the very conspicuous white colour of the turned-over leaves, which could indicate that someone has passed by. The genus name *Adenocaulon* comes from *adeno* (glandular) and *caulon* (a stem), and refers to the glandular hairs on the stem.

HOARY FALSE YARROW • *Chaenactis douglasii* var. *achilleaefolia*

GENERAL: Taprooted biennial, 15–60 cm tall, with a single leafy stem, **woolly hairy** and sometimes glandular above.

LEAVES: Fern-like, stalked basal leaves; stem leaves progressively reduced above.

FLOWERS: Composite heads, with 50–70 **white or sometimes pinkish disk flowers** and **no ray flowers**; involucre a single row of **glandular-hairy bracts**.

FRUITS: Densely hairy achenes, with a **pappus of 10–16 unequal scales**.

ECOLOGY: Scattered and infrequent at low to mid elevations on Thompson and Okanagan plateaus and in East Kootenays, on open, dry and often sandy or rocky sites.

SIMILAR SPECIES: A dwarf, subalpine/alpine phase, *C. douglasii* var. *montana*, is easily distinguished from the tall phase by its height (10–15 cm) and by its occurrence only at high elevations. It is rare in the southern mountain ranges of our region.

NOTES: The Nlaka'pmx made a decoction of this plant to cure swellings, and ingested it as a stomach tonic. The Okanagan used the steeped roots as an eyewash. • The Nlaka'pmx name for this plant, 'rattle-snake tail,' is derived from its leaf shape. This species is named after David Douglas (1798–1834), a Scottish plant collector.

PASTURE SAGE • *Artemisia frigida*

GENERAL: Often **mat-forming, woolly-hairy perennial**, 10–40 cm tall, with a stout stem base or woody crown; often shrubby at the base, **strongly aromatic**.

LEAVES: Mostly on the stem; both surfaces covered with **silvery-silky hairs**; **divided 2–3 times into 3s,** ultimately into narrow, linear segments.

FLOWERS: Several to many **composite heads** in a simple or branched, narrow cluster, with **yellow disk flowers** (often with a reddish tinge) and **no ray flowers**; involucre of several rows of overlapping bracts, loosely cottony-hairy and with brown edges.

FRUITS: Achenes, usually with **no pappus**.

ECOLOGY: Widespread and common at low to mid elevations throughout our plateaus, arid basins and southern Rocky Mountain Trench, on dry, rocky slopes and sandy terraces and in open Douglas-fir and ponderosa pine forests; especially common in dry grasslands; tends to become weedy in overgrazed grasslands.

SIMILAR SPECIES: Northern wormwood (*A. campestris*) also occurs in dry habitats at low to alpine elevations. Its leaves are primarily basal and are neither as small nor as divided as those of pasture sage. • Western mugwort (*A. ludoviciana*) is quite common at low to mid elevations in the mountains in the southern half of our region. Its leaves are mainly on the stem but again are not as finely divided as those of pasture sage.

NOTES: Southern Interior native peoples valued several species of *Artemisia* for ceremony and as medicine, for their pungent, aromatic fragrance. They burned pasture sage to drive away mosquitoes and other biting insects, and placed pieces of the plant in bedding to get rid of bedbugs, fleas and lice. The Okanagan used it to repel insects from drying racks of salmon. The Carrier sat in sweathouses with sage leaves on steaming rocks. The fragrant steam would alleviate local pains and 'nervous shooting' (Morice 1892).

TARRAGON • *Artemisia dracunculus*

GENERAL: Aromatic perennial, to 150 cm tall.

LEAVES: On the stem, **mostly linear** or the lower leaves divided into several linear segments.

FLOWERS: Several to many **composite heads** in a branched, spreading inflorescence, with **yellow disk flowers** and **no ray flowers**; involucre of several rows of overlapping bracts.

FRUITS: Achenes, usually with **no pappus**.

ECOLOGY: Widespread and common at low elevations on rocky slopes in dry grasslands.

NOTES: The Secwepemc used tarragon, mixed with white clematis (*Clematis ligustifolia*) to heal sprains, fractures and bruises. • The genus *Artemisia* includes several well-known, pungently aromatic species used as vermifuges, stimulants, and culinary herbs, such as tarragon, big sagebrush (*A. tridentata*), absinthe (*A. absinthium*), a weedy species of disturbed sites used to make a harmful liqueur, and Aleutian mugwort (*A. tilesii*) which has medicinal properties like codeine and is also reported to be an anti-tumour agent still used by northern groups such as the Tahltans.

MOUNTAIN SAGEWORT • *Artemisia norvegica* ssp. *saxatilis*
A. arctica

GENERAL: Perennial, 20–60 cm tall, with solitary or sometimes several stems from a short, branched stem base; often with **sterile rosettes on short runners**; sparsely or moderately hairy.

LEAVES: Mostly basal, long-stalked and **pinnately divided** into linear segments; a few smaller leaves on the stem.

FLOWERS: Many **composite heads nodding** in narrow inflorescences, with **yellowish disk flowers** (often tinged with red) and **no ray flowers**; involucre of several rows of overlapping bracts, greenish with dark brown edges.

FRUITS: Achenes, usually with **no pappus**.

ECOLOGY: Widespread and most common at subalpine and alpine elevations in rocky slopes and meadows.

SIMILAR SPECIES: Michaux's mugwort (*A. michauxiana*) may also be found at high elevations. Its leaves are primarily on the stem and are hairy underneath. Its flower clusters are usually considerably longer and have more heads than mountain sagewort's.

NOTES: Mountain sagewort, unlike many other species of *Artemisia*, does not have an aromatic sage smell. This is one of our circumboreal species, occurring throughout much of the northern hemisphere. • Sages are predominantly perennials. Close examination of the flower heads will show them to be composed entirely of disk flowers, generally brown or yellow in colour. The involucral bracts are dry and papery. The achenes are not hairy and have only a very short pappus of scales or awns or, more commonly, no pappus at all. Species identification depends primarily on the general form of the plants, the leaves and the shape of the flower cluster.

PINEAPPLE WEED • *Matricaria discoidea*
M. matricarioides

GENERAL: Pineapple-scented annual, 5–30 cm tall, from a short **taproot; stems highly branched from the base**.

LEAVES: Basal leaves usually withered (or have fallen off) by flowering time; stem leaves **fern-like, 1–3 times divided into short narrow segments**.

FLOWERS: Several to many **composite heads**, with **greenish-yellow disk flowers** on a **cone-shaped to narrowly dome-shaped base** (receptacle); **no ray flowers**; involucre of several rows of bracts with broad, pale edges, not strongly overlapping.

FRUITS: Achenes, with a **short, membranous pappus**.

ECOLOGY: Scattered and locally common at low to mid elevations on roadsides and waste areas in disturbed habitats, especially ground compacted from heavy trampling or machine traffic.

NOTES: The crushed leaves and flowers of this Eurasian weed emit a strong pineapple scent. This scent gives the plant both its common name and an easily recognizable characteristic. • The Okanagan used this plant as a medicine-charm to keep horses on their property. • The genus name *Matricaria* means 'mother-care,' and refers to this plant's former use in the treatment of uterine infections. The flower heads are disk-shaped, hence the species name *discoidea*.

COMMON TANSY • *Tanacetum vulgare*

GENERAL: Aromatic perennial, 40–150 cm tall, from a stout **rhizome** with branched stems.

LEAVES: Fern-like, with a broadly rounded or rounded-oblong outline, **deeply cleft to the midvein and again sharply toothed or cleft; midveins winged;** blade hairless and dotted with pits.

FLOWERS: Small, button-like composite heads, with densely packed, **yellow disk flowers and no ray flowers;** involucre of about 3 rows of overlapping bracts, the inner ones oblong, the outer ones lance-shaped with darkened edges; many heads, solitary at the ends of the branches in a **flat-topped, umbrella-shaped inflorescence.**

FRUITS: Glandular-dotted achenes; **pappus a very small, toothed crown.**

ECOLOGY: European weed; scattered at low to mid elevations in roadsides, pastures and disturbed sites.

NOTES: This species has traditionally been used as an insecticide or insect repellent, and it gives a pleasant orange colour when used as a dye. In Britain, the bitter juice of common tansy was used to flavour Easter cakes, and a piece of the plant was placed in the shoe to relieve ague. • 'Tansy' is from the Medieval Latin *anathasia* (later contracted to the French *tanacee*), which is from the Greek word for 'immortality.' The name may have been given to this plant because it has such long-lived, durable flowers. Common tansy was sold in 16th-century apothecaries as both 'anathasia' and 'tanacetum,' and was placed under the winding sheets of the dead to repel vermin. The genus name *Tanacetum* literally means 'a bed of tansy.'

LEAFY SPURGE • *Euphorbia esula*

GENERAL: Perennial, 20–90 cm tall, with heavy rootstocks and **milky juice;** stems divided into **umbrella-like branches.**

LEAVES: Lower leaves **smooth, long, narrow and nearly stalkless;** leaves in inflorescence very broadly **heart-shaped and borne in pairs.**

FLOWERS: Inconspicuous, greatly reduced; borne in clusters that appear to be a single flower, cluster has a **cup-shaped, green bract** with 4 brownish-green, **horned glands.**

FRUITS: Warty capsules.

ECOLOGY: Scattered and locally common throughout southern half of our region; weed of waste places and rangeland, but generally absent from our wet climates.

NOTES: Flowers of the spurge family are interesting because of their extremely reduced structure. What at first appears to be a small, green flower is actually a bract (involucre) that encloses a cluster of several male flowers and one female flower. The male flowers each consist of a single stamen, the female of a stalked pistil. None have petals or sepals. • This Eurasian introduction is becoming a serious threat to rangeland in our region. It is difficult to eradicate and **poisonous.** The milky-coloured latex can cause skin irritations in humans and poison livestock, although sheep can eat it with minimal effects. Sheep and beetles are being used to control leafy spurge. • The name 'spurge' comes from the old French *epurge*, from the Latin *espurgare* (to purge). This was the 'purging herb' because the fruits or seeds were taken like laxative pills. • The genus *Euphorbia* is most represented in the tropics. It was named in honour of Euphorbus, physician to King Juba II of Mauretania.

145

SEABLITE • *Suaeda depressa*

GENERAL: Taprooted annual, to 50 cm long; stems erect to **horizontal**, smooth, whitish, branched.

LEAVES: Fleshy and **linear**, somewhat **rounded in cross-section** and swollen at base; becoming smaller and broader within flowering head.

FLOWERS: Tiny and numerous, in **slender, leafy spikes**.

FRUITS: Small, hard, dry seeds.

ECOLOGY: Scattered and locally common at low to mid elevations throughout our dry climates, often around saline or alkaline wetlands and sloughs and on disturbed ground.

NOTES: In our area, the goosefoot family is a group of annual or perennial herbs of dry to alkaline places. It includes the familiar garden plants spinach and beets as well as a number of species found on seacoasts and in alkaline deserts. The species generally have fleshy or 'mealy' leaves and stems. Flowers are minute and inconspicuous, completely inscrutable without the aid of at least a 10x hand lens. • There appear to be some conflicting opinions on the origin of the name of this genus. One source says it is derived from the Arabic *suwayd* (a desert plant) and another from the Arabic word for salt. The species name *depressa* refers to its prostrate growth habit.

SUMMER CYPRESS • *Kochia scoparia*

GENERAL: Annual, 50–150 cm tall, with erect, branching stems, often covered with **silvery or rusty** hairs and usually reddish-tinged by fall.

LEAVES: Linear to narrowly lance-shaped, **prominently veined**, with **soft rusty hairs beneath** and hairless above.

FLOWERS: Very small, derive colour from rusty or silvery hairs; in clusters at bases of leaf-like bracts.

FRUITS: Winged, dry seeds.

ECOLOGY: Scattered and locally common at low elevations in our arid climates, in roadsides, ditches and waste places.

NOTES: Summer cypress is a Eurasian species that has become a common and troublesome weed in some areas of our region. It was originally introduced as a bedding plant for its red stems and foliage. In the horticultural trade, it is sometimes known as burning bush or red belvedere. (Belvedere is an architectural term applied to buildings commanding a fine prospect—a tribute to the handsome appearance of this plant.) • Some authors report that it may cause poisoning and photosensitization in livestock. • The scientific name *Kochia* honours W.D.J. Koch (1771–1849), a German botanist and director of the Erlangen Botanical Gardens, who wrote a flora of Germany and Switzerland.

LAMB'S-QUARTERS • *Chenopodium album*

GENERAL: Annual, 20–100 cm tall; stems branched, greenish to **greyish and mealy** (covered with flaky scales), often purple-striped with age.

LEAVES: Diamond- or lance-shaped with **irregular teeth or lobes**; somewhat firm and **fleshy**; lower surface greyish green and covered with **mealy particles**.

FLOWERS: Minute, greyish green, with little recognizable structure; in **dense clusters** in leaf axils and at stem tips.

FRUITS: Black, shiny, flattened, **circular nutlets**, often covered with a white, papery envelope.

ECOLOGY: Widespread and common at low to mid elevations throughout settled parts of our region in disturbed sites, especially cultivated land, gardens and roadsides.

SIMILAR SPECIES: Another large-leaved annual, red goosefoot (*C. rubrum*), occurs occasionally in saline or alkaline areas and on disturbed soil. Its smooth stems and leaves often turn reddish and have **no mealy or scaly covering**.

NOTES: Lamb's-quarters is a very characteristic and often abundant weed of agricultural areas. It is originally from Eurasia but is now naturalized in much of North America. Its leaves can be eaten raw or boiled. It was formerly an important potherb but has been replaced by its relative, spinach (*Spinacia oleracea*). Like spinach, it is an excellent source of iron but it should not be eaten in large quantities over extensive periods of time because its oxalates may interfere with calcium metabolism. A single plant can produce 50 to 70 thousand seeds the size and shape of poppy seeds. These may be used as a seasoning or coffee substitute, or ground and dried as a flour substitute. Napoleon is reported to have relied on ground lamb's-quarters seeds to make a 'black bread' to feed his troops. • The name 'lamb's-quarters,' or more correctly *lammas quarter*, was originally given to the related species *Atriplex patula*, because it bloomed about the first of August, which was the time of a traditional harvest festival. The leaves are supposedly shaped like the foot of a goose, giving rise to another common name, white goosefoot, and the genus name *Chenopodium* (from the Greek *chen*, 'a goose,' and *podos*, 'a foot').

STRAWBERRY-BLITE • *Chenopodium capitatum*

GENERAL: Annual, to 50 cm tall, usually with many smooth branches.

LEAVES: Fleshy, arrowhead-shaped, usually **shallowly lobed**, greenish on both surfaces.

FLOWERS: Tiny and **green, becoming deep red and very fleshy**; in **dense, spherical clusters** in leaf axils and in interrupted spikes at stem tips.

FRUITS: Red, fleshy, flattened, enclosing a **single, dry seed; in dense clusters resembling a strawberry both in colour and shape.**

ECOLOGY: Widespread and common at low to mid elevations throughout settled parts of our region in disturbed sites, especially cultivated land, gardens, and roadsides.

NOTES: Interior native peoples used the intensely red fruits of this plant as a source of red dye. Children often painted their cheeks with it for 'make-up.' • The leaves and flowers can be used as a salad ingredient—the colourful flower clusters are strikingly decorative. • Although frequently thought to mean disease, the word 'blite' actually comes from the Latin *blitum*, meaning 'insipid.' This name was originally given to the European species *C. bonus henricus*, an insipid herb!

EURASIAN WATER-MILFOIL •
Myriophyllum spicatum

GENERAL: Aquatic perennial from rhizomes; stems leafy, lax, 2–3 mm thick and 30 cm to 5 m long.

LEAVES: Whorled, 3–4 per whorl, 1–3 cm long, pinnately dissected into 14–24 pairs of thread-like segments.

FLOWERS: Tiny, unisexual, with 4 quickly deciduous, pinkish petals; single and stalkless in axils of **entire bracts**; inflorescence appears spike-like and often sticks up out of water.

FRUITS: 4 rounded achenes, about 2.5 mm long.

ECOLOGY: Introduced aquatic weed from Eurasia; scattered and often abundant at low to mid elevations, mostly in southern half of our region, in lakes, ponds, slough and slow-moving streams from 1–10 m deep.

SIMILAR SPECIES: Siberian water-milfoil (*M. sibericum*, also known as *M. spicatum* var. *exalbrescens*, **inset photo**) is one of our most common water-milfoils. It is very similar to Eurasian water-milfoil, but it has fewer leaf segments (5–12 pairs) and generally smaller floral bracts.

NOTES: This aquatic weed arrived in eastern North America in the late 1800s and spread across the continent. It is becoming a **serious threat** in warm lakes and waterways. It was first noticed in the Vernon arm of Okanagan Lake in 1970 and it has spread throughout the Okanagan and to lakes in the Shuswap and Kootenay areas. It spreads mainly by plant segments that break off, float away, sink and root. Boaters are reminded to clean their boats of any fragments when they leave infested lakes and to check them again before launching into a clean lake. • This species is also known as northern spiked water-milfoil. The species name *spicatum*, of course, refers to the spike-like inflorescence visible above the water.

WHORLED WATER-MILFOIL • *Myriophyllum verticillatum*

GENERAL: Aquatic perennial from rhizomes; stems leafy, lax, 2–3 mm thick and 30–100 cm long.

LEAVES: Whorled, 4–5 per whorl, 2–4.5 cm long, pinnately dissected into 9–17 pairs of thread-like segments.

FLOWERS: Tiny, unisexual; with 4 quickly deciduous, greenish-yellow petals; single and stalkless in axils of **pinnate bracts**; inflorescence appears spike-like and often sticks up out of water.

FRUITS: 4 rounded achenes, about 2.5 mm long.

ECOLOGY: Widespread and locally abundant at low to mid elevations in lakes and sloughs, usually less than 1 m deep (occasionally to 3 m).

NOTES: This is a common native water-milfoil. Its pinnately divided floral bracts distinguish it from Eurasian water-milfoil. • The genus name *Myriophyllum* is from the Greek *myrios*, 'thousand,' and *phyllon*, 'a leaf,' and it refers to the finely dissected leaf. The species name *verticillatum* means 'whorled' and gives rise to the common name.

COMMON MARE'S-TAIL • *Hippuris vulgaris*

GENERAL: Aquatic or amphibious perennial, 10–40 cm tall, from creeping rhizomes; stems hairless, leafy, **upright**, mostly unbranched **and usually partially submerged.**

LEAVES: Whorled, 6–12 per whorl, stalkless, **linear,** 0.5–3 cm long (sometimes to 5 cm) and 1–2 mm wide, **pointed;** leaves stiff above water but limp underwater.

FLOWERS: Tiny, inconspicuous; petals absent; **single and stalkless in axils** of upper whorls of leaves.

FRUITS: Nutlets, 1-seeded, about 2 mm long.

ECOLOGY: Scattered and locally common at low to mid elevations in shallow ponds and along lake-shores and streamsides.

SIMILAR SPECIES: Mountain mare's-tail (*H. montana*) grows in slow-moving shallow streams, ponds and wet meadows at mid to subalpine elevations. It is more terrestrial and smaller (usually less than 10 cm tall) than common mare's-tail, and its stems are about 0.5 mm thick and its leaves are 2–6 mm long (rarely to 1 cm). • Common mare's-tail looks much like a horse-tail (*Equisetum* sp.) but it is a flowering and seed-bearing plant and does not have jointed, hollow stems.

NOTES: The genus name *Hippuris* is from the Greek *hippos,* 'a horse,' and *oura,* 'a tail,' in reference to the brushy appearance of this plant.

COMMON DUCKWEED • *Lemna minor*

GENERAL: Minute, free-floating aquatic plant; single, short, white rootlet (to 2 cm) attached at centre of an often purplish underside; usually **forms dense colonies** covering large areas of water surface.

LEAVES: Single, flat, egg-shaped, **disk-like frond,** 2–5 mm long, obscurely 3-veined.

FLOWERS: Microscopic and rudimentary, occurring in pair of marginal pouches; rare because reproduction is mostly vegetative; young plants arise from a pair of marginal pouches near the narrow end of the plant.

FRUITS: Single, microscopic seeds.

ECOLOGY: Scattered and common at low to mid elevations in ponds and sluggish waters.

SIMILAR SPECIES: Ivy-leaved duckweed (*L. trisulca*) has a **more elongate frond that** tapers to a stem-like base, often with several generations of new plants attached to the parent plants by these long stalks. It usually floats just below the water's surface and often lies on the bottom in shallow water. It appears to have a preference for somewhat calcium-rich water and occurs most commonly on the Fraser and Thompson plateaus and in the southern Rocky Mountain Trench. • Great duckweed (*Spirodela polyrhiza*) resembles a large version of common duckweed (it is 4–8 mm long), but it has a bundle of **several rootlets** attached beneath the frond. Great duckweed has much the same distribution as common duckweed and occurs as isolated small groups among common duckweed. • Water-meal (*Wolffia borealis*) can be found in the Creston area. It consists of a **rootless ellipsoid frond** about 0.5–1.5 mm long—it is one of the smallest flowering plants in the world.

NOTES: Botanists recognize *Lemna* as one of the monocotyledon genera, but its very small flowers and round leaves make it difficult to identify as such. • Common duckweed, as its name implies, is an important food for many water-fowl species.

COMMON PLANTAIN • *Plantago major*

GENERAL: Perennial, to 30 cm tall, with a mass of fibrous roots and **leafless flowering stalks**.

LEAVES: All basal; blades broad and elliptic, with round to **heart-shaped bases** and **prominent parallel veins**; somewhat fleshy and more or less hairless.

FLOWERS: Tiny and greenish, in **long, dense spike** at top of flowering stalk.

FRUITS: Many-seeded capsules.

ECOLOGY: Widespread and common at low to mid elevations in weedy, often on disturbed ground and in waste places.

SIMILAR SPECIES: Indian wheat (*P. patagonica*) is a smaller (5–20 cm tall) species of dry, open grassland. It has narrow leaves and the whole plant is covered in woolly hairs.

NOTES: Plantain leaves are an effective poultice for infections and skin abrasions. Almost all Interior native peoples made a poultice from plantain leaves to soothe cuts, sores, burns and bee stings. They knew it as 'frog-leaf.' Placing plantain leaves in your hiking boots before a long trip may help prevent blisters and relieve foot pain. • The mature seed heads of plantain may be hung in bundles as food for caged birds. • The common name is from the Latin *plantago*, meaning 'foot-sole,' from the way some of the leaves lie flat on the ground as though they have been stepped on. Another common name, 'way-bread,' may originally have been 'way-broad,' meaning 'spread along the way,' and may refer to this species' habit of lining roadsides.

STINGING NETTLE • *Urtica dioica*

GENERAL: Perennial, 1–3 m tall, with thick, spreading rhizomes and armed with **stinging hairs**.

LEAVES: Paired, lance-shaped to oval or heart-shaped, with coarsely **saw-toothed edges**.

FLOWERS: Greenish and inconspicuous; no petals; clustered in **drooping bunches** from leaf axils.

FRUITS: Flattened seeds.

ECOLOGY: Widespread and common at low to mid elevations in meadows, thickets, open woods and streambanks; often in disturbed habitats, such as avalanche tracks, middens, slash piles, barnyards, and roadsides, **deep rich soil** and moist, shaded habitats.

NOTES: The stinging hairs, which are hollow, arise from a gland containing formic acid. As the brittle hair tips are broken, acid is secreted, causing an irritating rash on contact with skin. Nevertheless, the leaves can be cooked and eaten as greens when young. The cooked greens are a source of vitamins A, C and D as well as iron, calcium and potassium. • This plant was sometimes called Indian spinach, and its young leaves and stems were eaten by both Coastal and Interior native peoples, but it is questionable whether this use was traditional or introduced by Europeans. • Many Interior native groups plastered stinging nettles over sores and bruises. This treatment is very painful, but the pain goes away. They also used nettles medicinally as a counter-irritant and took decoctions of roots and leaves internally for a wide variety of ailments (such as those of the kidney, liver, gallbladder, lung and bladder and diabetes). • Although long considered an obnoxious weed by some, stinging nettle was revered as a sacred herb in the 10th century.

GOLDEN CORYDALIS • *Corydalis aurea*

GENERAL: Sprawling, taprooted annual or biennial, to 50 cm tall; stems hairless but with whitish bloom.

LEAVES: Highly divided, blue-green, usually with a whitish cast.

FLOWERS: Irregular, showy, yellow, with a **prominent spur**; several in loose clusters at branch ends.

FRUITS: Long, thin capsules constricted between seeds and usually curved; seeds black and shiny.

ECOLOGY: Scattered at low to mid elevations on our plateaus, arid basins and northern wet Columbia Mountains, in disturbed soil, clearings, burnt areas and thin soils.

SIMILAR SPECIES: Pink corydalis (*C. sempervirens*) has **pink flowers with yellow tips** and erect stems to 80 cm tall.

NOTES: The **flowers of the fumitory family have four petals arranged in two dissimilar pairs.** One or both of the outer petals (one in *Corydalis*) have a prominent spur at the base. The inner petals are joined at the tip. • *Corydalis* species are most common in disturbed areas. They apparently store their seeds in the soil for decades or even centuries, until a disturbance triggers their germination. • *Corydalis* is Greek for 'crested lark.' The rather ornate flowers were thought to resemble this bird.

CLUSTERED BROOMRAPE • *Orobanche fasciculata*

GENERAL: Parasitic perennial, 3–15 cm tall, with single or clustered pale yellow to purplish stems, **glandular** throughout.

LEAVES: Reduced to **brownish scales**.

FLOWERS: Irregular, purple or yellowish; tube-shaped corolla has 2 lips, upper lip 2-lobed and lower lip 3-lobed; inflorescence of 4–10 on long stalks forms a flat-topped cluster.

FRUITS: Capsules.

ECOLOGY: Scattered at low to mid elevations in arid basins and on dry Thompson and Okanagan plateaus, in grasslands and dry open forests; often with big sagebrush.

SIMILAR SPECIES: One-flowered cancer-root (*O. uniflora*), also called naked broomrape is parasitic on stonecrops (*Sedum* spp.) and alumroots (*Heuchera* spp.), and it is suspected of being parasitic on several other genera. It has a very short stem (1–5 cm tall) and 1–3 purple flowers, each on a long, bare stalk.

NOTES: The roots of clustered broomrape are parasitic on other plants, particularly sages (*Artemisia* spp.). • The genus name is from the Greek *orobos*, 'a vetch,' and *anchein*, 'to choke,' and alludes to the parasitic nature of this genus. A British species is parasitic on broom (*Cystisus scoparius*) and so plants of this genus are called broomrapes. The species name *fasciculata* refers to the arrangement of the flowers in 'fascicles,' or clusters.

Lamiaceae: Mint Family

The mint family (also called Labiatae) is one of the most easily recognized plant families. Nearly all members have **opposite leaves, square stems, irregular flowers and four seeds (nutlets)**. Their leaves seldom have lobes or divisions, but often have toothed edges. The showy flowers are composed of five sepals and five petals fused into a tubular corolla and calyx. The corolla separates at the top into five irregular lobes (four in *Mentha* species) that are often grouped into two sections or **'lips.'** The **lobes of the upper lip may be fused into a 'hood.'** The corolla tube encloses four stamens, or sometimes two.

FIELD MINT • *Mentha arvensis* M. canadensis

GENERAL: Rhizomatous perennial, 20–60 cm tall; **strong mint odour.**

LEAVES: Opposite, short-stalked, narrowly oval to broadly lance-shaped, short-hairy, with glandular dots on both surfaces and **sharply toothed edges.**

FLOWERS: Pale purple, pink or white; in **ball-shaped clusters around stem in leaf axils**; **corollas tubular** with 4 equal lobes; **4 stamens.**

FRUITS: 4 small nutlets.

ECOLOGY: Widespread and common at low and mid elevations in wet seepage sites, wetland edges and lakeshores.

NOTES: The nearly regular, 4-lobed corolla distinguishes *Mentha* species from other mints, which generally have irregular, 5-lobed corollas divided into two lips. • Interior native peoples made a tea from field mint to treat bad colds, pains and swelling. The Nlaka'pmx placed mint leaves around their dwellings to drive off insect pests. • Field mint is closely related to domesticated mints found in herb gardens. The mint family includes a number of cultivated plants, such as lavender, salvia and rosemary. The aromatic odours of these herbs are produced from glands dotted on the leaf surface. • Field mint is also known as Canada mint. 'Mint' comes from the Latin *mentha* (or *menta*) and the Greek *minthe*. Minthe was a nymph who was turned into a mint plant by Proserpina in a fit of jealousy.

WILD BERGAMOT • *Monarda fistulosa*

GENERAL: Perennial, 30–70 cm tall, with creeping **rhizomes**; **solitary flowering stems**, finely hairy throughout, with strong, pleasant odour.

LEAVES: Opposite, short-stalked, widely spaced along stem, triangular lance-shaped to oval, with **sharply toothed edges**.

FLOWERS: Bright mauve; in a showy **cluster at end of stem**; **corollas tubular**, opening into 2 unequal lips; **upper lip long and narrow**, forming a hood over **2 stamens**; lower lip 3-lobed.

FRUITS: 4 small nutlets.

ECOLOGY: Scattered and infrequent to locally common in Thompson and Okanagan basins, in mid-elevation grasslands, dry open forests, clearings and disturbed soils.

NOTES: The Ktunaxa made a tea from this plant. Other Interior peoples used it as an insect repellent and smudge. • The name 'wild bergamot' is derived from the plant's pleasant odour, which is reminiscent of 'essence of bergamot,' an essential oil extracted from oranges (*Citrus bergamia*) and used to flavour food, such as Earl Grey tea. • This species is also known as horse mint.

SELF-HEAL • *Prunella vulgaris*

GENERAL: Fibrous-rooted **perennial**, 10–50 cm tall, with solitary or clustered stems from a short woody base.

LEAVES: Opposite, elliptic, with rounded bases, smooth edges and **obvious stalks.**

FLOWERS: Purplish blue; in a short, dense, **squarish spike** with leafy bracts throughout; **corolla tubular**, opening into 2 unequal lips, **upper lip helmet-shaped,** lower lip 3-lobed **(middle lobe fringed); 4 stamens.**

FRUITS: 4 smooth nutlets.

ECOLOGY: Widespread at low to mid elevations in moist to wet meadows, streambanks, lakeshores, clearings cultivated areas and frequently in lawns.

NOTES: Self-heal is also known as heal-all, and it is widely distributed around the world. The traditional use of this plant for healing internal and external bleeding gives rise to the modern common names and to the old French proverb 'no one wants a surgeon who keeps *prunelle.*' *Prunella* (also spelled *Brunella*) is from the German *Bräune*, meaning 'quinsy' or 'angina,' which this plant was used to cure. Tests on the plant's extracts have not revealed any biochemical basis for the claims of healing. • The Nlaka'pmx used self-heal as a tonic a long time ago. • Old common names, such as 'hook-heal' and 'carpenter's herb,' refer to the use of this plant to heal wounds inflicted by sharp-edged tools.

MARSH SKULLCAP • *Scutellaria galericulata*

GENERAL: Perennial, 20–80 cm tall, with slender rhizomes; solitary, often branched flowering stems are **hairy on angles.**

LEAVES: Opposite, oval to lance-shaped with blunt-toothed blades, short-stalked, short-hairy below.

FLOWERS: Blue to pink-purple, marked with white, solitary on slender stalks and **paired** in leaf axils; both **calyx and corolla are tubular, opening into 2 short lips, upper lip helmet-shaped,** lower lip unlobed; **4 stamens.**

FRUITS: 4 small nutlets.

ECOLOGY: Widespread and common at low to mid elevations in wetlands, wet forest openings, lakeshores, streamsides and ditches.

NOTES: The genus name *Scutellaria* is from the Latin *scutella*, 'a tray,' and refers to a prominent ridge on the upper lip of the calyx. The species name *galericulata* is Latin for 'having a little helmet-like skull-cap,' hence the common names 'skull-cap' and 'helmet flower.'

Fabaceae: Pea Family

The pea (or legume) family, also called Leguminosae, is one of the largest plant families. Its many cultivated species, some dating back nearly 8,000 years, provide food, fodder, lumber and flowers in many parts of the world. Legume species range from herbs of alpine ridges to desert shrubs to some of the tallest trees of tropical forests. The wild legume species in our area are herbs, and most are perennials.

Legumes are most easily recognized by their flowers, whose distinctive 'pea-like' shape is called 'papilionaceous' (butterfly-like). The flowers are composed of five highly differentiated petals. The uppermost petal, called a '**banner**' or 'standard,' is usually the largest and showiest. Below it are two side petals, called '**wings**.' The two lowest petals are fused together, forming a '**keel**.' Enclosed within the keel are 10 stamens, nine of them generally fused into a tube.

Legume seeds are typically pea- or bean-like, enclosed within the characteristic seed pod, or 'legume.' The family name Leguminosae refers to the pods, which split in two at maturity.

Most legume species have compound leaves. They can be palmate, with leaflets arranged like fingers on a hand, or pinnate, with leaflets arranged in pairs along a central stalk. In some species, the uppermost leaflet is modified into a tendril. Each leaf usually has a pair of basal appendages called **stipules**.

The contribution of legumes to soil nutrients results from their relationship with nitrogen-fixing bacteria. These bacteria, which reside in nodules located on the roots, convert atmospheric nitrogen into compounds the plants can use. Nitrogen is in limited supply in most soils in our region, and species such as clovers, alfalfa, sweet-clovers and lupines increase soil fertility where they grow.

Key to the pea family genera

1a. Leaves with 3 leaflets 2
  2a. Fruits strongly curved to coiled .... *Medicago*
  2b. Fruits straight to slightly curved 3
    3a. 1–3 flowers in leaf axils .... *Lotus*
    3b. Flowers in clusters of more than 3 4
      4a. Flowers in long, narrow clusters .... *Melilotus*
      4b. Flowers in heads or short clusters .... *Trifolium*
1b. Leaves with more than 3 leaflets 5
  5a. Leaflets palmately arranged .... *Lupinus*
  5b. Leaflets pinnately arranged 6
    6a. Pods constricted between seeds .... *Hedysarum*
    6b. Pods not (or only slightly) constricted between seeds 7
      7a. Leaves with an even number of leaflets, and with a slender bristle or tendril instead of a leaflet at tip of leaf 8
        8a. Hairs all around tip of style (like a bottle brush) .... *Vicia*
        8b. Hairs on 1 side of style (like a toothbrush) .... *Lathyrus*
      7b. Leaves with an odd number of leaflets, and with a leaflet at end of leaf axis 9
        9a. 1–3 Flowers in leaf axils .... *Lotus*
        9b. Flowers usually in clusters of more than 3 10
          10a. Leaves mostly basal; keel petal abruptly narrowed to a beak-like pointed tip .... *Oxytropis*
          10b. Leaves mostly well distributed along stems; keel petal lacking a beak-like pointed tip .... *Astragalus*

Melilotus alba

Oxytropis campestris

Lathyrus ochroleucus

Trifolium pratense

Lotus denticulatus

Vicia americana

Medicago sativa

Lupinus sericeus

Astragalus collinus

Hedysarum sulphurescens

155

ALFALFA • *Medicago sativa*

GENERAL: Deep-rooted perennial; stems 30–100 cm tall.

LEAVES: 3 elliptic to oblong leaflets, slightly hairy, sharply toothed at tips.

FLOWERS: Pea-like, **blue to purple** (occasionally whitish); about 1 cm long, in short, oblong-shaped clusters.

FRUITS: Spirally coiled pods.

ECOLOGY: Scattered at low to mid elevations; locally common to infrequent in cultivated fields, escaping to roadsides and rights-of-way.

SIMILAR SPECIES: Black medick (*M. lupulina*) is another European introduction found in waste places and sandy or gravelly soils. Black medick is a 10–40 cm-tall annual with small (2–3 mm long), **yellow flowers** on loosely spreading stems. The pod is less tightly coiled than alfalfa's and turns black at maturity. • Alfalfa can often be found growing with sweet-clovers (*Melilotus* spp., p. 157), which have a similar growth form and three leaflets, but do not have coiled pods.

NOTES: Alfalfa is native to the Old World where it has long been cultivated as a forage crop. The Medes of ancient Persia are thought to have first domesticated it and the Greeks introduced it to Europe at the time of the Persian wars. The Latinized name translates as 'sown by the Medians.' The common name is a Spanish word originally derived from Arabic.

MEADOW BIRDS-FOOT TREFOIL • *Lotus denticulatus*

GENERAL: Annual, 10–55 cm tall; stems with few erect branches.

LEAVES: Pinnately compound with 3 or 4 **elliptic leaflets**, arranged with **a pair at end of stalk** and 1 or 2 on 1 side.

FLOWERS: Pea-like, **cream-coloured**; back of standard petal tinged purple; usually **solitary** in leaf axil.

FRUITS: Sparsely hairy pods with flattened seeds.

ECOLOGY: Scattered on our dry plateaus and in arid basins and southern Rocky Mountain Trench; common to infrequent in open, sandy fields, disturbed soils, dry open forests and grasslands.

NOTES: The genus name *Lotus* is Greek. Several species of *Lotus* are called bird's-foot trefoil because they resemble true bird's-foot (*Ornithopus perpusillus*), which has claw-like pods. 'Trefoil' is from the Latin *tria foliola*, 'three leaflets.'

WHITE SWEET-CLOVER • *Melilotus alba*

GENERAL: Tall annual (occasionally biennial), 1–2 m tall, with freely branching stems.

LEAVES: 3 oblong leaflets with finely toothed edges.

FLOWERS: Many, small (4–5 mm long), pea-like, **white; in long, tapering, slender, spike-like clusters.**

FRUITS: 1–2-seeded pods, hairless, black, with net-veined surfaces when ripe.

ECOLOGY: Scattered throughout low to mid elevations; common in waste places, roadsides, cultivated fields, wherever roads and settlement occur.

SIMILAR SPECIES: Yellow sweet-clover (*M. officinalis*) has yellow flowers, wide oblong-elliptic leaflets and yellowish-brown pods that are not strongly net-veined when ripe.

NOTES: Sweet-clovers are often responsible for the overwhelmingly sweet fragrance you might notice while driving on hot summer days. The sweet smell comes from coumarin, which also imparts a very pleasant smell to sweetgrass (*Hierochloe* spp.) and fresh-cut hay. If allowed to degrade (e.g., through rotting of hay), coumarin can break down into compounds which prevent blood from clotting, leading to hay-fed animals dying from even minor injuries. • Both species are weedy, introduced as forage crops from Europe (white sweet-clover) and the Mediterranean (yellow sweet-clover).

RED CLOVER • *Trifolium pratense*

GENERAL: Taprooted, short-lived perennial, 20–60 cm tall, somewhat soft-hairy, with several erect stems.

LEAVES: 3 leaflets (rarely 4—a sign of good luck), often with a white, crescent-shaped spot near base.

FLOWERS: Pea-like, **pinkish purple;** in **round, dense heads** at stem tops, with 2 leaves immediately below.

FRUITS: Small pods containing 2 seeds.

ECOLOGY: A European species now widely established at low to mid elevations; common in fields and grassy areas and on disturbed soils.

SIMILAR SPECIES: White clover (*T. repens*) and alsike clover (*T. hybridum,* inset photo) are the two other most common species. White clover has **creeping stems** and white to pinkish flower heads on long stalks. Alsike clover has **ascending stems** and pinkish white, stalked flower heads; it is a hybrid between red and white clover.

NOTES: Red clover is an introduced species and is one of several clovers that occur in our area. All have flowers in dense heads and leaves with three leaflets. They are found most commonly on disturbed sites, as agricultural escapes, or where they have been deliberately seeded for erosion control or to increase soil fertility. • The name 'clover' is from the Latin *clava,* 'a club,' as in the suit in cards, and describes the leaf shape.

ARCTIC LUPINE • *Lupinus arcticus*
L. latifolius var. *subalpinus*

GENERAL: Perennial, to 80 cm tall, with several smooth, hollow stems growing from a branched, woody rootstock.

LEAVES: Palmately compound, mostly on stem; with stalks **1–2 times as long as blade** and **6–8 lance-shaped leaflets** (3–6 cm long), smooth above and hairy below.

FLOWERS: Pea-like, **bluish** to occasionally pinkish (12–15 mm long); in an elongated cluster.

FRUITS: Hairy pods.

ECOLOGY: Widespread in moist climates of Fraser and Thompson plateaus and scattered in wet Columbia Mountains and southern Rocky Mountain Trench; common along roadsides, clearings, forests, high-elevation meadows and open subalpine forests.

SIMILAR SPECIES: Large-leaved lupine (*L. polyphyllus*) has large leaves with 10–17 leaflets. The lower stem leaves, at least, have **stalks 3–6 times as long as the longest leaflet**. Large-leaved lupine occurs naturally on moist, low- to mid-elevation sites, but it is also widely cultivated and often escapes into new areas where it can be seen on disturbed sites. The well-known 'Russel' lupine was developed from large-leaved lupine.

NOTES: Arctic lupine can form huge colonies in subalpine meadows, providing spectacular midsummer displays. • This and other lupines were considered a favourite food of marmots. Southern Interior native peoples noted that marmots were fat enough to eat when the lupines were in bloom. • In 1954, 10,000-year-old seeds of arctic lupine were found frozen in the Yukon in ancient lemming burrows—some of them successfully germinated.

DWARF MOUNTAIN LUPINE • *Lupinus lyallii*
L. lepidus var. *lobbii*

GENERAL: Perennial, **less than 10 cm tall**, with short, unbranched stems, **low to the ground and matted**; covered in **dense, silky, greyish or reddish hair**.

LEAVES: Palmately compound, mainly basal, with stalks much longer than leaflets; leaflets small (less than 15 mm long) lance-shaped, greyish-green, **very hairy** above and below.

FLOWERS: Pea-like, **deep to light blue** (occasionally pink), 8–13 mm long; arranged in whorls in a short (less than 5 cm), dense cluster.

FRUITS: Hairy pods, 1–2 cm long.

ECOLOGY: Scattered at high elevations in mountains of Coast/Interior Transition; locally common in dry to moist meadows and on gravelly alpine and subalpine slopes.

SIMILAR SPECIES: A hairy, dwarf form of arctic lupine (*L. arcticus*, above) may be encountered at high elevations, but it is never less than 10 cm tall.

NOTES: This tiny lupine is readily distinguished by its size and downy leaf surface. • The species name honours David Lyall (1817–95), a Scottish botanist who collected in North America.

SILKY LUPINE • *Lupinus sericeus*

GENERAL: Perennial, 20–60 cm tall, with simple or sparingly branched stems from a branching, woody crown, **covered with silky, silver- to rust-coloured hairs.**

LEAVES: Palmately compound, mostly on stem; stalks longer (up to 3 times) than leaflets; 7–9 **leaflets, appear greyish green from silky hairs** covering both surfaces.

FLOWERS: Pea-like, **deep blue to lavender** with whitish or yellow markings at base of wing petals; **banner petal is densely hairy on back;** inflorescence is a long, loose cluster.

FRUITS: Pods covered in **silky hairs.**

ECOLOGY: Scattered at low elevations on Thompson and Okanagan plateaus, in arid basins and in East Kootenays; common in dry grasslands, sagebrush flats, open ponderosa pine forests, clearings and disturbed soils.

NOTES: This is a variable species with many varieties. The long, silky hairs that give the plant its name are its most consistent character. • The Secwepemc report that chipmunks eat the seeds. • Several lupines are known to have caused **fatal poisoning in animals.** Although Alberta experts (Moss 1959; Cormack 1967) consider silky lupines to be a good cattle forage, it is on the U.S.D.A.'s list of the '10 most toxic' to sheep. • The common name 'silky' is a translation of the Latin *sericeus.*

SULPHUR LUPINE • *Lupinus sulphureus*

GENERAL: Perennial, 40–80 cm tall, with unbranched stems from a branching, woody crown, sparsely to densely covered with white to brown hairs.

LEAVES: Palmately compound, mostly on stem; stalks about equal to leaflets (basal ones much longer); 9–11 narrowly lance-shaped to oblong leaflets; usually hairy on both surfaces.

FLOWERS: Pea-like, **bright yellow**, sometimes white, blue or purple; inflorescence of many flowers in a long cluster.

FRUITS: Silky-hairy pods.

ECOLOGY: Scattered at low to mid elevations in Thompson and Okanagan basins and in Nicola valley; often common in dry grasslands and dry open forests.

NOTES: The lupines are easily recognized by their **palmately compound leaves and tall spires of brightly coloured flowers.** Differentiating between the species of this genus, however, is challenging, as they are highly variable and commonly hybridize. • Sulphur lupine will hybridize with other species, such as silky lupine (*L. sericeus,* above), producing intermediates in some areas. • There seems to be some confusion about the exact origin of the word 'lupine.' One source says it is derived from the Latin *lupinus* (from *lupus,* 'a wolf'), another that it is from the Greek *lopos,* 'a husk,' or *lepo,* 'a hull or peel,' in reference to the pod.

Vicia: the vetches and *Lathyrus:* the peavines

The vetches and peavines are very similar groups of weak-stemmed, viney plants. They can be recognized by their pinnately compound leaves which have an even number of leaflets and usually end in tendrils. They are often found among dense meadow vegetation, and they use their tendrils to climb up the stems of their stouter neighbours to avoid being overtopped. Although the groups include both annuals and perennials, the species common in our area are all perennial.

Peavine and vetch flowers are usually showy and brightly coloured. The flowers of the cultivated sweetpea (*Lathyrus odoratus*) exemplify the group. Closely examining the flowers provides the most reliable means of distinguishing between peavines and vetches. The styles of both have hairs at the tip which can usually be observed without magnification. The hairs on the styles of **peavines** are arranged on one side, so that **the style resembles a toothbrush**. The hairs on the **styles of vetches**, however, are distributed around the tip like a **bottle-brush**.

Although all species have pinnately compound leaves, leaflet shape is variable and can help to distinguish among the species. In most species, the base of the leaf stalk has a pair of prominent leafy appendages called **stipules**. The size and shape of the stipules also provide good clues to identification.

Livestock find peavines and vetches very palatable and several species are considered good natural fodder.

The genus name *Lathyrus* is from *la* and the Greek word *thouros*, meaning 'something exciting,' from the belief that the seeds had some medicinal value. The name 'vetch' is from the Latin *vicia* (also the genus name for vetches), which is thought to be derived from the Latin *vincio* (to bind), and refers to the climbing habit of these plants.

AMERICAN VETCH • *Vicia americana*

GENERAL: Rhizomatous perennial, 15–100 cm tall, with **trailing or climbing stems**, often in tangled masses.

LEAVES: Pinnately compound, with **8–18 smooth or hairy leaflets** with simple or forked tendrils; stipules are small, narrow and **sharply toothed**.

FLOWERS: Pea-like, **bluish to reddish purple**; in loose clusters of 3–9.

FRUITS: Hairless pods.

ECOLOGY: Widespread and common at low to mid elevations in fields, clearings and thickets, and moist and wet, open deciduous or mixed forest.

SIMILAR SPECIES: American vetch is often confused with purple peavine (*L. nevadensis*, p. 161). • Woolly vetch (*V. villosa*) is an introduced annual or biennial common in the southern third of our region along roadsides and in fields and waste places. Unlike American vetch, woolly vetch is very hairy throughout. Its flowers are 2-toned rosy-purple and white and occur in many-flowered, long, 1-sided spikes.

NOTES: American vetch can become a persistent garden weed. In pastures and rangeland, it provides fodder for livestock.

PURPLE PEAVINE • *Lathyrus nevadensis*
L. nuttallii

GENERAL: Rhizomatous perennial, 15–100 cm tall, often with free-standing stems.

LEAVES: Pinnately compound; **4–10 elliptic to oval leaflets** that are hairy below; tendrils usually branched; stipules are narrow and 2-lobed.

FLOWERS: Pea-like, bluish **purple to mauve-red**; in clusters of 2–7.

FRUITS: Hairless pods.

ECOLOGY: Widespread and locally common at low to mid elevations in moist to dry, open woods, clearings and open rocky slopes; absent from wet Columbia Mountains.

SIMILAR SPECIES: This herb is often confused with American vetch (*Vicia americana*, p. 160) because both have tendrils and purple flowers. Where they grow together, purple peavine generally appears more robust and has fewer and larger leaflets than American vetch. The **stipules of purple peavine have smooth or inconspicuously lobed edges,** whereas **American vetch stipules have jaggedly toothed edges.** There is also the generic distinction of 'bottle-brush' hairs on the style in *Vicia* and 'toothbrush' hairs on the style in *Lathyrus*.

NOTES: Purple peavine is also known as Nuttall's peavine.

CREAMY PEAVINE • *Lathyrus ochroleucus*

GENERAL: Rhizomatous perennial, 30–100 cm tall; stems smooth and somewhat angled.

LEAVES: Pinnately compound, with **3–4 pairs of leaflets** and well-developed, usually **branched tendrils; stipules are broad, oval,** often half as long as leaflets.

FLOWERS: Pea-like, **white to yellowish white**; in clusters of 6–15.

FRUITS: Hairless pods, turning brown and twisting open with age.

ECOLOGY: Widespread and often abundant at low to mid elevations in moist to dry, open woods (more abundant in deciduous and mixed stands than coniferous stands), rocky slopes and clearings.

SIMILAR SPECIES: Creamy peavine may be confused with purple peavine (*L. nevadensis*, above), especially when not in flower. Apart from the obvious differences in flower colour, these two species can be differentiated by their stipules, which are broad and oval in creamy peavine, and narrowly lance-shaped and 2-lobed in purple peavine. They often occur together throughout their range.

YELLOW HEDYSARUM • *Hedysarum sulphurescens*

GENERAL: Taprooted perennial, 17–90 cm tall, with several stems, sparsely hairy.

LEAVES: Pinnately compound; 9–21 **leaflets, elliptic to oblong,** with prominent veins and tiny points at tips, smooth above and sparsely grey-hairy below.

FLOWERS: Pea-like, **yellowish to nearly white,** 20–100, somewhat drooping, in an elongate, frequently 1-sided cluster.

FRUITS: Flattened pods with **conspicuous winged edges** and **constrictions between each of the 2–4 seeds**.

ECOLOGY: Scattered and locally common in Okanagan Basin and East Kootenays; along streambanks and in grasslands, clearings and open forests.

SIMILAR SPECIES: The fragrant, purple-flowered northern sweet-vetch (*Hedysarum boreale*) is also common in our region in grasslands and on dry hillsides, open slopes and gravel bars. Its leaflets are inconspicuously veined and its pods have 1–6 seeds. • The **pods** of yellow hedysarum, which **look like strings of flattened beads**, readily distinguish it from the milk-vetches (*Astragalus* spp., pp. 163–65).

NOTES: Yellow hedysarum is also called yellow sweet-vetch. The genus name *Hedysarum* is from the Greek *hedys*, 'sweet' and *aroma*, 'smell,' and refers to the sweet-smelling flowers.

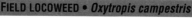

FIELD LOCOWEED • *Oxytropis campestris*

GENERAL: Taprooted perennial, 5–30 cm tall, with many short branches growing from a woody base; very variable in size and hairiness.

LEAVES: Pinnately compound, mainly basal and clustered, with 11 to many narrowly elliptic leaflets, and no tendrils; usually **densely silky-hairy**.

FLOWERS: Small (1–2 cm long), pea-like, **yellowish white**; in a cluster at the top of a hairy, leafless stem.

FRUITS: Pods, with black and white hairs; become **thin and papery when dry**.

ECOLOGY: Widespread and often common at low to alpine elevations on gravel bars, rocky outcrops, roadsides, dry open woodland, grasslands and meadows; in all but our wet climates.

SIMILAR SPECIES: Silky locoweed (*O. sericea*) also has pale yellow flowers. It is generally more grey silky-hairy than field locoweed and has fewer leaflets. Its pods are leathery and become **hardened and bony** when dry. It occurs throughout the southern half of our region at all elevations. • Two **purple-flowered species**, showy locoweed (*O. splendens*) and pendant-pod locoweed (*O. deflexa*), also occur in our area. Showy locoweed is also densely silvery-silky, but is distinguished by its many showy, reddish-purple flowers and it leaflets, which are in whorls of 2–6. Showy locoweed is infrequent along the slopes of the Rockies but common further north. More common

but scattered throughout our region is pendant-pod locoweed, identified by its leafy stipules and by pods that hang from tall, leafless stalks. • Locoweeds are quite similar to milk-vetches (*Astragalus* spp., pp. 163–65), but their leaf distribution is mostly basal in *Oxytropis*, while on the stems in *Astragalus*. The tip of the keel in *Oxytropis* is abruptly narrowed to a beak-like point.

NOTES: 'Locoweed' refers to the symptoms of staggering and loss of muscle control observed in livestock that have grazed on these plants.

Astragalus: the milk-vetches

The milk-vetches are a large group of perennial herbs found mostly in dry areas. They have **pinnately compound leaves with the leaflets arranged in pairs along the main stalk with one unpaired leaflet at the tip** and no tendrils. Each leaf usually has a pair of basal appendages called **stipules**. In some species, the stipules are joined on the side of the stem opposite the leaf blade, sometimes forming a collar around the stem. The flowers are generally borne in large, showy clusters on leafy stems.

ALPINE MILK-VETCH • Astragalus alpinus

GENERAL: Mat forming perennial, 4–25 cm long, with widespread rhizomes; stems are slender, creeping at base but becoming erect.

LEAVES: Pinnately compound, 4–15 cm long, with **11–23 oval to elliptic, silky-hairy leaflets**, each 0.5–2 cm long; stipules of at least the lowest leaves are joined.

FLOWERS: Pea-like, **2-toned bluish or pinkish purple, pale to white at base**, 7–12 mm long; calyx has black hairs; inflorescence of 5–25 small flowers in a **crowded cluster** at top of stalk.

FRUITS: Hanging, papery pods, **densely covered with black hairs.**

ECOLOGY: Scattered at mid to alpine elevations in northern part of our region and in Rockies, in moist thickets, gravel bars, swampy lake shores and open woods; locally common in alpine tundra, meadows and scree slopes.

SIMILAR SPECIES: Field milk-vetch (*A. agrestis,* also known as *A. dasyglottis*), another low-growing, purple-flowered milk-vetch, is common in the grasslands and open woods of the Fraser, Thompson and Okanagan basins and in the southern Rocky Mountain Trench. The flowers are erect and larger (1.5–2 cm long) than those of alpine milk-vetch. The inflated pods are also erect, not hanging.

NOTES: Alpine milk-vetch is not known to be toxic.

PULSE MILK-VETCH • Astragalus tenellus

GENERAL: Taprooted perennial, 20–60 cm tall, with several stems from a persistent, woody base.

LEAVES: Pinnately compound, with **11–25 linear or narrowly oblong leaflets**, finely hairy; stipules of at least the lowest leaves are joined.

FLOWERS: Pea-like, **yellowish-white**, sometimes pink-tinged with a purple-tipped keel, small (6–9 mm long); inflorescence a short, loose cluster of 7–20 flowers.

FRUITS: Hairless, papery, **strongly flattened pods**, hanging from short stalks.

ECOLOGY: Scattered and locally common at low to mid elevations throughout our dry climates in grasslands, dry slopes, eroded riverbanks and dry open forests.

NOTES: The term 'pulse' comes from the Latin *puls* and Hebrew *phul*. It was a cooked mixture of meal and peas that formed a staple food for Romans before the introduction of bread. After bread became common, this pottage was fed to the sacred chickens. The term is now confined to legumes and used mainly by agriculturists. • The species name *tenellus* is Latin for 'delicate,' which describes this slender plant.

PEA

TIMBER MILK-VETCH • *Astragalus miser*

GENERAL: Taprooted perennial, 10–40 cm tall, with many prostrate or erect stems; sparsely to densely hairy.

LEAVES: Pinnately compound, with **7–21 thin and needle-like to oval-shaped leaflets**; end leaflet is commonly longer than the adjacent pairs; stipules of at least the lowest leaves are joined.

FLOWERS: Pea-like, **white to lilac**, often with bluish penciling, 8–12 mm long; inflorescence of 2–20 flowers in a **loose, elongate cluster**.

FRUITS: Thin **pods hanging** directly from long flowering stalk.

ECOLOGY: Widespread and often common at low to mid elevations (sometimes to above timberline) in dry, warm climates of our region, in open ponderosa pine and Douglas-fir forests, clearings, grasslands and disturbed soils.

NOTES: Timber milk-vetch is considered poisonous and is most dangerous to lactating cows. There are taxonomic difficulties with milk-vetches, and a number of different species have the local common name 'timber milk-vetch,' some of which may not be poisonous. • When this plant was in bloom, the Okanagan knew pine cambium was ready to eat. They used timber milk-vetch in gathering pine cambium, to wipe off the turpentine-like juice, and their name for it means 'wipes off the inner side.' They ate the seeds as they came across them but did not gather them. The Nlaka'pmx sometimes used the leaves to cover cooking pits when they were cooking black lichen (*Bryoria* spp.) and wild onions.

AMERICAN MILK-VETCH • *Astragalus americanus*

GENERAL: Robust perennial, 30–100 cm tall, with a persistent woody base and usually unbranched stems.

LEAVES: Pinnately compound with **7–17 oval to elliptic leaflets**, 2–6 cm long; **stipules are long** (1–3 cm), **leaf-like**, bent downwards and not joined.

FLOWERS: Pea-like, **white**, turning yellowish with age, 1–1.5 cm long; inflorescence of 15–40 flowers in clusters at tips of stems.

FRUITS: Inflated, shiny, **drooping** pods.

ECOLOGY: Scattered and locally common at low to mid elevations on Fraser Plateau, in Fraser and Thompson basins and in southern Rocky Mountain Trench, in moist to wet soils along streams, wet seepage forests and at edge of wetlands.

SIMILAR SPECIES: Canada milk-vetch (*A. canadensis*) is another robust, yellowish- to white-flowered milk-vetch. It is found in moist habitats along riverbanks and in sandy soils. Its flowers are in an erect, spike-like cluster and the pods are erect with a tiny hook at the tip. Canada milk-vetch also has distinctive hairs, which if viewed under 10x magnification, appear pick-shaped, with two branches. • In flower, both *Astragalus* species superficially resemble yellow hedysarum (*Hedysarum sulphurescens*, p. 162) but the keel of hedysarum's flower is squared-off and there is a tiny point at the tip of each of its leaflets.

NOTES: The Okanagan soaked the tops of the plant in hot water to make a bathing solution for their sweatbath (see woollypod milk-vetch [*A. purshii*], p. 165). • This species is also known as arctic milk-vetch.

164

HILLSIDE MILK-VETCH • *Astragalus collinus*

GENERAL: **Robust, taprooted** perennial, 10–50 cm tall, with several spreading to erect stems; finely hairy.

LEAVES: Pinnately compound, with **11–21 linear to oblong leaflets**, often blunt or slightly **notched at tip;** stipules are small and spreading, not joined.

FLOWERS: Pea-like, **creamy white to yellowish**, 15 mm long; inflorescence of 15–40 flowers in a cluster at top of stalk; flower stalks are usually much longer than leaves.

FRUITS: Pods are **tapered at both ends**, drooping from **long stalks**.

ECOLOGY: Scattered and locally common at low to mid elevations in arid basins and on our dry plateaus, in grasslands, dry open forests and clearings.

NOTES: Several species of *Astragalus* are known to be toxic to livestock. The symptoms of poisoning include staggering and loss of muscle control, hence some species are called locoweeds. The symptoms could be caused either by locoine or by the accumulation in milk-vetches of large amounts of selenium, which is known to cause blind staggers. • *Astragalus* is an ancient Greek name, possibly from *astragulos*, 'ankle bone,' referring to the shape of the pods. Species of *Astragalus* were named 'milk-vetch' from the belief that a goat's milk supply increased if it ate these plants. The species name *collinus* means 'of hills.'

WOOLLYPOD MILK-VETCH • *Astragalus purshii*

GENERAL: **Taprooted, tufted to mat-forming** perennial, often with prostrate stems 5–10 cm long; **greyish-woolly.**

LEAVES: Pinnately compound, with **9–13 elliptic to almost round leaflets** with pointed tips, covered with **silky, white hairs**; stipules are small and spreading, not joined.

FLOWERS: Pea-like, **creamy yellow to deep reddish purple**, 1–3 cm long; inflorescence of 3–8 flowers in a loose cluster at top of short stalks.

FRUITS: Leathery, broad, flattened pods, covered in greyish, woolly hairs.

ECOLOGY: Scattered and infrequent at low to mid elevations in southern Okanagan and Nicola valleys, in grasslands, open ponderosa pine forests and openings and on sandy, gravelly soils and dry ridges.

SIMILAR SPECIES: Field locoweed (*Oxytropis campestris*, p. 162), which also has yellowish-white flowers and silky-hairy leaves, does not have the leafy flowering stalks of woollypod milk-vetch.

NOTES: The Nlaka'pmx used a bunch of these flower stems to bring luck back to fishing and hunting gear polluted or contaminated by bad medicine. The Okanagan used it to purify their sweatbaths. • The species is named in honour of F.T. Pursh (1774–1820), a German botanist who wrote one of the best-known floras of North America. Woollypod milk-vetch is also called Pursh's milk-vetch.

Scrophulariaceae: Figwort Family

The figworts are a large family of herbs and small shrubs. They have highly variable flowers, most of which exhibit some kind of irregularity in form. There are usually five petals and two to five sepals. The **petals are fused together into a tubular** corolla that divides at its top into two sometimes dissimilar segments or 'lips.' In some species, the upper lip is elongated and forms a hood that encloses the anthers. The number of anthers varies from two to five; most of our species have four. The fruit is a many-seeded capsule.

Figwort identification focuses on characteristics of the corolla, especially the presence or absence of the hooded upper corolla lip. Leaf shape and arrangement, including the leafy bracts often found within the flower cluster, are other useful characters. The number of anthers can narrow the possibilities in a specimen which has a different number than the usual four.

Many figworts are semi-parasites; that is, their roots may often be physically attached to the roots of other plants. Because all of these semi-parasitic species have green leaves, they are not considered to be true parasites.

Veronica wormskjoldii

Rhinanthus minor

Collinsia parviflora

Pedicularis bracteosa

Penstemon procerus

Verbascum thapsus

Castilleja miniata

Mimulus guttatus

Melampyrum lineare

Linaria genistifolia
spp. *dalmatica*

167

COMMON RED PAINTBRUSH • *Castilleja miniata*

GENERAL: Perennial, to 80 cm tall, with several usually unbranched flowering stems from a woody base.

LEAVES: Narrow and sharp-pointed, **linear to lance-shaped, usually without teeth or divisions,** but sometimes upper leaves have 3 shallow lobes.

FLOWERS: Showy, brush-like inflorescences with **hairy, bright red to scarlet bracts** partly concealing **greenish flowers with red tips; corollas are strongly 2-lipped; upper lip forms a hood** that is about as long as tubular part of corolla.

FRUITS: Capsules.

ECOLOGY: Widespread and most common at mid to high elevations in open dry to moist forests, open grassy slopes and disturbed soils, including roadsides.

SIMILAR SPECIES: Harsh paintbrush (*C. hispida*) has upper leaves that are deeply cleft into 3–7 linear lobes and its stems have stiff hairs. It occurs in dry, open forests and on grassy slopes at low to mid elevations, mostly in the dry climates of the southern half of our region.

NOTES: The Carrier Linguistic Committee (1974) reports that long ago, parents forbade children to pick red paintbrush because it was considered sacred. They often referred to it as 'fireweed.' The Nlaka'pmx knew it as 'hummingbird's sucking substance.' • The showy, red, leafy bracts, which are actually modified leaves, resemble a brush dipped in paint, hence the common name. It is also called Indian paintbrush. The species name *miniata* refers to the scarlet-red colour 'minium,' an oxide of lead.

ALPINE PAINTBRUSH • *Castilleja rhexifolia*

GENERAL: Perennial, 10–30 cm tall, with a cluster of stems from a woody base.

LEAVES: Linear to lance-shaped, **usually not toothed,** but upper leaves sometimes divided into 3 short, unequal lobes.

FLOWERS: Brush-like inflorescences with **crimson to scarlet, hairy, short-lobed bracts** (occasionally yellow) mostly concealing **fairly inconspicuous green flowers; corollas are strongly 2-lipped; upper lip forms a hood** that is usually shorter than tubular part of corolla.

FRUITS: 2-celled capsules.

ECOLOGY: Scattered at subalpine and alpine elevations throughout our region, mostly south of Williams Lake, in meadows and on rocky slopes.

SIMILAR SPECIES: Small-flowered paintbrush (*C. parviflora*) is also small (to 30 cm tall), has crimson to magenta flowers and is found at high elevations, but its bracts and leaves, except the few lowest ones, are deeply divided into 3–5 lobes.

• Alpine paintbrush is quite similar to common red paintbrush (*C. miniata*, above), but alpine paintbrush is restricted to high elevations, is smaller (less than 30 cm tall) and has blunt calyx lobes.

NOTES: The species name *rhexifolia* reflects the resemblance of the floral leaves to those of *Rhexia virginica*, the purple-coloured 'meadow beauty' of eastern North America.

FIGWORT

THOMPSON'S PAINTBRUSH • *Castilleja thompsonii*

GENERAL: Perennial, to 40 cm tall, with a cluster of hairy, **often branched stems** from a woody base.

LEAVES: Lower leaves are **linear, without lobes**; upper leaves have 1–2 pairs of long, narrow, **divergent lobes**.

FLOWERS: Brush-like inflorescences with **yellowish, hairy, lobed bracts**, broader than leaves **and greenish, inconspicuous flowers**, partly hidden among bracts; corollas are strongly 2-lipped; **lips nearly equal** to each other in length; **upper lip forms a hood.**

FRUITS: Many-seeded capsules.

ECOLOGY: Scattered and locally common at low to mid elevations in Thompson and Okanagan plateaus and basins and infrequent in southern Rocky Mountain Trench, in dry grasslands and open grassy slopes.

NOTES: The Okanagan dried and powdered the top of the plant and placed it on open cuts to draw out infections. • In many of our species the flowers are greenish and hidden among the bracts. The corollas are long and tubular, with the upper lip extended into a long, beaked hood that encloses the four anthers. The colour of the flower spike is helpful, but identification often depends on features that can be highly variable, such as the length of the upper corolla lip and the pattern of lobes on the leaves and bracts. • *Castilleja* species are extremely difficult to transplant because they are semi-parasitic on the roots of other plants. • The genus *Castilleja* was named after the Spanish botanist Domingo Castillejo.

YELLOW OWL-CLOVER • *Orthocarpus luteus*

GENERAL: Slender **annual**, to 40 cm tall, hairy, usually with a single **unbranched** stem.

LEAVES: Dark green, hairy and **linear**, usually **unlobed**.

FLOWERS: Brush-like inflorescences with broad, **3-lobed, green bracts with white or yellow tips, partially concealing golden yellow flowers**; corollas are 2-lipped, with a **sac-like lower lip**; upper lip forms a short, broad beak.

FRUITS: Many-seeded capsules.

ECOLOGY: Scattered at low to mid elevations of Fraser, Thompson and Okanagan basins, in grasslands and dry, open forests; less common in southern Rocky Mountain Trench.

SIMILAR SPECIES: Owl-clovers are very similar to paintbrushes (*Castilleja* spp., pp. 168–69) and may be readily confused with them. Like the paintbrushes, owl-clovers are also partial root-parasites. The main distinction between the two groups is that owl-clovers are annuals, while the paintbrushes in our area are all perennials. The corollas of owl-clover flowers differ slightly in that the upper lip does not extend much beyond the lower lip.

NOTES: The genus name is from the Greek *orthos* (straight) and *karpos* (fruit), and it refers to the symmetrical capsule. The species name *luteus* (Latin for 'yellow') refers to the flowers.

FIGWORT

BRACTED LOUSEWORT • *Pedicularis bracteosa*

GENERAL: Perennial, to 1 m tall, growing from a mix of coarse, fibrous and tuberous roots; with **unbranched stems**, hairless below inflorescence.

LEAVES: Finely divided or fern-like, with toothed edges, mostly **on flowering stems.**

FLOWERS: Yellowish, sometimes strongly **tinged red or purple**; with **2-lipped corolla**; **upper lip hooded,** beakless or with a short beak at tip; in a dense, **elongate cluster** above several hairy, leafy bracts.

FRUITS: Smooth, flattened, curved capsules.

ECOLOGY: Widespread and common, mostly at subalpine and alpine elevations, in moist open forest, openings, meadows and clearings; occasional in cool moist forests at mid elevations.

NOTES: Louseworts are perennial herbs that are mostly semi-parasitic on the roots of other species. Lousewort flowers are striking for their irregular forms. The strongly **two-lipped corollas are showy and they are not hidden by the leafy bracts**, as they are in paintbrushes. The upper lip forms a hood that arches over the four stamens and often extends into a prominent, sometimes spectacular beak. • Nlaka'pmx women incorporated the leaf pattern of bracted lousewort in basket designs. • Other common names for this plant are 'fernleaf' and 'wood betony.' 'Betony' comes from an old Gallic word meaning 'medicinal plant.' The species name *bracteosa* refers to the many bracts at the base of the flower cluster.

ELEPHANT'S HEAD LOUSEWORT • *Pedicularis groenlandica*

GENERAL: Perennial, 20–60 cm tall, with **clusters** of **unbranched**, sometimes reddish-purple stems, hairless.

LEAVES: Finely divided and fern-like with **sharply toothed divisions**; stem leaves are progressively smaller towards top of stem.

FLOWERS: Pink-purple to reddish, with 2-lipped corolla; **upper lip strongly hooded and beaked, resembling head and trunk of an elephant;** many flowers in a dense cluster at top of stem.

FRUITS: Smooth, flattened, curved capsules.

ECOLOGY: Scattered and infrequent at mid to subalpine elevations in wetlands, seepage areas and along streams.

SIMILAR SPECIES: Bird's-beak lousewort (*P. ornithorhyncha*) also has deeply divided, toothed leaves and reddish-purple flowers, but its **upper lip is extended into a straight beak**, 2–4 mm long, which resembles a bird's beak. It is primarily a coastal, high-elevation species, but it may be encountered in subalpine and alpine heaths and meadows along the western boundary of our region, and it is rare in the mountains to the east. • Langsdorf's lousewort (*P. langsdorfii*) also has purple flowers but its **upper lip is beakless and bears two slender teeth**. Its leaves bear coarse teeth and are almost the same size at the base and along the stem. This species occurs in alpine habitats in the northeastern part of our area.

NOTES: Elephant's head lousewort is one of the most peculiar of our flowers—its flower cluster truly resembles a cluster of pink elephant heads.

SICKLETOP LOUSEWORT • *Pedicularis racemosa*

GENERAL: Fibrous rooted perennial, 15–50 cm tall, with a **cluster of unbranched**, hairless to sparsely hairy stems.

LEAVES: Lance-shaped to linear, with **coarsely toothed edges**; lower leaves reduced in size.

FLOWERS: Creamy to pinkish white, with 2-lipped corolla; **upper lip strongly arched and tapering to a sickle-shape, down-curved beak;** in loose spike-like clusters, with lower flowers arising from bases of leaves.

FRUITS: Smooth, flattened, curved capsules.

ECOLOGY: Scattered and locally common at mid to subalpine elevations in coniferous forests, openings, and dry meadows.

SIMILAR SPECIES: Coil-beaked lousewort (*P. contorta*) is another lousewort with creamy-white flowers that is found at mid to high elevations. In our region it is restricted to the southern East Kootenays. The corollas of its flowers have strongly down-turned **upper lips which end in curved spurs.** The leaves are mainly basal and are deeply cleft.

NOTES: Many lousewort species are edible. Young stems and roots can be eaten raw or boiled until tender, but should only be eaten in an emergency. • The unmistakable sickle-shaped flowers give this plant its common name. The common name 'lousewort,' applied to most species of *Pedicularis*, dates back to the 17th century. It was formerly thought that cattle grazing in fields where lousewort (*P. sylvatica*) grew in abundance became infested with lice. It is more likely that these pastures were poor and supported weak, unhealthy and lice-ridden stock.

SMALL-FLOWERED BLUE-EYED MARY • *Collinsia parviflora*

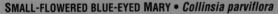

GENERAL: Slender annual, to 40 cm tall, with **long, weak stems,** covered with minute hairs.

LEAVES: Lower leaves are paired and spatula-shaped; upper leaves are often **in whorls** and linear to elliptic-shaped; edges are smooth or shallowly toothed.

FLOWERS: Very small, with 2-lipped corolla with pouch-like enlargement on upper side; upper lip **2-lobed, somewhat erect and pale blue to often white; lower lip 3-lobed and deep blue;** on hairy stalks arising from leaf axils as well as clustered at end of stem; blooms in spring.

FRUITS: Elliptic capsules, containing 1 to few seeds.

ECOLOGY: Widespread and locally common at low to mid elevations in Fraser, Thompson and Okanagan basins and southern Rocky Mountain Trench, in dry to moist ponderosa pine and Douglas-fir forests, openings and bunchgrass grasslands.

NOTES: *Collinsia* species are recognizable for the sharp bend at the base of the corolla tube. • This species is also called 'innocence.' The genus was named for the American botanist, Zacheus Collins (1764–1831). The species name *parviflora* means 'small-flowered.'

AMERICAN BROOKLIME • *Veronica americana*
V. beccabunga ssp. *americana*

GENERAL: Perennial, 10–70 cm long, from **shallow creeping rhizomes,** or rooting from **trailing stems**; flowering stems smooth, somewhat succulent and unbranched.

LEAVES: Opposite in **3–5 pairs on flowering stem, oval to lance-shaped**, with **toothed edges** and short stalks.

FLOWERS: Blue, violet or lilac; with **4 corolla lobes,** 1 noticeably the smallest; in **elongate clusters on long stalks** arising from leaf axils.

FRUITS: Round capsules.

ECOLOGY: Widespread at low to subalpine elevations and locally common on wet ground or in shallow water in wet forests, openings or clearings; absent from arid basins.

SIMILAR SPECIES: Marsh speedwell (*V. scutellata*) is also found in very wet areas at low to mid elevations. It has small blue flowers, its leaves are mainly stalkless and clasping and its flat, notched capsules are wider than long. • Speedwells are distinguished from other members of the figwort family by having two stamens.

NOTES: These leaves are edible and widely used as a salad vegetable and potherb. Care should be taken to avoid plants growing in polluted water. • Brooklimes have been used for centuries to treat urinary and kidney complaints and as a blood purifier. They have also been used to heal wounds and cure coughs. • The name 'brooklime' comes from Europe, where this plant grows along streams or brooks in wet mud where birds can become 'limed' (an expression for birds being trapped in sticky materials). The former species name *beccabunga* is from the Old German *Bachbungen*, meaning 'mouthsmart' or 'streamlet blocker.'

ALPINE SPEEDWELL • *Veronica wormskjoldii*

GENERAL: Perennial, 7–30 cm tall, from **shallow rhizomes**; flowering stems are unbranched, sparsely to densely **hairy, sticky among the flowers**.

LEAVES: Opposite along flowering stem, **elliptic to oval or lance-shaped,** rounded to pointed at tip, with **slightly toothed edges**.

FLOWERS: Blue-violet with cream-coloured centres; with **4 corolla lobes,** 1 noticeably the smallest, stalks sticky-glandular; few to several in a cluster at top of stem.

FRUITS: Heart-shaped, hairy capsules.

ECOLOGY: Scattered and locally common at low to high elevations in wetlands and seepage areas; absent from our warm, arid basins.

SIMILAR SPECIES: Cusick's speedwell (*V. cusickii*) is found on moist, open slopes at high elevations, often above timberline in Cathedral Lakes and Manning provincial parks. It has larger, showier flowers, with a protruding style, and hairless and more oval leaves than alpine speedwell.

NOTES: Speedwells are a group of annual or perennial herbs with **opposite leaves** and blue or white flowers. The flowers have four petals, usually with one noticeably smaller than the others. **There are only two stamens, a feature that distinguishes speedwells from other members of the figwort family in our area.** The mature seed capsules are often heart-shaped and strongly flattened. • The name 'speedwell' was applied originally to *V. officinalis*, which was used medicinally as a strengthening and wound-healing plant and against coughs. This species was named after Morten Wormskjold (1783–1845), a Danish lieutenant who collected the plant at Kodiak and Sitka.

YELLOW PENSTEMON • *Penstemon confertus*

GENERAL: Perennial, 20–50 cm tall, with **woody rhizomes**; flowering stems clustered, unbranched, smooth to finely hairy.

LEAVES: Oval to lance-shaped; **stem leaves opposite**, without stalks.

FLOWERS: Creamy white to pale yellow; with 2-lipped corolla; **lower lip is 3-cleft, hairy at the throat; upper lip is 2-cleft**; in 2–7 **whorl-like** clusters along upper stem.

FRUITS: Small capsules, with many small seeds.

ECOLOGY: Scattered at low to mid elevations throughout southern half of our region; common in open meadows and wetlands and on streambanks or seepage areas in forests.

NOTES: The Nlaka'pmx drank a decoction of the plant as a tonic and stomach remedy. • Beard-tongues are all perennials, easily appreciated for their showy, brightly coloured flowers. Beard-tongues have five petals fused into a corolla that **is tubular or trumpet-shaped with five flaring lobes at the tip. The lower three corolla lobes are grouped into a pronounced lip.** • The genus name *Penstemon* (five-thread) refers to the five stamens of the flowers, of which only four are fertile. The fifth, sterile stamen is often hairy and longer than the others. The throat and lower corolla lobes of many flowers are also very hairy, giving rise to another common name, 'beardtongue.' The species name *confertus* means 'crowded together.'

SMALL-FLOWERED PENSTEMON • *Penstemon procerus*

GENERAL: Perennial, to 40 cm tall, growing in clumps from a woody base.

LEAVES: Deep green, **oval to lance-shaped**, lacking teeth; **stem leaves opposite** and without stalks; basal leaves with short stalks.

FLOWERS: Blue-purple sometimes tinged pink (occasionally white), 8–12 mm long; corolla **small** and **not strongly 2-lipped**; in 1 to several tight clusters arranged in whorls around stem and at its tip.

FRUITS: Small capsules, with many seeds.

ECOLOGY: Scattered at low to alpine elevations; common in dry to moist open forests and clearings, grassy openings, meadows and disturbed areas; absent from our wet climates.

SIMILAR SPECIES: Chelan penstemon (*P. pruinosus*) has bigger blue flowers (over 13 mm long) and is generally hairier than small-flowered penstemon. Its leaves are sharply **toothed** and elliptic in shape. It occurs in sagebrush grasslands and dry, open forests in the southern Okanagan Basin and the southern Rocky Mountain Trench. • Coast penstemon (*P. serrulatus*) has even larger (17–28 mm long), deep blue to purple flowers. These are usually arranged in a **dense cluster at the top of the stem**, rather than in whorl-like clusters along the stem. It is uncommon along the western edge of our area at low to alpine elevations. • Richardson's penstemon (*P. richardsonii*) grows from a shrubby base with oval, **sharply serrated and pointed leaves** and has bright lavender flowers (22–32 mm long). It grows in dry, rocky places and cliff crevices in the south Okanagan valley.

NOTES: Small-flowered penstemon is also known as tall beard-tongue. The species name *procerus* means 'tall' in Latin.

173

YELLOW MONKEY-FLOWER • *Mimulus guttatus*

GENERAL: Annual or perennial, to 50 cm tall, **spreading by runners or by rooting along stem;** stems erect or trailing, but sometimes small and dwarfed.

LEAVES: Opposite, oval-shaped with **coarsely toothed edges,** smooth or covered with fine hairs; lower leaves are stalked; upper leaves clasp stem.

FLOWERS: Large, **bright yellow**, with **2-lipped, trumpet-shaped corolla** with **hairy throat;** lower corolla lobes have several crimson to brownish-red spots.

FRUITS: Many-seeded capsules, surrounded by **inflated calyx**.

ECOLOGY: Scattered at low to high elevations; commonly in wet seepage areas, wet shallow depressions and wet disturbed areas; absent from our arid climates.

SIMILAR SPECIES: Mountain monkey-flower (*M. tilingii*) is a small, perennial, somewhat creeping, alpine species with a few yellow flowers that are very much like those of yellow monkey-flower. The flowers look almost too big for the stems. Mountain monkey-flower occasionally grows in mossy seepage areas and along streambanks in the subalpine to alpine. • Purple-stemmed monkey-flower (*M. floribundus*), an annual, occurs infrequently in the southern half of our region. It has small, yellow flowers with red or maroon spots on a lower lip that is not noticeably larger than the upper. Its **leaves are densely hairy.** • Another lovely yellow-flowered species found in moist habitats in the southern half of our region is musk-flower (*M. moschatus*). Its leaves are covered in somewhat **slimy hairs and it is musk-scented.**

NOTES: Monkey-flowers can be recognized by their large flowers, which are borne on **stalks from the leaf bases.** The five petals are fused into tubular or trumpet-shaped corollas with five lobes flaring out from the top. The **five sepals are fused into a calyx that has a pleated appearance.** The leaves are opposite and may have toothed or smooth edges.

PINK MONKEY-FLOWER • *Mimulus lewisii*

GENERAL: Perennial, 30–80 cm tall, growing from **stout, branching rhizomes**; with clusters of robust,**sticky and softly hairy**, usually unbranched flowering stems.

LEAVES: Opposite, large, **oval**, with **sharply pointed tips, widely spaced teeth** along edges and conspicuous veins; upper leaves tend to clasp stem.

FLOWERS: Showy, large (3–5.5 cm long), rose-red to pale pink, with 2-lipped, trumpet-shaped corolla; lower **lobes marked with yellow** and a few hairs.

FRUITS: Oblong capsules.

ECOLOGY: Scattered at mid to subalpine elevations, mostly in wet Columbia Mountains and Coast/Interior Transition; locally common along streams and in wet, seepy, forest openings, clearings and along avalanche tracts.

SIMILAR SPECIES: Brewer's monkey-flower (*M. breweri*), a 15-cm-tall annual of dry, mid-elevation habitats near Rossland and Revelstoke, has narrow leaves and **small, pink to reddish** flowers, sometimes with yellow markings on the corolla lobes.

NOTES: Monkey-flowers have very sensitive, 2-lobed stigmas that will close if touched with a pin, straw, piece of grass or an insect's tongue, which is thought to help in pollination. • This species is sometimes called Lewis's monkey-flower. The genus name *Mimulus* means 'little actor.'

COW-WHEAT • *Melampyrum lineare*

GENERAL: Slender **annual**, 10–30 cm tall; stems simple or branched and glandular, especially in upper part.

LEAVES: Opposite, linear or lance-shaped, with short stalks.

FLOWERS: White or pinkish with a **yellow patch in throat**; **2-lipped corolla**; in axils of upper leaves or leafy bracts.

FRUITS: Curved, asymmetrical capsules, few-seeded.

ECOLOGY: Scattered and locally common at low to mid elevations on our plateaus and in wet Columbia Mountains, in dry to moist, somewhat open forests and grassy openings; commonly found under lodgepole pine on coarse, gravelly soils.

NOTES: Cow-wheat is host to stalactiform blister rust, which also attacks lodgepole pines in our area. • The name 'cow-wheat' was originally applied to the European species *M. arvense*, which was 'freely cropped by passing cattle, to which it was fed in times of scarcity.' Linnaeus claimed cows produced the yellowest butter after eating it. Another source says it is because the seed resembled wheat, but was useless to humans. Despite all this, our *M. lineare* is much too small and scattered to be a forage plant. The genus name *Melampyrum* is from the Greek *melas*, 'black,' and *pyros*, 'wheat,' and refers to the black seeds.

YELLOW RATTLE • *Rhinanthus minor*
R. crista-galli

GENERAL: Semi-parasitic **annual,** 15–80 cm tall, with **thinly hairy**, simple or few-branched stems.

LEAVES: Opposite, stalkless, all on stem, triangular-lance-shaped to oblong, with **toothed edges**.

FLOWERS: Yellow, with 2-lipped corolla; **upper lip forms a hood**; corolla is surrounded by a **flattened, inflated calyx**; arranged **in pairs** in a loose inflorescence at top of stem, with **leafy bracts below each pair**.

FRUITS: Round capsules inside **papery flattened calyx.**

ECOLOGY: Scattered at low to mid elevations mostly in our dry plateaus and East Kootenays; common in moist clearings, disturbed areas, grassy meadows and occasional in dry, open forests.

NOTES: Yellow rattle is semi-parasitic on the roots of neighbouring plants to obtain most of its water and minerals. • Yellow rattle, also called rattle box, gets its name from its yellow flowers and the rattling noise the mature seed capsules make when shaken. The genus name *Rhinanthus* is from the Greek *rhinos* (nose) and *anthos* (flower), in reference to the beak-like structure of the irregular flowers.

FIGWORT

GREAT MULLEIN • *Verbascum thapsus*

GENERAL: Coarse, taprooted **biennial**, to 2 m tall; single stem, **copiously hairy throughout**.

LEAVES: A **basal rosette of large, broadly lance-shaped, hairy** leaves; many stem leaves, **progressively smaller upwards**, stalkless and clasping stem.

FLOWERS: **Yellow, saucer-shaped**, with short corolla tubes and 5 spreading lobes; in a **dense, spike-like inflorescence** at top of stem.

FRUITS: Broadly **egg-shaped capsules**, with many minute seeds.

ECOLOGY: Widespread and common at low to mid elevations in disturbed, often gravelly sites, fields and pastures; mostly absent from wet Columbia Mountains.

NOTES: Great mullein is a biennial, living for two years. It produces a rosette of leaves in its first year and a tall flowering stalk in its second. It is of Eurasian origin and is widespread throughout much of our region. It can be recognized by its tall stalks, generally woolly demeanor and brown stalks that persist in winter. The soft-woolly leaves provide a good, natural toilet tissue! • Interior native peoples used to smoke the dried leaves. Greek legend has it that Ulysses, Hermes and Circe used this plant in their incantations and witchcraft. • 'Mullein' is from the Latin *mollis*, meaning 'soft,' and refers to the lovely, softly felted leaves. This species is also called woolly mullein. Two other common names, 'hedge-taper' and 'torch,' are derived from the practice of dipping the plant in suet and burning it as a candle or torch. The genus name *Verbascum is* from the Latin name for some species in this genus. It may be a corruption of *barbascum*, meaning 'bearded.' The species name *thapsus* is the name of an ancient town in the Mediterranean.

DALMATIAN TOADFLAX • *Linaria genistifolia* ssp. *dalmatica*

GENERAL: Robust perennial, 40–120 cm tall, with branched stem from a creeping root.

LEAVES: Numerous, **leathery**, **oval to broadly lance-shaped, clasp** stem.

FLOWERS: 2-lipped corolla, **bright yellow** with **hairy orange throats**; lower lip with a **long, narrow spur**; in a spike-like cluster.

FRUITS: Roundish capsules of winged seeds.

ECOLOGY: European native of low to mid elevations, especially with sandy soil; spreads rapidly on roadsides and dry, disturbed sites; a serious weed in some areas; generally absent from northern half of wet Columbia Mountains.

SIMILAR SPECIES: Common toadflax (*Linaria vulgaris*), also called butter-and-eggs, is another weedy Eurasian immigrant. Its **linear leaves do not clasp the stem**.

NOTES: The name 'toadflax' is thought to result from a mistake. It seems that common toadflax may have been used to treat 'buboes' (boils) and was known as *bubonio*. This somehow was transcribed as *bufonio*, meaning 'toad,' and from then on the plant became associated with toads. The genus name *Linaria* refers to the general similarity of the leaves of species in this genus to those of flax (*Linum* sp.). The species name *genistifolia* reflects the resemblance of the leaves to those of broom (*Genista* sp.). Dalmatian toadflax was originally given the scientific name *L. dalmatica* because it is thought to come from Dalmatia (on the eastern Adriatic coast).

Violaceae: Violet Family

The violets in our area are perennial herbs with showy, blue, violet, yellow or white flowers. The flowers have five petals, with **one petal typically developing into a spur-like pouch**. The leaves are broad, and they have rounded or heart-shaped bases and rounded or pointed tips. The leaf stalks usually have a pair of prominent basal appendages called **stipules**.

Violets occur in a variety of habitats, and in the field they are most easily distinguished on the basis of flower colour. If violets must be identified when they are not in flower, as is often the case, leaf and stem characteristics may be used. While all of our violets grow from an underground stem (rhizome), many also produce aerial stems which bear leaves and flowers. Some produce strawberry-like runners. The presence or absence of runners or aerial stems can help narrow down the number of possibilities.

The first showy blossoms of violets do not generally produce seeds. Most seeds are produced by flowers borne later in the season, either underground or right at the soil surface. These inconspicuous, greenish flowers do not open and are self-fertilized.

Violets have several unusual seed dispersal mechanisms. The capsule walls of some violet species (usually those with flowers held higher than the leaves) fold in on themselves as they dry, and eventually expel the seeds under pressure, catapulting them into the air. The seeds of other species have outgrowths that ants eat after carrying the seeds off and leaving them at some distance from the parent plant.

The leaves and flowers of all violet species can be eaten raw in salads, used as potherbs or made into a tea. Candied violet flowers are used for cake decorations. In the southern United States, the leaves are often added to soups as a thickening agent. The flowers and leaves of violets have long been used in various herbal remedies as poultices, laxatives for children and to relieve coughs and lung congestion.

Violets are associated with much folklore. If violets bloomed in August, it meant there was going to be a death or epidemic. It was also considered unlucky to bring only a small number of violets into the house because it was said to reduce the laying capacity of the hens. Spiteful neighbours might encourage children to take only one flower home so that only a single chick would hatch. Violets worn in a wreath around the neck were said to prevent drunkenness.

Pansies are violets; the name 'pansy' is from the French *pensée*, meaning a 'thought' or 'remembrance,' a notion similar to forget-me-not. The name 'violet' comes from the Latin *viola*.

Key to the violets

1a. Flowers yellow 2

    2a. Plants with leafy, aerial stems
from which flowers arise .... *V. glabella*

    2b. Plants with leaves and flowering
stems arising from a thickened stem base .... *V. orbiculata*

1b. Flowers white, blue or violet,
except at base of petals 3

    3a. Plants with leafy, aerial stems
from which flowers arise 4

        4a. Petals white to pale violet .... *V. canadensis*

        4b. Petals dark violet to purple .... *V. adunca*

    3b. Plants with leaves and flowering stems
arising from a thickened stem base or from runners 5

        5a. Plants with runners .... *V. palustris*

        5b. Plants lacking runners 6

            6a. Petals white .... *V. renifolia*

            6b. Petals bluish violet .... *V. nephrophylla*

VIOLET

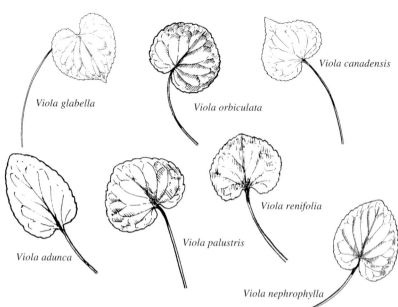

Viola glabella

Viola orbiculata

Viola canadensis

Viola adunca

Viola palustris

Viola renifolia

Viola nephrophylla

STREAM VIOLET • *Viola glabella*

GENERAL: Perennial, 5–30 cm tall, from **spreading, scaly, fleshy rhizomes**; with **aerial flowering stems**, leafless except on upper part.

LEAVES: Heart-shaped, with sharply **pointed tips**, and **toothed, usually hairy edges**.

FLOWERS: Yellow; 3 lower petals with purple lines; lowermost petal has a spur; lateral pair of petals white-bearded; flowers mostly on upper part of aerial stem.

FRUITS: Explosive capsules, containing brown seeds.

ECOLOGY: Scattered at low to subalpine elevations, mostly in moist and wet climates of our region; common in moist forests, openings, clearings and along streams; most abundant in wet subalpine.

NOTES: The species name *glabella* refers to the smooth leaves. Stream violet is also called yellow wood violet.

178

ROUND-LEAVED VIOLET • *Viola orbiculata*

GENERAL: Perennial, from **short, scaly rhizomes**; leafy aerial stems lacking or less than 5 cm tall.

LEAVES: Lying flat on ground, dark green, often remaining green over winter; **oval to nearly circular, heart-shaped at base, with toothed edges.**

FLOWERS: Lemon-yellow to gold; 3 lower petals with purplish pencil markings; lateral pair of petals yellow-bearded; lowest petal has a short, sac-like spur.

FRUITS: Capsules.

ECOLOGY: Widespread and common at low to subalpine elevations in moist coniferous forests, clearings and occasionally in meadows; absent from arid basins.

SIMILAR SPECIES: Trailing yellow violet (*V. sempervirens*) is found only in the Kootenay Lake area in our region. It generally has runners and thicker, leathery leaves which are often purple-spotted and also remain green through the winter.

NOTES: The species name *orbiculata* means 'round-leaved.'

CANADA VIOLET • *Viola canadensis*

GENERAL: Perennial, 10–40 cm tall, from **short, thick rhizomes, often with slender creeping runners; with leafy aerial stems.**

LEAVES: Heart-shaped, long stalked, with **sharply pointed tips** and **saw-toothed edges,** usually hairy on 1 or both surfaces.

FLOWERS: White with yellow bases; lower 3 petals with purple lines; upper 2 petals (sometimes all petals) **purplish tinged on back;** lateral petals bearded; flowers **borne on aerial stems.**

FRUITS: Capsules, containing brown seeds.

ECOLOGY: Scattered and locally common at low to mid elevations on our plateaus, in wet Columbia Mountains and in East Kootenays, in moist to fairly dry, usually deciduous, forests, often on floodplains and in clearings.

NOTES: These violets are easily propagated from runners or sections of rhizomes and are often invasive in a garden setting.

EARLY BLUE VIOLET • *Viola adunca*

GENERAL: Perennial, with slender **rhizomes** of variable length; **aerial stems usually lacking in early part of season, later developing to 10 cm tall.**

LEAVES: Generally **oval, with heart-shaped bases** and **finely round-toothed edges**.

FLOWERS: Blue to deep violet, 0.5–1.5 cm long; **lower 3 petals often white at base;** irregular; lowest petal **has a prominent slender spur half its length; style head bearded;** flowers borne on leafy aerial stems.

FRUITS: Small, 3-valved capsules.

ECOLOGY: Widespread at low elevations to near timberline but most frequent on our dry plateaus and in East Kootenays; common in various habitats, including dry to moist meadows, open woods, grasslands and open disturbed ground.

SIMILAR SPECIES: Alaska violet (*V. langsdorfii*) is also blue-flowered. Its flowers are larger (1.5–2.5 cm long) than early blue violet's, and have shorter, thicker spurs (less than half as long as the lowest petal). It also lacks the bearded styles.

NOTES: The species name *adunca* means 'hooked,' in reference to the slender spur.

KIDNEY-LEAVED VIOLET • *Viola renifolia*

GENERAL: Perennial, from short, generally erect **rhizomes, without** spreading runners or leafy aerial stems.

LEAVES: All basal, heart- to kidney-shaped, with round-toothed edges, hairy at least underneath.

FLOWERS: Pure white; lower 3 petals with purple pencil markings; all petals beardless; lowermost petal has a very short spur; flower stalks arise directly from base of plant, shorter than leaf stalks; blooming in spring and summer, very early after snowmelt.

FRUITS: Capsules.

ECOLOGY: Scattered at mid to subalpine elevations in our moist and wet climates; locally common in moist, cool, coniferous forests and forested wetlands.

SIMILAR SPECIES: Marsh violet (*V. palustris*) is also **white-flowered** and is found in moist, swampy habitats. Its flowers are similar in size (1–1.5 cm) to those of kidney-leaved violet, and its leaves are very similar in shape. Its petals are sparsely bearded and generally tinged with violet or blue on the back. The lowest petal has a conspicuous, sac-like spur. It also generally **has runners.** • Northern bog violet (*V. nephrophylla*) is a more robust species that has round to kidney-shaped leaves up to 7 cm broad with stalks 5–25 cm long. It has prominently bearded, **bluish-violet flowers** (the lower three petals can be more or less whitish at the base) and occurs in wet habitats at mid to high elevations.

NOTES: The species name *renifolia* means 'kidney-leaved.'

BUTTERWORT • *Pinguicula vulgaris*

GENERAL: Insectivorous perennial, 3–16 cm tall, with fibrous roots.

LEAVES: Greenish yellow and fleshy, in a **basal rosette,** broadly lance-shaped to elliptic with smooth, **inrolled edges; greasy-slimy on upper surface.**

FLOWERS: Irregular, solitary; lavender-purple, funnel-shaped **corolla** has unequal lobes, **prominent spurs** and white hairs in throat; nodding on a **leafless, sticky stem.**

FRUITS: Round capsules.

ECOLOGY: Scattered and infrequent at low to subalpine elevations in wet sites, including fens, swamps, bogs, mossy seeps, subalpine meadows and rocky drip-faces.

NOTES: Butterworts usually grow on sites that are low in available nutrients, and they supplement their diet with insects. Insects stick to the upper slimy surfaces of the leaves. The leaf edges tend to roll inward and prevent the insects from escaping. The plant secretes juices that digest an insect's soft tissues. • Butterwort supposedly encouraged or protected the milk-producing capacity of cows, ensuring a supply of butter. Yorkshire farm women anointed the chapped udders of cows with butterwort juice. Butterwort was also thought to protect cows from elf arrows, and human beings from witches and fairies. • The name 'butterwort' comes from the leaves, which feel as if melted butter has been poured over them. The genus name is from the Latin *pinguis*, 'fat.'

FLAT-LEAVED BLADDERWORT • *Utricularia intermedia*

GENERAL: Submerged aquatic perennial, with slender stems and **air bladders on specialized branches.**

LEAVES: 3-parted at base and then much divided into **unequal, linear segments.**

FLOWERS: Irregular, yellow corolla with 2-lips and a spur; lower lip covers throat opening, hiding stamens and pistil; **2–4 flowers nodding in a loose cluster** at top of a long bare stalk emerging above water.

FRUITS: Capsules.

ECOLOGY: Scattered at low to mid elevations in shallow, standing or slowly-moving water, commonly creeping along bottom.

SIMILAR SPECIES: Greater bladderwort (*U. vulgaris,* **photo**) has leaf segments that are rounded in cross-section, with the air bladders directly attached to them. The flowers are larger (lower lip 1–2 cm long) than those of flat-leaved bladderwort (lower lip 8–12 mm long). • Lesser bladderwort (*U. minor*) is a small species of bogs and lakes. It also has its air bladders on the leaves, rather than on specialized stems, and it has smaller flowers than either greater bladderwort or flat-leaved bladderwort (lower lip only 4–8 mm long).

NOTES: The genus name is from the Latin *utriculus*, 'a little bag,' and refers to the air bladders. The bladders are borne on specialized, leafless branches. They have trap doors and trigger hairs, which serve to trap aquatic insects that then provide the plants with a supplementary source of nitrogen.

Boraginaceae: Borage Family

The borages in our area are annual or perennial herbs with simple leaves. Most species are hairy, often coarsely so. Their flowers are regular in form, with a corolla of fused petals. The corolla is commonly funnel-shaped, with five spreading lobes at the top. There are often five hairy appendages (**fornices**) at the base of the corolla lobes. **The fruits are four nutlets, which may have distinctive ridges or prickles.**

TALL BLUEBELLS • *Mertensia paniculata*
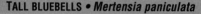

GENERAL: Tall perennial, 20–100 cm tall, with 1 to several stems from a somewhat woody base, hairy to hairless.

LEAVES: Basal leaves **long-stalked** and **heart-shaped** with **prominent veins**, often coarsely hairy on both sides; becoming more or less stalkless and lance- to egg-shaped upward.

FLOWERS: Blue, pinkish at first (rarely white), **bell-shaped** corolla, with style barely protruding from corolla tube; few to many-flowered, **drooping clusters** in an open, branching inflorescence.

FRUITS: 4 small **wrinkled nutlets**.

ECOLOGY: Scattered and infrequent at mid to subalpine elevations in moist open forest, streambanks, gravel bars, moist meadows and thickets.

SIMILAR SPECIES: Long-flowered mertensia (*M. longiflora*) is smaller (usually under 20 cm tall) than tall bluebells and blooms earlier. The leaves **lack distinct lateral veins**. It occurs in grasslands and open ponderosa pine forests in the southern half of our region.

NOTES: The leaves can be added to soups and casseroles and the flowers can be eaten fresh in salads. • Tall bluebells is sometimes called tall lungwort because of its similarity to the European lungwort (*Pulmonaria officinalis*), a plant believed to be good for lung diseases. The genus *Mertensia* was named for F.C. Mertens (1764–1831), a German botanist.

COMMON HOUND'S-TONGUE • *Cynoglossum officinale*

GENERAL: Coarse, **softly hairy biennial or short-lived perennial**, 30–90 cm tall, with a single stem.

LEAVES: Oblong to lance-shaped and **softly hairy**; upper leaves stalkless and clasping stem; basal rosette of large, oval and pointed, softly hairy leaves in first season.

FLOWERS: Reddish purple, funnel-shaped, with **prominent fornices**; in **long, 1-sided, often drooping clusters**.

FRUITS: 4 nutlets, densely covered with barbed prickles.

ECOLOGY: A serious weed introduced from Europe, reported at low to mid elevations in waste places, pastures and damp, semi-shaded areas.

NOTES: The hooked seeds are effectively dispersed by clinging to wool, hair and clothing. They can cause stress to cattle when large quantities attach to their faces. • In the old days hound's-tongue was used for skin diseases and dog bites. A piece placed in the shoe was believed to protect you from being barked at by strange dogs. • The name 'hound's-tongue,' from the Old English *hundes tunge*, was given to this species because the shape and rough texture of the leaves make them resemble a dog's tongue. The genus name is from the Greek *cynos*, 'a dog,' and *glossa*, 'a tongue.'

VIPER'S BUGLOSS • *Echium vulgare*

GENERAL: Bristly hairy, **taprooted biennial,** 30–60 cm tall, with a single, dark stem.

LEAVES: Bristly hairy, **narrow,** lance-shaped, stalked at base of stem, becoming smaller and stalkless upwards.

FLOWERS: Bright blue, funnel-shaped corolla opening into 5 **unequal lobes** (2 large and 3 small), with stamens protruding beyond lobes; **bristly hairy calyx;** inflorescence is an **elongated spike of small, bristly clusters** of flowers at base of upper stem leaves.

FRUITS: 4 **roughened** nutlets.

ECOLOGY: Introduced southern European weed, widely scattered at low elevations in waste places and roadsides.

NOTES: Viper's bugloss is also called blueweed. • The genus name is from the Greek, *echion*, which in turn comes from *echis*, meaning 'a viper.'

WESTERN STICKSEED • *Lappula redowskii*

GENERAL: Annual or occasionally biennial, 5–40 cm tall, with simple to branched stems, **short-hairy** throughout.

LEAVES: Linear to oblong; basal leaves often withering before flowers open.

FLOWERS: Small, **blue or white,** with **funnel-shaped** corolla; on short stalks at bases of stem leaves.

FRUITS: 4 nutlets, with **conspicuous barb-tipped prickles** on edges.

ECOLOGY: Scattered and often common at low elevations in our arid basins and southern Rocky Mountain Trench; often weedy, on dry to mesic disturbed sites, roadsides and overgrazed pastures.

SIMILAR SPECIES: Bristly stickseed (*L. echinata*) is common in our area on dry to moist, disturbed sites. It has nutlets with **two rows of prickles** along the edges rather than the single row found on western stickseed fruits.

NOTES: The genus name *Lappula* is the diminutive of the Latin *lappa* (a bur) and refers to the prickly fruits. The common name describes how the fruits catch readily on clothing and animal hair. The species name honours Ivan Redowski (1774–1807), a Russian botanist.

BORAGE

BLUE STICKSEED • *Hackelia micrantha*
H. jessicae

GENERAL: Taprooted, usually **coarsely hairy perennial, 30–100 cm tall, with several stems from a branching woody crown.**

LEAVES: Coarsely hairy, stalked and reverse lance-shaped to elliptic at base of stem, becoming smaller and stalkless upwards.

FLOWERS: Blue, with a yellow or whitish eye at centre; with short corolla tubes (4–7 mm long) opening abruptly into 5 lobes; many flowers in short, broad, loose clusters.

FRUITS: 4 nutlets with **barbed prickles** along edges and sides.

ECOLOGY: Scattered and infrequent at low to mid elevations on dry to moist sites, forest openings and clearings, mid-elevation grasslands and meadows.

SIMILAR SPECIES: Many-flowered stickseed (*H. floribunda*) is a hairy, **biennial** of moist to mesic sites at low elevations. It has blue flowers, with yellow eyes, borne in inflorescences that tend to be longer and narrower than those of blue stickseed. It has prickles only on the edges of the nutlets.

NOTES: Blue stickseed is also known as blue hackelia. • The genus is named in honour of Joseph Hackel (1783–1869), a Czech botanist.

MOUNTAIN FORGET-ME-NOT • *Myosotis alpestris*
M. asiatica

GENERAL: Low perennial, 10–30 cm tall, with more or less erect, densely clustered, hairy stems and withered leaves at base.

LEAVES: Basal leaves **spoon- to lance-shaped, stalked and hairy**; stem leaves shorter, more lance-shaped and **stalkless**.

FLOWERS: Bright blue (rarely white) **with a yellow centre**, corolla has short tube with erect fornices at bases of the 5 spreading lobes; all flowers arise **from 1 side of stem.**

FRUITS: 4 **black, shiny** and blunt nutlets.

ECOLOGY: Scattered in subalpine and alpine; often common in moist meadows and tundra.

SIMILAR SPECIES: Small-flowered forget-me-not (*M. laxa*) is found in moist, open areas, ditches and lake or stream sides at low elevations. It has small, pale blue flowers and thin, often prostrate stems.

NOTES: This attractive small, high-elevation plant is the state flower of Alaska. • One source says the common name 'forget-me-not' dates back to 1561. Traditionally a blue flower was worn to retain a lover's affection. Another source says the name was originally applied to the ground pine (*Ajuga chamaepitys*) because of the nauseating taste it left in one's mouth. There seems to be a great deal of confusion as to exactly how the name came to be transferred to *Myosotis* species. The genus name comes from the Greek *mus* (a mouse) and *ous* (an ear), in reference to the soft, long-hairy leaves.

SMALL-FLOWERED FIDDLENECK • *Amsinckia menziesii*

GENERAL: Taprooted, **bristly hairy annual, 15–70 cm tall,** with weak, simple to much-branched stems.

LEAVES: Linear to oblong, bristly hairy; basal leaves often drying before flowering.

FLOWERS: Small (2–3 mm wide), light yellow, with funnel-shaped corolla; in **coiled spikes.**

FRUITS: 4 egg-shaped, **wrinkled and warty** nutlets.

ECOLOGY: Scattered and infrequent at low to mid elevations in moist to dry disturbed sites and clearings.

SIMILAR SPECIES: Common fiddleneck (*A. intermedia*) is frequently found on roadsides and clearings at low to mid elevations. Its yellow to orange **flowers are larger** (0.5–1 cm wide) than those of small-flowered fiddleneck.

NOTES: The flowers are arranged like the **scroll-neck of a fiddle and unfurl with the youngest flowers at the tip.** • The genus was named for Wilhelm Amsinck, a patron of Hamburg Botanical Gardens in the 1800s, and the species was named for Archibald Menzies, an explorer of northwestern North America.

LEMONWEED • *Lithospermum ruderale*

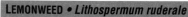

GENERAL: Hairy perennial, 20–60 cm tall, with several leafy stems clustered on a coarse **woody taproot.**

LEAVES: All on stem, linear to lance-shaped; **lower ones reduced** in size.

FLOWERS: Light yellow corolla with short tube (4–6 mm long) and 5 spreading lobes; in few-flowered clusters at bases of upper leaves.

FRUITS: 4 hard, smooth, **white** nutlets, with **prominent ridges** across top; often only 1–2 nutlets mature.

ECOLOGY: Widespread at low elevations in warm, dry parts of our region; locally common in open grasslands, open forests and rocky areas.

SIMILAR SPECIES: Yellow gromwell (*L. incisum*), typically a Great Plains species, occurs in the southeastern part and arid basins of our region. Its bright **yellow flowers are larger** (tubes 1.5–3 cm long) and more conspicuous than those of lemonweed. These flowers produce few nutlets. Inconspicuous flowers develop further down the stem later in the season and produce most of the nutlets. • The annual corn gromwell (*L. arvense*) is an introduced Eurasian weed. It has small, **white or bluish-white** flowers and wrinkled, pitted nutlets.

NOTES: The Okanagan drank an infusion of lemonweed roots to stop internal bleeding. They also used the plant as a charm to make it rain, while the Nlaka'pmx used the same plant to stop thunderstorms. The Nlaka'pmx also used the seeds as decorative beads. • The name 'lemonweed' refers to the pale lemon-coloured flowers. Another name, 'puccoon,' is from an Algonkian name given to many plants that were used to yield a red or yellow dye (from the word *pakon* or *pak* meaning 'blood'). The genus name *Lithospermum* comes from the Greek, *lithos* (a stone) and *sperma* (a seed) and refers to the hard nutlets. The species name *ruderale* is Latin for 'growing among rubbish.' Lemonweed is also called Columbia gromwell.

Campanulaceae: Harebell Family

In our region, the harebell family contains mostly perennial herbs with **blue to purple, bell-shaped flowers**. The flowers have tubular or bell-shaped corollas that may be divided and irregular. The leaves are simple, without lobes or divisions, but generally have toothed edges.

MOUNTAIN HAREBELL • *Campanula lasiocarpa*

GENERAL: Perennial, 2–15 cm tall **(usually less than 10 cm)**, with 1 to several flowering stems from a thin, branching rhizome.

LEAVES: Basal leaves small and more or less **egg-shaped** with **sharply toothed edges**; stem leaves narrower.

FLOWERS: Solitary, large (18–30 mm long), **bell-shaped, deep lilac-blue; calyx hairy**, with narrow, toothed lobes.

FRUITS: Erect, **papery capsules** covered with hairs.

ECOLOGY: Widespread and common in high subalpine and alpine areas, on stony slopes and scree in subalpine meadows, alpine tundra and heath.

SIMILAR SPECIES: Arctic harebell (*C. uniflora*) is a dwarf alpine species that grows to 10 cm tall. It is much less common than mountain harebell and has a flower that is smaller (6–12 mm long), much narrower and more funnel-shaped. The lobes of the calyx are smooth, and the leaves are not toothed but merely wavy around the edges.

NOTES: The flowers of mountain harebell are disproportionately large for such a tiny plant. • The genus name *Campanula* is the diminutive of the Latin *campana* (a bell) and refers to the shape of the flower.

COMMON HAREBELL • *Campanula rotundifolia*

GENERAL: Perennial, **10–50 cm tall**, with slender flowering stems from a slender, branched woody base or taproot.

LEAVES: Basal leaves oval to heart-shaped, long-stalked and coarsely toothed, usually **withering before flowers appear**; stem leaves are thin, **linear** or lance-shaped, smooth-edged or toothed.

FLOWERS: Purplish blue, rarely white, bell-shaped, with **hairless sepals**; nodding on thin wiry stems in a **loose cluster**.

FRUITS: Nodding oblong capsules.

ECOLOGY: Widespread and infrequent at low to subalpine elevations in a wide variety of habitats, including grassy slopes, gullies, moist forests, openings, clearings and rocky open ground.

NOTES: Common harebell is a very variable species. It ranges from 50 cm tall at low elevations to only 10 cm at high elevations. Its leaves are long and sparsely hairy on wet sites, but much shorter and hairier on dry ones. • The foliage contains alkaloids and is avoided by browsing animals. • The Nlaka'pmx used a concoction of this plant as an eyewash against sore eyes, and also used the flower as a charm.

KALM'S LOBELIA • *Lobelia kalmii*

GENERAL: Fibrous rooted perennial, 10–40 cm tall, with **slender, sometimes branched stems**.

LEAVES: Basal leaves are spatula-shaped, usually **withering before flowers appear**; stem leaves **thin and linear**.

FLOWERS: Blue with a white (sometimes yellow) eye; corolla 2-lipped; lower lip larger and 3-lobed; upper lip narrowly 2-lobed; 1 to few in a loose cluster at tip of stem.

FRUITS: Elliptic capsules.

ECOLOGY: Scattered and infrequent at mid elevations, mostly in southeastern part of our region, in wet areas, sphagnum bogs, stream and lake shores and wet meadows.

NOTES: The genus *Lobelia* was named after Mattias de L'Obel (1538–1616), a Flemish botanist who was a physician to James I. The species name honours Pehr Kalm (1716–79), a pupil of Linnaeus who travelled and collected extensively in Canada.

NORTHERN GENTIAN • *Gentianella amarella*
Gentiana acuta

GENERAL: Taprooted annual or biennial, 10–40 cm tall; erect, simple to branched stems.

LEAVES: Basal leaves **elliptic or lance- to spoon-shaped**; 5–8 **pairs of lance-shaped stem leaves**; often purplish in colour.

FLOWERS: Violet to pinkish, rarely white; **tubular corolla with a fringe of hairs in throat**; inflorescence of several to many flowers in clusters at ends of long, smooth branches.

FRUITS: Cylindrical capsules.

ECOLOGY: Widespread and common at low to subalpine elevations in open woods, thickets, meadows, clearings and generally moist areas.

SIMILAR SPECIES: Four-parted gentian (*Gentianella propinqua*) is a very similar plant. The main difference between these two little annual gentians is that the **flowers of four-parted gentian do not have a fringe of hairs** in their throats, and the tips of their petals have a much sharper point than those of northern gentian.

NOTES: The gentians are annuals or perennials with showy flowers and simple, paired leaves. The flowers have four or five united sepals and the same number of petals, which are fused into a tubular-shaped corolla. In some species the corolla has folds between the lobes or fringes in the throat.

Hydrophyllaceae: Waterleaf Family

The waterleaf family includes annual and perennial herbs. The plants are generally hairy throughout and often have compound leaves. The flowers have five sepals and petals. The sepals are usually narrow and hairy, joined only at the base. The petals are united into a funnel-shaped to almost tubular corolla with blunt lobes. **In many species the style and stamens extend beyond the corolla, giving the inflorescence a fuzzy look**.

BALLHEAD WATERLEAF • *Hydrophyllum capitatum*

GENERAL: Loosely hairy perennial, 10–40 cm tall, with a short, deep rootstock and slender fleshy roots, 1 or a few stems.

LEAVES: Mostly basal, on long stalks; blades large and **deeply divided** into 7–11 leaflets.

FLOWERS: Purplish blue, or occasionally white; **funnel-shaped, with style and stamens protruding** beyond corolla; inflorescence is a **compact round head** on a short stalk; blooms from early spring.

FRUITS: Capsules.

ECOLOGY: Scattered and infrequent at low to mid elevations in Thompson and Okanagan plateaus and East Kootenays, in thickets, grasslands, woodlands and moist slopes.

SIMILAR SPECIES: Ballhead waterleaf can be distinguished from the phacelias (*Phacelia* spp., below & p. 189) by its fuzzy, ball-shaped inflorescence.

NOTES: Native peoples of the Interior plateau ate the roots of ballhead waterleaf. • 'Ballhead' is a translation of *capitatum* and refers to the lovely, rounded heads of flowers. 'Waterleaf' is a direct translation of the Greek, *hydro* (water) and *phyllos* (a leaf).

SILVERLEAF PHACELIA • *Phacelia hastata*

GENERAL: Taprooted perennial, to 50 cm tall, from a woody branched base with several prostrate to almost erect, finely **silver haired** stems.

LEAVES: Elliptic, sometimes with a pair of small, lateral lobes near base, with **prominent veins**, mildly **silvery-bristly**.

FLOWERS: White to lavender, funnel-shaped with **stamens protruding** beyond corolla; inflorescence a **compact cluster**.

FRUITS: Capsules.

ECOLOGY: Scattered and locally common at low to subalpine elevations in arid basins and East Kootenays, in open, dry, gravelly sites, roadsides and railway rights-of-way.

SIMILAR SPECIES: Diverse-leaved phacelia (*P. heterophylla*) is 20–120 cm tall and has greyish-green (not silvery), bristly leaves, often with additional basal lobes. It grows in dry grasslands up to mid elevations in the southern part of our region.

NOTES: Species identification can be difficult in some of the highly variable *Phacelia*s. Our common species can be distinguished by their leaf and inflorescence shapes. The length of the stamens is also a useful character. • This plant is called 'silverleaf' because of the fine silvery pubescence on the leaves. The species name *hastata*, from the Latin *hastatus*, 'a spear,' suggests that the leaves, at least some of them, are shaped like a triangular spear-head.

THREAD-LEAVED PHACELIA • *Phacelia linearis*

GENERAL: Densely hairy annual, 10–50 cm tall.

LEAVES: Along stem, linear, often with a pair of lateral lobes near base.

FLOWERS: Bright lavender-blue, broadly funnel-shaped, with stamens about as long as petals; in **crowded clusters**; blooms from early spring.

FRUITS: Capsules, releasing coarsely pitted seeds.

ECOLOGY: Scattered and locally common at low elevations in Fraser, Thompson and Okanagan basins, in dry open forests, openings, sagebrush grasslands and alkaline flats.

NOTES: The genus name *Phacelia* is from the Greek *phakelos,* a 'fascicle' or 'dense bundle,' and refers to the tightly clustered flower heads on some species. The common name is a translation of the species name.

SILKY PHACELIA • *Phacelia sericea*

GENERAL: Taprooted perennial, 10–40 cm tall, with a branching woody base and several stems; stems and leaves covered in **silky, silver hairs**.

LEAVES: Deeply divided into many linear to oblong lobes, **feather-like**.

FLOWERS: Violet-blue, broadly funnel-shaped with **stamens protruding well past corolla**; inflorescence a **long dense cluster of coiled branches**.

FRUITS: Capsules, releasing pitted seeds.

ECOLOGY: Scattered at mid to high elevations on our plateaus, in wet Columbia mountains and in East Kootenays; locally abundant in dry, open, rocky places, open woods, ridges and meadows.

NOTES: The dense silky, silver hairs on the leaves provide a wonderful contrast for the deep purple flowers with their protruding, bright yellow stamens. • Many phacelias are well suited as rock garden ornamentals and are best propagated from seeds. • Another common name, 'scorpionweed,' may come from the resemblance of the coiled branches of flowers to a scorpion's tail.

SPREADING DOGBANE • *Apocynum androsaemifolium*

GENERAL: Rhizomatous perennial, 20–50 cm tall, branched stems with **milky sap**.

LEAVES: Opposite, simple, oval to oblong lance-shaped, spreading and drooping, hairless above.

FLOWERS: Small, pink, bell-shaped corolla with spreading lobes, showy and sweet-scented; in clusters at top of stem and on side branches.

FRUITS: Paired, long (5–12 cm), narrow, **cylindrical pods** that split lengthwise when mature, releasing many seeds with long t**ufts of cottony hairs**.

ECOLOGY: Scattered and often common at low to mid elevations in warm, well-drained soils, open hillsides, ridges, roadsides, clearings and dry open forest.

NOTES: A close look at the pink flowers will reveal deeper pink lines (honey guides) to lead insects into them. Inside the flowers are five peg-shaped nectaries that are visited by large butterflies and bees. • The plant is **toxic** to livestock, and sickness and death have been reported from its use for medicinal purposes. • The native peoples preferred to get fibre from the related hemp dogbane (*A. cannabinum*) because that bush is larger and the fibres are longer and tougher. But where hemp dogbane was not available, they would use spreading dogbane as a poor substitute. • The name 'dogbane' may come, in part, from the fact that the milky sap is very bitter and the plant is avoided by browsing animals.

HEMP DOGBANE • *Apocynum cannabinum*

GENERAL: Rhizomatous perennial, 30–100 cm tall, with smooth, often reddish, stems with **milky sap**.

LEAVES: Opposite, yellowish green, erect, oval to oblong lance-shaped, finely pointed at tips, short-stalked, hairless.

FLOWERS: Very small, greenish white, with a tube-shaped corolla and green calyx often more than half as long as corolla; in clusters at end of stems and in stem branches.

FRUITS: Pairs of very long (12–18 cm), narrow, **cylindrical pods**; many seeds with long **tufts of cottony hairs**.

ECOLOGY: Scattered and infrequent at low to mid elevations in arid basins and East Kootenays, in dry sites, roadsides and forest openings.

NOTES: Hemp dogbane contains very bitter glycosides and resins that discourage animals from browsing it. These substances are **toxic** to humans and livestock. • This plant was the most important source of fibre for Interior native groups. The stems were harvested in autumn and the inner fibrous parts of the bark removed and dried in the wind. The fibres were separated and formed into twine for a great variety of uses, such as fish nets, animal traps, sewing, weaving baskets and generally holding things together. Because of its importance in technology, hemp dogbane, also called Indian hemp, was a much-desired trade item among native peoples.

Polemoniaceae: Phlox Family

The phlox family consists of annual or perennial herbs and small shrubs. Phlox flowers are often showy. They are **regular and have five united sepals and five united petals**. The corolla lobes are generally rounded and spreading. The calyx lobes are often pointed and sometimes spiny. The leaves may be simple or pinnately compound and often narrow and linear. The fruits are capsules.

The family is generally easy to recognize. The calyx is either green throughout or consists of green ribs separated by nearly transparent sections. The stamens are borne on the inside of the corolla tube. In some species they are unequal in length and are inserted at uneven heights inside the tube.

NARROW-LEAVED COLLOMIA • *Collomia linearis*

GENERAL: Annual, 10–60 cm tall, with **hairy stems**, somewhat **sticky above**.

LEAVES: Along stem, **lance-shaped to linear**, almost stalkless; leaves beneath flower clusters are broader than those further down stem.

FLOWERS: Pink, bluish or white, in a cluster at top of stem; corolla has a slender tube and short lobes with **stamens unequally inserted** in tube; **calyx green throughout**.

FRUITS: Capsules, with 1 seed per chamber.

ECOLOGY: Scattered and infrequent at low to mid elevations, mostly in dry climates of southern half of region, in moist to dry forests, openings and moist meadows.

SIMILAR SPECIES: Large-flowered collomia (*C. grandiflora*) is frequently found in similar habitats in the southern part of our region. It is generally more robust than narrow-leaved collomia with **larger, salmon pink flowers**.

NOTES: Large-flowered collomia was used by the Okanagan as a laxative and purgative. A decoction of the leaves was used as an eyewash and skin toner. • The genus *Collomia* is named from the Greek *colla*, 'glue,' referring to the stickiness of the moistened seeds.

PINK TWINK • *Microsteris gracilis*

GENERAL: Taprooted **annual**, to 30 cm tall, with simple to much-branched stems.

LEAVES: Lowest leaves often oval and opposite, becoming linear to lance-shaped and alternate above; stalkless.

FLOWERS: White to yellowish corolla tube with **pink to lavender lobes**; **stamens unequally inserted** in tube; calyx glandular hairy with **5 green ribs separated by transparent segments**; flowers solitary or opposite at end of stem branches; blooms in spring.

FRUITS: Capsules.

ECOLOGY: Scattered and infrequent at low to mid elevations on Thompson and Okanagan plateaus and in arid basins, in dry to moderately moist open forests, floodplains, grasslands, streamsides and meadows.

NOTES: The genus *Microsteris* contains this single variable species. • Pink twink is also called pink microsteris. The genus name is from the Greek *mikros*, 'small,' and *sterizo*, 'to support,' and refers to the small size of the plant.

SCARLET GILIA • *Ipomopsis aggregata*
Gilia aggregata

GENERAL: Biennial or short-lived perennial, 20–100 cm tall, with 1 to several stems, **sticky hairy on upper part.**

LEAVES: Pinnately dissected into narrow segments, to 10 cm long; gradually reduced upwards; emit a strong skunk-like odour when crushed.

FLOWERS: Brilliant scarlet, showy, in a loose inflorescence; corolla is a **long tube** with spreading lobes; **calyx of short green ribs and transparent segments**.

FRUITS: Capsules.

ECOLOGY: Scattered and locally common at low to moderately high elevations in our arid climates south of Kamloops, in open, often rocky slopes, dry meadows, grasslands, open Douglas-fir or ponderosa pine forests and undisturbed roadsides.

NOTES: Scarlet gilia is a spectacular and unmistakable plant with its brilliant red, tube-shaped flowers clustered at the top of the stem. • The Okanagan used this plant in the same way they used large-flowered collomia (*Collomia grandiflora*). The Shoshone are reported to have boiled the plant, which they either drank or bathed in, to treat venereal diseases. • Scarlet gilia is also known as skyrocket. It was originally in the genus *Gilia,* which was named after the 16th-century Spanish botanist, Felipe Luis Gil (1756–1821). The genus name *Ipomopsis* means 'worm-like,' although why it is given to this plant is not clear. The species name *aggregata* refers to the clustered flowers.

SHOWY JACOB'S-LADDER • *Polemonium pulcherrimum*

GENERAL: Taprooted perennial, 5–35 cm tall, with several clustered stems; **leaves and stems have sticky hairs**.

LEAVES: Mainly **basal, pinnately compound**, with 11–25 paired, **egg-shaped to circular leaflets** with a strong **skunky odour**.

FLOWERS: Blue, with yellow centres, in showy, open clusters; **corolla is bell-shaped** with a short tube; **calyx is green throughout**.

FRUITS: Capsules.

ECOLOGY: Scattered and often common at mid to alpine elevations in dry to moist, often gravelly or sandy soils, open forests, meadows, roadsides, exposed slopes, alpine ridges; less common in areas of wet climates.

SIMILAR SPECIES: Elegant Jacob's-ladder (*P. elegans*) is a short, hairy plant with rounded heads of blue flowers. It is found in **alpine areas of the Cascade Mountains**. • Annual Jacob's-ladder (*P. micranthum*) occurs at low elevations in dry to vernally moist places in the southern part of our region. It lacks the dense basal rosette of leaves and its **flowers are white** and inconspicuous but the paired leaflets still look like a ladder.

NOTES: Alpine specimens of showy Jacob's-ladder are dwarfed. • Showy Jacob's-ladder is easily grown from seed, and once it is established it self-seeds. It does equally well in full sun or partial shade. • The common name refers to the ladder-like arrangement of the leaflets, and alludes to Jacob's ascent to heaven up a ladder, described in the *Book of Genesis*. The skunk-like smell of the bruised leaves earns this species another common name—skunk-weed. Despite the smell of the leaves, it lives up to its scientific name *pulcherrimum*, which means 'very handsome.' The genus name *Polemonium* comes from the Greek *polemos* (war) and refers to a legend about two kings who apparently took to the battlefield to prove who first discovered the (alleged) medicinal properties of Jacob's-ladder.

SPREADING PHLOX • *Phlox diffusa*

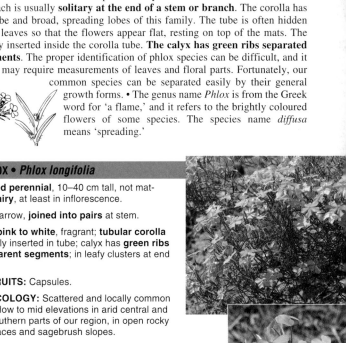

GENERAL: Taprooted, mat-forming perennial, rarely to 10 cm tall; foliage is often nearly **hidden by the blooms**.

LEAVES: Opposite, **narrowly linear, with cobwebby hairs** along edges at base.

FLOWERS: Showy; **white to pinkish or light blue tubular corollas**, with stamens unequally inserted in tube; calyx has **green ribs separated by transparent segments** and is covered with **cobwebby hairs**.

FRUITS: Capsules.

ECOLOGY: Scattered at low to mid elevations in southern half of wet Columbia Mountains, on Thompson and Okanagan plateaus, and in East Kootenays; locally abundant in open forests and rocky slopes.

SIMILAR SPECIES: Tufted phlox (*P. caespitosa*) is found on dry slopes and open forests in the southeastern part of our region. It does not form the dense mats typical of spreading phlox and its leaves are firmer. It has long **glandular hairs on the calyx**.

NOTES: The phloxes are typically mat-forming plants of rocky habitats, although some species have upright stems. Their leaves are **opposite, narrow and needle-like** in most species. They often **have**

many flowers, but each is usually **solitary at the end of a stem or branch**. The corolla has the typical narrow tube and broad, spreading lobes of this family. The tube is often hidden within the calyx and leaves so that the flowers appear flat, resting on top of the mats. The stamens are unequally inserted inside the corolla tube. **The calyx has green ribs separated by transparent segments**. The proper identification of phlox species can be difficult, and it may require measurements of leaves and floral parts. Fortunately, our common species can be separated easily by their general growth forms. • The genus name *Phlox* is from the Greek word for 'a flame,' and it refers to the brightly coloured flowers of some species. The species name *diffusa* means 'spreading.'

LONG-LEAVED PHLOX • *Phlox longifolia*

GENERAL: **Taprooted perennial**, 10–40 cm tall, not mat-forming; **glandular-hairy**, at least in inflorescence.

LEAVES: Long and narrow, **joined into pairs** at stem.

FLOWERS: Showy, **pink to white**, fragrant; **tubular corolla** with stamens unequally inserted in tube; calyx has **green ribs separated by transparent segments**; in leafy clusters at end of stem.

FRUITS: Capsules.

ECOLOGY: Scattered and locally common at low to mid elevations in arid central and southern parts of our region, in open rocky places and sagebrush slopes.

NOTES: The Okanagan steeped the whole plant in hot water and gave the infusion to anaemic children. • Several phlox species are desirable as garden ornamentals and rock garden plants, but they generally require good soil drainage and cold, dry winters. They can be propagated from seed, layering or from new-growth cuttings.

Primulaceae: Primrose Family

The primroses are annual or perennial herbs with attractive, often showy flowers. They have simple leaves with neither lobes nor teeth. The leaves are most commonly basal. Where there are leaves on the stems, they are usually paired or in whorls. The **flowers are regular, and the petals are fused into a tubular to saucer-shaped corolla with five lobes.** The sepals are also fused into a deeply 5-lobed calyx.

FEW-FLOWERED SHOOTING STAR • *Dodecatheon pulchellum* D. *pauciflorum*

GENERAL: Perennial, 5–40 cm tall, with leafless flowering stalks, hairless to very glandular-hairy throughout.

LEAVES: In a **basal rosette**, oblong **lance- to spatula-shaped**, tapering gradually to **winged stalks**.

FLOWERS: Purple-lavender, with **corolla lobes turned backwards**; the 5 **stamens are united into a yellow to orange tube** from which style and anthers protrude; 1 to several flowers **nodding** on leafless stalks.

FRUITS: Cylindrical to egg-shaped capsules.

ECOLOGY: Scattered and locally common at low to alpine elevations, mostly in our warm dry climates, in grasslands, mountain meadows, streambanks and sites that are moist when the plants are in bloom.

NOTES: The Okanagan used an infusion of this plant as an eyewash. The Nlaka'pmx used the flowers as a charm to obtain wealth. • Note the similarity in flower shape to a closely related, cultivated, potted plant, cyclamen (*Cyclamen* sp.). Some shooting stars make good rock garden ornamentals and are available commercially. They can be propagated from seeds but transplants from the wild usually fail. • This species is also called pretty shooting star. The common name is an apt description of the flowers, whose stamens lead the way as the turned-back petals stream behind like the tail of a shooting star. The genus name is from the Greek *dodeka* (twelve) and *theos* (god) and means 'the plant protected by twelve gods.'

FAIRY CANDELABRA • *Androsace septentrionalis*

GENERAL: Hairy, annual or short-lived perennial, 3–25 cm tall, with 1-several flowering stalks.

LEAVES: All in a basal rosette, often toothed, roughly **lance-shaped**.

FLOWERS: Small, **white**, with a **tubular, 5-lobed corolla** inside a **funnel-shaped calyx**; in **umbrella-like clusters** at tops of leafless stalks.

FRUITS: Round capsules, with dark brown seeds.

ECOLOGY: Widespread and locally common at low to high elevations in dry to moist open sites, often with disturbed soil; frequently a weed in gardens.

NOTES: In gardening circles, *Androsace* species are called rock jasmine, and they make very attractive rockery plants. • Rosamund Pojar writes that she can find no reference to the source of the name 'fairy candelabra' although it aptly describes how the tiny, white, perfect flowers are arranged in what could be interpreted as an inverted candelabra that is about the right size for fairy banquet halls. • The genus is from *androsakes* the Greek name for a marine plant.

FRINGED LOOSESTRIFE • *Lysimachia ciliata*

Steironema ciliatum

GENERAL: Perennial, 30–120 cm tall, with **creeping rhizomes**; stems leafy and erect.

LEAVES: Opposite on stems, oval to broadly lance-shaped; on short leafstalks with **long hairs on the edges**.

FLOWERS: Yellow corolla is a **short tube** with **spreading, oval lobes**; **solitary on slender stalks** from leaf axils.

FRUITS: Egg-shaped capsules.

ECOLOGY: Scattered and locally common at low to mid elevations in central part of our region south of Kamloops, in wet to moist sites, including damp meadows, marshes, ponds and stream edges.

SIMILAR SPECIES: Tufted loosestrife (*L. thyrsiflora*) is purple-dotted throughout. Its yellow flowers have narrow petals and are in crowded heads in the leaf axils.

NOTES: Loosestrife apparently deters gnats and flies, which may be why it was attached to harnesses to quiet 'quarrelsome beasts,' such as horses and oxen, at the plough. It also used to be burned inside houses to drive out serpents, flies and gnats. • Do not confuse this species with purple loosestrife (*Lythrum salicaria*), which is a noxious weed. • The genus name may be derived from the Greek *lysis,* 'a loosing,' and *mache*, 'strife,' which reflects the common name. Pliny, however, says that it was named after the Thracian king Lysimachus (c. 360–281 BC), a companion of Alexander. The fringe of hairs at the base of the leaves gives rise to both the 'fringed' part of the common name and the species name *ciliata*. The genus was formerly called *Steironema* from *steros*, 'sterile,' and *nema*, 'a thread,' in reference to the sterile stamens (staminodia).

BROAD-LEAVED STARFLOWER • *Trientalis latifolia*
T. europaea var. *latifolia*

GENERAL: Perennial, 5–20 cm tall, with slender rhizomes with **thickened erect tubers**; stems slender and unbranched.

LEAVES: Oval-elliptic, usually 4–8 in a **whorl at top of stem**; stem leaves reduced to small bracts.

FLOWERS: Pinkish to rose; **saucer-shaped corolla,** deeply divided into 6–7 sharply pointed lobes; each flower is **borne on a thin curved stalk** arising from centre of leaf whorl.

FRUITS: Spherical capsules, splitting into 5 parts when dry.

ECOLOGY: Scattered and locally common at low to mid elevations in southern half of our region, in shady, moist forests, forest openings and seepage sites.

SIMILAR SPECIES: Northern starflower (*T. arctica*) is found in wet and boggy areas. It has small leaves along the stem below the main whorl of leaves and fewer **white** flowers than broad-leaved starflower.

NOTES: The Nlaka'pmx used the flower of broad-leaved starflower to obtain good luck in gambling. • Broad-leaved starflower is also called western starflower. Plants of this genus are called starflowers because the flower stalks are very thin, leaving the flowers apparently hanging in the air like tiny stars. *Trientalis* means 'one-third of a foot,' which aptly describes the plant's height. The species name *latifolia* means 'broad-leaved.'

Rubiaceae: Madder Family

Madders are members of the same family as coffee plants (*Coffea* spp.), and their fruits can be roasted and used as a coffee substitute. This large, mainly tropical family has two common species in our area, both from the genus *Galium* (the bedstraws).

The bedstraws are annual or perennial herbs with **square, slender stems and whorls of simple leaves**. The flowers have **four petals that are united at the base into a short tube** with broadly spreading lobes. The fruits are often covered with hooked hairs and have two lobes, each of which contains a single seed.

NORTHERN BEDSTRAW • *Galium boreale*

GENERAL: Perennial, mostly 20–60 cm tall, from creeping rhizomes; with clusters of **square** stems, 1 to few branches.

LEAVES: In whorls of 4 on stems, narrowly lance-shaped, pointed with **minutely rounded tips, strongly 3-nerved**.

FLOWERS: White to slightly creamy, small but **numerous in a showy cluster at top of stem; very fragrant** when in full flower.

FRUITS: Pairs of dry nutlets, covered with **straight or curly (not hooked) hairs**.

ECOLOGY: Widespread and common at low to alpine elevations in open, often fairly dry forests, grassy meadows, clearings and roadsides.

SIMILAR SPECIES: Small bedstraw (*G. trifidum*) is somewhat similar with its four leaves in a whorl, but it is **prostrate and generally smaller, has 1-nerved leaves** and smooth nutlets, lacks showy flower clusters and grows in wet habitats.

NOTES: 'Bedstraw' is shortened from 'Our Lady's bedstraw,' the common name of the European species, *G. verum*. Legend has it that the Virgin Mary lay on a bed that was a mixture of bracken (*Pteridium aquilinum*) and *G. verum*. The bracken did not acknowledge the child's birth and lost its flowers, but the bedstraw welcomed the child and blossomed. • The genus name is from the Greek *gala*, 'milk,' in reference to the use of bedstraw to curdle milk when making cheese.

SWEET-SCENTED BEDSTRAW • *Galium triflorum*

GENERAL: Rhizomatous perennial, 20–80 cm long, with **strongly hooked-bristly stems, prostrate or ascending and scrambling on other vegetation**.

LEAVES: Mostly 6 (rarely 5) in a **whorl**, narrowly elliptic, **1-nerved**, with **hooked hairs on underside of midrib** and a **sharp-pointed tip**.

FLOWERS: Greenish white, in open **clusters of 3** on stalks from leaf axils.

FRUITS: Paired nutlets covered with **hooked bristles**.

ECOLOGY: Widespread and common at low to subalpine elevations in moist open forest, openings, clearings and thickets, usually in partial shade; generally absent from our arid climates.

NOTES: The plant smells strongly of **vanilla** (coumarin), especially when dry, hence the name 'sweet-scented bedstraw.' The Secwepemc used it as a special scent and charm. The roots of bedstraw species are a source of dyes—the Okanagan used them to make red and blue dyes. If the roots are boiled too long, the dye turns yellow.

SITKA VALERIAN • *Valeriana sitchensis*

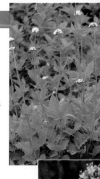

GENERAL: Perennial, 30–120 cm tall, from a stout, branched rhizome or woody stem-base; somewhat succulent, squarish stems.

LEAVES: In 2–5 pairs on stem, **long-stalked**, divided into **3–7 coarsely toothed leaflets**; end leaflet is largest and broadest.

FLOWERS: Pale pink, fading to white; corolla tubular and 5-lobed, with **style and 3 stamens protruding** from tube; inflorescence of many small flowers arranged in a **dense, hemispherical to flat-topped cluster**; sweet scented.

FRUITS: Many **ribbed** achenes, each topped by tuft of **feathery plumes** that aid wind dispersal.

ECOLOGY: Widespread and often abundant at mid to (more commonly) high elevations in moist and wet climates, in moist meadows, clearings, openings, streambanks and open subalpine forest.

SIMILAR SPECIES: Marsh valerian (*V. dioica*) is a smaller (usually less than 40 cm tall) and less common species found in wet places at low to mid elevations. It is distinguished from Sitka valerian by its simple basal leaves and much smaller flowers, as well as its generally smaller size.

NOTES: Sitka valerian is responsible for the strong, sour odour detected in subalpine meadows after the first frost. • The Carrier, Secwepemc and Nlaka'pmx used Sitka valerian as a medicine and disinfectant. The Secwepemc used it for colds and bathed their racehorses with it. Some Nlaka'pmx men mixed the dried, powdered root with tobacco for flavouring. • One source says that 'valerian' may be named for Valeria, a part of Hungary where valerian (*V. officinalis*) grew. Another proposes that the name comes from the Latin *valere*, which means 'to be healthy,' and refers to its medicinal properties.

BUCKBEAN • *Menyanthes trifoliata*

GENERAL: Aquatic to semiaquatic perennial, 10–30 cm tall, with thick, submerged **rhizomes**; flowering stalks stout and smooth.

LEAVES: In a cluster, clasping base of flowering stalk, each divided into **3 elliptic, long-stalked leaflets** with smooth or slightly crinkly edges.

FLOWERS: White, usually tinged purplish pink, **showy**; corolla 5-lobed, with long**, white hairs on inner surface**; in clusters at tip of long, leafless stalks.

FRUITS: Round to oval capsules.

ECOLOGY: Common at low to mid elevations in wetlands and at edges of water bodies.

NOTES: The rhizomes can be made into an emergency food. Finns and Lapps called bread made from buckbean 'missen' or 'famine' bread. The rhizomes are dried, ground, washed in several changes of water (to remove the bitterness) and then dried again. • The leaves have been used to make a bitter tonic

which, taken in large doses, has a cathartic and emetic effect. Buckbean tea was also used to relieve fever and migraine headaches, for indigestion, to promote appetite and to eliminate intestinal worms. It was used externally to promote the healing of ulcerous wounds. The dry leaves have been used as a substitute for hops in brewing. • The foliage is similar to that of broad beans, which may have given rise to the 'bean' part of the common name. Another common name is bogbean. The original name may have meant 'goat's bean,' with 'buck' deriving from the French *bouc*, 'goat'. The genus name *Menyanthes* is from the Greek *men* (a month) and *anthos* (a flower), either because flowering was said to last one month or because it was once used medicinally to bring on menstruation.

Santalaceae: Sandalwood Family

The sandalwood family has only two members in our area, but there are many species worldwide. Many of these, including ours, are **parasitic on the roots of other plants.** Our two species are perennial herbs with fleshy or leathery leaves. Their flowers are small, but they are distinctive when examined closely. They **lack petals but have five sepals** that are **fused into a lobed cup** enclosing five hairy-based stamens.

PALE COMANDRA • *Comandra umbellata*
C. pallida

GENERAL: Perennial **root parasite,** 5–35 cm tall, with rhizomes and clustered stems.

LEAVES: Rather **thick and fleshy**, with a whitish cast; **lance-shaped to oblong or elliptic.**

FLOWERS: Greenish white to purplish, in a compact cluster at **top of stem.**

FRUITS: Dry to somewhat fleshy and **berry-like, blue to purplish brown,** 1-seeded.

ECOLOGY: Scattered and infrequent at low to mid elevations in our arid climates, in dry grasslands and on sagebrush slopes.

NOTES: The genus name *Comandra* is from the Greek *kome*, 'hair,' and *andros*, 'a man,' and refers to the hairs at the base of the stamens. The common name refers to the whitish cast on the leaves.

BASTARD TOAD-FLAX • *Geocaulon lividum*
Comandra livida

GENERAL: Perennial **root parasite**, 10–25 cm tall, with single or clumped stems growing from creeping, **thread-like, reddish rhizomes**.

LEAVES: Fleshy, oval, bright green or frequently yellow-variegated.

FLOWERS: Greenish purple, in slender-stalked, 2–4 flowered **clusters in axils of upper leaves**; usually only centre flower is fertile.

FRUITS: Scarlet to fluorescent orange, **succulent and berry-like;** edibility is questionable, not recommended.

ECOLOGY: Scattered and locally common at low to subalpine elevations on our plateaus, in East Kootenays and in wet Columbia Mountains, in dry to moist, forests, openings and bog forests.

NOTES: Bastard toad-flax is parasitic on the roots of other plants, including forest trees. The yellow variegation in the leaves is a condition caused by lodgepole pine's comandra blister rust, of which *Geocaulon* species are the alternate host. • *G. lividum* is called 'bastard' toad-flax because it looks like true toad-flax, the European species *Linaria vulgaris*. The name 'toad-flax' refers in part to the similarity of *L. vulgaris* leaves to those of flax (*Linum usitatissimum*). The 'toad' part may be an error in translation from an old herbal in which toad-flax was described as a plant used to treat *buboes* (boils). The Latin word for 'boil' is *bubonio*, whereas the word for 'toad' is *bufo*.

Polygonaceae: Buckwheat Family

The buckwheat family plants generally have many flowers, individually small and inconspicuous, that may be clustered into showy inflorescences. The flowers are composed of a **single set of three to six petal-like parts**, sometimes referred to as **tepals**, that are usually fused at the base, but in most cases they appear to be separate. The leaves of buckwheat family plants do not have lobes or divisions and usually are not toothed. In most species, the leaf bases (stipules) form papery sheaths that surround the stems. Unfortunately, the largest group in our area, the buckwheats (*Eriogonum* spp.), lack this distinctive feature.

MOUNTAIN SORREL • *Oxyria digyna*

GENERAL: Taprooted perennial, 5–40 cm tall, with several clustered stems, smooth, often reddish-tinged.

LEAVES: Many, **mainly at base of stems, kidney- to heart-shaped**, with **long stalks**, somewhat **succulent**; single leaf on stem below flower head.

FLOWERS: Tiny, green to reddish-coloured, in a long, narrow inflorescence; each flower composed of 4 tepals, 2 narrow and 2 broad.

FRUITS: Oval, **flattened seeds** with **broad translucent wings**.

ECOLOGY: Scattered and infrequent at high elevations in moist rock crevices or talus slopes, meadows and seepage sites.

SIMILAR SPECIES: Mountain sorrel may be confused with docks (*Rumex* spp., p. 200), which have similar inflorescences. The kidney-shaped leaves of mountain sorrel readily distinguishes it from our docks, which have arrow-shaped leaves.

NOTES: The fruits appeared bright red because of the persistent and enlarged tepals that surround them and quiver in the faintest breeze. • Mountain sorrel is rich in vitamin C. The Okanagan ate the fresh leaves raw, but only in moderation because the **oxalic acid they contain may be harmful in quantity**.

ALPINE BISTORT • *Bistorta vivipara*
Polygonum viviparum

GENERAL: Perennial, mostly 10–30 cm tall, from a short, thick **rhizome**; 1 to several flowering stems with **several prominent joints**.

LEAVES: Basal, often only a single leaf **on a long stalk**; blade narrowly oblong to lance-shaped, smooth, dark green and shiny above, greyish below; 2–4 smaller leaves on stem.

FLOWERS: Small and white (to pink) with greenish bases, 5 tepals; in a **dense, spike-like cluster** at top of stem; lower flowers are replaced by purplish bulblets (which sometimes sprout while still on the mother plant).

FRUITS: Brown, shiny, **3-angled seeds** (nutlets).

ECOLOGY: Scattered and infrequent, mostly at high elevations, in open woods, moist meadows and streambanks, alpine tundra and heath.

SIMILAR SPECIES: American bistort (*B. bistortoides,* also known as *Polygonum bistortoides*) is found in moist to wet subalpine and alpine areas in our region. Its flowering head is broader and more compact than in alpine bistort and it never bears bulblets.

NOTES: Alpine bistort was used as an emergency food all across the northern hemisphere. Black and grizzly bears commonly eat the roots. • You can often find small pink bulblets clustered at the bases of the stem leaves and in the lower part of the inflorescence. These are dislodged by the wind and roll away to form new plants, hence the species name *vivipara*, which means 'producing live young.' • The genus name means 'twice twisted,' and refers to the contorted, snake-like underground stem, which led to the belief that bistort was an antidote for snake-bites.

FRAGILE SOUR WEED • *Rumex acetosella*

GENERAL: Perennial, 20–30 cm tall, with **long, slender roots**; 1 to several stems, smooth and unbranched below flower clusters.

LEAVES: Arrow-shaped basal leaves with long stalks and a **pair of outward-flaring lobes**; smaller stem leaves with shortened stalks.

FLOWERS: Many, **tiny** and **reddish**, with 6 tepals; in a **long, narrow inflorescence**; male and female flowers on separate plants.

FRUITS: Smooth, **winged seeds**, reddish brown and shiny, triangular in cross-section.

ECOLOGY: Scattered and locally common at low to mid elevations in waste places, roadsides, meadows, cultivated fields, pastures, rangeland and other open habitats; prefers acid soils.

SIMILAR SPECIES: Curly dock (*R. crispus*) is another widespread, introduced, weedy species, but it is larger (to 1 m tall) and has oblong leaves with crisped edges. • Green sorrel (*R. acetosa* ssp. *alpestris*) also has leaves that are shaped like an arrowhead, but with basal lobes that curve downward. It is a native species of low to alpine elevations.

NOTES: Fragile sour weed, also called sheep sorrel, is a Eurasian native that can be a troublesome weed. It often forms large patches from long, underground roots. • The young, fleshy leaves of sour weed are tart and rich in vitamin C. The sour taste is due to the presence of oxalic acid, which can interfere with the body's calcium metabolism and therefore should be eaten in moderation. • *Rumex* was Pliny's name for sorrel.

SNOW BUCKWHEAT • *Eriogonum niveum*

GENERAL: Taprooted perennial, to 14 cm tall, with woody, mat-forming or erect stems.

LEAVES: Oblong to broadly lance-shaped, on stalks as long as or longer than blades; **greyish hairy below**, less so above.

FLOWERS: Tiny, cup-shaped, **cream or pink**, with 6 tepals; in **small clusters** in freely branching, leafy inflorescences; bloom into autumn.

FRUITS: Hard, dry seeds.

ECOLOGY: Widespread and locally common at low to mid elevations in our plateaus, arid basins and southern Rocky Mountain Trench, in sagebrush grasslands and dry, open ponderosa pine forests.

NOTES: The Okanagan used this plant medicinally in much the same way as they used parsnip-flowered buckwheat (*E. heracleoides*, p. 201). • Buckwheats are plants of dry, rocky places. They **do not have the papery sheaths (stipules) around the stems** that are characteristic of the other members of the buckwheat family. Buckwheat flowers are cup-shaped, with six petals (tepals) and nine stamens. Although the flowers are individually tiny, they are often grouped into dense, showy inflorescences. **The flowers sit on short stalks extending out of a woolly, bell-shaped cup (involucre) with sepal-like lobes**. • True buckwheats (*Fagopyrum* spp.), also in the Polygonaceae family, are widely cultivated in Europe for fodder and flour. • The common name 'buckwheat' is thought to be derived from the middle-Dutch *boecweite*, meaning 'beech-wheat,' because the fruits resemble beech nuts. The genus name *Eriogonum* comes from the Greek *erion*, 'wool,' and *gonu*, 'a knee' or 'a joint,' and refers to the woolly, jointed stems. The species name *niveum*, 'snow,' refers to the whitish flowers.

PARSNIP-FLOWERED BUCKWHEAT • *Eriogonum heracleoides*

GENERAL: Clump-forming perennial, stems 10–40 cm tall, with a branched, woody base, **woolly hairy throughout.**

LEAVES: Linear to lance-shaped, in whorls at base of stem; **greyish woolly on both surfaces**; usually a second whorl of **leaf-like bracts about mid-length on stem.**

FLOWERS: Tiny, cup-shaped, **white to yellowish white**, occasionally rose tinged, with 6 tepals; in **compact spherical clusters** (umbels), all in a compound umbel.

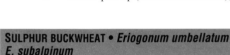

FRUITS: Hard, dry seeds.

ECOLOGY: Scattered and locally common at low to high elevations in sagebrush grasslands, dry, open forests, grassy openings and open, steep, warm slopes in mountains; absent from wet Columbia Mountains.

NOTES: The flowers of buckwheat species provide excellent nectar for honey-bees. • The Okanagan made a tea from the roots to cure diarrhea. They boiled the roots and stems to treat infected cuts, colds, blood poisoning, tuberculosis, cancer, and all types of sickness and made the leaves into a poultice for cuts. • The flowers are somewhat similar in appearance to those of cow-parsnip (*Heracleum lanatum*), hence the species name *heracleoides*.

SULPHUR BUCKWHEAT • *Eriogonum umbellatum* *E. subalpinum*

GENERAL: Taprooted, mat-forming perennial, 10–30 cm tall, usually with prostrate branches; flowering stems usually leafless.

LEAVES: Oblong to spatula-shaped, in whorls at base of stems, **densely grey-woolly below and hairless to woolly above**; occasionally 1 leaf-like bract near middle of flowering stems.

FLOWERS: Tiny and cup-shaped, **creamy white or yellow**, tinged with pink on aging, with 6 petals; in **compact spherical clusters** (umbels), all in a compound umbel.

FRUITS: Hard, dry, **3-angled seeds** with hairy tips.

ECOLOGY: Scattered and locally common at low to alpine elevations in dry climates of our region, in dry sagebrush flats, steep, warm grassy slopes, alpine ridges and talus slopes.

SIMILAR SPECIES: Cushion buckwheat (*E. ovalifolium*) is a mat-forming species, 1–6 cm high, which also ranges from sagebrush deserts to alpine ridges. It has a single head of creamy white flowers on a leafless stalk. The basal leaves vary from oval to spatula-shaped and are silvery-white.

NOTES: Buckwheats are tempermental plants that are best suited to dry, sunny rock gardens. They are difficult to propagate and best results are attained from seed. • During autumn, clumps of the bright red leaves of sulphur buckwheat form showy patches in high-elevation grasslands. • The inverted umbrella-shaped clusters of sulphur-yellow flowers give rise to the species and common names.

Ranunculaceae: Buttercup Family

The buttercup family is one of the most interesting of our native groups. It contains such a diversity of growth habits, flower structures, leaf forms and fruits that it is nearly impossible to characterize. Its flower structure varies from a ring of simple petals in the buttercups (*Ranunculus* spp.) to the highly modified flowers of the larkspurs (*Delphinium* spp.), monkshoods (*Aconitum* spp.) and columbines (*Aquilegia* spp.). The flowers typically contain a **large number of stamens and pistils**. They are often nectar producing. Fruits vary from simple seeds (or achenes), which are usually borne in large clusters, to follicles or berries.

The genera of the buttercup family are often easy to recognize. Individual species within the genera can be more difficult to distinguish, however, especially in large groups, such as buttercups, which show little floral variation among their species.

All of our Ranunculaceae species are perennials. They are predominantly herbaceous, although several are vines (such as *Clematis* spp.). Many species are related to familiar garden plants.

Some members of Ranunculaceae, such as marsh marigold (*Caltha palustris*) and several buttercups, contain chemicals that can severely irritate and blister the skin, or, if they are swallowed, inflame the tissues of the mouth, throat and digestive tract.

Key to the buttercup family genera

1a. Flowers not radially symmetrical 2
    2a. Upper sepal spurred but not hooded; 4 petals, not covered by sepals .... ***Delphinium***
    2b. Upper sepal hooded but not spurred; 2 petals, covered by hood .... ***Aconitum***
1b. Flowers radially symmetrical 3
    3a. Petals with long spurs that are swollen at tip; flowers very showy .... ***Aquilegia***
    3b. Petals lacking prominent spurs; flowers showy or not 4
        4a. Fruits are red or white berries; 1 ovary per flower .... ***Actaea***
        4b. Fruits are achenes or follicles, but not berries; generally more than 1 ovary per flower 5
            5a. Fruits are 1-seeded achenes, not opening when mature. 6
                6a. Flowers with both petals and sepals; petals more showy than sepals; flowers generally yellow .... ***Ranunculus***
                6b. Petals usually lacking (sepals sometimes petal-like), if present, petals less showy than sepals; flowers generally white 7
                    7a. Sepals small and less showy than stamens (or ovaries if stamens absent); stem leaves alternate, if present. 8
                        8a. Leaves simple, palmately lobed .... ***Trautvetteria***
                        8b. Leaves 2 or 3 times compound .... ***Thalictrum***
                    7b. Sepals petal-like, more showy than stamens; stem leaves opposite or whorled 9
                        9a. Plants vine-like; leaves opposite .... ***Clematis***
                        9b. Plants not vines; stem leaves usually in a whorl of 3 .... ***Anemone***
             5b. Fruits are follicles with 2 to many seeds; opening when mature 10
                10a. Leaves simple, with toothed edges, not lobed. .... ***Caltha***
                10b. Leaves deeply lobed to compound 11
                    11a. Leaves divided into 3 main segments or leaflets .... ***Coptis***
                    11b. Leaves palmately lobed or divided into more than 3 (usually 5) main segments .... ***Trollius***

Delphinium
nuttalli

Aconitum
columbianum

Aquilegia
formosa

Ranunculus
eschscholtzii

Actaea rubra

Thalictrum
occidentale

Clematis
occidentalis

Anemone multifida

Caltha
leptosepala

Coptis trifolia

Trollius laxus

UPLAND LARKSPUR • *Delphinium nuttallianum*

GENERAL: Perennial, 15–40 cm tall, from a **fleshy, tuberous rootstock**, with **single stems**.

LEAVES: Mostly basal, long-stalked and **palmately divided or lobed into linear segments**; stem leaves smaller, with fewer segments.

FLOWERS: Irregular; petals whitish to bluish; **sepals blue to violet**, uppermost sepal with **long spur**; 3–15 on stalks in a loose, elongate cluster; blooms in spring.

FRUITS: Clusters of 3 erect capsules (follicles), releasing blackish and partly winged seeds.

ECOLOGY: Scattered and locally common at low to mid elevations in our arid basins and in areas with dry climates on Fraser Plateau, in dry grasslands, sagebrush slopes and open ponderosa pine and Douglas-fir forests.

SIMILAR SPECIES: Montana larkspur (*D. bicolor*) is found in dry places at low to subalpine elevations. The two species can be separated by examining the **lowest two petals, which are deeply notched in upland larkspur and only shallowly lobed in Montana larkspur**. Also, Montana larkspur has fibrous roots and the ultimate leaf segments are broad.

NOTES: Larkspurs are easily recognized for their showy, highly modified flowers and usually palmately divided leaves. The showy part of the flower is actually composed of the five sepals, with the four petals forming a small cluster in the centre of the flower. The uppermost sepal forms a hollow, nectar-producing spur. Because of the depth of the spur, the nectar is accessible only to insects with long feeding structures, such as butterflies and bumble bees. • Larkspurs contain delphinine, which is **poisonous** to cattle but apparently not to sheep; so sheep can be used to eradicate larkspurs from range in restricted areas. These plants are very toxic in spring and less so at flowering and maturity, but the seeds are highly toxic. Larkspurs are also **highly toxic to humans**. • This species is also known as Nuttall's larkspur.

TALL LARKSPUR • *Delphinium glaucum*

GENERAL: Perennial, 1–2 m tall, from a **thick, short rootstock; stems hollow and stout**, with a whitish cast, usually unbranched below flowers.

LEAVES: Many, **palmately divided into 5–7 lobes**, with **each lobe 2–3 times subdivided or toothed**, smooth to sparsely hairy.

FLOWERS: Irregular, deep purple (pale blue within), small (12–24 mm across); uppermost sepal forms a **long spur; numerous in a long cluster**.

FRUITS: Clusters of 3 erect capsules (follicles), smooth to slightly hairy.

ECOLOGY: Scattered and infrequent at low to alpine elevations in our moist and wet climates, especially in eastern parts of our region, in open, deciduous or mixed forest, aspen parkland, forest edges, moist meadows, subalpine parkland, avalanche tracts and tundra.

NOTES: Poisonous. Tall larkspur, also known as tall delphinium, is among the first plants to emerge in spring, and it is most toxic in its youngest growth. It is quite palatable to livestock, leading to cattle losses on range where it is a major component. • The Nlaka'pmx and Okanagan extracted a blue dye from the flowers of tall larkspur. • The name 'larkspur' is derived from French *pied d'alouette*, meaning 'foot of the lark,' or *eperon d'alouette*, meaning 'spur of the lark,' and it refers to the projecting spur of the flowers.

COLUMBIAN MONKSHOOD • *Aconitum columbianum*

GENERAL: Perennial, 0.5–2 m tall, from **tuberous roots**, with several sturdy, **hollow stems**.

LEAVES: Mostly on stem, palmately divided into 5 coarsely toothed lobes; lower leaves with long stalks; upper leaves almost stalkless.

FLOWERS: Irregular, dark blue to purple, sometimes tinged with green, yellow or white; upper sepal modified into **hood-like structure that is higher than wide**.

FRUITS: Clusters of 3–5 **erect capsules** (follicles) with sculptured seeds.

ECOLOGY: Scattered and infrequent at low to subalpine elevations, mostly in moist and wet climates in southern half of our region, in moist, open, often deciduous forests, moist thickets, openings, meadows and streambanks.

SIMILAR SPECIES: Mountain monkshood (*A. delphiniifolium*) occurs in the Rocky Mountains and the northern part of our region. The **hood of the flower is wider than high** in side view. At alpine elevations mountain monkshood is usually dwarfed (10 cm tall), but it can attain heights of 1 m in valley bottoms.

NOTES: The deep blue, hooded flowers of *Aconitum* species cannot be confused with any other group. The hood is actually formed by the uppermost of five sepals. The petals are reduced in size and concealed by the hood. • **All parts of the plant are highly poisonous**, especially to livestock. The tubers contain aconitin, which, according to folklore, was an essential ingredient of the 'flying ointment' that witches smeared over themselves before taking flight. It would cause heart fibrillation and, together with belladonna, which causes delirium, could give the sensation of flying. • The most likely explanation for the genus name *Aconitum* is that it derives from the Greek word for 'without a struggle,' which aptly describes the deadly poisonous nature of the plant.

RED COLUMBINE • *Aquilegia formosa*

GENERAL: **Taprooted** perennial, to 1 m tall, with unbranched stems, smooth below, sparsely hairy above.

LEAVES: Mainly basal, long-stalked, **2 or 3 times divided into 3s**.

FLOWERS: Irregular; red sepals; yellow petals, each bearing a **long, erect, reddish spur with a bulbous tip**; central tuft of stamens and styles protrudes from ring of petals; **drooping**, usually in clusters of **2–5** (sometimes more on vigorous plants).

FRUITS: Clusters of 5 erect capsules (follicles), with hairy, spreading tips.

ECOLOGY: Widespread and common at low to subalpine elevations in moist, open forests, openings, meadows, roadsides and avalanche tracts.

SIMILAR SPECIES: Yellow columbine (*A. flavescens*) is similar except that its whole flower is yellow. Its range overlaps with red columbine, but yellow columbine occurs primarily at subalpine to alpine elevations.

NOTES: Columbines are among the most familiar of our native plants, and their complex and distinctive floral structure is unmistakable. Although the leaves resemble those of the meadowrues (*Thalictrum* spp.), there is no possibility of confusing their flowers. • Columbine flowers attract hummingbirds and butterflies with the sweet nectar at their spur bases. • Native peoples in our region used columbine as a good luck charm for gambling and love, and used a decoction of the plant as a hair-wash. • The common name is derived from the Latin *columbina*, meaning 'dove-like.' The arched petals

and spurs of the flowers resemble a quintet of doves arranged in a ring around a dish (a favourite device of ancient artists). An old name for columbine is 'culverwort,' which comes from the Anglo-Saxon *culfre*, 'pigeon' and *wort*, 'plant,' because the flowers resemble the heads of pigeons feeding together. The genus is named from the Latin *aquila*, 'eagle,' because the petals are like eagle's talons. This species is also called Sitka columbine.

Ranunculus: the buttercups

The buttercups in our area have shiny, yellow, regular flowers with five petals and sepals, and a nectar-producing scale (nectary) at the petal bases. The flowers produce many seeds in spherical or cylindrical clusters. The seeds (achenes) usually have a beak and may also have ribs.

There are several aquatic buttercups in our area, most of which have floating or creeping stems. Their submerged leaves, if present, are generally more finely divided than the floating leaves. Another common name for aquatic buttercups is 'water-crowfoot,' from the supposed resemblance of the floating leaves to a crow's feet.

Buttercup flowers do not vary much from species to species, so identification can sometimes be difficult. Growth habit can be helpful, as can the pattern of leaf divisions. The shapes of the seed clusters and of the individual seeds are also useful characters.

Key to the buttercups

1a. Leaves entire to shallowly lobed 2

    2a. Achenes finely hairy; plants of dry habitats .... *R. glaberrimus*

    2b. Achenes without hairs; plants of very wet habitats 3

        3a. 50–200 achenes in a columnar cluster;
        leaves often toothed or shallowly lobed .... *R. cymbalaria*

        3b. Less than 60 achenes in a rounded
        cluster; leaves entire .... *R. flammula*

1b. Leaves deeply lobed to compound 4

    4a. Plants aquatic or semi-aquatic 5

        5a. Plants annual, erect, not rooting at nodes .... *R. sceleratus*

        5b. Plants perennial, floating to creeping, rooting at nodes 6

            6a. Leaf blades 2–8 cm long, divided
            into many narrow (generally less than
            2 mm wide) segments .... *R. flabellaris*

            6b. Leaf blades usually less than 2 cm long,
            lobed to divided into a few segments that
            are often greater than 2 mm wide .... *R. gmelinii*

    4b. Plants neither aquatic nor semi-aquatic,
    but sometimes occurring in quite moist habitats 7

        7a. Achenes finely hairy
        and only moderately flattened .... *R. eschscholtzii*

        7b. Achenes lacking hairs and
        strongly flattened, often disk-shaped 8

        8a. Petals shorter than to slightly
        longer than sepals, usually less than 7 mm long 9

            9a. Leaf blades compound; beak
            of achene nearly straight .... *R. macounii*

            9b. Leaf blades deeply lobed but
            not compound; beak of achene hooked .... *R. uncinatus*

        8b. Petals considerably longer than sepals,
        usually much longer than 7 mm 10

            10a. Achenes less than 2.5 mm long; sepals spreading;
            leaf blades divided into many segments .... *R. acris*

            10b. Achenes more than 2.5 mm long;
            sepals generally turned downward;
            leaf blades divided into only
            a few main segments .... *R. occidentalis*

SAGEBRUSH BUTTERCUP • *Ranunculus glaberrimus*

GENERAL: Low perennial with several **stems growing from thick, fleshy roots**; stems 5–15 cm long, often prostrate, but not rooting at nodes.

LEAVES: Mainly basal; blades rather **fleshy**, elliptic to **lance-shaped, often with 2 shallow notches at tip**; stem leaves sometimes 3-lobed.

FLOWERS: Yellow, often purplish-tinged, 2.5 cm wide; **bloom in spring**.

FRUITS: Semi-spherical clusters of 30–150 seeds with **short hairs** and straight, short, flattened beaks.

ECOLOGY: Scattered and locally common at low elevations in arid basins, in dry ponderosa pine and Douglas-fir forests, grasslands, sagebrush slopes, moist meadows and dry, rocky ridges.

NOTES: This delightful little buttercup is one of our earliest spring-blooming wildflowers. Its shiny, bright flowers peep out from the dead winter foliage of dry hillsides. By midsummer, the leaves have often withered and all signs of the plant have disappeared. • Sagebrush buttercup is known to be **poisonous** and Okanagan children were warned not to touch or pick it. The Nlaka'pmx used it as poison on their arrowheads. The blooming of this little buttercup announced the arrival of spring, to the Secwepemc. • The species name *glaberrimus* means 'very smooth' or 'smoothest,' and refers to the shiny, hairless leaves.

SUBALPINE BUTTERCUP • *Ranunculus eschscholtzii*

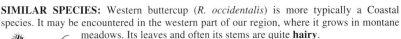

GENERAL: Perennial, 10–25 cm tall, from a **woody base with fibrous roots**; 1 to several small stems.

LEAVES: Mostly basal, slender-stalked, **kidney-shaped** to oval in outline, **usually deeply 3-lobed and then divided again**; all leaves hairless.

FLOWERS: Yellow, 1.5–3 cm wide; **sepals often with yellowish or brownish hairs**, dropping off soon after flower opens; 1–3 at tops of stem.

FRUITS: Elongate clusters of 20–80 **finely hairy seeds** with **short, slender, straight to somewhat curved beaks**.

ECOLOGY: Widespread and common at subalpine and alpine elevations in mountain meadows, avalanche tracks, talus slopes, streambanks and open forests; **often blooms at edges of melting snowbanks.**

SIMILAR SPECIES: Western buttercup (*R. occidentalis*) is more typically a Coastal species. It may be encountered in the western part of our region, where it grows in montane meadows. Its leaves and often its stems are quite **hairy**.

NOTES: All buttercups contain alkaloid compounds that are **poisonous** to grazing cattle. Despite the common occurrence of buttercup in pastures, poisonings are rare because most of the plants are distasteful to animals. Buttercups are considered to be harmless in hay, however, because the poisonous material is volatile and 'evaporates' when the hay is cured. • The genus was named *Ranunculus* (little frog) presumably because the first species described grew where frogs are found. 'Buttercup' comes from *button-cop*, from the French *button d'or*, 'golden button,' and the Anglo-Saxon *cop*, 'head.' This species was named for Johann Frederich Eschscholtz (1793–1831), the surgeon and naturalist on Kotzebue's explorations to California in 1816 and 1824. Subalpine buttercup also called mountain buttercup.

BUTTERCUP

LITTLE BUTTERCUP • *Ranunculus uncinatus*

GENERAL: Annual or perennial, 20–60 cm tall; **stem single, hollow.**

LEAVES: Mostly basal, long-stalked; blades **heart- to kidney-shaped** in outline, **deeply divided into 3 lobes** and **again divided and coarsely toothed**; 1–2 stem leaves, with lance-shaped lobes.

FLOWERS: Pale yellow and very small (3–8 mm wide); in few-flowered clusters above leafy bracts at end of stem.

FRUITS: Rounded clusters of 5–30 small seeds, each with a **small, hooked beak**.

ECOLOGY: Scattered and common at low to mid elevations on our plateaus, in Coast/Interior Transition and in wet Columbia Mountains, in shady, moist forests, wet openings, meadows and disturbed, trampled areas.

SIMILAR SPECIES: Macoun's buttercup (*R. macounii*) also has small flowers, and it is found in similar habitats. Its leaves are divided at the base into three leaflets. The two lateral leaflets usually have two main lobes and the middle one has three lobes. The stems are often prostrate and rooting at nodes. • The leaves of little buttercup are somewhat similar to those of meadow buttercup (*R. acris*, below) but they are not as finely or deeply divided.

NOTES: The Nlaka'pmx used little buttercup as a body wash for purification in the sweathouse. • Little buttercup is also known as small-flowered buttercup. The species name *uncinatus* is Latin for 'hooked at the point' and describes the **hooked seeds that readily attach to fur and clothing**.

MEADOW BUTTERCUP • *Ranunculus acris*

GENERAL: Hairy perennial, 30–80 cm tall, with **slender fibrous roots**; 1 to several **hollow** stems.

LEAVES: Densely hairy; blades broadly 5-sided or **heart-shaped in outline, deeply lobed and divided nearly to base,** so that whole leaf blade has a ragged appearance.

FLOWERS: Glossy yellow, 1–3.5 cm wide; sepals greenish and hairy, dropping off soon after flower opens; several in loose clusters on **hairy stalks**.

FRUITS: Spherical clusters of 25–40 smooth, flattened seeds with tiny, flattened, curved beaks.

ECOLOGY: Scattered and locally abundant at low to mid elevations in well-drained soils, moist meadows, pastures, clearings and roadsides.

NOTES: Meadow buttercup is a widely established, weedy, European species. • According to folklore, Irish farmers rubbed their cows' udders with buttercups on May Day to increase the milk supply. Buttercup flowers were woven into May Day garlands. • The species name *acris* refers to the acrid-tasting juice of this plant, which is **poisonous** to cattle.

SMALL YELLOW WATER-BUTTERCUP • *Ranunculus gmelinii*

GENERAL: Aquatic perennial; **stems floating in water or creeping on mud and rooting at nodes.**

LEAVES: Mainly on stem, small and more or less **circular in outline, deeply divided into 3 lobes,** further divided into **linear, elongate segments**; lobes of submerged leaves delicate and often narrower than those of floating leaves (sometimes almost thread-like).

FLOWERS: Small (6–15 mm wide); **petals yellow; solitary** on hairy stalks.

FRUITS: Short-beaked seeds.

ECOLOGY: Widespread and often common at low to mid elevations in arid basins and on our plateaus, in mud flats, shallow water in ponds, ditches, drained beaver ponds and along lakeshores.

SIMILAR SPECIES: Yellow water-crowfoot (*R. flabellaris*) is closely related to small yellow water-buttercup. Although rare in our region, it shares similar habit requirements and is distinguished by its leaves, which are repeatedly 3–5 times divided into threes; in the submerged leaves, the resulting segments are thread-like. The seeds have prominent keels and a large beak. • Cursed crowfoot (*R. sceleratus*), also called celery-leaved buttercup, is an annual that occupies similar habitats. However, it is **erect**, its creeping stems do not root at the nodes, and it has larger clusters of seeds.

NOTES: The species name *gmelinii* honours Johann Georg Gmelin (1709–55) who explored Siberia and the Bering area in 1730s and 1740s.

LESSER SPEARWORT • *Ranunculus flammula*

GENERAL: Perennial; **stems creeping** (usually on wet mud), rooting at nodes, to 50 cm long.

LEAVES: Blades **lance-shaped to linear, without teeth or lobes,** scarcely broader than the long stalks.

FLOWERS: Yellow, small (8–10 mm wide); sepals hairy; **solitary.**

FRUITS: Spherical clusters of 5–25 seeds; each small and smooth with a very short, stout beak.

ECOLOGY: Widespread and common at low to mid elevations in shallow lake and stream edges, ditches and wet ground in marshes and meadows.

SIMILAR SPECIES: Shore buttercup (*R. cymbalaria*) is another common amphibious or aquatic species with simple, long-stalked leaves and creeping stems. Its leaves are more rounded than those of lesser spearwort and have scalloped edges. Shore buttercup can be easily distinguished in fruit by its **column of 50–200 ribbed seeds,** each with a conspicuous beak. • Kidney-leaved buttercup (*R. abortivus*) can be found in similar habitats. It has basal, **kidney-shaped,** toothed leaves, yellow to white petals that are shorter than the sepals and a cylindrical column of seeds.

NOTES: This is one of the most **poisonous** of our buttercups. • Lesser spearwort is also called creeping spearwort. 'Spearwort' aptly describes the shape of the leaves. It has also been called banewort because it was supposed to 'bane' (poison) sheep by causing ulcerated entrails.

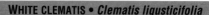

WHITE CLEMATIS • *Clematis ligusticifolia*

GENERAL: Robust, **woody climbing vine**; stems to 20 m long.

LEAVES: Opposite, pinnately compound; 5–7 **leaflets, oval to heart-shaped, toothed**.

FLOWERS: 4 white sepals around a **cluster of stamens and styles**; no petals; few to many in abundant small clusters on short stems in leaf axils; **male and female flowers usually on separate plants.**

FRUITS: Clusters of seeds, each with a **long, feathery tail** (style).

ECOLOGY: Widespread and frequent, mostly at low elevations in arid basins, in damp places, such as along streams and ditches in grasslands and ponderosa pine and Douglas-fir forests.

NOTES: Virgin's bowers are unique within the buttercup family because they grow as climbing or trailing vines. Their **paired compound leaves** are also distinctive. *Clematis* flowers are showy, composed of four or five petal-like sepals surrounding many stamens and pistils. As they mature, they produce equally showy clusters of feathery, plumed seeds, which give the plant a white-bearded appearance in autumn. • The St'at'imc, Secwepemc and Nlaka'pmx mixed white clematis with wild tarragon to make a poultice that was used to alleviate pain from bruises, sprains and broken bones. The Nlaka'pmx also used the fluffy seeds as infant diapers. The Okanagan used the bark to weave mats, garments, bags and other items. • The species name *ligusticifolia* means 'having leaves like *Ligusticum*,' which is a member of the carrot family (Umbelliferae). Other common names are 'virgin's bower' and 'traveller's joy' because it forms bowers along fences and hedges that provide shade and shelter for maidens and travellers alike.

BLUE CLEMATIS • *Clematis occidentalis C. columbiana*

GENERAL: Climbing or trailing vine of variable length, 0.5–5 m long.

LEAVES: Opposite, divided into **3 oval to lance-shaped, toothed leaflets,** thinly hairy.

FLOWERS: Solitary; 4 blue sepals around a cluster of **yellow stamens and styles;** no petals; on long, leafless stalks arising from leaf axils.

FRUITS: Mop-shaped clusters of seeds, each with a **long, feathery tail** (style).

ECOLOGY: Scattered and fairly common at low to mid elevations on our plateaus, arid basins and East Kootenays, in moist to dry sites in open woods or rocky open areas, frequently in mixed deciduous and coniferous forests.

NOTES: The Nlaka'pmx made a medicine for scabs and skin sores from this plant, but they considered it less effective than white clematis (*C. ligustifolia*). • Blue clematis makes a good garden ornamental for our area. It is easily propagated from fresh seeds sown in autumn, or by layering a section of the vine. Like many horticultural varieties of clematis, it grows well in full sun as long as the base of the plant is shaded. • The genus name *Clematis* is from the Greek *kematis*, from *kema*, meaning 'vine-shoot.' The species name *occidentalis* means 'western' and refers to its distribution.

WESTERN MEADOWRUE • *Thalictrum occidentale*

GENERAL: **Rhizomatous** perennial, 40–100 cm tall; stems leafy and purplish when young.

LEAVES: Mostly along stem, with thin stalks; smooth, **bluish green, divided 3–4 times into 3s**; each leaflet 3-lobed.

FLOWERS: Small and **inconspicuous**; **sepals greenish white**, 2–5 mm long; no petals; in loose clusters at tops of stems; **male flowers with prominent, purplish, hanging stamens**; **male and female flowers on separate plants.**

FRUITS: Short-stalked, **long-pointed seeds** with 3 prominent ridges on each side; arranged in star-like clusters.

ECOLOGY: Widespread and common at low to high elevations in moist, often deciduous, open forests, thickets, grassy openings, slide tracks and clearings.

SIMILAR SPECIES: Veiny meadowrue (*T. venulosum*) has **prominent, much-raised** veins on the lower surface of its leaflets.

NOTES: The Nlaka'pmx used a decoction of western meadowrue as a tonic, and they also used it externally as a wash or bathwater to remove stiffness and pains. Turner (1979) notes that the Flathead of Montana 'dried seeds [of western meadowrue], chewed them until pulverized, then rubbed them on the hair and body as perfume.' Some species of meadowrue contain thalictrine, which is a very active **cardiac poison**. • The genus name *Thalictrum* is from the Greek *Thaleia*, 'the blooming one,' the muse of pastoral poetry and comedy. The common name 'meadowrue' refers to the similarity of the leaves to those of rue (*Ruta graveolens*).

BANEBERRY • *Actaea rubra*
A. arguta

GENERAL: **Rhizomatous** perennial, 40–100 cm tall; 1 to several stems, branched, leafy.

LEAVES: All on stems; 2–3 times divided into 3s; **segments coarsely toothed and lobed**.

FLOWERS: Small, **white**, **numerous**; 5–10 petals and 3–5 sepals soon falling; **in rounded clusters** at ends of long stalks.

FRUITS: Smooth, **glossy white or more often red berries**.

ECOLOGY: Widespread at low to subalpine elevations; common in moist, shady forest, along streambanks and in clearings; especially common on rich alluvial sites.

SIMILAR SPECIES: False bugbane (*Trautvetteria caroliniensis*) grows in shady, moist forests and streambanks in the **extreme western and southeastern** parts of our region. Its leaves are deeply palmately lobed and coarsely toothed and it has a showy cluster of white flowers. The flowers are unusual because they have tiny sepals and no petals; their showiness results from tufts of white stamens. • The leaves of baneberry are similar in shape to those of sweet-cicely (*Osmorhiza* sp., p. 247).

NOTES: The berries, foliage and roots are all **highly poisonous**. As few as two berries can induce vomiting, bloody diarrhea and finally cardiac arrest or respiratory system paralysis. The rootstock is a violent purgative and emetic. • The St'at'imc name for this plant means 'sick.' 'They used it sparingly as a physic and tonic boiled in water, but anyone taking it had to suffer the consequences of being severely ill' (Turner 1978). Among the Nlaka'pmx, it was said to cure rheumatism, arthritis, venereal disease and other ailments. • The common name 'baneberry' obviously refers to the plant's severely poisonous nature and comes from the Anglo-Saxon *bana,* meaning 'murderous.'

211

Anemone: the anemones

Anemones are also called windflowers, from their plumed or woolly seeds, which are dispersed by the wind. The several alpine species are among the earliest flowers of the mountain meadows, often flowering even before the snow is completely gone.

Anemones are perennials. Most have highly divided leaves and a solitary flower on each stem, and they are generally hairy throughout. The leaves are primarily at the base of the stem, but most species also have a **whorl of three stalkless leaves on the stem** below the flower. The flowers are showy and consist of a cup of **five or six coloured sepals**, which are usually **hairy on the undersides**. The flowers have **no petals**. Each flower produces many hairy seeds. As the seeds mature, the flowers of some species develop a distinctive shaggy ball or 'mop-head' look. These seed heads are usually a good key to species identification.

Anemone is from the Greek *anemos,* 'wind.' According to one myth, the anemone sprang from the tears that Venus shed over the body of Adonis.

Key to the anemones

1a. Leaves divided into 3 parts, each part only shallowly lobed .... *A. parviflora*
1b. Leaves divided into many, often narrow segments 2

    2a. Styles lacking hairs and less than 2 mm long;
    fruit forming a compact, hairy cluster less than 2 cm across .... *A. multifida*
    2b. Styles feathery-hairy, more than 15 mm long at maturity;
    fruit forming a large silky cluster more than 4 cm across 3

        3a. Sepals white to purplish tinged .... *A. occidentalis*
        3b. Sepals usually blue to purplish .... *A. patens*

CUT-LEAF ANEMONE • *Anemone multifida*

GENERAL: Hairy, clumped perennial, 15–50 cm tall; from a thickened, commonly branched base; 1 to many stems.

LEAVES: Many, long-stalked basal leaves, with roundish outlines, **divided into 3 leaflets and again divided 2 or 3 times**; **leaves on flower stem in a whorl of 3**, divided like basal leaves.

FLOWERS: Creamy white, yellowish or pinkish, tinged with red, blue or purple, particularly on outer surface of the 5–6 sepals; petals absent; **solitary** or less commonly in clusters of up to 4 on long stalks.

FRUITS: Silky-woolly seeds, borne in tight, **egg-shaped or spherical clusters** less than 2 cm across.

ECOLOGY: Widespread and common at low to high elevations in our dry climates in grasslands, open forests, scrub and dry meadows; restricted to dry, rocky, exposed slopes and steep, warm aspects in moist and wet climates.

SIMILAR SPECIES: Northern anemone (*A. parviflora*) is 10–30 cm tall and typically occurs in subalpine and alpine habitats, such as moist tundra, heaths, seepage areas, snowbeds and screes. It has basal leaves with **3 wedge-shaped, broadly lobed leaflets** and its solitary, frosty-white flowers are often tinged with blue on the outside.

NOTES: A strong decoction of cut-leaf anemone was used to kill fleas and lice. The Ktunaxa, St'at'imc and Nlaka'pmx used it as a counter-irritant poultice for cuts, bruises and muscular pains, but only in very small doses and for very short periods. The Nlaka'pmx used the leaves to stop nosebleeds.

PRAIRIE CROCUS • *Anemone patens* ssp. *multifida*
Pulsatilla patens, A. nuttalliana

GENERAL: Perennial, 5–40 cm tall, with several stems from a branched woody base; usually with abundant **long, silky, greyish hairs** throughout.

LEAVES: Many basal leaves developing after earliest flowers; blades **palmately divided into 3 main leaflets** and again divided into **narrow linear segments; leaves on flower stem in a whorl of 3**, divided like basal leaves.

FLOWERS: Solitary, blue to purple, cup-shaped; 5–6 sepals, 5–7 cm long; no petals; blooms in spring soon after, or even before, snowmelt.

FRUITS: Large spherical clusters of **silky-haired, long-plumed seeds**.

ECOLOGY: Scattered in southern Rocky Mountain Trench; locally common in grasslands, dry meadows and mountain slopes.

NOTES: The Ktunaxa used prairie crocus as a counter-irritant in much the same way as other native groups used cut-leaf anemone (*A. multifida*, p. 212). • Prairie crocus is a desirable ornamental and can be propagated without much difficulty from autumn-sown seed. It is often difficult to cultivate successfully, but where conditions are right, it will increase through self-seeding. • Despite the similarities in appearance and name, prairie crocus is not remotely related to true crocuses (*Crocus* spp.), which are in the iris family (Iridaceae). Prairie crocus is also known as pasqueflower.

WESTERN PASQUEFLOWER • *Anemone occidentalis*
Pulsatilla occidentalis

GENERAL: Perennial, 20–50 cm tall, with stout, often branched, woody base; **greyish green and densely hairy** throughout.

LEAVES: Many basal leaves, long-stalked, triangular in outline, **pinnately divided** and again **divided into narrow linear segments; 3 leaves in a whorl** on flower stem, divided like basal leaves.

FLOWERS: Solitary, white or purplish-tinged; 5–6 sepals; no petals; blooms in spring soon after snowmelt.

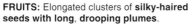

FRUITS: Elongated clusters of **silky-haired seeds with long, drooping plumes**.

ECOLOGY: Widespread and common in subalpine and alpine meadows and subalpine forest openings.

NOTES: Poisonous when fresh. • The Nlaka'pmx used western pasqueflower as an eyewash and as medicine for rheumatism and stomach and bowel troubles. • Western pasqueflower is also called western anemone. Two other common names, 'tow-headed babies' and 'mop-tops,' aptly describe the conspicuous heads of soft, whitish, hairy seed heads which appear after the flowers fall. • The name 'pasqueflower,' originally *passeflower*, is from the boiling of their roots with the *passum* (Latin for 'raisin-wine'). In 1597 the name was changed to 'pasqueflower' because they 'flower for the most part about Easter' (*pasque* being the Old French word for Easter).

WHITE MARSH-MARIGOLD • *Caltha leptosepala*

GENERAL: **Fleshy** perennial, 5–20 cm tall, from a short, erect rootstock with fleshy roots.

LEAVES: **Waxy green, fleshy**, growing from plant base; **oblong-oval**, with somewhat **heart- or arrowhead-shaped bases**; **edges smooth or blunt-toothed.**

FLOWERS: A **single**, showy flower on a smooth stem; 5–12 **sepals, white or greenish** (often **tinged with blue on back**); no petals; centre greenish yellow.

FRUITS: Compact clusters of spreading, **single-chambered capsules** (follicles).

ECOLOGY: Widespread and common at subalpine and alpine elevations in wet meadows, seepage areas, streambanks and snowbeds.

NOTES: This plant was not used by native peoples in our region, but in Alaska, native peoples ate the leaves and flower buds. They also boiled the long, white roots which look like sauerkraut when cooked. If soaked in saltwater and vinegar, the flower buds apparently make an acceptable substitute for capers. The leaves are **toxic** if eaten raw but cooking or drying renders them safe. They contain chemicals that can severely irritate and blister the skin, or inflame tissues of the mouth, throat and digestive tract when swallowed. • This species is also called elkslip. The name 'marigold' appears to come from the Anglo-Saxon *meargealla*, meaning 'horse-gall,' presumably because the unopened buds resemble galls. The species name *leptosepala* means 'with slender sepals.'

GLOBEFLOWER • *Trollius laxus* T. albiflorus

GENERAL: Perennial, 10–40 cm tall, from a short rootstock with strong, fibrous roots; 1 to several stems.

LEAVES: Mostly basal with long stalks; blades **palmately divided into 5 oval main segments** that are further **deeply toothed**; 2–3 short-stalked stem leaves.

FLOWERS: Solitary, showy, long-stalked; **5 sepals, greenish white to creamy white** (sometimes with a pinkish tinge); no petals.

FRUITS: Cone-shaped heads composed of several **single-chambered capsules** with many seeds.

ECOLOGY: Widespread and common at high elevations in wet meadows, seepage areas, streambanks and snowbeds; along streams and seepage areas in subalpine; usually blooms just as snow recedes.

SIMILAR SPECIES: Globeflower can be confused with marsh marigold (*Caltha leptosepala*, above) or white *Anemone* species (pp. 212–13), which usually have a bluish tinge on the outside of the flowers.

NOTES: The centre of the flower contains the many stamens typical of the buttercup family. Globeflowers are unusual however, because the outer ring of stamens are modified into oblong, flattened structures (staminodia) that bear nectar instead of pollen. • The common name 'globeflower' is derived from the globular shape of the flower, at least of the European species *Trollius europaeus*. The genus name *Trollius* is a Latinized rendition of the Swiss-German common name *trollblume* (troll flower). It was supposedly named after the Swedish *troll*, a malignant supernatural being, because the plant contains **acrid, poisonous substances**.

THREE-LEAVED GOLDTHREAD • *Coptis trifolia*

GENERAL: Low perennial, 4–12 cm tall, from slender, **bright yellow rhizomes.**

LEAVES: Evergreen; **3 leaflets, shiny, leathery, fan-shaped and sharp-toothed.**

FLOWERS: White; 5–8 narrow sepals; 5–7 **petals, fleshy, hollow**, about half as long as sepals; **solitary on leafless stalks.**

FRUITS: Long-stalked follicles with erect beaks.

ECOLOGY: Scattered and infrequent at low to mid elevations in northern wet Columbia Mountains in damp, mossy forests, bogs and wet sites.

NOTES: The distinctive, tubular petals of three-leaved goldthread produce nectar at their tips. • In the early 1800s, three-leaved goldthread was sold in large quantities in Boston druggist's shops because it was thought to be good against mouth ulceration (hence an alternative name, mouthwort). It appears to have lost favour by 1884. • The genus name is from the Greek *kopto*, 'to cut,' and *trifolia*, 'three leaves,' which both refer to the divided leaves. The bright yellow rhizomes give rise to the common name 'goldthread.'

WILD GINGER • *Asarum caudatum*

GENERAL: Evergreen perennial with extensive rhizomes; **flowering stems trailing**, freely rooting, sometimes forming large mats.

LEAVES: Opposite, heart- to kidney-shaped, dark green, leathery, long-stalked, finely hairy on veins.

FLOWERS: Solitary, purplish brown, bell-like; composed of **3 wide-spreading sepals,** each tapering to a long point; often hidden beneath leaves and close to ground.

FRUITS: Fleshy capsules; seeds roundish with prominent fleshy appendages.

ECOLOGY: Scattered and locally common at low to mid elevations in Coast/Interior Transition and wet Columbia Mountains, in rich, moist, shaded forests, seepage sites and floodplains.

NOTES: Wild ginger is an inconspicuous but striking plant that is often missed by the casual observer. • When crushed, the whole plant has a strong smell of lemon-ginger. This scent was valued by the Nlaka'pmx and Okanagan, who mixed it with sphagnum moss to make a soft, sweet-smelling bedding for infants. The roots can be eaten fresh, or they can be dried and ground as a ginger substitute. The Nlaka'pmx used the

leaves of wild ginger as a poultice for sprains and cuts, and they drank a rhizome decoction for stomach troubles and indigestion. The Secwepemc chewed the roots as a cold remedy, or they drank a decoction made from the roots for colds and flu. • This plant would make a good shade-garden ground cover, but its southern relative, *A. marmoratum*, which has boldly mottled leaves, is superior. Wild ginger is easily propagated from a section of the rhizome. • The word 'ginger' dates back to the 13th century. It means 'horn-root' or 'root with a horn shape,' and it has generally been applied to plants with this particular flavour or smell.

YELLOW WATERLILY • *Nuphar polysepalum*
N. luteum ssp. *polysepalum*

GENERAL: Aquatic perennial with massive, submerged, prehistoric-looking rhizomes; stems thick and fleshy.

LEAVES: Floating (sometimes partially or wholly submerged), **leathery, round or heart-shaped**; stalks to 2 m long.

FLOWERS: Floating, solitary, cup-shaped; 8–17 sepals (**usually 9**), large, **yellow** (tinged with green or red); petals narrow, yellow or greenish, hidden by **many reddish or purplish stamens**; flower centre dominated by **large, knob-like stigma**.

FRUITS: Many-seeded, **oval, leathery, ribbed capsules**.

ECOLOGY: Widespread and locally common at low to mid elevations in ponds, shallow lakes and sluggish streams.

SIMILAR SPECIES: Pond-lily (*N. variegatum,* also known as *N. luteum* ssp. *variegatum*) has yellow stamens and its leaf stalks are rather flattened with lateral ribs. It occupies much the same distribution and habitats.

NOTES: The large, floating leaves and yellow, cup-shaped flowers are unmistakable. The conspicuous flower parts are the larger of two rings of sepals. The outer ring of sepals is smaller and greenish. The petals are small and inconspicuous. • The Carrier still use the rhizomes medicinally. The rhizomes are peeled, sliced, air-dried and stored sliced or powdered. Rehydrated slices are applied as a poultice to aching joints, broken bones and skin ulcers. The powder is sprinkled on food and eaten. A weak decoction of fresh rhizome can be drunk as an appetite stimulant or tonic. The Nlaka'pmx also used the plant for ulcers, and mixed it into salves for bites, swellings and infections. • Yellow waterlily is also called spatterdock. The genus name *Nuphar* is from the Greek name for waterlilies.

COMMON ST. JOHN'S-WORT • *Hypericum perforatum*

GENERAL: Taprooted perennial, 30–100 cm tall, with short rhizomes.

LEAVES: Opposite, lance-shaped, with **purplish-black dots**.

FLOWERS: Yellow petals with **purplish-black spots** along edges; **linear sepals**; **75–100 stamens, divided into 3 distinct groups**; **pistil cone-shaped,** prominent; in loose clusters at ends of paired stalks.

FRUITS: Pointed capsules releasing pitted, brown seeds.

ECOLOGY: A serious European weed established in southern half of our region on waste land, roadsides and pastures.

SIMILAR SPECIES: Western St. John's-wort (*H. formosum*) is found infrequently on moist to boggy sites at low to subalpine elevations in the southern part of our region. Its **triangular sepals** distinguish it from common St. John's-wort. The showy flowers of western St. John's-wort open to display a brush of golden yellow stamens.

NOTES: Common St. John's-wort is **poisonous** to livestock and difficult to eradicate. It contains a photosensitizing pigment in the glands of its leaves and flowers, and livestock, especially those with white skin, may develop skin lesions after ingesting the plant. Black-skinned animals or even unshorn white sheep are rarely affected. Insects that feed exclusively on common St. John's-wort have been released to control it. • St. John's-wort is named after St. John the Baptist. The bright spots seen when the leaf is held up to the light were believed to ooze blood on the day he was executed (August 27th or 29th). Folklore holds that if this plant was gathered on the eve of St. John's birthday (June 24th) and hung in the windows, it would protect the house against thunder and evil spirits. • This plant is also known as Klamath weed.

BLAZING-STAR • *Mentzelia laevicaulis*

GENERAL: Taprooted **biennial or short-lived perennial**, 30–100 cm tall; stems usually angular; covered in **stiff, grey hairs**.

LEAVES: Lance-shaped with **deep sinuous lobes**; upper leaves stalkless, less deeply lobed and covered with barbed hairs.

FLOWERS: Lemon yellow, large and showy; 5 pointed petals, 2–8 cm long; many **long** stamens, with 5 **outer ones narrowly expanded and petal-like**.

FRUITS: Capsules.

ECOLOGY: Scattered and locally common at low elevations in arid basins in dry, often disturbed grasslands.

SIMILAR SPECIES: The **annual** small-flowered evening star (*M. albicaulis*) occurs at low elevations in the Thompson and Okanagan basins, usually on dry, sandy soils. Its flowers are much smaller (the petals are 2–6 mm long) than those of blazing-star, and its stem is whitish and shining.

NOTES: The five petal-like outer stamens give the flower the appearance of having 10 petals. • The northern Cheyenne of Montana apparently used the root as an ingredient in medicinal preparations for fevers and complicated illnesses. • The common name aptly describes the brilliant, golden, star-shaped flowers with their central puff of many long stamens. The species name *laevicaulis* suggests a smooth stem, but it is actually quite rough to the touch. The genus was named for the German botanist C. Mentzel (1622–1701).

BRITTLE PRICKLY-PEAR CACTUS • *Opuntia fragilis*

GENERAL: Prostrate perennial, forming 5–20-cm-tall mats of spiny, jointed, **succulent**, dark green stems; individual sections of stem are often nearly **as thick as broad**, usually less than 5 cm long and easily detached.

LEAVES: Reduced to **large, strongly barbed spines**, 1–3 cm long.

FLOWERS: Yellow (often peach-coloured when first flowering), showy; **petals** many, **thin**; stamens many, **reddish–stalked**.

FRUITS: More or less **pear-shaped berries**, dry and somewhat spiny.

ECOLOGY: Widespread and often abundant at low elevations in arid basins, southern Rocky Mountain Trench and driest parts of our plateaus, in dry grasslands, sagebrush slopes, openings in ponderosa pine forests and on rocky outcrops.

SIMILAR SPECIES: Many-spined prickly-pear cactus (*O. polyacantha*) is also found in dry, open places, but it is restricted to the southern Okanagan Basin in our area. Its stem sections are conspicuously flattened and larger than those of brittle prickly-pear cactus, and its flowers may have a reddish tint.

NOTES: Many Interior native peoples gathered the stems, mainly in spring. They ate the inner stem boiled, roasted or pit-cooked, used it in soup or mixed it with fat and berries to bake in cakes. Brittle prickly-pear cactus was an important food in times of famine. The Secwepemc also boiled the flesh into a syrup for use as a cough medicine. • The name 'cactus,' from the Greek *kaktos* (any kind of prickly plant), was originally ascribed to the prickly 'cardoon' or thistle, (*Cynara cardunculus*). Theophrastus originally described a plant (probably a *Euphorbia* species) from the Locris Opuntia area of central Greece, which became known by herbalists as Opuntium. When the prickly-pear was introduced from North America, herbalists thought it was the same plant and gave it the name Opuntium, which was subsequently Latinized to *Opuntia*.

Rosaceae: Rose Family

The rose family is a highly diverse group that includes trees and shrubs as well as herbs. Among its members are many commercially valuable tree fruits (e.g., apples, cherries and pears), berries (e.g., blackberries, raspberries and strawberries) and flowers (e.g., roses and spireas). Many of these commercial species have wild relatives that also produce edible fruits, such as salmonberry, thimbleberry and wild blackberries, raspberries, strawberries and roses.

Rose family flowers are most commonly white, but they can vary through shades of pink, red or yellow. The flowers are symmetrical and generally consist of **five separate petals,** five sepals (often fused into a cup-shaped calyx) and **many stamens**. The petals of the different family members do not show a great deal of variation ('a rose is a rose' from the standpoint of petal form).

The general form of the plants often provides some clues to identification. Many have compound leaves, and the shape and arrangement of the leaflets will help to identify many species. Some groups, such as roses and raspberries, have thorns or spines on the stem.

One of the most useful characteristics for identification is the type of fruit. In many species, parts of the flower become swollen and fleshy. These fleshy fruits may surround the seeds, as in apples, cherries and roses, or they may bear the seeds on their surfaces, as in strawberries. The fruits of raspberries are actually clusters of small, fleshy fruitlets. Other species, such as avens, have 1-seeded, dry fruits often found in clusters.

GOAT'S-BEARD • *Aruncus dioicus*
A. sylvester

GENERAL: Perennial, 1–2 m tall, from a stout, short **rhizome**; with several robust flowering stems.

LEAVES: Lower leaves **large, compound** (usually **3 times compound**); leaflets sharply toothed with tapering tips, dark green and usually hairless above, hairy and paler below; upper stem leaves smaller.

FLOWERS: Tiny, white; **densely packed in long, semi-drooping clusters on branched, spike-like inflorescence**; male and female flowers on separate plants.

FRUITS: Small, erect **follicles** with **spreading tips** on long, drooping branches.

ECOLOGY: Scattered and locally common at low to subalpine elevations in wet Columbia Mountains and Coast/Interior Transition, in moist forests, openings, seepage areas and moist clearings.

NOTES: The Nlaka'pmx prepared a decoction from the root to treat internal ailments, swelling, broken ribs and colds. They also applied it as a poultice for swollen limbs. Goat's-beard was also an important medicine for the Lil'wet'ul. • The genus name *Aruncus* is derived from the Greek *aryngos*, which means 'goat's beard' and refers to the long, fluffy, white flower clusters.

WILD STRAWBERRY • *Fragaria virginiana*

GENERAL: Low-growing perennial; stems (**runners**) usually several, trailing, weakly hairy, reddish.

LEAVES: Bluish green, on long stalks arising directly from rootstock, **divided into 3 leaflets with toothed edges**, hairless above but hairy below.

FLOWERS: White; 2–15 in open clusters on **stems that are usually shorter than surrounding leaves**.

FRUITS: Small strawberries, juicy, delicious and much richer in flavour than domestic species; on stems shorter than the leaves.

ECOLOGY: Widespread and common at low to subalpine elevations in dry and moist forests, openings and disturbed areas.

SIMILAR SPECIES: Wood strawberry (*F. vesca*) is less common than wild strawberry in our area. Its leaves are bright yellow-green and hairy above, and the runners are green to reddish. The **flowers and fruits are usually on stems which are longer than the leaves**.

NOTES: The fruit of both wood strawberry and wild strawberry were highly prized by all Interior native peoples. They usually ate the berries fresh, although some people mashed and dried them in cakes, uncooked, for winter use. The dried leaves were steeped to make a tea for diarrhea, or they were used to flavour cooked roots. In folk medicine, the tea from leaves is a remedy for diarrhea and a gargle for sore throats. • Wild strawberry is the original parent of nine-tenths of all the cultivated strawberries now grown. • Wild strawberry is also called blue-leaved strawberry. The name 'strawberry' could be derived from the practice of spreading the dried runners on the ground (like straw), or from the Old English word for 'straw,' which also means 'mote' or 'chaff,' in reference to the small seeds embedded in the surface of the berry. The genus name *Fragaria* is from the Latin *fragra*, meaning 'fragrant.'

SIBBALDIA • *Sibbaldia procumbens*

GENERAL: Dwarf, **mat-forming** perennial, with **prostrate stems and rhizomes**; stiff, flat-lying hairs throughout; flowering stems erect and leafless.

LEAVES: Mainly on prostrate stems, stalked and divided into **3 sparsely hairy leaflets with 3–5 teeth across tip**.

FLOWERS: Pale yellow, saucer-shaped; 5 petals, shorter than the 5 hairy sepals; **in small clusters** at tops of flowering stems.

FRUITS: Clusters of small **dry seeds**.

ECOLOGY: Scattered at subalpine and alpine elevations in open, often rocky, areas and meadows; infrequent at mid elevations in northern half of our region, in moist, open forests and on disturbed soils.

SIMILAR SPECIES: Sibbaldia somewhat resembles wild strawberry (*Fragaria virginiana*, above), but it has blunter leaf tips, yellow flowers and produces a head of dry seeds instead of an edible, juicy berry. • Sibbaldia may be distinguished from the cinquefoils (*Potentilla* spp., pp. 224–28) by the number of stamens—it has **five or 10 stamens** while cinquefoils usually have more than 10.

NOTES: The genus and common name honour Sir Robert Sibbald (1641–1722), a Scottish physician and botanist.

PARTRIDGEFOOT • *Luetkea pectinata*
Spiraea pectinata

GENERAL: Semi-shrub, to 15 cm tall, **prostrate, mat-forming,** with erect flowering stems.

LEAVES: Evergreen, crowded in **thick basal tufts** and along flowering stems, **fan-shaped and much-divided** into several linear segments.

FLOWERS: Small, white; in a dense, showy cluster at tops of leafy stems.

FRUITS: Several-seeded follicles.

ECOLOGY: Widespread and common at subalpine and alpine elevations in open, moist and wet areas and seepage sites; indicator of late snowmelt patches.

NOTES: Partridgefoot is the sole member in the genus *Luetkea.* • It is a superior ground cover in moist rock gardens, and it is extremely easy to propagate. Although it takes readily from seed, it is most easily propagated from a small section of stem and rhizome rooted in moist sand. • The common name 'partridgefoot' refers to the finely divided leaves, which somewhat resemble the footprint of a partridge or ptarmigan. It is also called creeping spirea. The genus name commemorates Count F. P. Lütke, a 19th-century Russian sea captain and explorer. The species name *pectinata* means 'pectinate' (like the teeth of a comb) and here refers to the leaves.

SITKA BURNET • *Sanguisorba canadensis*
S. sitchensis

GENERAL: Rhizomatous perennial, 25–100 cm tall.

LEAVES: Mostly basal, pinnately divided into **9–17 egg-shaped to oblong, coarsely toothed leaflets**; 1–3 stem leaves, with fewer leaflets and 2 leaflet-like stipules where leaves join stem.

FLOWERS: Greenish or yellowish white, many, small; in a **dense, cylindrical head**.

FRUITS: Single, dry seeds, slightly winged.

ECOLOGY: Scattered at subalpine and alpine elevations in Coast/Interior Transition and northern half of wet Columbia Mountains, in wetlands, moist forests and seepage areas; often abundant in wet clearings.

NOTES: Herbalists recommend using the leaves to make an herbal tea and the roots for a decoction for internal and external bleeding, dysentery or genital discharges. Indeed, the genus name *Sanguisorba* and the alternative common name 'burnet bloodwort' both refer to the plant's supposed power to stanch blood. (*Sanguisorba* literally translates as 'blood absorber.') • This species is also known as Canada burnet. The name 'burnet' comes from the Old French word *brunette*, meaning 'brown,' and is applied to European species of *Sanguisorba* because their flowers are a rich red-brown colour.

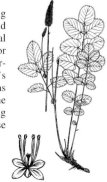

YELLOW MOUNTAIN-AVENS • *Dryas drummondii*

GENERAL: Prostrate, **evergreen semi-shrub**; stems freely rooting, trailing, woody; often forming extensive, low mats.

LEAVES: Oblong to oval, to 2 cm long, broadest above middle and wedge-shaped at base, leathery, wrinkly; edges scalloped; either hairless and dark green above or hairy and white above, **densely covered in white hairs below**; withering but not dropping off immediately.

FLOWERS: Pale yellow, 2–3 cm across; **oval sepals with dark glandular hairs**; nodding; single on hairy, leafless stalks.

FRUITS: Many achenes, each with a silky golden-yellow, **feathery plume** which becomes twisted around the others and later opens into a fluffy mass.

ECOLOGY: Scattered at low to alpine elevations in open gravelly (frequently calcium-rich) areas.

SIMILAR SPECIES: Two varieties occur commonly in B.C.—*D. drummondii* var. *drummondii* has a dark green upper leaf surface while *D. drummondii* var. *tomentosa* has a whitish upper leaf surface.

NOTES: The Secwepemc used yellow mountain-avens as a heart medicine and the Nlaka'pmx drank a decoction against kidney and bladder trouble. • Yellow mountain-avens is valued as a dwarf rock-garden plant, and it can be propagated by layering and by cuttings. It is often available commercially. • The species is named for Thomas Drummond (1780–1835), an early Canadian botanist.

WHITE MOUNTAIN-AVENS • *Dryas octopetala*
D. hookeriana

GENERAL: Low, prostrate, **evergreen semi-shrub**; stems freely rooting, trailing, woody; often forming large patches.

LEAVES: Oblong to lance-shaped; to 3 cm long, leathery, wrinkly, **dark green**, leaf base rounded or heart-shaped; **edges coarsely scalloped** and often rolled under; **densely white-hairy below**, hairless but often studded with warty glands above.

FLOWERS: Creamy white, 2–3 cm across; **lance-shaped sepals**; solitary on hairy, leafless stalks.

FRUITS: Many achenes, each with a silky, golden-yellow, **feathery plume** which becomes twisted around others and later opens into a fluffy mass, becoming detached and dispersed by wind.

ECOLOGY: Scattered and often abundant at alpine elevations on open sites with gravelly soils.

NOTES: White mountain-avens is widely available as a rock-garden plant and thrives in sunny, well-drained sites. Many commercial varieties were developed from European stock. • The genus name *Dryas* is from the Greek for 'wood-nymph.'

Geum : the avens

This group of herbaceous species can be difficult to identify because of the similarity of their flowers to those of several cinquefoils (*Potentilla* spp., pp. 224–28) and buttercups (*Ranunculus* spp., pp. 206–09).

The identification of species emphasizes the leaves, especially the cluster of large, compound leaves located at the base of the flowering stem. These leaves are 'pinnately' compound, meaning they are composed of many leaflets arranged in rows on either side of the leaf stalk. In most species, the leaflet at the top of the stalk is noticeably the largest.

Avens flowers are yellow, pink or purplish. They are composed of five petals, five sepals and many stamens. The **sepals are arranged alternately with five bracts, making it appear as though the flowers have 10 sepals**. Examining the flowers under 10x magnification reveals distinctively hooked or kinked styles that may also be visible on the seeds. The seed shape and the hooked style will usually separate the avens from genera with similar flowers.

The fruits are usually a ball-shaped cluster of seeds that are dry, hard and generally hairy, often with a long plumy 'tail.' In **most species the seeds retain the hooked styles**. These fruits have a 'stick-tight' mode of dispersal, and they cling to any rough surface, such as animal fur and human clothing.

The name 'avens' appears to come from the Old French *avence* or medieval Latin *avancia*. These in turn may have been derived from the Greek word for 'antidote,' because avens was supposed to ward off 'the devil and evil spirits, venomous serpents and wild beasts.'

The Nlaka'pmx and Okanagan boiled and steeped the roots to make a tea that was used as a beverage or appetizer and as a medicine for colds and fever.

OLD MAN'S WHISKERS • *Geum triflorum*

GENERAL: Rhizomatous perennial, to 40 cm tall, often forming **clumps, covered in old leaf-bases**; flowering stems softly hairy.

LEAVES: Basal leaves in a cluster, long-stalked, **compound, divided into many crowded leaflets and divided again into narrow, sometimes toothed segments**; stem leaves few, small, usually divided into linear lobes.

FLOWERS: Urn-shaped; pink to yellow petals; purplish sepals; in clusters of 1–5 (usually 3); blooms in early spring at low elevations.

FRUITS: Feathery clusters of seeds with **plume-like, bronze to purplish styles**.

ECOLOGY: Widespread at low to subalpine elevations on our dry plateaus, in arid basins and in East Kootenays, in dry, open forests, grasslands and openings; often common on dry gravelly soils.

NOTES: The Okanagan prepared an infusion from the plant to treat vaginal yeast infections, and they also used it as a women's love potion. The Nlaka'pmx boiled the roots to make a drink and to make a decoction which they used as a body wash in sweathouses. • The species name *triflorum* (3-flowered) refers to the flowers, which are usually in clusters of three. This species is also called purple avens and prairie smoke. When there are many plants growing together, the colour and texture of the feathery styles on the fruits suggest a haze of low-lying smoke.

LARGE-LEAVED AVENS • *Geum macrophyllum*

GENERAL: Rhizomatous perennial, 30–70 cm tall, with hairy stems.

LEAVES: Basal leaves in a cluster, **long-stalked, compound; top leaflet heart- to kidney-shaped, shallowly lobed and toothed, many times larger** than the several smaller leaflets below it; few stem leaves, small, 3-lobed.

FLOWERS: Bright yellow, saucer-shaped; solitary or in a few-flowered cluster at tip of stem.

FRUITS: Clusters of hairy seeds, with persistent styles bearing an **S-shaped bend (hook) near tip.**

ECOLOGY: Scattered at low to subalpine elevations in moist and wet forests, seepage areas, openings and clearings.

NOTES: After childbirth Okanagan women drank a tea made from the roots of large-leaved avens. The Nlaka'pmx drank a decoction of the plant against rash-causing diseases, including smallpox. It was also used as a charm. • The species name *macrophyllum* (large leaf) refers to the size of the leaflet at the tip of the compound leaf. The leaflet pattern should readily distinguish large-leaved avens from any of the other avens in our area.

WATER AVENS • *Geum rivale*

GENERAL: Perennial, 40–60 cm tall, with short, thick rhizomes; flowering stems hairy.

LEAVES: Basal leaves in a cluster, **long-stalked, compound,** divided into unequally sized leaflets with **saw-toothed edges; uppermost leaflet largest, lyre-shaped, usually deeply 3-lobed;** several smaller stem leaves.

FLOWERS: Yellow to **pinkish, cup-shaped;** petals **purple-veined,** shorter than sepals; **sepals reddish purple,** erect to spreading; in clusters of 3–7 at tips of stems.

FRUITS: Clusters of **hairy seeds** with persistent styles, **hooked at tip.**

ECOLOGY: Frequent at low to subalpine elevations in wet, forested sites, seepage areas and non-peaty wetlands.

SIMILAR SPECIES: Yellow avens (*G. aleppicum*) has a similar distribution and is found in similar habitats. It is distinguished from water avens by its **green sepals, which turn downward, and by its yellow petals**.

NOTES: The species name *rivale* means 'of riverbanks' and refers to this plant's habitat.

Potentilla: the cinquefoils

The cinquefoils are a large group of mostly herbs that can be recognized by their five yellow (occassionally white or deep red), broadly heart-shaped petals. In our region there is one shrub, shrubby cinquefoil (*P. fruticosa*, p. 66). The **five lance-shaped sepals alternate with five very similar bracts, so that there appear to be 10 sepals**.

Cinquefoil leaves are always compound. The arrangement of the leaflets, however, varies widely and is not always consistent within a species. The common leaflet arrangements are referred to as **pinnate** or **palmate**. In **palmately compound** leaves, **all the leaflets originate from a single point on the leaf stalk**. In **pinnately compound** leaves, the **leaflets are arranged in opposite pairs along the leaf stalk**. Leaflet arrangement, whether pinnate or palmate, is generally best expressed in the basal leaves.

Some cinquefoils may be confused with the yellow-flowered species of avens (*Geum* spp., pp. 222–23), but most of these cases can be resolved on the basis of leaf shape. Examination of the flowers under 10x magnification will also show that cinquefoils lack the hairy, kinked styles typical of the avens.

Key to the cinquefoils

1a. Petals dark red to purple; plants with trailing stems; very wet habitats .... *P. palustris*

1b. Petals yellow to white; stems erect to sometimes trailing; dry to wet habitats 2

  2a. Flowers solitary on leafless stems; plants with long runners .... *P. anserina*

  2b. Usually several to many flowers on generally leafy stems; plants lacking runners 3

    3a. Basal leaves with 3 leaflets 4

      4a. Plants annual to biennial; lower surface
of leaves somewhat hairy but not white-woolly .... *P. norvegica*

      4b. Plants perennial; lower surface of leaves white-woolly 5

        5a. Scales at stem base very dark brown; leaves
somewhat leathery; flowers usually more than 2 cm across .... *P. villosa*

        5b. Scales at stem base reddish brown; leaves
not leathery; flowers less than 2 cm across .... *P. uniflora*

    3b. Basal leaves with more than 3 leaflets 6

      6a. Leaflets palmately arranged 7

        7a. Leaves mostly along stems; mature achenes
with ridges; stems with long, coarse, spreading hairs .... *P. recta*

        7b. Leaves mostly basal; mature achenes smooth;
stems often hairy, but usually not with long, coarse, spreading hairs 8

          8a. Leaflets mostly more than 3 cm long, paler
on lower surface than upper; plants lowland to montane .... *P. gracilis*

          8b. Leaflets mostly less than 3 cm long, of similar
colour on both surfaces; plants subalpine to alpine .... *P. diversifolia*

      6b. Leaflets pinnately arranged 9

        9a. Styles tapered at both ends, attached near
middle or on lower half of achene 10

          10a. Flower clusters dense, with nearly erect branches .... *P. arguta*

          10b. Flower clusters open, with somewhat spreading branches .... *P. glandulosa*

        9b. Styles tapering, thickest near base, often attached near top of achene 11

          11a. Leaflets attached near each other, so that
leaf appears almost palmately divided .... *P. diversifolia*

          11b. Leaflets not all attached near each other, leaves clearly pinnate 12

            12a. Style thickened and roughened near base .... *P. pensylvanica*

            12b. Style slender and smooth 13

              13a. Stems and leaves hairless or with a few hairs, green ..... *P. drummondii*

              13b. Stems and leaves densely hairy, greyish .... *P. hippiana*

MARSH CINQUEFOIL • *Potentilla palustris*

GENERAL: Perennial with long, **creeping rhizomes**, often with floating stems that can root at nodes; flowering stems frequently reddish, horizontal to erect, to 1 m long.

LEAVES: Mainly on flowering stems, pinnately compound; lower leaves with 5–7 **oblong and coarsely toothed leaflets**, light green above and paler below; upper leaves smaller, with fewer leaflets.

FLOWERS: Reddish purple; arranged in loose clusters at top of flowering stems.

FRUITS: Many plump, **brownish-purple** achenes.

ECOLOGY: Widespread at low to mid elevations, usually partly submerged in wetlands and in shallow pond and lake edges; generally absent from our arid basins.

NOTES: The reddish-purple flowers distinguish marsh cinquefoil from the other yellow-flowered cinquefoils. The flowers emit a fetid odour that attracts carrion-feeding insects as pollinators. • 'Cinquefoil' literally means 'five leaves' and refers to the five leaflets of the compound leaves of many species of *Potentilla*.

SILVERWEED • *Potentilla anserina*

GENERAL: Generally **hairy** perennial with **long, strawberry-like runners**.

LEAVES: In a **basal cluster**, long-stalked, pinnately compound; **10–25 leaflets, oval to oblong, coarsely toothed**; varying from **silky grey-hairy** on both surfaces to smooth and green above and hairy below.

FLOWERS: Solitary, yellow, saucer-shaped; on a long, **leafless stalk**; bloom in spring.

FRUITS: Corky achenes, wrinkled on back and top.

ECOLOGY: Scattered and often common at low to mid elevations on our dry plateaus, in arid basins and in East Kootenays, in non-peaty wetlands, moist places in grasslands and alkaline meadows.

NOTES: Silverweed is sometimes also called Indian sweet potato, because many Interior peoples ate the long fleshy roots cooked or raw. The roots are said to have a pleasant, slightly bitter taste. The Blackfoot of Alberta used the runners as ties for leggings and blankets (Turner 1979). • The common name 'silverweed' describes the silky grey-hairy appearance of this plant. In Europe, it is known as 'powerful little one' and was used as a remedy against witches and as a love divination. The genus name *Potentilla*, Latin for 'quite powerful,' refers to its use as a medicinal herb.

VILLOUS CINQUEFOIL • *Potentilla villosa*

GENERAL: Perennial, 3–15 cm tall, with **thick, scaly root-stock** and branched crown; **greyish-hairy throughout**, usually with **woolly stems**.

LEAVES: Mostly basal, divided into **3 dark green leaflets**; leaflets strongly veined, coarsely toothed, silky-hairy above and **white-woolly below**.

FLOWERS: Yellow; **petals shallowly notched**, 5–8 mm long, longer than **woolly sepals**; 2–5 in an open cluster.

FRUITS: Clusters of achenes with slightly ridged surfaces.

ECOLOGY: Scattered on dry, gravelly and rocky alpine sites.

SIMILAR SPECIES: One-flowered cinquefoil (*P. uniflora*) can be mistaken for a small version of villous cinquefoil. It is wide-spread at alpine elevations and grows in similar habi-

tats, but is less hairy and has smaller flowers (the petals are 4–5 mm long) than villous cinquefoil.

NOTES: The species name *villosa* is not a reference to villainy or anything vile, but to the shaggy hairs that cover the plant.

SULPHUR CINQUEFOIL • *Potentilla recta*

GENERAL: Stiffly erect perennial, 30–80 cm tall, with a woody base; **hairy** and sometimes glandular throughout.

LEAVES: Mostly on stem, palmately divided into **5–7 deeply toothed and strongly veined leaflets**.

FLOWERS: Many **showy, yellow flowers** in flat-topped clusters.

FRUITS: Clusters of dark, **wrinkled** achenes.

ECOLOGY: Scattered and often abundant, mostly at low elevations in southern part of our region in disturbed ground, grasslands and pastures.

SIMILAR SPECIES: Norwegian cinquefoil (*P. norvegica*) is an **annual or biennial** species of similar habitats. It is a hairy (but never glandular) plant, and its leaves are usually divided into oval, blunt-toothed leaflets. The flowers are spread along the stem.

NOTES: This troublesome weed, introduced from Eurasia, is now widely established in east-ern North America and parts of the Pacific Northwest. • The Okanagan used sulphur cinquefoil internally and externally as a medicine. The leaves were steeped in hot water and were said to alleviate stomach trouble. The leaves and stems were also pounded and applied as a poultice to wounds.

ELBE

GRACEFUL CINQUEFOIL • *Potentilla gracilis*

GENERAL: Perennial, 40–80 cm tall, from a thick, woody base; with several variably hairy stems.

LEAVES: Mostly basal, long-stalked and **palmately divided into 5–9 sharply toothed leaflets**; usually pale and **densely hairy** (often woolly) below; 1–2 small stem leaves.

FLOWERS: Yellow, **showy**; **heart-shaped petals**; several to many in open clusters at top of stem.

FRUITS: Many small, smooth, **greenish** achenes.

ECOLOGY: Common at low to mid elevations, mostly on our dry plateaus, in grasslands, dry, open forests and on disturbed ground.

NOTES: Graceful cinquefoil is highly variable in its hairiness and leaflet shape. • The Okanagan made a tea from the roots as a tonic for blood, aches and pains, and as a cure for diarrhea and gonorrhea. The tea was also used to wash sores. The Nlaka'pmx made a salve from graceful cinquefoil mixed with pitch, which they used to heal wounds and draw out pain.

DIVERSE-LEAVED CINQUEFOIL • *Potentilla diversifolia*

GENERAL: Tufted perennial, 15–40 cm tall, from a stout, branched rootstock; with slender stems.

LEAVES: Mostly basal, long-stalked and mostly **palmately compound** with **5–7 deeply toothed leaflets,** sparsely hairy below.

FLOWERS: Yellow, showy; petals notched at tips; on long stalks in an open cluster.

FRUITS: Cluster of small, dry achenes.

ECOLOGY: Widespread and common in subalpine meadows and alpine tundra; in Chilcotin it descends into dry, open forests and openings at mid elevations.

SIMILAR SPECIES: See sticky cinquefoil (*P. glandulosa*, p. 228).

NOTES: Some plants have a distinct bluish- or greyish-green appearance. Although the leaflets are most commonly palmately arranged, individuals with a pinnate arrangement may be encountered.

STICKY CINQUEFOIL • *Potentilla glandulosa*

GENERAL: Perennial, 15–40 cm tall, from a branched rootstock; flowering stems covered with **sticky, often reddish hairs**.

LEAVES: Mainly basal, pinnately divided into **5–9 sharply toothed, oval leaflets**.

FLOWERS: Deep yellow to pale cream; in small, open clusters on branches at top of stem.

FRUITS: Loose clusters of smooth achenes.

ECOLOGY: Scattered at low to mid elevations in our dry and moist climates in open forests and meadows.

SIMILAR SPECIES: There are several other *Potentilla* species in our area that have mainly pinnately compound leaves. • White cinquefoil (*P. arguta*) grows in similar habitats to sticky cinquefoil. Its pinnately compound leaves (with 7–9 leaflets) are densely sticky-hairy, as are its stems and flowers. It can be distinguished by its **short, narrow, dense clusters of pale yellow to whitish flowers** and by its stout stems (30–100 cm tall). • Drummond's cinquefoil (*P. drummondii*) has distinctly pinnately compound leaves that are **often hairless** or have just a few soft hairs. It occurs in wet areas and meadows at mid to **high** elevations. • Woolly cinquefoil (*P. hippiana*) has pinnately compound leaves that tend to be **white-hairy all over**. It occurs on dry, rocky slopes, grasslands, sagebrush and open woods at low to mid elevations, mostly on the Fraser Plateau and in the southern Rocky Mountain Trench.

NOTES: The Nlaka'pmx used a decoction of the whole plant as a tonic and stimulant.

PRAIRIE CINQUEFOIL • *Potentilla pensylvanica*

GENERAL: Tufted perennial, 20–50 cm tall, from a stout, branched rootstock; 1 to several flowering stems, sparsely to thickly hairy.

LEAVES: Pinnately compound; 5–9 leaflets (sometimes 11), deeply toothed to more than halfway to middle; lower leaflet often reduced; upper 3 leaflets largest; greenish, densely covered with hairs above and white-woolly below.

FLOWERS: Yellow, showy; petals notched at tips; style thickened and rough; several on long stalks in open cluster.

FRUITS: Cluster of small, dry achenes.

ECOLOGY: Scattered at low to mid elevations on our dry plateaus, in arid basins and in southern Rocky Mountain Trench, in dry grasslands and rocky slopes.

NOTES: Prairie cinquefoil, as its name suggests, is also a species of the prairies east of the Rockies.

Brassicaceae: Mustard Family

The mustard family (also called Cruciferae) is a large family of annual, biennial or perennial herbs with considerable economic importance, having been developed into many commonly used edible plants and ornamentals. In addition to table mustard, food crops include cabbage, cauliflower, broccoli, kohlrabi, Brussels sprout (all developed from *Brassica oleracea*), turnip (*Brassica rapa*), radish (*Raphanus sativus*), and watercress (*Rorippa nasturtium aquaticum*). 'Flowering Kale,' wallflower (*Erysimum cheiri*), 'Silver Dollar,' stocks (*Matthiola*), rocket (*Hesperis*), sweet alyssum (*Lobularia maritima*) and rockcress (*Arabis*) commonly provide colour in flower gardens.

Many of our common, persistent weeds are introduced mustards, including shepherd's-purse (*Capsella bursa-pastoris*), flixweed (*Descurainia sophia*) and tumble-mustards (*Sisybrium* spp.). Many of these weedy mustards are actually winter annuals. Their seeds germinate in autumn, forming a hardy seedling or rosette. These overwinter, ready for a quick start in spring, and they are often the first green plants in your garden.

Members of the mustard family can be recognized by the typical mustard flower, which has **four coloured petals, four sepals and six stamens** (four of them long, and two short on opposite sides of the pistil). The four small petals are arranged in a cross, or an 'X.' Mustard flowers are yellow, white or pink to purple.

In most mustards the fruits are pod-like, similar to a pea or bean, but with a thin partition down the middle. Upon maturing, the pods often pop open and release a spray of tiny seeds. Mustards can be prolific seed producers; a single plant may produce as many as 10,000 tiny seeds.

The plants continue to blossom at the stem tips long after the lower flowers have developed into mature pods. Thus, during much of the growing season, plants will have a cluster of flowers at the top of the stems with an array of pods in different stages of development distributed downwards.

Many species of butterflies use mustard flowers for nectar. Some groups of butterflies, especially the marblewings, whites and orangetips, depend on mustard species as their specific host plants. The emergence of the attractive Sara orangetip coincides every year exactly with the early spring flowering time of native mustards, particularly *Arabis* spp. The cabbage white, an introduced 'weedy' butterfly, is familiar to any gardener who has a patch of broccoli or cabbage, although its main sustenance is from introduced, weedy mustard plants.

The identification of mustard species involves checking the shape, size and orientation of the seedpods, as well as flower colour and leaf shape. Mustard species fall into two general groups based on the outline of their seed pods. One group has rounded pods (**silicles**), the other has long, narrow pods (**siliques**). Within these groups there is further variation in outline and cross-section and in whether the pods are held upright or bend downwards. To assist in identification, a picture key to the flower colour, leaf and seedpod shape of common mustards is provided.

Picture-key to the common mustards

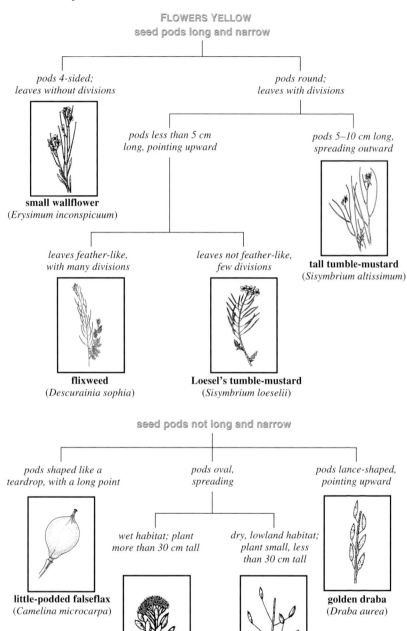

FLOWERS YELLOW
seed pods long and narrow

*pods 4-sided;
leaves without divisions*

*pods round;
leaves with divisions*

*pods less than 5 cm
long, pointing upward*

*pods 5–10 cm long,
spreading outward*

small wallflower
(*Erysimum inconspicuum*)

*leaves feather-like,
with many divisions*

*leaves not feather-like,
few divisions*

tall tumble-mustard
(*Sisymbrium altissimum*)

flixweed
(*Descurainia sophia*)

Loesel's tumble-mustard
(*Sisymbrium loeselii*)

seed pods not long and narrow

*pods shaped like a
teardrop, with a long point*

*pods oval,
spreading*

*pods lance-shaped,
pointing upward*

little-podded falseflax
(*Camelina microcarpa*)

*wet habitat; plant
more than 30 cm tall*

*dry, lowland habitat;
plant small, less
than 30 cm tall*

golden draba
(*Draba aurea*)

marsh yellow-cress
(*Rorippa palustris*)

woods draba
(*Draba nemorosa*)

FLOWERS WHITE OR PURPLE
seed pods long and narrow

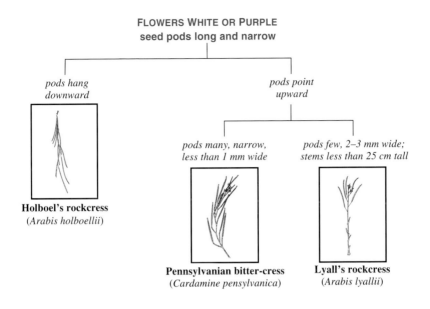

*pods hang
downward*

Holboel's rockcress
(*Arabis holboellii*)

*pods point
upward*

*pods many, narrow,
less than 1 mm wide*

Pennsylvanian bitter-cress
(*Cardamine pensylvanica*)

*pods few, 2–3 mm wide;
stems less than 25 cm tall*

Lyall's rockcress
(*Arabis lyallii*)

seed pods not long and narrow

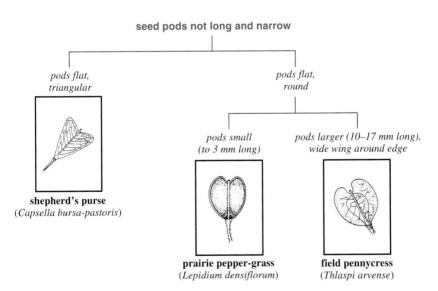

*pods flat,
triangular*

shepherd's purse
(*Capsella bursa-pastoris*)

*pods flat,
round*

*pods small
(to 3 mm long)*

prairie pepper-grass
(*Lepidium densiflorum*)

*pods larger (10–17 mm long),
wide wing around edge*

field pennycress
(*Thlaspi arvense*)

HOLBOELL'S ROCKCRESS • *Arabis holboellii*

GENERAL: Taprooted **biennial**, 20–80 cm tall, with solitary or few stems, hairy near base.

LEAVES: A basal cluster of lance-shaped, **finely hairy** leaves, tapering to slender stalks; stem leaves smaller towards top of stem, often with ear-like **lobes** (auricles) **that clasp stem**.

FLOWERS: Small, **pink or pinkish-purple**, varying to white; in clusters at top of stem, which become longer as they mature.

FRUITS: Long, narrow, flattened pods; on short stalks that **bend downward**.

ECOLOGY: Widespread at low to subalpine elevations in grasslands, open forests, openings, dry, gravelly sites and rocky south slopes.

SIMILAR SPECIES: There are five or six relatively common species of rockcress in our region. • Drummond's rockcress (*A drummondii*) is similar to Holboell's rockcress in both general appearance and habitat, but Drummond's rockcress is shorter, it has white or pinkish petals, and its pods are stiffly erect or slightly spreading. • Tower mustard (*A. glabra*) is a tall (to 1.5 m), stout, introduced weed with bluish-green, unbranched stems that are hairy only at the base, creamy-white flowers and stiffly erect pods. It occurs only in disturbed habitats at low elevations.

NOTES: The Nlaka'pmx chewed the raw leaves of Holboell's rockcress to prevent toothaches. • Cress leaves are widely used for salads, and the name 'cress' derives from an old Indo-European word meaning 'to nibble' or 'to eat.' *Arabis* species are closely related to other cresses (such as watercress [*Rorippa nasturium-aquaticum*]), but grow in dry, rocky places—hence 'rockcress.'

LYALL'S ROCKCRESS • *Arabis lyallii*

GENERAL: Taprooted, tufted **perennial**, 10–25 cm tall, with several **short, mostly smooth stems** from a branched, woody base.

LEAVES: A basal rosette of fleshy, narrow leaves, **without toothed edges**; several stem leaves with tiny ear-like **lobes** (auricles) **that clasp stem**.

FLOWERS: Small, **pale purple**; 3 or more flowers per stem.

FRUITS: Long, narrow, flattened pods; **held upright** on short stalks, and **slightly spreading away from stem**.

ECOLOGY: Widespread and infrequent at subalpine and alpine elevations in fairly dry meadows, scree slopes and rock outcrops.

SIMILAR SPECIES: Several other species of small rockcresses occur in our region, and they also have erect, slightly spreading pods. • Littleleaf rockcress (*A. microphylla*) has basal leaves that are toothed and covered with grey hairs. • Nuttall's rockcress (*A. nuttallii*) has stem leaves without auricles, and it is frequently found in shrub-carrs in the northern part of our region.

SMALL WALLFLOWER • *Erysimum inconspicuum*

GENERAL: Perennial, 20–60 cm tall, usually with a single, branched stem.

LEAVES: Long and narrow, mainly on stem.

FLOWERS: Pale yellow, 6–12 mm long.

FRUITS: Long, narrow pods, 2.5–5 cm long; held stiffly **erect**.

ECOLOGY: Widespread and infrequent at low to mid elevations in grasslands and dry, open forests; often on alkaline soils.

SIMILAR SPECIES: This native species is easily confused with wormseed mustard (*E. cheiranthoides*), which has smaller petals (less than 6 mm long) and shorter seedpods (1.5–3 cm long). Wormseed mustard is a weedy annual that is often found in moist disturbed sites, such as roadsides.

NOTES: The genus name *Erysimum* is from *erysio*, meaning 'to draw' (as in drawing out pain or causing blisters), because it was often used as a poultice.

FLIXWEED • *Descurainia sophia*

GENERAL: Branched **annual**, 30–100 cm tall, with a **greyish-green colour** caused by a dense covering of **fine, star-shaped hairs**.

LEAVES: Mainly along stem, oval, **divided 2–3 times into very narrow segments** (almost feather-like).

FLOWERS: Very small, **pale yellow**; clustered at ends of branches.

FRUITS: Long, narrow pods; held **erect** and nearly parallel to stem on short stalks.

ECOLOGY: Scattered and often common at low to mid elevations in dry disturbed soils (often around human habitation) and overgrazed grasslands.

SIMILAR SPECIES: Western tansy-mustard (*D. pinnata*) also has finely divided leaves, but it is greenish in colour and has glandular hairs, and its seedpods are shorter (about the same length as the stalks). • Richardson's tansy-mustard (*D. richard-*

sonii) is generally grey-hairy, with leaves that are less finely divided than those of flixweed. It is distinguished from flixweed and western tansy-mustard by its pointed seedpods.

NOTES: Flixweed is a vigorous, introduced weed that is found where native vegetation has been removed. The two other species of *Descurainia* are native to our region, and all three species abound in disturbed grassland sites. • The species name *sophia* means 'wisdom' or 'skill,' and comes from the wise use of this plant to treat the disease 'flix' (dysentery), and as an antiputrid, a vulnerary (for healing wounds) and a vermifuge (to expel intestinal worms). It is also appropriately called fluxweed. The genus is named after François Descourain (1658–1740), a French apothecary and botanist.

TALL TUMBLE-MUSTARD • *Sisymbrium altissimum*

GENERAL: Coarse **annual**, to 1.5 m tall, with many spreading branches; stems are hairy mainly at their bases.

LEAVES: Finely divided into slender segments; lower leaves hairy, divided into broad segments with a small triangular end lobe, usually shrivelling long before pods are formed.

FLOWERS: Pale yellow; clustered at tips of branches.

FRUITS: Long, very slender pods, 5–10 cm long; **spreading** and almost branch-like, on stalks of about same thickness as pods.

ECOLOGY: Widespread and common at low to mid elevations in southern part of our region on disturbed soils and cultivated ground; scattered and infrequent farther north.

SIMILAR SPECIES: Loesel's tumble-mustard (*S. loeselii*, below) has deeper yellow flowers, and shorter, more upright pods, and it is a generally taller, narrower plant. Both species are rapid colonizers of barren, dry soils.

NOTES: In late summer this introduced weed dries into a spherical, woody, light brown skeleton. Eventually, the weakly anchored plant breaks loose and tumbles freely in the wind, scattering seeds as it goes.

LOESEL'S TUMBLE-MUSTARD • *Sisymbrium loeselii*

GENERAL: Coarse **annual**, to 120 cm tall; stems strongly branched, with prominent, down-pointing hairs on lower parts.

LEAVES: Coarsely lobed, with a large, triangular end lobe; basal leaves withering by flowering time.

FLOWERS: Bright yellow; in loose clusters at branch tips.

FRUITS: Long, slender pods, 2–3.5 cm long; held **erect** on narrow stalks.

ECOLOGY: Scattered and common at low to mid elevations, particularly in northern part of our region, on disturbed soils and cultivated fields.

SIMILAR SPECIES: Field mustard (*Brassica campestris*) also has bright yellow flowers, but it has bristly, unlobed but wavy leaves that clasp the stem, and pods with beak-like tips. • When the plants are young, Loesel's tumble-mustard is very similar to tall tumble-mustard (*S. altissimum*, above), but the mature plants are easily distinguished (see 'Similar Species' for tall tumble-mustard).

NOTES: Introduced from Eurasia, this weedy mustard often appears like a yellow blanket covering fields and roadsides in early summer. • Because Loesel's tumble-mustard is taller and narrower than tall tumble-mustard it is a much less efficient tumbleweed.

WOODS DRABA • *Draba nemorosa*

GENERAL: Small, **taprooted annual**, 5–25 cm tall.

LEAVES: Mostly basal, with a few on the lower third of the stem, covered with both simple and branched hairs.

FLOWERS: Pale yellow; in a long, open inflorescence, 2/3 the length of the plant; bloom in spring.

FRUITS: Oval to **elliptic** pods; on **long, spreading stalks.**

ECOLOGY: Scattered and frequent at low to mid elevations in arid basins, southern Rocky Mountain Trench and dry plateaus; primarily in grasslands.

NOTES: This native draba is a common grassland plant that is often overlooked because of its diminutive size. It flowers in early spring while there is still moisture left in the soil from snowmelt. • Woods draba is also called wood whitlow-grass.

GOLDEN DRABA • *Draba aurea*

GENERAL: Perennial, 10–50 cm tall; stems often branched at base.

LEAVES: A basal rosette of overlapping leaves and **more than 6 stem leaves,** covered with **cross-shaped hairs.**

FLOWERS: Yellow; in a long inflorescence.

FRUITS: Lance-shaped, flattened pods, sometimes twisted; on short stalks.

ECOLOGY: Scattered and locally common at mid to alpine elevations in dry, semi-open areas, meadows and talus slopes.

SIMILAR SPECIES: Tall draba (*D. praealta*) can be distinguished by its white flowers and few (1–6) stem leaves.

NOTES: The drabas (also called whitlow-grasses) constitute a small but distinctive group in the mustard family, with 14 or so species in our region. A few species, such as woods draba (*D. nemorosa*) and tall draba (*D. praealta*), can be found in lowland habitats, but most are small, tufted or cushion-like alpine species. As most draba species are restricted to mountain habitats, they are unfamiliar to many people, although anyone hiking in the high country is sure to come across their bright yellow mats clinging to rock crevices where there is hardly any soil. • Golden draba is also called golden whitlow-grass.

PAYSON'S DRABA • *Draba paysonii*

GENERAL: Low, **densely matted perennial**, 0.5–3 cm tall.

LEAVES: All basal, arranged in tight spirals; narrow (less than 2 mm broad) and **covered with simple or forked hairs**.

FLOWERS: Many tiny, **yellow** flowers; clustered at tops of short, leafless stems.

FRUITS: Small, slightly flattened, **egg-shaped pods**, covered with simple or branched hairs.

ECOLOGY: Scattered in subalpine and alpine areas, particularly in dry Chilcotin Ranges, on rocky slopes and crevices.

NOTES: The genus name *Draba* is from the Greek *drabe*, meaning 'bitter' or 'acrid.' Payson's draba is named after Edwin Blake Payson (1893–1927) a professor of botany (specializing in the Cruciferae) in Wyoming.

YELLOWSTONE DRABA • *Draba incerta*

GENERAL: Small, **loosely tufted perennial**, usually 1–3 cm tall (occasionally to 20 cm), with short stems and many overlapping leaves.

LEAVES: All basal; narrow, covered with both simple and **feather-shaped hairs** that stand up from the surface (visible at 10x magnification).

FLOWERS: Yellow, fading to white; clustered near end of stem.

FRUITS: Egg-shaped pods, usually covered with stiff hairs; on stalks about equal in length to pods.

ECOLOGY: Scattered in subalpine and alpine areas on rocky slopes, cliffs and crevices.

SIMILAR SPECIES: Other widespread, mat-forming alpine draba species in our region are Payson's draba (*D. paysonii*, above), few-seeded draba (*D. oligosperma*), lance-fruited draba (*D. lonchocarpa*), and snow draba (*D. nivalis*). Examination of the shape and arrangement of the hairs, along with a key to draba species, is required for positive identification of these delightful, high-elevation drabas.

NOTES: The species name *incerta*, meaning 'uncertain,' suggests the difficulty in identifying this draba.

PRAIRIE PEPPER-GRASS • *Lepidium densiflorum*

GENERAL: Bushy-shaped **annual**, 25–50 cm tall, with many-branched stems, densely covered with short hairs.

LEAVES: Small, linear stem leaves, occasionally with toothed edges, stalkless and not clasping stem; basal leaves soon falling off.

FLOWERS: White and inconspicuous, often without petals.

FRUITS: Nearly round, flattened pods, with a narrow notch at the top.

ECOLOGY: Widespread and common at low to mid elevations, mostly in arid basins, southern Rocky Mountain Trench and dry parts of our plateaus, in dry sites in grasslands and disturbed soil.

SIMILAR SPECIES: Field pepper-grass (*L. campestre*) is an introduced weedy species. It has clasping leaves and is usually single-stemmed.

NOTES: Prairie pepper-grass is native to our region. • The genus name *Lepidium* is from the Greek, *lepis*, 'a scale,' and refers to the small, scale-like fruit.

FIELD PENNYCRESS • *Thlaspi arvense*

GENERAL: Taprooted annual, 10–50 cm tall, with simple or branched stems.

LEAVES: Small stem leaves, with irregularly toothed edges and basal lobes that clasp stem; rosette of stalked basal leaves, shrivel before flowers appear.

FLOWERS: White, inconspicuous; in rounded clusters at stem tips.

FRUITS: Flat, circular pods, 10–17 mm wide, with **wide wings around edges and** a deep notch at top; bright green, becoming yellowish with age.

ECOLOGY: Scattered and locally abundant at low to mid elevations in cultivated areas and moist waste places, wherever bare soil occurs.

SIMILAR SPECIES: The large, penny-sized, mature pods distinguish field pennycress from the pepper-grasses (*Lepidium* spp., above), which have tiny pods when ripe.

NOTES: Like most weedy mustards, field pennycress blooms continually from early spring until frost. • The seeds of this Eurasian weed have a potent mustard flavour, but the green buds and flowers are milder and more salad-like. • This species earned the name 'pennycress' from it large, penny-sized pods. The strong odour that comes from the crushed green leaves gave it another common name—'stinkweed.' The genus name *Thlaspi* is apparently from the Greek *thlao*, 'to compress,' and presumably describes the flattened fruits.

LITTLE-PODDED FALSEFLAX • *Camelina microcarpa*

GENERAL: Annual, to 90 cm tall, with sparsely branched stems, rough-hairy on lower portion.

LEAVES: Upper stem leaves **arrowhead-shaped, rough-hairy, clasp stem.**

FLOWERS: Small, **pale yellow.**

FRUITS: Inflated, **pear-shaped pods**, less than 6 mm long; on slender, spreading stalks.

ECOLOGY: Scattered and locally common at low to mid elevations in disturbed soil in grasslands and along roadsides; usually in dry, sandy soil.

SIMILAR SPECIES: Columbia bladderpod (*Lesquerella douglasii*), a native grassland perennial, is somewhat similar in appearance, but it has narrow, non-clasping stem leaves and round, inflated pods that have long, slender styles (equal in length to the pods).

NOTES: This introduced weedy species appears to be on the increase in grassland areas. Little-podded falseflax can be distinguished from most other mustards that have small, nearly round pods, by its smooth, teardrop-shaped seedpods, arrowhead-shaped stem leaves, and rough-hairy stems and leaves.

SHEPHERD'S PURSE • *Capsella bursa-pastoris*

GENERAL: Annual, or winter annual, 10–50 cm tall; stems often branched at base, covered with fine grey hairs.

LEAVES: Basal leaves in a rosette flat on the ground; leaf edges vary from almost smooth to deeply lobed; upper leaves are smaller, with toothed edges and lobes that clasp stem.

FLOWERS: Small, **white.**

FRUITS: Many **flattened, triangular to heart-shaped pods**, with many seeds.

ECOLOGY: Widespread and common at low to mid elevations wherever there is long-term soil disturbance, such as roadsides and fields.

NOTES: Originally from Europe, shepherd's-purse has become a widespread weed in much of North America. • The seeds are sticky when wet and attract insects, such as ants, which stick tight to the seed, die, and serve as a nutrient source for the developing seedlings. • The distinctive fruits are responsible for both the scientific and common names, due to the resemblance of the pod to a little box (*capsella*), or the purse (*bursa*) of a shepherd (*pastor*).

MARSH YELLOW-CRESS • *Rorippa palustris*
R. islandica

GENERAL: Many-branched **annual or biennial**, 30–100 cm tall.

LEAVES: Deeply lobed, with toothed edges; upper stem leaves becoming simply toothed and clasping stem.

FLOWERS: Light yellow.

FRUITS: Oval pods; on **spreading stalks** that are longer than the pods.

ECOLOGY: Scattered and locally common at low to mid elevations at marsh edges and in moist, disturbed soil.

NOTES: This native marsh plant turns a golden colour in autumn. It is a western North American mustard species that may colonize moist waste areas, but does not invade cultivated lands. • The genus name *Rorippa* is from the Old Saxon name for this plant, *rorippen*. The species name *palustris* describes this species' preference for marshy places.

PENNSYLVANIAN BITTER-CRESS • *Cardamine pensylvanica*

GENERAL: Taprooted annual, 10–30 cm tall, usually with many-branched stems.

LEAVES: Compound, with narrow side leaflets and a larger leaflet at the tip; leaf stalks hairless.

FLOWERS: White, very small.

FRUITS: Long, narrow pods, less than 1 mm thick; held **erect**.

ECOLOGY: Widespread and frequent at low to mid elevations in moist sites in open forests, lakeshores and moist waste places.

SIMILAR SPECIES: Little western bitter-cress (*C. oligosperma*), a weedy species, is very similar, but it has wider leaflets, hairy leaf stalks, and thicker seed pods than Pennsylvanian bitter-cress.

NOTES: This small, somewhat succulent annual is edible, and it has a refreshing peppery flavour. • The seed pods become explosive as they dry, and burst when touched, propelling the tiny seeds up to 1 m away.

Onagraceae: Evening-primrose Family

This family includes annual or perennial herbs with **4-parted flowers** (2-parted in *Circaea* spp.). The flowers are regular in form, often with notched or lobed petals. The leaves are usually simple, but sometimes have lobes (especially in *Oenothera* spp.). The fruits are capsules that develop below the petals from long, narrow ovaries, which in most species look much like flower stalks.

ALPINE WILLOWHERB • *Epilobium anagallidifolium* E. alpinum

GENERAL: Low, usually matted perennial, 5–30 cm tall, spreading by extensive **rhizomes and runners**; stems often reddish purple and branched.

LEAVES: 2–3 **pairs**, oblong to egg-shaped, with smooth to wavy edges.

FLOWERS: Few, **small, pink to rose-purple** (occasionally white).

FRUITS: Long, thin capsules, beneath each flower.

ECOLOGY: Widespread and common, mostly at mid elevations to above timberline, in moist seepage areas in open forests, openings, clearings and alpine meadows.

SIMILAR SPECIES: The pink- to purplish-flowered Hornemann's willowherb (*E. hornemannii*) is 10–40 cm tall, has toothed leaves and is found at low to mid elevations. • Small-flowered willowherb (*E. minutum*) is an **annual** of rocky bluffs and temporarily wet spots at low to mid elevations. It is 3–40 cm tall and has white to rose, notched petals that are only 2–4 mm long.

NOTES: The Okanagan knew alpine willowherb to be eaten by deer and horses. • The almost-impossible-to-pronounce species name of alpine willowherb means 'with leaves like *Anagallis*.' Pimpernels (*Anagallis* spp.) are small, low-growing plants of the primrose family (Primulaceae); their leaves are egg-shaped.

PURPLE-LEAVED WILLOWHERB • *Epilobium ciliatum* E. watsonii

GENERAL: Perennial, **0.5–1.5 m tall**, sometimes with bulb-like buds (offsets) from short rhizomes; stems simple, or branched above, hairy on upper parts.

LEAVES: Opposite, lance-shaped to oval or elliptic, with pointed tips and toothed edges, more or less stalkless.

FLOWERS: Small, white, pink, or rose-purple; in a **leafy-bracted cluster** at top of stem.

FRUITS: Long, narrow capsules.

ECOLOGY: Scattered and fairly common at low to subalpine elevations in moist habitats, coniferous forests, openings, clearings and other moist, disturbed sites.

NOTES: Purple-leaved willowherb is part of a large complex of small-flowered *Epilobium* species, including what some taxonomists distinguish as *E. adenocaulon*, *E. glandulosum* and *E. watsonii*. All are highly variable, with a great range in several morphological features. • Willowherbs got their name from the resemblance of their leaves to those of the weeping willow (*Salix babylonica*).

FIREWEED • *Epilobium angustifolium*

GENERAL: Perennial, 1–3 m tall, with **wide-spreading horizontal roots** that produce small buds (plantlets); flowering stems usually **unbranched**; upper stem often purplish.

LEAVES: Alternate, narrowly lance-shaped, 5–20 cm long, **distinctly veined below**; crowded along stem on very short stalks.

FLOWERS: Large, rose to purple; several (**more than 15**) in an elongate and striking inflorescence at top of stem.

FRUITS: Long, green to red capsules, with **abundant, fluffy seeds**.

ECOLOGY: Widespread and common at low to subalpine elevations in disturbed areas, especially recently burned sites; also in open forests and openings; generally absent from arid parts of our region.

NOTES: Fireweed is sometimes grown as an ornamental, but it is apt to become a bothersome weed. It can form extensive stands that produce clouds of woolly seeds in late summer. • Among Interior peoples, fireweed was used externally as a medicine against eczema, sometimes mixed with other plants. Many Interior native peoples peeled young stems of fireweed and ate the succulent marrow (pith) raw. Sometimes they boiled or steamed whole stems. After eating the marrow, some Coastal peoples dried the stem peelings and twisted them into a type of twine used for fishing nets. Some mixed the seed 'fluff' with hair from mountain goats or dogs and used it for weaving or padding. • Dried fireweed leaves have been used as a tea substitute in England and Russia, but they may have a laxative effect. The flowers produce a lot of nectar, which makes an excellent honey. • The name 'fireweed' refers to this plant's almost ubiquitous occurrence in burned areas. Fireweed is also called rosebay willowherb from its resemblance to rosebay (*Nerium oleander*).

BROAD-LEAVED WILLOWHERB • *Epilobium latifolium*

GENERAL: Low-growing, matted perennial, 5–30 cm tall, with a **stout, woody base**; stems semi-upright, **branched**.

LEAVES: Opposite, lance-shaped to elliptic or oval, **somewhat fleshy**, with **indistinct veins below**, and often with a white-grey bloom, stalkless.

FLOWERS: Large and showy, pink to rose-purple; 3–12 in a loose, short, leafy inflorescence.

FRUITS: Long, slender, **hairy capsules**, often purplish.

ECOLOGY: Scattered and locally common at mid to alpine elevations in sandy and gravelly soils on riverbars, streambanks and disturbed areas; generally absent from our arid climates.

NOTES: Within this species there is considerable variation in the size and shape of the leaves. An albino-flowered form is also encountered quite often. • Alaskan Inuit picked young broad-leaved willowherbs before flowering and mixed them with other greens. The central pith in the stem can also be peeled and eaten. • Broad-leaved willowherb is also known as river-beauty. The genus name *Epilobium* is from the Greek *epi*, 'upon,' and *lobos*, 'a pod,' and refers to the flower being placed above the seed pod.

ENCHANTER'S NIGHTSHADE • *Circaea alpina*

GENERAL: Tender perennial, 10–30 cm tall, with simple or branched stems from a slender, tuberous rootstock.

LEAVES: Opposite, heart- to egg-shaped, stalked, with pointed tips and toothed edges.

FLOWERS: Small, **white to pink, with 2 petals and 2 sepals**; petals deeply 2-lobed; in clusters of 8–12 on long stalks.

FRUITS: Oblong, **pear-shaped capsules**, covered with hooked hairs.

ECOLOGY: Scattered and often common at low to subalpine elevations, mostly in wet Columbia Mountains, in moist, cool forests, moist, rich openings and clearings.

NOTES: Enchanter's nightshade can be distinguished from the rest of the evening-primrose family by its flowers, which are 2-parted, and by its oblong seed capsules. • The name 'enchanter's nightshade' results, in part, from some confusion. The genus *Circaea* was named after the Greek goddess Circe—the enchantress—who supposedly used this plant 'as a tempting powder in some amorous concerns' (Hitchcock et al. 1961). The application of 'nightshade' to this plant is, however, a mystery. It was originally applied to the plants deadly nightshade (*Atropa belladonna*) and woody nightshade (*Solanum dulcamara*). Somehow, it was subsequently transferred to *Circaea*. The origin of the name 'nightshade' in relation to these two other species is in itself a mistake. An old herbal describes *Atropa belladonna* as a *solatrum* or soothing anodyne. In translation this was mistaken for the words *solem atrum*, which mean 'black sun' or 'eclipse.'

YELLOW EVENING-PRIMROSE • *Oenothera villosa* *O. depressa, O. strigosa*

GENERAL: Biennial or short-lived perennial, 30–100 cm tall, from a stout taproot; stems simple to branched, usually covered with **dense, stiff hairs**.

LEAVES: Narrowly lance-shaped to oblong, hairy; lower leaves with stalks, becoming stalkless on upper stem.

FLOWERS: Large, **bright yellow**; in a **crowded, leafy cluster**.

FRUITS: Linear to spindle-shaped, **hairy capsules**.

ECOLOGY: Scattered and infrequent at low elevations, mostly in Thompson and Okanagan basins, in sagebrush grasslands, dry, open forests and dry, disturbed places with well-drained soils.

SIMILAR SPECIES: Pale evening-primrose (*O. pallida*), a perennial, white-flowered species, may be found on dry hill slopes among sagebrush in the southern Okanagan Basin. Yellow evening-primrose has often been misidentified as common evening-primrose (*O. biennis*) which is primarily a species of eastern North America. Common evening-primrose is more glandular hairy and has longer free sepal tips than yellow evening-primrose.

NOTES: Common evening-primrose is the commercial source of evening-primrose oil • Evening-primrose flowers are seldom seen at their best because they open just before sundown and fade in the morning light. They are pollinated by several species of moths.

Apiaceae: Carrot Family

The carrot family, (also known as Umbelliferae) is a group of mostly perennial herbs with hollow stems. Members of this family encompass the entire range of edibility from highly edible (carrots, parsnips, caraway) to deadly poisonous (poison-hemlock).

The alternate family name Umbelliferae comes from '**umbel**,' the technical term for the type of inflorescence found in species of this family. The family can easily be recognized by these umbrella-shaped clusters of small, usually white flowers. The inflorescences are generally compound, being composed of a number of smaller clusters of flowers. Because the inflorescences are so similar among the species they are often of little help in distinguishing among them. Species identifications are most readily based on characteristics of the leaves or the fruits.

The fruits, technically known as **schizocarps**, are another distinctive feature of this family. These small, dry fruits divide at maturity into two seeds that have variously shaped ribs or prickles. The backs of the seeds are rounded or flattened. In many species, some of the ribs have broad, flat wings.

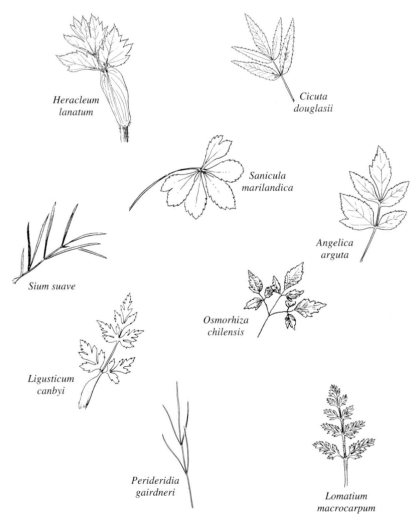

Heracleum lanatum

Cicuta douglasii

Sanicula marilandica

Angelica arguta

Sium suave

Osmorhiza chilensis

Ligusticum canbyi

Perideridia gairdneri

Lomatium macrocarpum

243

COW-PARSNIP • *Heracleum lanatum*
H. sphondylium

GENERAL: Large robust, hairy perennial, 1–3 m tall, from a stout taproot or cluster of fibrous roots; **stems single, hollow**, with a **strong, pungent odour** when mature.

LEAVES: Large, **compound**, divided into **3 large, stalked segments, each coarsely toothed and lobed**; leaf base conspicuously inflated and winged.

FLOWERS: Large, **flat-topped, compound inflorescence** of small, **white** flowers.

FRUITS: Oval to heart-shaped seeds, with **flattened backs**, visible oil tubes and **2 broad wings**; aromatic.

ECOLOGY: Widespread and common at low to subalpine elevations in moist and wet, open forests, seepage areas and moist, disturbed ground; often abundant in moist deciduous forests.

NOTES: Cow-parsnip is also known as Indian celery and Indian rhubarb, and it is still widely used as a green vegetable. Nearly every native group reports harvesting the young stalks and leaf stems, peeling off the fibrous outer layer, and eating them raw. Sometimes they boiled, steamed or roasted the stems. Several groups made toy flutes and whistles out of the dry hollow stems. • **Caution:** Be sure to distinguish this species from the violently poisonous water-hemlocks (*Cicuta* spp.) and poison-hemlock (*Conium maculatum*), which are described on page 245. • The name 'parsnip' comes from *pastnip*, a corruption of *pastinaca*, the Latin name for the cultivated parsnip (*Pastinaca sativa*). The genus name *Heracleum* was the name given to this plant by Theophrastus, a Greek philosopher and scientist (372–287 BC), and it means 'Hercules' healer'—presumably because of its medicinal properties and giant proportions.

WATER PARSNIP • *Sium suave*

GENERAL: Semiaquatic perennial, mostly 50–120 cm tall, from fibrous roots, with roots often emerging from lower stem nodes; **stems stout, hairless, hollow, strongly ridged**; thickened stem base is **not chambered**.

LEAVES: Emergent leaves divided into **7–13 lance-shaped to linear leaflets**, hairless and glossy, with **finely saw-toothed edges**; submerged leaves much narrower.

FLOWERS: White; in **tight clusters** in open, **umbrella-like inflorescences**, with a ring of bracts at their base.

FRUITS: Oval to elliptic seeds, with **rounded backs** and **prominent ribs**, but without wings.

ECOLOGY: Scattered and locally common at low to mid elevations in shallow water of swamps, marshes, lakeshores and ditches.

SIMILAR SPECIES: This plant is very similar in habitat and appearance to the extremely poisonous water-hemlocks (*Cicuta* spp., above) and special care must be taken to avoid accidental poisoning. The leaves of water parsnip are once-divided, while those of water-hemlock are divided several times.

NOTES: Water parsnip is also called swamp parsnip, wild carrot and wild saccharin. The sweet, finger-like roots were eaten by many Interior natives. They were dug up in spring, before the plants bloomed, and again in summer, and they were eaten raw, fried or steamed. They have a distinct carrot flavour. • **Caution:** The young shoots are also edible, but older plants and flowers are toxic and have been implicated in livestock poisonings.

DOUGLAS'S WATER-HEMLOCK • *Cicuta douglasii*

GENERAL: Robust perennial, 0.5–2 m tall, with 1 to several **stout, often purplish stems** from a **tuberous-thickened and chambered base**.

LEAVES: Compound, divided several times into many **lance-shaped to oblong leaflets**; leaflets **sharp-pointed, toothed; side veins end in notch between teeth rather** than at tips of teeth (as in some similar species).

FLOWERS: Flat-topped, compound inflorescence of small, **white to greenish** flowers.

FRUITS: Egg-shaped to circular seeds, with **rounded backs** and **corky-thickened ribs**.

ECOLOGY: Scattered and locally common at low to mid elevations in marshes, streams edges, ditches and other wet places.

SIMILAR SPECIES: Bulbous water-hemlock (*C. bulbifera*) has bulblets in the axils of the leaflets of its upper leaves, and the leaflets are narrowly linear. It occupies similar habitats, but it is less common in our region. **It is also very poisonous.** • Poison-hemlock (*Conium maculatum*), another **deadly poisonous** species, was introduced from Eurasia and is found in moist, disturbed sites, such as ditches. It is a coarse, freely branching biennial from a stout taproot, with highly dissected, feathery leaves and purple-spotted stems.

NOTES: Extremely poisonous. Even small amounts can be deadly. Its toxin, cucutoxin, acts on the central nervous system and causes violent convulsions, followed by paralysis and respiratory failure. It causes many deaths among cattle, especially in early spring when they can easily pull up the shallow roots along with the young tops. All parts of the plant are poisonous, but the tuberous-thickened roots are especially so. • The Okanagan used the powdered roots as an arrow poison and the Carrier applied the fresh roots as a poultice for rheumatism. • Important features to help distinguish Douglas's water-hemlock from the similar angelicas (*Angelica* spp., p. 246) and cow-parsnips (*Heracleum* spp., p. 244) are the narrower leaflets and the arrangement of the leaf veins. In Douglas's water-hemlock, the side veins of the leaflets end between the teeth rather than at their points. Another distinguishing feature is the chambered stem base. This feature must be observed with care, however, due to the poisonous juice produced when the stem is cut. **Wash your hands and cutting knife immediately!**

BLACK SANICLE • *Sanicula marilandica*

GENERAL: Perennial, 40–120 cm tall, with **solitary stems** from a cluster of fibrous roots.

LEAVES: Deeply lobed or divided into **5–7 lance-shaped, sharp-toothed segments**; lower leaves long-stalked; upper leaves nearly stalkless and smaller.

FLOWERS: Greenish white; in **compound inflorescences of rounded clusters**.

FRUITS: Oval burs, covered with many **hooked prickles**.

ECOLOGY: Scattered and infrequent at low to mid elevations in wet to moist, open forests and openings.

NOTES: Black sanicle is also called snake-root. The genus name *Sanicula* comes from the Latin *sanare*, 'to heal.' This species was thought to have curative properties, as indicated by the proverbial axiom, 'He who keeps sanicle has no business with a doctor,' and Lyte (1578) wrote that 'the iyce of Sanicle dronken, doth make whole and sound all inward, and outwarde woundes and hurtes.'

SHARPTOOTH ANGELICA • *Angelica arguta*

GENERAL: **Robust, taprooted** perennial, 30–200 cm tall, usually with a single stem and with a **disagreeable odour**.

LEAVES: Compound, with **major divisions in turn divided into toothed leaflets,** hairy below on veins; bases of leaf stalks inflated, surrounding main stem.

FLOWERS: Large, **compound, umbrella-shaped inflorescence** of small, **white flowers**.

FRUITS: Elliptic seeds, with **flattened backs** and **2 broad wings**.

ECOLOGY: Widespread and common at low to mid elevations in moist streambanks, wet meadows, marshes and wet, seepy forests; absent from our arid basins.

SIMILAR SPECIES: Kneeling angelica (*A. genuflexa*) has leaves that bend downwards above the first pair of leaflets. • Care must be taken not to confuse angelicas with the poisonous water-hemlocks (*Cicuta* spp., p. 245) which have similar leaves.

NOTES: The St'at'imc chewed kneeling angelica to relieve colds and sore throats. • The genus name *Angelica* is from the Latin *angelus* (an angel). This name was given to a plant that was reputedly revealed to Matthaeus Sylvaticus by the archangel as a medicinal plant and *Angelica* is therefore believed to have healing powers. The species name *arguta*, Latin for 'sharp-tooth,' refers to the serrations on the leaflets, which also give the species its common name.

CANBY'S LOVAGE • *Ligusticum canbyi*

GENERAL: Taprooted perennial, 50–120 cm tall, smooth or slightly rough to the touch.

LEAVES: Compound, divided into **3 main parts,** then again into **small, deeply cleft leaflets**.

FLOWERS: Compound, umbrella-shaped inflorescences of small, **white** flowers.

FRUITS: Oblong to elliptic seeds, with **rounded backs** and **narrow wings**.

ECOLOGY: Scattered and infrequent, mostly at mid elevations, in moist and wet meadows, streambanks and boggy slopes.

NOTES: The pungent-smelling root was smoked, usually mixed with tobacco, by the Eastern Secwepemc and Okanagan. It was also chewed to relieve coughs and colds. • 'Lovage' seems to have derived from *love-ache*, meaning 'love-parsley,' which appeared in a translation of Pliny, a Roman naturalist (23–79 AD). However, the hint of an amorous connection is misleading as it is more likely that there was a misspelling or corruption of *levisticum*, which was derived from *ligusticum*. The latter name, from the Greek *ligustikon*, was the name used by the Greek physician Dioscorides (40–70 AD) for a related plant from the region of the Ligurians, the present province of Liguria in Italy plus a portion of south-eastern France. Canby's lovage is named for William Marriott Canby (1831–1904), a Delaware businessman and collector of a large herbarium.

MOUNTAIN SWEET-CICELY • *Osmorhiza chilensis*

GENERAL: Taprooted perennial, 30–100 cm tall, with 1–3 slender stems.

LEAVES: Pale, **thin**, hairy, **twice divided into 3 parts,** for a total of **9 deeply cleft and toothed leaflets**; several, long-stalked basal leaves; 1–3 stalkless to short-stalked stem leaves.

FLOWERS: Small, greenish white; in **compound, umbrella-shaped inflorescences**.

FRUITS: Black, needle-like, narrowing below tips and broadening into a short 'beak,' **bristly-hairy** (often catch on clothing).

ECOLOGY: Widespread and common, mostly at low to mid elevations in moist and wet, open forests, meadows and clearings.

SIMILAR SPECIES: Blunt-fruited sweet-cicely (*O. depauperata*) can be distinguished from mountain sweet-cicely by a close examination (with a hand lens) of the mature fruits. In blunt-fruited sweet-cicely the fruits are shaped like a club or baseball bat, without a 'beak.' Blunt-fruited sweet-cicely also tends to be smaller—usually less than 60 cm tall. • Purple sweet-cicely (*O. purpurea*) can easily be confused with both mountain and blunt-fruited sweet-cicely. In flower, the purple colour is usually a give-away, but purple sweet-cicely sometimes has greenish-white flowers. Purple sweet-cicely is often hairless, unlike the other two species, both of which usually have hairy leaves.

NOTES: The Lil'wet'ul and Nlaka'pmx ate the thick, aromatic root. They dug it up in early spring and steamed it or boiled it in stews. The root was known for its delicate, sweet flavour, which is reminiscent of baby carrots. The Nlaka'pmx also chewed the root as a cold remedy. Their name for it, 'dry-land parsnip,' distinguishes it from water parsnip (*Sium suave*). • 'Cicely' is from *seseli*, the ancient Greek name for a related plant used in medicine. The genus name *Osmorhiza* means 'scented root,' and plants of this genus are called sweet-cicely because of the licorice-like odour of the root and green fruits when crushed.

YAMPA • *Perideridia gairdneri*

GENERAL: Caraway-scented perennial, 40–120 cm tall, with **solitary, slender stems** from more or less tuberous roots.

LEAVES: Divided into **long, narrow segments**; frequently dried by the time the flowers open.

FLOWERS: Small, white; in small, compact heads forming a loose, **flat-topped, umbrella-shaped, compound inflorescence**.

FRUITS: Circular-shaped seeds, with **rounded backs** and **prominent ribs**, but no wings.

ECOLOGY: Scattered and locally common at low to mid elevations in southern half of our region, in moist, open forests, moist meadows and open, grassy slopes.

NOTES: The Okanagan and Ktunaxa widely used this plant. The edible roots, known as 'yampah,' were pounded to make a flour, which Lewis and Clark described as having a flavour 'not unlike anise seed.' This species is also known as wild caraway, in reference to its similarity in appearance and smell to caraway (*Carum carvi*). • Heinrich Reichenbach of Dresden named the genus *Perideridia*, but no one knows what it means. It may have been derived from the Greek *peri*, 'around,' and *derris*, 'leather coat,' in reference to the tough-coated root. The species name, and the alternate common name 'Gairdner's yampah,' honour Meredith Gairdner (1809–37), a surgeon to the Hudson's Bay Company who collected plants in the American Northwest.

FERN-LEAVED DESERT-PARSLEY • *Lomatium dissectum*

GENERAL: **Robust** perennial, 30–150 cm tall, from a large, **woody taproot**; several **hollow stems**, purple at the base.

LEAVES: **Finely dissected and fern-like**, rough-surfaced, with a **spicy fragrance**.

FLOWERS: **Compound, umbrella-shaped inflorescences** of **yellow or deep-purple** flowers on tall stalks; blooms in spring.

FRUITS: **Elliptic seeds**, with **flattened backs** and **narrow, corky-thickened wings**.

ECOLOGY: Widespread and locally common at low to mid elevations in Fraser, Thompson and Okanagan basins and southern Rocky Mountain Trench, on rocky slopes and dry grasslands; commonly among bunchgrasses and sagebrush.

SIMILAR SPECIES: Barestem desert-parsley (*L. nudicale*) is a yellow-flowered species with a blue-white bloom on its compound leaves. Its leaves are not fern-like, but are composed of well-defined leaflets. As both the common and botanical name suggest, there are no leaves on the flower stalks.

NOTES: The Secwepemc, Nlaka'pmx and St'at'imc ate the young shoots and roots, although they reported them to be bitter. The dried roots were often steam-cooked together with the bulbs of yellow glacier lily (*Erythronium grandiflorum*). • Fern-leaved desert-parsley makes an interesting rock garden plant. • The desert-parsleys differ from most of the Umbelliferae in that many of the species have yellow flowers. The leaves are mostly basal and compound, and they are often highly dissected. The many species of *Lomatium* found in the Pacific Northwest are notoriously difficult to separate. Fortunately, the common species in our area can be distinguished by a combination of leaf shape and flower colour. • The species name *dissectum* refers to the finely divided, fern- or parsley-like leaves, which are also the source of the common name. A much more charming name is 'chocolate-tips,' which refers to the often purplish-chocolate flowers.

LARGE-FRUITED DESERT-PARSLEY • *Lomatium macrocarpum*

GENERAL: **Low-growing** perennial, less than 25 cm tall, from an elongated, **thickened taproot**; leaves and flower stalks clustered close to the ground.

LEAVES: **Dissected into fern-like segments**; **greyish and hairy**, with purple on the stalks and undersides when young.

FLOWERS: **White to purplish white**; in **tight, fuzzy clusters** with conspicuous, linear bracts on 1 side, **in a larger, umbrella-shaped inflorescence**; bloom in spring.

FRUITS: Narrow, **linear seeds**, with **flattened backs** and **thin wings**.

ECOLOGY: Scattered and locally common, mostly at low elevations in our dry climates, on warm open slopes, dry gravelly areas and grasslands.

SIMILAR SPECIES: Another white flowered desert-parsley of dry slopes and sagebrush flats is Geyer's lomatium (*L. geyeri*). It is taller than large-fruited desert-parsley and has **dark-green** (not grey) carrot-like foliage.

NOTES: All the native people in our area used the desert-parsleys. They dug up the roots in spring before the plants flowered. The root has a strong peppery taste and was eaten raw, boiled, cooked in pits or dried for later use. An infusion could be made to treat heart problems. • In Secwepemc, the plant is called *qweq'wile*, and the meadow lark sings, 'Don't hide my *qweq'wile*.' • The genus name *Lomatium* comes from the Greek *loma* (border) and refers to the well-developed wings on the seeds of most desert-parsley species.

NARROW-LEAVED DESERT-PARSLEY • *Lomatium triternatum*

GENERAL: Perennial, 20–80 cm tall, from a simple or sparingly branched crown on an **elongated taproot**.

LEAVES: Divided several times into long, narrow segments; stalks winged.

FLOWERS: Yellow; in tight **umbrella-shaped clusters** on unequal-length stem branches; blooms in spring.

FRUITS: Oblong to elliptic seeds, with **flattened backs** and **broad wings**.

ECOLOGY: Scattered and locally common at low to mid elevations in arid basins and driest parts of plateaus, mostly south of Kamloops, on dry open slopes and grasslands.

SIMILAR SPECIES: Swale desert-parsley (*L. ambiguum*) is another yellow-flowered species with a swollen taproot and leaves divided into narrow segments. It is found on dry, rocky slopes and on sagebrush flats up to mid elevations.

NOTES: The Okanagan dried the flowers and upper leaves in June to flavour meats, stews and salads. They also used it to make an infusion for sore throats and colds. • 'Cous' (also 'couse' or 'cows') was a native word for the fleshy, tuberous roots of several species of *Lomatium*. The Lewis and Clark journals describe how the roots were ground into a meal that was then shaped into large flat cakes. • The species name *triternatum* means 'divided three times in threes,' and refers to the finely divided leaves. This species is also called nineleaf biscuitroot, a name that refers to both the form of leaf division and the use of the ground roots as flour.

SHOWY MILKWEED • *Asclepias speciosa*

GENERAL: Rhizomatous perennial, 40–120 cm tall, **softly greyish-hairy throughout**; stout, **hollow stems with milky juice**.

LEAVES: Opposite, oblong lance-shaped, with a pinkish midrib and conspicuous cross veins.

FLOWERS: Pink to reddish purple; 5 petals, bent sharply backwards; 5 stamens, joined to form a tube with 5 erect, horn-like appendages; on downy stems, in **large umbrella-shaped heads**.

FRUITS: Hairy pods, opening along 1 side to reveal long, silky-haired seeds.

ECOLOGY: Widely scattered and locally common at low elevations in dry climates in southern half of our region, in moist, sandy or gravelly open areas near streams and ditches and along roadsides and railways.

SIMILAR SPECIES: Oval-leaf milkweed (*A. ovalifolia*) is rare in our region—it is known only from the Revelstoke area. It is smaller than showy milkweed and has a more oval leaf shape and greenish-white flowers.

NOTES: The intricate flower structure of the milkweeds is arranged to attract insects and then hold their feet in such a way that they will pick up masses of pollen as they escape. • Milkweed stems produce a milky sap that contains poisonous resinoids and cardiac glycosides. Monarch butterflies lay their eggs on milkweeds. As the larvae feed on the plants, they accumulate the glycosides, to which they are immune. The glycosides however, are distasteful to birds, which learn to avoid eating the monarch larvae and butterflies. • The Secwepemc treated warts with the milky sap, and the Nlaka'pmx used it as a face-cream. • The genus *Asclepias* is named for the Greek physician and god of medicine, Asklepios.

249

WILD SARSAPARILLA • *Aralia nudicaulis*

GENERAL: Perennial, with widely creeping rhizomes and short, stout, woody stems; often forms large clones in undisturbed forests.

LEAVES: Solitary, compound, with 3 main divisions, each with **3–5 finely toothed leaflets**.

FLOWERS: Small, greenish white; in 3–7 umbrella- or ball-shaped clusters, hidden from sight beneath leaves; male and female flowers on separate plants.

FRUITS: Dark purple, plump berries, greenish white when young; edible, but not very palatable.

ECOLOGY: Widespread and common at low to mid elevations in moist, shady forests, openings and floodplains; generally absent from our arid climates.

NOTES: The Nlaka'pmx drank a root decoction as a tonic for purifying the blood, and the Secwepemc made a tea to treat colds. The rhizomes have a spicy fragrance and were once used to make a refreshing drink as a substitute for true sarsaparilla. • The common name refers to the medicinal properties, which are similar to those of sarsaparilla (*Smilax officinalis*), a tropical, prickly vine. 'Sarsaparilla' comes from the Spanish *zarza parilla*, meaning 'little prickly vine,' though our wild sarsaparilla has no thorns or prickles.

BUNCHBERRY • *Cornus canadensis*

GENERAL: Low perennial, 5–20 cm tall, somewhat woody at base, with widely spreading **rhizomes**.

LEAVES: Evergreen, 4–7 in a whorl at top of stem, oval-elliptic; hairless, whitish beneath, with mostly parallel veins.

FLOWERS: 4 white to purplish-tinged, petal-like bracts surrounding a central cluster of small greenish-white to purplish flowers.

FRUITS: Clusters of **bright red, fleshy, berry-like** drupes.

ECOLOGY: Widespread and common at low to subalpine elevations in dry to moist, forests and clearings; generally absent from our arid climates.

NOTES: The four bracts are easily mistaken for petals. A close look will show that they have no floral parts of their own, but surround a cluster of tiny true flowers. • Bunchberry is reported to have an explosive pollination mechanism, whereby the petals of the mature, but unopened, flower buds suddenly reflex and the anthers spring out simultaneously, catapulting their pollen loads into the air. The trigger for this explosion appears to be a tiny 'antenna' (just over 1 mm long) that projects from near the tip of one of the four petals in bud. • The berries are sweet, although pulpy. The Lil'wet'ul and Coastal native peoples ate bunchberries raw or cooked. Generally, Interior people did not use them and some even considered them poisonous. • Bunchberry makes a very attractive ground-cover plant in shady gardens. It prefers soil with coarse humus or rotting wood. • Bunchberry is also called dwarf dogwood. The name 'bunchberry' comes from the fact that the berries are all bunched together in a terminal cluster.

Caryophyllaceae: Pink Family

The pink family is known for some widely cultivated plants such as carnation (*Dianthus caryophyllus*; *Dianthus* is Greek for 'flower of the gods') as well as for the ineradicable garden chickweed (*Stellaria media*). The native species, while often not particularly showy, include some interesting plants, such as the campions (*Silene* spp.), in which the sepals are fused into an inflated, bladder-like tube.

The common species in our area are mostly perennial herbs, although the family as a whole includes many annuals. Members of the family can usually be recognized by their narrow leaves, arranged in pairs or whorls, and by their slender stems, which are swollen at the points of attachment of the leaves. Many species have distinctively shaped petals consisting of a long, narrow basal section (called a **claw**) that widens into an expanded, often lobed blade. The sepals are often fused. Although the **petals and sepals come in fives, the petals are often so deeply notched at the tip that there appear to be 10.**

Characteristics of the flowers are useful in distinguishing among the species. The presence of a calyx tube is a useful characteristic. Petal shapes, particularly the notches at the tips and the narrow claws, should also be noted. Other distinguishing features include the number of styles and the general hairiness (or stickiness) of the plant.

Members of the pink family in our area include a number of dwarf, tufted, alpine species of starworts (*Stellaria* spp.), chickweeds (*Cerastium* spp.) and sandworts (*Minuartia* spp.). Most have small, narrow leaves and fairly small, white flowers. The starworts and chickweeds have deeply notched or bilobed petals, whereas the sandworts and pearlworts have entire or shallowly notched petals.

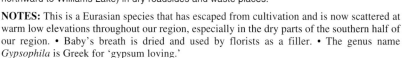

BABY'S BREATH • *Gypsophila paniculata*

GENERAL: Perennial, 40–80 cm tall, from a thick root, with **delicate, freely branching stems**.

LEAVES: Opposite, lance-shaped to linear with pointed tips, bluish.

FLOWERS: Many, **tiny, white; massed in airy clusters**; each flower on a thin stalk 2–4 times its length; **calyx lobes are purplish and edged in white; 2 styles**.

FRUITS: Capsules, with 2–5 black seeds.

ECOLOGY: Scattered and infrequent in Thompson and Okanagan basins and southern Rocky Mountain Trench (although sporadically northward to Williams Lake) in dry roadsides and waste places.

NOTES: This is a Eurasian species that has escaped from cultivation and is now scattered at warm low elevations throughout our region, especially in the dry parts of the southern half of our region. • Baby's breath is dried and used by florists as a filler. • The genus name *Gypsophila* is Greek for 'gypsum loving.'

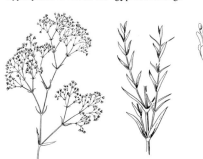

THREAD-LEAVED SANDWORT • *Arenaria capillaris*

GENERAL: Perennial, to 30 cm tall, in **loose mats** to 20 cm wide; stems slender and often whitish, covered with **glandular hairs.**

LEAVES: A cluster of **narrowly linear** leaves, 2–4 cm long, **at base of stem**; 2–5 pairs of short leaves on flowering stem.

FLOWERS: 5 white petals, about **twice as long as purplish-tinged sepals**; 3 styles; in a small, **flat-topped inflorescence** at end of flowering stalk.

FRUITS: Egg-shaped capsules, opening by **6 teeth**.

ECOLOGY: Common in our dry climates from sagebrush grasslands to rocky, subalpine slopes.

SIMILAR SPECIES: Thyme-leaved sandwort (*A. serpyllifolia*) is a common weedy annual found on dry roadsides and disturbed places in our area. It has tiny leaves (3–7 mm long) and does not form tufts or mats.

NOTES: The genus name *Arenaria*, from the Latin *arena*, 'sand,' and the common name 'sandwort' reflect the preference of these plants for often sandy habitats. The term 'wort' is often found in the common names of plants. It is derived from the old English *wyrt*, which was a general name for a plant or vegetable and was often applied to plants having some medicinal value. The species name *capillaris* refers to the slender, hair-like leaves.

BLUNT-LEAVED SANDWORT • *Moehringia lateriflora*
Arenaria lateriflora

GENERAL: Perennial, 5–20 cm tall, from **runners or rhizomes**; minutely hairy flowering stems arise singly or in small clumps.

LEAVES: Opposite, **egg-shaped to oblong or lance-shaped, rounded at tip,** minutely hairy; smaller leaves at base of flowering stem.

FLOWERS: Small, with 5 **white, 3–8-mm-long petals** (2–3 times longer than the **white-edged sepals**); 3 styles; solitary or in clusters of 2–5 at tip of stem.

FRUITS: Rounded capsules, opening by **6 teeth**; few seeds.

ECOLOGY: Scattered and often common at low to mid elevations (occasionally to subalpine) in meadows, grassy slopes, clearings and dry, open deciduous and mixed forests, often with trembling aspen.

NOTES: This genus is named for P.H.G. Moehring (1710–92), a German naturalist.

ALPINE SANDWORT • *Minuartia obtusiloba*
Arenaria obtusiloba

GENERAL: Perennial, 1–6 cm tall, in **loose to dense mats** (up to 40 cm wide) of trailing stems that are covered with persistent leaves; flowering stems slender and hairy, with **glands** near tip.

LEAVES: A cluster of **narrowly linear** leaves at **base of stem**; 1–2 pairs of leaves on flowering stem.

FLOWERS: 5 white petals, much longer than **purplish-tinged sepals; 3 styles; solitary** at end of flowering stalk.

FRUITS: Egg-shaped capsules, opening by **3 teeth.**

ECOLOGY: Scattered at subalpine and alpine elevations on dry gravelly slopes and in meadows.

SIMILAR SPECIES: Boreal sandwort (*M. rubella,* also known as *Arenaria rubella*) is also found on dry sites in subalpine and alpine areas. It is densely hairy and covered with glands, and its white petals are shorter than the purplish sepals.

NOTES: The genus *Minuartia* is named after Juan Minuart (1693–1768), a Spanish botanist.

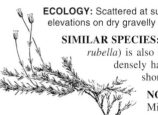

FIELD CHICKWEED • *Cerastium arvense*

GENERAL: Perennial, 10–30 cm tall, in **loose mats with trailing stems;** flowering stems **greyish-hairy** on upper part and among flowers.

LEAVES: Narrow, with **pointed tips, finely hairy and greyish green;** stem leaves **opposite,** most have **secondary leafy tufts in their axils.**

FLOWERS: 5 white petals with **deeply notched** tips, 2–3 times longer than sepals; **5 styles;** 5 to many flowers on hairy stalks in an **open, flat-topped inflorescence;** uppermost leafy bracts on flowering stems have whitish, papery edges.

FRUITS: Cylindrical, many-seeded capsules, opening by **10 teeth.**

ECOLOGY: Scattered at low to alpine elevations; locally common on rock outcrops, scree, grassy slopes, meadows, dry open forest and clearings; absent from our wettest climates.

SIMILAR SPECIES: Mouse-ear chickweed (*C. fontanum,* also known as *C. vulgatum*), is an introduced weed common on roadsides, and in waste places, lawns and gardens. This **sprawling, small, hairy biennial has oblong leaves** along the stem, which ends in a cluster of small, white flowers. • Bering chickweed (*C. beeringianum*) is common on dry slopes and cliffs in subalpine and alpine areas. It forms dense to sprawling mats, and it has **broader leaves with rounded tips** and fewer flowers than field chickweed and it lacks the papery edges on its flowering bracts.

NOTES: The name 'chickweed' comes from the practice of feeding this species and garden chickweed (*Stellaria media*), a garden weed, to chickens, goslings, and cage birds, especially if they were ill. The genus name *Cerastium* is Latin for 'horned,' referring to the shape of the fruits.

MOSS CAMPION • *Silene acaulis*

GENERAL: Perennial, 3–6 cm tall, in **compact, hemispherical or flat mats** up to 50 cm broad; stems have densely crowded branches.

LEAVES: Mostly basal, linear to narrowly lance-shaped, stiff, sharp-pointed, stalkless and hairless; withering and persisting for many years.

FLOWERS: Showy, pink, lilac, or pale purple (rarely white), with 5 petals inside an **inflated, bladder-like calyx**; **3 styles**; **borne singly** on very short stalks.

FRUITS: 3-chambered capsules.

ECOLOGY: Scattered and often common at high elevations in moist but well-drained rock crevices, cliffs and ledges, gravelly exposed ridges and turfy tundra barrens.

NOTES: This is one of our most beautiful alpine cushion plants and it is an excellent plant for rock gardens. It does best in well-drained, sunny locations, and it is easily propagated from seed. • The species name *acaulis* means 'without a stem' and refers to the moss-like, low-growing cushion habit of the plant. The common name 'campion' (or 'champion') comes from Europe, where flowers of red campion (*S. dioica*) were used to adorn chaplets (wreaths) placed on heads of champions at public games.

PARRY'S CAMPION • *Silene parryi*

GENERAL: Perennial, 20–50 cm tall, with several **unbranched, hairy and more or less sticky stems** from a thickened, branched base.

LEAVES: Mostly basal, narrowly **spatula-shaped**; leaves on flowering stem are opposite and narrow.

FLOWERS: White, sometimes green or purple tinged, with 5 petals flaring out above a **tubular** and somewhat **inflated calyx** with 10 prominent greenish to purplish ribs; **petals have 4 lobes and 2 appendages**, which give the appearance of a frill at the mouth of the calyx tube; **3 styles**.

FRUITS: 1-celled capsules.

ECOLOGY: Scattered and locally common at subalpine and alpine elevations in moist to dry meadows and open subalpine forests.

SIMILAR SPECIES: The campions include a number of species that were introduced from Europe and have become weedy. The weedy species are mostly annuals. Bladder campion (*S. vulgaris*, also known as *S. cucubalus*), a widely distributed weed of waste places, is one of the most common of these. **Its inflated calyx is hairless and its petals usually do not have any appendages**. The long, often leafy stem branches freely.

NOTES: The campions are among the showier members of the pink family. They are most notable for their **sepals, which are fused together and often inflated** to form a distinctive bladder-like calyx. The **petals have a long narrow basal section** (a **claw**) and a broad blade that extends out of the calyx. The petals generally also have some type of appendage where the claw and blade join. • This species was named after Charles Christopher Parry (1823–90), a Colorado and Iowa botanist who worked on the Mexican Boundary Survey.

MENZIES'S CAMPION • *Silene menziesii*

GENERAL: Low, somewhat matted perennial, 5–30 cm tall, with long, slender rootstock and many prostrate to erect, **finely sticky-hairy stems**.

LEAVES: Opposite, mostly on stem, lance-shaped, almost stalkless, 2–6 cm long.

FLOWERS: White, with **5 rounded, deeply notched petals** flaring out above an **inflated, tubular to bell-shaped calyx; 3 styles**; in loose, leafy clusters at tips of stems.

FRUITS: 1-celled capsules.

ECOLOGY: Scattered and infrequent at low to mid elevations in dry climates of southern half of our region, in meadows and open forests.

SIMILAR SPECIES: Douglas's campion (*S. douglasii*) is a more robust species, common on dry sites at low to montane elevations. It has showy, white flowers with bilobed petals and a **large, white calyx that is inflated and papery** in fruit.

NOTES: The Okanagan use Menzies's campion to make eye-drop medication for cataracts. • Menzies's campion is also known as small-flowered catchfly. The derivation of the genus name *Silene* is uncertain. It is believed to be from the Greek *seilenos*, a type of woodland satyr (Silene was one of Bacchus's companions). The species name honours Archibald Menzies, an explorer of the Pacific Northwest.

NIGHT-FLOWERING CATCHFLY • *Silene noctiflora*

GENERAL: Annual, 20–60 cm tall, with 1–3 simple to freely branching stems, **hairy throughout and sticky above**.

LEAVES: Opposite, broadly **lance-shaped to elliptic**; lower leaves with broad stalks; upper leaves nearly stalkless.

FLOWERS: White to pinkish, with 5 petals flaring out above a **tubular to bell-shaped and prominently ribbed calyx tube; petals are deeply notched and bear 2 appendages**, which give the appearance of a frill at the mouth of the tube; **3 styles; arranged in sparse clusters.**

FRUITS: 3-chambered capsules.

ECOLOGY: Introduced weed of fields and waste places, widely scattered throughout warm dry climates of our region.

SIMILAR SPECIES: Night-flowering catchfly could be confused with the less common white cockle (*S. alba*, also known as *Lychnis alba*). White cockle is much more rank in growth, and it **usually has five styles in contrast to the three of most *Silene* species**.

NOTES: The flowers open in the evening and are pollinated by moths. During the day, the petals are shriveled, giving the appearance of being past their prime. • The Nlaka'pmx used night-flowering catchfly as a charm for wealth, good health, and good luck in hunting and gambling. • The common name 'catchfly' refers to the sticky stems.

CRISP STARWORT • *Stellaria crispa*

GENERAL: Low, spreading perennial, 5–30 cm long, from slender rhizomes, often clumped or matted; stems, weak and mostly unbranched.

LEAVES: In many **pairs, lance- or egg-shaped,** with sharp-pointed tips; **edges thin and minutely wavy,** like potato chips.

FLOWERS: Greenish to whitish, very small; petals are usually lacking, if present they are shorter than the sepals; **solitary,** from the leaf axils.

FRUITS: Straw-coloured or brownish capsules, nearly twice as long as the sepals, opening by **6 teeth.**

ECOLOGY: Scattered at low to subalpine elevations mostly in our moist and wet climates, on streambanks and in seepage areas, clearings and wet seepage forests.

SIMILAR SPECIES: Northern starwort (*S. calycantha*) is another low, often matted plant, but its **flowers are in clusters** on leafy stems and its leaves are more narrowly lance-shaped. • Garden chickweed (*S. media*) is a widespread introduced weed of cultivated fields, gardens, lawns and pastures. It is not as delicate as our native species and has lines of hairs on its stems and leaf stalks.

NOTES: The common name 'starwort' and the genus name *Stellaria*, from the Latin *stella*, 'a star,' refer to the star-shaped flowers.

LONG-STALKED STARWORT • *Stellaria longipes*

GENERAL: Perennial, 5–30 cm long, in small to large **tufts or mats**; stems slender and **square.**

LEAVES: Opposite, linear to narrowly lance-shaped, 1–3 cm long, sharp-pointed, **stiff and shiny.**

FLOWERS: White, with 5 deeply notched, small petals, as long as the sepals; **solitary** or several in loose clusters, on **slender, erect stalks.**

FRUITS: Shiny, **purplish to black capsules,** opening by 6 teeth.

ECOLOGY: Scattered at low to high elevations on streambanks, lakeshores, rocky slopes, alpine scree, mountain meadows, and open forest; also weedy in disturbed areas, such as roadsides.

NOTES: This species represents a complex of forms (many of which have been called separate species by some taxonomists) that vary in colour, hairiness and number of flowers. • The starworts are **thin-stemmed, delicate plants with narrow, paired, stalkless leaves and small, white flowers.** Their five petals are usually **deeply bilobed** (appearing as 10), but may be very small, or missing altogether. Flowers of our species have **three styles.**

Portulacaceae: Purslane Family

The purslanes are annual or perennial herbs with **fleshy stems and leaves**. The leaves are simple and smooth, without lobes or toothed edges, and they are often opposite. Purslane flowers are regular in form and often showy, and they usually have **two sepals**, which distinguishes them from flowers of the pink family (Caryophyllaceae).

BITTERROOT • *Lewisia rediviva*

GENERAL: Fleshy perennial, 1–3 cm tall, flowering stalks arise from a deep, thick, branched **taproot** and a short, simple or branched woody base.

LEAVES: All basal, linear, round in cross section, usually **drying and withering** by flowering time.

FLOWERS: Solitary, deep pink to sometimes white; about **15 narrow petals**; **6–9 oval sepals**; on a short stalk close to soil surface.

FRUITS: Capsules, with dark brown, shiny seeds.

ECOLOGY: Scattered and locally frequent in southern Okanagan Basin and rarely in southernmost Rocky Mountain Trench, in dry grasslands and sagebrush slopes.

SIMILAR SPECIES: Alpine lewisia (*L. pygmaea*) is found at high elevations in the southern half of our region. It has **two sepals** and fewer petals (5–9) than bitterroot, and its narrow leaves are often longer than the flowering stalks.

NOTES: The spectacular 'water-lily' flowers of bitterroot open only in the sun. • Many southern Interior peoples ate the roots. They dug them in early spring as the leaves were developing and before the root became bitter. The roots were peeled and cooked or dried for

winter use. Bitterroot was considered a valuable plant and it figured prominently in trade. A favourite dish of Interior peoples was a pudding of bitterroot, saskatoon berries and salmon eggs. • Lewis and Clark reported that the prepared root was still too bitter for their taste; hence it was called 'bitter-root.' Meriwether Lewis first collected it in 1806 in Montana. When his pressed, dried specimen was examined months later, it still showed signs of life and when planted, it promptly grew; so it was called *rediviva* meaning 'restored to life.'

OKANOGAN FAMEFLOWER • *Talinum sediforme*
T. okanoganense

GENERAL: Fleshy perennial; thick, branched taproot; woody base and many **branching stems, in cushions** less than 15 cm broad.

LEAVES: Greenish red, linear, almost round in cross section; soon falling off, leaving behind the basal portion of the midrib, which looks like a curved bristle.

FLOWERS: White, sometimes yellowish or pinkish tinged, with 5 petals and **2 sepals, which fall off soon after flowers open**; 3–9 flowers in flat-topped, showy clusters.

FRUITS: Firm-walled capsules, with 6 teeth.

ECOLOGY: Scattered and infrequent at low to mid elevations in Thompson and Okanagan basins, on exposed slopes and ledges, dry grasslands and sagebrush steppes.

NOTES: The origin of the name 'fameflower' is not clear, but this plant was originally described from Okanogan County in Washington State. It is also called rock pink. The origin of the genus name *Talinum* is also mysterious; it is thought to be from Senegal (Africa). The species name *sediforme* describes the fleshy leaves and growth form, which resemble those of stonecrops (*Sedum* spp.).

WESTERN SPRING BEAUTY • *Claytonia lanceolata*

GENERAL: Somewhat fleshy perennial, 5–20 cm tall, with a rounded, easily detached **marble-sized corm**; 1 to several stems.

LEAVES: 1 to few lance-shaped **basal leaves**, with **largely underground stalks** (sometimes withering or lacking); flowering stems have a single **pair of stalkless leaves below flowers**.

FLOWERS: White to pinkish, often with **deep pink veins**; **2 sepals** and 5 petals; in a cluster of 3–20 flowers.

FRUITS: Egg-shaped capsules, each with **3–6 black, shiny seeds**.

ECOLOGY: Widely scattered at mid to high elevations in open, moist, grassy slopes; sometimes among deciduous shrubs or in areas of late snowbeds.

NOTES: Western spring beauty often forms large patches. At timberline in moist meadows, near snowbanks and in upper elevation grasslands, it flowers soon after snowmelt and wilts as soon as the capsules mature. In general, alpine plants are smaller, with fewer smaller flowers, and they have smaller but broader leaves. • The leaves are a source of vita-

mins A and C. The corms, which taste like potatoes when cooked— they are often referred to as Indian potato—were an important source of carbohydrates for Interior native people. They were dug in June, just after flowering. Large quantities were harvested near Lytton and in the Potato Mountains of the southern Chilcotin. The Secwepemc stored them in deep earthen pits, just like potatoes. Native people ensured sustained yields by replanting the smaller corms to grow for next year's crop. Browsing by livestock and the invasion of weedy plants have caused a deterioration in the habitat of this fragile plant.

MINER'S-LETTUCE • *Claytonia perfoliata*
Montia perfoliata

GENERAL: Somewhat fleshy annual, 3–35 cm tall, with a slender taproot; generally with several stems, often branched at base.

LEAVES: Many basal leaves, varying from **linear spatula-shaped** to oval, with long stalks; upper flowering stem has a pair of leaves which are usually joined into a **single disk-like leaf** below the flowers.

FLOWERS: White to pinkish, with **2 sepals** and 5 petals; several nodding flowers in a cluster above leaf disk.

FRUITS: Egg-shaped capsules, each with 3 black, shiny seeds.

ECOLOGY: Scattered and infrequent at low to mid elevations, mostly on Thompson and Okanagan plateaus; usually in moist (at least in spring) open to shady woods and thickets.

SIMILAR SPECIES: Siberian miner's-lettuce (*C. sibirica*, also known as *Montia sibirica*) is often rhizomatous and persists for more than one year. It has larger flowers than miner's-lettuce (its petals are 6–12 mm long, rather than 2–8 mm) and the **pair of opposite leaves on the stem is never joined into a disk**. It is common in moist, usually shaded areas in the Coast/Interior Transition of the Cascade Mountains and less common further eastward.

NOTES: The disk-like leaf surrounding the stem below the flowers immediately identifies this woodland herb. • The Nlaka'pmx used this plant as a medicine for sore eyes. • Miner's-lettuce, as the name implies, was used by early prospectors as a salad green or lettuce. Its leaves are a source of vitamins A and C.

NARROW-LEAVED MONTIA • *Montia linearis*

GENERAL: Low growing annual, 5–20 cm tall, sometimes with a single, branching, erect to ascending, leafy stem.

LEAVES: Alternate, linear, all borne on stem.

FLOWERS: White, small, 3–4 mm long; 5 petals, about same length as the **2 sepals;** 5–12 in a loose, 1-sided inflorescence.

FRUITS: Egg-shaped capsules, opening into 3 segments, bearing 2 black shiny seeds.

ECOLOGY: Scattered and infrequent at low to mid elevations, mostly on Thompson and Okanagan plateaus; usually in moist (at least in spring) and often sandy, open to shady woods and thickets.

NOTES: The genera *Claytonia* and *Montia* are very similar in their above-ground appearance. Both have the typical purslane characteristics of flowers with two sepals and fleshy leaves and stems. Their flowers are white to pinkish, and are borne in a loose, unbranched inflorescence. The two groups are best distinguished by examining their roots. The *Claytonia* species grow from an edible tuber (corm) or thick taproot, while the *Montia* species always have fibrous roots.

SMALL-LEAVED MONTIA • *Montia parvifolia*

GENERAL: Somewhat fleshy perennial, 10–20 cm tall, with long spreading rootstocks and horizontal vegetative stems; 1 to several flowering stems.

LEAVES: Lance-shaped to **round or spoon-shaped** basal leaves with stalks about as long as blades; several **alternate,** smaller stem leaves.

FLOWERS: Showy, light to deep pink, with **2 sepals** and 5 petals; on long stalks in an open inflorescence.

FRUITS: Capsules, each bearing 2 black shiny seeds.

ECOLOGY: Scattered and infrequent at low to mid elevations in southern half of our region in moist, often rocky sites.

SIMILAR SPECIES: Blinks chickweed (*M. fontana*), also called water chickweed, is an uncommon annual of wet meadows or shallow water at low to mid elevations in our region. Unlike small-leaved montia, blinks chickweed has **several opposite, lance-shaped leaves** along its stems and its small, white flowers usually have only **two petals.**

NOTES: The long, slender rootstocks of small-leaved montia can spread extensively, creating large patches. • The species name *parvifolia* means 'small-leaved.' The genus *Montia* was named for the Italian botanist Guiseppe Monti (1682–1760). Small-leaved montia is also called spring beauty.

259

Crassulaceae: Stonecrop Family

The stonecrop family consists of succulent herbs that grow mostly in rocky places. Our species are all in the genus *Sedum*. These low-growing perennials have thick, fleshy leaves and dense, showy clusters of small flowers. The flowers have five petals and five sepals that are separate, or joined only at the base. The **fruits are distinctive, five-parted capsules with pointed tips**.

The leaves of all stonecrops are edible, but they should be eaten only in moderation as some have emetic and cathartic properties and can cause headaches.

The genus name *Sedum* comes from the Latin *sedeo*, 'to sit,' and refers to the low growth form. 'Stonecrop' is from the Old English *stancrop*, meaning 'that which is cropped, cut, or gathered off stone.' Prior (1874) claims that 'crop' means a 'top, or bunch of flowers.'

'Orpine,' another name for this family, was originally given to the yellow-flowered species of this genus, but ironically it is now mainly used for the pink-flowered *S. telephium* of Europe. It is from the French *orpin* or Latin *auropigmentum*, meaning a 'gold-pigment.'

The charming name 'livelong' refers to the plant's ability to remain alive (green) long after it has been picked. It was once used to test a lover's fidelity. On Midsummer's Eve, a young girl would pick two pieces, one representing herself and one her lover. These were set on a slate or trencher and the length of time his piece lived and whether or not it turned towards hers indicated the strength of his fidelity. These plants were also called 'lovelong' and 'midsummer men.'

If stonecrop grew on a roof it was believed to protect a house from fire and lightning. Some species were used in a vermifuge, and were known as 'trip-madam,' 'prick-madam' or 'pricket'—all corruptions of 'triacle-madame,' which was from the French *triacque* and *triaquette*, for an antihelminthic medicine.

ROSEROOT • *Sedum integrifolium*
S. roseum, Rhodiola integrifolia

GENERAL: Succulent perennial, 5–20 cm tall, with fleshy rootstocks; flowering stems clothed with **many persistent leaves**.

LEAVES: Oval to oblong, flattened and fleshy, distributed along length of flowering stems, smallest at base.

FLOWERS: Usually **dark purple** (occasionally rose-coloured) with **oblong petals**; in short, dense clusters at tip of stems.

FRUITS: Red or purplish, 5-parted capsules, with more or less **erect sections with curved tips**.

ECOLOGY: Scattered and locally common at high elevations, but most abundant on less acidic bedrock types; subalpine to alpine scree, talus, cliffs and ridges (usually where moist in spring), or sometimes in grassy tundra.

NOTES: The Nlaka'pmx bathed babies in a solution made from *Sedum* species, and it was said to soothe them. As a poultice, it was used to treat haemorrhoids. • The common name 'roseroot' derives from the rose-like fragrance produced when the roots are cut or bruised. Another common name, 'king's crown,' may refer to the flowers, which are arranged in a dense, crown-like inflorescence at the tip of the stem.

LANCE-LEAVED STONECROP • *Sedum lanceolatum*

GENERAL: Succulent perennial, 5–20 cm high, with clusters of flowering stems and short, sterile shoots.

LEAVES: Alternate, succulent, narrowly lance-shaped, rounded in cross-section; mostly clustered near base; stem leaves tend to drop off before flowering.

FLOWERS: Bright yellow, with **narrowly lance-shaped petals**; in dense, flat-topped clusters at tip of stem.

FRUITS: 5-parted capsules, with **erect-tipped sections**.

ECOLOGY: Scattered and often common at low to subalpine elevations on dry, open slopes, ridges and rock outcrops; usually on very dry, thin or gravelly soils; especially common on dry, rocky, south-facing slopes.

SIMILAR SPECIES: Spreading stonecrop (*S. divergens*) may be confused with lance-leaved stonecrop. Spreading stonecrop is mat-forming, with prostrate stems and ascending flowering branches. It has berry-like, egg- to spoon-shaped, often bright red **leaves that are opposite rather than alternate**. Spreading stonecrop grows at moderate to alpine elevations, often in temporarily moist, gravelly habitats.

NOTES: The Okanagan made an infusion from the stems, leaves and flowers and used it as a laxative or to clean out the womb after childbirth. • Stonecrops are some of the easiest plants to grow, and many are suitable for use in rock gardens or as house plants. They do best in sunny locations on well-drained soils. A small piece of leafy stem potted in soil will usually root.

WORM-LEAVED STONECROP • *Sedum stenopetalum*
S. douglasii

GENERAL: Succulent perennial, 5–20 cm tall, with clusters of flowering stems and short leafy sterile shoots.

LEAVES: Mostly basal, linear and reddish, prominently keeled and tapering to a slender point; upper leaves generally shrivel or fall before flowering time, but some may persist and bear little **bulbils** at their bases.

FLOWERS: Yellow, with **narrowly lance-shaped petals**; in crowded flat-topped clusters at tip of stem.

FRUITS: 5-parted capsules, with **nearly horizontal sections**.

ECOLOGY: Scattered and locally common at low to subalpine elevations in grasslands, sagebrush flats, ponderosa pine parkland, dry rocky openings, cliffs and talus slopes.

SIMILAR SPECIES: Lance-leaved stonecrop (*S. lanceolatum*, above) can be distinguished from worm-leaved stonecrop by its blunt leaves, which are rounded in cross section, and by its capsules, which have erect sections.

NOTES: The species name *stenopetalum* means 'narrow-petalled,' and this species is sometimes called narrow-petalled stonecrop.

Geraniaceae: Geranium Family

Geraniums are herbs that usually have palmately compound leaves (with the leaflets arranged around a central point), but pinnately compound leaves (with the leaflets in pairs) are found in the genus *Erodium*. A **column of fused styles**, which develops soon after the flowers open, is an immediately identifiable feature of this family. The flowers are regular in structure, with five petals, and five generally bristle-tipped sepals. It is useful to note the quantity of hairs on the petals, and the colour of the flowers.

BICKNELL'S GERANIUM • *Geranium bicknellii*

GENERAL: Taprooted, annual or biennial, 20–60 cm high, with **much-branched** straggly stems, hairy and somewhat **sticky**.

LEAVES: Small, 2–7 cm broad, **deeply 5-lobed**; lobes further divided into pointed, narrow segments; hairy on veins.

FLOWERS: Small, pale pink-purple, usually 2 per stalk.

FRUITS: 5-parted capsules, with **long beaks** shaped like a stork's or crane's bill.

ECOLOGY: Scattered and common at low to mid elevations on roadsides, recent clearings, burns and disturbed soils.

NOTES: The stalked capsules open explosively, splitting the beak lengthwise from the bottom, and flinging the seeds away from the parent plant. • Bicknell's geranium, pink corydalis (*Corydalis sempervirens*) and golden corydalis  (*C. aurea*) are often abundant for a few years after disturbances, such as wildfires or clear-cutting followed by slash-burning. Apparently, its seeds remain on the forest floor for decades or even centuries, and germination is triggered by disturbance. • This species was named for E.P. Bicknell (1858–1925), a New York banker and amateur botanist.

STICKY GERANIUM • *Geranium viscosissimum*

GENERAL: Perennial, 40–90 cm tall; stems and leaves densely covered with **sticky, glandular hairs**.

LEAVES: Basal leaves on **long stalks**; blades 5–12 cm broad and **deeply palmately lobed** into 5 sharply toothed divisions.

FLOWERS: Pinkish-lavender to deep purple-magenta petals, softly hairy on lower half and strongly **veined with purple**.

FRUITS: Elongated, **glandular** hairy capsules, with a **long beak** shaped like a stork's or crane's bill.

ECOLOGY: Scattered and locally abundant at low to mid elevations in dry parts of our plateaus, arid basins and East Kootenays, in grasslands, open forests and occasionally moist meadows; most common in dry Douglas-fir forests and associated grassland slopes.

NOTES: The Okanagan made a warm poultice from the leaves to treat sores, and they held a leaf between sore lips to relieve the pain. The Nlaka'pmx considered it a woman's love charm. • Herbalists apply powdered roots to cuts to help blood clotting or use it internally to stop bleeding. • **Caution:** Geranium leaves resemble those of mountain monkshood (*Aconitum delphiniifolium*, p. 205), which is **poisonous**, so care should be taken to collect only during flowering time. • This species is also called pink geranium. The genus name *Geranium*, from the Greek *geranos*, 'a crane,' refers to the fruit, which has a central, pointed column of fused styles thought to resemble the long bill of a crane. Many species of *Geranium* have the name 'crane's-bill' or 'stork's-bill.'

WHITE GERANIUM • *Geranium richardsonii*

GENERAL: Perennial, 40–80 cm tall, with hairy stems from a short, woody stem-base.

LEAVES: Basal leaves long stalked; stem leaves paired, stalkless; blades 6–14 cm broad, **sparsely hairy on veins** and deeply divided into 5–7 irregularly lobed main segments.

FLOWERS: White or sometimes pinkish, **with purple veins**, 2–3.5 cm across; petals have **long hairs at base**.

FRUITS: 5-parted capsules, with **long beaks** shaped like a stork's or crane's bill.

ECOLOGY: Scattered at low to mid elevations in moist meadows, glades, thickets, and open, usually deciduous forests, especially aspen groves; generally absent from our wet climates.

SIMILAR SPECIES: Sticky geranium (*G. viscosissimum*, p. 262) has leaves that are sticky-hairy all over, whereas the leaves of white geranium are hairy only along the veins of the lower sides of the leaves.

NOTES: The capsules open explosively, with the beak splitting lengthwise from the bottom and flinging the seeds away from the parent plant. • Occasionally, light lavender-flowered specimens of white geranium are found, which could be the result of hybridization with sticky geranium. • Both of our large wild geraniums are easily propagated from fall-sown seed. White geranium prefers partially shaded locations rich in humus, whereas sticky geranium thrives in dry locations with full sun. • This species was named for Sir John Richardson (1787–1865), the Scottish botanist assigned to Sir John Franklin's expedition to Arctic America.

STORK'S-BILL • *Erodium cicutarium*

GENERAL: Annual, 3–30 cm tall, prostrate, mat-forming with more or less reddish stems with swollen joints.

LEAVES: Mainly in a **basal rosette, pinnately compound**; segments **deeply cut and fern-like**.

FLOWERS: Few, **small, pink**; in umbrella-shaped clusters; 5 fertile stamens.

FRUITS: Capsules, with **long beaks** shaped like a stork's or crane's bill.

ECOLOGY: Scattered, mostly at low elevations in southern half of our region, on dry plains, hillsides and waste places.

NOTES: A European species now naturalized in dry grasslands, stork's-bill is considered palatable and nutritious for stock, especially sheep. • The beaked fruits identify stork's-bill as a member of the geranium family, and its pinnately compound leaves distinguish it from the geraniums. There are usually 10 stamens, but only five of them are fertile in *Erodium* species. • This species is also called crane's-bill. A more correct common name would be 'heron's-bill,' since the genus name *Erodium* is from *erodios*, the Greek name for a heron. Both names refer to the long beaks on the fruits, which resemble the bills of these birds. Very old names include 'pink-needle,' 'powke-needle' and 'pick-needle,' because the beaks on the fruits resemble the needles used for pinking (making eyelet holes, called pinks) in muslin for ladies' dresses.

263

WILD BLUE FLAX • *Linum perenne* ssp. *lewisii*

GENERAL: Perennial, 10–60 cm tall, with slender, branching stems from a woody crown.

LEAVES: Linear, 1–3 cm long, along stem.

FLOWERS: Sky-blue, saucer-shaped; 5 separate petals, soon falling, leaving **5 persistent sepals**; in a few-flowered, open inflorescence at tip of stem.

FRUITS: Rounded capsules, splitting to disperse flattened seeds.

ECOLOGY: Scattered and frequent at low to (less commonly) mid elevations throughout dry climates of our region, in dry grasslands, sagebrush steppes and open ponderosa pine and Douglas-fir forests.

NOTES: The Nlaka'pmx used a decoction to rinse their hair and scalp. • Wild blue flax is a suitable garden ornamental. • The genus name *Linum* is from the Greek *linon*, meaning 'a thread, rope, linen, or flax.' Flax has been cultivated for about 4,000 years in Africa and Eurasia for the production of linen thread. The word 'flax' is from the Old English *fleax* and German *flachs*, both meaning 'a thread' (originally from Latin *filum*, 'a thread'). This subspecies was named after the U.S. explorer Meriwether Lewis (1774–1809).

FRINGED GRASS-OF-PARNASSUS • *Parnassia fimbriata*

GENERAL: Perennial, 15–30 cm tall, with 1 to several flowering stems from a short rhizome.

LEAVES: Mostly basal, on long stalks, **broadly kidney-shaped** and glossy green; **a single leaf clasps flowering stem** about half-way up.

FLOWERS: Single, showy, white, with greenish or yellowish veins; lower edges of petals are **fringed with hairs**; 5 fertile stamens alternating with 5 broad, greenish-yellow, sterile stamens that are divided into **5–9 finger-like lobes**.

FRUITS: Capsules, with many seeds.

ECOLOGY: Widespread and common at mid to alpine elevations in damp meadows, streamsides, and open and forested seepage areas.

SIMILAR SPECIES: Northern grass-of-Parnassus (*P. palustris*), also found in wet places, has leaves that are heart-shaped at the base. Its **petals lack the fringe of hairs** that distinguishes fringed grass-of-Parnassus.

NOTES: Alternating fertile and sterile stamens are characteristic of the genus *Parnassia*. The shapes and colours of the sterile stamens (staminodia) vary among the species. • The genus and common names come from a confusion about a grass-like plant Dioscorides described from Mount Parnassus. When the Greek description was translated, this 'grass' was taken to be *P. palustris*. This was obviously a mistake, because *Parnassia* species are not even remotely grass-like, but the name stuck.

Saxifragaceae: Saxifrage Family

The saxifrage family is a large group of plants often associated with rocky habitats. A large number of the species are alpine. All of our species are perennial herbs with simple to compound, primarily basal leaves. The flowers are mostly small and delicate, but they can be highly intricate.

The flowers often provide the best clue to identification, but they must be looked at closely, preferably under 10x magnification. The five sepals form a bell- to saucer-shaped cup (calyx) from which the five separate petals project. The petals can be highly intricate and are well worth a close look. In most of our species, they have narrow, stalk-like bases called **claws**. In some species, most notably the mitreworts (*Mitella* spp.), the petals are finely lobed or dissected. The number of stamens (usually five or 10) is also a useful identifying feature.

Without flowers, it can be very difficult to distinguish among the several genera and species of the Saxifragaceae that have similar foliage (such as *Mitella*, *Heuchera*, *Tellima*, *Tiarella*).

Key to the saxifrage family genera

1a. 5 stamens 2

    2a. Petals entire, not lobed (sometimes lacking) .... *Heuchera*

    2b. Petals divided into at least 3 lobes .... *Mitella*

1b. 10 stamens 3

    3a. Leaves mostly in a basal rosette;
    flowering stem leafless or with only a few small leaves 4

        4a. Petals divided into lobes .... *Mitella*

        4b. Petals entire, not lobed 5

            5a. Ovaries separated almost
            to base; leaves leathery, elliptic,
            generally more than 5 cm long .... *Leptarrhena*

            5b. Ovaries united to well above base;
            leaves not leathery (but sometimes thick
            and fleshy), variable in size and shape,
            but often very small .... *Saxifraga*

    3b. Leaves frequent along flowering stems,
    often forming a basal rosette as well 6

        6a. Petals lobed or divided 7

            7a. 3 styles; leaves deeply cleft or lobed .... *Lithophragma*

            7b. 2 styles; leaves
            shallowly lobed .... *Tellima*

        6b. Petals entire, not lobed 8

            8a. Ovary and capsule with
            1 chamber; leaves shallowly to
            deeply lobed, or divided into leaflets .... *Tiarella*

            8b. Ovary and capsule with 2 chambers;
            leaves various, but often entire .... *Saxifraga*

ROUND-LEAVED ALUMROOT • *Heuchera cylindrica*

GENERAL: Robust perennial, 15–90 cm tall, with a branching crown and a short, thick rhizome; stems more or less **glandular-hairy.**

LEAVES: All basal on long stalks, usually hairy; blades **heart- or kidney-shaped**, with 5–9 broadly rounded, shallow lobes and round teeth.

FLOWERS: Cream to greenish-yellow flowers; in a long, narrow inflorescence; with a **bell-shaped calyx; petals (often lacking) with narrowed bases**; 5 stamens.

FRUITS: Many-seeded capsules.

ECOLOGY: Widespread and often common at all elevations, mostly in our dry plateaus, arid basins and East Kootenays, in dry open forests and grasslands, exposed bedrock outcrops and talus slopes; scattered elsewhere in our moist and wet climates on dry, warm sites.

SIMILAR SPECIES: Smooth alumroot (*H. glabra*) has sparsely hairy, more sharply toothed leaves and a more **spreading inflorescence.** It inhabits rocky meadows, mossy talus slopes, moist slabs and boulders (as in the spray zone near waterfalls), at mid to high elevations. • Meadow alumroot (*H. chlorantha*) looks much like round-leaved alumroot, but it is larger (40–100 cm tall) and hairier, and it has bright green sepals.

NOTES: The alumroots were important medicinal species for North American native people and herbalists. The root is a very intense astringent (like alum) that was reportedly used to treat cancer in the 18th century. The roots of several *Heuchera* species were pounded and dried to apply as poultices on cuts and sores to stop bleeding and promote healing. A root infusion was used to treat sore throats and liver disorders. Interior peoples used alumroot widely to treat wounds and sores. The Secwepemc also added the leaves to make a solution to bathe sore feet and used it to treat diarrhea. • Alumroot is commonly used as a mordant to fix dyes. Many crafts people prefer it to manufactured alternatives.

FRINGECUP • *Tellima grandiflora*

GENERAL: Perennial, to 80 cm tall, with a short creeping rhizome; **flowering stems unbranched and very hairy below.**

LEAVES: Heart- to kidney-shaped basal leaves, shallowly lobed with irregular, round teeth, **on long hairy stalks**; 1–3 smaller leaves on flowering stem.

FLOWERS: Small, **greenish white**, often turning deep reddish with age, very fragrant; **5 fringe-tipped petals** spreading from cup-shaped calyx; 10–35 flowers in a **narrow, glandular spike**.

FRUITS: Capsules.

ECOLOGY: Scattered and infrequent at low to subalpine elevations in wet Columbia Mountains, in moist open forests, seepage areas and clearings.

NOTES: The genus name *Tellima* is an anagram of *Mitella*, the genus under which it was first described. The species name *grandiflora* means 'large-flowered.' The highly divided petals form a fringe around the edge of the floral disk (the cup), which gives rise to the common name.

BREWER'S MITREWORT • *Mitella breweri*

GENERAL: Perennial, 15–30 cm tall, hairless or sparsely hairy below to **densely hairy above**; with generally leafless flowering stems.

LEAVES: Basal, **heart- to kidney-shaped** with round-toothed edges, hairless or with sparse white or brown hairs.

FLOWERS: Greenish yellow, with a saucer-shaped calyx; **petals pinnately dissected into 5–9 pairs of thread-like segments**; 5 stamens, attached between petals.

FRUITS: Capsules open widely to expose **shiny black seeds in a shallow cup.**

ECOLOGY: Locally common at low to (more commonly) subalpine elevations, mostly in wet Columbia Mountains, in moist forests, wet openings and clearings.

SIMILAR SPECIES: Five-stamened mitrewort (*M. pentandra*) is found in similar habitats. It also has **five stamens**, but they are **attached at the bases of the petals, not between them**. Its leaves are elongated heart-shaped and are often coarsely hairy on both sides.

NOTES: The intricate floral structure in this group of common woodland and streambank plants is familiar only to those who look closely. The tiny green or yellow flowers scattered along a slender and generally leafless stem do not attract the attention of the unaided eye. The sepals form a bell- or vase-shaped calyx typical of the family. Extending outwards from the calyx are five finely wrought, lattice-like petals. At the base of the petals are five or 10 stamens. The details of the lattice work and the number and arrangement of the stamens are distinctive for each species.

COMMON MITREWORT • *Mitella nuda*

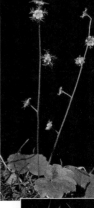

GENERAL: Rhizomatous perennial, 3–20 cm tall, with some creeping stems; finely hairy, leafless flowering stalks.

LEAVES: A few small **basal** leaves, 1–3 cm long, kidney- to **heart-shaped**, with round-toothed edges and **stiffly erect hairs on upper surface**.

FLOWERS: Greenish yellow, with a saucer-shaped, 5-lobed calyx; **petals pinnately dissected**, with 4 **pairs of thread-like segments** and a single terminal segment; **10 stamens.**

FRUITS: Capsules open widely to expose **shiny black seeds in a shallow cup.**

ECOLOGY: Widespread and common at low to subalpine elevations in moist forests, clearings, seepage areas and wetlands.

NOTES: This is the **only species of mitrewort in B.C. with 10 stamens.** All others have five. • Seed dispersal is (at least partly) by a 'splash-cup' mechanism by which direct hits from rain drops eject the small seeds. • Several *Mitella* species make attractive ground cover plants in shaded gardens. • The common and Latin names come from the diminutive of *mitra*, which means 'a cap' or 'a mitre.' Presumably, the cupped seed capsule was thought to resemble a little cap. Mitreworts have also been called 'snowflake' because the finely divided petals are reminiscent of the intricate designs of some snowflakes. The name 'coolwort' has also been applied to these plants, supposedly because a tea made from the leaves was used to treat a fever.

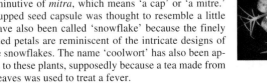

ONE-LEAVED FOAMFLOWER • *Tiarella unifoliata*
T. trifoliata var. *unifoliata*

GENERAL: Perennial, 15–50 cm tall, from short rhizomes, with slender, hairy flowering stems.

LEAVES: Broadly **heart-shaped, unequally 5-lobed** and **coarsely toothed,** with long stalks; 1–3 smaller stem leaves, with short stalks and sometimes 3-lobed.

FLOWERS: Tiny, delicate, white; narrow, thread-like petals are surpassed by the **10 stamens;** several to many flowers on short, wiry stalks, scattered in groups of 3 along stem.

FRUITS: Few-seeded capsules, **divided into 2 unequal parts,** opening to form structures that **resemble sugar scoops.**

ECOLOGY: Widespread and common at low to subalpine elevations mostly in wet Columbia Mountains, moist climates of our plateaus and Coast/Interior Transition, in moist, shady coniferous forests, openings and clearings.

T. trifoliata

SIMILAR SPECIES: Three-leaved foamflower (*T. trifoliata*) is very similar in general appearance, floral characters and habitat to one-leaved foamflower, and some taxonomists think that these two are varieties of the same species. The leaves of three-leaved foamflower are divided into three stalked leaflets.

NOTES: The name 'foamflower' presumably arose because the flowers appear like specks of foam. The plant is sometimes called 'sugar-scoops' in reference to the unusual shape of the opened capsules. This capsule was also thought to resemble the upright headdress worn by ancient Persian kings—the tiara—hence the genus name *Tiarella*. Foamflowers were also called 'coolwort' or 'coolworth' by early pioneers near Cooperstown, New York, because the leaves were laid on scalds and burns (also see the mitreworts [*Mitella* spp.] on page 267).

T. unifoliata

SMALL-FLOWERED WOODLAND STAR • *Lithophragma parviflorum*

GENERAL: Perennial, 10–30 cm tall, with **rice-like bulblets** among thin rhizomes; stems **slender, glandular-hairy,** often purplish.

LEAVES: Mostly basal, circular to kidney-shaped, with **deeply cleft and divided blades,** long-stalked; stem leaves stalkless, divided into narrow segments.

FLOWERS: White to pink-tinged; 5–11 in a cluster at tip of stem; **cone-shaped calyx; petals divided into 3–5 linear segments; 10 stamens;** blooms in spring.

FRUITS: 3-valved capsules.

ECOLOGY: Scattered at low elevations in Thompson and Okanagan basins, in grasslands, sagebrush slopes and open ponderosa pine and Douglas-fir forests.

SIMILAR SPECIES: Smooth woodland star (*L. glabrum*) is also found in open ponderosa pine stands, grasslands and sagebrush areas in our region. It often bears **bulblets at the bases of the stem leaves,** is covered in purple-tipped hairs and has 2–5 flowers.

NOTES: The flowers of small-flowered woodland star appear early in spring and quickly disappear. • The genus name is derived from the Greek *lithos,* 'a stone,' and *phragma,* 'a wall,' and refers to the habitat of some species, but not of those that occur in our area! Small-flowered woodland star is also called fringe-cup, and both common names describe the delicate star-like flowers with their divided (fringed) petals.

LEATHERLEAF SAXIFRAGE • *Leptarrhena pyrolifolia*

GENERAL: Perennial, 20–40 cm tall, with wide-spreading, robust rhizomes and unbranched, **sticky-hairy** flowering stems.

LEAVES: Mostly basal, oval-oblong, deeply veined, with round-toothed edges, **leathery** and rough; 1–3 smaller leaves on flowering stem.

FLOWERS: Small, white; in a tight cluster at stem tip; bell-shaped calyx; petals with narrowed bases; **10 stamens.**

FRUITS: Paired, purplish-red, single-chambered capsules, in a dense cluster at tip of a purplish-red stem.

ECOLOGY: Scattered and often common at subalpine and alpine elevations in wet, open, subalpine forests, wet meadows, streambanks and seepage areas.

NOTES: Hitchcock et al. (1977) notes that leatherleaf saxifrage 'takes well to cultivation and, because of its deep, green leathery leaves and usually reddish follicles, is well worth a place in the native garden or in a moist spot in the rockery.' It can be propagated from seeds or rooted pieces of rhizome. • The genus name is derived from the Greek *leptos*, 'fine,' and *arrhen*, 'male,' and refers to the slender filaments of the stamens. The species name means '*Pyrola*-like leaves,' in reference to the leathery, bright green leaves.

PURPLE MOUNTAIN SAXIFRAGE • *Saxifraga oppositifolia*

GENERAL: Densely to loosely matted, **cushion-forming** perennial, from a taproot, with crowded or trailing branches and **very short, leafy flowering stems**.

LEAVES: Very small and **scale-like,** 1–5 mm long, **leathery, opposite,** overlapping, oblong to oval, with **bristly-hairs along edges.**

FLOWERS: Single, showy, lilac or purple (rarely white); at tip of stem; one of the earliest-flowering species of the alpine zone.

FRUITS: Capsules, with slender, spreading tips.

ECOLOGY: Scattered in alpine, most commonly on calcium-rich substrates, on moist but well-drained alpine cliffs, ledges, gravelly ridges, scree slopes and exposed tundra.

NOTES: This is the only purple-flowered saxifrage in our area. It frequently grows on inaccessible cliffs high in the mountains. Its spectacular mass of flowers appear very early in the mountain spring and are often over before many of us can enjoy their beauty. • The species name *oppositifolia* refers to the opposite leaves. This feature is also unique among our *Saxifraga* species, but is not easy to see because of the densely crowded leaves. The common name describes the colour and habitat of this flower.

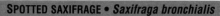

SPOTTED SAXIFRAGE • *Saxifraga bronchialis*

GENERAL: Densely matted, cushion-forming perennial, 5–13 cm tall; flowering stems hairy.

LEAVES: Evergreen, leathery, closely crowded and overlapping, linear lance-shaped to oblong, with small, **spiny tips** and **coarsely hairy edges**; lower portions of branches with withered persistent leaves.

FLOWERS: Creamy-white petals, usually **spotted with purple, orange and yellow**; few to several in a branched inflorescence at tip of stem.

FRUITS: 2-pointed capsules.

ECOLOGY: Widespread and common at mid to high elevations in dry, gravelly and rocky places, such as cliffs, crevices and ridges; usually in non-forested habitats.

SIMILAR SPECIES: Evergreen saxifrage (*S. aizoides*) is another mat-forming species that is often found on streambanks and moist talus slopes high in the Selkirk and Rocky Mountain ranges. It has **yellow flowers dotted with orange** and stalkless, linear leaves, usually without stiff hairs. • Tufted saxifrage (*S. caespitosa*) also forms dense mats on dry to moist rocky ledges, cliffs and banks as well as in open gravelly places at low to high elevations. Its flowers are **white, spotted with purple**, and its **leaves have three lobes**.

NOTES: The spots on the petals often range through a progression of colours from purple or crimson at the tip through orange to yellow at the base. • The dense mat-forming habit makes this a desirable ornamental for rock gardens. • This species is also called prickly saxifrage, from the spiny tips on its leaves. The species name *bronchialis* is from the Greek *bronchos*, 'a windpipe,' because the branches of the inflorescence were likened to the forked branches of the bronchia.

RED-STEMMED SAXIFRAGE • *Saxifraga lyallii*

GENERAL: Perennial, 8–25 cm tall, with well-developed rootstocks; flowering stems leafless, **reddish to purplish**.

LEAVES: Basal, fan-, wedge- or spoon-shaped, with **coarsely toothed edges, abruptly narrowing to long stalks**, hairless to sparsely hairy.

FLOWERS: White, often aging to pinkish; few to several along upper stem.

FRUITS: 2–4-pointed capsules, **often bright red**.

ECOLOGY: Scattered mostly in alpine, primarily in Coast/Interior Transition and wet Columbia Mountains, on streambanks, seepage areas, snowbeds and other wet places; also along shaded streams in high sub-alpine areas.

NOTES: This species is also called Lyall's saxifrage. • The saxifrages are common in rocky places, especially in the alpine, although there are several woodland and streambank species. Growth form, habitat, leaf shape and floral characteristics are all useful in identifying species. They all have slender stems and the tiny, intricate flowers that are typical of the family. The flowers are most commonly white, but they can be greenish, yellow or purple. The petals often have narrowed bases (claws) and many have coloured spots. The leaves are generally basal, but there are often a few small leaves or bracts on the flowering stems.

ALASKA SAXIFRAGE • *Saxifraga ferruginea*
S. newcombei

GENERAL: Perennial, 15–50 cm tall, with a short, woody base or thick rootstock; 1 to several hairy, leafless flowering stems.

LEAVES: Basal, broadly lance- to **wedge-shaped**, with sharply toothed edges, tapering gradually into broad, **winged stalks**, hairy.

FLOWERS: Many, **white**; in an open inflorescence; 3 upper petals abruptly narrowed at base and have **2 yellow spots**; some flowers may be replaced by **pink, leafy bulblets** that drop from plant before fruits mature.

FRUITS: 2-pointed capsules.

ECOLOGY: Scattered at low to subalpine elevations mostly in wet Columbia Mountains on moist rock outcrops, damp soil and streambanks.

SIMILAR SPECIES: Western saxifrage (*S. occidentalis*) is a variable species, but it generally has compact clusters of white flowers, lacks bulblets, and has oval leaves with irregular teeth and reddish glands.

NOTES: An old European belief is that the fresh roots of saxifrages are supposed to remove freckles and relieve toothaches. • Another common name, 'rusty saxifrage,' and the species name *ferruginea*, refer to the rusty-coloured calyx.

NODDING SAXIFRAGE • *Saxifraga cernua*

GENERAL: Perennial, 10–15 cm tall, in **tufts** from a fibrous rootstock; with 2 to several unbranched, thickly **glandular-hairy**, leafy flowering stems.

LEAVES: Basal and on flowering stem, kidney-shaped, with large, rounded teeth or shallow lobes; basal leaves often have **rice-like bulblets** at their bases.

FLOWERS: White; in a spike-like inflorescence; all but uppermost flower often **replaced by bulblets**.

FRUITS: Mature capsules, not seen.

ECOLOGY: Scattered, mostly in alpine areas of Selkirk and Rocky Mountain ranges, on streambanks, moist scree and ledges.

SIMILAR SPECIES: Wood saxifrage (*S. mertensiana*) is often found on streambanks and moist rocky places in the central parts of our region. It also has round to kidney-shaped leaves and some of its flowers are replaced by bulblets, but the plant is quite robust (15–40 cm tall), with large leaves (blades 3–10 cm across), and its flowers are in an open, branched inflorescence.

NOTES: Apparently, this species almost always reproduces vegetatively. The capsules and seeds have not been described botanically. • The species name *cernua* means 'nodding,' a reference to the drooping flowers. The name *Saxifraga* comes from the Latin *saxum*, 'a rock,' and *frangere*, 'to break,' because these plants were thought to break the rocks upon which they grow. Saxifrage plants were ground up and fed to patients with gallstones as a supposed cure. Hence saxifrages may also be called 'breakstone.'

Ericaceae: Heath Family

The heath family is arguably the most varied family of plants in our area. It includes some of our most common shrubs (blueberries and huckleberries [*Vaccinium* spp.] and rhododendrons [*Rhododendron* spp.]) and a group of botanical curiosities—the saprophytic Indian-pipes and their relatives. The herbaceous members of the heath family are generally separated into two subgroups. Most of the saprophytes fall into the Indian-pipe subfamily (Monotropae), and the semi-saprophytic herbs with green leaves belong to the wintergreen subfamily (Pyrolae).

Pyrolae: Wintergreen Subfamily

The wintergreens are perennial, evergreen herbs with leathery, generally basal leaves. Their single flowering stems are unbranched and lack leaves. The flowers are borne at the tip of the stem and have five sepals and petals. The style and stigma are large and generally project out of the flower. The shape of the style and stigma can help to distinguish among the very similar species.

Key to the wintergreens

1a. Flowers single .... *Moneses uniflora*

1b. 2 or more flowers per stem. 2

    2a. Flowers on 1 side of stem;
    style straight; leaves often in more than 1 whorl .... *Orthilia secunda*

    2b. Flowers arranged all around stem; style bent
    or straight; leaves usually in 1 whorl at base of stem 3

        3a. Style straight and short (2 mm long or less) .... *Pyrola minor*

        3b. Style bent and relatively long
        (generally more than 3 mm) 4

            4a. Flowers whitish; leaves usually
            less than 3 cm long .... *Pyrola chlorantha*

            4b. Flowers pink to reddish; leaves
            usually more than 3 cm long .... *Pyrola asarifolia*

*Pyrola
chlorantha*

*Pyrola
minor*

*Pyrola
asarifolia*

*Moneses
uniflora*

*Orthilia
secunda*

GREEN WINTERGREEN • *Pyrola chlorantha*
P. virens

GENERAL: Perennial, with long, slender rhizomes and leafy sterile shoots; **flowering stems to 25 cm tall.**

LEAVES: Evergreen, 1 to few in a **basal rosette, circular to broadly oval,** with slightly round-toothed edges; **stalks longer than blades;** pale green above, darker below.

FLOWERS: Pale yellowish to greenish white; in a **long, straight inflorescence of 3–10 nodding flowers;** long style bends downward and sideways.

FRUITS: Spherical capsules.

ECOLOGY: Scattered and infrequent at low to mid elevations on humus in dry to moist coniferous and mixed forest; absent from arid basins.

SIMILAR SPECIES: Lesser wintergreen (*P. minor*) has white to pinkish flowers with **short, straight styles,** its **leaf stalks are shorter than the blades,** and it is frequent in similar habitats.

NOTES: Wintergreen leaves contain acids which are effective in the treatment of skin eruptions. Mashed leaves of several *Pyrola* species have traditionally been used by herbalists in skin salves or poultices for snake and insect bites. • The *Pyrola* species are true wintergreens, but they are not the plants from which oil of winter-

green is obtained. The oil comes from the eastern North American plant, false wintergreen (*Gaultheria procumbens*). • The common name 'wintergreen' appears to have originally been applied to ivy (*Hedera helix*), because it stayed green throughout the winter. The name has subsequently been applied to the *Pyrola* species because they are also evergreen. The genus name *Pyrola* comes from the Latin *pyrus*, 'a pear,' because *Pyrola* leaves are often pear-shaped.

PINK WINTERGREEN • *Pyrola asarifolia*

GENERAL: Rhizomatous perennial; **flowering stems to 40 cm tall**.

LEAVES: Evergreen, few to many in a **basal rosette, circular to elliptic,** with slightly toothed edges, on long stalks, shiny, dark green above, purplish below; flowering stems bear a few papery bracts.

FLOWERS: Pinkish to purplish red, saucer-shaped; style long, curved and bent downward; **10–25 flowers in a long, loose inflorescence.**

FRUITS: Spherical capsules.

ECOLOGY: Widespread and common at low elevations to near timberline in moist to wet, usually wooded, sites, thickets and meadows; absent from arid basins.

NOTES: This is the largest and most handsome wintergreen in our forests. Though some of the other wintergreens may have flowers tinged with pink, only pink wintergreen has truly pink to red flowers. • Some Interior native groups know the plant as 'beaver's ears' and used it as a kidney medicine. It was apparently used by the Nlaka'pmx as a medi-

cine for women in childbirth. • This attractive, shade-loving plant is very difficult to transplant and cultivate, probably due a dependent association with fungi and decaying humus. • The species name *asarifolia* refers to the resemblance of the leaves to those of wild ginger (*Asarum caudatum*).

SINGLE DELIGHT • *Moneses uniflora*
Pyrola uniflora

GENERAL: Perennial, from creeping rhizomes; slender flowering stalks **to 10 cm tall**.

LEAVES: Evergreen, small, thin, oval to circular, with toothed edges and prominent veins; on short stalks.

FLOWERS: Single, white, waxy; nodding on a leafless stalk; prominent style is tipped with a 5-toothed stigma.

FRUITS: Spherical, erect capsules, split lengthwise into 5 parts when dry.

ECOLOGY: Scattered and sometimes common at low to mid elevations throughout moist and wet climates of our region, on humus or rotting wood in open to dense, usually moist, mossy coniferous forests.

SIMILAR SPECIES: One-sided wintergreen (*Orthilia secunda*, below) looks very similar when the flowers are absent, but its leaves are less veined.

NOTES: Single delight is a very distinctive and attractive plant when in flower. It has a lovely fragrance similar to that of lily-of-the-valley (*Convallaria majalis*). • Single delight is not known to be used by southern Interior native peoples, but it was considered a powerful medicine by the Haida. A weak tea made from the whole plant was drunk for many ailments, including diarrhea, smallpox and cancer, as well as for 'power' and good luck. • Because most members of the Pyrolae are semi-saprophytes, they are exceptionally difficult to transplant and should be left in their native habitat. • This species is also called one-flowered wintergreen. The delicate, waxy-white, fragrant, solitary flowers justly deserve the name 'single delight.' The genus name *Moneses* derives from the Greek *monos,* 'one,' and *hesia,* 'delight.'

ONE-SIDED WINTERGREEN • *Orthilia secunda*
Pyrola secunda

GENERAL: Rhizomatous perennial; flowering stems **to 20 cm tall, leafy on lower half, often woody towards base**.

LEAVES: Evergreen, many, **oval-elliptical**, with toothed edges, dark green above, paler below.

FLOWERS: Pale green to white, bell-shaped, with a straight style; **6–20 nodding flowers** in an **elongated inflorescence, with flowers directed to 1 side**.

FRUITS: Spherical capsules.

ECOLOGY: Widespread and common at low to subalpine elevations in dry to moist, usually mossy, coniferous or mixed forests; also persists in clearings.

NOTES: One-sided wintergreen can be distinguished from other Pyrolae by its leafy stem and 1-sided inflorescence. • The genus name *Orthilia* means 'straight,' in reference to the style, and the species name *secunda* means 'directed to one side,' in reference to the inflorescence.

Monotropae: Indian-pipe Subfamily

The subfamily Monotropae includes the **leafless, saprophytic** species of the heath family. These are among the oddest members of our flora, including some species that are so unusual that they might not be taken for flowering plants at all. These plants do not have green leaves or chlorophyll and cannot manufacture their own food. Instead, they obtain their food from decaying material in the litter and humus. Because they require a well-developed humus layer, but do not depend on the sun, they are most often encountered in the deep shade of mature coniferous forests.

The **Monotropae are most noticeable for their lack of green leaves.** Most have small, leaf-like bracts along their unbranched flowering stems. The four or five petals are usually separate and in a bell-shaped arrangement. In some species, most notably pinedrops (*Pterospora andromedea*), the petals are united into an urn-shaped corolla.

PINEDROPS • *Pterospora andromedea*

GENERAL: Saprophytic perennial, 30–100 cm tall, with **reddish brown,** unbranched flowering stems, **sticky-hairy** all over, fleshy at flowering, then turning fibrous and persisting as dried stems for over a year.

LEAVES: Scale-like bracts, narrow, lance-shaped, crowded near base of stem.

FLOWERS: Pale yellow, with 5 petals fused into an **urn-shaped corolla;** nodding in a long, **upright, spike-like inflorescence.**

FRUITS: Rounded capsules.

ECOLOGY: Locally common at low to mid elevations, mostly in Thompson and Okanagan plateaus, southern Rocky Mountain Trench and southern half of wet Columbia Mountains, in shaded humus under conifers.

NOTES: This spectacular plant, with its tall, leafless stalks and nodding, urn-shaped flowers, is unmistakable. It is the tallest saprophyte in our region, and its reddish-brown stems are often persistent through winter. • The Flathead and some Okanagan peoples called it 'coyote's arrow.' The common name comes from a supposed resemblance of the flowers to drops of resin from the pines (and other conifers) under which it grows. The genus name is from the Greek *pteron*, 'a wing,' and *sporos*, 'a seed,' in reference to the broad, net-like wing attached to one end of the seed. The species name *andromedea* refers to the resemblance of the flowers to those of bog-rosemary (*Andromeda* sp.) which is also in the Ericaceae.

INDIAN-PIPE • *Monotropa uniflora*

GENERAL: **Saprophytic** perennial, 5–25 cm tall, with clusters of fleshy, **waxy-white or pinkish** flowering stems, **turning black** with age.

LEAVES: **Scale-like** bracts along entire stem, linear or lance-shaped.

FLOWERS: Single, white, bell-shaped; 1 per stem, at first **nodding or curved to 1 side**; petals somewhat sac-like at base.

FRUITS: Erect, oval to circular capsules, brown, split open when mature.

ECOLOGY: Widely scattered and infrequent at low to mid elevations on humus in shaded, usually mature, coniferous forests.

NOTES: Note that while the flower hangs down, the fruit eventually points up! • The Nlaka'pmx used ashes or a powder from the plant medicinally to rub on sores that would not heal. • The Nlaka'pmx name for this plant translates as 'wolf-urine' be-

cause it is said to grow wherever wolves urinate. The common name 'Indian-pipe' refers to the pipe-like flowering stalks. It is also called ghost-flower, corpse plant and ice plant—names inspired by the unusual colour and texture of the plant. The genus name *Monotropa* comes from the Greek *monos* (one) and *tropos* (direction), in reference to the way the flower turns to one side.

PINESAP • *Hypopitys monotropa*

GENERAL: **Saprophytic** perennial, to 30 cm tall; fleshy, **yellowish to pinkish** flowering stems, usually solitary, hairy, **turning black** with age.

LEAVES: **Scale-like** bracts, linear or lance-shaped, crowded near base of stem.

FLOWERS: Yellowish to pinkish; petals somewhat sac-like at base and hairy on 1 or both surfaces; **in a cluster** at tip of stem, at first **nodding** and more or less bent to 1 side.

FRUITS: Erect, oval to round capsules, brown, split open when dry.

ECOLOGY: Widely scattered and locally common at low to mid elevations in our moist and wet climates; on humus in deep shade in coniferous forests.

NOTES: The roots of pinesap share the same mycorrhizal fungus as some pine and spruce trees. Nutrients from the conifers can pass through the fungus to pinesap. The interactions among pinesap, its fungus and coniferous trees appear to be quite complex. There is evidence that substances in the fungus may help trees fight some rots. • The name 'pinesap' refers to the fact that the plants often grow under pines and perhaps because the colour and texture of the nodding flowers resemble con-gealed pine resin. The genus name *Hypopitys* comes from the Greek *hypos* (beneath) and *pitys* (a tree).

Droseraceae: Sundew Family

The sundews (*Drosera* spp.) are insectivorous plants. They are small and similar in colour to the sphagnum moss on which they often grow. Their flowers are inconspicuous and infrequently produced. The leaves, however, borne in a basal rosette, are unmistakable. **Along the leaf edges are hairs, or tentacles, tipped with glands that produce drops of red-coloured, sticky juice** (the 'dew' of sundew). Insects, attracted by the juice, adhere to it and are trapped when the tentacles and leaf edges curl in around them. The leaves then secrete digestive enzymes that extract nutrients from the trapped insects.

LONG-LEAVED SUNDEW • *Drosera anglica*

GENERAL: Small **insectivorous** perennial, 5–25 cm tall.

LEAVES: In a basal rosette, erect to spreading, with **spoon-shaped to oblong or linear, glandular,** often reddish blades, at least twice as long as broad, with **gland-tipped hairs on edges.**

FLOWERS: Small, white, fully open only in strong sunlight; 3–10 flowers in a spike uncoiling from the tip, **all on 1 side of stem.**

FRUITS: Capsules, with spindle-shaped seeds.

ECOLOGY: Scattered and locally common at low to mid elevations in fens, swamps and wet lakeshores; less commonly in acid sphagnum bogs.

SIMILAR SPECIES: Long-leaved sundew is more common in our region than round-leaved sundew (*D. rotundifolia*, below). Long-leaved sundew tends to grow in lower, wetter, mucky parts of the wetlands, whereas round-leaved sundew is found on higher sites in bogs that are wet but not usually flooded.

NOTES: Sundews are commonly pollinated by the same insects they use for food—mosquitoes, midges and gnats! • A Mediterranean drink called 'Rossolis' is made from a mixture of sundew blended with raisins and brandy. • This species is also called great sundew. 'Sundew' is thought to come from a misspelling of the Saxon word *sin-dew*, which means 'always dewy'—which indeed it is! The genus name *Drosera* comes from the Greek *drosos*, 'dew.'

ROUND-LEAVED SUNDEW • *Drosera rotundifolia*

GENERAL: Small, fibrous-rooted, **insectivorous** perennial, 5–25 cm tall, with a single flowering stalk.

LEAVES: In a basal rosette, long-stalked, flat-lying to erect; **round to broadly egg- or wedge-shaped glandular blades,** with **glandular hairs on edges.**

FLOWERS: Small, white, fully open only in strong sunlight; inflorescence of 3–10 flowers in a spike uncoiling from tip, **all on 1 side of stem.**

FRUITS: Many-seeded, partitioned capsules.

ECOLOGY: Scattered at low to mid elevations in sphagnum bogs, fens and wet meadows; most frequently on higher parts of bog surface, which are wet but not usually flooded; mostly rooted in sphagnum moss.

NOTES: The sap of round-leaved sundew is acrid and has the reputation for curdling milk. Fresh leaves were used in Europe in the preparation of cheeses and junkets and for the removal of warts. The sap also contains an antibiotic that is effective against several bacteria and was used to treat tuberculosis, asthma, bronchitis and coughs.

PURPLE LOOSESTRIFE • *Lythrum salicaria*

GENERAL: Perennial, 50–200 cm tall, more or less downy-hairy, with **square** stems.

LEAVES: Opposite or sometimes in 3s, **lance-shaped, with rounded to heart-shaped bases,** soft to stiffly hairy.

FLOWERS: Magenta-purple; in **crowded, elongated clusters** at tips of stems; 5–7 petals attached to top of a **tubular, purple-veined** cup around ovary (the hypanthium).

FRUITS: Elongated capsules.

ECOLOGY: Introduced weed of swamps and marshes; potentially occurring throughout our region at low to subalpine elevations.

NOTES: Purple loosestrife, a Eurasian species, is becoming a serious pest that chokes out native wetland flora. Classified as a weed, this very invasive species should be diligently dug up and destroyed. Attempts are underway to introduce biological control agents. • This plant appears to have some effect against gnats and flies, and it was reputed to calm quarrelsome beasts of burden at the plough if placed upon the yoke. • The name 'loosestrife' derives from *lysimachia,* meaning 'to deliver from strife,' and was given by early botanists to plants of both *Lythrum* and *Lysimachia* genera. For a fuller discussion see fringed loosestrife (*Lysimachia ciliata,* p. 195). The genus name *Lythrum* is from the Greek *luthron,* 'blood,' which may refer either to its use as a dye or to the colour of its flowers.

MOUNTAIN HOLLYHOCK • *Iliamna rivularis*

GENERAL: Perennial, 1–1.8 m tall, with woody, rigid, coarsely hairy stems.

LEAVES: Large, maple-leaf shape with 5–7 lobes, 5–15 cm long, on short stout stalks, variably hairy.

FLOWERS: Rose pink, large and showy; with 5 petals and many **stamens fused into a tube** below the **club-shaped stigma;** in loose spikes in leaf axils.

FRUITS: Hairy capsules.

ECOLOGY: Scattered and infrequent at low elevations in Thompson and Okanagan basins and southern Rocky Mountain Trench, in dry open forests, openings, moist grassy roadsides and streamsides.

NOTES: Mountain hollyhock is closely related to the garden hollyhock (*Malva* sp.) and also makes an attractive garden ornamental. Both prefer full sun and moist locations in the home garden. Seed germination is poor. • This species is also known as wild hollyhock.

Key to the monocotyledon families

1a. Flowers generally showy
(except for some small, greenish orchids),
or with a showy bract 1

    2a. Flowers bilaterally symmetrical,
    small and greenish to very showy .... **Orchidaceae** (p. 280)

    2b. Flowers radially
    symmetrical;
    generally showy .... **Liliaceae, Iridaceae, Alismataceae, Araceae** (p. 291)

1b. Flowers not showy,
greenish to brown, small 3

    3a. Plants floating, small,
    not differentiated into stem and leaf .... **Lemnaceae** (p. 149)

    3b. Plants with stem and leaves 4

        4a. Leaves divided into a blade
        and long sheath surrounding the stem;
        stems round; flowers in open
        or dense clusters .... **Poaceae** (p. 308)

        4b. Leaves absent or
        having only a small sheath;
        stems round or triangular;
        flowers usually in dense clusters 5

            5a. Stems triangular;
            leaves present .... **Cyperaceae** (p. 339)

            5b. Stems round;
            leaves often absent
            or small .... **Juncaceae, Juncaginaceae, Typhaceae** (p. 356)

Orchidaceae: Orchid Family

The orchids of British Columbia, while not as spectacular as the tropical or cultivated orchids, include some of the most attractive and unusual members of our flora. The family includes such diverse members as the delicate twayblades (*Listera* spp.), the ladyslippers (*Cypripedium* spp.) and the saprophytic coralroots (*Corallorhiza* spp.). The rattlesnake plantains (*Goodyera* spp.) and several species of the rein-orchids (*Platanthera* spp.) have such small, unremarkable flowers that they might not be recognized as orchids. Some of the most attractive of the orchids are also quite rare.

The flowers of the orchids are highly varied and are among the most specialized of all flowers. The flowers are composed of **three sepals and three petals.** In many species there will appear to be fewer than three because the lowest petal is so highly modified that it appears to be a completely different structure. This petal, or **lip**, is generally larger than the other petals and sepals. It is often coloured differently and more conspicuously than the others and its shape may be modified with lobes, forks, pouches or spurs. This elaborate lip acts to attract pollinating insects and to guide them to a nectary at its base. Associated with the nectary are the reproductive organs (stamens and style), which have been reduced and fused into an elongated organ called the **'column.'** The column is arranged to deposit sacs of pollen precisely on the head or proboscis of the visiting insect as it drinks from the nectary and at the same time to receive pollen from a previously visited flower.

Seeds are borne in capsules and are distinctive for their profusion. A single capsule may contain more than a million microscopic seeds. The seeds of orchids are also unusual in that they contain no food reserves. Successful germination and establishment depends on an ideal combination of conditions, often including an association with fungi. These demanding requirements make propagation difficult and rarely successful.

Many species are becoming rare due to urban development, cultivation, logging and cattle grazing. They should not be picked for flowers or collected for garden cultivation unless it is a last-ditch effort to save them from the bulldozer.

Key to the orchid family genera

1a. Plants without green stems and leaves .... *Corallorhiza*
1b. Plants with green stems
and leaves (leaves may be withered at flowering) 2
  2a. Lip of flower inflated and pouch- or slipper-like 3
    3a. Plant with a single, basal leaf; flower rose-purple .... *Calypso*
    3b. Plant with several leaves along stem;
flowers white to yellow .... *Cypripedium*
  2b. Lip of flower not inflated or pouch-like 4
    4a. Lip of flower with spur at base 5
      5a. Flowers white to pale pink, with dark red spots .... *Amerorchis*
      5b. Flowers white to green, not spotted 6
        6a. Sepals with 1 nerve; basal leaves
usually withered at flowering .... *Piperia*
        6b. Sepals with 3 nerves; basal leaves
still green at flowering .... *Platanthera*
    4b. Lip of flower lacking spur 7
      7a. Leaves all basal, evergreen
and mottled or veined with white .... *Goodyera*
      7b. Leaves at least in part on
flower stem, not evergreen,
neither mottled nor veined with white 8
        8a. 2 leaves, paired .... *Listera*
        8b. Several leaves, alternate along flower stem .... *Spiranthes*

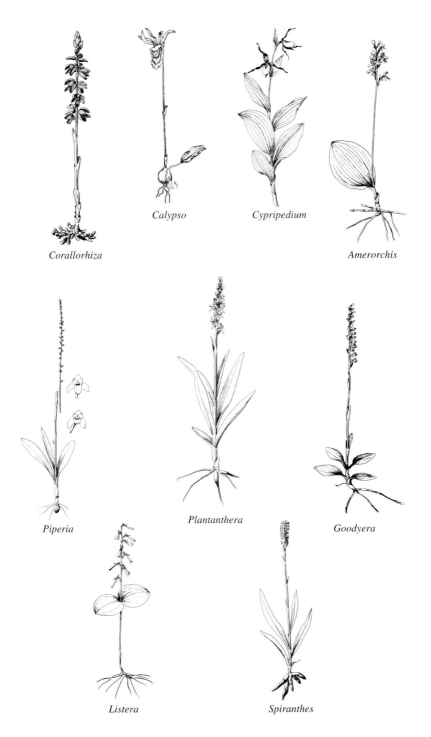

Corallorhiza

Calypso

Cypripedium

Amerorchis

Piperia

Plantanthera

Goodyera

Listera

Spiranthes

Corallorhiza: the coralroots

Members of the genus *Corallorhiza* are **saprophytic**. They derive their nutrients from decaying organic matter and lack the green pigment (chlorophyll) used by most plants for food production. All coralroots grow in close symbiotic association with soil fungi, and, as with most saprophytes, they cannot be cultivated. Because of their dependency on decaying matter, **the coralroots may be relatively abundant in one part of the forest floor one year and completely absent the next.**

You can recognize coralroots by their yellow, purple or brownish stems and their lack of any green parts. The vestiges of leaves can be seen as membranous sheaths or scales surrounding the stem. The four species in our area can be distinguished by the pattern of striping or spotting on the petals.

These peculiar plants are often encountered in large groups in deep coniferous forests. Their clumps of purple or yellow stems provide an unexpected contrast to the dark greens and browns of their surroundings.

The genus name *Corallorhiza* comes from the Greek *korallion,* 'coral,' and *riza,* 'a root,' and refers to the distinctive, **coral-like appearance of the rhizome.** Coralroots are sometimes inelegantly referred to as 'chicken-toes.'

YELLOW CORALROOT • *Corallorhiza trifida*

GENERAL: Perennial **saprophyte,** 10–25 cm tall, from coral-like rhizomes; stems **slender, pale yellow to greenish yellow.**

LEAVES: A few fleshy scales on stem, same colour as stem.

FLOWERS: Irregular, **yellow or greenish yellow to nearly white;** lowest petal forms an **unequally 3-lobed lip,** nearly white, sometimes lightly red-spotted; 3–15 flowers per stem.

FRUITS: Drooping, ellipsoid capsules.

ECOLOGY: Widespread and infrequent at low to subalpine elevations in moist to dry forests and some wetlands.

SIMILAR SPECIES: The 3-lobed lip resembles that of spotted coralroot (*C. maculata* ssp. *maculata,* p. 283) but is quite different from the unlobed lip of striped coralroot (*C. striata,* p. 283).

NOTES: Yellow coralroot is the most common saprophytic orchid in North America. • Unlike the other coralroots, yellow coralroot has a slight greenish tinge, especially in its seed capsules, which suggests it has some chlorophyll and is capable of manufacturing a small part of its food. Another common name for this species is pale coralroot. The species name *trifida* refers to the 3-lobed lip.

SPOTTED CORALROOT • *Corallorhiza maculata* ssp. *maculata*

GENERAL: Perennial **saprophyte**, 20–40 cm tall, from coral-like rhizomes; **stems purplish to reddish brown**, sometimes light yellow to tan (albino form).

LEAVES: A few fleshy scales on stem, same colour as stem.

FLOWERS: Irregular, **reddish purple and pink, with wine-red spots**; lowest petal forms an **unequally 3-lobed lip**, white and spotted with purple; 10–30 flowers per stem.

FRUITS: Nodding, oval capsules.

ECOLOGY: Widespread and common at low to mid elevations in moist and wet climates, in thick humus in moist to fairly dry forests.

SIMILAR SPECIES: Western coralroot (*C. maculata* ssp. *mertensiana*) lacks the wine-red spotting on the petals and is less common in our area than spotted coralroot.

NOTES: An albino form of spotted coralroot often occurs among normal plants. Albinos are pale yellowish and have a white lip that lacks spots. • The species name *maculata* means 'spotted' and refers to the spotting on the floral parts.

STRIPED CORALROOT • *Corallorhiza striata*

GENERAL: Perennial **saprophyte**, 15–50 cm tall, from coral-like rhizomes; **stems shiny, purplish-tinged.**

LEAVES: A few fleshy scales on stem, same colour as stem.

FLOWERS: Irregular, **pink to yellowish pink, with 3 purplish stripes** on each sepal; lowest petal forms a **tongue-shaped lip**, without lobes; 7–25 flowers per stem in fairly loose arrangement; blooms in spring and summer.

FRUITS: Nodding, ellipsoid capsules.

ECOLOGY: Scattered and infrequent at low to mid elevations in moist and wet climates, in moist humus in shady forests.

NOTES: An albino form of striped coralroot, pale yellow throughout, is occasionally found. • Striped coralroot takes its name from the stripes on the sepals and petals. This species is also known as madder-stripes, in reference to the flower colour, which is sometimes described as 'madder-purple.' Madder (*Rubia tinctorum*) is a climbing plant that was formally cultivated for the reddish-purple dye obtained from its roots.

MOUNTAIN LADYSLIPPER • *Cypripedium montanum*

GENERAL: Perennial, 15–60 cm tall, from cord-like roots; **leafy stems.**

LEAVES: Broadly lance-shaped to egg-shaped; all along stem, bases of lowest leaves wrapped around stem.

FLOWERS: Irregular, lowest petal forms a **prominent, pouch-shaped lower lip, white** with purple veins; upper petals and sepals **copper-coloured, long and twisted;** 1–3 **fragrant** flowers per stem.

FRUITS: Erect to ascending oblong capsules, 2–3 cm long.

ECOLOGY: Widely scattered and infrequent at low to subalpine elevations in dry to moist, open areas and open woods on rich humus.

SIMILAR SPECIES: Mountain ladyslipper flowers resemble those of the sparrow's-egg ladyslipper (*C. passerinum*), which is only 15–30 cm tall and usually has a single, relatively small flower with a **creamy-white pouch that is purple spotted inside.** It occurs in moist, shaded, mossy coniferous forests, in swamps and fens, on gravelly outwash and streambanks. It is uncommon throughout most of our region but becomes more common along the Rocky Mountains.

NOTES: The ladyslippers have showy flowers that are easily recognized by their strongly inflated lip, which forms a distinctive slipper-like pouch. The flowers appear to have only four sepals and petals because two sepals are fused together and one petal has been modified to become the lip. • The Nlaka'pmx and possibly the Secwepemc called this plant 'buck (plant),' because the lance-shaped brown sepals resemble a buck's antlers. The Okanagan called them 'moccasins' or 'giant baby's footwear,' and used the steeped stalks and leaves as a medicine. Pregnant women drank this medicine to ensure having a small baby.

YELLOW LADYSLIPPER • *Cypripedium calceolus*

GENERAL: Perennial, 15–40 cm tall, somewhat rhizomatous; **stems leafy** and glandular-hairy.

LEAVES: Broadly lance-shaped, softly hairy with bases somewhat wrapped around stem.

FLOWERS: Irregular, lowest petal forms a **prominent pouch-shaped, golden-yellow lip;** upper petals and sepals **greenish yellow to purplish bronze, slightly twisted** with wavy edges; usually a single flower per stem.

FRUITS: Erect to ascending oblong capsules.

ECOLOGY: Widely scattered and infrequent at low to mid elevations in moist rich woods, seepage areas and wetlands.

SIMILAR SPECIES: The leafy-stemmed yellow ladyslipper and mountain ladyslipper (*C. montanum*, above) have much larger flowers than fairyslipper (*Calypso bulbosa*, p. 285), which has no leaves on its stem.

NOTES: The ladyslippers and many of our other native orchids are very attractive and the temptation to pick the flowers or transplant them to the home garden is great. Our orchids are extremely difficult to propagate and transplants seldom survive more than a few seasons. More importantly, overcollecting has eliminated many of these plants from their former habitats. • Yellow ladyslipper was originally known as *Calceolus mariae* (St. Mary's little shoe). It is also called golden slipper. The genus name *Cypripedium* comes from the Greek *kupris* (Aphrodite) and *pedilion* (a shoe) and means 'Aphrodite's shoe.' The species name *calceolus* means 'slipper-shaped.'

FAIRYSLIPPER • *Calypso bulbosa*

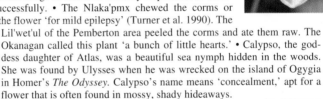

GENERAL: Perennial, 10–25 cm tall, with a **round or oval bulb-like corm**; flowering stalk delicate, yellow- to brown-purple, covered with thin, leaf-like bracts.

LEAVES: Solitary, broadly egg-shaped, dark green and pleated, produced at top of bulb in autumn, persists through winter and withers the following summer.

FLOWERS: Solitary, showy, fragrant, rose-purple; lowest petal forms a **large slipper-like lip,** yellowish purple to lavender, spotted with magenta and with a cluster of golden hairs; **sepals and 2 upper petals narrow, pointed and twisted,** sitting erect above lip.

FRUITS: Erect capsules.

ECOLOGY: Widespread and locally common at low to mid elevations in moist to dry forests, often in soil with abundant leaf mould; generally absent from our hot arid and very wet climates.

NOTES: This beautiful (and deliciously perfumed) little orchid, although widespread, is rapidly being exterminated in populated areas through trampling and picking. The bulbs are attached by delicate roots that are easily broken by even the lightest touch or tug on the stem. Hence, when the flower is picked, the plant usually dies. As well, it grows in association with specific fungi so that it is virtually impossible to transplant successfully. • The Nlaka'pmx chewed the corms or sucked the flower 'for mild epilepsy' (Turner et al. 1990). The Lil'wet'ul of the Pemberton area peeled the corms and ate them raw. The Okanagan called this plant 'a bunch of little hearts.' • Calypso, the goddess daughter of Atlas, was a beautiful sea nymph hidden in the woods. She was found by Ulysses when he was wrecked on the island of Ogygia in Homer's *The Odyssey*. Calypso's name means 'concealment,' apt for a flower that is often found in mossy, shady hideaways.

ROUND-LEAVED ORCHIS • *Amerorchis rotundifolia*
Orchis rotundifolia

GENERAL: Perennial, 10–30 cm tall, from **rhizomes or runners;** flowering stalks smooth and sometimes reddish.

LEAVES: Basal, solitary, broadly elliptic, 3–9 cm long, with short stalk or stalkless.

FLOWERS: Irregular, with 3 white to pink sepals; upper sepal combines with upper 2 purple-veined petals to form a hood; 2 lateral sepals are wing-like; lowest petal forms a **white to pink, oblong, 3-lobed lip, spotted with dark red and spurred;** inflorescence of 2–15 flowers in a short cluster at top of stem.

FRUITS: Ellipsoid capsules, to 15 mm long.

ECOLOGY: Scattered and locally common at low to mid elevations, mostly on Fraser and Thompson plateaus and in southern Rockies, in well-drained parts of bogs and swamps, and in cold, moist, mossy coniferous forests.

NOTES: Occasionally a plant with white flowers will be seen as well as a variety with two broad magenta-purple strips on the lip instead of the usual dark red spots. • The former genus name, *Orchis,* is from the Greek word for a testicle, and it refers to the round tubers of some species. The species name *rotundifolia* is an obvious reference to its round leaves.

285

Platanthera: the rein-orchids and bog-orchids

The rein-orchids (bog-orchids) comprise the largest group of orchids in British Columbia and include some of the most common orchid species. They are typically found in wet or boggy habitats, as the common name 'bog-orchid' indicates.

Rein-orchid flowers are small and white to greenish. Its most **distinguishing feature is the spur, a narrow sack-like projection at the base of the lip.** The upper sepal (and often the upper petals) forms a hood over the lip. The rein-orchid species are distinguished primarily by the characteristics of the spur and lip and the shape and distribution of the leaves.

The genus *Platanthera is* referred to in some guides as *Habenaria.* The common name 'rein-orchid' comes from the Latin *habenas,* 'a strap' or 'a rein,' and refers to the shape of the lip and spur. *Platanthera* is Latin for 'flat anthers.'

ONE-LEAVED REIN-ORCHID • *Platanthera obtusata*
Habenaria obtusata

GENERAL: Perennial, 8–20 cm tall, from fleshy, tuber-like roots; **stems leafless** except for 1 leaf and 1–2 sheathing bracts at base.

LEAVES: Solitary, at base of flowering stalk, **narrowly elliptic to oblong** but broadest above middle, blunt-tipped, surrounding stem.

FLOWERS: Irregular, **pale green or yellowish green**, with whitish petals; lowest petal forms a **narrowly lance-shaped lip,** straight to slightly curved upwards with a **slender, tapering spur as long as lip**; inflorescence of 3–12 flowers in loose clusters at top of stem.

FRUITS: Erect capsules.

ECOLOGY: Widespread and infrequent at low to mid elevations in wetlands and cool, moist to wet forest.

SIMILAR SPECIES: Another one-leaved, spurred orchid of similar sites in our region is round-leaved orchid (*Amerorchis rotundifolia*, p. 285), which has showy, white, dark-red spotted flowers.

NOTES: This species is regularly pollinated by mosquitoes. • One-leaved rein-orchid is also called blunt-leaved orchid (*obtusata* means 'blunt') because of its single, blunt-tipped leaf.

ROUND-LEAVED REIN-ORCHID • *Platanthera orbiculata*
Habenaria orbiculata

GENERAL: Perennial, 20–60 cm tall, from fleshy tuber-like roots; flowering **stalks leafless,** but with 1–5 lance-shaped bracts.

LEAVES: Usually 2, lying flat on ground; **round, glossy** and somewhat fleshy, clasping at base.

FLOWERS: Irregular, **whitish green**; lowest petal forms a straight, **linear or strap-shaped lip** with a long, **cylindrical spur** tapering and **curving upward at tip;** inflorescence of 5–25 flowers in a loose, elongated cluster at top of stem.

FRUITS: Erect, curved capsules.

ECOLOGY: Widespread and infrequent at low to mid elevations in moist, mossy forest and wetlands; less common in dry forests.

NOTES: The species name *orbiculata* means 'round' and refers to the large, round leaves.

WHITE BOG-ORCHID • *Platanthera dilatata*
Habenaria dilatata

GENERAL: Perennial, to 1 m tall, from fleshy tuber-like roots; **leafy stems.**

LEAVES: Oblong to broadly lance-shaped; **leaf base surrounds stem;** upper leaves smaller and grading into bracts in inflorescence.

FLOWERS: Irregular, **white to greenish-tinged,** waxy, small but very fragrant; lowest petal forms a lip (to 1 cm long) that widens at base and bears a **slender, curved spur** that can be up to twice as long as the lip; numerous and loosely to densely packed along upper stem.

FRUITS: Ellipsoid capsules.

ECOLOGY: Widespread and common at low to high elevations in wetlands, seepage areas, subalpine meadows, wet coniferous forests and clearings.

NOTES: The tall green stalks of white bog-orchid provide a stunning display, with their dense whitish inflorescences rising nearly a metre out of a marsh or bog. • Some Interior native peoples believed the plant to be poisonous to humans and animals. The Secwepemc used extracts as poison to sprinkle on baits for coyote and grizzlies. It is an important charm for Interior Salish people. • This very fragrant species is often smelled before it is seen. Other common names are 'fragrant white rein-orchid' and 'scent-candle.' Szczawinski (1959) describes the perfume as a mix of cloves, vanilla and mock-orange! • The species name *dilatata* means 'expanded,' referring to the base of the lip.

GREEN-FLOWERED BOG-ORCHID • *Platanthera hyperborea*
Habenaria hyperborea

GENERAL: Perennial, 20–50 cm tall, from thickened, tuber-like roots; **succulent stems.**

LEAVES: Several, usually **on lower half of stem,** narrowly **elliptic to lance-shaped.**

FLOWERS: Irregular, **pale to deep green,** often purplish-tinged or veined; upper sepal curves over 2 lateral petals to form a **distinct hood;** lowest petal forms a **narrowly lance-shaped lip,** rather fleshy and sometimes **upturned,** with a **cylindrical spur;** inflorescence a densely packed spike-like cluster at top of stalk; not scented.

FRUITS: Ellipsoid capsules.

ECOLOGY: Widespread and common at mid to alpine elevations in moist to wet forests (tolerant of deep shade), wetlands and wet clearings.

SIMILAR SPECIES: Slender bog-orchid (*P. saccata*) can be distinguished by the short, **sac-shaped spur.** The spur is long and cylindrical in green-flowered bog-orchid. • Both species resemble white bog-orchid (*P. dilatata*, above), but unlike that species they have green flowers and fewer leaves that are more rounded at the tip.

NOTES: The species name *hyperborea* means 'beyond the north' and refers to this species' occurrence in muskeg north of the Arctic Circle.

ORCHID

ALASKA REIN-ORCHID • *Piperia unalaschensis*
Platanthera unalaschensis

GENERAL: Perennial, to 60 cm tall, from 1–3 fleshy, spherical to egg-shaped tuberous roots; **leafless flowering stalks** with inconspicuous bracts.

LEAVES: 2–4 at base of flowering stalk and sheathing it; **lance-shaped,** withering at time of flowering.

FLOWERS: Irregular, **greenish white to white,** small and moderately fragrant; lowest petal forms a **short, fleshy, narrowly lance-shaped to triangular lip** (to 5 mm long) with a **spur about equal to lip** in length; inflorescence of many, spirally arranged flowers.

FRUITS: Ellipsoid capsules.

ECOLOGY: Widespread and common at low to mid elevations south of Williams Lake in dry to moist forests and on open, often rocky slopes that are often dry by midsummer.

SIMILAR SPECIES: Elegant rein-orchid (*Piperia elegans*, also known as *Platanthera unalaschensis* ssp. *elata*) has larger flowers and the **spur is 1–2 cm long, at least twice as long as the lip**. It occurs in similar habitats as Alaska rein-orchid but primarily in the southern half of our region.

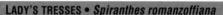

LADY'S TRESSES • *Spiranthes romanzoffiana*

GENERAL: Perennial, 10–60 cm tall, from enlarged, fleshy roots.

LEAVES: Several near **base of stem**, **linear to lance-shaped**; changing abruptly along stem to short, lance-shaped bracts that surround stem.

FLOWERS: Irregular, **creamy white to straw-coloured,** densely crowded in **1–4 rows that spiral** around stem; **sepals and petals form a hood over lip,** which curves downward with almost a pointed tip; sweet scented.

FRUITS: Dry, many-seeded capsules.

ECOLOGY: Widely scattered and infrequent at low to mid elevations in dry to moist forests, wetlands and moist open gravelly areas; occasionally on fairly dry sites.

NOTES: You can easily recognize lady's tresses by the spiralling rows of flowers. • The genus name *Spiranthes* is derived from the Greek *speira* (a coil) and *anthos* (a flower), referring to the distinctive spiral arrangement of the flowers. The flowers are supposed to resemble a lady's braided hair (called 'traces' or 'tresses'), although the name is more appropriate for its original owner, *Neottia spiralis*, a Eurasian species. The species name *romanzoffiana* honours Nikolei Rumliantzev (1754–1826), Count Romanoff, the Russian patron of science who financed Otto von Kotzebue's exploration of the Alaskan coast.

RATTLESNAKE PLANTAIN • *Goodyera oblongifolia*

GENERAL: Evergreen perennial, 20–40 cm tall, from short **creeping rhizomes**, sometimes forming extensive colonies; flowering stems stout, stiff and hairy.

LEAVES: In basal rosette, often strikingly patterned with **white mottles or stripes**, **especially along midrib**, against dark green background; oval or oblong to narrowly elliptic in shape.

FLOWERS: Irregular, **dull white to greenish**, upper petals and 1 sepal form **hood over lip**; many flowers in a **long, hairy, cluster** at top of flowering stem, with most flowers oriented to 1 side.

FRUITS: Erect capsules.

ECOLOGY: Widespread and common at low to subalpine elevations in mossy dry to moist, shady coniferous forests.

NOTES: The St'at'imc and Okanagan made a poultice from rattlesnake plantain to apply to cuts and sores. Apparently, if the leaf is crushed by a sideways motion between thumb and forefinger it divides in two, and it can then be applied to cuts and bruises, with the raw side of the leaf placed next to the wound. Children used to make 'balloons' from the leaves by rubbing them gently to separate the top and bottom, and then blowing them up. The St'at'imc also used rattlesnake plantain to make a concoction for ulcer and stomach trouble. Nlaka'pmx women chewed the plants to ease childbirth. The Secwepemc, however, considered this plant as 'Indian Doctor Medicine' and advised not to touch it.

DWARF RATTLESNAKE PLANTAIN • *Goodyera repens*

GENERAL: Evergreen perennial, 10–15 cm tall, from slender **creeping rhizomes**.

LEAVES: Narrow, oval-shaped, green with darker green veins.

FLOWERS: Irregular, **white or pale green**, upper petals and 1 sepal form a **hood over lip**; all flowers oriented to 1 side of stalk.

FRUITS: Dry, many-seeded capsules.

ECOLOGY: Scattered and infrequent at low to mid elevations throughout northern parts of our region and in Rockies, in dry to moist forests; rare elsewhere.

SIMILAR SPECIES: The lack of white mottling on the leaves, and the generally smaller size of this plant distinguish it from rattlesnake plantain (*G. oblongifolia*, above).

NOTES: You can recognize the rattlesnake plantains by their generally thick and dark **evergreen leaves, which usually form a rosette** at the base of the flowering stalk. The flowers are numerous, small, dull greenish white and distributed along the upper half of the flowering stem. The two upper petals and one sepal form a hood over the sac-shaped lip. • These orchids undergo vigorous vegetative multiplication with their rhizomes, and they can cover a large piece of ground without re-establishing from seeds. In fact, the species name *repens* refers to the creeping habit of the rhizomes. • According to the 'Doctrine of Signs,' early settlers believed that because the markings on rattlesnake plantain leaves resemble snake-skin markings, this plant could be used to treat (rattle) snake bites. Presumably, it was also thought to resemble a plantain (*Plantago* sp.) because of the similarity of the flattened basal leaf clusters of the two genera. • The genus name *Goodyera* honours John Goodyer (1592–1664), an English botanist.

ORCHID

BROAD-LEAVED TWAYBLADE • *Listera convallarioides*

GENERAL: Perennial, 10–35 cm tall, from slender, **creeping rhizomes**; stems smooth at base but hairy above leaves.

LEAVES: Single pair near mid-length of stem, oval to oblong, with rounded to abruptly pointed tips, not heart-shaped.

FLOWERS: Irregular, **yellow-green**; lowest petal forms a **broad, wedge-shaped lip** that projects forward almost horizontally; lip has a shallow notch at tip, small hair-like projections along edges and a short triangular tooth on each side of its base; inflorescence of 5–35 flowers in a loose cluster at top of stem.

FRUITS: Many-seeded capsules.

ECOLOGY: Scattered and infrequent at low to mid elevations in our moist and wet climates, in moist, shaded, mossy woods and wet openings.

SIMILAR SPECIES: Two other twayblades are also widely scattered and infrequent in our region, and like broad-leaved twayblade, both have flowers with a wedge-shaped lip. • Northwestern twayblade (*L. caurina*) has long slender teeth at the base of the lip but no hair-like projections along its edges, and the lip angles downward instead of being horizontal (as in broad-leaved twayblade). • Northern twayblade (*L. borealis*) has flower lips with a deep, bilobed cleft at the tip and hair-like projections along the edges, but without the pair of teeth at the base.

NOTES: The twayblades are a common but inconspicuous group of orchids. You can identify them by the presence of a **single set of paired leaves near the middle of the stem**. The flowers are small and greenish, with an elongated lip that is usually cleft or lobed. • The broad leaves of this species resemble those of lily-of-the-valley (*Convallaria* sp.), hence the species name *convallarioides*.

HEART-LEAVED TWAYBLADE • *Listera cordata*

GENERAL: Perennial, 6–15 cm tall, from slender, **creeping rhizomes**; stems smooth below leaves, hairy above.

LEAVES: Single pair near mid-length of stem, broad and **heart-shaped**.

FLOWERS: Irregular, **pale green to purplish brown**, unpleasant odour; lowest petal forms a **lip, divided into 2 linear or lance-shaped lobes** and with a **pair of horn-like teeth at base**; inflorescence of 5–16 flowers in an elongated cluster at top of flowering stem.

FRUITS: Many-seeded capsules.

ECOLOGY: Widespread and locally common at low to subalpine elevations in our moist and wet climates (especially in wet Columbia Mountains), in moist to wet, mossy coniferous forests and seepage areas.

NOTES: Heart-leaved twayblade is our most common twayblade. The two lobes on the lip give the flowers a 'forked-tongue' appearance. • The intricate pollination mechanisms of *Listera* species fascinated Darwin, who studied them intensively. The pollen mass is blown out explosively within a drop of viscous fluid that glues the pollinia to unsuspecting insects (or to your finger if you touch the top of the column!). • The name 'twayblade' (two blade) refers to the two small leaves found on the flowering stem. The genus *Listera* is named for English naturalist M. Lister (1638–1712). The species name *cordata* means 'heart-shaped' and refers to the leaves. This plant is also called mannikin twayblade, 'mannikin' meaning a dwarf or little man.

Liliaceae: Lily Family

The lily family includes many familiar ornamental species and some of the most attractive members of our flora. Our native species of *Lilium, Trillium* and *Fritillaria* rival the large, showy lilies available at flower shops. Although the family contains some poisonous species, such as meadow death-camas (*Zigadenus venenosus*) and Indian hellebore (*Veratrum viride*), other species were used extensively for food or medicine by native groups.

Lilies typically have **parallel-veined leaves** and (except for *Maianthemum* species) the **flowers are 3-parted**. In most of our species, however, the sepals and petals are so similar that the flowers appear to be composed of six petals (often referred to as tepals). The exceptions are *Trillium* and *Calochortus* species, which clearly have three petals and three sepals.

Our lily species are all perennial herbs. Many lilies grow from bulbs, which vary from being onion-like (including the smell) to clusters of many small bulblets. Other lilies grow from rhizomes.

Most lily species are not difficult to identify. The number and arrangement of the leaves will usually limit the number of possibilities. Flower colour, size and arrangement are other useful characteristics. Taylor (1966) provides further information about our lilies.

Key to the lily family genera

10b. Flowers occurring singly along stems or in small clusters at stem tips 12

12a. Flowers scattered along lower side of stem, often under leaves .... *Streptopus*

12b. 1–3 flowers at tips of branches .... *Disporum*

5b. Leaves mostly basal; flower stems lacking leaves
or with leaves greatly reduced in size upward 13

13a. Leaves grass-like, stiff, tough and evergreen;
inflorescence often very large,
with many flowers (more than 100) .... *Xerophyllum*

13b. Leaves soft and not lasting more than 1 year;
inflorescences generally small,
with less than 50 flowers (flowers often single) 14

14a. Generally 2 leaves (sometimes 3),
fairly wide (less than 8 times
as long as wide); usually 1–2 flowers 15

15a. Flowers white, generally single;
leaves hairy; plants with long rhizomes .... *Clintonia*

15b. 1 or more flowers, yellow;
leaves lacking hairs; plants with bulb .... *Erythronium*

14b. 3 or more leaves, narrow, generally
more than 10 times as long as wide; flowers single to numerous 16

16a. 1 style; 1 flower, or sometimes 2 .... *Lloydia*

16b. 3 styles; generally 3 or more flowers 17

17a. Leaves in 2 ranks; plants with rhizomes .... *Tofieldia*

17b. Leaves not in 2 ranks; plants with bulbs 18

18a. Stems slender; flowers tubular
to bell-shaped, nodding on slender
stalks; tepals greenish yellow to
purplish green, lacking gland at base .... *Stenanthium*

18b. Stems stout; flowers saucer-shaped,
fairly erect, not nodding; tepals white to
greenish white, with gland at base .... *Zigadenus*

Trillium

Calochortus

Allium

Brodiaea

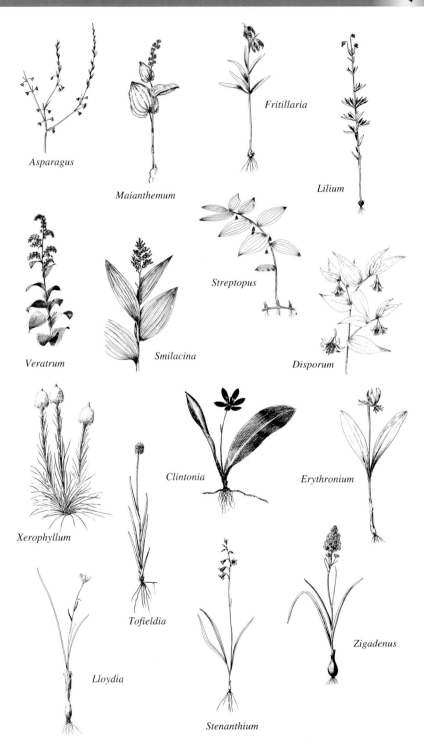

Asparagus

Maianthemum

Fritillaria

Lilium

Veratrum

Smilacina

Streptopus

Disporum

Xerophyllum

Tofieldia

Clintonia

Erythronium

Lloydia

Stenanthium

Zigadenus

WESTERN WHITE TRILLIUM • *Trillium ovatum*

GENERAL: Perennial, to 45 cm tall, from short, stout rhizomes.

LEAVES: Triangular-oval, in **whorl of 3 just below flower**.

FLOWERS: Solitary, 3 broad, white petals and **3 narrow, green sepals** beneath; blooms in spring.

FRUITS: Oval, green, **berry-like capsules**, seeds have oily appendage.

ECOLOGY: Scattered and locally common at low to mid elevations south of Shuswap Lake and in East Kootenays, in moist to wet woods and open seepage areas.

NOTES: The single white flower sitting above the three broad leaves identifies this familiar plant. • Ants provide a dispersal mechanism by carrying the oil-rich seeds to their nests. The seeds later germinate after being discarded underground. • The Nlaka'pmx used an infusion or powder from the roots as eye medicine. • The common and genus names, from the Latin *trillium,* 'in threes,' refer to the leaves, petals, sepals and stigmas. Another name is 'wake robin,' presumably in reference to its early blooming.

GARDEN ASPARAGUS • *Asparagus officinalis*

GENERAL: Perennial, 1–1.5 m tall, from cord-like rhizomes; stems fleshy and **unbranched when young**, becoming **freely branching and fern-like with age**.

LEAVES: Short and scaly; upper stems with clusters of short, green, flattened leaf-like branches.

FLOWERS: Small, **greenish white and bell-shaped**; borne singly, hanging downwards on slender stalks; male and female flowers on separate plants.

FRUITS: Red berries.

ECOLOGY: Scattered and locally common, mostly at low elevations in Thompson and Okanagan plateaus and basins and southern Rocky Mountain Trench, in moist disturbed sites near settled areas; an escapee from cultivation.

NOTES: This is the common garden asparagus extensively grown in the southern half of our region. The older, highly branched stems have clusters of short, greenish branchlets that function as leaves and give the plant a fern-like appearance, completely unlike the young stalks seen on supermarket shelves. • Although this plant was introduced as a garden and crop plant, it naturalized in some locations, and it was gathered by some Nlaka'pmx and Secwepemc people in late spring. The native people apparently adapted its use from Chinese and European settlers. • The origin of the genus name *Asparagus* is obscure. It may have derived from the Greek *asparagos,* meaning 'to sprout' or 'a plant with edible shoots.' The species name *officinalis* (of the shop) reflects the long time this plant has been sold for medicinal and culinary use.

THREE-SPOT MARIPOSA LILY • *Calochortus apiculatus*

GENERAL: Perennial, 10–30 cm tall, from **deep-seated, fleshy bulbs**.

LEAVES: Single, grass-like basal leaf; shorter than flowering stem.

FLOWERS: Saucer-shaped, yellowish white, sometimes pencilled with purple; petals **fringed along sides** and hairy on lower half, with **small purple spot near base**; sepals small and green, **shorter and narrower than petals**; borne in clusters of 1–5.

FRUITS: Hanging oval capsules, with 3 lengthwise ridges.

ECOLOGY: Infrequent at low elevations in East Kootenays and Okanagan Basin, on dry grassy slopes and in open woodlands.

SIMILAR SPECIES: Lyall's mariposa lily (*C. lyallii*) is a smaller white mariposa lily, distinguished by the moon-shaped spot at the base of the petals, often with a broad purple crescent above it. It has an upright capsule. It is rare in our region, being restricted to the southernmost Okanagan.

NOTES: Mariposa lilies are magnificent flowers of grassy meadows and dry hillsides. They differ from most members of the lily family in that they have **distinctly different sets of three petals and three sepals**. The flowers are saucer-shaped with large, broad petals at the base of which is a **distinctive coloured spot (gland) that is heavily bearded**. • The Ktunaxa dug and ate the corms or roots of three-spot mariposa lily. • Cultivated mariposa lilies are sold through garden outlets. Wild mariposa lilies do not transplant well and should be left alone, but they will propagate freely from seed. It takes 3–5 years of exacting care, however, to produce a flowering bulb. • The common name refers to the three distinct purplish spots (glands) at the base of the petals. The species name *apiculatus* means 'with pointed tips' and refers to the end of the petals.

SAGEBRUSH MARIPOSA LILY • *Calochortus macrocarpus*

GENERAL: Perennial, 20–50 cm tall, from **deep-seated, oval bulbs**; stems stout and often bear bulblets at base of leaves.

LEAVES: Grass-like, decreasing in size along stem.

FLOWERS: Pale to dark lavender; petals have a **long green stripe** and sometimes a **purple band** over an **arrow-shaped spot**, moderately hairy above spot; sepals narrow and **longer than petals**; 1–3 flowers per stem.

FRUITS: Thin **upright capsules**, with 3 lengthwise ridges; straw-coloured seeds.

ECOLOGY: Widespread and common at low elevations in Fraser, Thompson and Okanagan basins and southern Rocky Mountain Trench, in dry grasslands and open ponderosa pine forests.

NOTES: Sagebrush mariposa lily is highly palatable to livestock and it will disappear from heavily grazed areas. **This species was once widespread, but it is now considerably less common and harvesting the flowers or bulbs is discouraged because it destroys the entire plant.** • Native people and early settlers harvested the thick, fleshy bulbs in early spring and ate them raw, steamed, boiled or pit-cooked. They were dug before the plants flowered in late spring and early summer. The Okanagan mashed the bulbs and applied the poultice to soothe poison-ivy blisters. • The genus derives its name from the Greek *kalo,* 'beautiful,' and *chortos,* 'grass,' referring to the lovely flowers of nearly all the species. 'Mariposa' is Spanish for butterfly—the wide, spreading petals resemble broad-winged butterflies. Another name for this group is 'sego-lily' from the Shoshonean *seego* (an edible bulb).

NODDING ONION • *Allium cernuum*

GENERAL: Perennial, to 50 cm tall, from **oval bulbs**; slender, **leafless flowering stalks**; entire plant **smells strongly of onion**.

LEAVES: Grass-like, several per bulb, often keeled; **remains green during flowering**.

FLOWERS: Pink to rose-purple, small and bell-shaped; inflorescence a **nodding, umbrella-shaped cluster** at top of stalk.

FRUITS: 3-lobed capsules.

ECOLOGY: Widespread and common at low to mid elevations in dry open woods (often Douglas-fir), dry rocky sites and grasslands; generally absent from our wet climates.

SIMILAR SPECIES: Wild chives (*A. schoenoprasum*) are found in wet meadows, rocky or gravelly streambanks and lake edges in the Kootenays. They **have round, hollow leaves** and an upright rather than drooping head. Their flowers are arranged in a densely packed ball. • Alp lily (*Lloydia serotina*) may be found in the alpine tundra of the western part of our region. It has small, very narrow, onion-like leaves that do not smell of onions. Its **flowers are generally single** (instead of clustered, as in *Allium* species), and they are creamy white and purple-lined and appear very soon after snowmelt. • **CAUTION:** Wild onion bulbs can be confused with those of death-camas (*Zigadenus* sp., p. 305) but the latter do not have an onion odour.

NOTES: All *Allium* species smell strongly of onion and have small flowers in a cluster at the top of a leafless stalk. Nodding onion is the most common species in our region, and it is readily identified by its pink, drooping or nodding inflorescence. • Onions, garlic, leeks and chives are some of the cultivated *Allium* species. • All Interior native peoples used wild onion bulbs. They harvested the bulbs before flowering and ate them raw (with the leaves), steamed, boiled or roasted, or for flavouring other foods, such as salmon and meat. The bulbs were also dried for later use. Wild onions make an excellent substitute for green onions and chives. • The crushed bulb has been used as a disinfectant and as a poultice to alleviate pain and swelling from insect bites. • The genus name *Allium* is from the Latin name for garlic.

LARGE-FLOWERED TRITELIA • *Brodiaea douglasii* Triteleia grandiflora

GENERAL: Perennial, 20–70 cm tall, from **deep-seated, fibrous-coated bulbs**; **leafless flowering stalk**.

LEAVES: Basal, grass-like, 1–4 per bulb, green at flowering time.

FLOWERS: Light to deep blue, vase-shaped; inflorescence of 6–20 flowers arranged in a loose **umbrella-shaped cluster** at top of stem.

FRUITS: Capsules.

ECOLOGY: Scattered and infrequent at low elevations in Thompson and Okanagan basins east to southern Rocky Mountain Trench, in grasslands and dry ponderosa pine woodlands.

SIMILAR SPECIES: Harvest brodiaea (*B. coronaria*), mainly a Coastal species, occurs as an isolated population near Spences Bridge. It has three anthers (large-flowered tritelia has six anthers) and its leaves wither before flowering. • *Brodiaea* species resemble *Allium* species (above), but they do not have the distinctive onion smell.

NOTES: The Okanagan, Nlaka'pmx and St'at'imc ate the bulbs of *Brodiaea* species. They were one of the earliest bulbs harvested, and were dug in April along with those of yellow bell (*Fritillaria pudica*). • This species is also called Douglas's brodiaea. The genus *Brodiaea* was named for James L. Brodie, a Scottish botanist. The species name *douglasii* refers to David Douglas of the Royal Horticultural Society of England, who collected plants in North America in the 1800s.

CHOCOLATE LILY • *Fritillaria lanceolata*
F. affinis

GENERAL: Perennial, to 80 cm tall, from **small, scaly bulbs and many bulblets**; **stems leafy** and unbranched.

LEAVES: **Linear to lance-shaped**, mostly **on stem** in widely spaced **whorls** of 3–4.

FLOWERS: **Bell-shaped** and **purplish, faintly to strongly mottled with green or yellow**; commonly 2–5 per stem.

FRUITS: Erect, many-seeded capsules with **broad wings**.

ECOLOGY: Scattered and infrequent at low to low subalpine elevations in grasslands, meadows and open woodlands.

SIMILAR SPECIES: Northern rice-root (*F. camschatcensis*) is also widely scattered in our region. It is distinguished from chocolate lily by the compactness of its inflorescence, the **absence of mottling on the flowers** and the wingless capsule.

NOTES: The fritillaries have one to several showy flowers, which are usually bell-shaped and hang downward from an unbranched, leafy stem. In our species, the **curved flower stalks straighten as the fruit matures, so that the seed capsules eventually stand erect.** • The 'dirty socks' or 'rotting meat' odour of the flowers attracts flies, which pollinate them. • The southern Secwepemc, St'at'imc and Nlaka'pmx dug chocolate lily bulbs between early spring and late summer and boiled or pit-cooked them. • The bulblets around the main bulb help propagate more plants vegetatively. The rice-like appearance of the bulblets give fritillaries the alternative common name 'rice-root.' Chocolate lily, also called checker lily, is named for its dark, mottled flowers.

YELLOW BELL • *Fritillaria pudica*

GENERAL: Perennial, 10–25 cm tall, from **small scaly bulbs**.

LEAVES: Usually a **pair** or sometimes 3, more or less in a whorl about halfway up stem, **linear to lance-shaped**.

FLOWERS: **1 or rarely 2, bell-shaped** and **drooping, yellow**, often faintly striped with purple or brown at base; blooms in spring.

FRUITS: Erect, cylindrical capsules, with many flat seeds.

ECOLOGY: Scattered and locally common at low to mid elevations in Thompson and Okanagan basins and southern Rocky Mountain Trench, in dry grasslands and dry open ponderosa pine forests.

NOTES: Yellow bell is a small, delicate flower that appears soon after snowmelt. Its yellow flowers are among the loveliest signs of early spring in sagebrush country. The flowers turn orange to brick-red with age. • The Secwepemc, Nlaka'pmx and Okanagan ate yellow bell bulbs. The Nlaka'pmx dug them in early spring along with *Brodiaea* species, but the Secwepemc and Okanagan harvested them, along with western spring beauty (*Claytonia lanceolata*), in the late spring or summer. They were eaten raw, boiled or steamed. • The fritillaries are treasured as cultivated plants, but they should only be propagated from seed or obtained from nursery stock. • The genus name *Fritillaria* comes from the Latin *fritillus*, 'a dice box,' and refers to the appearance of the fruit. The species name *pudica* means 'bashful.'

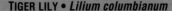
TIGER LILY • *Lilium columbianum*

GENERAL: Perennial, to 1 m tall, from a **cluster of scaly bulbs**; **unbranched stems**.

LEAVES: Narrowly lance-shaped, usually arranged in **several whorls of 6–9** leaves each; upper leaves may also be scattered along stem.

FLOWERS: Large, showy, bright orange, with deep red or purple spots near centre, **petals curled backward**; few to many, **nodding** at top of stem.

FRUITS: Barrel-shaped capsules with flat seeds.

ECOLOGY: Widespread and common at low to subalpine elevations, mostly on southern plateaus and in wet Columbia Mountains and East Kootenays, in moist, open forests, openings and clearings.

NOTES: You can recognize true lilies by their **large, showy flowers, smooth, unbranched stems and whorls of narrow, lance-shaped leaves.** • Tiger lilies can have up to 30 flowers per stem. The downward-hanging flowers and curled-back petals are distinctive. • Although they have a peppery or bitter taste, the large bulbs of tiger lily were eaten by all Interior peoples. They were often used as a condiment to add a peppery flavour to other roots or foods, including pudding made from saskatoons, bitter root, salmon eggs, tree lichen and sometimes other foods. • The name 'tiger' probably comes from the spots on the petals. The spots also give rise to the superstition that smelling the tiger lily will give you freckles! Another common name is Columbia lily.

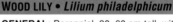
WOOD LILY • *Lilium philadelphicum*

GENERAL: Perennial, 30–60 cm tall, with a cluster of **thick, white, pointed bulb scales**.

LEAVES: Narrowly lance-shaped, lower stem leaves overlapping, upper leaves usually arranged in 1–2 whorls on stem.

FLOWERS: Large and showy, orange to red with yellowish to maroon spots near base; **usually single,** but sometimes 2–3; **stiffly erect.**

FRUITS: Egg-shaped capsules.

ECOLOGY: Scattered but often abundant at low to mid elevations in southern Rocky Mountain Trench, in meadows, open forest and clearings.

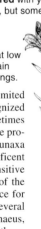

NOTES: This striking lily, which has a limited distribution in our region, is easily recognized by its erect, red flowers, and it is sometimes called red lily (or Philadelphia lily). It is the provincial flower of Saskatchewan. • The Ktunaxa ate the bulbs of wood lilies. • This magnificent species is in decline because it is very sensitive to picking, which results in non-renewal of the bulb for the next season. • The name 'wood lily' comes from its preference for open woods, although it often grows in open, grassy places. There are several explanations of the species name *philadelphicum*. Kalm, a student of Linnaeus, collected near Philadelphia, and he may have collected the first specimen there. Alternatively, however, it may have been named to honour the pharaoh Ptolemy Philadelphus. A third possibility is that it is from *philos* (love) and *delphicus* (the ancient wooded oracle at Delphi), hence 'wood-lover.'

STAR-FLOWERED FALSE SOLOMON'S-SEAL • *Smilacina stellata*

GENERAL: Perennial, 20–60 cm tall, from **long, pale rhizomes**, forms **dense colonies**, often in partial shade; stems finely hairy, unbranched, **erect to arching**.

LEAVES: Arranged in **2 rows along stem**; narrowly **lance-shaped**, with **prominent veins** and somewhat clasping bases, sometimes folded down centre; **leaf edges are hairless**, but leaf undersides are finely hairy.

FLOWERS: Small, **creamy white, star-like**; borne in a **short, unbranched cluster** at end of stem.

FRUITS: Round berries, greenish yellow with **6 blue-purple stripes**, becoming **dark blue or reddish black** at maturity.

ECOLOGY: Widespread and common at low to mid and occasionally subalpine elevations in moist (less commonly dry) forests, clearings and moist openings.

SIMILAR SPECIES: When star-flowered false Solomon's-seal is not in flower or fruit, it can be distinguished from rosy twisted stalk (*Streptopus roseus*, p. 300) by the stiff, forward-pointing hairs on the leaf edges of rosy twisted stalk.

NOTES: You can most easily recognize false Solomon's-seals by their **clusters of small, white, star-like flowers, which are borne at the end of the flowering stems**. When not in flower or fruit, they may be confused with some of the twisted stalks (*Streptopus* spp., pp. 300–01) or fairybells (*Disporum* spp., p. 301). • The Nlaka'pmx used star-flowered false Solomon's-seal as a rheumatism medicine, or against colds. Some Nlaka'pmx, St'at'imc, Okanagan and Secwepemc people also ate the berries. • Star-flowered false Solomon's-seal is easily propagated from a section of rhizome. It prefers a moist shady location in the home garden.

FALSE SOLOMON'S-SEAL • *Smilacina racemosa*

GENERAL: Perennial, 30–100 cm tall, from **stout, fleshy rhizomes**, often growing in clumps; **stems erect to stiffly arched**, unbranched.

LEAVES: Arranged in **2 rows along stem**; **broad and elliptic**, with pronounced parallel veins and somewhat clasping bases.

FLOWERS: Small, **creamy white and star-like**; borne in large, **showy, egg- or pyramid-shaped inflorescence** at end of flowering stem; strongly perfumed.

FRUITS: Red, fleshy, round berries, sometimes dotted with purple.

ECOLOGY: Widespread and common at low to subalpine elevations in moist forests, openings and clearings.

NOTES: When false Solomon's-seal is in flower, the large showy inflorescences easily distinguish it from the other white-flowered members of the lily family. • The Secwepemc used the roots as a blood purifier, and the Nlaka'pmx used them as an internal medicine and 'woman's medicine.' The young greens and fleshy rhizomes were eaten by the Secwepemc and others. The Secwepemc, Nlaka'pmx, Okanagan and Lil'wet'ul also ate the berries. In spring, the St'at'imc gathered the rhizomes and berries to make a cleanser for fishing nets. • The name 'Solomon's-seal' (first given to *Polygonatum multiflorum*) is thought to refer to the rhizomes, which, when cut, bear surface scars or markings that resemble the seal of Solomon, a 6-pointed star. • **CAUTION:** When first emerging, this plant resembles the **poisonous** Indian hellebore (*Veratrum viride*, p. 303).

CLASPING TWISTED STALK • *Streptopus amplexifolius*

GENERAL: Perennial, 0.5–1 m tall, from thick, short rhizomes that are covered with fibrous roots; **stems branched**, usually with slight bend or kink above each leaf.

LEAVES: Oval to lance-shaped, with pointed tips and **grey-green undersides**; **base clasps and surrounds stem**.

FLOWERS: Greenish white, bell-shaped, with flaring tips; solitary (occasionally 2) at base of each leaf, hanging from **slender, curled or twisted stalk with a distinct joint or kink about mid-length**.

FRUITS: Yellow to red, oval-oblong berries (sometimes turning dark purple).

ECOLOGY: Widespread and common at low to high elevations in our moist and wet climates, in moist, rich seepage forests and openings or clearings with seepage.

NOTES: The **branched stem separates clasping twisted stalk from other twisted stalks**. In this species the flower stalks and the main stem are bent or twisted. • The Nlaka'pmx used a decoction of the roots as a remedy for internal pains, stomachaches or loss of appetite. The edible shoots were eaten by some Alaskan native people, but not by peoples of the Interior. • **CAUTION: The young shoots of twisted stalk are easily confused with those of the extremely toxic Indian hellebore (*Veratrum viride*, p. 303), which can cause severe poisoning, even death, when eaten.** • Another common name is large twisted stalk. The name *amplexifolius* means 'clasping leaf,' from the Latin *amplexor* (to surround) and *folius* (a leaf).

ROSY TWISTED STALK • *Streptopus roseus*

GENERAL: Rhizomatous perennial, 15–30 cm tall; stems **usually unbranched** and not as conspicuously bent as in other twisted stalks, with sparse fringe of hairs at stem where leaves arise.

LEAVES: Oval to elliptic, with **tiny, irregularly spaced, forward-pointing hairs** along edges; leaf bases **do not clasp stem**.

FLOWERS: Bell-shaped, rose-coloured with white tips, (sometimes greenish yellow streaked with reddish purple), **usually solitary from leaf axils** on a **curved, not kinked, stalk**.

FRUITS: Red, round to oblong berries.

ECOLOGY: Widespread and common at mid to high elevations in our moist and wet climates, in moist forests, forest openings and clearings.

SIMILAR SPECIES: The arrangement of the flowers distinguishes twisted stalks from the quite similar fairybells (*Disporum* spp., p. 301) and false Solomon's-seals (*Smilacina* spp., p. 299). **Twisted stalk flowers arise from leaf axils along the stem, while fairybells flowers appear as a pair at the tip of the stem, and false Solomon's-seal flowers are in a cluster at the tip of the stem.**

NOTES: A decoction of the root of rosy twisted stalk was used as a medicine by the Nlaka'pmx. Most Interior native groups considered the berries inedible or poisonous and referred to them as 'grizzly bear's favourite food.'

SMALL TWISTED STALK • *Streptopus streptopoides*

GENERAL: Perennial, 10–20 cm tall, from very slender, creeping rhizomes; **stems unbranched**, with fringe of coarse hairs opposite leaf bases.

LEAVES: Small, **oval to lance-shaped**, with sharp-pointed tips; edges with tiny, closely crowded teeth (visible with hand lens); leaf bases **do not clasp stem**.

FLOWERS: Rose to greenish purple, **saucer-shaped**, with **curled-back petal tips**; usually **solitary in leaf axils** on slender, drooping stalk.

FRUITS: Red, round berries.

ECOLOGY: Scattered and infrequent at mid to subalpine elevations in wet Columbia Mountains and East Kootenays, in shady, coniferous forests, especially in areas with heavy snowfall.

NOTES: Although the twisted stalks are named for their zigzag stems, you can also recognize them by the solitary (or sometimes paired) **flowers that hang on slender stalks from the leaf axils, and by their large red berries**. • Small twisted stalk is recognizable by its small size and purple-tinged, saucer-shaped flowers with their curled-back petal tips. • Small twisted stalk is suitable for groundcover in a shady garden. All our twisted stalks are easily propagated from pieces of rhizome or from seed. • The genus name *Streptopus* comes from the Greek *streptos* (twisted) and *podus* (foot), and it refers to the zigzag bends in the stem, which are fairly distinctive for the group. *Streptopus streptopoides* means the '*Streptopus* that's like *Streptopus*'!

HOOKER'S FAIRYBELLS • *Disporum hookeri*

GENERAL: Rhizomatous perennial, to 75 cm tall; stems with a few branches.

LEAVES: Oval to lance-shaped, with **pointed tips** and slightly hairy upper surfaces; bases somewhat clasping stem; **edges with hairs that point toward leaf tip**.

D. trachycarpum

FLOWERS: Creamy white, narrowly bell-shaped; usually 2 **nodding** beneath leaves at tip of each branch.

FRUITS: Lemon-yellow to red (when mature), **egg-shaped berries** with 4–6 seeds.

D. hookeri

ECOLOGY: Scattered and locally common at low to mid elevations, mostly in wet Columbia Mountains, Rocky Mountains and moist climates on our plateaus, in moist shady forests, openings and clearings.

SIMILAR SPECIES: Rough-fruited fairybells (*D. trachycarpum*) is very similar, but the hairs on its leaf edges spread outward (not forward), and its fruits have a rough, warty and velvety surface and contain 6–12 seeds. Rough-fruited fairybells occurs most commonly throughout our plateaus in dry to moist forests.

NOTES: Most native people of the Interior regard the berries of Hooker's fairybells as inedible and call them 'snakeberries,' although Nlaka'pmx elder Annie York considered them edible (Turner et al. 1990). • The plant is used successfully as a garden ornament. • The genus name *Disporum* means 'two seeded,' referring to the two seeds in each division of the fruit in some species. The species name *hookeri* honours the European botanist Joseph Hooker.

WILD LILY-OF-THE-VALLEY • *Maianthemum canadense*

GENERAL: Perennial, 5–25 cm tall, from creeping rhizomes; stems **hairy** (at least in upper parts).

LEAVES: Broadly **heart-shaped** to oval with pointed tips, 2–3 borne **on flowering stem**.

FLOWERS: Small and white; **4 petals**; in a **cylindrical cluster**.

FRUITS: Small round berries, hard, green, shiny and **mottled with brown when young**, becoming **red and soft when mature**.

ECOLOGY: Scattered and locally common in moist to dry, usually shady woods and mossy clearings in northeastern part of our region.

NOTES: Wild lily-of-the-valley spreads vigorously from its creeping rhizome. It is not unusual to find large colonies on the forest floor, forming a sea of the distinctive, heart-shaped leaves but few flowers. • Although Coastal native people gathered and ate the berries of the similar false lily-of-the-valley (*M. dilatatum*), there are no reports of Interior peoples eating berries of wild lily-of-the-valley. • This species is called wild lily-of-the-valley because of its similarity to the true lily-of-the-valley (*Convallaria majalis*), a European species. Wild lily-of-the-valley is sometimes called mayflower from the genus name *Maianthemum* (literally, 'May flower').

QUEEN'S CUP • *Clintonia uniflora*

GENERAL: Perennial, to 15 cm tall, from slender rhizomes; flowering stalks short and **leafless**.

LEAVES: 2–3 oblong or elliptic leaves at **base of flowering stalk**; slightly fleshy and shiny with noticeably hairy edges.

FLOWERS: Solitary (sometimes 2), **white, cup-shaped** at top of erect, hairy stalk.

FRUITS: Bright **metallic-blue berry**.

ECOLOGY: Widespread and common at low to subalpine elevations in moist forests, openings and clearings; absent from our hot arid climates.

NOTES: Turner (1978) notes that queen's cup 'was not generally recognized by contemporary native peoples.' However, the leaves were used by the Lil'wet'ul as an eye medicine and by the Okanagan to stop bleeding. The Lower Nlaka'pmx used the fruit for a blue dye. • The berries are considered unpalatable, although grouse reportedly eat them. • This plant is easily grown in woodland gardens, and the foliage and berries are especially attractive. • The beautiful, pure white, cup-shaped flower, with its crown of golden stamens, justly deserves the name 'queen's cup.' It is also called blue-bead clintonia and blue-bead lily, referring to the single blue berry. The genus *Clintonia* is named in memory of New York State governor and botanist DeWitt Clinton (1769–1828).

YELLOW GLACIER LILY • *Erythronium grandiflorum*

GENERAL: Perennial, to 30 cm tall, from a **long, slender, scaly bulb**; **flowering stalk leafless** and unbranched.

LEAVES: Single pair at **base** of stem, oblong to oval.

FLOWERS: Usually a **single golden-yellow flower** at top of stalk; **petals curve backward**.

FRUITS: Spindle-shaped capsules.

ECOLOGY: Widespread and common in subalpine and alpine meadows and wet, open high subalpine forests; rare in mid-elevation openings and aspen groves.

NOTES: Yellow glacier lily was a very important root vegetable, and the dried bulbs were also an important trading item for Interior Salish peoples. They gathered the bulbs in June to August. These bulbs are inedible when raw, but prolonged steaming, such as in pit-cooking, converts their indigestible carbohydrate, inulin, into edible fructose. Drying also helps this process. Kuhnlein and Turner (1991) note that a St'at'imc man observed grizzlies digging yellow glacier lilies and letting them wilt on the ground, then returning a few days later to eat them. Evidently bears were aware of the increased sweetness of the lilies after exposure to air. • Yellow glacier lily blooms soon after snowmelt, often at the edges of retreating snowbanks, which gives rise to the common name and the alternate name 'yellow avalanche lily.' The genus name is from the Greek *erythro,* meaning 'red,' and refers to the pink flowers of some species. The species name *grandiflorum* refers to the large flowers.

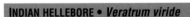

INDIAN HELLEBORE • *Veratrum viride*

GENERAL: Robust perennial, **to 2 m tall**, from a short, stout rhizome; stems unbranched and robust, leafy and hairy throughout.

LEAVES: Large (10–25 cm long), **oblong to elliptic**, with pointed tips and clasping bases, **prominently ribbed** (accordion pleated), hairy below.

FLOWERS: Star-shaped, yellow-green with dark green centres; in long inflorescence of **thin, drooping tassels** at top of stem; musky odour.

FRUITS: Oblong or oval capsules, straw-coloured to dark brown.

ECOLOGY: Widespread and most abundant at subalpine elevations (less common at low elevations) in wet Columbia Mountains, on wet seepage sites in moist and wet forests, openings and clearings.

NOTES: Poisonous. Plants of this genus are powdered to form the garden insecticide 'hellebore.' The native people recognized its poisonous nature but also used it as an important remedy for advanced stages of serious illness, such as cancer or tuberculosis. It was administered under very controlled conditions by specialists only. • **All parts of the plant are toxic to humans and livestock.** People who drank water in which Indian hellebore was growing reported stomach cramps. Other symptoms of hellebore poisoning include frothing at the mouth, blurred vision and 'lock-jaw,' as well as vomiting and diarrhea. Native people considered a salmon-head soup and salmon oil to be the only antidote. • The genus name *Veratrum* presumably refers to the blackish rhizome (from *vera,* 'true,' and *atrum,* 'black'). The species name *viride* means 'green.' The origin of the name 'hellebore' is obscure. The true hellebores (*Helleborus* spp.) are not much similar to *Veratrum* species, which may give rise to its other common name, 'false hellebore.'

BEAR-GRASS • *Xerophyllum tenax*

GENERAL: Perennial, to 1.5 m tall, from a short, thick rhizome; **robust flowering stems**.

LEAVES: **Wiry, grass-like**, in **dense basal clump and on stem**; rough with sharp edges, covered with many small hairs.

FLOWERS: Numerous **tiny, white flowers** in **large, showy head on long stem**; sweet smelling.

FRUITS: Small, dry, 3-lobed capsule with 2–5 seeds per chamber.

ECOLOGY: Locally abundant, especially at mid to high elevations in East Kootenays and southern parts of wet Columbia Mountains, in open woods, meadows and clearings; prefers heavy clay or peaty soils.

NOTES: Poisonous. Bear-grass is the only evergreen member of the lily family in our region. The dense clumps of basal leaves persist for several years. The flowering stems are produced from off-shoot plants growing at the base of the clump. These off-shoot plants die after flowering. Plants seem to flower every 5–10 years. • The Ktunaxa used the tough leaves of this plant to ornament baskets (hence its other common name, 'Indian basket-grass'), and they also traded the leaves to the Nlaka'pmx and Okanagan, who used them for the same purpose. • This plant is very difficult to cultivate in gardens and should be left undisturbed. • Bears are reported to eat the fleshy leaf bases in the spring and presumably this is how the plant got its common name. The genus name is from the Greek *xeros*, 'dry,' and *phyllon*, 'a leaf.' The species name *tenax* means 'holding fast' or 'tenacious,' and it refers to the tough pliable leaves.

BRONZE BELLS • *Stenanthium occidentale*

GENERAL: Perennial, 25–40 cm tall, from a **small, oval bulb**.

LEAVES: **Narrowly lance-shaped**, 2–3 at **base of stem**, to 30 cm long.

FLOWERS: **Narrow and bell-shaped**, pale **green-brown to deep purplish green**, **nodding** on slender stalks in a **long, narrow inflorescence**.

FRUITS: Small, 3–beaked capsules with winged seeds.

ECOLOGY: Scattered and infrequent at mid to alpine elevations in Kootenays and southern Coast/Interior Transition and occasionally on southern Okanagan Plateau, in moist forests and openings.

NOTES: Poisonous. This species is easily recognized by the drooping bronze bells that give it its common name. It is also called mountain-bells. The genus name is from the Greek *stenos*, 'narrow,' and *anthos*, 'a flower,' and refers to the flower's narrow tepals.

MOUNTAIN DEATH-CAMAS • *Zigadenus elegans*

GENERAL: Perennial, 15–70 cm tall, from a **scaly bulb**; stems often pinkish.

LEAVES: Mainly basal, but with 1–2 on stem, greyish green, linear, with prominent, keeled midrib.

FLOWERS: Greenish to yellowish white; bases of petals have green and **bilobed spots (glands);** in upright clusters; foul smelling.

FRUITS: 3-lobed capsules, form beneath flower.

ECOLOGY: Frequent at low to alpine elevations in southern half of our region, most commonly in Kootenays, in open montane forests, damp meadows and rocky or grassy slopes.

NOTES: Poisonous. The bulb and leaves contain an alkaloid, zigadenine, that is poisonous to humans and grazing animals. Symptoms include vomiting, lowered body temperature, difficult breathing and finally coma. • The Interior native peoples recognized the poisonous nature of the death-camases and were extremely cautious not to confuse them with nodding onion (*Allium cernuum*, p. 296), which in some places grows in the same locations. • The genus name means 'joined glands' and refers to the pair of glands in the perianth.

MEADOW DEATH-CAMAS • *Zigadenus venenosus*

GENERAL: Perennial, 20–60 cm tall, from a **scaly bulb**; stems often pinkish.

LEAVES: Mostly basal, linear, with keeled midrib; 3–4 on lower part of stem.

FLOWERS: Creamy white; bases of petals have **yellowish-green, oval spots** (glands); foul smelling.

FRUITS: Small, dry, many-seeded capsules, form above flower.

ECOLOGY: Frequent in our dry plateaus, arid basins and East Kootenays, on dry, grassy hillsides that are wet in spring, in pockets of soil between rock outcrops and in meadows at all elevations.

SIMILAR SPECIES: Meadow death-camas can be distinguished from mountain death-camas (*Z. elegans*, above) by its more compact spike of small flowers.

NOTES: The death-camases, as the name implies, are a group of **highly poisonous** perennial herbs. They grow from an **oval bulb** that is **covered with blackish scales**. The leaves are mostly basal, linear and grass-like. The flowers are white to greenish in an open, branched inflorescence. The petals (**tepals**) have a yellow or greenish spot (**gland**) at their base. • Meadow death-camas is one of the first plants to push through and turn green in spring. Serious losses can occur to stock grazing in meadows and grasslands where it is common. • The Okanagan and St'at'imc used the mashed bulbs as arrow poison.

STICKY FALSE ASPHODEL • *Tofieldia glutinosa*

GENERAL: Perennial, to 40 cm tall, from fairly **stout rhizomes** covered with fibrous remains of old leaf bases; stems **very sticky on upper part of stem.**

LEAVES: Grass-like; 2–4 at base of stem, growing to half length of stem; 1–2 smaller leaves on stem.

FLOWERS: Small, **white or greenish white**, often with **conspicuous purplish anthers**; in a dense cluster at top of stem.

FRUITS: Large, erect, **reddish-purple capsules**, with spongy seeds.

ECOLOGY: Scattered and infrequent from valley bottoms to alpine areas in peaty wetlands and open seepage areas; absent from our hot arid climates.

NOTES: The sticky stem topped by a cluster of small white flowers or red capsules distinguishes this bog plant. • The origin of the name 'asphodel' is ancient and obscure. It is the flower of the Elysian Fields, as in Homer's 'meadows of asphodel' inhabited by the souls of the dead, and may be from the Greek *a* (not) and *spodos* (ashes). Another source says it is from the Greek *a* (not) and *sphallo* (I surpass), meaning 'a stately plant of great beauty.' The genus *Tofieldia* is named for the English botanist Thomas Tofield (1730–79).

IDAHO BLUE-EYED-GRASS • *Sisyrinchium idahoense* S. angustifolium

GENERAL: Short, **stiff, tufted perennial**, to 30 cm tall.

LEAVES: Grass-like, **basal**, shorter than stems.

FLOWERS: Blue, often with yellow eye, shallowly **saucer-shaped**, petals with pointed tips; 1 to few on slender stalks near top of **flattened main stem with winged edges**; blooms in spring.

FRUITS: Egg-shaped capsules, with black seeds.

ECOLOGY: Scattered and locally common at low to mid elevations in our plateaus and East Kootenays, in dry to moist (at least during spring) grassy openings.

SIMILAR SPECIES: Mountain blue-eyed-grass (*S. montanum* inset photo) is also found in our region. Its blue flowers resemble Idaho blue-eyed-grass, but its petals are somewhat rounder. It is best distinguished from Idaho blue-eyed-grass by the **unequal length of the upper leaves**, which occur just below the slender flower stalk.

NOTES: According to Hitchcock et al. (1969), the classification of the blue-flowered *Sisyrinchium* species is somewhat chaotic. • The genus name *Sisyrinchium* is from Theophrastus's name for an iris.

WAPATO • *Sagittaria latifolia*

GENERAL: Semiaquatic perennial, to 90 cm tall, **from tuber-bearing rhizomes**; flowering stalks leafless.

LEAVES: Arrowhead-shaped, at **base** of flowering stalk, on long stalks that hold blades above water; submerged leaves sometimes lance-shaped to linear.

FLOWERS: 1–3 cm across; **3 white** petals, twice length of sepals, **soon falling off**; 3 greenish sepals; sexes often in separate flowers; in several whorls of 3 flowers in a long, narrow terminal cluster.

FRUITS: Flattened, winged **achenes**, with **sharp beak at right angles** to main body; usually more than 20 in round clusters.

ECOLOGY: Scattered and infrequent at low to mid elevations in marshes, ponds, lakes edges and wet ditches.

SIMILAR SPECIES: Arum-leaved arrowhead (*S. cuneata*) is found in similar habitats. It is smaller than wapato—its leaf blades are to 12 cm long (versus 25 cm), and its flowering stalks are to 50 cm long (versus 90 cm). The three sepals of the flowers are about two-thirds as long as the petals, and the achenes have an erect beak.

NOTES: Both species have starchy tubers that are eaten by ducks and muskrats. • Interior native peoples collected the tubers, which they called 'lower valley wild potato' or 'swamp potato.' The tubers were baked and have a sweet taste somewhat like chestnuts. • The common name 'wapato' comes from the Chinook of the lower Columbia River. Wapato is also called arrowhead.

SKUNK CABBAGE • *Lysichiton americanum*

GENERAL: Perennial, 30–150 cm tall, from fleshy, upright **rhizomes**; entire plant has a **swampy odour**.

LEAVES: Lance-shaped to broadly elliptic, often **huge** (30–120 cm long), on stout stalks.

FLOWERS: Hundreds of tiny, **greenish-yellow flowers**, sunken into thick, fleshy stalk (spadix) **surrounded by a bright yellow hood** (spathe).

FRUITS: Greenish to reddish, berry-like and pulpy, 1–2 seeded.

ECOLOGY: Widespread and locally common at low to mid elevations in the wet Columbia Mountains and Coast/Interior Transition; in very wet, swampy or peaty sites in forests and openings.

SIMILAR SPECIES: Water arum (*Calla palustris*) is another member of the arum family. It occurs sporadically in the northern part of our region in swamps, bog pools and often along the edges of ponds and sloughs. It has a long thick rhizome, heart-shaped leaves, a white spathe and red berries.

NOTES: The huge leaves and bright yellow spathe identify this swamp plant. Skunk cabbage grows in large patches. The spathes almost glow against the deep green of the leaves—it is also called swamp lantern. • Some native people refer to skunk cabbage as 'Indian wax paper' because all groups with access to the large shiny leaves traditionally used them in many of the same ways as waxed paper, such as lining food-steaming pits, and wrapping or covering food. Turner (1978) notes that only the Lil'wet'ul ate the rootstocks and that their name for the plant means 'hot' (as in spicy). Crystals of calcium oxalate in skunk cabbage

leave a burning sensation in the mouth, but drying or roasting the rootstocks destroys the crystals. Skunk cabbage was an important source of starch for local native peoples. Oinments prepared from the rhizome have been used for skin tumours and ulcerous sores. • The genus name *Lysichiton* (spelled *Lysichitum* in some works) is from the Greek *lysis* (loosening) and *chiton* (a tunic) and refers to the spathe.

Poaceae: Grass Family

Of all the world's flowering plants, the grasses (family Poaceae, also called Gramineae) are undoubtedly the most useful to humankind. They supply cereal grains, such as wheat, barley, oats, corn and rice, and sugar from sugar cane, as well as forage and turf. Interior native peoples used grasses widely for lining steam-cooking pits, wiping fish, covering berries, stringing food for drying, spreading on floors or as bedding. Many species of wildlife, from large grazing mammals to waterfowl, depend on grasses in grasslands or wetland habitats. In British Columbia, there are over 300 grass species. Only the most common species encountered in our region are presented here.

Although the grasses are generally easy to recognize, take care to distinguish them from the sedges (family Cyperaceae) and the rushes (family Juncaceae). These three main groups of grass-like plants can usually be separated on the basis of stem structure. Grass stems are round in cross section, are almost always hollow, and are jointed. Rush stems are also round in cross section, but they lack joints. Sedge stems are triangular in cross section.

The leaves of most grasses sheath the stem before diverging as a blade. At the point where the sheath and the blade join, there are two distinctive organs that useful for identification, the **ligule** (a thin membrane or fringe of hairs forming a collar around the stem) and the paired **auricles** (ear-like lobes), which may or may not be present. Leaf blades may be flat, folded or rolled.

Grass flowers are small but complex, and familiarity with their structure is essential for identification. The tiny flowers are borne in the axils of a small inner bract (**palea**), and a larger outer bract (**lemma**), which often bears a bristle-like **awn**. The flower, lemma and palea together are called a **floret**. Below the florets is an additional pair of bracts, the **glumes**. The florets and glumes together are called a **spikelet**.

You should note whether the spikelets are borne in an open, branching inflorescence (a **panicle** or a **raceme**) or directly on the stem (a **spike**). In several species, such as timothy (*Phleum pratense*), although the inflorescence appears to be a spike, the spikelets are actually borne on short stalks, not directly on the stem. You will need to determine if each spikelet has one, two, or more than two florets, and if its glumes are longer or shorter than the first floret. If the lemmas are awned, you should look to see if the awn originates from the tip of the glume, from below the tip, or from between the teeth of a divided tip.

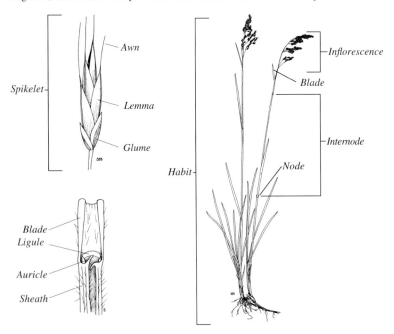

Key to the common grass tribes

1a. Inflorescence of 1 or
more spikes (spikelets without stalks) 2

2a. Inflorescence a single spike .... **Hordeae**

2b. Inflorescence of several
1-sided spikes .... **Chlorideae**

1b. Inflorescence a panicle (spikelets with
stalks; stalks are occasionally short
and panicle compressed) 3

3a. Each spikelet with 1 floret; glumes small .... **Agrostideae**

3b. Each spikelet with 2 to many florets 4

4a. Glumes shorter than 1st floret (lowest
enclosed lemma) lemmas awnless,
or awned from near their tip .... **Festuceae**

4b. Glumes equal to, or longer than 1st floret
(lowest enclosed lemma) 5

5a. Glumes narrow; lemmas
awned from their back, or awnless .... **Aveneae**

5b. Glumes broad, boat-shaped; lemmas
awned from a notched tip, or awnless .... **Phalarideae**

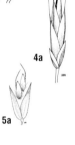

Picture-key to common genera of the grass tribes

HORDEAE (Barley Tribe)

inflorescence a single spike

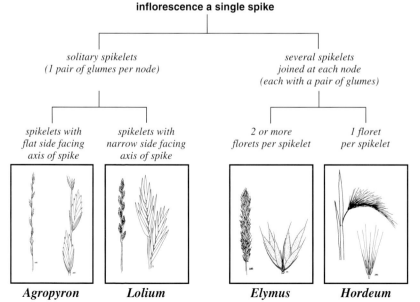

solitary spikelets *(1 pair of glumes per node)*		several spikelets *joined at each node (each with a pair of glumes)*	
spikelets with flat side facing axis of spike	*spikelets with narrow side facing axis of spike*	*2 or more florets per spikelet*	*1 floret per spikelet*
Agropyron	**Lolium**	**Elymus**	**Hordeum**

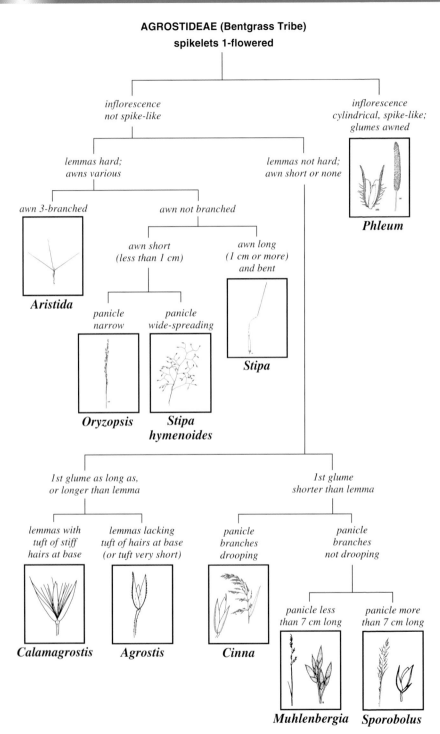

AGROSTIDEAE (Bentgrass Tribe)

spikelets 1-flowered

inflorescence not spike-like

inflorescence cylindrical, spike-like; glumes awned

lemmas hard; awns various

lemmas not hard; awn short or none

Phleum

awn 3-branched

awn not branched

Aristida

awn short (less than 1 cm)

awn long (1 cm or more) and bent

panicle narrow

panicle wide-spreading

Stipa

Oryzopsis

Stipa hymenoides

1st glume as long as, or longer than lemma

1st glume shorter than lemma

lemmas with tuft of stiff hairs at base

lemmas lacking tuft of hairs at base (or tuft very short)

panicle branches drooping

panicle branches not drooping

Calamagrostis

Agrostis

Cinna

panicle less than 7 cm long

panicle more than 7 cm long

Muhlenbergia

Sporobolus

FESTUCEAE (Fescue Tribe)

spikelets 2- to many-flowered;
glumes shorter than 1st floret

lemmas with awns
or awn-tipped

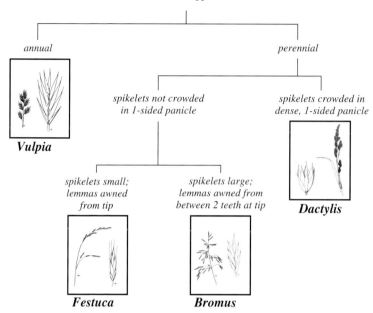

annual

perennial

spikelets not crowded
in 1-sided panicle

spikelets crowded in
dense, 1-sided panicle

Vulpia

spikelets small;
lemmas awned
from tip

spikelets large;
lemmas awned from
between 2 teeth at tip

Dactylis

Festuca

Bromus

lemmas without awns

plants of
saline habitats

plants not
of saline habitats

panicle dense;
male and female heads
on separate plants

panicle open; male
and female flowers
on same plant

spikelets usually small;
lemmas with or without
curly hair at base

spikelets large; lemmas
with tuft of straight
hair at base

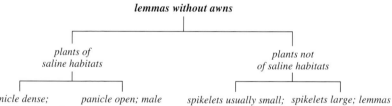

Distichlis

Puccinellia

Poa

Scolochloa

AVENEAE (Oat Tribe)

**spikelets 2- to many-flowered;
glumes equal to or longer than 1st floret**

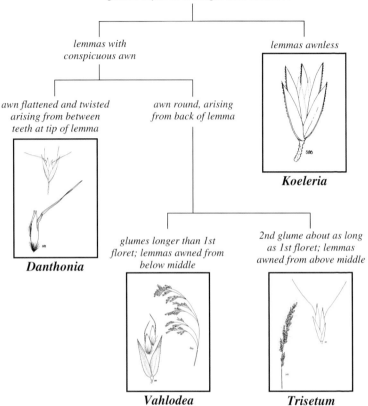

*lemmas with
conspicuous awn*

lemmas awnless

*awn flattened and twisted
arising from between
teeth at tip of lemma*

*awn round, arising
from back of lemma*

Koeleria

Danthonia

*glumes longer than 1st
floret; lemmas awned from
below middle*

*2nd glume about as long
as 1st floret; lemmas
awned from above middle*

Vahlodea

Trisetum

PHALARIDEAE (Canarygrass Tribe)

**spikelets 3-flowered;
glumes broad, boat-shaped**

CHLORIDEAE (Grama Tribe)

**inflorescence of
several 1-sided spikes**

*panicle open
or tufted*

*panicle compact; spikelets crowded,
all turned in same direction*

*spikes alternating
along stem*

Hierochloe

Phalaris

Spartina

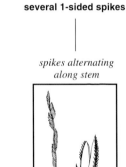

BLUEBUNCH WHEATGRASS • *Agropyron spicatum* *Elymus spicatus*

GENERAL: Perennial bunchgrass, 60–100 cm tall; many stems, often **forms large clumps**.

LEAVES: Flat or loosely inrolled blades, hairy above; **claw-like auricles** and short (1 mm), collar-like ligules; **previous year's leaves persist**.

INFLORESCENCE: Slender stiff spike of stalkless spikelets with **1 spikelet per node; spikelets usually shorter than internodes (not overlapping)**; lemmas usually without awns, but may have awns 1–2 cm long.

ECOLOGY: Widespread and common in grasslands and dry open forests at low elevations in Fraser, Thompson and Okanagan basins and southern Rocky Mountain Trench; otherwise scattered on warm southerly slopes at low to mid elevations on our dry plateaus and in East Kootenays.

NOTES: The Okanagan recognized this grass as a medicinal plant for sores and arthritis. They spread it on floors of pithouses and also used it as tinder and for stuffing moccasins in winter. All Interior native peoples used layers of this grass for drying soopolallie berries (*Sheperdia canadensis*). • This native grass is excellent forage for both domestic stock and wildlife, but is susceptible to damage or local extinction from overgrazing in spring. • The genus name *Agropyron* is from the Greek *agrios,* 'wild,' and *pyros* (or *puros*), 'wheat.'

CRESTED WHEATGRASS • *Agropyron cristatum*

GENERAL: Perennial bunchgrass, 0.5–1 m tall; forms dense tufts.

LEAVES: Flat blades, hairy above; slender, **claw-like auricles** and short (to 1 mm), collar-like ligules.

INFLORESCENCE: Crowded, flattened spike; **spikelets spreading**, several times longer than internodes; glumes and lemmas with **short awns** (2–4 mm).

ECOLOGY: Scattered and frequent at low to mid elevations in grasslands and on roadsides, where it is often seeded.

NOTES: Crested wheatgrass was introduced from Russia. This drought-tolerant species is seeded for forage and for erosion control on dry, disturbed sites. It frequently becomes established and replaces native species. The flattened, frequently crested shape of the seed head is distinctive.

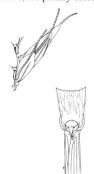

QUACKGRASS • *Agropyron repens* *Elymus repens*

GENERAL: Sod-forming perennial, to 1 m tall, from long, deep-penetrating **rhizomes.**

LEAVES: Broad, flat blades (to 1 cm wide), rough and often **sparsely hairy above**; slender, **claw-like auricles**, to 3 mm long; short, collar-like ligules.

INFLORESCENCE: Erect stiff spike of stalkless spikelets with **1 spikelet per node; spikelets overlapping, about twice as long as internodes**; lemmas awnless, or with awns up to 1 cm long.

ECOLOGY: Widespread and well established on disturbed sites (especially gardens and roadsides) in settled areas.

SIMILAR SPECIES: Slender wheatgrass (*A. trachycaulum*, also known as *Elymus trachycaulus*), a native, loosely tufted bunchgrass, has a similar inflorescence but lacks rhizomes and occurs in drier, less disturbed sites.

NOTES: Quackgrass was introduced from Eurasia and can be an extremely troublesome weed in cultivated fields and gardens. It is used for stabilizing embankments, and is also palatable to livestock. • The Okanagan reportedly used this grass as a liner in pit-cooking ovens in recent times, and as a substitute for bluebunch wheatgrass (*Agropyron spicatum*). • Quackgrass is also called couchgrass.

BLUE WILDRYE • *Elymus glaucus*

GENERAL: Perennial, 0.5–1.5 m tall; usually forms small clumps.

LEAVES: Broad and flat, usually lax, with **rough surfaces** and slightly in-rolled edges; **claw-like, clasping auricles** and short (about 1 mm), collar-like ligules.

INFLORESCENCE: Erect, **stiff spike**, usually with **2 stalkless spikelets at each node**; spikelets with 2 or more florets; lemmas hairless to sparsely short-hairy, with awns up to 2 cm long.

ECOLOGY: Widespread and common at low to mid elevations in open (often deciduous) forests, openings and clearings.

SIMILAR SPECIES: Hairy wildrye (*E. hirsutus*) has flexible, drooping spikes and lemmas fringed with long hairs. It is frequently seen in the western and central parts of our region, in open forests, meadows, streambanks, avalanche tracks and mountain gullies. It hybridizes with blue wildrye.

NOTES: This species is one of our tallest grasses, and it provides forage for both domestic stock and wildlife. • The blue-grey colour accounts for the species name *glaucus*.

GIANT WILDRYE • *Elymus cinereus*
Leymus cinereus

GENERAL: Robust **perennial**; forms **large clumps up to 1 m broad and 1–2 m high.**

LEAVES: **Broad**, very tough and stiff, greyish green, smooth; **well-developed auricles** at base of some blades; long ligules (3–7 mm).

INFLORESCENCE: An erect, **stiff spike**, with **3 or more spikelets at each node;** spikelets with a pair of **very narrow, 1–2-cm-long glumes**; 4–6 florets with **short-awned lemmas**.

ECOLOGY: Scattered and infrequent at low to mid elevations in Fraser, Thompson and Okanagan basins and southern Rocky Mountain Trench, in grasslands, open forests and open areas where sub-surface moisture is present.

NOTES: The Nlaka'pmx and other Interior peoples split the stems of giant wildrye and used them to decorate split cedar-root baskets. The Okanagan and St'at'imc used the leaves to line steam-pits and food caches, and to cover the floors of winter houses. They also used it to make a drink to treat gonorrhea and to prevent internal bleeding. • The species name *cinereus* means 'ash-coloured.'

SQUIRRELTAIL GRASS • *Elymus elymoides*
Sitanion hystrix

GENERAL: Densely tufted **perennial**, 10–60 cm tall, from fibrous roots.

LEAVES: Flat to rolled, with finely hairy surfaces; **claw-like auricles** at base of some blades; short ligules (0.5 mm).

INFLORESCENCE: Bristly spike, with **2 or more spikelets at each node**, breaking apart easily; spikelets with very narrow glumes; glumes and lemmas extending into **long** (3–10 cm), **spreading awns**.

ECOLOGY: Scattered on dry to moist sites in open forests and grasslands at all elevations, and on steep, rocky slopes in alpine areas.

SIMILAR SPECIES: The spikes of both squirreltail grass and foxtail barley (*Hordeum jubatum*, p. 316), with their long awned lemmas and glumes, look like bushy tails, but squirreltail grass has stiff, spreading awns, while foxtail barley has soft purplish, more compact awns. Squirreltail grass grows scattered here and there in dry forests, while foxtail barley is often seen blanketing the edge of wetlands.

315

FOXTAIL BARLEY • *Hordeum jubatum*

GENERAL: Tufted perennial, 30–60 cm tall; erect stems, curved at base.

LEAVES: Greyish green, rough in texture, hairy; short ligules (to 1 mm).

INFLORESCENCE: Nodding spike, with **3 or more spikelets at each node**; spikelets with **awn-like glumes** and 1 floret with a **long** (2–6 cm) awn at tip of lemma.

ECOLOGY: Very common weedy species at low to mid elevations in meadows and disturbed sites.

SIMILAR SPECIES: Meadow barley (*H. brachyantherum*) has a narrower spike with awns that are less than 2 cm long.

NOTES: Foxtail barley is easily recognized by its 'foxtail' of long purplish awns. The barbed awns of this species can become embedded in grazing animals, sometimes leading to considerable irritation of their mouths, ears or eyes. • The genus name *Hordeum* is from the Latin for barley.

PERENNIAL RYEGRASS • *Lolium perenne*

GENERAL: Tufted, short-lived **perennial**, 30–80 cm tall; stems smooth, curved at base.

LEAVES: Flat to folded; **smooth, glossy, claw-like auricles** at base of most leaves and short (1 mm) ligules.

INFLORESCENCE: Erect **stiff spike**, with a **single stalkless spikelet attached edgewise to stem at each node**; spikelets with **long, narrow glumes** and 6–10 florets; **lemmas** sharp-pointed but **awnless**.

ECOLOGY: Widespread on disturbed sites at low to mid elevations.

SIMILAR SPECIES: Both *Lolium* and *Agropyron* (pp. 313–14) species have one spikelet per node, but the spikelet is joined edgewise to the stem in *Lolium* species and flat to the stem in *Agropyron* species.

NOTES: This Eurasian species is used in grass-seed mixtures for lawns, clearings and as a cover crop. • The genus name *Lolium* is Latin for a 'darnel,' a weed of corn (or wheat) fields.

TIMBER OATGRASS • *Danthonia intermedia*

GENERAL: Densely tufted **perennial**, 5–40 cm tall.

LEAVES: Mainly basal, with hairs below and **tufts of long hair where blade joins stem**; ligule is a fringe of hairs.

INFLORESCENCE: Dense panicle, with few spikelets; spikelets with **2 or more florets** and **glumes about as long as spikelet**; **lemmas hairy at base and edges**, with a **twisted awn** (to 1 cm long) originating from below their tip.

ECOLOGY: Common at mid to high elevations in grasslands, meadows, wetlands and open forests; also in alpine areas.

SIMILAR SPECIES: Poverty oatgrass (*D. spicata*) has lemmas that are less than 6 mm long and are hairy on their backs and edges. It is common in open forests at low to mid elevations in the southern part of our region.

NOTES: Timber oatgrass is one of the first grasses to start growing in spring. It is a distinctive grass with large, oat-like spikelets that often turn purplish at high elevations. • The genus was named for Etienne Danthione, a French botanist of the early 19th century.

MOUNTAIN HAIRGRASS • *Vahlodea atropurpurea*
Deschampsia atropurpurea

GENERAL: Loosely tufted **perennial**, 40–80 cm tall.

LEAVES: Flat, soft, deep green, with more or less prow-like tips; hairy ligules, 1.5–3.5 mm long.

INFLORESCENCE: Open panicle, often nodding; spikelets quite large and often **purplish** at maturity; lemmas with stout, **bent awns** from below tips.

ECOLOGY: Scattered and locally abundant at high elevations in mountain meadows and open subalpine forests in areas of heavy snowfall.

NOTES: The species name means 'dark purple,' in reference to the colour of the spikelets.

NODDING TRISETUM • *Trisetum cernuum*

GENERAL: Tufted **perennial**, 60–120 cm tall.

LEAVES: Flat and lax, 0.5–1 cm broad, with thin prominent tips; ligules collar-like, 1.5–3 mm long, with fringed tips.

INFLORESCENCE: Open, very loose panicle, often nodding; lemmas 5–6 mm long, with **long bent awns** from below tips; **2nd glume wider than 1st**, with a sharp tip.

ECOLOGY: Common in moist forests, clearings and streambanks at low to subalpine elevations in wet parts of our region.

SIMILAR SPECIES: Nodding trisetum could be confused with false melic (*Schizachne purpurascens*) which lacks a sharp tip on the larger glume, has longer lemmas (1 cm long) and narrower leaves (3–5 mm wide).

NOTES: The inflorescence is nodding, hence the species name *cernuum*.

SPIKE TRISETUM • *Trisetum spicatum*

GENERAL: Densely tufted **perennial bunchgrass**, 10–50 cm tall.

LEAVES: Stiff and flat, quite short, finely hairy; ligules mostly 1 mm long.

INFLORESCENCE: Dense, spike-like panicle, with short branches, often turning purple or silvery; glumes slightly unequal in size; lemmas 4–5 mm long, with **long** (5–6 mm) **bent awns** from below divided tips.

ECOLOGY: Widespread but rarely abundant on dry open sites at low to high elevations.

NOTES: This species is often somewhat weedy in disturbed sites. It is a widely distributed, highly variable species that is not only found in the cold areas of North America and Eurasia (a common distribution pattern for arctic-alpine species), but it also occurs in southern South America (a very unusual discontinuous distribution).

JUNEGRASS • *Koeleria macrantha*
K. cristata

GENERAL: Densely tufted perennial, 20–50 cm tall; stems smooth to downy.

LEAVES: Slightly in-rolled, bluish green and usually covered in short hairs; hairy ligules, 0.5–2 mm long, with fringed tips.

INFLORESCENCE: Dense, spike-like panicle, with short branches; spikelets with 2–4 florets; **lemmas awnless** or with a very short awn.

ECOLOGY: Scattered but locally abundant at low to high elevations in grasslands, open forests and on well-drained soils.

NOTES: This species is a good forage grass, but the plants are usually widely spaced. • It is called junegrass because it flowers briefly in June. The genus is named after L. Koeler, a German botanist.

TIMOTHY • *Phleum pratense*

GENERAL: Short-lived perennial, to 1 m tall, forms large clumps; stems with bulbous bases.

LEAVES: Wide (4–8 mm) and **flat; ligules 2–3 mm long**.

INFLORESCENCE: Dense, cylindrical, spike-like panicle, to 10 cm long, with very short branches; spikelets flattened, with **1 floret** enclosed within glumes; glumes equal, flattened, **strongly ciliate along keels** and with **short, stiff awns**.

ECOLOGY: Common at low to mid elevations wherever it has been introduced.

SIMILAR SPECIES: Alpine timothy (*P. alpinum*), a common native grass in subalpine and alpine areas, is smaller (to 50 cm tall), does not have a bulbous base, and has a shorter (less than 5 cm), wider inflorescence than timothy.

NOTES: Timothy was introduced from Eurasia and is now partly naturalized near settled areas. This palatable, leafy grass is one of the more important domestic hay grasses in North America, and one of our more common causes of hay fever. Timothy does well in cold climates. • Early New England settlers called this species 'herd grass' after John Herd, who found it growing near Portsmouth, New Hampshire, in 1711. It was subsequently named 'timothy' after Timothy Hanson, the 18th-century U.S. agrologist who championed its use in domestic pastures in the early 1700s. The genus name *Phleum* is from *pleos*, the Greek name for a reedy grass.

319

HAIR BENTGRASS • *Agrostis scabra*

GENERAL: Densely tufted perennial, 20–50 cm tall; **rough stems, leaves and inflorescences**.

LEAVES: Mainly basal, **narrow (1–3 mm wide), fine and short**; ligules 2–3 mm long.

INFLORESCENCE: Large, delicate panicle; spikelets borne near branch tips, often purplish; spikelets with **1 floret** enclosed within small, equal glumes; delicate **lemma awnless** or with a fine awn.

ECOLOGY: Common at low to mid elevations in meadows, forest openings and disturbed sites.

SIMILAR SPECIES: Redtop (*A. gigantea*, below) differs from hair bentgrass by having rhizomes and a panicle with stiff branches bearing spikelets throughout their length.

NOTES: The inflorescence breaks away with age and rolls along the ground like a tumbleweed in the wind. • Hair bentgrass is also called ticklegrass. The species name *scabra* means 'rough' or 'scurfy,' referring to the feel of the stems, leaves and inflorescence branches.

REDTOP • *Agrostis gigantea*
A. alba

GENERAL: Long-lived, loosely tufted, **rhizomatous perennial**, 50–130 cm tall; often forms dense stands.

LEAVES: Broad (2–10 mm wide), smooth and **usually flat**; ligules of upper leaves 2–6 mm long.

INFLORESCENCE: Open and spreading panicle, often purplish, with whorls of stiff branches bearing spikelets throughout their length; spikelets with **1 floret** enclosed within small glumes; **lemma awnless**.

ECOLOGY: Common at low to subalpine elevations on disturbed sites.

SIMILAR SPECIES: Redtop was formerly combined with creeping bentgrass (*A. stolonifera*) under the name *A. alba*. Redtop is distinguished from creeping bentgrass by its underground horizontal stems (rhizomes), its open inflorescence, and its tolerance of much drier conditions than creeping bentgrass. Creeping bentgrass has above-ground, horizontal stems (stolons) and a more constricted inflorescence.

NOTES: Both redtop and creeping bentgrass are widespread turf grasses that have been introduced from Europe. Redtop is valued in grass seed mixtures. It grows quickly and vigorously, forming an initial turf that protects the soil from erosion until slower-growing grasses become established. • The reddish colour of the seed head accounts for the common name.

BLUEJOINT • *Calamagrostis canadensis*

GENERAL: Coarse, **tussock-forming perennial**, to 2 m tall, from creeping **rhizomes**.

LEAVES: Long, wide and **rather lax**; collar-like ligules, 3–10 mm long, with fringed tips.

INFLORESCENCE: Panicle, narrow and rather dense to loose and relatively open; spikelets with **1 floret** enclosed within glumes; **lemma** with a usually **straight awn** and many **long hairs at base, nearly as long as lemma**.

ECOLOGY: Common and often locally abundant at low to high elevations in moist to wet forests, wetlands and clearings.

SIMILAR SPECIES: The lemmas of pinegrass (*C. rubescens*, below) have short hairs at the base and a bent awn. Unlike bluejoint, however, pinegrass rarely forms heads.

NOTES: Bluejoint is a very aggressive colonizer after disturbances. • Bluejoint is also called Canada reedgrass or bluejoint reedgrass. The genus name is from the Latin *calamos*, 'a reed,' and *agrostis*, 'grass.'

PINEGRASS • *Calamagrostis rubescens*

GENERAL: Perennial, 60–100 cm tall, from long **rhizomes**; stem bases reddish; usually forms extensive cover.

LEAVES: Long, flat or rolled blades, distinctly hairy at base; collar-like ligules, 5 mm long.

INFLORESCENCE: Dense panicle, yellowish green to purple; spikelets with **1 floret** enclosed by glumes; lemma has a **bent awn** and **hairs at base** less than half its length.

ECOLOGY: Common and often abundant at low to mid elevations in dry to mesic forests and clearings; generally absent from wet Columbia Mountains.

SIMILAR SPECIES: Purple reedgrass (*C. purpurascens*) has well-spaced plants with fewer leaves and a denser panicle than pinegrass.

NOTES: Pinegrass and other similar grass and sedge species were called 'timbergrass' by Interior native peoples, and they used it to make soapberry beaters, in the preparation of dried soapberry cakes, or for lining cache pits and pit-cooking ovens. The Okanagan, Nlaka'pmx and Secwepemc wove socks and insoles from it for their moccasins. • This common yellow-green grass carpets the dry coniferous forests of our region, rarely forming heads except in open, sunny areas. • Pinegrass is not very palatable to grazing animals except for new spring growth.

ROUGH-LEAVED RICEGRASS • *Oryzopsis asperifolia*

GENERAL: Tufted perennial, 20–40 cm long; **stems spreading or prostrate**; plants usually solitary.

LEAVES: Wide, flat, firm and rather lax, rough in texture, tapered at both ends; short ligules (0.5 mm).

INFLORESCENCE: Narrow panicle, with a few spikelets on short branches; spikelets with **1 floret** enclosed within 6–8-mm-long glumes; **lemma hard** with an awn (0.5–1 cm long) at tip.

ECOLOGY: Widespread and scattered at low to mid elevations in dry to moist open forests and clearings.

NOTES: Rough-leaved ricegrass can dominate dry forested sites, the clusters of spreading leaves forming characteristic circles on herb-poor forest floors. • The genus name *Oryzopsis* comes from the Greek *oruza*, 'rice,' and *opsis*, 'like,' although the resemblance to rice (*Oryza sativa*) is weak. The leaves are rough to the touch, hence the species name *asperifolia*.

SHORT-AWNED RICEGRASS • *Oryzopsis pungens*

GENERAL: Tufted perennial, 15–30 cm tall, usually loosely clumped.

LEAVES: Long, slender and rather stiff.

INFLORESCENCE: Narrow panicle, with spikelets borne at branch tips; spikelets with **1 floret** enclosed within wide glumes; **lemma hard and cylindrical**, with a short awn (1–2 mm) that is usually absent at maturity.

ECOLOGY: Scattered at low to mid elevations in very dry forests and openings, usually on sandy or rocky soils, particularly in the northern part of our region.

SIMILAR SPECIES: Little-seeded ricegrass (*O. micrantha*) has a spreading panicle and long, persistent awns. This attractive grass, with its yellow-green tufts and delicate heads, is quite conspicuous growing on dry forest slopes.

NOTES: The small, fine short-awned ricegrass is easily overlooked. It increases in abundance in disturbed areas.

STIFF NEEDLEGRASS • *Stipa occidentalis*

GENERAL: Strongly **tufted, robust perennial**, 40–80 cm tall; **erect flowering stalks**.

LEAVES: Thin, stiff and usually **in-rolled**, with white hairs above; ligules 0.5 mm long.

INFLORESCENCE: Narrow, lax panicle; spikelets with **1 floret** enclosed within glumes; lemma sharp-pointed at base with a **bent, corkscrew-twisted awn** (3–4 cm long).

ECOLOGY: At low to mid elevations on dry grassy ridges and in dry, open forests and grasslands.

NOTES: The genus name *Stipa* comes from the Greek *stupe*, meaning 'tow' (the fibre of flax, hemp or jute, used for spinning), and refers to the feathery awns of some species.

SPREADING NEEDLEGRASS • *Stipa richardsonii*

GENERAL: Tufted perennial, 40–100 cm tall; **flowering stalks arched near top**.

LEAVES: Mostly basal, with **in-rolled edges**; ligules to 0.5 mm long.

INFLORESCENCE: Loose and open, slender spikelets borne at tips of drooping branches; spikelets with **1 floret** enclosed within glumes; lemmas with a **bent corkscrew-twisted awn** (3 cm long).

ECOLOGY: Common at low to mid elevations in grasslands and forest openings; often forming solid stands at forest edges.

NOTES: The short awns and open, drooping head distinguishes this needlegrass from all others. • It was named after Sir John Richardson of Franklin's Arctic expedition.

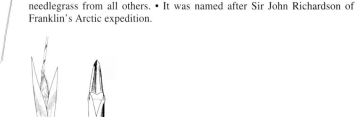

GRASS

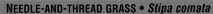

NEEDLE-AND-THREAD GRASS • *Stipa comata*

GENERAL: Densely **tufted perennial bunchgrass**, 30–60 cm tall.

LEAVES: Narrow with rolled edges, somewhat rough; **membranous ligules**, 3–6 mm long, very noticeable at base of leaves.

INFLORESCENCE: Open panicle, with a mass of curly-awned spikelets on short branches; spikelets with **1 floret** enclosed by 2 narrow glumes, 2 cm long; lemma firm and sparsely hairy all over, ending in a very long **twisted awn** (10–15 cm long).

ECOLOGY: Very common at low to mid elevations in grasslands and on south-facing slopes in dry forest openings.

SIMILAR SPECIES: Porcupine grass (*S. curtiseta,* below) has larger glumes, and its lemmas have a single line of hairs.

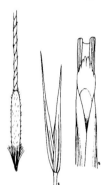

NOTES: Native children of the Interior played with the seeds of this grass, called 'speargrass' or 'coyote's needle,' by throwing them like darts. • Seeds of needle-and-thread grass are very sharp, and they can burrow through socks or injure the mouths of grazing animals. However, this grass provides forage in spring and autumn, before the 'needles' are formed, and again after they are shed. Like most range grasses, it should only be grazed to a point where about half the total season's growth is left, leaving the plant with adequate food reserves for winter. • The species name *comata* means 'with hair.'

PORCUPINE GRASS • *Stipa curtiseta*
S. spartea var. *curtiseta*

GENERAL: Densely **tufted perennial bunchgrass**, 30–80 cm tall.

LEAVES: Long, flat or rolled, rough above; short ligules (2 mm).

INFLORESCENCE: Panicle, with a mass of curly-awned spikelets on short, upright branches; spikelets with **1 floret** enclosed within a pair of 2–3-cm-long glumes; lemma firm, hairy at base and smooth above, except for a **single line of hairs on the back**, ending in a **long twisted awn (6–9 cm)**.

ECOLOGY: Common at low to mid elevations in grasslands on dry to moist sites, particularly in northern part of our region, where it is often the dominant grass.

NOTES: Both porcupine grass and needle-and-thread grass (*S. comata*, above) have awns that twist and untwist as the humidity varies, helping to bury the sharp-pointed seeds deep into the soil (or into your socks). • The grasslands on the upper plateau above the Fraser and Chilcotin river canyons, in the Cariboo/Chilcotin area, are unique in having porcupine grass as the dominant vegetation. Late in the season these grasslands become golden prairies.

INDIAN RICEGRASS • *Stipa hymenoides*
Oryzopsis hymenoides

GENERAL: Densely **tufted perennial**, 30–60 cm tall; stiff stems.

LEAVES: Long, narrow and coarsely ridged, usually with **in-rolled edges**; conspicuous ligules (about 6 mm long).

INFLORESCENCE: Large, open panicle with spikelets borne at tips of widely spreading, slender branches; spikelets with **1 floret** enclosed within **abruptly pointed glumes**; lemma **dark and densely covered by white hairs**, with a **short, stout awn** (4–6 mm).

ECOLOGY: Scattered and locally common at low elevations in our arid basins, in grasslands on dry slopes and sandy soils.

NOTES: This attractive grass is a delight to watch swaying in the breeze. It is an important forage grass in dry areas.

RED THREE-AWN • *Aristida longiseta*

GENERAL: Tufted perennial, 20–50 cm tall, forming large clumps.

LEAVES: Narrow, stiff and very rough; **short ligules** (0.5 mm), with a **tuft of fine hairs** (2–3 mm long) at front edges.

INFLORESCENCE: Narrow, few-flowered, bristly panicle; spikelets with **1 floret** enclosed within a pair of **long, narrow glumes**; lemma long and hard, with **3 long** (5–8 cm), **spreading awns**.

ECOLOGY: Locally common at low elevations, scattered throughout dry grassland sites, especially on bare ground and shallow rocky soils.

NOTES: This native grass is distinctive with its feathery mass of long, reddish awns. The sharp awns and hard, pointed florets can injure the mouths of grazing animals. • The genus name comes from the Latin *arista*, meaning 'awn.'

SAND DROPSEED • *Sporobolus cryptandrus*

GENERAL: Tufted perennial, 30–70 cm tall.

LEAVES: Flat, tapering to a fine point; **conspicuous tufts of long white hairs** where leaf joins stem; **ligules short, fringed**.

INFLORESCENCE: Mature panicles, moderately open, with **small, pale spikelets** crowded along upper part of main branches; spikelets with **1 floret** enclosed within tiny glumes; **awnless** lemma; seeds fall readily at maturity.

ECOLOGY: Locally abundant at low elevations, widely distributed in grasslands on open, south-facing slopes; often on sandy soil.

NOTES: During most of the growing season, the inflorescences are typically partly covered by a leaf sheath. Late in the season, patches of dormant sand dropseed stand out, in contrast to other grasses, with their pale, arched sheaths. Historically, the seed grains were collected for food. • The common name comes from a translation of the genus name *Sporobolus* which is from the Greek *sporos,* 'a seed,' and *ballein,* 'to throw,' because the seeds often 'drop' from the pericarp. The species name means 'hidden stamens.'

MAT MUHLY • *Muhlenbergia richardsonis*

GENERAL: Low, matted perennial, 5–30 cm tall, from extensive creeping **rhizomes**.

LEAVES: Narrow and rolled; ligules 1–2 mm long.

INFLORESCENCE: Narrow, spike-like panicle, with small spikelets on short branches; spikelets with **1 floret** within a pair of 1-mm-long glumes.

ECOLOGY: Common, especially in northern part of our region, in grasslands, shrub-carrs and meadows, often on alkaline soils.

NOTES: The matted, low growth form makes mat muhly distinct from most other grasses. This species furnishes considerable erosion protection to vulnerable soils. • The common name is an abbreviation of the genus name, which honours G.H.E. Muhlenberg (1753–1815), a minister from Pennsylvania who studied grasses.

NODDING WOOD-REED • *Cinna latifolia*

GENERAL: Rhizomatous perennial, 60–120 cm high; bases sometimes bulbous.

LEAVES: Thin, **rough and wide, rapidly narrowing to a sharp tip**, borne at right angles to stem; hairy ligules, 4–8 mm long.

INFLORESCENCE: Open, loose panicle, with small spikelets on drooping branches; spikelets with **1 floret**; lemma with a short, straight awn, or awnless.

ECOLOGY: Widespread at low to mid elevations in moist forests and moist disturbed areas.

NOTES: Nodding wood-reed increases tremendously on disturbed sites. • There is no reported use of it by Interior native peoples, but the Alaskan Tlingit used this and other species as decorations in woven baskets. • The genus name *Cinna* is from *kinni*, the ancient Greek name of a grass.

NUTTALL'S ALKALIGRASS • *Puccinellia nuttalliana*

GENERAL: Tufted perennial, 40–80 cm tall.

LEAVES: Short, smooth and **flat (becoming rolled)**; ligules 1–3 mm long.

INFLORESCENCE: Large, open, spreading panicle; tiny, narrow spikelets with **4–7 florets** with small glumes; lemmas blunt-tipped, **awnless**.

ECOLOGY: Common at low to mid elevations in wetlands, usually where alkaline.

NOTES: Continuous stands of Nuttall's alkaligrass provide considerable forage in wetlands. It is often found growing with alkali saltgrass (*Distichlis stricta*). • The genus and species names honour Benedetto Puccinelli (1808–50), an Italian botanist, and naturalist Thomas Nuttall.

PUMPELLY BROME • *Bromus inermis* ssp. *pumpellianus*

GENERAL: Rhizomatous, generally sod-forming perennial, 50–80 cm tall; stems hairy at joints.

LEAVES: Flat and wide, with prominent veins; ligules 0.5–2.5 mm long; **auricles** usually present.

INFLORESCENCE: Large panicle, with large and often purplish-tinged spikelets on short branches; spikelets with **7–11 florets**; **lemmas fuzzy-hairy**, with **short awns** (2–3 mm) from between 2 small teeth at tip.

ECOLOGY: Scattered at low to subalpine elevations on grassy slopes and at edges of dry forests.

SIMILAR SPECIES: This native species can be distinguished from the introduced smooth brome (*B. inermis* ssp. *inermis*) by the presence of hairs on the lemmas and at the stem nodes. Smooth brome is well established in disturbed areas and is an important component of hayfields and pastures.

FRINGED BROME • *Bromus ciliatus*

GENERAL: Loosely tufted perennial, 70–120 cm tall; stems often hairy.

LEAVES: Flat, broad and drooping, sometimes hairy above; **short ligules** (1 mm); no auricles.

INFLORESCENCE: Nodding panicle, with slender spikelets at ends of drooping branches; each spikelet with **7–10 florets** supported by a pair of smooth glumes; lemmas with coarse, stiff hairs along edges (sometimes over the back), and a **short awn** (3–5 mm) at tip.

ECOLOGY: Common at mid to subalpine elevations in moist forests (particularly deciduous forests) and wetlands.

SIMILAR SPECIES: This species is very similar to Columbia brome (*B. vulgaris*) which has longer awns (more than 5 mm long) and longer ligules (3–5 mm long). Columbia brome is also common throughout our region.

328

NODDING BROME • *Bromus anomalus*

GENERAL: Tall **perennial**, to 1 m tall, from fibrous roots.

LEAVES: Flat and stiff; short ligules (1–1.5 mm); no auricles.

INFLORESCENCE: Nodding panicle, with large, fuzzy spikelets at ends of drooping branches; each spikelet with **7–11 florets** and hairy glumes; **lemmas densely hairy**, with a short **awn** (2–3 mm) at tip.

ECOLOGY: Widespread at low to high elevations on Fraser Plateau and in Rocky Mountains, in grasslands, open forests and moist meadows and fields.

NOTES: The large, attractive, nodding head with fuzzy spikelets distinguishes this grass. • The species name *anomalus* means 'out of the ordinary.'

CHEATGRASS • *Bromus tectorum*

GENERAL: Tufted annual, 20–60 cm tall; hairy stems.

LEAVES: Flat, with long, soft hairs; ligules to 3 mm long; no auricles.

INFLORESCENCE: Open panicle, with many spikelets on drooping branches; each spikelet with **3–6 florets** with **hairy glumes and lemmas**; **long awns** (12–15 mm) from between 2 small teeth at tip of lemmas.

ECOLOGY: Widespread at low to mid elevations on dry, disturbed sites in grasslands and forest openings.

NOTES: Cheatgrass is an introduced, weedy annual, that can be very prolific, rapidly covering disturbed ground. • The species name *tectorum* literally means 'of tiles' or 'growing on rooftops,' implying that it is a weedy species that grows on sod roofs. The common name 'cheatgrass' suggests that it is a grass with little nutrient value.

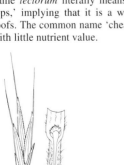

329

ROCKY MOUNTAIN FESCUE • *Festuca saximontana*
F. ovina var. *rydbergii*

GENERAL: Small, densely tufted perennial, 25–50 cm tall.

LEAVES: Erect, **slender and tightly rolled**, in a distinct, short **basal cluster**; ligules short (to 0.4 mm), with a fine fringe at top, higher at sides.

INFLORESCENCE: Narrow panicle, with short branches; spikelets with **3–5 florets**; lemmas 4–5 mm long, taper to a **short awn** (1–2 mm).

ECOLOGY: Common at mid to high elevations in grasslands and dry open forests; absent from areas of wet climate.

SIMILAR SPECIES: Alpine fescue (*F. brachyphylla*, also known as *F. ovina* var. *brachyphylla*) is a dwarf (5–15 cm tall) alpine species that is common throughout our region at high elevations.

NOTES: This variable species has been divided by some taxonomists into several varieties, each growing to different heights and with different leaf lengths.

WESTERN FESCUE • *Festuca occidentalis*

GENERAL: Tufted perennial, 25–70 cm tall; stems few, slender.

LEAVES: Narrow and soft, in lax basal tufts; ligules short (to 0.5 mm), fringed, higher at sides.

INFLORESCENCE: Open panicle, usually drooping at top; spikelets with **3–5 florets**; lemmas about 5 mm long, taper to a long (4–10 mm), **slender awn.**

ECOLOGY: Widespread and common at low to mid elevation in dry to moist forests and clearings.

NOTES: Western fescue can be distinguished from other fescues by the tuft of long, soft, narrow leaves and the long, slender awn.

ROUGH FESCUE • *Festuca campestris*
F. scabrella var. *major*

GENERAL: Densely tufted perennial, 60–100 cm tall, often forming large clumps; old sheaths and leaf bases persist for many years in thick mats.

LEAVES: Narrow and stiff, with a **rough surface**; ligules short, fringed, higher at sides.

INFLORESCENCE: Loose panicle with large spikelets at end of long branches; spikelets with **5–7 florets**; lemmas 7–8 mm long, taper to a sharp point (or tiny awn).

ECOLOGY: Common at low to mid elevations south of 51°N on dry to moist sites in forest openings and grasslands.

SIMILAR SPECIES: Altai fescue (*F. altaica*) has lemmas with transparent edges, which gives a sheen to the spikelets. In our region it occurs only at high elevations north of 51°N.

NOTES: Rough fescue, like other fescues, is a 'cool season' grass, attaining maturity in early to midsummer. • When protected from grazing, single plants can often grow to 30 cm or more across. • The genus name *Festuca* is from an ancient word meaning 'a straw' or 'a mere nothing.'

IDAHO FESCUE • *Festuca idahoensis*

GENERAL: Densely tufted perennial bunchgrass, 30–90 cm tall.

LEAVES: Many, long, narrow, very rough in texture, often bluish green; ligules short (0.5 mm), finely fringed, higher at sides.

INFLORESCENCE: Slender panicle, with few spikelets; spikelets with **5–7 florets**; lemmas about 6 mm long, taper to a **stout awn** (2–5 mm long).

ECOLOGY: Frequent at low to subalpine elevations south of 50°N in cool grasslands, particularly on north-facing slopes; infrequent in open forests.

SIMILAR SPECIES: Idaho fescue can be confused with Rocky Mountain fescue (*F. saximontana* p. 330), which is generally smaller and has shorter lemmas and awns.

NOTES: Idaho fescue often decreases greatly in abundance with heavy grazing, and in many areas it is not nearly as common now as it was 150 years ago.

ALPINE BLUEGRASS • *Poa alpina*

GENERAL: Short, tufted perennial, 5–30 cm tall, forming mats of basal leaves.

LEAVES: At base of stem, **short** and **flat**, tips curved upwards and prow-like; persistent light-coloured sheath; ligules 1–3 mm long.

INFLORESCENCE: Short, open panicle, about as long as it is broad; spikelets large, with **3–6 florets**; lemmas **hairy on lower half**, but with no cobwebby hairs at base.

ECOLOGY: Common throughout our region at high elevations in meadows and tundra, and on rocky slopes; often abundant on disturbed sites.

NOTES: *Poa* is a difficult genus taxonomically, and some of the 20 or so species that occur in our region are difficult to tell apart. • The bluegrasses rank high both as forage plants for wild and domestic animals, and as cultivated pasture and turf grasses.

ARCTIC BLUEGRASS • *Poa arctica*
P. grayana

GENERAL: Loosely tufted perennial, 10–40 cm tall, from creeping **rhizomes**; stems purplish and curved at base.

LEAVES: Flat or folded, with rough edges and tips curved upwards and prow-like; ligules pointed, 1–3 mm long.

INFLORESCENCE: Open, loose, pyramidal panicle; **often purplish spikelets** with 3–4 florets; lemmas usually hairy on the back, with a **tuft of cobwebby hairs at base**.

ECOLOGY: Common in subalpine and alpine meadows.

NOTES: This variable species has been divided into several varieties.

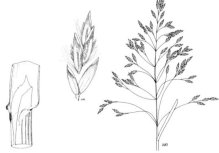

KENTUCKY BLUEGRASS • *Poa pratensis*

GENERAL: Sod-forming perennial, 30–80 cm tall, from long creeping **rhizomes**.

LEAVES: Flat to folded, tips curved upwards and prow-like; ligules 1–3 mm long.

INFLORESCENCE: Open, pyramidal panicle, tending to be curved and 1-sided when mature, usually with 3–5 branches at each joint; spikelets with **3–5 florets**; lemmas about 3.5 mm long, with **cobwebby hairs at base**, awnless.

ECOLOGY: Widespread at low to high elevations throughout most of our region, in grasslands, open forests, wetlands and disturbed areas.

SIMILAR SPECIES: Fowl bluegrass (*P. palustris*), a native wetland species, resembles Kentucky bluegrass but has shorter lemmas (about 2.6 mm long). • Canada bluegrass (*P. compressa*) has stems that are strongly flattened and 2-edged. It is sometimes seeded as a substitute for Kentucky bluegrass.

NOTES: Kentucky bluegrass, extensively used as lawn and pasture grass, is highly tolerant of close grazing and mowing. This introduced Eurasian species is the state flower of Kentucky.

ALKALI BLUEGRASS • *Poa juncifolia*
P. secunda ssp. *juncifolia*

GENERAL: Tall, strongly tufted perennial, 40–100 cm tall.

LEAVES: Narrow, smooth and rolled; **ligules thickened, hairy**, 0.5 mm long at plant base to 2 mm long on upper stem leaves.

INFLORESCENCE: Narrow panicle; spikelets with **3–6 florets**; lemmas 4 mm long, awnless, rough near base, without basal cobwebby hairs.

ECOLOGY: Common at low to mid elevations in alkaline meadows, grasslands and dry open forests.

SIMILAR SPECIES: Sandberg's bluegrass (*P. secunda* p. 334) is a much smaller plant, with shorter stems (under 30 cm tall) and longer ligules on the upper stem leaves (more than 2 mm long).

NOTES: The stems and leaves of alkali bluegrass usually have a blue-grey appearance.

WHEELER'S BLUEGRASS • *Poa wheeleri*
P. nervosa var. *wheeleri*

GENERAL: Slender perennial, 30–70 cm tall, from creeping **rhizomes**; smooth stems.

LEAVES: Flat or folded; ligules notably thickened, upper ligules rounded, 1–2 mm long.

INFLORESCENCE: Open panicle, with spreading or upright branches that support fairly large spikelets; lemmas 4.5–5 mm long, awnless.

ECOLOGY: Widespread but never abundant at low to subalpine elevations in dry, open, coniferous forests.

SIMILAR SPECIES: Cusick's bluegrass (*P. cusickii*, p. 335) lacks the open panicle and thick ligules of Wheeler's bluegrass.

NOTES: This species is unusual in that the plants are all female—the pollen is non-functional and the seeds appear to be produced asexually.

SANDBERG BLUEGRASS • *Poa secunda*
P. sandbergii

GENERAL: Low tufted perennial, to 30 cm tall, often purplish-tinged.

LEAVES: In a basal tuft, short (2–3 cm) and narrow, with rough surfaces, often curled; ligules generally short (1 mm) but sometimes over 3 mm long on stem leaves.

INFLORESCENCE: Narrow panicle, with short, ascending branches; spikelets with **3–5 florets**; lemmas about 4 mm long, awnless, with fine **hairs on lower half**.

ECOLOGY: Widespread at low to mid elevations on well-drained soils; common in low-elevation grasslands.

NOTES: This species now includes most of the species in the Scabrellae subgroup of the genus *Poa*, namely *P. sandbergii*, *P. canbyi*, *P. gracillina* and *P. scabrella* ssp. *secunda*. • Sandberg bluegrass is distinguished from other similar bluegrass species by its low stature, narrow short leaves, purplish colour, and somewhat smaller spikelets. • Sandberg's bluegrass seedheads mature early, before July.

CUSICK'S BLUEGRASS • *Poa cusickii*

GENERAL: **Densely tufted perennial**, 20–60 cm tall, from fibrous roots.

LEAVES: In a **basal tuft**, very **narrow** and **rough** in texture; ligules thin, 1–3 mm long.

INFLORESCENCE: Compact, oblong panicle, pale or purple-tinged; spikelets with **3–5 florets**; lemmas 4.5–6 mm long.

ECOLOGY: Widespread at low to high elevations in grasslands and alpine meadows.

SIMILAR SPECIES: Wheeler's bluegrass (*Poa wheeleri*, p. 334) has a more open panicle, thicker ligules and creeping rhizomes.

NOTES: Also known as skyline bluegrass, this plant was named after plant collector William Conklin Cusick (1842–1922).

SPANGLE-TOP • *Scolochloa festucacea*

GENERAL: Tall, stout perennial, 1–1.5 m tall, from extensive, thick, creeping **rhizomes**.

LEAVES: Stiff and **flat,** tapering to a **slender tip**; ligules large (2–8 mm long) and torn.

INFLORESCENCE: Spreading, with stiff branches supporting large spikelets; each spikelet with **3–5 florets**; lemmas 6 mm long, with a **tuft of hairs at base**.

ECOLOGY: Scattered at low to mid elevations in shallow water and marshes.

NOTES: This stout marsh grass often forms a tall border around shallow open water, providing habitat for many birds and animals. • Spangle-top is so called because the whitish colour of the empty heads can be readily identified from a distance ('spangle' means 'gleam,' or 'glitter'). The genus name comes from the Greek *scolops,* 'a prickle,' and *chloa,* 'grass,' although it is not clear why it is applied to this plant. The species name *festucacea* indicates that this species looks like a *Festuca* species.

SIX-WEEKS FESCUE • *Vulpia octoflora*
Festuca octoflora

GENERAL: Slender, low annual, 15–30 cm tall, from a shallow root system.

LEAVES: Narrow, in a **short basal tuft**; ligules short (1 mm), higher at sides.

INFLORESCENCE: Narrow, erect panicle, with very short branches; spikelets with **8–12 florets**; **awn-tipped lemmas**.

ECOLOGY: Scattered at low to mid elevations in southern part of our region on disturbed, open ground on dry to moist sites.

NOTES: This is a weedy species. • The common name 'six-weeks' refers to its habit of appearing, producing seeds and drying out, all within a short period of time. The genus is named after J.S. Vulpius (1760–1846), a German botanist. The species name *octoflora* means '8-flowered,' and it refers to the average number of florets per spikelet.

ALKALI SALTGRASS • *Distichlis stricta*
D. spicata var. *stricta*

GENERAL: Short, sod-forming perennial, 10–30 cm tall, from vigorous, scaly **rhizomes**.

LEAVES: Yellowish green, **stiff** and **erect**, **closely 2-ranked**; **old leaves persist**; ligules short (0.5 mm) with tufts of long hairs at front.

INFLORESCENCE: Compact, with large, **flattened spikelets** on short branches; spikelets with **7–9 florets**; lemmas **hardened**, **awnless**; male and female flowers on separate plants.

ECOLOGY: Common at low to mid elevations in arid basins and adjacent plateaus, in saline or alkaline meadows.

NOTES: This low, coarse grass often forms a uniform cover over large areas of wetlands. • The genus name *Distichlis* is from the Greek *distichos*, '2-ranked,' and refers to the two rows of leaves.

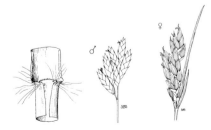

ORCHARDGRASS • *Dactylis glomerata*

GENERAL: Strongly tufted perennial, to 1.2 m tall.

LEAVES: Flat, broad and rough, early growth light bluish green; **ligules 3–10 mm long**, somewhat hairy.

INFLORESCENCE: Panicle, with spikelets borne at end of stiff branches in **congested 1-sided heads; spikelets flattened**, with **3–5 florets**; lemmas **stiffly hairy on the back**, with an **awn-tip** (to 1 mm long); outer glume **also stiffly hairy on the back**.

ECOLOGY: Widespread and often locally abundant at low to mid elevations near areas of human habitation or disturbance.

NOTES: This Eurasian species is cultivated for hay, and it is also used in grass-seed mixtures on clearings and for erosion control along road cuts. • The genus name is from the Greek *dactylos* (a finger), perhaps in reference to the stiff branches of the panicle.

ALKALI CORDGRASS • *Spartina gracilis*

GENERAL: Perennial, 30–60 cm tall, from creeping rhizomes; stems well spaced, upright.

LEAVES: Stiff and flat, to curled at edges, rough in texture, tapering to a pointed tip; ligules a dense fringe of fine hairs, 1 mm long.

INFLORESCENCE: Narrow, with 4–8 spikes alternating along stem, each spike with a double row of crowded spikelets; spikelets with **1 floret**; lemmas and glumes with a fringe of stiff hairs on the back; **lower glume is twice as long as upper one**.

ECOLOGY: Scattered and locally common in our dry climates at low to mid elevations, in dry to moist meadows and grasslands, usually where alkaline.

NOTES: This wiry grass is very distinctive with its flattened, cord-like seed head. • The genus name *Spartina* is from *spartine*, the Greek name for cord made from the European species *S. juncea*, which is also the source of the common name 'cordgrass.'

337

COMMON SWEETGRASS • *Hierochloe odorata*

GENERAL: Rhizomatous perennial, 30–60 cm tall; **stems purplish at base**; sweet smelling.

LEAVES: Short, broad stem leaves; non-flowering shoots often with long blades; ligules 3–5 mm long.

INFLORESCENCE: Open, **pyramidal panicle; spikelets a lustrous golden yellow**, tulip-shaped; broad glumes equal in length to florets; lemmas hairy and awnless.

ECOLOGY: Widely scattered at low to high elevations in wetlands.

NOTES: The sweet, lingering fragrance of this grass comes from the presence of coumarin, which was formerly used as a flavouring agent. • This grass was widely used by native people across North America to make fragrant baskets and as a body wash. Interior native people, however, did not use it in the same way as Plains people.

REED CANARYGRASS • *Phalaris arundinacea*

GENERAL: Perennial, to 1.7 m tall, from long scaly pinkish **rhizomes**; hollow stems.

LEAVES: Flat and roughened; sheath open, edges overlapping; ligules 4–9 mm long, usually tattered and turned backward.

INFLORESCENCE: Panicle compact, to 15 cm long, with spikelets crowded on branches; spikelets with **3 florets** enclosed within broad glumes; 1 fertile floret with 2 sterile ones below it.

ECOLOGY: Scattered, often locally abundant, at low to mid elevations in marshes, disturbed wet sites and streambanks; often around areas of agricultural activity.

NOTES: The Okanagan used reed canarygrass to make mats for eating on and for drying food, and peaked hats for native doctors. A rope was also made from this grass for binding fish weirs. The Nlaka'pmx used the whitish flowering stems to weave decorative patterns into split cedar root baskets. • Reed canarygrass is a very useful, high yielding hay grass for moist river valleys and marshy land.

Cyperaceae: Sedge Family and Juncaceae: Rush Family

Sedges (family Cyperaceae) and rushes (family Juncaceae) resemble perennial grasses in their long, narrow, parallel-veined leaves and inconspicuous flowers with several scale-like bracts. They are most easily distinguished by their stems, which in sedges are generally triangular in cross-section and solid (not hollow), with the leaves in three rows (versus two rows for grasses), and in rushes are round and solid (pithy). Remember: 'sedges have edges and rushes are round.' Both provide important forage and habitat for a variety of wildlife species.

The sedge family has several genera. The largest is *Carex*, which has its ovary and 1-seeded fruit (**achene**) enclosed in a membranous sac (the **perigynium**) in the axil of a single, scale-like bract. In addition to sedges (*Carex* spp.), the sedge family also includes bulrushes (*Scirpus* spp.), spike-rushes (*Eleocharis* spp.), cotton-grasses (*Eriophorum* spp.), clubrushes (*Trichophorum* spp.) and kobreseias (*Kobresia* spp.).

The rush family includes two genera, *Juncus* and *Luzula*, both of which have two series of three scale-like floral bracts. Each fruit (capsule) of *Juncus* has many seeds while the fruit of *Luzula* contains only three seeds.

Features of sedges (*Carex* spp.)

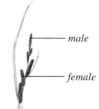

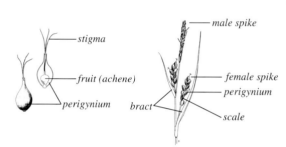

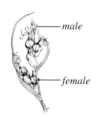

long inflorecence with cylindrical spikes

short inflorescence; more than one spike per stem; each spike many flowered; male and female flowers on same spike

each spike few flowered; male spike separate at tip of stem

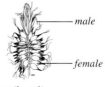

spike solitary

perigynium covered with hairs

sheath (at base of leaf) shedding, becoming web-like

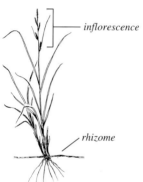

339

Key to the common sedges

1a. Long inflorescence (more than 5 cm); cylindrical spikes 2

  2a. Spikes nodding on long stalks 3

    3a. Roots covered with yellowish woolly hair .... *C. paupercula*

    3b. Roots without a yellowish woolly covering .... *C. spectabilis*

  2b. Spikes not nodding (spikes with short stalks, or stalkless) 4

    4a. Perigynia covered with hair .... *C. lanuginosa*

    4b. Perigynia smooth 5

      5a. Perigynia with a prominent beak (1–2 mm long) .... *C. rostrata*

      5b. Perigynia with a short beak (0.3 mm) .... *C. aquatilis*

1b. Short inflorescence (less than 5 cm); spikes various 6

  6a. Spike solitary 7

    7a. Perigynia covered with hairs .... *C. scirpoidea*

    7b. Perigynia without hairs 8

      8a. Plants growing in tufts, without rhizomes;
leaves narrow (1.5 mm wide or less) .... *C. pyrenaica*

      8b. Plants growing from rhizomes 9

        9a. Leaves more than 1.5 mm wide .... *C. nigricans*

        9b. Leaves 1.5 mm wide, or less .... *C. obtusata*

  6b. More than 1 spike per stem 10

    10a. Spikes few-flowered (each with less than 15 perigynia) 11

      11a. Perigynia hairless 12

        12a. Perigynia with a prominent beak .... *C. deweyana*

        12b. Perigynia with barely noticeable beak .... *C. disperma*

      11b. Perigynia covered with hairs 13

        13a. A few spikes near base of plant,
widely separated from upper spikes .... *C. rossii*

        13b. All spikes at top of plant, high above the leaves 14

          14a. Male spikes small (3–6 mm long) .... *C. concinna*

          14b. Male spikes large (8–20 mm long) .... *C. concinnoides*

    10b. Spikes many-flowered (each with more than 15 perigynia) 15

      15a. Scales black (or dark brown) 16

        16a. Perigynia green or bronze .... *C. media*

        16b. Perigynia blackish purple .... *C. albonigra*

      15b. Scales brown 17

        17a. Male flowers above female, or on separate spike 18

          18a. Top spike male, female spikes below .... *C. viridula*

          18b. Male and female spikes on separate plants,
or occasionally a few male flowers above the female ones .... *C. praegracilis*

        17b. Male flowers below female, in each spike 19

          19a. Plants alpine .... *C. phaeocephala*

          19b. Plants not alpine 20

            20a. Lower bract longer than inflorescence .... *C. athrostachya*

            20b. All bracts short 21

              21a. Perigynia more than 1 mm wide .... *C. petasata*

              21b. Perigynia 1 mm wide, or less .... *C. crawfordii*

LOW NORTHERN SEDGE • *Carex concinna*

GENERAL: **Small, loosely tufted,** to 20 cm tall, from slender, scaly rhizomes; stems slender, smooth, arching, brownish, somewhat shredded at base.

LEAVES: Narrow (about 2 mm wide), clustered near base, much shorter than stem.

INFLORESCENCE: Unisexual spikes; **male spike, 3–6 mm long,** at top of stem, surrounded by 2–3 **few-flowered female spikes**.

PERIGYNIA: **Hairy** and plump, with a dark reddish-brown scale, 3-angled, with a very short beak and **3 short, dark stigmas**.

ECOLOGY: Widespread and common at mid elevations in open coniferous forests; also in shrub-carrs and clearings.

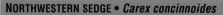

SIMILAR SPECIES: Northwestern sedge (*C concinnoides,* below) closely resembles low northern sedge, but it is larger and has a longer male spike (8 mm or more in length).

NOTES: The species name is from the Latin *concinnus,* which means 'well proportioned,' 'neat' or 'elegant,' and may refer to the tidy inflorescence.

NORTHWESTERN SEDGE • *Carex concinnoides*

GENERAL: **Loosely tufted,** 15–23 cm tall, from slender, scaly rhizomes; stems slender, **smooth,** erect to curved, bases dark purplish brown.

LEAVES: Clustered near base and usually shorter than stem, **2–5 mm wide**.

INFLORESCENCE: Unisexual spikes; **stalkless male spike, 8–22 mm long,** at top of stem, with 1–2 few-flowered female spikes below it.

PERIGYNIA: **Hairy** and plump, wider and longer than the dark, purplish-red scale, obscurely 3-angled, usually with **4 long, brownish stigmas**.

ECOLOGY: Widespread and common at low to high elevations in our dry plateaus and East Kootenays, in dry, open coniferous forests and openings.

SIMILAR SPECIES: Richardson's sedge (*C. richardsonii*) is similar in appearance and habitat, but it has **rough** stems and longer leaves, and the **male spike is stalked**.

NOTES: This sedge is one of the species called 'timbergrass' by Interior native peoples. It was commonly used for lining pit-cooking ovens, cache pits and moccasins, and for covering and lining berry baskets.

ROSS'S SEDGE • *Carex rossii*

GENERAL: Low, **dense tufts,** 10–30 cm tall; clusters of slender stems.

LEAVES: Narrow (1–2.5 mm wide) and thin but firm, with **purplish sheaths at base**, at least some longer than stem.

INFLORESCENCE: Unisexual spikes; male spike at **top of stem** with 2–3 few-flowered female spikes below it; well-developed, leaf-like bracts, usually longer than the inflorescence; **additional female spikes borne on long stalks near stem base**, widely separated from terminal spike.

PERIGYNIA: Few per spike, **hairy** and plump, 3-angled, with a stalk-like base and narrow, elongate beak; 3 stigmas.

ECOLOGY: Widespread and common at low to high elevations in dry, open forests and disturbed areas, often where gravelly.

SIMILAR SPECIES: Peck's sedge (*C. peckii*) is somewhat similar in appearance and habitat. It has hairy perigynia and purplish leaf sheaths, but unlike Ross's sedge it lacks the additional stalked spikes near the base of the stem. • Bent sedge (*C. deflexa*) is closely related to Ross's sedge and is sometimes considered the same species.

NOTES: To the Nlaka'pmx, some sedges that occur in the same habitats as bighorn sheep were known as 'mountain sheep plant,' indicating their use as an ecological indicator. • Ross's sedge is named in honour of Sir James Clark Ross (1800–62) who explored the Arctic and Antarctic.

GREEN SEDGE • *Carex viridula*
C. oederi var. *viridula*

GENERAL: Densely tufted, to 40 cm tall, in small clumps with stiff stems; last year's leaves remain conspicuous at base.

LEAVES: Flat to folded, yellowish green, 1–4 mm wide.

INFLORESCENCE: Unisexual spikes; long, narrow **male spike at top of stem**, and 2–6 female spikes below it, each with a **long, leaf-like bract**.

PERIGYNIA: Yellowish green, 2–3 mm long, plump, with many ribs; **spreading at maturity**; scale reddish or straw-coloured, shorter and narrower than perigynium; 3 stigmas.

ECOLOGY: Scattered at low to mid elevations in wetlands, particularly alkaline sites.

SIMILAR SPECIES: Yellow sedge (*C. flava*, **photo on right**) resembles green sedge and is found in similar habitats, but it has larger perigynia (4.5–6 mm long) with longer, **curved beaks**.

Conspectus of large water sedges

species	perigynium	inflorescence	leaves	plant
C. rostrata	inflated, narrowing abruptly to a beak with short teeth	spikes thick, cylindrical and erect	**yellowish-green**; sheaths brown	in clumps from stout, long, scaly rhizomes
C. atherodes	inflated, gradually tapering to a long beak with long teeth	spikes thick, cylindrical and erect	**hairy**; sheaths reddish, hairy, shedding and becoming web-like	in clumps from long, slender, scaly rhizomes
C. aquatilis	small, flattened, egg-shaped, with very short beak	spikes narrow, with short stalks or stalkless, erect	**bluish-green**; sheaths reddish, not shedding	in clumps from stout, long, scaly rhizomes
C. sitchensis	small, flattened, egg-shaped, with very short beak	**lower spikes drooping on long stalks; scales white-tipped**	sheaths reddish, not shedding	tufted, with short rhizomes (sometimes lacking)
C. exsiccata	inflated, **gradually tapering to a long beak**	spikes thick, **reddish**, cylindrical and erect	sheath reddish, shedding and becoming web-like	in clumps from short rhizomes (sometimes lacking)
C. retrorsa	inflated, narrowing abruptly to a beak with short teeth	spikes thick, with long stalks; **perigynia reflexed at maturity**	sheath reddish, shedding and becoming web-like	tufted, from very short rhizomes

SEDGE

BEAKED SEDGE • *Carex rostrata*
C. utriculata

GENERAL: In large clumps, to 120 cm tall, from short stout rhizomes and **long creeping runners**, sometimes forming dense sod; stems thick, bases light brown, spongy, conspicuously clothed with old leaves; **sheaths not shedding nor becoming web-like.**

LEAVES: Upper leaves longer than stems, thick and flat, to 12 mm wide, yellowish green, conspicuously partitioned by **whitish, knot-like crosswalls** between veins.

INFLORESCENCE: Long, cylindrical, unisexual spikes; 2–4 overlapping, male spikes at top of stem with densely flowered, erect female spikes below; lowest bract leaf-like and longer than spikes.

PERIGYNIA: Yellowish green to straw-coloured and **shiny**, egg-shaped and **inflated, with several ribs**, abruptly constricted to a **beak with 2 short points** and **3 stigmas**; spreading at maturity.

ECOLOGY: Widespread and very common at low to mid elevations; prefers perennially wet areas.

SIMILAR SPECIES: Beaked sedge is one of six common species of large water sedges in our region, which all have the same general appearance and smooth perigynia. The characteristics that can be used to distinguish among these species are described in the conspectus on page 343.

NOTES: The Nlaka'pmx ate the fleshy leaf bases of beaked sedge, and they also knew it as muskrat food. Interior native peoples sometimes used it as a brush for cleaning things.

WATER SEDGE • *Carex aquatilis*

GENERAL: Dense clumps, to 1 m tall, from deep-buried, scaly, **cord-like rhizomes**; slender stems, with bases reddish-tinged, surrounded by long brown scales and clothed with old leaves.

LEAVES: Bluish green, flat or somewhat channeled at base, as long as or shorter than stems and up to 8 mm wide.

INFLORESCENCE: Long, cylindrical, unisexual spikes; 1–3 male spikes at top of stem with several **erect female spikes** below; lowest bract is leaf-like and longer than inflorescence.

PERIGYNIA: Small (2–3 mm long), light green, with blackish scales; egg-shaped and **flattened**; with a very short beak and 2 stigmas.

ECOLOGY: Widespread and very common at low elevations to timberline in wetlands.

SIMILAR SPECIES: Water sedge is one of six common species of large water sedges in our region which have the same general appearance. Characteristics that can be used to distinguish among these species are described in the conspectus on page 343.

NOTES: Water sedge and beaked sedge (*C. rostrata*, above) often grow in solid stands in shallow water or very wet soil, forming a dense sod. They are a common component of wetland hay in ranching country, and they are valued as food for waterfowl.

WOOLLY SEDGE • *Carex lanuginosa*

GENERAL: Loose tufts, to 1 m tall, from long, creeping, scaly rhizomes; stems stiff, upright, with reddish bases.

LEAVES: Often longer than stem, **flat** and rough on edges, **2–5 mm wide**.

INFLORESCENCE: Unisexual spikes; 1–3 male spikes at top of stem with 2–3 female spikes widely separated below; lowest bract long and leaf-like.

PERIGYNIA: Leathery, dull brownish green, with a reddish-brown scale, **densely covered with soft hairs**; egg-shaped and inflated, with a **beak divided into 2 slightly spreading points** and 3 stigmas.

ECOLOGY: Common at low to mid elevations in wetlands.

SIMILAR SPECIES: Slender sedge (*C. lasio-carpa*) is similar in appearance and habitat, but it has **narrower** (less than 2 mm wide), **in-rolled leaves**, and its perigynia have two upright, slightly shorter points.

NOTES: The species name *lanuginosa* means 'woolly' or 'downy,' and it refers to the dense covering of soft hairs on the perigynia.

POOR SEDGE • *Carex paupercula*
C. magellanica ssp. *irrigua*

GENERAL: Clustered in tufts, to 80 cm tall, with **many stems** from long slender rhizomes; stems slender, reddish brown and clothed with old leaves at base; **roots covered with yellowish felt**.

LEAVES: Shorter than stem, 2–4 mm wide, **flat**, with **slightly in-rolled edges**.

INFLORESCENCE: Unisexual spikes; short (4–12 mm long), single **male spike at top of stem**, with 3–4 female spikes below, **nodding on long slender stalks**; lowest bract long and leaf-like.

PERIGYNIA: Bluish green to brown and leathery, broadly egg-shaped to elliptic, 3-angled but flattened, with 3 stigmas and **no beak; scales brown, taper to a short point, narrower and longer than perigynia**.

ECOLOGY: Widespread and common at low to subalpine elevations in fens.

SIMILAR SPECIES: Shore sedge (*C. limosa*) and large-awned sedge (*C. macrochaeta*) both have the same characteristic nodding spikes and yellow-felted roots as poor sedge. However, shore sedge has broad-tipped, brown scales covering the perigynia, and large-awned sedge has black scales with long awns (to 1 cm), compared to poor sedge's brown scales with short points (to 1 mm long).

NOTES: Poor sedge is often found growing with shore sedge.

SOFT-LEAVED SEDGE • *Carex disperma*

GENERAL: Loosely tufted, 10–40 cm tall, from long slender **rhizomes; stems very slender and weak, usually nodding**, clothed with old leaves at base.

LEAVES: Narrow (about 1–2 mm wide), **thin and soft**, mostly shorter than stem, light green.

INFLORESCENCE: Very small, greenish, bisexual spikes, well separated from each other; spikes **few-flowered** (2–6) with **male flowers at top of each spike**.

PERIGYNIA: Plump, greenish to brownish and shining at maturity, small (but longer and wider than the whitish-green scales), 2-angled, with a very short beak and 2 stigmas.

ECOLOGY: Widespread and very common at low to mid elevations in moist to wet forests and wetlands.

SIMILAR SPECIES: This species can be confused with ryegrass sedge (*C. loliacea*), which also has few-flowered, well-separated spikes. However, ryegrass sedge spikes have **male flowers at the base** and their strongly lined perigynia spread at right angles to the stem. It occupies similar habitats as soft-leaved sedge but is less common.

DEWEY'S SEDGE • *Carex deweyana*

GENERAL: Loose to dense clumps, 30–80 cm tall, without rhizomes; **stems weak, spreading out from base**.

LEAVES: Thin, flat and soft, 2–5 mm wide, shorter than stems.

INFLORESCENCE: 2–6 **well-separated**, few-flowered, bisexual spikes form a head 2–6 cm long; **male flowers at base of each spike**; lowest spike has a long, narrow bract.

PERIGYNIA: Pale green or tan, flat on 1 side and rounded on the other, about 5 mm long, **tapering to a beak almost half the total length, thin and papery**, thus breaking easily and exposing the seed.

ECOLOGY: Common at low to mid elevations in moist to wet forest edges.

NOTES: Dewey's sedge is distinguished from similar sedges by its well-separated spikes and the long beak on the perigynia.

FIELD SEDGE • *Carex praegracilis*

GENERAL: Many stems, to 70 cm tall, from **stout, black, scaly rhizomes**; old leaf sheaths dark like the rhizomes.

LEAVES: Several, arising from near base of stem, shorter than stem, 1–3 mm wide, flat and firm.

INFLORESCENCE: Oblong head of several closely packed spikes; most plants **unisexual, with only female or only male flowers**; occasionally bisexual spikes with male flowers at top and female flowers below.

PERIGYNIA: Dark brown and leathery at maturity, concealed by a chestnut-coloured scale; flat on 1 side and rounded on the other, tapering to a prominent, narrow beak with 2 stigmas.

ECOLOGY: Scattered at low to mid elevations; common in alkaline meadows.

SIMILAR SPECIES: Douglas's sedge (*C. douglasii*) and hay sedge (*C. siccata*, also known as *C. foenea*) resemble field sedge but are less common. Douglas's sedge has dark slender rhizomes, and hay sedge has fine, light brown rhizomes, compared to the stout, black, scaly rhizomes of field sedge.

PASTURE SEDGE • *Carex petasata*

GENERAL: Densely tufted, to 80 cm tall, without creeping rhizomes; stiffly erect stems.

LEAVES: Narrow and shorter than stems.

INFLORESCENCE: 3–6 overlapping bisexual spikes in a stiff upright head; male flowers at base of each spike.

PERIGYNIA: Brownish green to yellowish brown, narrow, **to 8 mm long**, egg-shaped, with flattened edges, tapering to a long, slender beak with 2 stigmas; **scale light reddish brown, with silvery edges**, concealing perigynium.

ECOLOGY: Common at low to subalpine elevations in grasslands and openings in dry forests.

SIMILAR SPECIES: Meadow sedge (*C. praticola*) resembles pasture sedge but has smaller perigynia (less than 6 mm long) and a slightly nodding head. • Dry-land sedge (*C. xerantica*), a less common species, is similar to pasture sedge in appearance and habitat, but it is rhizomatous and has a perigynium with a more flattened, broadly edged beak.

NOTES: Pasture sedge is usually found as isolated plants scattered among other grassland vegetation.

SLENDER-BEAKED SEDGE • *Carex athrostachya*

GENERAL: Clustered in tufts, 20–90 cm tall, without rhizomes, usually with many stems.

LEAVES: Flat and shorter than stem, 1.5–4 mm wide, usually clustered on lower third of stem.

INFLORESCENCE: Several small, bisexual spikes crowded into a short (1–2 cm) head; male flowers at base of each spike; a **long, leaf-like bract sticks out sideways from base of lowest spike**.

PERIGYNIA: Light green to straw-coloured, **narrow and thin-edged**, tapering to a well-defined beak; scale shorter and narrower than perigynium; 2 stigmas.

ECOLOGY: Widespread at low to mid elevations in moist meadows; often increasing where the soil is disturbed.

SIMILAR SPECIES: Many-headed sedge (*C. sychnocephala*) occurs in similar habitats, but it is less common and has **several leaf-like bracts** that are **much longer than the head**.

NOTES: Slender-beaked sedge is distinguished from other sedges with similar heads by its **single, long, leaf-like bract**, which extends far to the **side of the head**.

CRAWFORD'S SEDGE • *Carex crawfordii*

GENERAL: Densely tufted, to 70 cm tall, without rhizomes; rather stiff stems.

LEAVES: Flat, 1–3 mm wide, from lower part of stem, almost as long as stem.

INFLORESCENCE: Greenish to pale orange; several bisexual spikes crowded into a dense oblong head; **male flowers at base of each spike**.

PERIGYNIA: Slender (less than 1 mm wide), 3–4 times as long as wide, tapering to a long, flat beak with 2 stigmas.

ECOLOGY: Scattered at low to mid elevations on wet to moist sites.

SIMILAR SPECIES: Bebb's sedge (*C. bebbii*) closely resembles this sedge, but it has shorter, wider perigynia (more than 1 mm wide).

NOTES: Its **orange-tinged mass of heads** distinguishes Crawford's sedge from all other sedges. • Crawford's sedge frequently forms large clumps with many stems, and it often grows in profusion on disturbed ground.

TWO-TONED SEDGE • *Carex albonigra*

GENERAL: Loosely tufted, 10–30 cm tall, from short, slender rhizomes; stems stiff, red-tinged and clothed with old leaves at base.

LEAVES: Clustered near base of stem and much shorter than stem, flat, firm, 2–5 mm wide.

INFLORESCENCE: 2–4 **crowded, black spikes** on short stalks; **uppermost spike bisexual, with female flowers at top** and **male flowers at base**; lower spikes with female flowers only.

PERIGYNIA: Dark reddish brown to purplish black, about 3 mm long, **egg-shaped**, **strongly flattened**, abruptly short beaked, with 3 stigmas; **reddish-black scales** with conspicuous pale edges and tips.

ECOLOGY: Widely distributed at alpine and upper subalpine elevations on exposed wind-swept areas.

NOTES: The crowded black spikes and 2-toned scales make this mountain sedge distinctive.

SCANDINAVIAN SEDGE • *Carex media*

GENERAL: Loosely tufted, 10–70 cm tall, from short, slender rhizomes; stems slender and purplish red, with old leaves at base.

LEAVES: Clustered towards base of stem, much shorter than stem, flat, 2–3 mm wide.

INFLORESCENCE: 3–4 **short (3–8 mm) spikes closely packed at top of stem**; uppermost spike bisexual, with male flowers at base; lower spikes with female flowers only.

PERIGYNIA: Bluish green when young, maturing to bronze, with **purplish-black scales**; **2–3 mm long**, oblong to egg-shaped, 3-angled, abruptly short-beaked, with 3 stigmas.

ECOLOGY: Widespread at mid to high elevations in moist shrubby habitats.

SIMILAR SPECIES: Black-scaled sedge (*C. atrosquama*, also known as *C. atrata*) has larger spikes (more than 1 cm long) and larger perigynia (more than 3 mm long) than Scandinavian sedge.

NOTES: Scandinavian sedge was previously included with *C. norvegica*, a species of eastern and southern North America.

349

BLACK ALPINE SEDGE • *Carex nigricans*

GENERAL: Tufted, 5–30 cm tall, **from stout creeping rhizomes**, often forming **hummocky mats**; stems stiff, light brown and clothed with old leaves at base.

LEAVES: Densely packed near base of stem, usually shorter than stem, stiff, 1–2.5 mm wide.

INFLORESCENCE: Solitary, bisexual spike, with **male flowers at top** and female flowers below.

PERIGYNIA: Brownish, with dark brown scales; 3–4.5 mm long, lance- to narrowly egg-shaped, **stalked at base** and tapering at tip into a **short beak** with **3 stigmas**; **spreading at maturity and soon falling off**.

ECOLOGY: Widespread and common in high-elevation wetlands.

SIMILAR SPECIES: Black alpine sedge could be confused with Pyrenean sedge (*C. pyrenaica*, p. 352), but that species lacks a rhizome and has less widely spreading perigynia. • Spikenard sedge (*C. nardina*), another alpine species, has leaves that are longer than its wiry, curved stems, an oblong spike and lance-shaped perigynia that are narrowed to a stubby base.

DUNHEAD SEDGE • *Carex phaeocephala*

GENERAL: Densely tufted, 10–30 cm tall, without rhizomes, often forming large clumps; stems slender but stiff, clothed in **old leaves at base**.

LEAVES: Shorter than stem, stiff and usually channeled, about 2 mm wide.

INFLORESCENCE: 2–6 bisexual spikes crowded into a **stiff, straw-coloured head**; male flowers at base of each spike.

PERIGYNIA: Straw-coloured to dark brown, with **green-winged edges** and a large **reddish-brown scale**; up to 6 mm long, oval to egg-shaped, **flattened**, abruptly tapering into a short beak with 2 stigmas.

ECOLOGY: Common at high elevations on rocky slopes.

SIMILAR SPECIES: Two-parted sedge (*C. bipartita*, also known as *C. lachenalii*) is a similar alpine species of wet tundra and snowbeds. It has 1–4 spikes, and perigynia without winged edges.

SHOWY SEDGE • *Carex spectabilis*

GENERAL: Loosely tufted, 30–80 cm tall, from stout, matted, branching rootstocks; slender stems.

LEAVES: Flat, 2–7 mm wide, arising from lower half of stem, shorter than stem.

INFLORESCENCE: Unisexual spikes; top spike with all male flowers; lower spikes female, usually nodding on slender stalks.

PERIGYNIA: Pale green or blackish-tinged, egg-shaped and flattened, with a stout beak; **dark scale with a conspicuous pale midrib extended into a 1 mm awn**; 3 stigmas.

ECOLOGY: Widely distributed but sporadic in moist subalpine and lower alpine meadows.

SIMILAR SPECIES: Graceful mountain sedge (*C. podocarpa*) is similar in appearance and habitat, but its scales have a barely noticeable midrib that does not extend into an awn. It is more common in the northern part of B.C. • Mertens's sedge (*C. mertensii*) has many more (6–10) large drooping spikes, and it forms large clumps in moist forest openings and disturbed areas at mid to subalpine elevations.

SINGLE-SPIKED SEDGE • *Carex scirpoidea*

GENERAL: Stiff stems, to 40 cm tall, from short, stout, scaly rhizomes.

LEAVES: Firm, flat, to 3 mm wide, arising from near base of stem, shorter than stem.

INFLORESCENCE: Solitary spikes, male and female flowers on separate plants; each spike contains many flowers.

PERIGYNIA: Straw-coloured and **covered with short white hairs**, oval, with a short, slender beak and 3 stigmas; **dark, hairy scale**.

ECOLOGY: Scattered at alpine and higher subalpine elevations.

NOTES: Single-spiked sedge is recognized by its dark, slender, solitary spike, which is either all male or all female.

351

SEDGE

PYRENEAN SEDGE • *Carex pyrenaica*

GENERAL: Small, densely tufted, to 20 cm tall, without rhizomes; stems slender and upright, clothed with **old leaves at base**.

LEAVES: Stiff and hair-like, 1 mm wide and nearly as long as stem.

INFLORESCENCE: Single bisexual spike, with **male flowers at top** and female flowers below.

PERIGYNIA: Dark brown to straw-coloured, glossy, egg-shaped, with a short stalk at base and tapering at tip to a **short beak** with 3 stigmas; scale dark chestnut, shorter and wider than perigynium.

ECOLOGY: Widespread at alpine elevations on rocky exposed sites.

SIMILAR SPECIES: Pyrenean sedge can be confused with the other alpine species that have solitary spikes. • Spikenard sedge (*C. nardina*) also has fine leaves, but the perigynia do not have the extended beak and stalk at the base. • Black alpine sedge (*C. nigricans*, p. 350) has stout, creeping rhizomes and widely spreading perigynia.

BLUNT SEDGE • *Carex obtusata*

GENERAL: Small stems, **10–20 cm tall**, scattered at more or less regular intervals along a slender, **dark rhizome**.

LEAVES: Several per stem, arising from near base, shorter than stem, flat, narrow (about 1 mm wide).

INFLORESCENCE: 1 spike per stem; spikes few-flowered (6 or less), **bisexual**, with male flowers at top and female flowers below.

PERIGYNIA: Dark, leathery, **plump and glossy when mature**, oval and ribbed, about same length as scale; 3 stigmas.

ECOLOGY: Widespread at low to alpine elevations mainly in Cariboo/Chilcotin area, in grasslands and dry, open forests.

SIMILAR SPECIES: Narrow-leaved sedge (*C. eleocharis*, also known as *C. stenophylla*) is somewhat similar in both habitat and appearance, but it has four or more spikes densely clustered into a single head, and it has light brown perigynia.

NOTES: Both blunt sedge and narrow-leaved sedge mature early in the season.

SEDGE

TUFTED CLUBRUSH • *Trichophorum cespitosum*
Scirpus cespitosus

GENERAL: Densely tufted, 10–40 cm tall, from a short rhizome, often **forming tussocks**; stems smooth, slender, circular in cross-section, clothed with leaf sheaths at base.

LEAVES: Several light brown, scale-like leaves at base of stem; **single stem leaf, about 1 cm long**.

INFLORESCENCE: Single, 2–4 flowered spike at top of stem; 2–3 small bracts below inflorescence; midvein of lowest bract prolonged into a blunt awn (about as long as spike).

FRUITS: Brown, oval, 3-angled achenes, **each surrounded by 6 delicate white bristles** about **twice as long (3 mm) as achene**; scales brown.

ECOLOGY: Scattered at low to alpine elevations in peaty wetlands.

SIMILAR SPECIES: Hudson Bay clubrush (*T. alpinum*, also known as *Scirpus hudsonianus*) has stems that arise in a row from a short rhizome, and the perigynium is surrounded by six white bristles that are much longer (to 2.5 cm long).

NOTES: Clubrush derives its name from the shape of its inflorescence. The Latin *Trichophorum* means 'hair-carrier,' referring to the long bristles surrounding the fruits. The species name *cespitosum* means 'tufted,' which describes the growth form of the plant.

BELLARD'S KOBRESIA • *Kobresia myosuroides*
K. bellardii

GENERAL: Densely tufted in **compact clumps**, 5–40 cm tall, sometimes forming large mats; stems slender and wiry; many **old brown sheaths at base of stems**.

LEAVES: Very narrow (about 0.5 mm) and wiry, equalling or somewhat shorter than stems.

INFLORESCENCE: Solitary, narrow spikes, 1–3 cm long, seldom more than 2 mm thick; each spikelet with a female and a male flower.

FRUITS: Shiny brown, oval achenes, **loosely wrapped by light brown scales**; 3 stigmas.

ECOLOGY: Scattered on dry alpine sites.

NOTES: This plant is easily mistaken for a sedge (*Carex* sp.), but it can be distinguished by the exposed achenes and conspicuous brown leaf sheaths. The small scales that partially wrap the achenes are similar to the perigynia of true sedges, but they do not completely enclose the achene.

NARROW-LEAVED COTTON-GRASS • *Eriophorum angustifolium* E. *polystachion*

GENERAL: Stems to 70 cm tall, arising singly or a few together from widely **spreading rhizomes**; stems rounded, clothed at base with dark brown sheaths.

LEAVES: Both at base and along stem; flat below middle, **triangular and channeled toward tip**, 2–6 mm wide.

INFLORESCENCE: 2–8 drooping, **cottony spikelets** at top of stem; 2 or more **long leafy bracts** below inflorescence.

FRUITS: Dark brown to black, 3-angled achenes, each surrounded by **many, long (2–3.5 cm) white bristles**, and with a brownish or greyish scale at base, **slender midrib of scale not reaching tip**.

ECOLOGY: Widespread and common at low to high elevations in peaty wetlands.

SIMILAR SPECIES: Green-keeled cotton-grass (*E. viridi-carinatum*) closely resembles this species in appearance and habitat, but its bracts are shorter than the inflorescence, and the midrib of the scale extends to its tip. • Chamisso's cotton-grass (*E. chamissonis*) is distinguished from other single-headed cotton-grasses by the rust-coloured bristles and spreading rhizomes.

NOTES: The Nlaka'pmx used a decoction of this plant as a medicine for ulcers. • The long bristles surrounding the achene, the remnants of sepals and petals, form the distinctive cottony tufts that give the cotton-grasses their common and botanical names. The genus name *Eriophorum* is Latin for 'wool-bearer.'

COMMON SPIKE-RUSH • *Eleocharis palustris*

GENERAL: Perennial, usually 20–80 cm tall; stems round, arising singly or in clusters from long, **creeping rhizomes**; often growing in dense stands.

LEAVES: All basal, reduced to mere sheaths.

INFLORESCENCE: Solitary spikelet at top of stem, **covered with several overlapping scales**; lowest scales are empty; upper ones each cover an achene and a male flower.

FRUITS: Small (1.5–2.5 mm long), egg-shaped achenes, with a distinct **pyramidal cap at top**, surrounded by **4 white, barbed bristles**, each slightly longer than achene; 2 stigmas.

ECOLOGY: Widespread at low to mid elevations in wetlands; often in alkaline sites.

SIMILAR SPECIES: Needle spike-rush (*E. acicularis*) and few-flowered spike-rush (*E. quinqueflora*, also known as *E. rostellata*) are shorter, with fewer flowers per spikelet, and they have three stigmas.

NOTES: Common spike-rush is widespread throughout the cool regions of the Northern Hemisphere. • The Okanagan used common spike-rush as bedding, for pillows and as a ground cover in sweathouses. • The species name *palustris* means 'marsh-loving.'

GREAT BULRUSH • *Scirpus lacustris*

GENERAL: Stout, red-scaly, **rhizomatous perennial**, to 3 m tall; stems round, 1–2 cm thick at base and tapering to top; often growing in dense stands.

LEAVES: Few, all basal, mostly reduced to brownish sheaths.

INFLORESCENCE: Flowers borne in **many compact brown spikelets**, clustered at ends of short, recurving branches; a **single long bract at base of inflorescence** appears to be an extension of stem.

FRUITS: Many small, shiny **achenes**, about 2 mm long, each **surrounded by fragile hooked bristles**, and covered by a reddish-brown or pale grey scale.

ECOLOGY: Common at low to mid elevations in wetlands with standing water.

SIMILAR SPECIES: Alkali bulrush (*S. maritimus*), Nevada bulrush (*S. nevadensis*) and American bulrush (*S. americanus*) are all similar in appearance and habitat, but they are usually much shorter than great bulrush, and they have inflorescences of a few stalkless spikelets. • Great bulrush includes two subspecies—hard-stemmed bulrush (*S. lacustris* ssp. *glaucus*, also known as *S. acutus*), which has greyish-brown spikelets and stems that are not easily crushed between the fingers, and soft-stemmed bulrush (*S. lacustris* ssp. *validus*, also known as *S. validus*), which has reddish-brown spikelets and soft stems that are easily crushed between the fingers.

NOTES: Interior native peoples used this bulrush, sewn together with stinging nettle or hemp fibre, to make mats and roofs and wall-coverings for summer lodges or tents. Bulrush mats were also used for drying berries and as ground-covers on which to eat. • The abundant nut-like seeds produced by bulrush stands are an important food source for waterfowl. • This species is also known as tule.

SMALL-FLOWERED BULRUSH • *Scirpus microcarpus*
S. sylvaticus

GENERAL: Robust, **leafy-stemmed perennial**, to 1.5 m tall, from a sturdy **rhizome**; stout, **triangular stems**, usually in a cluster.

LEAVES: From base and stem, flat to somewhat keeled, 1–1.5 cm wide; **leaf sheaths often purplish-tinged**.

INFLORESCENCE: Many short spikelets **in small clusters at end of spreading branches**; **several leaf-like bracts** below inflorescence.

FRUITS: Pale, lens-shaped **achenes**, each **surrounded by 4–6 bristles** and covered by greenish-black scales.

ECOLOGY: Common at low to mid elevations in wetlands.

NOTES: Interior native peoples, especially the Okanagan, used this bulrush to weave light baskets for carrying berries and roots. • 'Bulrush' is a corruption of 'pole-rush' or 'pool-rush' (describing the habitat of the plant). The genus name *Scirpus* is from an ancient name for rush-like plants. The common name 'small-flowered' is a translation of the species name *microcarpus*.

BALTIC RUSH • *Juncus balticus*
J. arcticus ssp. *ater*

GENERAL: Robust perennial, 10–80 cm tall, with **rows of stems** from a **thick horizontal rhizome;** stems **rounded in cross-section.**

LEAVES: All basal, mostly reduced to pointy-tipped sheaths.

INFLORESCENCE: Many flowers in a loose, short-branched inflorescence clustered **on 1 side of stem;** a **long** (5–20 cm) **rounded bract** at base of inflorescence appears to be a continuation of stem.

FRUITS: Oval **capsules,** with a small tip and many small seeds.

ECOLOGY: Scattered and infrequent at low to mid elevations, often in saline or alkaline wetlands; locally common on Fraser Plateau.

SIMILAR SPECIES: Thread rush (*J. filiformis*) grows in similar habitats, but the bract of its inflorescence is longer (about as long as the stem). • Chestnut rush (*J. castaneus*) is often found in similar habitats. It has leaves along the stem and large chestnut-brown capsules.

NOTES: The long bract below the inflorescence, plus the many flowers per stem, help distinguish Baltic rush from other rushes. • The Blackfoot of Alberta obtained a brownish-green dye from the stems of this plant.

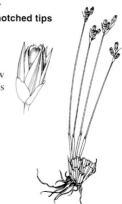

DRUMMOND'S RUSH • *Juncus drummondii*

GENERAL: Perennial, 5–40 cm tall, in **small mats** of tufted stems from **short rhizomes;** stems **rounded in cross-section.**

LEAVES: All basal, reduced to sheaths with short bristle tips.

INFLORESCENCE: 1–4 flowers, loosely grouped together at **top of each stem;** short bract (1–2 cm) **at base of inflorescence** appears to be a continuation of stem.

FRUITS: Capsules, with **rounded, notched tips** and many small seeds.

ECOLOGY: Common on moist sites at mid to high elevations.

NOTES: The short bract and the few flowers per stem help distinguish this species from other low rushes.

MERTENS'S RUSH • *Juncus mertensianus*

GENERAL: Perennial, **10–25 cm tall**, with closely clustered stems from **creeping rhizomes**; stems **oval in cross-section**.

LEAVES: 1–4 per stem, semicircular, with **2 rounded, membranous ears** (1–2 mm long) at base of leaf.

INFLORESCENCE: Single, dark, spherical head at top of stem; many-flowered, each flower with 6 **deep brown, pointed petals**.

FRUITS: Small, **dark capsules**, with many tiny seeds.

ECOLOGY: Common at mid to alpine elevations in wet areas.

NOTES: The **single head** at the top of the stem distinguishes Mertens's rush from other rush species. • This species was named for Karl Franz Mertens (1764–1831), a German botanist.

SPIKED WOOD-RUSH • *Luzula spicata*

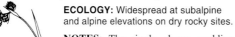

GENERAL: Perennial, usually less than 40 cm tall; **stems solitary or in small tufts**, round in cross-section.

LEAVES: Narrow (1–4 mm), with a **fringe of fine hairs at base**.

INFLORESCENCE: Single, spike-like cluster, 1–3 cm long, usually **nodding on a slender stalk**; flowers with **6 dark brown petals** that taper to fine points, and a **strongly fringed bract** at base.

FRUITS: Dark capsules, each containing 3 small seeds.

ECOLOGY: Widespread at subalpine and alpine elevations on dry rocky sites.

NOTES: The single, dense, nodding head distinguishes spiked wood-rush from all other rushes in our region.

PIPER'S WOOD-RUSH • *Luzula piperi*
L. wahlenbergii ssp. *piperi*

GENERAL: Perennial, usually less than 30 cm tall, from a short rhizome; **stems solitary or in small tufts**, round in cross-section.

LEAVES: Flat and flexible, found at base of plant and (2–3) along stem; **less than 5 mm wide.**

INFLORESCENCE: Solitary flowers, with 6 **purplish-brown petals**, in a nodding, open inflorescence; each flower with a **finely fringed bract** at its base.

FRUITS: Small (less than 2.5 mm long), **dark capsules**, each with 3 small seeds.

ECOLOGY: Common at alpine and higher subalpine elevations on moist sites.

SIMILAR SPECIES: Piper's wood-rush is shorter than small-flowered wood-rush (*L. parviflora*, below) and has fewer, narrower leaves and more shredded, frilly bracts. • Smooth wood-rush (*L. hitchcockii*), another high-elevation species, is quite similar, but it has a longer capsule (2.8–3.8 mm long) with a distinct beak.

NOTES: The genus name *Luzula* is from *Gramen luzulae,* an ancient Latin name that means 'grass of light,' supposedly because of the tendency for the plants to shine when covered with dew. This species was named for Charles Vancouver Piper (1867–1953), an agrologist with the U.S.D.A. and the author of *The Flora of Washington*.

SMALL-FLOWERED WOOD-RUSH • *Luzula parviflora*

GENERAL: Perennial, 20–80 cm tall, from a rhizome; **stems solitary or in small tufts**, **round in cross-section**, sometimes tending to become horizontal.

LEAVES: Both basal and (**4 or more**) along stem, **large (0.5–1 cm wide)** and flat, with a few long white hairs on edges.

INFLORESCENCE: Solitary flowers, with 6 **purplish-brown petals** in a nodding, open inflorescence.

FRUITS: Brown **capsules**, each with 3 small seeds.

ECOLOGY: Widespread and common at mid to high elevations in open forests and disturbed sites.

NOTES: This species can be distinguished from other open-flowered wood-rushes by its height (usually more than 30 cm) and by the presence of four or more broad stem leaves. • 'Rush' is from the Old English *rysc*, from a German word meaning 'to bind' or 'to plait.' Rushes were often braided into mats.

SEASIDE ARROW-GRASS • *Triglochin maritimum*

GENERAL: Perennial, 20–120 cm tall, **from a stout, often woody rhizome**, often covered with whitish fibrous remains of old leaf bases, sometimes forming large clumps; flowering stems leafless.

LEAVES: All basal, upright to spreading, **long and linear,** rounded to **somewhat flattened,** hairless, with sheathing bases.

FLOWERS: Small, inconspicuous and greenish, but with 6 feathery, reddish stigmas, 6 flower scales and 6 stamens; short-stalked and numerous in a long, narrow, spike-like cluster, often as much as half the plant's total length.

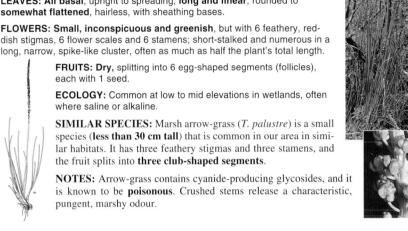

FRUITS: Dry, splitting into 6 egg-shaped segments (follicles), each with 1 seed.

ECOLOGY: Common at low to mid elevations in wetlands, often where saline or alkaline.

SIMILAR SPECIES: Marsh arrow-grass (*T. palustre*) is a small species (**less than 30 cm tall**) that is common in our area in similar habitats. It has three feathery stigmas and three stamens, and the fruit splits into **three club-shaped segments**.

NOTES: Arrow-grass contains cyanide-producing glycosides, and it is known to be **poisonous**. Crushed stems release a characteristic, pungent, marshy odour.

CATTAIL • *Typha latifolia*

GENERAL: Perennial, to 2 m tall or more, with coarse **rhizomes**; flowering stems **stiff, cylindrical, pithy** at centre.

LEAVES: Flat, slender, long and somewhat spongy.

FLOWERS: Tiny, numerous, borne in a densely crowded, **cylindrical spike at top of stem;** lower portion **dark brown and velvety,** bearing female flowers; upper portion cone-shaped, bearing male flowers, disintegrates to leave a section of bare stem.

FRUITS: Dry, ellipsoid seeds, with **many long slender hairs** at base.

ECOLOGY: Scattered and locally abundant at low to mid elevations in wetlands with slow-moving or standing water.

SIMILAR SPECIES: Great bulrush (*Scirpus lacustris*, p. 355) grows in similar habitats and often forms large colonies, like cattail, but it has open flower clusters and lacks the wide, flat leaves.

NOTES: Cattail often forms dense, exclusive patches. You can recognize it easily by its tall stalks topped by 'cattail' inflorescences. • This species provides important habitat and food for many marsh animals, including wrens, blackbirds, waterfowl and muskrats. • The Nlaka'pmx, Okanagan, Lil'wet'ul and Tsilhqot'in ate the starchy rhizomes, leaf blades and young flower spikes and peeled and ate the white lower stem. • Other native uses were for making mats for bedding, sitting or kneeling on in canoes, as insulation for winter homes, or for capes, hats, blankets or bags. Cattail seed fluff was used as stuffing for pillows and mattresses, as wound dressing and for diapers. • The sticky juice found between cattail leaves may be rubbed on the gums to relieve toothaches.

Ferns and Their Allies

This section describes of a fairly diverse group of plants referred to as the ferns and their 'allies.' These are vascular plants, so they have internal tubes for transporting fluids (in common with all other plants in this guide except the bryophytes and lichens). However, they reproduce not by seeds but by spores (in common with the bryophytes and lichens). This places them in a position morphologically intermediate between flowering plants and bryophytes.

Reproduction in this group of plants is a complex and intriguing process. The ordinary green fern plant represents an asexual (sporophyte) generation. It produces minute spores that germinate to form small, inconspicuous plants (thalli) that are the sexual (gametophyte) generation. These thalli, which are rarely seen by most people, bear the sex organs that produce the eggs and the swimming sperm that fertilize the eggs on the same plant. The fertilized eggs give rise to the leafy green plant we recognize as a fern, thus completing the cycle.

Because this group of plants depends on swimming sperm for sexual reproduction, most species require moist environments. Those that have evolved to inhabit drier environments have done so by reproducing during seasons when moisture (from dew and rainfall) are likely to be most plentiful.

Key to the ferns and their allies

1a. Leaves pinnatifid (divided or cut into many segments, or lobes on 2 sides of a common axis), feather-like or fan-shaped .... **ferns** (below)

1b. Leaves simple and small 2

    2a. Branches and leaves whorled; stems ribbed and jointed .... **horsetails** (p. 370)

    2b. Branches and leaves alternate or opposite; stem not ribbed .. **clubmosses and spikemosses** (p. 373)

Ferns

The ferns can be divided into five major groups, only two of which, the adder's-tongues and the 'true' ferns, are common in our area.

Ferns in the adder's-tongue family—grape ferns (*Botrychium* spp.) in our region—are relatively small, and they have fleshy roots and short, vertical, underground stems (**rhizomes**). Their single leaf (**frond**) is divided into a sterile expanded blade and a branched, leafless, fertile blade. The spore sacs (**sporangia**) are globe-shaped and are borne in grape-like clusters on the fertile stalk, rather than on green leaves as in most of the true ferns. The genus name *Botrychium* is from the Greek *botryos* (a bunch of grapes), in reference to the clustered spore sacs.

True ferns have creeping or erect rhizomes, which are often very scaly, and often large, stalked, erect or spreading leaves. The leaf blades are curled as buds (in 'fiddleheads') and they are usually lobed or divided or variously compound. The fertile and sterile leaves are usually alike, but they are dissimilar in some genera. The spore sacs are grouped together in **sori**, which are sometimes enclosed or covered by a membranous **indusium**.

At first glance many ferns appear quite similar, especially those with clumps of lance-shaped, pinnately divided leaves, but the shape of the blades and leaflets and the number of times the blades are divided can help separate the species. Confident identification, however, often requires an examination of the reproductive structures. The shape and location of the sori, presence or absence of an indusium and its point of attachment are usually good diagnostic features. The absence of an indusium should be interpreted with caution, however, as these structures often fall off older leaves.

Key to the fern genera

1a. Spore sacs in clusters on a leafless stalk that projects from upper side of leaf .... *Botrychium*

1b. Spore sacs borne on underside of leaves, or on separate, modified, fertile leaves (true ferns) 2

2a. Leaves of 2 distinct types; spore sacs on separate leaves 3

> **3a.** Fertile leaves shorter and less divided
> than sterile leaves, eventually dark brown .... *Matteucia*

> **3b.** Fertile leaves taller than sterile leaves, remaining green 4

>> **4a.** Leaves once pinnately divided .... *Blechnum*

>> **4b.** Leaves 2–3 times pinnate;
>> sterile leaves parsley-like .... *Cryptogramma*

2b. Leaves of 1 type, fertile and sterile leaves similar 5

> **5a.** Spore sacs in clusters (sori) along leaflet edges,
> covered (at least when young) by rolled-under edge of leaflet 6

>> **6a.** Sori distinct; indusium (protective
>> membrane over sori) formed by rolled-under
>> flaps of pinnules (ultimate divisions of leaf) .... *Adiantum*

>> **6b.** Sori continuous; indusium formed
>> by continuous rolled-under edge .... *Pteridium*

> **5b.** Sori not along leaflet edges, naked or covered by indusia 7

>> **7a.** Sori naked, indusia absent or reduced to slender, inconspicuous rays 8

>>> **8a.** Frond evergreen, merely pinnately lobed,
>>> not divided all the way into leaflets .... *Polypodium*

>>> **8b.** Fronds deciduous, 2-4 times pinnate 9

>>>> **9a.** Leaves in dense tufts, covered at base
>>>> with conspicuous, persistent bases of stipes of past years 10

>>>>> **10a.** Sori elongate; leaves relatively large
>>>>> (2–8 cm long), forming a vase-like tuft;
>>>>> base of stalk coarse, flattened, 3 mm wide or more .... *Athyrium*

>>>>> **10b.** Sori round; leaves smaller (0.5–3.5 cm long),
>>>>> not forming vase-like tuft; base of stalk slender
>>>>> and wiry, not more than 2 mm wide .... *Woodsia*

>>>> **9b.** Leaves scattered or in small tufts, lacking
>>>> conspicuous, persistent leaf stalk bases of past years 11

>>>>> **11a.** Leaves 2–3 times pinnate, hairless,
>>>>> lacking fringe of hairs on edges .... *Gymnocarpium*

>>>>> **11b.** Leaves 1–2 times pinnate,
>>>>> hairy along main axis and midribs,
>>>>> with fringe of hairs on edges .... *Thelypteris*

>> **7b.** Sori covered (at least when young) by indusia 12

>>> **12a.** Indusium long, flap-like, attached along the edge .... *Athyrium*

>>> **12b.** Indusium attached at a point 13

>>>> **13a.** Indusium circular, centrally attached;
>>>> leaves evergreen, often sharp-toothed .... *Polystichum*

>>>> **13b.** Indusium attached on the side;
>>>> leaves deciduous or evergreen 14

>>>>> **14a.** Indusium hood-like, delicate, soon
>>>>> shrivelling, its free tip thrown back as sori mature .... *Cystopteris*

>>>>> **14b**. Indusium kidney- or horseshoe-shaped 15

>>>>>> **15a.** Leaves twice pinnate, hairy at least
>>>>>> along main axis and midveins; indusium
>>>>>> (when present) small and inconspicuous .... *Thelypteris*

>>>>>> **15b.** Leaves 2–3 times pinnate, hairless or
>>>>>> merely scaly, not hairy; indusium well
>>>>>> developed and persistent .... *Dryopteris*

BRACKEN • *Pteridium aquilinum*

GENERAL: Large, solitary leaves (often in dense colonies), to 2 m tall, from deep, spreading, much-branched, hairy rhizomes.

LEAVES: Sterile and fertile leaves alike, **deciduous**; stalks stout, straw-coloured to greenish, smooth, **longer than blades**; blades **triangular, 2–3 times pinnately divided** into round-toothed leaflets with **edges rolled under.**

SORI: Continuous along leaflet edges, partly covered by rolled-under leaf edges; **indusium not evident.**

ECOLOGY: Scattered and locally common at low to mid elevations, mostly in moist and wet climates, in pastures, roadsides, moist forests, openings and clearings; often weedy.

NOTES: Bracken is one of the most widespread vascular plants on our planet. It is a very aggressive weedy species that often invades disturbed areas. • **Caution: may be poisonous.** Although bracken fiddleheads are popular with the Japanese, they have been implicated in livestock poisonings and stomach cancer, so they probably should not be eaten. Furthermore, a South American study found a three-fold higher incidence of gastric cancer in humans who drank untreated milk from cattle that habitually ingested bracken. • Both the Lil'wet'ul and Lower Nlaka'pmx who live close to the Coast ate the long, black rhizomes, but Interior peoples did not. The rhizomes were roasted until the outer skin was burned off and then pounded to separate the whitish edible part. It was eaten like candy or in loaves. Some Secwepemc people used bracken to cover berry baskets and as a bedding in camp.

OAK FERN • *Gymnocarpium dryopteris*

GENERAL: Usually **solitary leaves** (but often in large continuous colonies), to 35 cm tall, from slender, long creeping rhizomes with a few brown scales.

LEAVES: Sterile and fertile leaves **alike, deciduous**; stalks shiny, straw-coloured, with scaly bases; blades **broadly triangular, 2–3 times pinnate** into **rounded leaflets; lowest pair of main branches triangular** and asymmetrical, with 2 basal segments noticeably larger than others.

SORI: Small, **circular**, borne on undersides of leaflets; **indusium absent.**

ECOLOGY: Widespread and common at low to subalpine elevations throughout our moist and wet climates; often abundant in moist seepage forests and openings.

NOTES: Oak fern is characteristic of moist forest sites. • The Okanagan dipped the leaves in water and used them to cover food being cooked in pits. • Oak fern's spreading rhizome makes it very amenable to transplanting. Small pieces of rhizome dug from the wild transplant easily into moist shady gardens. • The genus name *Gymnocarpium* means 'naked fruit,' because the sori lack an indusium. The close relationship of oak fern to the genus *Dryopteris* is reflected by its species name, and some taxonomists even include it in that genus under the name *Dryopteris disjuncta*. The common name 'oak fern' is a translation of *dryopteris*.

LADY FERN • *Athyrium filix-femina*

GENERAL: Many erect to spreading leaves in a **vase-like cluster**, to 1.5 m tall, with old leaf stalks at base, from a **stout, scaly rhizome**.

LEAVES: Leaves all fertile, deciduous; stalks short, **fragile, with scaly bases**; blades **soft**, narrowly to broadly lance-shaped, **tapering at both ends (with a diamond-shaped profile)**, pinnately divided 2–3 times.

SORI: Elongate and curved, borne on undersides of leaflets, partly covered by a **flap-like indusium** attached at side of sorus.

ECOLOGY: Widespread and locally abundant at low to subalpine elevations, mostly in Coast/Interior Transition and wet Columbia Mountains, in moist to wet forests, thickets, openings, slide tracks, streambanks, meadows and clearings.

SIMILAR SPECIES: Lady fern is similar to spiny wood fern (*Dryopteris expansa*, below), but the leaves of that species are broadly triangular in outline, with the blade not tapering to the base. • Alpine lady fern (*A. distentifolium*, also known as *A. alpestre*) is smaller (to 80 cm tall) and has more crowded, finely dissected leaflets and an inconspicuous indusium. Alpine lady fern is a high-elevation species, and it occurs in our region in the southern Columbia Mountains.

NOTES: The Nlaka'pmx used lady fern as a medicine. They ate the fiddleheads, boiled, baked or raw with grease, in early spring. • Lady fern is an excellent fern for moist gardens. • The genus name *Athyrium* is Greek for 'without a shield,' perhaps because the indusium is ultimately forced open. The species name *filix-femina* means 'lady fern,' and at one time it was believed to sneak around at night to mate with male fern (*Dryopteris filix-mas*).

SPINY WOOD FERN • *Dryopteris expansa*
D. assimilis, D. austriaca, D. dilatata

GENERAL: Clusters of somewhat evergreen leaves, to 1 m tall, from a stout rhizome with large papery scales.

LEAVES: Sterile and fertile leaves **alike, mostly deciduous**; stalks short, with scaly bases; blades **broadly triangular**, egg-shaped or broadly oblong, **3 times pinnate**, with **stiffly toothed leaflets; lowest leaflet pair broadly triangular and asymmetrical**, with 2 basal segments noticeably larger than the others.

SORI: Rounded, on undersides of leaflets, partially covered by a rounded indusium attached at side of sorus.

ECOLOGY: Widespread and locally abundant at low to subalpine elevations, most often in East Kootenays and wet Columbia Mountains, in moist to wet forests, thickets, openings, slide tracks, streambanks, meadows and clearings.

SIMILAR SPECIES: Lady fern (*Athyrium filix-femina*, above) can be distinguished from spiny wood fern by its diamond-shaped leaf outline. Also, the secondary leaflets of spiny wood fern are noticeably longer on the lower side of the primary leaflet. • Male fern (*D. filix-mas*) is a large fern with deciduous leaves that are 1–2 times pinnate and have a broadly lance-shaped outline similar to that of lady fern. Male fern occurs sporadically at low to mid elevations in the Selkirk Mountains, on wooded slopes and in avalanche track thickets and shaded talus.

NOTES: The creeping stems of spiny wood fern were an extremely important starch for many Interior native groups, especially the Nlaka'pmx, Lil'wet'ul and Tsilhqot'in. They were dug in autumn or early spring, baked in pits overnight and then peeled like bananas and eaten. They taste a little like coconut. • Spiny wood fern enjoys a cool, moist site in the home garden. • Spiny wood fern is also called shield fern.

OSTRICH FERN • *Matteucia struthiopteris*

GENERAL: Large, **vase-shaped clumps**, to 2 m tall, with old leaf stalks at base, from deep, creeping rhizomes with many brown scales; a circle of **tall sterile leaves** surrounds **shorter fertile leaves**.

LEAVES: Sterile and fertile leaves **markedly different, deciduous**; stalks dark green to black; **sterile blades lance-shaped, tapering at both ends** and **pinnately divided** into pinnately lobed leaflets; **fertile leaves** shorter, becoming dry, **stiff and dark brown**, persisting through winter; fertile blades **oblong**, **once divided** into crowded pairs of **pod-like leaflets**, with **edges rolled under**.

SORI: Elongated, on undersides of leaflets, **covered by rolled-under leaf edges**; indusium is hood-like, but soon deciduous.

ECOLOGY: Widely scattered and locally abundant at low elevations in moist to wet forests along major streams and rivers and at edges of swamps and lakes.

NOTES: Of all our ferns, the fiddleheads of the ostrich fern are the largest, tastiest and safest to eat. • Ostrich fern is used extensively in gardens throughout North America, and it is generally available from nurseries. It thrives best in moist shady locations rich in humus where it often 'seeds' itself. • The genus *Matteucia* is named for Italian physicist Carlo Matteuci (1800–68). The common name 'ostrich fern' refers to the plume-like appearance of the sterile leaf.

MOUNTAIN HOLLY FERN • *Polystichum lonchitis*

GENERAL: Close **clusters of leaves**, to 60 cm tall, with old leaf stalks at base, from a stout, chaffy rhizome.

LEAVES: Sterile and fertile leaves **alike**, shiny, **evergreen and leathery**; stalks very short (about 1/6 the length of blade, or less) with abundant brown scales; blades **narrow and linear**, **pinnately divided** into many, pointed **leaflets with sharp, spine-like teeth** (holly-like); lower leaflets nearly triangular in outline.

SORI: Large and **circular, usually in 2 rows** on undersides of leaflets, partly covered by a large, centrally attached, round indusium with irregularly toothed edges.

ECOLOGY: Scattered and infrequent at mid to high elevations in wet Columbia Mountains, in rock crevices, shaded talus and rocky slopes.

SIMILAR SPECIES: The holly ferns (*Polystichum* spp.) are mostly big, tufted evergreen ferns with round sori that have centrally attached indusia. • Braun's holly fern (*P. braunii*) has bipinnate leaves, and it is found sporadically in moist (especially deciduous) woods, shaded rocky slopes and streamsides at low to subalpine elevations in the southeastern part of our region. • Kruckeberg's holly fern (*P. kruckebergii*) is smaller than mountain holly fern and its leaflets are conspicuously cleft on the upper edge. It is widely scattered in our region on ultrabasic rock outcrops. It is thought to be a self-perpetuating hybrid of mountain holly fern and Lemmon's holly fern (*P. lemmonii*), which principally occurs south of our region, also on ultrabasic rock outcrops.

NOTES: Holly ferns are difficult to grow, and as most are quite uncommon, they are best left in the wild. • The name 'holly fern' refers to the prickly, spear- or lance-shaped leaves of these species. The genus name *Polystichum* means 'many-rows,' referring to the sori, and the species name *lonchitis* refers to the lance-shaped leaves.

WESTERN LICORICE FERN • *Polypodium hesperium* P. vulgare var. columbianum

GENERAL: Scattered leaves, to 20 cm tall, from a thick, creeping, reddish-brown, scaly, sweet, **licorice-flavoured rhizome**.

LEAVES: Sterile and fertile leaves **alike, evergreen**; stalks **smooth**, straw-coloured, usually shorter than blades; blades lance-shaped, pinnately divided into leaflets with **rounded tips** and fairly smooth edges.

SORI: Oval to round, **in 2 rows** on either side of main vein on undersides of leaflets; **indusium absent**.

ECOLOGY: Widely scattered and infrequent at low to mid elevations in moist and wet climates, on dry to moist rock faces and crevices.

NOTES: *Polypodium* ferns have evergreen leaves that (for a fern) are relatively little-divided. The genus name is derived from *poly*, 'many,' and *podium*, 'a foot,' and refers to the creeping, hairy rhizomes, which look like animal feet, found in several species in this genus.

DEER FERN • *Blechnum spicant*

GENERAL: Clusters of spreading sterile leaves and erect fertile leaves, 20–80 cm tall, from a short, stout rhizome.

LEAVES: Sterile and fertile leaves **different**; **sterile leaves** often **pressed to the ground, evergreen and leathery**, on purplish-brown stalks; sterile blades **linear**, tapered at both ends, **pinnately divided** into oblong leaflets; **fertile leaves** similar but often longer, **upright, deciduous**, with much **narrower leaflets** (to 2 mm wide) **with edges rolled under**.

SORI: In continuous lines on both sides of midribs on undersides of leaflets, protected by a **continuous, translucent, brown indusium** attached close to leaflet edge.

ECOLOGY: Infrequent at low to mid elevations in Coast/Interior Transition and Revelstoke area of wet Columbia Mountains, in moist and wet forests and under alders in wet slide areas; occasionally in bogs.

NOTES: This fern is more abundant in wet forests of the Coast than in our area. • On the west coast of Vancouver Island, the leaves were used as a medicine for skin sores, a use said by Hesquiat elders to have been learned by watching deer rub their antler stubs on this plant after their antlers had fallen off. • Although deer fern is relatively easily propagated from spores and transplanted young plants, its scarceness in the Interior and its rigid climatic requirements dictate that it is best enjoyed in the wild. • The name 'deer fern' comes from its importance as a major winter food source for animals in coastal areas. The genus name *Blechnum* is from the Greek name for a fern. The species name *spicant* means 'tufted,' referring to the way the leaves arise from the same point as a tuft.

OREGON WOODSIA • *Woodsia oregana*

GENERAL: Clusters of leaves, to 30 cm tall, **with old leaf stalks** at base, from short, creeping, scaly rhizomes.

LEAVES: Sterile and fertile leaves **alike, deciduous**; stalks short, stiff, brown near base, straw-coloured upwards, shorter than blades; blades **lance-shaped, tapering at both ends**, 1–2 times pinnately divided into **hairless**, round–toothed leaflets.

SORI: Round, on undersides of leaflets, partially enclosed by minute, deeply divided, **thread-like indusium** centrally attached below sorus.

ECOLOGY: Scattered and often common at low to high elevations on dry cliffs, crevices, rock slides and talus slopes (often of calcareous materials).

SIMILAR SPECIES: Rocky Mountain woodsia (*W. scopulina*, below) is found in similar habitats. It has many white hairs and stalked glands on the lower surface of its blades, and it has more closely and evenly spaced leaflets than Oregon woodsia. • Oregon woodsia may also be confused with fragile fern (*Cystopteris fragilis*, p. 367) which lacks the conspicuous, persistent leaf stalks and has crescent-shaped, hooded indusia.

NOTES: The Secwepemc used the leaves of Oregon woodsia and other ferns to pack down berries in their baskets and prevent them from spilling. The Okanagan considered this and other ferns to indicate water.

ROCKY MOUNTAIN WOODSIA • *Woodsia scopulina*

GENERAL: Clusters of brittle leaves, to 40 cm tall, with **persistent old leaf stalks** at base, from shallowly creeping rhizomes covered with **hair-tipped scales**.

LEAVES: Sterile and fertile leaves **alike, deciduous**; stalks **short, stiff**, brown near base, straw-coloured upwards, shorter than blades; blades **oblong, lance-shaped, tapering at both ends**, 1–2 times pinnately divided into densely to sparsely **white-hairy and glandular leaflets**.

SORI: Rounded, on undersides of leaflets, partially enclosed by arms of a deeply **linear-lobed indusium** centrally attached below sorus.

ECOLOGY: Scattered and locally common at low to high elevations, mostly throughout southern half of our region, on dry cliffs, crevices, rock slides and talus slopes.

SIMILAR SPECIES: Oregon woodsia (*W. oregana*, above) and fragile fern (*Cystopteris fragilis*, p. 367) are similar. See the notes under Oregon woodsia for their distinguishing features.

NOTES: The creeping stems of Rocky Mountain woodsia were eaten by some Interior peoples. • The genus *Woodsia* is named in honour of English botanist Joseph Woods (1776–1864). The species name *scopulina* (of the rocks or cliffs) describes the habitat of this fern.

FRAGILE FERN • *Cystopteris fragilis*

GENERAL: Leaves **usually clustered**, to 30 cm tall, from short, densely scaly rhizomes.

LEAVES: Sterile and fertile leaves **alike, deciduous**; stalks short, brittle, **straw-coloured**, equal to or shorter than blades; blades lance-shaped, **tapering at both ends**, 2–3 times pinnately divided into irregularly toothed leaflets.

SORI: Small and **round**, on undersides of leaflets, partially covered with a **hood-like, somewhat toothed or lobed indusium** attached beneath sorus.

ECOLOGY: Widespread and common at low to high elevations on moist to dry, rocky forests and openings, rock cliffs, crevices, ledges and talus slopes.

SIMILAR SPECIES: Fragile fern is sometimes confused with Oregon woodsia (*W. oregana*, p. 366), a fern with many old leaf bases and an indusium with radiating, hair-like segments. • Mountain bladder fern (*C. montana*) is a sporadic and often overlooked species of shady, moist to wet forests, glades, rocky slopes and streambanks. It occurs at mid to subalpine elevations in the Rocky Mountains, typically on nutrient-rich or calcareous sites. Mountain bladder fern looks more like a *Gymnocarpium* or *Dryopteris* species, with triangular-egg-shaped, twice-pinnate leaves, but it has a hood-like indusium.

NOTES: This delicate, lacy fern is easily grown from spores. • The genus name *Cystopteris* is from the Greek *kystos* (a bladder) and *pteris* (a fern), referring to the hood-like indusium. The species name *fragilis* means 'brittle,' referring to the stems.

PARSLEY FERN • *Cryptogramma crispa*
C. acrostichoides

GENERAL: Small, dense clusters of tall fertile leaves, to 30 cm tall, **and shorter sterile leaves** with old leaf stalks at base, from short, stout, **erect rhizomes** covered with scales.

LEAVES: Sterile and fertile leaves markedly different, ever-green; sterile leaves thick and crisply firm, finely divided and parsley-like, on straw-coloured to greenish stalks longer than blades; blades egg-shaped and divided into 3–10 pairs of finely toothed leaflets; fertile leaves taller, broadly lance-shaped, divided into 3–10 offset pairs of leaflets with rolled edges.

SORI: Continuous along length of fertile leaflets, **covered by rolled leaflet edges**; indusium not well defined.

ECOLOGY: Scattered and infrequent at mid to high elevations on fairly dry rocky, open sites (cliffs, ledges, crevices, talus slopes).

SIMILAR SPECIES: Slender rock-break (*C. stelleri*) is another small fern of rock crevices and cliffs. Its few scattered sterile leaves are delicate, thin and membranous and arise from a slender rhizome. It frequents mid to alpine elevations on calcareous rock in the Rockies.

NOTES: The St'at'imc ate the raw roots of parsley fern to cure colds. • Parsley fern, with its yellow-green foliage, makes an attractive addition to a rock garden. • The genus name *Cryptogramma* is from the Greek *krypto* (hidden) and *gramma* (a line), referring to the way the rolled leaf edges hide the sori. The species name *crispa* refers to the irregularly curled (crisped) leaflet edges. The name 'parsley fern' refers to the resemblance of the sterile leaves to parsley.

MAIDENHAIR FERN • *Adiantum pedatum*
A. aleuticum

GENERAL: Delicate, **palmately branched leaves**, usually solitary but often in colonies, from stout, scaly, creeping rhizomes.

LEAVES: Sterile and fertile leaves alike, deciduous; stalks lustrous, dark brown or black, erect, 15–60 cm tall, forked above into 2 branches, each with 2 to several leaflets (pinnae) that are more or less parallel to the ground; each leaflet with oblong or fan-shaped ultimate segments (pinnules) that are smooth and straight along their lower edge and cleft into ragged, rectangular lobes on upper edge.

SORI: Oblong, **along edges of upper lobes of leaflets**, covered by a **flap-like, false indusium** formed by **rolled lobe edges**.

ECOLOGY: Scattered and quite uncommon at low to mid elevations (occasionally in subalpine) in Coast/Interior Transition and wet Columbia Mountains, in shady, moist forests, streambanks, cliffs, waterfall spray zones, occasionally in dry forests on ultrabasic soils.

NOTES: In Europe maidenhair fern was used by herbalists as cough medicine. It was also boiled with sugar to make the syrup called 'capillaire,' which has some emetic properties. • The Nlaka'pmx noted that maidenhair fern is associated with grizzly-bear habitat. • Maidenhair fern is used in shaded gardens as a foliage plant, and it responds very vigorously to cultivation. It is sold in some nurseries and includes a dwarf variety. • The name 'maidenhair fern' refers to the very fine, hair-like stalks. This genus is named *Adiantum*, meaning 'unwetted,' because the leaves stay dry underwater. The species name *pedatum* refers to the palmate arrangement of the leaves.

BEECH FERN • *Thelypteris phegopteris*
Phegopteris connectilis

GENERAL: Scattered, erect leaves, to 40 cm tall, from slender, sparsely scaly rhizomes.

LEAVES: Sterile and fertile leaves **alike, deciduous**; stalks slender, scaly, straw-coloured, equal to or more usually longer than blades; blades **narrowly triangular to egg-shaped**, pinnately divided into pinnately lobed, hairy leaflets; **lowest pair of leaflets usually curving downward**.

SORI: Small, more or less **circular**, near edges on undersides of leaflets; **indusium absent**.

ECOLOGY: Scattered and locally common at low to subalpine elevations, mostly in northern half of wet Columbia Mountains, in moist, rich forests, streambanks, wet cliffs and rocky seepage slopes; most abundant on basic or calcium-rich soils.

NOTES: The common name 'beech fern' is the result of a confusing and deliberate mistranslation of *phegopteris*, which means 'oak fern.' Because there is already an oak fern, *phegopteris* was treated as if *phegos* was the same as *fagus* (beech) when the name was anglicized. This species is also called cowboy fern because the lowest pair of leaflets resemble the chaps on the legs of a bowed-legged cowboy. The genus name *Thelypteris* is from the Greek *thelus* (female) and *pteris* (a fern).

COMMON MOONWORT • *Botrychium lunaria*

GENERAL: Small, single, **yellowish- or bluish-green** frond, 10–20 cm tall.

LEAVES: Oblong, sterile blade; stalk equal to or longer than blade; blade pinnately divided into **2–7 pairs** of **round to fan-shaped**, somewhat leathery, overlapping **leaflets**, 1 cm wide.

REPRODUCTIVE: Stalk equal to or longer than spike; fertile spike 1–7 cm long, pinnately branched, with many, large, stalkless, **globular spore sacs** on branches.

ECOLOGY: Widespread but infrequent and scattered at low to high elevations in grassy slopes, meadows, turf ledges, open deciduous forests and hayfields; often overlooked.

SIMILAR SPECIES: Mingan moonwort (*B. minganense*) closely resembles common moonwort but it has narrower leaflets (about 3.5 mm wide) with wedge-shaped bases. Also, the leaflets of Mingan moonwort are well separated and not overlapping. It is uncommon, and it occurs at the edge of woods and in damp, grassy areas.

NOTES: Common moonwort also occurs in the southern hemisphere (in Australia, New Zealand and Patagonia). • The genus name *Lunaria* and the common name 'moonwort' both refer (presumably) to the crescent-shaped leaflets.

RATTLESNAKE FERN • *Botrychium virginianum*

GENERAL: Single hairless to sparsely hairy frond, 15–60 cm tall; stalk equal to or longer than sterile leaf.

LEAVES: Sterile blade thin, **triangular in outline, 2–4 times compound** and much-divided, **fern-like**, stalkless.

REPRODUCTIVE: Fertile spike arising from sterile frond, 2–15 cm long, 2–3 times **pinnately compound**, with many large, stalkless, **globular spore sacs** on branches; on a stalk 3–20 cm long.

ECOLOGY: Scattered and locally common at low to mid elevations in moist, often deciduous forests, damp open places and wet alluvial forests.

SIMILAR SPECIES: Leathery grape fern (*B. multifidum*) has stalked, fleshy and leathery leaves with the previous year's leaf persisting. It occurs in wet meadows, lake edges, grassy slopes and alluvial forests. • Northwestern moonwort (*B. boreale*, also known as *B. pinnatum*) has an egg-shaped, stalkless blade with broader, oblong segments and a fertile spike that is longer than the sterile leaf. Its habitat is similar to that of common moonwort (*B. lunaria*, above).

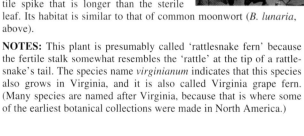

NOTES: This plant is presumably called 'rattlesnake fern' because the fertile stalk somewhat resembles the 'rattle' at the tip of a rattlesnake's tail. The species name *virginianum* indicates that this species also grows in Virginia, and it is also called Virginia grape fern. (Many species are named after Virginia, because that is where some of the earliest botanical collections were made in North America.)

Equisetaceae: Horsetail Family

The horsetails are all perennials with both underground and aerial stems. The aerial stems are usually hollow, grooved, jointed and impregnated with silica, making them harsh to the touch. Aerial stems may be annual (deciduous) or perennial and evergreen. The branches and leaves are borne in whorls at the conspicuous nodes. The leaves are reduced to a series of teeth united by a sheath, and they often lack chlorophyll (the stems and branches are photosynthetic). The spores are produced in cones at the top of the stem, often on a stalk that appears as an extension of the stem. The cone-producing (fertile) stems are often different in colour or branching from the sterile stems.

The horsetail family has a single genus, *Equisetum*, with about 20 species worldwide. Branched species of *Equisetum* are called horsetails because the stems and branches resemble a horse's tail, and the unbranched species are called scouring rushes.

Key to the horsetails and scouring rushes

1a. Stems evergreen and perennial, usually unbranched;
cones sharp-pointed at tip (scouring rushes) 2

    2a. Stems low and flexible, rather bent and twisted;
    central cavity lacking; sheaths with 3 teeth .... *E. scirpoides*

    2b. Stems stout, 20–150 cm tall, 3–10 mm thick,
    with 14–50 ridges; central cavity taking up 3/4 or
    more of stem diameter; sheaths with many teeth .... *E. hyemale*

1b. Stems annual, usually with regularly
whorled branches; cones blunt at tip (horsetails) 3

    3a. Branches themselves branched; ridges on
    sterile stems with 2 rows of minute, delicate,
    curved spines; stem sheaths brownish,
    with teeth united in several broad lobes .... *E. sylvaticum*

    3b. Branches usually not again branched;
    sterile stems with blunt bumps or cross-ridges
    on ridges; stem sheaths greenish, with
    dark teeth that are free or nearly so 4

        4a. Fertile stems white to brownish and without
        branches, soon withering; sterile stems smooth
        or with inconspicuous low bumps; 1st segments
        of branches much longer than stem sheath .... *E. arvense*

        4b. Fertile stems becoming green, branched, persistent;
        sterile stems with conspicuous bumps; 1st segments of
        branches shorter than or equal to length of stem sheath .... *E. pratense*

*Equisetum
hyemale*

*Equisetum
arvense*

*Equisetum
scirpoides*

*Equisetum
sylvaticum*

*Equisetum
pratense*

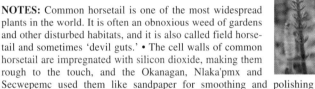

COMMON HORSETAIL • *Equisetum arvense*

GENERAL: Sterile and fertile stems **dissimilar**, **annual** from creeping, dark-felted underground stems with tubers; **fertile stems unbranched**, to 30 cm tall, usually thick and succulent, **brownish to whitish**, soon withering; **sterile stems** solitary or clustered, to 50 cm tall, slender, **green, with many simple branches** in whorls; central cavity about half stem diameter; sheaths green, pressed to stem, with 10–12 brownish or blackish teeth; **1st segment of branches longer than stem sheath**.

CONES: Stalked, blunt-tipped, **persistent**.

ECOLOGY: Widespread and common at low to alpine elevations in moist to wet forests, meadows, swamps, fens and alpine seepage areas; often weedy (as on roadsides and cutbanks); absent from arid basins.

SIMILAR SPECIES: The sterile stems are easily confused with those of meadow horsetail (*E. pratense*, below). • The sterile shoots of swamp horsetail (*E. palustre*) are also similar, but the stems have a smaller central cavity (about one-sixth the stem diameter), and the first branch segments are shorter than the adjacent stem sheaths.

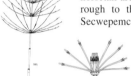

NOTES: Common horsetail is one of the most widespread plants in the world. It is often an obnoxious weed of gardens and other disturbed habitats, and it is also called field horsetail and sometimes 'devil guts.' • The cell walls of common horsetail are impregnated with silicon dioxide, making them rough to the touch, and the Okanagan, Nlaka'pmx and Secwepemc used them like sandpaper for smoothing and polishing surfaces. They also boiled the stems and drank the water for kidney problems and as a diuretic. The liquid was used to treat poison ivy rashes and skin sores. The dark underground stems were used as decorative imbrications in woven baskets.

MEADOW HORSETAIL • *Equisetum pratense*

GENERAL: Sterile and fertile stems **dissimilar**, deciduous, to 50 cm tall, from creeping, black underground stems; **fertile stems green, unbranched when young**, later with branches similar to sterile stems; **sterile stems** mostly solitary, with **inflated sheaths** (with 8–10 white-edged teeth), and **many, fine, simple branches**; branch sheaths pale green, **inflated,** with 3 white-edged teeth; **1st segment of branches equal to or shorter than stem sheath**.

CONES: Stalked, blunt-tipped, soon deciduous.

ECOLOGY: Scattered and often abundant at low to mid elevations in moist and wet forests, meadows, streambanks, and clearings; generally absent from arid basins.

SIMILAR SPECIES: Meadow horsetail is most commonly confused with common horsetail (*E. arvense*, above) which has a coarser appearance and lacks inflated sheaths on the branches. The first branch segment (internode) in common horsetail is longer than the stem sheath, and in meadow horsetail it is shorter.

NOTES: Meadow horsetail may have been used by native peoples as a type of sandpaper.

WOOD HORSETAIL • *Equisetum sylvaticum*

GENERAL: Sterile and fertile stems **dissimilar**, **deciduous**, to 70 cm tall, from deep, creeping underground stems; **fertile stems** green to flesh-coloured, **unbranched when young**, later with **compound branches**; **sterile stems** green, mostly solitary, with **compound branches**; ultimate branches delicate, tending to droop at ends.

CONES: Long-stalked, blunt-tipped, **soon deciduous**.

ECOLOGY: Scattered and often abundant at low to mid elevations in moist to wet meadows, shady forests, swamps, bog edges, recent burns and clearings; usually in more acid, lower-nutrient conditions than common or meadow horsetails.

SIMILAR SPECIES: Common horsetail (*E. arvense*, p. 371) and meadow horsetail (*E. pratense*, p. 371) are of similar size, but they have simple branching. Wood horsetail is our only species with multiple branching.

NOTES: The species name *sylvaticum* means 'of the forests,' emphasizing that this species is most commonly found in forested habitats.

SCOURING-RUSH • *Equisetum hyemale*

GENERAL: Sterile and fertile stems **similar**, unbranched, **evergreen**, to 1.5 m tall, rough to touch, from felted, blackish underground stems, sometimes forming dense colonies; stem sheaths green to ashy grey, usually with **2 black bands** and dark brown to whitish teeth.

CONES: Short-stalked, pointed, **persistent**.

ECOLOGY: Scattered and common at low to mid elevations in wet habitats, especially along major streams and rivers, on open sandbars and in shaded alluvial forests; occasionally on dry, upland, sandy soils.

SIMILAR SPECIES: Smooth scouring-rush (*E. laevigatum*) is another stout, stiffly erect scouring-rush. Its aerial stems are annual and have sheaths with only a single black band. Smooth scouring-rush is common on dry soils in the hot, dry valleys of the Thompson and Okanagan basins.

NOTES: Young St'at'imc men rubbed the silicon-impregnated stems on their skin to keep from growing whiskers. Stem segments were filled with water that was used to treat sore eyes. The Nlaka'pmx used the ashes from burnt stems to treat burns. Both the Nlaka'pmx and Secwepemc used scouring-rush as a woman's medicine to ease labour. • The name 'scouring-rush' was given to this species because it was used in Europe for scouring utensils made of wood or pewter.

DWARF SCOURING-RUSH • *Equisetum scirpoides*

GENERAL: Sterile and fertile stems alike, **evergreen, slender** (0.5–1 mm thick), **flexuous, unbranched**, evergreen, without a central cavity, growing in large clusters from shallow, brown underground stems; to 20 cm long.

CONES: Small (3–5 mm long), black, **very short-stalked, pointed, persistent**.

ECOLOGY: Scattered and often common at low to subalpine elevations among mosses and in humus on wet to moist sites, in forests, hummocks in swamps, streambanks, fen or bog edges to alpine tundra; particularly common in cold coniferous forests; absent from arid basins.

NOTES: The **thin, flexible, zigzag stems** and small size are characteristic of dwarf scouring-rush, and this is the only *Equisetum* species in our area without a large central cavity in the stems. • The species name *scirpoides* means 'rush-like,' echoing the common name 'scouring-rush.' This species is called goosegrass in some areas.

Lycopodiaceae: Clubmoss Family and Selaginellaceae: Spikemoss Family

The clubmosses (*Lycopodium* spp.) and spikemosses (*Selaginella* spp.) are mainly low-growing plants with small, evergreen leaves. They commonly have long, horizontal, main stems with erect, aerial stems that can be simple to highly branched. The horizontal stems are often leafy and may trail along the ground for considerable distances. The spores develop inside spore sacs (**sporangia**), which sit at the base of more or less modified leaves (**sporophylls**). In most species, the spore sacs and sporophylls are collected into cone-like structures at the ends of aerial branches. In the clubmosses, the cones are generally cylindrical, while in the spikemosses, they are sharply 4-angled.

While there are no reports of local native groups using the spores of *Lycopodium* species, other North American natives supposedly used the spore powder (known as vegetable sulphur) as a drying agent for wounds, nosebleeds and diaper rash. The spores may also be used today as a body powder for bedridden patients. *Lycopodium* spores contain much oil and are very flammable. Powdered spores were once used for flash photography, fireworks and special lightning effects on stage.

The 'resurrection plant' available in many nurseries is a little spikemoss (*Selaginella lepidophylla*) from the southern U.S. and Mexico. Although many clubmosses form attractive ground cover in their natural settings, they are difficult to propagate and are best left to be admired in the wild.

Lycopodium is from the Greek *lycos* (a wolf) and *podos* (a foot) after a fancied resemblance of clubmoss leaves to a wolf's paw. *Selaginella* is the diminutive of *selago*, Pliny's original name for the clubmosses. Thus, *Selaginella* translates as 'little clubmoss,' which is another common name for the spikemosses.

Key to the clubmosses and spikemosses

1a. Stems long-creeping; branches (or stems) erect,
tufted and forking, or single from a stout rhizome;
cones (when present) cylindrical, usually conspicuous (clubmosses) 2

    2a. Spore sacs in axils of ordinary
    green leaves, not forming definite cones .... *L. selago*

    2b. Spore sacs in conspicuous terminal cones 3

        3a. Cones stalkless 4

            4a. Leaves in 4 rows, flattened against stem,
            with free portion usually less than 3 mm long .... *L. alpinum*

            4b. Leaves in 6 or more rows, spreading,
            with free portion usually 4 mm long or more 5

                5a. Aerial branches simple or few-forked;
                horizontal stems creeping on ground .... *L. annotinum*

                5b. Aerial branches much-branched
                above, tree-like; horizontal stems
                spreading below-ground .... *L. dendroideum*

        3b. Cones stalked 6

            6a. Leaves awl-shaped, with long hair-tips,
            spreading; aerial stems round and few-branched .... *L. clavatum*

            6b. Leaves scale-like, not hair-tipped,
             flattened against stem; aerial stems much-branched
            (bush-like), with flattened branchlets .... *L. complanatum*

1b. Stems usually short-creeping, often mat-forming;
branches prostrate, not forking; cones
usually 4-angled, inconspicuous (spikemosses) 7

    7a. Stems slender, creeping, not
    mat-forming; rootlets few; leaves
    soft; cones not 4-angled, thicker than stem .... *S. selaginoides*

    7b. Stems mat-forming; leaves thick, firm; freely rooting
    along stem; cones 4-angled, not appreciably thicker than stem 8

        8a. Plants usually forming loose mats;
        branches not at all flattened; stem leaves
        overlapping, not fused to stem at base .... *S. wallacei*

        8b. Plants usually forming densely tufted,
        cushion-like mats; branches somewhat flattened;
        leaves crowded, fused to stem at base .... *S. densa*

STIFF CLUBMOSS • *Lycopodium annotinum*

GENERAL: Main stems **leafy, creeping** on or near surface of ground, to 1 m long; aerial stems **erect, shiny, simple or once- to twice-forked**, to 25 cm tall.

LEAVES: Narrow and pointed, crowded, **whorl-like** in 8 ranks, usually spreading.

CONES: Cylindrical, **solitary** and **stalkless** at branch tips; sporophylls rounded, toothed along edge and tapering to a slender point.

ECOLOGY: Widespread and common at low to subalpine elevations throughout moist and wet parts of our region in moist forests, thickets, bog edges and subalpine heaths.

SIMILAR SPECIES: Stiff clubmoss somewhat resembles running clubmoss (*L. clavatum*, below) which has leaves with soft, white bristle tips and 2–4 cones on long stalks.

NOTES: In recent times stiff clubmoss has been used to make Christmas decorations.

RUNNING CLUBMOSS • *Lycopodium clavatum*

GENERAL: Main stems **leafy, creeping** on ground surface and rooting at intervals, to 1 m long or more; aerial stems **erect, irregularly branched**, to 25 cm tall.

LEAVES: Bright green, lance-shaped, with soft, white bristle tips (at least when young), **crowded** in about 10 ranks.

CONES: Cylindrical, 2–4 on a **long, forked stalk** with a **few scale-like leaves**; sporophylls pale green, tapered (often hair-tipped), with torn edges.

ECOLOGY: Scattered and infrequent at low to mid elevations throughout moist and wet climates of our region, on moist to dry open forests, edges of swamps and bogs, openings, clearings and roadcuts (often on sandy soil); sometimes in high-elevation heaths and tundra.

SIMILAR SPECIES: Stiff clubmoss (*L. annotinum*, above) is distinguished from running clubmoss by the lack of soft white bristle tips on the leaves and by its single stalkless cone.

NOTES: Running clubmoss was used in modern times by the Bella Coola and Nootka for making Christmas wreaths. The Gitksan recognize this plant and call it 'otter belt.' It may have been used in medicinal preparations. The Nlaka'pmx, however, thought that it brought bad luck.

GROUND-CEDAR • *Lycopodium complanatum*

GENERAL: Main stems **creeping** on or near ground surface, to 1 m long, rooting throughout; aerial stems **erect, highly branched**, to 35 cm tall; branchlets whitish green, **flattened and strongly constricted between each year's growth**.

LEAVES: In **4 ranks, scale-like** (resembling redcedar leaves), **some fused to stem** for more than half their length; often somewhat bluish white.

CONES: Cylindrical, usually **2–3** on a **long, forked, nearly leafless stalk** arising from tips of aerial stems; sporophylls fan-shaped, with an abrupt, sharp point, toothed except for base.

ECOLOGY: Scattered and infrequent at low to mid elevations throughout moist and wet climates in our region, in moist to dry forests, rocky slopes and sandy openings; often in deciduous forests.

SIMILAR SPECIES: Alpine clubmoss (*L. alpinum*) somewhat resembles ground-cedar, but it is generally smaller (to 15 cm tall) with **solitary, stalkless cones** and leaves that are free from the stem for more than half their length. Alpine clubmoss occurs at high elevations, often in subalpine meadows or alpine tundra.

NOTES: The foliage of this species somewhat resembles that of western redcedar, hence the common name. The species name *complanatum* refers to the flattened branchlets.

GROUND-PINE • *Lycopodium dendroideum*
L. obscurum

GENERAL: Stems **erect**, irregularly branched, bushy, **tree-like**, to 30 cm tall, from deep, creeping, **underground stems**.

LEAVES: Many, **6–9 ranked**, long-pointed and prickly.

CONES: Cylindrical, **stalkless**, **solitary** at branch tips; with broadly egg-shaped, pointed sporophylls.

ECOLOGY: Scattered and sometimes common at low to subalpine elevations, mostly in wet Columbia Mountains, in dry to moist coniferous and deciduous forests, thickets, openings and bog edges.

NOTES: Ground-pine, ground-cedar (*L. complanatum*) and running clubmoss (*L. clavatum*) have been observed forming 'fairy rings' when growing in openings or old fields. • The name 'ground-pine' refers to the resemblance of the plant to a miniature conifer.

FIR CLUBMOSS • *Lycopodium selago*
Huperzia selago

GENERAL: Aerial stems **erect, simple or** equally forked and **branched**, often forming **tight, more or less flat-topped tufts**, to 20 cm tall, from short, withering horizontal stems.

LEAVES: Lance-shaped to nearly linear, pointed, crowded in **8 ranks.**

CONES: Spore sacs borne at bases of sporophylls that resemble **ordinary leaves** at or near branch tips, **not aggregated into cones.**

ECOLOGY: Scattered and rarely abundant, mostly at high elevations, in moist, open, usually subalpine forests, parklands, heaths, bogs, shaded, acid cliffs and boulders, alpine heaths and tundra.

SIMILAR SPECIES: Alpine clubmoss (*L. alpinum*, p. 376) is another clubmoss that grows at high elevations. Its branches are somewhat flattened and its spore cases are borne in solitary, **stalkless cones** at the branch tips.

NOTES: Fir clubmoss is the only species in our area in which the reproductive structures (the sporophylls and spore sacs) are not clustered into obvious cones. It is also our only common species in which the sporophylls resemble sterile leaves. • It can be propagated, with difficulty, from its tiny vegetative propagules (gemmae) which can be found scattered among the upper leaves. • Fir clubmoss contains a chemical that is being investigated for use in the treatment of Alzheimer's disease. • Fir clubmoss is also known as mountain clubmoss.

COMPACT SELAGINELLA • *Selaginella densa*

GENERAL: Short, creeping main stems, with many, short branches (mostly less than 2.5 cm long), forming **dense, low, greyish-green mats**, often 10 cm or more wide.

LEAVES: Lance-shaped, to 2.5 mm long, with **long, yellowish hair-points**, often fringed with hairs, **crowded** and pressed to stem, forming tufts at ends of branches.

CONES: 4-angled, stalkless and **stiffly erect** at branch tips; sporophylls egg-shaped, with pointed tips and fringed edges.

ECOLOGY: Widespread and common from valley bottoms to alpine on dry, exposed ridges, grasslands and rock outcrops; occasionally in dry forests.

SIMILAR SPECIES: Low selaginella (*S. selaginoides*) also occurs sporadically throughout our region. It is easily distinguished by its **more open habit** and its shorter, softer, more prominently toothed leaves that lack hair-points. It differs from other spikemosses in our area in that its **cones are not 4-angled**. This circumboreal species occurs on wet sites, such as seepage areas, streambanks, fens and bogs, and it is uncommon south of our region.

NOTES: Compact selaginella is also called dense spikemoss.

WALLACE'S SELAGINELLA • *Selaginella wallacei*

GENERAL: Main stems prostrate, rooting sparsely and forming **loose, tangled mats**; aerial stems erect, irregularly branched, to 4 cm long.

LEAVES: Long (2.5 mm) and narrow, with **tips extended into bristles**, **closely overlapping** and pressed to stem.

CONES: Many, 1–3 cm long, **4-angled, slightly curved**, stalkless at branch tips; sporophylls egg-shaped, with pointed tips and fringed edges.

ECOLOGY: Scattered and fairly common at low to mid elevations, mostly in southern half of our region, on rocky cliff-faces and ledges, dry, exposed rock outcrops and rocky soils.

SIMILAR SPECIES: Compact selaginella (*S. densa*, p. 377) can be distinguished from Wallace's selaginella by its short, tufted branches and by its 'denser' (more compactly branched) habit, forming small 'cushions' on the ground.

Bryophytes: Mosses and Liverworts

'Bryophytes' is a general term for a large group of plants—the mosses, liverworts and hornworts—that have intriguing habitat requirements, unusual distributions and richly detailed beauty. Nearly 1,000 bryophytes occur in British Columbia (probably at least 500 of them in our region), so there is a rich array of interesting species available to us, each with its own biological peculiarities.

Bryophytes are characterized by an independent green plant (**gametophyte**) that produces the sex organs. This is generally leafy, with very small leaves, but hornworts and some liverworts are strap-shaped (**thallose**). The gametophyte usually lives for many years. The spore-producing organ (**sporophyte**) is parasitic on the gametophyte, and it usually survives for less than a year. The sporophyte produces a single capsule (the spore-producing sac) usually at the tip of an elongate stalk. The stalk pushes the maturing capsule upward from the gametophyte so that the spores can be carried away by air currents.

In mosses, the stalk of the sporophyte is usually green when it is immature, and it is held rigid by thick-walled cells. The tip of the stalk is protected by a hood (**calyptra**) until the stalk has reached its maximum length and the capsule develops. The capsule usually has a lid (**operculum**) that falls off when mature. Around the mouth of the capsule are teeth that curve in and out with changing moisture conditions, drawing out the spores from within.

In liverworts, the whole sporophyte matures before the stalk elongates, and the calyptra is left at the base of the colourless stalk. The capsule usually opens by four longitudinal lines and elongate coiled cells (**elaters**) help scatter the spores. The stalk, held rigid by water within its cells, collapses soon after the spores are released. The immature sporophyte is often protected within a sleeve, which in leafy liverworts is usually green and is called a **perianth**.

Mosses can form extensive carpets in forests and wetlands. They are significant in the mineral and water economy of the vegetation that occurs with them and often generate the conditions that favour its growth. Liverworts are less common than mosses as extensive coverage, and in our area they are best represented at subalpine elevations. Mosses and liverworts occur on living trees, decaying logs and rocks and submerged in lakes and streams.

Bryophytes depend on water to dissolve the minerals they need and to create the proper conditions for sexual reproduction, since their sperm are mobile. Bryophyte sperm can only swim short distances, however, which is why the plants are small.

Identifying bryophytes depends on the careful observation of very small features, and a hand lens increases the characters available for identification. The presence of capsules adds to the features available for initial recognition, but with experience many bryophytes can be recognized without capsules.

Key to the bryophytes

1a. Plant a strap-shaped thallus or with leaves in 2 or 3 rows .... **Liverworts** (p. 407)
1b. Plant always leafy, with leaves in more than 3 rows .... **Mosses** (below)

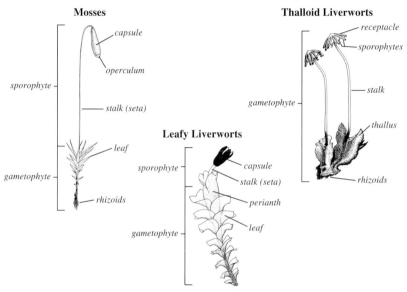

Key to the mosses

Note: This key is based as much as possible on features visible to the naked eye, but a 10x hand lens makes many features easier to see. This key includes only the primary species in this book, and a similar species in the region may key out to one of the species included here.

1a. Plants resemble small trees, with an erect 'trunk' and a tuft of branches at tip 2

    2a. Leaves of 'trunk' heart-shaped .... *Climacium dendroides*

    2b. Leaves of 'trunk' egg-shaped .... *Philonotis fontana*

1b. Plants never resemble small trees 3

    3a. Plants with cluster of branches at tip; tufts of side branches
spirally arranged lower on stem; leaves lacking midribs .... *Sphagnum squarrosum*

    3b. Plants lacking cluster of branches at tip; lower branches not in side tufts 4

        4a. Calyptra sheathing most of capsule 5

            5a. Calyptra elongate, never hairy or pleated, with nearly
straight, parallel sides and definite snout at tip .... *Encalypta rhaptocarpa*

            5b. Calyptra hairy or pleated, swollen to accommodate swollen capsule 6

                6a. Calyptra pleated, lacking hairs or bristles 7

                    7a. Peristome teeth 4 .... *Tetraphis pellucida*

                    7b. Peristome teeth more than 4 .... *Coscinodon calyptratus*

                6b. Calyptra with hairs or bristles 8

                    8a. Calyptra with erect bristles on surface .... *Orthotrichum speciosum*

                    8b. Calyptra completely sheathed with long interwoven hairs 9

                        9a. Leaves with red tips; leaf edges lacking teeth
and curved inward over upper surface .... *Polytrichum juniperinum*

                      9b. Leaves with green tips; leaf edges flat and with teeth .. *Polytrichastrum alpinum*

        4b. Calyptra absent or sheathing only fraction of upper part of capsule 10

29a. 4 peristome teeth .... *Tetraphis pellucida*

29b. More than 4 peristome teeth 30

30a. Plants forming cushions or turfs of
erect non-glossy plants, growing on rock .... *Dicranoweisia crispula*

30b. Plants creeping, with erect shiny branches,
growing on poplar and aspen trees .... *Pylaisiella polyantha*

25b. Sporangium inclined or curved when peristome is exposed 31

31a. Sporangium with membrane across mouth, ringed by short peristome teeth 32

32a. Sporangium 4-angled in cross-section
when mature and hood has fallen .... *Polytrichum juniperinum*

32b. Sporangium circular in cross-section .... *Polytrichastrum alpinum*

31b. Sporangium lacking membrane across mouth 33

33a. Plants with complex branching, with branchlets bearing branchlets 34

34a. Plants producing annual, arching, step-like branch systems;
this year's shoot extension arising from near middle of preceding
year's branch system; stems reddish .... *Hylocomium splendens*

34b. Plants with branch systems continuous with previous year's
system, yellow-green to dark green with green stems .... *Thuidium recognitum*

33b. Plants unbranched or with branches seldom bearing branchlets 35

35a. Plants erect with few or no irregular branches 36

36a. Leaves not glossy when dry 37

37a. Plants pale yellow-green; leaves closely overlapping
and erect to slightly divergent when moist; stem with
many woolly red rhizoids .... *Aulacomnium palustre*

37b. Plants dark green to reddish purple; leaves strongly
divergent when moist; stem with inconspicuous rhizoids .... *Ceratodon purpureus*

36b. Leaves glossy when dry 38

38a. Leaves long lance-shaped, more than 1 cm long,
many curved to 1 side of shoot .... *Dicranum scoparium*

38b. Leaves ovate to broadly ovate, pointing upward on all sides of shoot 39

39a. Leafy plants short, stout and bud-like, firmly attached
to soil by rhizoids; capsule grooved when mature .... *Funaria hygrometrica*

39b. Leafy plants long and slender, loosely attached to
organic substrate; capsule smooth when mature .... *Calliergon stramineum*

35b. Plants reclining or erect, with regular side branches 40

40a. Leaves C-shaped and hook-like, with many points
facing to 1 side of leafy shoot 41

41a. Plants dark green to purplish or dark brown;
aquatic or growing in very wet habitats .... *Drepanocladus exannulatus*

41b. Plants light green to yellow or golden green;
growing in well-drained habitats 42

42a. Many branches, closely spaced, forming strongly
feather-like leafy shoot; leaves lacking midrib .... *Ptilium crista-castrensis*

42b. Branches widely spaced; shoot not markedly
feather-like; leaves with midrib .... *Sanionia uncinata*

40b. Leaves not C-shaped in outline, points facing in all directions from leafy shoot 43

43a. Leaves with midrib 44

44a. Plants dark green to brownish, glossy when dry 45

45a. Plants growing in wet sites, forming dense
interwoven mats of erect to nearly erect shoots .... *Cratoneuron filicinum*

45b. Plants growing in well-drained sites, sometimes
epiphytic, forming loose mats of creeping shoots .... *Pseudoleskea baileyi*

44b. Plants yellow-green to golden, glossy when dry 46

46a. Plants with many, often regular, branches; branches and stems
curling upward from substrate when dry .... ***Homalothecium aeneum***

46b. Plants with few irregular branches
never coiling up from substrate when dry .... ***Brachythecium albicans***

43b. Leaves lacking midrib 47

   47a. Leaves strongly squarrose (base somewhat clasping with
tapering leaf tip abruptly bending outward) .... ***Campylium stellatum***

   47b. Leaves not squarrose 48

      48a. Leaves lacking wrinkles or pleats 49

         49a. Plants pinnately branched; leaves straight; stems red-brown ...... ***Pleurozium schreberi***

         49b. Plants irregularly branched;
leaves sometimes curved; stems green .... ***Hygrohypnum duriusculum***

      48b. Leaves with wrinkles on surface or pleats through part of their length 50

         50a. Leaves with wrinkles on surface and tips somewhat curved .... ***Rhytidiopsis robusta***

         50b. Leaves with basal pleats or pleats whole length of leaf 51

            51a. Pleats basal; leaves at stem tip sometimes
C-shaped; stems red brown .... ***Rhytidiadelphus loreus***

            51b. Pleats extending most of leaf length; stem tips blunt
with leaves diverging outwards untidily at all angles .... ***Rhytidiadelphus triquetrus***

10b. Sporangium absent 52

52a. Plants with gemma-bearing, erect shoots, with dusty gemmae at shoot tip 53

   53a. Gemmae exposed in dark-green mass at slenderly tapering shoot tip .... ***Aulacomnium palustre***

   53b. Gemmae in cup-like 'nest' of leaves at shoot tip .... ***Tetraphis pellucida***

52b. Plants lacking gemmae on erect shoot tips 54

   54a. Leaves with pronounced, white hair-point or tip abruptly different from body of leaf 55

      55a. Leaves lacking midrib; only leaf tip white .... ***Hedwigia ciliata***

      55b. Leaves with midrib, with or without hair-point 56

         56a. Hair-point abruptly extending from otherwise blunt leaf tip;
leaves squarrose when moist .... ***Tortula ruralis***

         56b. Tip gradually tapering to white point; leaves spreading
but not squarrose when moist 57

            57a. Plants worm-like in appearance, whitish green .... ***Bryum argenteum***

            57b. Plants neither worm-like nor whitish green 58

               58a. Plants less than 1 cm tall, attached to soil by rhizoids,
unbranched or irregularly branched .... ***Funaria hygrometrica***

               58b. Plants more than 1 cm tall, loosely attached
to substrate, usually with many short side branches .... ***Racomitrium ericoides***

   54b. Leaves lacking white hair-point or tip 59

      59a. Leaves with sheathing base and long, lance-shaped blade
flaring outward at strong angle from stem 60

         60a. Leaves with rusty sheathing base; leaf blade
transparent green, lacking lamellae on upper surface .... ***Timmia austriaca***

         60b. Leaves with white sheathing base; leaf blade opaque with longitudinal lamellae 61

            61a. Leaves with flattened, toothed edges .... ***Polytrichastrum alpinum***

            61b. Leaves with incurved edges, lacking teeth on edges .... ***Polytrichum juniperinum***

      59b. Leaves without sheathing base, or if with sheathing base,
rest of blade squarrose (arching outward, then tip curving downward) 62

         62a. Plants erect to nearly erect, without branches
or with a few at acute angles to main shoot 63

            63a. Leaves 1–2 cm long, long lance-shaped,
many strongly curved to 1 side of shoot .... ***Dicranum scoparium***

            63b. Leaves usually less than 1 cm long, not curved to 1 side of shoot 64

64a. Leaves dark green to nearly black, with blunt tip and blunt teeth along edge ... ***Racomitrium aciculare***

64b. Leaves light to yellow green, with pointed tip and obscure (or no) teeth along edge 65

65a. Leaves lance-shaped, dark green to reddish green; sporophytes usually present, with red stalks and inclined, red-purple, grooved capsule when mature .... ***Ceratodon purpureus***

65b. Leaves ovate to broadly lance-shaped, yellow-green; sporophytes infrequent, if present not grooved or red-purple 66

66a. Leafy shoots 0.5–1 cm wide; leaves not glossy (except for conspicuous midrib), strongly divergent when moist .... ***Aulacomnium palustre***

66b. Leafy shoots 0.5–1 mm wide; leaves glossy (with conspicuous midrib), closely overlapping like tiles when moist .... ***Calliergon stramineum***

62b. Plants creeping to nearly erect, with many side branches arising regularly at wide angles from main shoot 67

67a. Leaves decidedly squarrose below tip (with partly sheathing base and upper fork of leaf bent outward with point curved slightly downward) .... ***Campylium stellatum***

67b. Leaves not squarrose 68

68a. Leaves C-shaped or hook-like in appearance 69

69a. Plants with many regular side branches emerging at right angles from main stem, making shoot appear feather-like .... ***Ptilium crista-castrensis***

69b. Plants with few side branches arising irregularly at acute angles 70

70a. Plants aquatic or growing in wet sites, dark green to red-purplish or brown .... ***Drepanocladus exannulatus***

70b. Plants growing in well-drained sites, yellow to golden green .... ***Sanionia uncinata***

68b. Leaves straight or tip somewhat curved to 1 side 71

71a. Plants with very complex branching; branches with branchlets also branching 72

72a. Annual increments of growth marked by arching, step-wise branch system; stems red-brown; leaves glossy when dry .... ***Hylocomium splendens***

72b. Annual increments of growth not obvious; stems green; leaves not glossy when dry .... ***Thuidium recognitum***

71b. Plants usually once branched; branchlets rarely branched 73

73a. Leaves lacking pleats or wrinkles 74

74a. Plants growing in wet or seepy habitats, often splashed or partly submerged 75

75a. Plants firmly attached to rocks, only edges of colony pinnately branched; leaves with inconspicuous midribs .... ***Hygrohypnum duriusculum***

75b. Plants not firmly attached to substrate; shoots regularly pinnately branched erect to suberect; midrib apparent .... ***Cratoneuron filicinum***

74b. Plants growing in well-drained habitats, never splashed or submerged 76

76a. Leaves with midrib; plants usually dark grey to dark brownish green .... ***Pseudoleskea baileyi***

76b. Leaves lacking single midrib, 2 obscure midribs instead; plants golden green to brownish green .... ***Hypnum revolutum***

73b. Leaves with pleats or longitudinal wrinkles 77

77a. Branches and plants coiling upward when dry .... ***Homalothecium aeneum***

77b. Branches and plants not coiling upward when dry 78

78a. Leaves 1 mm or less, on main stem .... ***Brachythecium albicans***

78b. Leaves 1.5–2 mm long, sometimes longer on main stem 79

79a. Pleats confined to leaf base; leaves near shoot yet sometimes curved to one side .... ***Rhytidiadelphus loreus***

79b. Pleats or wrinkles extending most of leaf length 80

80a. Leaves with straight pleats; main shoots with leaves untidily divergent in all directions ... ***Rhytidiadelphus triquetrus***

80b. Leaves with irregular wrinkles; main shoots with neatly overlapping leaves (like roof tiles) with points curving downward .... ***Rhytidiopsis robusta***

SHAGGY PEAT MOSS • *Sphagnum squarrosum*

GENERAL: In loose mats; shoots erect, whitish to yellow-green (sometimes dark green in shade), 5–20 cm tall, with **clusters of branches on main stem** and **head of short, densely clumped branches**.

LEAVES: Ovate, with tapering upper portions, 2–3 mm long; **upper half abruptly bent outward from stem**.

SPOROPHYTES: Capsules nearly **spherical**, dark brown when mature, 2 mm long; stalks leafless, **whitish**, 0.6–1.5 cm long; maturing in summer; occasional.

ECOLOGY: Low to subalpine elevations; seepy areas in woodlands; also in wetlands, but **not a bog species**.

SIMILAR SPECIES: There are several other species of *Sphagnum* in our region. A pinkish to reddish species at high elevations is most likely to be Warnstorf's peat moss (*S. warnstorfii*).

NOTES: The erect shoot with clusters of branches topped by a dense head of short branches is typical of peat mosses. The pale yellow-green mats of large, coarse plants, and the way the leaves abruptly bend backward make shaggy peat moss the easiest peat moss to identify. • The native peoples of B.C., including the peoples of the Interior, recognized the soft, absorbent qualities of sphagnum moss. They used it widely for bedding, sanitary napkins and baby diapers. • The species name *squarrosum* describes the leaves, which bend outward abruptly from a somewhat sheathing base on the stem.

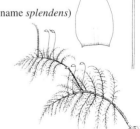

STEP MOSS • *Hylocomium splendens*

GENERAL: Extensive, loose, rusty green to dark green carpets, 2–20 cm long; stems red-brown, in complex, **arching, step-like branch systems**.

LEAVES: Main stem leaves ovate, 1–3 mm long, **with extended, often wavy tips**, and 2 red midribs; branch leaves shorter, with pointed tips and less apparent midribs.

SPOROPHYTES: Capsules egg-shaped, brown, 2–3 mm long, arising from main shoot, **inclined** on red-brown stalks (1–1.5 cm long); maturing in spring to autumn; infrequent.

ECOLOGY: Predominantly on forest floors, especially in coniferous forests where extensive mats often occupy low to subalpine elevations; also on open slopes and tundra in alpine sites, cliff shelves and boulders near streams.

NOTES: Step moss is a beautiful moss (hence the species name *splendens*) that is distinctive for its red-brown, arching shoots and complex feathery branches. Each year's growth is marked by a new shoot extension and triangular mass of branches. At high elevations, step moss sometimes forms turfs of semi-erect shoots, with less obvious step-like increments. • The Nlaka'pmx steeped step moss in hot water and used it as a poultice for sores.

KNIGHT'S PLUME • *Ptilium crista-castrensis*

GENERAL: In yellow-green to golden mats; shoots nearly erect, loosely interwoven, **regularly pinnately branched**, 3–9 cm long.

LEAVES: Ovate and markedly pleated, 1–2 mm long, with **tips strongly curved downward**.

SPOROPHYTES: Capsules cylindrical, red-brown, curved when mature, 2–3 mm long, **inclined** on red brown stalks (3–5 cm long); maturing in summer; occasional.

ECOLOGY: Extensive carpets or mats, mainly on coniferous forest floors; also on decaying logs and over rocks.

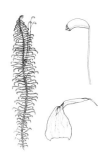

SIMILAR SPECIES: *Hypnum* species (p. 391) superficially resemble knight's plume, but they do not have the regular branching or the pleated leaves. • Sickle moss (*Sanionia uncinata*, p. 386) has pleated leaves (like knight's plume), but the leaves are decidedly curved and have a single midrib (absent in knight's plume). Branching in sickle moss is rarely as regular as in knight's plume.

NOTES: Knight's plume can be recognized by its regular pinnate branching and its pleated, yellow- to golden-green leaves with down-curved tips. • The species name *crista-castrensis* refers to a military plume of headgear.

LACY FERN MOSS • *Thuidium recognitum*

GENERAL: In loosely interwoven carpets; plants dull **yellow-green to dark green**, reclining, 4–9 cm long, with bluntish-tipped main stems and **complex branching**.

LEAVES: Main stem leaves are broadly triangular, 0.6–1 mm long, with **tips spreading strongly outward**; branch leaves are smaller and more narrowly triangular, pressed close to stem when dry, more spreading when moist.

SPOROPHYTES: Capsules cylindrical, curved, red-brown when mature, 2–3.5 mm long, **inclined** on red brown stalks (2–4 cm long); maturing in summer; rare.

ECOLOGY: Coniferous forest floors, cliff ledges, moist slopes; mainly at low elevations.

SIMILAR SPECIES: *Claopodium bolanderi* and *Helodium blandowii* are similar mosses, but they lack the complex branching found in lacy fern moss.

NOTES: The dull, yellowish-green colour, complex branching and broadly triangular, divergently pointed stem leaves are distinguishing features of lacy fern moss.

SICKLE MOSS • *Sanionia uncinata*
Drepanocladus uncinatus

GENERAL: In thin, **pale to golden-green** mats or creeping strands, or shoots sometimes erect, inter-woven, 2–10 cm long, with **regularly to irregularly pinnate branching**.

LEAVES: Lance-shaped from ovate base, 1–4 cm long, **strongly curved and hook-like**, with most points facing to 1 side of shoot; midrib present but obscured by **many pleats**.

SPOROPHYTES: Capsules cylindrical, curved, brown when mature, 3–4 mm long, **nearly erect** to erect on red-brown stalks (1–3 cm long); maturing in summer; occasional.

ECOLOGY: Extremely variable; tree trunks, extensive carpets on coniferous forest floors, cliff shelves, bogs, tundra and rotten logs; low grasslands to alpine elevations.

SIMILAR SPECIES: *Hypnum* species (p. 391) and knight's plume (*Ptilium crista-castrensis*, p. 385) are superficially similar, but their leaves lack a central midrib.

NOTES: The generally pinnate branching, the strongly curved leaves that hook to one side of the shoot, the obvious pleats in the leaves and the presence of a midrib are all useful identifying features. • When it grows over the ground, sickle moss is loosely attached, but when it grows on tree trunks it is often firmly attached by rhizoids. • The species name *uncinata* means 'hooked.'

HOOKED SPRING MOSS • *Drepanocladus exannulatus*

GENERAL: In floating or submerged mats of dark green to brownish plants, 4–15 cm long (sometimes longer), with **irregularly pinnate stems**; or in reddish-purple to brownish mats with densely interwoven shoots in wet depressions or seepage areas.

LEAVES: Strongly curved, 2–3.5 mm long, with midrib, shiny when dry, **most leaf tips facing to 1 side of shoot**.

SPOROPHYTES: Capsules curved, cylindrical, brown when mature, 2–3 mm long, **inclined** on red-brown stalks (4–8 cm long); maturing in summer; usually absent but sometimes abundant.

ECOLOGY: Aquatic, either float-ing or submerged; also growing loosely in wet depressions or seepage sites; common in lakes and swampy areas; can coat ba-sins of small subalpine and alpine pools; also at low elevations.

SIMILAR SPECIES: Without a microscope, hooked spring moss cannot be readily distinguished from other *Drepanocladus* species in our area, in particular *D. crassicostatus* and *D. fluitans*.

NOTES: The genus name *Drepanocladus* derives from Greek words meaning 'sickle-branched,' in reference to the curved leaves.

HANGING BASKET MOSS • *Rhytidiadelphus loreus*

GENERAL: In loose brownish-green to dark green, interwoven carpets; stems **red**, arching and reclining, 5–20 cm long, with widely spaced and **regularly pinnate branching.**

LEAVES: Broadly triangular, 3–4 mm long, tapering to point, **often curved, with pleated lower parts** and **no midribs.**

SPOROPHYTES: Capsules nearly **spherical**, red-brown when mature, 1.2 mm long, **inclined** on wiry stalks (3–5 cm long); maturing in spring; occasional.

ECOLOGY: Logs of coniferous forest floors; also on humus over rock of cliffs and boulders, usually in shaded sites; low to subalpine elevations.

SIMILAR SPECIES: *R. squarrosus* is similar in size and colour, but the leaves of that species are squarrose (the upper part of the leaf bends abruptly outward, then downward at the tip), giving the leafy shoot, in sectional view, a star-like outline. The leaves of hanging basket moss are not squarrose and the leaves at the stem tips are often curved to one side.

NOTES: This moss is commonly used to line hanging baskets of ornamental plants. • The species name *loreus* means 'striped,' perhaps in reference to the pleats of the leaves.

ELECTRIFIED CAT'S TAIL MOSS • *Rhytidiadelphus triquetrus*

GENERAL: In loose carpets of nearly erect to reclining, coarse, dull yellowish-green shoots, 5–15 cm long, with **untidily diverging leaves**; irregular or regular branches often to 3 cm long; loosely attached to substrate.

LEAVES: Ovate to broadly triangular, 3–5 mm long, not glossy, **deeply pleated**, with 2 relatively obvious midribs.

SPOROPHYTES: Capsules short-cylindrical, red-brown when mature, 3 mm long, **inclined to nodding** on red-brown stalks (2–3 cm long); maturing in spring; occasional.

ECOLOGY: Open to shaded sites; also on cliffs, boulders and rotten logs, both in forests and grasslands; mainly in lowlands.

NOTES: Electrified cat's tail moss is distinguished by its coarse yellow-green stems with untidy, tufted, blunt, leafy stem tips and non-glossy, deeply pleated leaves. • The species name *triquetrus* means 'in three rows,' in reference to the 3-rowed leaves found on some shoots.

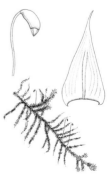

387

SCHREBER'S RED STEM • *Pleurozium schreberi*

GENERAL: In loose, glossy yellow-green to dull green mats; usually reclining, **regularly side-branched**, interwoven, **red shoots**, 10–15 cm long; not firmly attached to substrate.

LEAVES: Ovate, with somewhat blunt tips, 2–2.5 mm long, **lacking obvious midribs**.

SPOROPHYTES: Capsules curved, cylindrical, dark brown when mature, 1.5–2 mm long; stalks red-brown, 3–6 cm long; maturing in summer; infrequent.

ECOLOGY: Mainly on coniferous forest floors; also on humus, logs and cliff shelves; extensive carpets in humid as well as relatively dry forests; lowlands to low subalpine elevations.

SIMILAR SPECIES: *Calliergonella cuspidata* is superficially similar, but it has green stems and is restricted to wet sites.

NOTES: The red, pinnately branched stems with shiny, ovate, yellow-green leaves and loosely attached shoots are reliable features of Schreber's red stem. • This moss, which is also called red-stemmed feathermoss, is extremely common throughout the north temperate region. • The species name honours the German botanist J.C. Schreber (1739–1810).

PIPECLEANER MOSS • *Rhytidiopsis robusta*

GENERAL: In deep, **golden-green carpets** of interwoven, **fat, reclining shoots**, 3–12 cm long, with few branches; loosely attached to substrate.

LEAVES: Ovate and tapered to tips, 5 mm long, **curved to 1 side of shoot**; **2 midribs**.

SPOROPHYTES: Capsules curved, cylindrical, 3 mm long, inclined on pale to red-brown stalks (2–3 cm long); maturing in autumn; infrequent.

ECOLOGY: Abundant on humus and logs on subalpine forest floors, often in extensive carpets; also on subalpine heath slopes; also common at low elevations to mid-elevation montane forests in areas of high snowfall.

NOTES: The golden-green colour and irregularly wrinkled leaves that curve to one side of the shoot serve as useful diagnostic features. The swollen leafy shoots resemble fat yellow caterpillars. • The species name *robusta* refers to the large size of this species when compared with the superficially similar *Rhytidium rugosum*, which is found in calcium-rich, dry sites.

COMMON LAWN MOSS • *Brachythecium albicans*

GENERAL: In pale **yellowish** to whitish-green mats of nearly erect to creeping, **irregularly branched** shoots.

LEAVES: Triangular, about 1 mm long, **sharply pointed and pleated**, with obscure midribs; closely pressed to stems when dry.

SPOROPHYTES: Capsules brown, to 1 mm long, nearly erect on smooth, red-brown stalks (to 2 cm long); maturing in summer; infrequent.

ECOLOGY: Open, dry sites of poor pastures; also on road and trail edges; mainly in non-forested sites.

SIMILAR SPECIES: Common lawn moss can be confused with many other species in the genera *Brachythecium* and *Homalothecium* (below).

NOTES: Common lawn moss is the common *Brachythecium* species of the dry grasslands, but also occurs at high elevations, especially in grassy areas. It can be a troublesome species. • This species is named *albicans* for the whitish-yellow colour of the plant.

GOLDEN CURLS MOSS • *Homalothecium aeneum*

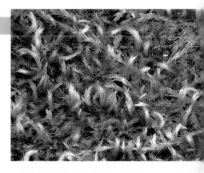

GENERAL: In glossy, yellow-green mats of interwoven, **irregularly pinnately branched** shoots, 2–8 cm long; upper portions of shoots and branches **curl upward when dry**; loosely attached to substrate.

LEAVES: Narrowly ovate, 1.5 mm long, **with midribs and longitudinal pleats** (use hand lens); diverging from stem when moist, held tightly to it when dry.

SPOROPHYTES: Capsules cylindrical, brown, slightly curved, 4 mm long, **inclined** on rough, red-brown stalks (1–1.5 cm long); maturing in spring; occasional.

ECOLOGY: Sheltered rocky outcrops and soil in open woodlands; mainly on lowlands, especially in dry grasslands.

SIMILAR SPECIES: The similar *Homalothecium nevadense* is confined to rock surfaces and has long, **nearly erect**, cylindrical capsules. • *Homalothecium fulgescens* grows mainly on tree trunks and also has long, cylindrical capsules.

NOTES: The yellow-green glossy plants that coil upward when dry identify golden curls moss. • The species name *aeneum* is from the Latin for 'bronze coloured,' and refers to the colour of this moss under some conditions.

SPRING CLAW MOSS • *Cratoneuron filicinum*

GENERAL: In dense mats of erect to reclining, dark green to **brownish-green** to golden-brown shoots, 4–10 cm long or longer, usually **pinnately branched and fern-like** in outline.

LEAVES: Narrowly triangular to broadly triangular, **1.5–2 mm long**, with **obvious midrib**, sharp pointed and often curved at tip.

SPOROPHYTES: Capsules cylindrical, curved, 2 mm long, brown, **inclined** on red-brown stalks (3–3.5 cm long); maturing in summer; infrequent.

ECOLOGY: Sometimes forming extensive mats, commonly in seepage sites, especially in calcium-rich areas; low to sub-alpine elevations.

SIMILAR SPECIES: Other mosses of similar sites include *Drepanocladus* species (p. 386), which have sickle-shaped leaves, and *Calliergon* species (p. 392), in which the leaves have a less apparent midrib and are glossy (wet or dry).

NOTES: The **seepage habitat**, the fern-like form of the branched shoots, the conspicuous midrib of the narrowly triangular leaves and the growth into extensive mats readily identify spring claw moss. • The species name *filicinum* is from the Latin *filix*, 'a fern,' and refers to the fern-like appearance of this moss.

RIGID BROOK MOSS • *Hygrohypnum duriusculum*

GENERAL: In reclining, rusty to **dark green mats**, 1–4 cm long, with many erect and nearly erect, **irregular branches**; firmly attached to substrate.

LEAVES: Ovate, 1–2 mm long, often with curved tips and **no apparent midribs**.

SPOROPHYTES: Capsules cylindrical, curved, brown when mature, 1.5–2 mm long, **inclined** on red brown stalks (1.5–2 cm long); maturing in summer, locally abundant to rare.

ECOLOGY: Boulders and outcrops in or near cascading streams; also sometimes on logs in streams; always within splash zone or in shallow, rapidly moving water.

SIMILAR SPECIES: Rigid brook moss resembles several other species of *Hygrohypnum* that occupy the same habitat. It also resembles *Scleropodium obtusifolium*, but in that species the leafy stems are worm-like and the leaves have a midrib.

NOTES: The genus name *Hygrohypnum* is from the Greek for 'aquatic *Hypnum*,' which describes both the habitat of this species and the similarity of other species in this genus to *Hypnum* species.

RUSTY CLAW MOSS • *Hypnum revolutum*

GENERAL: In reclining mats of **pinnately branched**, rusty-green to golden-green shoots, 2–6 cm long; loosely attached to substrate.

LEAVES: Ovate, with edges curved under, 1–2 mm long, **tips mainly curving in 1 direction**, **without obvious midribs.**

SPOROPHYTES: Capsules cylindrical, somewhat curved, brown when mature, 1–3 mm long, **nearly erect** on red-brown stalks (1–2 cm long); maturing in summer; occasional.

ECOLOGY: Common on mineral soil in open dry forests; rock and soil of dry grasslands where it is most common on rock outcrops and cliffs; especially in **calcium-rich terrain**; low to subalpine elevations.

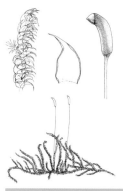

SIMILAR SPECIES: Sickle moss (*Sanionia uncinata*, p. 386) is similar, but in that species the leaves have a midrib and pleats, and are more strongly curled and almost C-shaped in outline.

NOTES: *Hypnum* is easy to recognize as a genus, but the species are not readily separated except on microscopic features. The creeping, regularly branched shoots and curved leaves that lack an obvious midrib are useful identifying features. • The genus name *Hypnum* is from the Greek *hypnos*, 'sleep,' apparently in reference to an ancient use of some mosses.

RUSTY MOUNTAIN HEATH MOSS • *Pseudoleskea baileyi*
Lescuraea baileyi

GENERAL: Loosely interwoven, **regularly to irregularly branched**, rusty brown to **dark green** shoots, 3–8 cm long, sometimes longer; loosely or firmly attached to substrate.

LEAVES: Narrowly ovate, 1.5–2 mm long, with midribs; divergent when moist, pressed closely to stem when dry.

SPOROPHYTES: Capsules cylindrical, 1–1.5 mm long, **inclined** on red-brown stalks (1–2 cm long); maturing in summer; uncommon.

ECOLOGY: Upper subalpine forests and heath zones; often in loose mats among mountain-heathers (*Cassiope* and *Phyllodoce* spp.), but also on lower stems of blueberries (*Vaccinium* spp.), and other shrubs within forests, **especially in areas where snow remains long into summer.**

SIMILAR SPECIES: *P. stenophylla* is much smaller than rusty mountain heath moss, is usually tightly epiphytic, and is more firmly attached to the plants on which it grows.

NOTES: Rusty mountain heath moss is distinguished by its rusty brown, creeping shoots, which are somewhat irregularly branched, and by its unusual ecology (see above). • The species name honours the amateur bryologist, J.W. Bailey.

GOLDEN STAR MOSS • *Campylium stellatum*

GENERAL: In shiny golden green to dark green mats of **erect, irregularly branched**, loosely interwoven shoots.

LEAVES: Triangular, about 2 mm long, **without obvious midribs**; leaf bases compressed against stem and with sharply tapering **points arching abruptly outward**, making **leafy shoot appear star-like in outline**.

SPOROPHYTES: Capsules curved-cylindrical, light to dark brown when mature, about 2 mm long; on elongate, red to reddish-yellow stalks; maturing in summer; infrequent.

ECOLOGY: Usually in open sites, but also in subalpine forest openings; often in calcium-rich seepage areas; widespread at low to high elevations.

SIMILAR SPECIES: Golden star moss can be confused with *Rhytidiadelphus squarrosus* (p. 387), which often occurs in the same habitats. However, *R. squarrosus* has reddish stems (golden star moss has yellowish-green stems) and its uppermost leaves flare outward (in golden star moss they tend to be erect).

NOTES: The species name *stellatum* is from the Latin for 'a star.'

STRAW MOSS • *Calliergon stramineum*

GENERAL: Shiny, slender, yellow-green, unbranched or irregularly branched strands, nearly erect or reclining; **loosely attached** to other mosses or to humus.

LEAVES: Narrowly ovate, 0.8–1.2 mm long, with thin midribs and blunt tips; **closely overlapping**, giving stem a string-like appearance.

SPOROPHYTES: Capsules cylindrical, curved, brown and smooth when mature, 2–3 mm long, with **cone-shaped lids**; on long, red-yellow to red stalks; maturing in summer; infrequent.

ECOLOGY: Bogs, rich fens, lakeshores and ditches that are wet much of year; usually in open areas from valley bottoms to subalpine elevations.

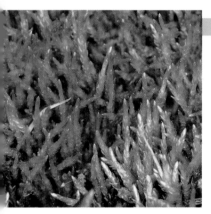

NOTES: Straw moss can be identified by its slender, often unbranched, shiny yellow-green shoots and its damp habitat. • The species name *stramineum* is from the Latin for 'straw.'

RED-TOOTHED ROCK MOSS • *Schistidium apocarpum* *Grimmia apocarpa*

GENERAL: In reddish-brown to dark green cushions or mats of irregularly branched, erect to creeping shoots, 1–11cm long; firmly attached to substrate.

LEAVES: Ovate, 1–2 mm long, narrowing to sharp points, with keel-like midribs; spreading when moist, pressed close to stem when dry.

SPOROPHYTES: Capsules short, cylindrical, 1–1.5 mm long, red-brown when mature, with **bright, red peristome teeth, which flare outward when dry**; mainly **immersed among surrounding leaves**; maturing in spring to summer; frequent.

ECOLOGY: Boulders, cliffs, open sites; low to alpine elevations.

SIMILAR SPECIES: Hedwig's rock moss (*Hedwigia ciliata*, below) can be distinguished from red-toothed rock moss by the absence of leaf midribs and the lack of red peristome teeth.

NOTES: Red-toothed rock moss is distinguished by its growth into usually low mats or cushions, the sporophyte capsules, which are immersed in the surrounding leaves, and the flaring, red peristome teeth. • This moss represents a complex of related species.

HEDWIG'S ROCK MOSS • *Hedwigia ciliata*

GENERAL: In **whitish-green to yellow-green mats**, 1–6 cm long, of irregularly branched, reddish, nearly erect shoots; firmly attached to rock.

LEAVES: Ovate, 1–2.5 mm long, **no midribs**, decidedly **whitish at tips** and not glossy; diverging from stem when moist, but held tightly to it when dry; leaves around capsules with **hairy edges**.

SPOROPHYTES: Capsules spherical, red-brown when mature, 0.5–1 mm long, **lacking peristome teeth**; **immersed among leaves** on extremely short stalks; maturing in spring; common.

ECOLOGY: Sunny acid rocks (not on limy rock); mainly in lowlands.

SIMILAR SPECIES: The superficially similar *Racomitrium elongatum* has leaves with midribs and hair-points that curve outward untidily on the stem when dry.

NOTES: Hedwig's rock moss can be distinguished by its white tipped, yellowish-green leaves that lack midribs and by its spherical capsules without peristome teeth, hidden among the hair-fringed leaves. • The genus is named for Johannes Hedwig (1730–99), the 'father' of moss study. The species name *ciliata* describes the hairy-fringed leaves that envelop the capsule.

SHAGGY YELLOW SAND MOSS • *Racomitrium ericoides*

GENERAL: In dense mats of **short-branched**, yellow-green (when moist) to whitish-green (when dry), leafy shoots, 2–6 cm tall; loosely attached to substrate.

LEAVES: Ovate, with **pointed tips**, obvious midribs, and **white hair-points flaring outward untidily** and accentuating whitish appearance.

SPOROPHYTES: Capsules red-brown, cylindrical, 2 mm long, **erect** on twisted, red-brown stalks (1–2 cm tall); maturing in spring; occasional.

ECOLOGY: Open dry areas, rocks, pebbly and sandy sites near roadsides, watercourses and stabilized lake beaches; low to subalpine and alpine elevations.

SIMILAR SPECIES: Shaggy yellow sand moss is very hard to distinguish from *R. elongatum* (p. 393). • *R. muticum*, found at subalpine elevations, lacks hair-points on the leaves, among other features, and grows in late-snow areas.

NOTES: Shaggy yellow sand moss has distinctive shoots with stubby branches and untidily diverging white hair-points.

BLACK BROOK MOSS • *Racomitrium aciculare*

GENERAL: In dark green to nearly black turfs of erect plants, 1.5–4 cm tall; firmly attached to rock.

LEAVES: Broadly lance- to tongue-shaped, 2–2.5 mm long, with **blunt tips** and obvious midribs; flaring outward when wet, pressed close to stem when dry.

SPOROPHYTES: Capsules red-brown to black, cylindrical, 1.5–3 mm long, **erect** on **red-brown to black stalks** (0.5–1.5 cm long) that are twisted when dry; maturing in spring to summer; common.

ECOLOGY: Splashed or irrigated rocks of streams and lake edges; low to alpine elevations.

SIMILAR SPECIES: *Scouleria aquatica* has a similar colour and ecology, but the leaves diverge almost at right angles to the stem when wet, while those of black brook moss diverge at an acute angle. Also, *S. aquatica* has near-spherical capsules with virtually no stalks.

NOTES: The blackish plants with flaring, blunt leaves, the splashed-rock habitat, and the erect, cylindrical capsules on elongate stalks identify black brook moss. • The species name *aciculare*, 'needle-like,' may refer to the sharp snout on the capsule lid.

HOODED MOSS • *Orthotrichum speciosum*

GENERAL: In yellowish-green tufts or loose turfs of erect, branched plants, 2–4 cm tall.

LEAVES: Lance-shaped, 3–5 mm long, not glossy, with keel-like midribs; widely flaring when moist.

SPOROPHYTES: Capsules short cylindrical, grooved when mature, 1.5–2.4 mm long, mostly **covered by short-bristled hood**; yellow to brownish **peristome teeth in 2 series**; outer teeth curving outward, **inner teeth bending into capsule mouth**; **stalks short, concealed by leaves**; maturing in late spring to summer; common.

ECOLOGY: Usually on somewhat shaded rock surfaces at edges of dry grasslands and in open forests; also on tree trunks; mainly at low elevations.

NOTES: Many species of *Orthotrichum* in our region are not easy to distinguish from one another without microscopic examination and experience. Of these, hooded moss is the most common. • The genus name *Orthotrichum* is from the Greek *orthos*, 'straight,' and *trichos*, 'a hair,' and refers to the short bristles on the surface of the hood.

APPLE MOSS • *Bartramia pomiformis*

GENERAL: In **bluish- to yellowish-green** tufts of unbranched stems with **red fuzzy rhizoids**; sometimes forming turfs of densely bound shoots, 2–6 cm tall.

LEAVES: Narrowly lance-shaped, 3–7 mm long, with midribs forming a green ridge on back of leaf; diverging outward nearly at right angles to the stem when moist; **very twisted when dry**.

SPOROPHYTES: Capsules **spherical**, smooth and green when immature, but strongly **grooved** and light brown when mature and dry, about 2 mm long; usually abundant in late spring and summer; old capsules remain for more than a year.

ECOLOGY: Moist cliff shelves, especially near streams, mainly in forested areas at low elevations.

SIMILAR SPECIES: *B. halleriana*, a rare species in our area, resembles apple moss but has its capsules on very short stalks that seem to be embedded within the turf. • *B. ithyphylla,* mainly an alpine species, has a very shiny, sheathing base to its leaves, which are not strongly twisted when dry.

NOTES: The species name *pomiformis* is Latin for 'apple-shaped,' and refers to the spherical capsules.

FLAPPER MOSS • *Mnium spinulosum*

GENERAL: In **dark green to bluish-green**, loose turfs of unbranched shoots, 2–3 cm tall; attached to substrate by rhizoids at base of shoots.

LEAVES: Inverted ovate (widest near tip), 2–2.5 mm long abruptly tapered to a point; toothed edges form **small, colourless or red ridges around leaves**; midribs obvious, occasionally red-brown.

SPOROPHYTES: Capsules yellowish, cylindrical, 2–3 mm long, often **red-brown at neck and mouth**, **nodding** on red-brown stalks (1.5–3 cm long); **often several on each shoot**; maturing in late spring to summer; frequent.

ECOLOGY: Humus or rotten logs, often near tree bases, usually in coniferous forests, on slopes; low to subalpine elevations.

SIMILAR SPECIES: *M. arizonicum* is usually smaller than flapper moss and is found at subalpine to alpine elevations.

NOTES: Flapper moss is the only true *Mnium* species of forest floors, although others are found on rocks in forested areas. • As the capsule ripens, the mouth turns dark brown, an unusual characteristic. • The common name, coined by the bryologist Howard Crum, comes from the reddish colour around the mouth of the capsule, which is reminiscent of the style among 'flappers' of the 1930s. This moss is also called Menzies's red-mouth mnium. The species name *spinulosum* refers to the spine-like teeth along the leaf edges.

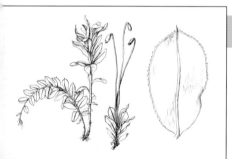

TRAILING LEAFY MOSS • *Plagiomnium medium*

GENERAL: In loose turfs of condensed, erect, dark to light green plants, 2–4 cm tall, also produce extensive **unbranched, creeping shoots** (to 6 cm long), with horizontally flattened leaves.

LEAVES: Ovate to inverted ovate, 4–7 mm long, with pointed tips; edges toothed, with border of long cells; flat when moist, contorted when dry.

SPOROPHYTES: Capsules light to **yellow-brown**, 3–4 mm long, **nodding** on **yellowish-green stalks** (3–5 cm long); **1–3 on each leafy shoot**; maturing in summer; relatively common.

ECOLOGY: Wet areas, near streams and lakes, and in forest depressions; low to subalpine elevations.

SIMILAR SPECIES: Several other species of *Plagiomnium* occur in our region, and trailing leafy moss can be distinguished from them by its usually abundant creeping shoots. • *P. insigne* (**photo**) is less common than trailing leafy moss and has arched, rather than creeping, shoots. • *Mnium rostratum*, usually found in limy, wet sites, has creeping shoots, but its leaves become extremely contorted and greatly reduced in size when dry. • The leaves of *M. medium*, although contorted when dry, do not shrink as drastically in size.

NOTES: • The genus name *Plagiomnium* refers to the obliquely oriented shoots in some species of this *Mnium*-related genus.

GLOW MOSS • *Aulacomnium palustre*

GENERAL: In bright **yellow-green turfs** of **erect** plants, often bound together by **red-brown fuzz of stem rhizoids**; often with short, leafless stalks bearing lance-shaped **gemmae**.

LEAVES: Closely **overlapping**, broadly lance-shaped to **ovate**, 3–5 mm long, pointed, with **shiny, whitish midribs**; **spreading when moist**, becoming contorted when dry.

SPOROPHYTES: Capsules **nearly erect** and smooth when immature, **curved, longitudinally grooved** and light brown when mature and dry, 3–4 mm long; maturing spring to summer; often absent.

ECOLOGY: Mostly on organic soil in seepy, swampy or boggy areas; lowlands to subalpine elevations; best developed in non-forested sites.

SIMILAR SPECIES: *A. androgynum*, a smaller species than glow moss, is often found on humus or on decaying logs and not in swamps. Its gemmae, which are common in spring and autumn, form **spherical clusters** on the tips of elongated shoots; in **glow moss the gemmae clusters are elongated**.

NOTES: Glow moss often produces masses of dark green dusty gemmae on elongate shoots. • The species name *palustre* is from the Latin for 'a marsh.'

FIRE MOSS • *Ceratodon purpureus*

GENERAL: In velvety, **dark green to reddish-green** turfs of **erect**, unbranched, tightly packed shoots, 1–3 cm tall; firmly attached to mineral soil.

LEAVES: Lance-shaped, keeled with strong midribs; spreading from stem when moist, **somewhat twisted to curled when dry**.

SPOROPHYTES: Capsules **cylindrical**, smooth and green when immature, horizontal, chestnut-brown and **grooved** when mature, 2–3 mm long, **erect** on elongate, **shiny, red-purplish stalks** (to 3 cm long); maturing spring to summer; common.

ECOLOGY: Very common in disturbed sites; often frequent in logged and burned areas; also a roadside weed; low to subalpine elevations.

NOTES: Fire moss is easily recognized by its green or reddish turfs growing on mineral soil, its purplish-red stalks, and its glossy, grooved, chestnut-brown capsules (when mature). • The species name *purpureus* refers to the purplish-red stalks.

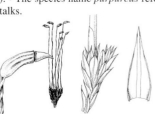

PALM MOSS • *Climacium dendroides*

GENERAL: In loose stands of tiny, **tree-like** plants, 3–6 cm tall, arising from underground creeping stem, varying in colour from dark to yellowish green; firmly attached to substrate by rhizoids at stem base.

LEAVES: Narrowly **ovate** (2–3 mm long) on branches, **broadly ovate** (4–4.5 mm long) on main stem, both with midribs.

SPOROPHYTES: Capsules cylindrical, red-brown when mature, about 4 mm long, **erect** on red stalks (3–4 cm long); maturing spring to summer; not frequent.

ECOLOGY: Most frequent in wetlands, including swamps and lake or stream edges; usually in open sites; low to subalpine elevations.

SIMILAR SPECIES: Palm moss is one of two erect, tree-like mosses in our area. The other species, *Leucolepis acanthoneuron*, is infrequent and grows in more shaded sites and not in wetlands. *L. acantho-neuron* has narrowly triangular stem leaves (not broadly ovate) and its capsules are nodding (not erect).

NOTES: The species name *dendroides* is from the Greek for 'tree-like.'

SEEPAGE APPLE MOSS • *Philonotis fontana*

GENERAL: In turfs of yellow- or golden-green to dark green, **unbranched** or **tree-like** shoots, 3–6 cm tall, bearing tuft of branches at tip; lower portions of **shoots often heavily clothed in red-brown rhizoids** that bind shoots together.

LEAVES: Broadly to narrowly **ovate**, 1–1.5 mm long, tapered to tip; **small teeth along edges**; obvious midrib; flaring when moist, somewhat twisted and overlapping when dry.

SPOROPHYTES: Capsules almost **spherical** when young, becoming stoutly short-cylindrical and **grooved** when mature, 1–3 mm long; red-brown stalks, 2–5 cm long; maturing in spring to late summer; common.

ECOLOGY: Frequent on rock and mineral soil of seepage sites, streamsides, lake edges and ditches; low to high elevations; sometimes in extensive patches along snowmelt streamlets in alpine terrain (where it is often intermixed with *Pohlia wahlenbergii*).

SIMILAR SPECIES: *Pohlia wahlenbergii* (p. 400) looks similar when the sporophytes are absent, but its shoots lack the abundant rhizoids of seepage apple moss. When the sporophyte capsules are present, their cylindrical form and nodding attachment readily distinguish *P. wahlenbergii*.

NOTES: The seepage habitat, the nearly spherical capsule and the tufts of branches radiating from male shoots distinguish seepage apple moss. • The genus name *Philonotis* is from the Greek *philos*, 'love,' and *notios*, 'moisture.' The species name *fontana* is from the Latin for 'of fountains or springs' and describes the habitat of this species.

BRISTLY HAIRCAP MOSS • *Polytrichastrum alpinum* *Polytrichum alpinum, Pogonatum alpinum*

GENERAL: In tall turfs of dark green, erect plants, 1–20 cm tall, with branched or unbranched shoots; lower portions of shoots red-brown; firmly attached to substrate by rhizoids at base of shoot.

LEAVES: Long, lance-shaped, 0.5–2 cm long, opaque with many longitudinal flaps covering most of midrib; **strongly toothed edges**; base colourless to reddish, **sheathing stem**; stiff when moist, somewhat twisted when dry; **leaves on lower part of stem scale-like and lacking blades**.

SPOROPHYTES: Capsules cylindrical to nearly spherical (circular in cross-section), 5–7 mm long; peristome teeth short, overarching edge of a **membrane that covers most of capsule mouth**; young capsule **partially covered by hairy hood; inclined** on red-purple stalks (1–4 cm long); maturing in summer to autumn; frequent.

ECOLOGY: Usually on mineral soil; overturned tree roots, banks, cliff shelves; low to high elevations.

SIMILAR SPECIES: *Polytrichum commune* (**photo**) and *Polytrichum formosum* are superficially similar to bristly haircap moss, but both these species have leaves with blades along the entire stem length and their capsules are almost square in cross-section. • False haircap moss (*Timmia austriaca*, p. 400) differs in having a nodding capsule and leaves with exposed midribs, among other obvious features.

NOTES: Bristly haircap moss can be identified by its long, opaque, dark green leaves (the lowermost of which are bladeless), its sheathing leaf bases, its toothed leaf edges, and its cylindrical capsules that are circular in cross-section.

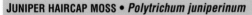

JUNIPER HAIRCAP MOSS • *Polytrichum juniperinum*

GENERAL: In tall to short, **bluish-green turfs** of usually densely packed, erect, unbranched, red shoots, 2–10 cm tall; firmly attached to substrate by rhizoids at stem base.

LEAVES: Rigid, 7–10 mm long, with **reddish, bristle-like tips, white, sheathing bases**, and **edges curved over longitudinal flaps**; strongly **diverging from stem when moist**, somewhat upright when dry.

SPOROPHYTES: Capsules are rectangular boxes with **circular lids**, erect and green when immature, red-brown and **inclined** when ripe, 2–3 mm long; peristome teeth small, overarching edge of **white membrane that closes much of capsule mouth**; capsules **completely sheathed in hairy hoods** until mature; on wiry, red-brown stalks (2–6 cm long); maturing in summer to autumn; common.

ECOLOGY: Mainly on soil in open, well-drained sites; also humus, cliff shelves and forests; low-elevation grasslands to alpine tundra.

SIMILAR SPECIES: *P. strictum* is commonly found in boggy sites, usually has leaves half as long as those of juniper haircap moss, and has stems that are densely covered in whitish rhizoids.

NOTES: Juniper haircap moss can be recognized by its bristly, bluish-green leaves with reddish tips, its box-like capsules, and its generally well-drained habitat. • The species name refers to the resemblance of this moss to young juniper (*Juniperus* sp.) seedlings.

FALSE HAIRCAP MOSS • *Timmia austriaca*

GENERAL: In tall turfs of dark green to brownish-green, erect, unbranched plants, 1–10 cm tall.

LEAVES: Lance-shaped, 3–6 mm long, sometimes reddish brown, with obvious midribs, toothed edges, and **sheathing bases**; **widely spreading when moist**; pressed closely to stem and somewhat contorted when dry, with leaves somewhat folded and midribs more obvious.

SPOROPHYTES: Capsules cylindrical, light brown, 4 mm long, **nodding** on red-brown stalks (3–3.5 cm long); maturing in summer; occasional.

ECOLOGY: Well-drained sites: forest floors, cliff shelves, rotten logs and banks; low to subalpine elevations.

SIMILAR SPECIES: This moss superficially resembles the true haircap mosses (*Polytrichum* spp., p. 399) but its leaves are not rigid, nor do they have flaps (lamellae) on the upper surface. The nodding capsules also separate false haircap moss from true haircap mosses and related mosses.

NOTES: The species name *austriaca* means 'from Austria,' and refers to the locality from which it was first described.

COMMON NODDING POHLIA • *Pohlia nutans*

GENERAL: In short turfs of dark to light green, erect, unbranched plants, 7–12 mm tall; firmly attached to substrate by rhizoids.

LEAVES: Lance-shaped, 1.5–2 mm long, with **small teeth near tips** and obvious midribs; spreading when moist, slightly contorted and overlapping when dry.

SPOROPHYTES: Capsules cylindrical to slightly pear-shaped, dull red-brown when mature, about 3 mm long, **nodding** on **red-brown stalks** (2–4 cm long); maturing in spring to autumn, depending on elevation; common.

ECOLOGY: Generally mineral soil, also humus, logs and rocks, in somewhat shaded to open sites; low to high elevations; often abundant in logged areas.

SIMILAR SPECIES: Common nodding pohlia is a very abundant moss that strongly resembles the common and difficult genus *Bryum* (p. 401). No single, non-microscopic character can be used to discriminate these genera. • *P. wahlenbergii*, a common moss of damp sites, is yellow-green and has reddish stems and a capsule that shrinks to half its length when dry (common nodding pohlia capsules are essentially unaltered). • *P. cruda* grows in more shaded sites, has capsules that are usually not nodding and leaves with a slight metallic sheen.

NOTES: The species name *nutans* is Latin for 'nodding' and refers to the attachment of the sporophyte capsule.

SILVER MOSS • *Bryum argenteum*

GENERAL: In short, **silvery green** turfs of erect, **worm-like shoots**, usually less than 0.5 cm tall.

LEAVES: Ovate, **pointed**, 0.5 mm long or less, closely overlapping on shoots, with midribs; **tip is often white** and sharply pointed, especially on dry sites.

SPOROPHYTES: Capsules bright red, 1–2 mm long, **nodding** on red stalks; maturing in spring to summer; common.

ECOLOGY: Common in mineral soil of dry grasslands; also around buildings, especially on concrete; to subalpine areas in well-drained, non-forested sites.

SIMILAR SPECIES: *Plagiobryum zierii*, usually found on humid cliffs, has capsules that have long necks and are never red when mature. Its gametophytes are also much larger than those of silver moss.

NOTES: Silver moss is a very distinctive, small, silvery green moss. The contrasting bright red sporophytes are very striking. • The species name *argenteum* is from the Latin for 'silver' and refers to the silvery green colour of this moss, caused by a scarcity of chlorophyll in most of the upper leaf cells.

PEAR MOSS • *Leptobryum pyriforme*

GENERAL: In shiny, low, silky, yellow-green turfs, 0.5–1.5 mm tall; usually overlooked when sporophytes are absent.

LEAVES: Lance-shaped, **very narrow and hair-like**, 3–4 mm long; strongly divergent from stem and somewhat twisted when moist, **strongly twisted when dry**.

SPOROPHYTES: Capsules glossy red-brown to rusty brown, **pear-shaped**, 2–2.5 mm long, with elongate necks, **nodding** on yellowish to brownish stalks (1–3.5 cm long); maturing spring to summer; often abundant.

ECOLOGY: Disturbed mineral soil, sometimes peaty soil; low to subalpine elevations; sometimes abundant in burned over forests.

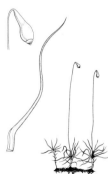

SIMILAR SPECIES: Pear moss is distinguished from *Pohlia* species (p. 400) and *Bryum* species (above) by its glossy, pear-shaped, nodding capsules, especially in association with the silky, narrow, yellow-green leaves.

NOTES: The species name *pyriforme*, Latin for 'pear shaped,' refers to the shape of the capsules.

BROOM MOSS • *Dicranum scoparium*

GENERAL: In glossy, dark green to yellow-green **tufts**, 2–8 cm tall, often with abundant, whitish to red-brown masses of woolly rhizoids on lower parts of shoots.

LEAVES: Lance-shaped, 5–12 mm long, **shiny** when dry; usually **strongly curved, with most leaf tips facing to 1 side of shoots**.

SPOROPHYTES: Capsules curved, brown, smooth, with **long-snouted hood**, 5–6 mm long (including hood), **inclined** on red-brown stalks (1.5–3 cm long); usually only 1 per shoot; maturing late spring to summer; common.

ECOLOGY: Decaying logs, cliff shelves, forest floors; also on trunks of living trees; sometimes in wetlands (especially bogs); lowlands to alpine elevations; in both open and shaded sites.

SIMILAR SPECIES: *D. polysetum* has many sporophytes on each shoot and wavy leaves. • *D. fuscescens* has leaves that are not glossy and become very contorted when dry.

NOTES: The glossy curved **leaves, in which the tips are swept to one side of the shoot**, are frequent in species of this genus. • Broom moss, also called heron's bill moss, is a common and variable species. • The species name *scoparium*, from the Latin *scopa*, 'a broom,' refers to the swept appearance of the leaves on the stem.

YELLOW-GREEN CUSHION MOSS • *Dicranoweisia crispula*

GENERAL: In green to yellow-green (occasionally black) **tufts**, 1–4 cm tall, somewhat taller when in deep crevices; somewhat loosely attached to substrate.

LEAVES: Lance-shaped, 1.5–4 mm long, with conspicuous, keel-like midribs; nearly straight when moist, **strongly twisted when dry**.

SPOROPHYTES: Capsules cylindrical, 1–1.5 mm long, smooth and pale brown (occasionally black) when mature, **erect** on long, yellowish to brown stalks (1–1.5 cm long); maturing summer to autumn; common.

ECOLOGY: On rocks, usually in crevices; subalpine and alpine elevations; sometimes abundant in areas where snow remains late into summer.

SIMILAR SPECIES: *Kiaeria* species occur in similar habitats, but their leaves are not strongly twisted when dry and their capsules are usually slightly inclined and curved.

NOTES: Yellow-green cushion moss can be distinguished from most similar mosses of high elevations by its crevice habitat, twisted leaves (when dry), and erect capsules on elongate stalks. • The species name *crispula* refers to the leaves, which become 'crisped' or twisted when dry.

CORD MOSS • *Funaria hygrometrica*

GENERAL: In loose, short turfs, 3–5 mm tall of pale green, somewhat glossy, **rosette- or bulb-like plants**; **firmly attached** to soil by **rhizoids**.

LEAVES: Ovate, 2–4 mm long, with **obvious midrib** and **sharp tip**; forming clusters at shoot tip.

SPOROPHYTES: Capsules inverted egg-shaped (narrowest near base), pale yellow-green when young, **grooved** and red-brown when mature, 2–3 mm long; peristome teeth rich red-brown; **pale yellowish hood with inflated base** and tiny beak; **inclined to nodding** on **twisted, yellow stalks** (1–4 cm long); maturing in spring or summer; common.

ECOLOGY: Mainly in disturbed habitats, especially roadsides and burned forest sites (where it appears soon after fire); common also on bonfire sites; low elevations; a greenhouse 'weed.'

NOTES: Cord moss is not easily recognized without its sporophyte capsules, but it is unmistakable when they are present. The asymmetrically egg-shaped capsule that curves downward when mature and the unusual, inflated-based, beaked hood make it distinctive. • The sporophyte stalks twist and untwist rapidly with changes in moisture, which gave rise to the species name *hygrometrica* and the common name 'cord moss.'

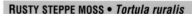

RUSTY STEPPE MOSS • *Tortula ruralis*

GENERAL: In tall or short turfs of reddish brown to dark green, erect, unbranched shoots, 1–8 cm tall.

LEAVES: Tongue-shaped, 1–4 mm long, with **colourless bases** and opaque upper portions; midribs extending into abrupt, **white hair-point**; **broadly flaring when moist**.

SPOROPHYTES: Capsules cylindrical, brown, 5–8 mm long; **peristome teeth reddish, corkscrewtwisted**, extend from distinct, **white, sleeve-like tubes** at top of capsules; **erect** on smooth stalks (2–4 cm long); maturing spring to summer; occasional.

ECOLOGY: Common on mineral soil among grassland plants, also on outcrops along watercourses; mainly at low elevations.

SIMILAR SPECIES: In subalpine and alpine slopes, rusty steppe moss is replaced by *T. norvegica*, in which the hair-points are at least partly reddish brown, especially near the base.

NOTES: The strongly flaring leaves, the white hair-points that extend abruptly from the leaf blades, and the erect, unbranched plants that grow on mineral soil (especially calcium-rich soil) make rusty steppe moss very distinctive. The peristome, with its white, basal sleeve bearing corkscrew-twisted teeth, is also distinctive. • The genus name *Tortula*, Latin for 'a small twist,' refers to the twisted peristome teeth; the species name *ruralis* means 'from the countryside.'

COMMON DUNG MOSS • *Tetraplodon mnioides*

GENERAL: In cone-shaped to rounded, compact tufts, 2–4 cm tall, of light green, erect, unbranched shoots, firmly interwoven with rhizoids.

LEAVES: Broadly ovate, 2–5 mm long, with distinct midribs and abruptly tapered points; diverging slightly when moist, twisted when dry.

SPOROPHYTES: Capsules red-brown to nearly black, cylindrical, 1–2 mm long, often with somewhat **bulging lower portions; peristome teeth bright red-brown**, flare outward from top of capsule and expose dusty mass of green spores; **erect** on stout, red-brown to nearly black stalks (1–6 cm long); maturing in summer; frequent.

ECOLOGY: On dung (usually of carnivorous animals), sometimes on bones and owl regurgitation pellets; open forests, bogs and tundra; low to subalpine elevations.

SIMILAR SPECIES: *T. angustatus* has leaves with toothed edges, and its capsules are usually on very short stalks.

NOTES: Common dung moss is a distinctive moss recognized by its stiff, cone-shaped colonies on dung, its erect, basally swollen capsules with striking, red-brown stalks (when young) and its flaring, red-brown peristome teeth. • The species name *mnioides*, meaning 'resembling *Mnium*,' is a rather misleading name.

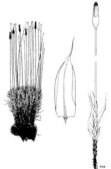

ASPEN MOSS • *Pylaisiella polyantha*

GENERAL: In yellow-green to dark green, turf-like mats of creeping shoots, 1–4 cm long, with upright, sometimes slightly curved branches (3–10 mm tall); tightly attached to substrate.

LEAVES: Ovate to lance-shaped, 0.6–1.2 mm long, without obvious midribs; spreading when moist, pressed closely to stem when dry.

SPOROPHYTES: Capsules light brown, cylindrical, 1.2–2 mm long, **erect** on 6–12 mm long stalks; maturing in summer; abundant.

ECOLOGY: Mainly on trunks of cottonwoods and aspens, especially near base; sometimes on coniferous trees and on rocks.

NOTES: This is the moss most commonly encountered on cottonwood and aspen trees in our area. • The yellowish to dark green colonies, with many short, upright branches on creeping shoots, the leaves lacking obvious midribs and the erect, cylindrical capsule are good diagnostic characters. • The species name *polyantha*, 'many flowers,' refers to the many female branches.

COMMON LANTERN MOSS • *Andreaea rupestris*

GENERAL: In small **black to dark or red-brown tufts**, 1–2 cm tall, tightly attached to rock, sometimes forming short turf.

LEAVES: Ovate, with blunt tips (0.5 mm long) and no midribs; spreading when moist.

SPOROPHYTES: Capsules dark brown to black, elliptic, 0.5 mm long, with **4 longitudinal gaps that open when ripe**; **stalkless** but extending on a length of leafless stem; maturing spring to summer; common.

ECOLOGY: Confined mainly to igneous rocks; most frequent at mid to high elevations on exposed to somewhat shaded rock surfaces.

SIMILAR SPECIES: There are 10 species of *Andreaea* in B.C., but only four have been noted in our region. Both *A. blyttii* and *A. nivalis* are found in late-snow areas and have midribs in

their leaves. *A. nivalis* tends to be larger and softer than *A. blyttii* or common lantern moss, and its leaves are strongly curved to one side of the shoot.

NOTES: This moss genus has a unique capsule which resembles a tiny lantern (the capsule wall arches out to form the four openings). • The species name *rupestris* is from the Latin, *rupes*, meaning 'rock.'

WOOLLY CATERPILLAR MOSS • *Pterygoneurum subsessile*

GENERAL: In short, **white-haired turfs**, 1–3 mm tall; barely visible unless moist.

LEAVES: Ovate, with **long hair-points** (0.5–2 mm long); greyish green when moist, almost white when dry, dominated by the long hair-points.

SPOROPHYTES: Capsules spherical, yellow-brown when mature, 0.5–1 mm long, **without peristome teeth**, on very short stalks **immersed among leaves** at shoot tips; maturing in spring; common.

ECOLOGY: Stable, fine-textured soil among herbs and shrubs in grasslands; also on banks; confined to low elevations.

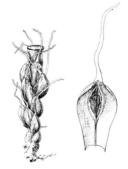

SIMILAR SPECIES: Other species of *Pterygoneurum* are similar, but *P. lamellatum* and *P. ovatum* have more obvious sporophyte stalks (2–4 mm long) that raise the capsules above the leaves. These mosses are also found in dry grasslands.

NOTES: This tiny plant is tolerant of long periods of drying, but it is generally found in sites where the night-time dew lasts longer into the day than in more exposed sites. • The species name *subsessile* describes the capsule immersed among the leaves.

GROOVED GNOME-CAP MOSS • *Encalypta rhaptocarpa*

GENERAL: In short, **loose turfs** of **light green** to yellowish-green **plants**, 3–6 mm tall.

LEAVES: Oblong ovate, 1–2 mm long, not glossy, with **obvious midribs and hair-points**; broadly flaring when moist, slightly shrinking when dry; leaf bases are constructed of colourless thin-walled cells.

SPOROPHYTES: Capsules cylindrical, brown, **grooved when mature**, 3–4 mm long; brown peristome teeth; capsules **completely sheathed by long, smooth hood; erect** on reddish stalks (0.5–1.5 cm long); maturing in late spring to summer; common.

ECOLOGY: On mineral soil, mainly in calcium-rich sites, also in cliff and rock crevices; dry grasslands at low elevations to tundra at high elevations.

SIMILAR SPECIES: There are many other species of *Encalypta* in our region. A common species, *E. vulgaris*, has capsules lacking grooves, as do some other species of *Encalypta*.

NOTES: *Encalypta* is a distictive genus with light green, short, leafy plants and erect capsules completely sheathed by a smooth hood with a snout at the tip. • The genus name *Encalypta* derives from the Greek *kalyptos*, 'covered' or 'hidden,' referring to the hood-shaped calyptra. The common name 'gnome-cap' likewise refers to the hood.

FOUR-TOOTHED LOG MOSS • *Tetraphis pellucida*

GENERAL: In short, dark green turfs of erect plants, 0.5–1.5 cm tall; in spring, many shoots are topped by enlarged, spreading leaves that enclose a **mass of pale green, disk-shaped gemmae**, or shoots have a short upper leafless portion bearing cluster of unprotected gemmae; firmly attached to substrate by rhizoids at stem base.

LEAVES: Lower leaves are ovate, 0.5–1 mm long, with obvious midribs, tapering to tips, diverging outward slightly from shoot; upper leaves of sporophyte-bearing shoots are lance-shaped, 1.5–3 mm long, erect, with bases that sheathe stalks; **leaves at tips of gemmae-producing shoots are often blunt**, 0.5–1 mm long, forming cups.

SPOROPHYTES: Capsules cylindrical, **red-brown** when mature, 2–3 mm long, **covered by pleated hood; with 4 triangular peristome teeth; erect** on red-brown stalks (0.6–2 cm long); maturing late spring to summer; common.

ECOLOGY: Usually on rotten logs and stumps in coniferous forests; low to subalpine elevations.

SIMILAR SPECIES: *T. geniculata* has sporophyte stalks that are rough and have a distinct angular kink near their middle.

NOTES: Four-toothed log moss is very distinctive, and it is easily recognized by its erect cylindrical capsule with four peristome teeth, its erect gemmae-bearing shoots and its occurrence on rotten logs. • The species name *pellucida*, from the Latin 'clear' or 'transparent,' describes the leaves of this moss when wet.

STEPPE MOUSE-MOSS • *Coscinodon calyptratus*

GENERAL: In rounded, **greyish to whitish** tufts or compact, **rounded cushions**, 1–2.5 cm tall.

LEAVES: Narrowly ovate to lance-shaped, with obvious midribs and long, **conspicuous, white hair-points**, 1–3 mm long (including hair-point); somewhat twisted when dry.

SPOROPHYTES: Capsules cylindrical, 1.5–2.5 mm long, pale brown and smooth to slightly wrinkled when dry, **completely sheathed by pleated, whitish to pale yellow hood** with darkened tip; stalk straight, yellowish to brown, 2–3 mm long; maturing in spring; common.

ECOLOGY: Dry rocks and outcrops in semi-arid grasslands; low elevations.

SIMILAR SPECIES: *Grimmia pulvinata* has partly sheathing, smooth hoods, and curved stalks, generally more than 3 mm long. • *Racomitrium* species (p. 394) also occur on rocks, but they do not grow in rounded cushions.

NOTES: Steppe mouse-moss can be distinguished by its growth in rounded, greyish to whitish tufts on rocks, and the pleated hood completely sheathing the capsule. • The species name *calyptratus* describes the hood-like structure that sheathes the capsule until it matures.

Key to the liverworts

1a. Plants thallose (strap-shaped), lacking leaves 2

    2a. Obvious pattern of many-angled chambers outlined in plant surface; gives off spicy odour when crushed .... *Conocephalum conicum*

    2b. Obscure pattern of chambers in plant surface; no spicy odour when crushed .... *Marchantia polymorpha*

1b. Plants with stems, bearing small leaves 3

    3a. Leaves with more than 2 lobes 4

        4a. Leaf edges with long, ciliate hairs throughout .... *Ptilidium ciliare*

        4b. Leaf edges lacking ciliate hairs, except at base of marginal lobe .... *Barbilophozia hatcheri*

    3b. Leaves not lobed or with 2 lobes 5

        5a. Leaves not lobed .... *Plagiochila asplenioides*

        5b. Leaves 2-lobed 6

            6a. Lobes of equal size 7

                7a. Lobes divided to more than half of leaf length; leaves light green .... *Cephalozia bicuspidata*

                7b. Lobes shallowly divided at leaf tip; leaves dark green to rusty or red-brown .... *Marsupella emarginata*

            6b. Lobes of unequal size 8

                8a. Smaller lobe on under surface of stem .... *Porella cordaeana*

                8b. Smaller lobe on upper surface of stem 9

                      9a. Both lobes tongue-shaped; smaller lobe oriented parallel to stem length; leaves yellow-green .... *Diplophyllum taxifolium*

                    9b. Larger lobe kidney-shaped; smaller lobe rounded; leaves dark green to reddish .... *Scapania undulata*

SPICY CONEHEAD • *Conocephalum conicum*

GENERAL: Thallose, yellowish green to dark green, broadly strap-shaped, irregularly branched, 4–6 cm long and 0.5–1.5 cm broad; **upper surface marked by regular, many-angled outlines of air chambers**, each perforated by tiny, white-ringed hole; firmly attached to substrate by whitish to greyish rhizoids.

SPOROPHYTES: Capsules, black, cylindrical, 0.5–1 mm long, hanging down from **underside of stalked, conical heads** near erect branch tips (to 4 cm tall); maturing spring to summer; occasional.

ECOLOGY: Usually on damp, somewhat shaded cliffs, often near streams and waterfalls in our area.

NOTES: The thalli have the appearance of reptilian skin, with the very obvious chamber out-

lines resembling scales. The cone-shaped heads that bear the sporophytes are also unmistakable, when present. • When crushed, this species has a spicy odour not noted in other local thallose liverworts.

GREEN TONGUE WORT • *Marchantia polymorpha*

GENERAL: Thallose, with flattened, dark green, forking branches, 4–10 cm long and 5–10 mm wide; upper surface marked by **cell-like pattern, with each 'cell' bearing 1 central pore**, often also bearing frilled gemmae cups containing 'nests' of tiny, lens-shaped, pale green gemmae; firmly attached to substrate by white rhizoids.

SPOROPHYTES: Capsules, spherical, light brown, 0.5 mm long, **hidden beneath conspicuous, umbrella-like receptacle borne on elongate, erect shoot** (0.5–2 cm tall); maturing in summer, occasional to abundant.

ECOLOGY: Common on mineral soil in burned, deforested lands; also on disturbed banks and in seepage sites; low to subalpine elevations.

NOTES: The male and female sex organs are on separate plants (the photograph shows male plants) on striking, umbrella-like stalks. These differ from the reproductive structures of any other liverwort in the province. The rounded, frilled gemmae cups (one is shown on the male plant in the illustration), are also characteristic of this genus. • The species name *polymorpha* means 'many forms,' reflecting the differences among male, female and gemmae-producing thalli.

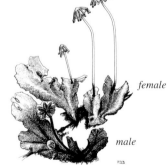

female

male

ORANGE TALUS WORT • *Ptilidium ciliare*

GENERAL: Leafy, forming loose, rusty to orange-brown patches of erect, much-branched, 'fuzzy' shoots, 4–10 cm tall.

LEAVES: In 3 rows; 2 rows of side leaves, 1–2 mm long and 2.2–3 mm wide, with **4–5 lobes** bearing **many ciliate teeth**; 1 row of smaller underleaves, with many short, ciliate-edged lobes.

SPOROPHYTES: Not seen in local populations; capsules spherical, pale brown, 0.5–1 mm long, barely emerging from swollen tube of fused leaves with a puckered mouth.

ECOLOGY: Most frequent among large boulders of stable boulder slopes; also on forest floors and cliff shelves; mid to subalpine elevations.

NOTES: This liverwort can be recognized by its much-branched, fuzzy masses of shoots and its many-lobed leaves with ciliate edges.

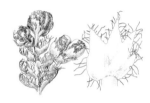

HATCHER'S FAN WORT • *Barbilophozia hatcheri*

GENERAL: Leafy, forming loose, pale green to brownish turfs or mats of erect to reclining, mainly unbranched, flattened shoots, 2–5 cm long.

LEAVES: In 3 rows; side leaves flattened horizontally and attached at oblique angle, **3–4 lobed,** with lobes sharply pointed and broadly triangular (0.7–1.5 mm wide and slightly less long), divided 1/3 the leaf length; upper leaves sometimes misshapen and bearing dusty masses of red-brown gemmae; underleaves visible with hand lens, 0.5 mm long, deeply 2-lobed with ciliate edges.

SPOROPHYTES: Capsules spherical, 0.5–1 mm long, dark brown to black; white stalks, 0.5–1.5 cm long; maturing in summer; uncommon.

ECOLOGY: Logs, forest floors, cliff ledges and humus over boulders in humid coniferous forests; low to subalpine elevations.

SIMILAR SPECIES: Hatcher's fan wort resembles other species of *Barbilophozia* and *Lophozia*, especially *B. barbata*, which is one-third to twice as large, is generally creeping and lacks gemmae.

NOTES: The often-abundant, red-brown gemmae and the obliquely attached side leaves with 3–4 pointed, broad lobes usually identify this liverwort. • Hatcher's fan wort is named for its spreading, fan-like leaves.

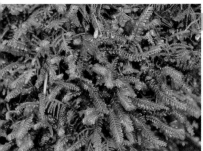

CEDAR-SHAKE WORT • *Plagiochila asplenioides*

GENERAL: Leafy, forming dull green to somewhat rusty green turfs of erect to semi-erect shoots, sparsely branched, 1–10 cm long; loosely attached to substrate.

LEAVES: In 2 rows, broadly ovate, 2–4 mm long; edges curved downward, sometimes strongly toothed.

SPOROPHYTES: Capsules egg-shaped, brown, 1.5–2 mm long; on white stalks, 1.5–5 cm long, emerging from club-shaped tube of fused leaves, swollen at base but compressed at toothed mouth (4–7 mm long); maturing in spring to summer; occasional.

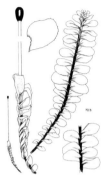

ECOLOGY: Cliff shelves, tundra banks, rotten logs and moist depressions in forests; low to alpine elevations.

NOTES: The two rows of ovate, unlobed leaves with downward-curving edges make this a very distinctive liverwort. • The species name is from the fancied resemblance to the fern *Asplenium.*

SLENDER TWO-TOOTHED WORT • *Cephalozia bicuspidata*

GENERAL: Leafy, dark green to light green, 2–2.5 cm long, forming depressed, creeping patches or nearly erect, loose strands that are sometimes mixed with other bryophytes.

LEAVES: In 2 side rows, attached at oblique angle, **equally 2-lobed** with sharply pointed tips, 0.2–0.5 mm long.

SPOROPHYTES: Capsules cylindrical, dark brown to black, 0.3–0.5 mm long; on white stalks, 0.5–1 mm tall; emerging from pale green cylindrical tubes of fused, pleated, leaves with whitish, toothed mouths (1–1.5 mm long); maturing spring to summer; common, especially when growing over rotten logs.

ECOLOGY: Logs without bark, damp depressions; mainly in forests but also in the alpine.

NOTES: This tiny liverwort is identified by its dark to pale green colour, its sharply 2-lobed leaves, its cylindrical, pleated sporophyte tube (perianth) and its occurrence on damp logs or in moist depressions. • Slender two-toothed wort is so named for the sharply 2-lobed leaves.

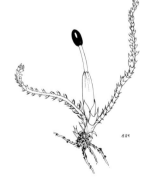

RUSTY ROCK WORT • *Marsupella emarginata*

GENERAL: Leafy, forming rusty brown, reddish-purple to dark green turfs of erect, usually unbranched shoots, 0.3–3 cm tall; firmly attached to rock.

LEAVES: In 2 rows, closely appressed and curving outward from stem, with **2 rounded to broadly obtuse lobes** with somewhat downward-curving edges, 0.7–1.5 mm long and slightly wider.

SPOROPHYTES: Capsules spherical, 0.5–0.8 mm long; on white stalks, 0.3–1 mm long; maturing spring to summer; occasional.

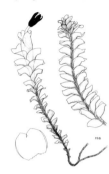

ECOLOGY: Rock faces and splashed boulders near streams and lakes; occasionally on boulders in woodlands and tundra.

SIMILAR SPECIES: In our region, most other *Marsupella* species are either soil-dwelling and loosely attached, or are smaller.

NOTES: The dark colour, the occurrence on rock and the obtusely 2-lobed leaves with slightly down-curved edges are distinguishing features of rusty rock wort.

DULL SCALE FEATHER WORT • *Porella cordaeana*

GENERAL: Leafy, forming masses of flattened, pinnately-branched, dull dark green shoots, 1–10 cm long, with tips pointing downward and branches arching outward; loosely attached to substrate.

LEAVES: In 3 rows; 2 rows of overlapping leaves on upper surface of stem, circular to ovate, 1–2 mm long, **unequally 2-lobed**, with **smaller, tongue-shaped lobes on underside of stem**; 1 row of ovate, unlobed leaves on under surface of stem, with ruffled to toothed lower edges.

SPOROPHYTES: Capsules spherical, light brown, 2–3 mm long; stalks short, barely emerging from flattened tubes of fused leaves (1–2.5 mm long); maturing in spring, occasional.

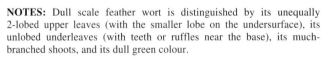

ECOLOGY: Confined to shaded rocks in our region; also on trees and shrubs elsewhere in B.C.

NOTES: Dull scale feather wort is distinguished by its unequally 2-lobed upper leaves (with the smaller lobe on the undersurface), its unlobed underleaves (with teeth or ruffles near the base), its much-branched shoots, and its dull green colour.

YELLOW DOUBLE-LEAF WORT • *Diplophyllum taxifolium*

GENERAL: Leafy, forming thin patches of ascending to reclining, unbranched, flattened, bright yellow-green to yellowish brown shoots, 1–5 cm long.

LEAVES: In 2 rows, spreading strongly outward from stem; **unequally 2-lobed**, with large, **strap-shaped**, outward arching lobe beneath (0.3–0.7 mm long), and **smaller lobe** (0.1–0.4 mm long) **above it**, oriented nearly parallel to stem; clusters of green gemmae sometimes frequent on upper leaves.

SPOROPHYTES: Capsules spherical, brown, 1–1.5 mm long; stalks 4–6 mm long, emerging from short, pleated tubes of fused leaves; maturing in summer; infrequent.

ECOLOGY: Shaded cliffs, rocks and tundra, occasionally on trees; low to subalpine and alpine elevations.

SIMILAR SPECIES: *Scapania* species (below) also have 2-lobed leaves, but in none of these is the narrow, larger lobe so long and narrow.

NOTES: The bright yellow-green, flattened plants with unequally 2-lobed leaves make *Diplophyllum* species very distinctive. • The species name *taxifolium* describes the flaring leaf arrangement, which resembles that of yew (*Taxus* sp.). The common name comes from the way each strongly 2-lobed leaf looks like two parallel leaves emerging from the same spot.

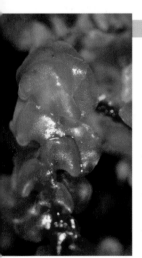

WATER MITTEN-LEAF WORT • *Scapania undulata*

GENERAL: Leafy, forming mats of robust, ascending to erect, irregularly branched shoots, 2–10 cm long, varying from dark green or reddish purple to almost black; usually firmly attached to substrate.

LEAVES: In 2 rows, **unequally 2-lobed**; larger lobe **kidney-shaped**, 0.3–0.7 mm high, 0.5–1.7 mm wide; **smaller lobe similar but on upper surface of stem**; both lobes sometimes with small teeth; leaves spreading outward when moist, contorted and wavy when dry.

SPOROPHYTES: Capsules dark brown, egg-shaped, 0.3–0.5 mm long; on white stalks, 0.8–1.5 cm long, emerging from flattened tube of fused leaves (5–6 mm long); maturing in summer, occasional.

ECOLOGY: On rocks, wood and soil, often submerged in streams and along lake edges, especially at high elevations; submerged plants tend to be dark green, whereas those in sunny sites tend to be red-purple to nearly black.

SIMILAR SPECIES: Several species of *Scapania* occur in our area and they are difficult to tell apart without a microscope. • *Diplophyllum* species (above) have less rounded leaf lobes.

Lichens

More than a thousand different kinds of lichens make their home in British Columbia. Only a few hundred, however, are widespread and conspicuous. In southern British Columbia, the richest habitats for lichens include open forests, rocky outcrops and the alpine. Undisturbed grasslands and old-growth forests also appear to be important for many species.

Lichens are the banners of the fungal kingdom. Think of them as fungi that have discovered agriculture. Instead of invading or scavenging for a living like moulds, mildews, mushrooms or other fungi, lichen fungi cultivate algae within themselves. Algae are photosynthesizers, and so supply the fungus with carbohydrates, vitamins and proteins. In return, the fungus appears to provide the alga with protection from the elements. A lichen is simply the physical manifestation of this relationship, much as a gall is the manifestation of, for example, a larval insect feeding on a leaf.

Most lichen fungi cultivate algae, though in some cases the photosynthesizing partner (**photobiont**) is a cyanobacterium. In a few lichen species, both types of photobionts are present, with the paler (green) alga scattered throughout, and the darker (blue-green) cyanobacterium localized in small colonies called **cephalodia**.

Lichens reproduce in several ways. Sometimes the fungal partner produces saucer-like fruiting bodies (**apothecia**). In some species the inner 'stuffing' (**medulla**) of the lichen becomes exposed at the surface as clusters of tiny powdery balls (**soredia**). In other species, the upper surface bears tiny wart-like outgrowths (**isidia**). When soredia and isidia are carried to new locations, as by birds, they may develop into new lichens.

Lichen life forms

Lichens come in many different shapes, but they never form leafy stems, as mosses do. The following account encompasses seven growth forms—dust, crust, scale, leaf, club, shrub and hair.

Dust: Intimately attached; composed entirely of tiny powdery granules, rubbing off on the fingers like chalk dust.

Crust: Intimately attached; lower surface absent; hard upper surface present.

Scale: Tiny, shell-like lobes with a typically loose, cottony lower surface; usually forming overlapping colonies.

Leaf: Small to large, leaf- or strap-like lobes, usually with holdfasts and a hard (non-cottony) lower surface.

Club: Unbranched or sparsely branched cylindrical stems, usually upright.

Shrub: Much-branched, cylindrical stems, usually tufted.

Hair: Intricately branched filaments, tufted to pendent.

LIME DUST • *Chrysothrix chlorina*

GENERAL: Continuous dust lichen consisting of tiny, powdery, **bright 'fluorescent' greenish-yellow** granules (soredia).

REPRODUCTIVE: No sexual fruiting bodies.

HABITAT: On shaded, vertical rock outcrops in humid localities and less frequently on sheltered conifer trunks; common.

SIMILAR SPECIES: Gold dust (*C. candelaris*) has a more orangish-yellow thallus and usually grows on tree trunks. Also similar are various species of *Lepraria* and *Leproloma*. In those genera, however, the thallus is usually whitish, bluish or greenish, not orangish or yellowish.

NOTES: Typically growing in habitats sheltered from rain, these lichens satisfy their moisture requirements directly from the air. Most species do not produce fruiting bodies; they reproduce by disseminating the powdery granules of which they are comprised. • The genus name *Chrysothrix* is Greek for 'golden thread,' while the species name *chlorina* is Greek for 'pale green.'

COW PIE • *Diploschistes muscorum*

GENERAL: Continuous to somewhat chinky crust lichen with a finely cracked, creamy or **whitish-grey upper surface**.

REPRODUCTIVE: Many, tiny, **black, sunken, crater-like apothecia** always present.

HABITAT: Over soil and humus in open, often exposed localities; most abundant in lowland grasslands; common.

NOTES: Cow pie, as unmistakable as its name, often begins life as a parasite of *Cladonia* species, especially ribbed cladonia (*C. cariosa*, p. 416), though it later becomes free-living. • This is one of dozens of soil-dwelling species of lichens, mosses, liverworts, cyanobacteria and microfungi that collectively help to hold many native grassland communities together, both by checking erosion and by sealing the soil against invasive annual and biennial weeds. Trampling by cattle and other livestock has contributed to a gradual decline in these 'cryptogamic crusts' throughout many portions of their former range. • The genus name *Diploschistes* is Greek for 'twice divided,' probably in reference to the spores, one of which is illustrated schematically.

BLOODY HEART • *Mycoblastus sanguinarius*

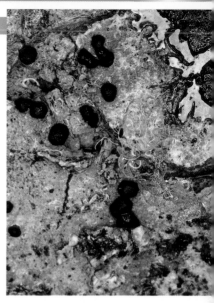

GENERAL: Continuous crust lichen with a **pale greyish** to pale greenish or pale bluish upper surface.

REPRODUCTIVE: Tiny, **black, hemispherical apothecia, usually red within** (use a pocket knife and hand lens), always present.

HABITAT: Over **conifer bark** (also over birch) in open to shady forests; common.

NOTES: Until the fruiting bodies of this species are sliced open and examined for their 'bloody hearts,' this lichen is easily mistaken for any of several bark-dwelling crust lichens having black fruiting bodies (apothecia). Occasionally a fruiting body will be found that has been exposed by a grazing insect or other invertebrate, evidence that even crust lichens have their devotees. As with most other lichens, each apothecium bears thousands of tiny flasks or 'asci.' Bloody heart differs from most other lichens in that it has only a single spore per ascus, while most other lichens have several. • Appropriately, the species name *sanguinarius* is Latin for 'bloody.'

GREEN MAP • *Rhizocarpon geographicum*

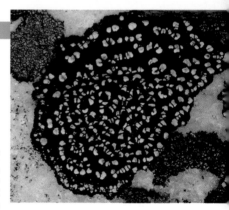

GENERAL: **Mosaic crust** lichen consisting of tiny **yellowish-green 'tiles'** (areoles) set against a **black background** (prothallus).

REPRODUCTIVE: **Black apothecia** always present.

HABITAT: Forming **roughly circular colonies over acid rock** in open sites; more frequent at upper elevations; common.

NOTES: Green map belongs to a group of closely related species notoriously difficult to tell apart without a microscope. Although green map may grow only a few centimetres in a century, it is an extraordinarily long-lived species. Some colonies in the Canadian Arctic are estimated to be many thousands of years old—older even than the fabled bristlecone pine. This is one of a handful of crust lichens used for dating rock surfaces (for example, when studying the advances and retreats of glaciers), a technique known as lichenometry. • The scientific name *Rhizocarpon geographicum* is from the Greek and Latin for 'mapped root-fruit.'

SOCKEYE PSORA • *Psora decipiens*

GENERAL: Appressed scale lichen with **small**, discrete, shell-like lobes (to about 5 mm long); upper surface **pinkish red** to brownish red, usually **whitish near edges**; lower surface white and cottony.

REPRODUCTIVE: Tiny, **black, hemispherical apothecia usually present, located near lobe edges.**

HABITAT: Forming scattered colonies over **calcium-rich soil** in open, often exposed sites, most abundant in undisturbed grasslands and in the alpine; frequent.

SIMILAR SPECIES: Sockeye psora might be confused with other *Psora* species, but is readily distinguished by its reddish lobes and eyeball-shaped apothecia. • In dry grassland communities, watch also for brain scale (*P. cerebriformis*), with its tiny, cracked, yellowish cream-coloured scales.

NOTES: This species is generally slow to colonize after disturbance, and so is most common in 'old-growth' grasslands. • 'Sockeye' refers to the pinkish-red colour, which resembles the colour of spawning sockeye salmon. The genus name *Psora* is Greek for 'mange,' and the species name *decipiens* is Latin for 'deceptive.'

RIBBED CLADONIA • *Cladonia cariosa*

GENERAL: Small to medium-sized **scale** lichen consisting of **colonies of upright scales**; **lobes small**, to about 2–3 mm long; upper surface pale greyish green to brownish green; lower surface white and cottony.

REPRODUCTIVE: Brown apothecia, located on tips of upright clubs, often absent.

HABITAT: Forming loosely overlapping colonies over humus and soil in open, dry forests and grasslands at all elevations; best developed in disturbed sites; common.

SIMILAR SPECIES: The scales (squamules) of other soil-dwelling *Cladonia* species, including *C. symphycarpa*, may be similar, but are usually somewhat larger and less consistently upright.

NOTES: Like other *Cladonia* species, ribbed cladonia often gives rise to pale whitish or greenish clubs (podetia) which, in this case, are vertically 'ribbed' and bear dark brown fruiting bodies at their tips. • In rather dry ecosystems, this pioneer species is among the first soil-dwelling lichens to colonize after disturbance. • For more on this species, see notes under cow pie (*Diploschistes muscorum*, p. 414). • The species name *cariosa* is Latin for 'decay.'

PUNCTURED ROCKTRIPE • *Umbilicaria torrefacta*

GENERAL: Medium-sized, **circular, few-lobed leaf lichen**, 1.5–4 cm across, attached centrally by a **single holdfast**; upper surface **dark brown**, apparently chinky-cracked, abundantly and **minutely perforate** toward edges (best viewed against the sky); lower surface brown or blackish, often platy in part, lacking holdfasts.

REPRODUCTIVE: Much-fissured **apothecia** often present.

HABITAT: Over acid to somewhat calcium-rich **rock** in open sites at all elevations; frequent.

SIMILAR SPECIES: Blistered rocktripe (*U. hyperborea*) is similar in habit and ecology, but has a 'blistered' upper surface and lacks the tiny perforations of punctured rocktripe. • Peppered rocktripe (*U. deusta*) bears minute, grainy isidia over its upper surface (use a hand lens).

NOTES: Rocktripes were used by Sir John Franklin and other early northern explorers as an emergency food. They are best prepared for this purpose by being soaked in soda water (or ashes) to remove acids that can cause severe intestinal discomfort. Stewing them with a pair of old hiking boots may possibly improve the flavour! Rocktripes were also once important as a source of scarlet dyes, and they are known as *corkir* in Scotland, where they were used for dyeing tartan cloth.

FROSTED ROCKTRIPE • *Umbilicaria vellea*

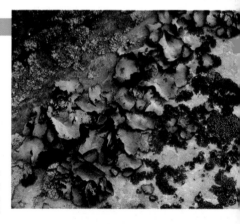

GENERAL: **Medium-sized** to large, **circular, few-lobed leaf lichen**, 4–10 cm or more across, attached centrally by a **single thickened holdfast**; upper surface pale **whitish grey**, smooth and dull; lower surface black and **densely covered in short holdfasts**.

REPRODUCTIVE: Usually absent.

HABITAT: Over **vertical, acid rock faces in sheltered, often somewhat shady sites** at all elevations; frequent.

SIMILAR SPECIES: The only species likely to be confused with frosted rocktripe is *U. americana*, a widespread lowland species in which only stubby, black, essentially unbranched holdfasts are present.

NOTES: Frosted rocktripe is easily recognized by its central umbilicus (characteristic of all *Umbilicaria* species), as well as by its pale greyish or frosted upper surface, and black lower surface covered in short holdfasts. Some of these holdfasts are short, black and unbranched, while others are long, pale and copiously branched. • The scientific name *Umbilicaria vellea* means, approximately, 'woollen belly button,' which is not a bad description, we think.

FRECKLE PELT • *Peltigera aphthosa*

GENERAL: Large, **loosely appressed leaf lichen**, with **broad** lobes, 2–5 cm wide; upper surface **pale greyish green** (dry) **to bright green** (moist), bearing scattered 'warts'; lower surface cottony and pale, **blackening abruptly** inward of lobe edges, without veins or with only broad, **inconspicuous veins**; holdfasts scarce.

REPRODUCTIVE: Erect, flattened, **brown apothecia** usually present.

HABITAT: Over moss, humus, rocks, and decaying logs in open forests; common.

SIMILAR SPECIES: The broad, green, 'warted,' ground-dwelling lobes of freckle pelt are likely to be confused, in our region, only with those of other freckle pelts, including *P. leucophlebia* and *P. britannica*. *P. leucophlebia*, however, has well-developed veins that darken gradually inward. *P. britannica* is restricted to very humid regions and produces loosely appressed 'warts' (cephalodia) that are readily dislodged with the flick of a fingernail. • Apple pelt (*P. malacea*) is also similar in general appearance, but is more bluish, has a blue-green photobiont and lacks cephalodia.

NOTES: The 'warts' on the upper surface contain tiny colonies of blue-green cyanobacteria, which supply the lichen fungus and its green algal partner with nitrogen. Freckle pelt is thus a symbiosis among representatives of three of the five kingdoms of life: Protista, Fungi and Monera. • The genus name *Peltigera*, from Greek and Latin, means 'shield bearing'; the species name *aphthosa*, from Greek, means 'thrush'—the disease, not the bird.

DOG PELT • *Peltigera canina*

GENERAL: Medium-sized or large, **loosely appressed leaf lichen**, with **broad** lobes, 1.5–2 cm wide; upper surface pale brownish or greyish, thinly covered in **fine, appressed hairs**, especially toward edges (visible with a hand lens), with **downturned lobe tips**; lower surface cottony and pale, bearing narrow, **brownish veins** and dark, **flaring holdfasts**.

REPRODUCTIVE: Erect, brown, longitudinally folded **apothecia** often present.

HABITAT: Over mineral soil and humus, moss or decaying wood in open places at all elevations; common.

SIMILAR SPECIES: Dog pelt is often difficult to distinguish from related pelts, especially those with a finely hairy upper surface. Of these, *P. rufescens* and *P. ponojensis* are smaller and have upturned lobe tips, and *P. membranacea* and *P. praetextata* have thinner lobes and finely fuzzy veins (use a hand lens), and are restricted to somewhat humid areas. Only dog pelt combines downturned lobe tips, an appressed-hairy upper surface, non-hairy veins and flaring holdfasts (illustrated).

NOTES: Dog pelt was used in former times to treat rabies, apparently because the fruiting bodies were thought to resemble dogs' teeth or, possibly, ears.

FROG PELT • *Peltigera neopolydactyla*

GENERAL: Medium-sized to large, **loosely appressed leaf lichen** with **broad lobes**, 1–2.5 cm wide; upper surface **hairless**, olive green to pale or dark **bluish grey**; lower surface whitish and **cottony**, bearing low, broad, brownish or blackish veins and **long, slender holdfasts**.

REPRODUCTIVE: Brownish, tooth-like apothecia often present, located on raised lobes along lobe edges.

HABITAT: Over rock, moss, soil and logs in open to shady forests, especially in somewhat humid areas; common.

SIMILAR SPECIES: Frog pelt's broad lobes, naked upper surface, veins and long, slender holdfasts are distinctive, and it is not likely to be confused with any other lichen except, perhaps, *P. polydactylon*, which has smaller lobes with frilly edges, *P. neckeri*, which has black, vertical apothecia, and *P. elisabethae* and *P. horizontalis*, in which the apothecia are flattened and horizontally oriented and the outermost holdfasts are concentrically arranged.

NOTES: *Peltigera* species are among the most conspicuous of ground-dwelling lichens. Nowhere are they more varied than in B.C., which is home to at least 30 species.

FAN PELT • *Peltigera venosa*

GENERAL: Small, **circular to fan-shaped leaf lichen**, 1–1.5 cm across, attached at edge by a **single thickened holdfast**; upper surface hairless, **pale bluish green** when dry, apple green when moist; lower surface white and cottony, bearing many flat, broad, **dark brownish veins** that lack holdfasts.

REPRODUCTIVE: Brown, flat, horizontally oriented **apothecia**; always 1 or several borne along lobe edges.

HABITAT: Over calcium-rich soil along streambanks, sheltered road cuts and other **steep, recently disturbed sites**, especially in somewhat humid areas; common.

NOTES: With its highly contrastive, 'Tudor-style' veins, fan pelt is unlikely to be confused with any other lichen. • Careful inspection of the veins will usually reveal the presence of many tiny, blackish 'warts' (cephalodia), which contain small colonies of cyanobacteria. Under certain conditions, these warts may become detached and develop into tiny, blackened, tar-papery lobes (use a hand lens) growing unattached at the base of a fan pelt. Because these

lobes share the same fungal partner as fan pelt, and because lichens are named for their fungal partner (not their 'algal' partner), they have the same scientific name as fan pelt—*Peltigera venosa*.

LUNGWORT • *Lobaria pulmonaria*

GENERAL: Large, **loosely attached leaf lichen** with **broad** lobes, to 2–3 cm wide; upper surface **pale bluish green (bright green when moist)**, strongly ridged, **deeply indented between ridges**; lower surface brownish and finely hairy, with scattered **whitish, naked** patches.

REPRODUCTIVE: Soredia or isidia borne along ridges of upper surface and lobe edges; apothecia infrequent.

HABITAT: On **trees**, both coniferous and deciduous, in humid forests at low elevations; occasional over mossy rock; common.

SIMILAR SPECIES: Cabbage lung (*L. linita*) lacks soredia and isidia and occurs primarily over mossy rocks at upper forested elevations.

NOTES: Lungwort's large, broad, greenish, loosely hanging lobes and tree-dwelling ecology are unmistakable. • Lungwort was used by early physicians in the treatment of pneumonia and other lung diseases, on the basis of its resemblance to that part of the body! Nowadays this species is still considered to be good for the lungs, at least in the sense that it grows only where the air is pure; in polluted areas, lungwort sickens and dies. • As a rhyming scientific name, *Lobaria pulmonaria* is second only to *Chrysanthemum leucanthemum* (the former scientific name of oxeye daisy).

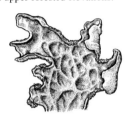

GREEN PAW • *Nephroma arcticum*

GENERAL: Large, loosely appressed leaf lichen, with broad lobes, 5–8 cm wide; upper surface **pale yellowish green to lime green**, smooth, shiny and hairless; lower surface pale creamy, becoming blackish toward centre, thinly covered in **fine hairs**.

REPRODUCTIVE: Large **apothecia**, generally 1–3 cm across, usually present positioned; **near lobe tips on lower surface**.

HABITAT: Over mossy rock outcrops or on moss and decaying wood in open, usually coniferous forests; scattered in sheltered sites at mid to upper elevations, especially in snowy subalpine forests.

NOTES: The large lobes, green upper surface, paw-like apothecia and ground-dwelling ecology are distinctive. Some *Peltigera* species are similar in habit and habitat, but have cottony, veined lower surfaces. • Green paw bears internal colonies of cyanobacteria, which, viewed from above, somewhat resemble liver spots. • The apothecia in this species are the largest of any lichen, occasionally measuring to 5 cm across. • Green paw is also sometimes called green kidney lichen, owing perhaps to the kidney-like outline of the apothecia or to the kidney-brown colour of many other species in this genus. The genus name *Nephroma* is Greek for 'sick kidney.'

BLISTERED PAW • *Nephroma resupinatum*

GENERAL: Medium-sized, **loosely appressed leaf lichen**, with **broad lobes**, 0.5–1 cm wide; upper surface **brownish grey**, smooth, and minutely hairy toward edges; lower surface minutely felty, pale creamy to brownish, bearing a few **naked protuberances** (papillae) visible to the naked eye.

REPRODUCTIVE: Brown apothecia, located **near lobe tips on lower surface**; frequent.

HABITAT: Forming colonies over trees and mossy logs and rocks in open to somewhat shady, humid forests at lower elevations; frequent.

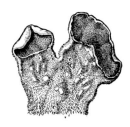

SIMILAR SPECIES: Dog paw (*N. helveticum*) differs in the presence of marginal lobules, as well as in the lack of papillae over the lower surface.

NOTES: What physiological or reproductive function, if any, blistered paw's papillae perform is unknown, but they do make this species easy to identify. Blistered paw appears to be most common in young forest types. • The species name *resupinatum* is Latin for 'bent back,' probably in reference to the typically raised and reflexed lobes on which the apothecia are positioned.

POWDERED PAW • *Nephroma parile*

GENERAL: Medium-sized, **loosely appressed leaf lichen** with **broad lobes**, to 0.5–1 cm wide; upper surface **brownish**, smooth, naked or minutely felty; **lower surface usually minutely hairy**, pale creamy to brownish, **lacking protuberances**.

REPRODUCTIVE: Soredia borne over upper surface and especially along lobe edges; **apothecia** located near lobe tips on lower surface, **rare**.

HABITAT: Over trees, decaying logs and mossy rocks, especially in humid forests at lower elevations; shade tolerant, but apparently unable to withstand exposed conditions; common.

SIMILAR SPECIES: Some forms of powdered paw are close to peppered paw (*N. isidiosum*), an uncommon species with a dark, densely hairy lower surface and abundant isidia. • Also similar

is tree pelt (*Peltigera collina*), which differs, however, in having a distinctly veined lower surface.

NOTES: The dark lobes, sorediate lobes and pale, minutely hairy lower surface are distinctive. The upper surface of powdered paw is sometimes speckled with tiny, dark or pale 'blisters.' These are the fruiting bodies of parasitic fungi that make a living siphoning off carbohydrates from the cyanobacterial partner in this lichen.

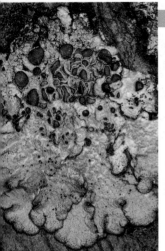

MOUNTAIN CANDLEWAX • *Ahtiana sphaerosporella*

GENERAL: Medium-sized, **closely appressed leaf lichen** with proportionately broad lobes, 2–5 mm wide; upper surface **yellowish green**, naked and finely wrinkled; lower surface pale, bearing several holdfasts.

REPRODUCTIVE: Disk-like, pale brownish **apothecia (common)** and many **black dots** (pycnidia) located over upper surface; soredia lacking.

HABITAT: Over conifers, **especially whitebark pine**, in open, usually rather exposed sites at upper forested elevations; locally frequent.

NOTES: Mountain candlewax is unlikely to be confused with any other lichen, owing to its appressed, yellowish lobes and subalpine distribution. The usual association with whitebark pine, at least in B.C., is exceptional among tree-dwelling lichens, which typically have broader ecologies. On the other hand, in California this species is said to be 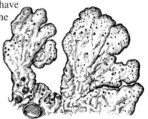 associated almost exclusively with fir trees! No satisfactory explanation has been offered for either observation. • The genus name *Ahtiana* honours the well-known Finnish lichenologist Teuvo Ahti; the species name *sphaerosporella*, 'tiny round spores,' aptly describes this species' spores.

BROWN-EYED SUNSHINE • *Vulpicida canadensis*
Cetraria canadensis

GENERAL: Small to medium-sized, **loosely attached leaf lichen** with proportionately broad lobes, 2–4 mm wide; upper and lower surfaces wrinkled, **strong lemon yellow** and essentially lacking holdfasts.

REPRODUCTIVE: Brown apothecia usually present; **black dots** (pycnidia) along lobe edges.

HABITAT: Over conifers, especially pines, in open forested sites at low elevations; common.

SIMILAR SPECIES: Powdered sunshine (*V. pinastri*) bears soredia and is restricted to the lower trunks and branches of conifers in more humid sites.

NOTES: Brown-eyed sunshine is one of the most brightly coloured lichens. The yellow colour derives primarily from two **poisonous** substances, pinastric and vulpinic acids. These acids occur only in lichens, and they are thought to deter grazing by insects and other invertebrates. There is evidence that native people in B.C. may have used *Vulpicida* species as a source of yellow dye.

SHADOW RUFFLE • *Cetraria chlorophylla*
Tuckermannopsis chlorophylla

GENERAL: Small, **loosely attached leaf lichen** with rather narrow lobes, 1–3 mm wide; upper and lower surfaces smooth and **brownish**, essentially lack holdfasts.

REPRODUCTIVE: Greyish or whitish soredia borne along lobe edges; apothecia very rare.

HABITAT: Over conifers and, less frequently, deciduous trees in open to somewhat shady sites at all forested elevations; most well developed in rather humid areas; common.

NOTES: The brown, narrow lobes and sorediate lobe edges are diagnostic. Shadow ruffle is unlikely to be confused with any other tree-dwelling species. • Though it is seldom abundant, shadow ruffle is among the most widespread of tree-dwelling lichens in southern B.C. • The genus name *Cetraria* is from Latin and

means 'resembling a leather shield.' The species name *chlorophylla* is Greek and means 'green leaf,' presumably in reference to this species' rather greenish colour when wet. Some Coastal forms are greenish even when dry.

WEATHERED RUFFLE • *Cetraria platyphylla*
Tuckermannopsis platyphylla

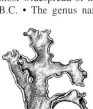

GENERAL: Small to medium-sized, **loosely attached leaf lichen** with **broad lobes**, to 4–10 mm wide; upper and lower surfaces **wrinkled and brownish**, essentially lacking holdfasts.

REPRODUCTIVE: Usually bearing **apothecia** and black dots (pycnidia) along lobe edges; **lacking soredia**.

HABITAT: Over conifers in open sites at all forested elevations; most well developed in rather dry areas; common.

SIMILAR SPECIES: Fringed ruffle (*C. ciliaris*) is smaller and bears sparse 'eyelashes' (cilia) along the edges. • *C. orbata* is also similar, but its lobes are comparatively small and narrow (1–5 mm wide at maturity).

NOTES: Weathered ruffle may be distinguished from other brown tree-dwelling species by its broad, wrinkled lobes and abundant apothecia. • Weathered ruffle is restricted to western North America. • The scientific name *platyphylla*, Greek for 'broad leaves,' nicely captures the appearance of this species.

ICELANDMOSS • *Cetraria ericetorum*

GENERAL: Medium-sized, **upright leaf lichen**, to 2–5 cm tall, with **narrow** lobes, to 2–4 mm wide; surfaces **brownish** and **strongly folded lengthwise**, often bearing **tiny spines** along edges; lower surface bears a **thin white line of 'breathing pores' (pseudocyphellae) along each of the lobe edges** (use a hand lens).

REPRODUCTIVE: Apothecia occasionally present, located on lobe tips.

HABITAT: Over soil and humus in open, rather well-drained sites at all elevations; restricted to windswept sites and upper portions of logs in areas of prolonged snowcover; common.

SIMILAR SPECIES: In the related *C. islandica*, the pseudocyphellae take the form of tiny white patches scattered over the lower surface.

NOTES: Three subspecies of *C. ericetorum* are recognized world-wide. The fact that one of these occurs only in southern South America, whereas the others are restricted to the northern hemisphere, suggests that Icelandmoss may be a very ancient species that may have evolved before the breakup of Pangaea 200 million years ago. • In exposed alpine areas, Icelandmoss may occasionally be blown about in the wind like tumbleweed. • The species name *ericetorum* is Latin for 'of the heaths.'

RAGGED SNOW • *Cetraria nivalis*
Flavocetraria nivalis

GENERAL: Medium-sized, **upright leaf lichen**, to 2.5–4 cm tall; lobes narrow, to 2–3 mm wide; upper and lower surfaces **whitish green** to yellowish green, often becoming **yellowish orange at base**, **weakly folded lengthwise**, somewhat ridged, with somewhat frilly edges.

REPRODUCTIVE: Apothecia usually absent.

HABITAT: Forming colonies over soil or humus in open sites, especially **at or above treeline**, but also on north-facing outcrops in low, semi-arid areas; frequent.

SIMILAR SPECIES: Curled snow (*C. cucullata*) is similar in colour, size and habitat, but it has nar-rower, much more strongly folded lobes that discolour to red, not yellow-orange, toward the base. • Limestone sunshine (*Vulpicida tilesii*) has bright yellow lobes and is restricted to calcium-rich habitats.

NOTES: Ragged snow tolerates prolonged snowcover to an extent unusual among ground-dwelling lichens. • The species name *nivalis* is Latin for 'of the snow,' an apt description of the ecology of this species. Ragged snow is also called ragged paperdoll.

COLORADO ROCKFROG • *Xanthoparmelia coloradoensis*

GENERAL: Medium-sized or large, orbicular, **loosely appressed leaf lichen**; lobes proportionately rather broad, 2–5 mm wide; upper surface **pale yellowish green** and shiny; lower surface pale brown and somewhat shiny, bearing many holdfasts.

REPRODUCTIVE: Apothecia often present, borne on upper surface; soredia and isidia lacking.

HABITAT: Over rock in open sites, mostly at lower elevations; common.

SIMILAR SPECIES: The related *X. cumberlandia* is more closely attached and has somewhat more rounded lobe tips; chemical tests, however, may sometimes be required to distinguish with certainty between these two species. • Rippled rockfrog (*Arctoparmelia centrifuga*) is also similar, but it has narrower lobes and a dull lower surface, and it is restricted to cooler, usually somewhat sheltered sites.

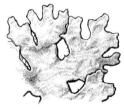

NOTES: Colorado rockfrog is one of very few non-sorediate, non-isidiate, rock-dwelling lichens with broad, yellowish lobes. • *Xanthoparmelia* is a widespread genus consisting of more than 400 species worldwide. Most, however, are restricted to arid or semi-arid regions; only eight species are currently known from B.C. • Colorado rockfrog is sometimes called questionable rockfrog.

POWDERED ORANGE • *Xanthoria fallax*

GENERAL: Small, **loosely appressed leaf lichen**, forming small, scattered colonies; lobes proportionately **broad**, to 0.5–1 mm wide, **blunt-tipped**; upper surface pale or **bright orange**.

REPRODUCTIVE: Soredia borne on undersides of lobe edges; apothecia usually absent.

HABITAT: Over trees and shrubs, especially deciduous, in open sites, also over rock, restricted mostly to low elevations; frequent.

SIMILAR SPECIES: The related shrubby lichen (*X. candelaria*) will often be found growing with powdered orange. Its lobes are narrower, long, thin, upright and end in soredia or isidia.

NOTES: Powdered orange is the only orange-coloured lichen bearing soredia on the lower surface of its lobe tips. • *Xanthoria* species benefit from the presence of calcium or nitrogen, and they thrive near barnyards and in sites regularly manured by bird droppings. • The genus name *Xanthoria* is from both Greek and Latin and means 'pertaining to the colour yellow.' The species name *fallax* is Latin for 'deceptive.'

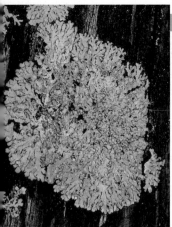

GREY STARBURST • *Parmeliopsis hyperopta*

GENERAL: Small, **closely appressed leaf lichen** with very narrow lobes, 0.5–0.8 mm wide; upper surface **pale greyish, weakly shiny toward lobe tips**; lower surface pale or darkening, with sparse holdfasts (use a hand lens).

REPRODUCTIVE: Soredia in many **hemispherical clusters** over upper surface; apothecia uncommon.

HABITAT: Forming rosettes over **conifers** and other acid-barked trees and shrubs in humid sites at all forested elevations; also over logs and stumps with or without bark; common.

SIMILAR SPECIES: Grey starburst (**on left** in photo) often grows together with green starburst (*P. ambigua*, **on right** in photo), a closely related species that is identical in all respects except in being greenish, not greyish. Interestingly, green starburst is less tolerant of humidity than grey starburst, and it usually extends somewhat higher on tree trunks. • Another similar tree-dwelling lichen is salted starburst (*Imshaugia aleurites*). However, the upper surface of that lichen is covered with tiny, whitish, granular isidia.

NOTES: The genus name *Parmeliopsis* means 'resembling *Parmelia*,' which these lichens most certainly do.

POWDERED SHIELD • *Parmelia sulcata*

GENERAL: Medium-sized, **loosely appressed leaf lichen** with narrow lobes, 1–3 mm wide; upper surface **pale greyish**; lower surface black, with many **copiously branched, black holdfasts**.

REPRODUCTIVE: Soredia in long narrow cracks on upper surface; apothecia rare.

HABITAT: Over trees and rock in forests and in open sites alike, present at all elevations; common.

SIMILAR SPECIES: The salted shields (*P. saxatilis* and *P. hygrophila*) have un-branched holdfasts and produce granular or branched isidia, not powdery soredia.

NOTES: Powdered shield is one of the most common, widespread and easily identified lichens. • Powdered shield has long been used by north Europeans and Canadian Inuit as a natural dyestuff, yielding a variety of hues, from yellowish brown to dark or even rusty brown. Brown dyes from *Parmelia* species were called *crottle* in Scotland. • This species is commonly used by rufous hummingbirds to decorate and camouflage the outsides of their nests. • The genus name *Parmelia* derives from Latin, and appears to mean 'small round shield.' The species name *sulcata*, also from Latin, means 'furrowed,' apparently in reference to the cracks in which the soredia are formed.

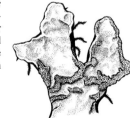

RAGBAG • *Platismatia glauca*

GENERAL: Large, **loosely attached leaf lichen** with **broad lobes, to 1–2 cm wide**; upper surface pale bluish green to **whitish** grey, often with **frilly edges**; lower surface white to black, **shiny**, typically **lacking holdfasts.**

REPRODUCTIVE: Soredia or isidia borne mostly on lobe edges; apothecia rare.

HABITAT: On trees in open and shady forests alike, occurring at all forested elevations; common.

SIMILAR SPECIES: Yellow rag (*Esslingeriana idahoensis*) has uniformly long, narrow lobes with a uniformly black lower surface, a faint yellowish cast on the upper surface and many tiny, black dots (pycnidia).

NOTES: Though few species are likely to be confused with it, ragbag is a bewilderingly variable

species in which some forms have a very, very unkempt appearance. • Ragbag has a remarkably broad distribution, occurring on every continent except Antarctica; it may possibly be of great evolutionary age. • The genus name *Platismatia* is Greek for 'plate-like,' while the species name *glauca*, also Greek, means 'silvery' or 'gleaming.'

ABRADED BROWN • *Melanelia subaurifera*

GENERAL: Small to medium-sized, **appressed leaf lichen**; lobes narrow to proportionately broad, to **1–4 mm wide**; upper surface flat, **olive brown**, and shiny toward lobe edges; lower surface pale to dark, shiny and bearing scattered holdfasts.

REPRODUCTIVE: Minute, scattered, granular or cylindrical isidia (visible only through a hand lens) on upper surface; apothecia generally lacking.

HABITAT: Over deciduous trees and shrubs, less often on conifers, in open to somewhat sheltered forests at low elevations; scattered.

NOTES: Abraded brown is one of several isidia-bearing *Melanelia* species occurring over the trunks and branches of trees. It differs from related species in having granular or cylindrical isidia that are so minute they are virtually invisible to the naked eye. When these are rubbed with a forefinger, the distinctly yellowish underlying medulla is clearly exposed, thus providing yet another diagnostic feature. • The isidia are this species' hope for the future. Help create a new generation of abraded browns by simply rubbing an isidia-laden forefinger (see above) over a nearby branch. • The genus name *Melanelia* is a portmanteau word intended to convey the meaning 'black *Parmelia.*' The species name *subaurifera* is Latin for 'bearing gold below,' and refers to the pale yellow colour of the medulla.

GREY-EYED ROSETTE • *Physcia aipolia*

GENERAL: Small to medium-sized, **closely appressed leaf lichen** with narrow lobes, to 1–2 mm wide; upper surface **pale greyish** with small white spots; lower surface tan with many pale holdfasts.

REPRODUCTIVE: Many apothecia on upper surface, usually with a **frosted** appearance; soredia lacking.

HABITAT: Forming rosettes on bark of **deciduous trees** and shrubs, especially aspen and willow; widespread at low to mid elevations; common.

SIMILAR SPECIES: Black-eyed rosette (*P. phaea*) is usually darker and colonizes acid rock in open sites.

NOTES: The genus name *Physcia* is from the Greek for 'a sausage,' 'a blister' or 'the large intestine.' The species name *aipolia*, also Greek, appears to mean 'forever grey,' probably in reference to the fact that this species, unlike other related species, remains the same colour whether wet or dry.

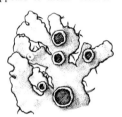

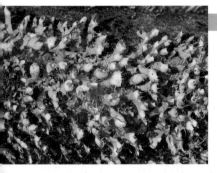

HOODED ROSETTE • *Physcia adscendens*

GENERAL: Small, **loosely appressed leaf lichen**; lobes narrow, to 0.5–1 mm wide, with **long, slender 'eyelashes'** (cilia) on edges, ending in **hood-shaped tips**; upper surface dull **pale greyish** with small white spots; lower surface white.

REPRODUCTIVE: Powdery soredia (use a hand lens) **on inside of hood-shaped swellings** on lobe tips; apothecia uncommon.

HABITAT: Over deciduous trees and shrubs in open or somewhat shady sites at lowland elevations; common.

SIMILAR SPECIES: Monk's-hood (*Hypogymnia physodes*, p. 430) and the rare *H. vittata* (p. 430) are the only other lichens with hood-shaped lobe tips. In the *Hypogymnia* species, however, the lobes are hollow, the lower surface is black, and there are no cilia. • The closely related *P. tenella* is also similar to hooded rosette, but it lacks the hood.

NOTES: Recent studies have shown that the algal partners in the soredia of various *Physcia* species are sometimes commandeered by the germinating spores of other lichens, particularly *Xanthoria* species. This may be part of the answer to an intriguing question: how do lichen spores find an appropriate algal partner with which to form a new lichen?

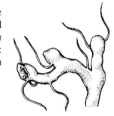

POWDERED ROSETTE • *Physcia caesia*

GENERAL: Small, **closely appressed leaf lichen** with narrow lobes, 0.5–1 mm wide; upper surface **dull pale greyish**; lower surface pale, with sparse holdfasts (use a hand lens).

REPRODUCTIVE: Many **hemispherical clusters of soredia** on upper surface; apothecia uncommon.

HABITAT: Forming rosettes over **calcium-rich rock** (including rocks enriched by bird droppings) in sheltered or, more often, well-illuminated sites at all elevations.

SIMILAR SPECIES: The only other common, rock-dwelling leaf lichen with tiny, dull, whitish lobes **and** soredia is *P. dubia*. In that species, however, the soredia are located on the lower surface of the lobe tips, not over the upper surface as they are in powdered rosette.

Specimens in which the soredia's position is intermediate must be checked for the presence of the chemical atranorin, which is present in powdered rosette but absent in *P. dubia*.

NOTES: The species name *caesia* is Latin for 'pale grey,' though this species can be darker when it grows under exposed conditions—an instance of lichen suntanning!

GROUND FROST • *Physconia muscigena*

GENERAL: Medium-sized, **loosely appressed leaf lichen** with **narrow lobes**, 1–1.5 mm wide (sometimes to 2 mm); upper surface dull pale brownish or nearly whitish, with a **distinctly 'frosted'** appearance; lower surface pale or darkening toward thallus centre, densely covered in dark, **copiously branched holdfasts** (use a hand lens).

REPRODUCTIVE: Soredia lacking; apothecia uncommon.

HABITAT: Over moss, humus and mossy rock, also occasionally over bases of shrubs, in open to somewhat sheltered calcium-rich sites at lowland elevations; most common in grassland ecosystems.

SIMILAR SPECIES: The bordered frosts (*P. perisidiosa* and *P. enteroxantha*) both bear powdery soredia: over the lower surface of the lobe tips in *P. perisidiosa*, and along the edges in *P. enteroxantha*.

NOTES: The 'frosted' upper surface and dark, densely branched holdfasts are diagnostic. The 'frost' in this species is actually a deposit of minute, white crystals of calcium oxalate, believed to deter grazing by insects and other animals. • The genus name *Physconia* emphasizes this genus's general resemblance to *Physcia*. The species name *muscigena* is Latin for 'arising from moss.'

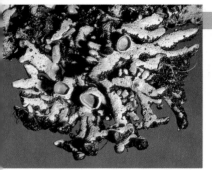

LATTICE PIPE • *Hypogymnia occidentalis*

GENERAL: Medium-sized, appressed or pendent **leaf lichen; lobes narrow, 1.5–2.5 mm wide** (sometimes to 3 mm), with irregular, **hollow** branches with dark interiors (check upper portions) and **constricted bases**; upper surface **pale greyish** to pale greenish; lower surface black, **without holdfasts.**

REPRODUCTIVE: Apothecia often present on upper surface; soredia absent.

HABITAT: Over trees, especially conifers, in humid, somewhat sheltered forests at all forested elevations; common.

SIMILAR SPECIES: Some forms of deflated pipe (*H. metaphysodes*) and forking pipe (*H. imshaugii*) are similar, but in deflated pipe the lobes are flattened and appressed to the substrate, while in forking pipe the branching is more regular and the interiors of the lobes are white.

NOTES: Lattice pipe may be distinguished from most other non-sorediate tree-dwelling lichens by its pale upper surface and hollow lobes. • Lattice pipe is restricted to western North America. • The genus name *Hypogymnia* is Greek for 'naked bottom,' in reference to the lack of holdfasts. A gymnasium, by the way, was originally a place in ancient Greece where men exercised naked.

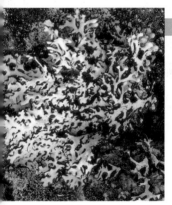

MONK'S-HOOD • *Hypogymnia physodes*

GENERAL: Medium-sized, **appressed leaf lichen**; lobes narrow, 1–2 mm wide, **hollow** with pale interiors (check upper portions) and **hood-shaped tips**; upper surface pale greyish to pale greenish white; lower surface black, **without holdfasts.**

REPRODUCTIVE: Powdery soredia on insides of burst lobe tips; apothecia rare.

HABITAT: On nearly all available surfaces, including trees, moss and boulders; common and widespread, at low to subalpine elevations.

SIMILAR SPECIES: *H. vittata* is the only other *Hypogymnia* species with hood-shaped, soredia-bearing lobe tips. It is restricted to humid areas, especially old-growth forests, and it has a dark, rather than pale, central cavity. • *H. tubulosa* is also somewhat similar; however, its soredia are located externally, not internally, over the tips of the lobes. It is also much less common than monk's-hood.

NOTES: Monk's-hood is among the most pollution-tolerant of the macrolichens, and it is a familiar species of city parks and boulevards. • The species name *physodes* means 'inflated-looking' or 'puffed out.'

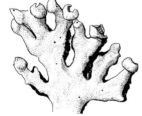

GREEN STUBBLE • *Calicium viride*

GENERAL: Tiny, upright **club lichen** arising from a thin, **bright green crust**, to 0.5–1.5 mm tall; **clubs black**, solid, unbranched, arranged in colonies.

REPRODUCTIVE: Minute, black, powdery, **ball-like fruiting bodies** (mazaedia) at ends of clubs (use a hand lens), always present.

HABITAT: Over sheltered trunks and branches of old conifers in humid forests at all forested elevations; common.

NOTES: Though tiny, and thus easily overlooked, this lichen is unlikely to be mistaken for any other species. Green stubble belongs to a distinctive group of lollipop-like lichens, the Caliciales. Most Caliciales are restricted to old-growth forests, and in eastern North America they have been used to estimate the relative ages of very old woodlands. • Green stubble produces its spores in loose, upwelling chains, which is why gently rubbing the mazaedia with a forefinger produces a black, sooty smudge.

DEVIL'S MATCHSTICK • *Pilophorus acicularis*

GENERAL: Medium-sized, **upright club lichen**, to **1–3 cm tall**, often arising from thin, whitish crust; clubs **clustered, whitish** to pale greenish, **solid** and mostly unbranched.

REPRODUCTIVE: Tiny, black, ball-like apothecia at club tips, always present.

HABITAT: Over rocks in cool, moist forests, often near creeks and waterfalls, at all forested elevations; scattered.

SIMILAR SPECIES: Pink beret (*Baeomyces rufus*) also produces solid, unbranched, upright clubs, but its apothecia are pinkish or brownish, never black.

NOTES: Devil's matchstick, which is unmistakable, is typical of many club lichens in that it combines two very different growth forms: a sterile basal crust and a fertile, apothecia-bearing club. • The genus name *Pilophorus* is Greek for 'ball-bearing'; the species name *acicularis* is Latin for 'a small pin.'

PIXIE-CUP • *Cladonia pyxidata*

GENERAL: Small, **upright club lichen**, to **1–1.5 cm tall**, arising from clusters of tiny, greenish basal scales; clubs greyish green, hollow and unbranched, **covered in 'warts'** and **flaring upward to a broad cup.**

REPRODUCTIVE: Brown apothecia often present on rims of cups; **soredia absent.**

HABITAT: Forming colonies on mineral soil and humus in open forests, grasslands and alpine at all elevations; common.

SIMILAR SPECIES: *C. borealis* is yellowish and has red apothecia. • *C. chlorophaea* and *C. pleurota* are the soredia-bearing counterparts of pixie-cup. *C. chlorophaea* has brown apothecia, and *C. pleurota* has red apothecia.

NOTES: All of the *Cladonia* species mentioned above are called pixie-cups or fairy-cups because of their resemblance to tiny goblets. Perhaps surprisingly, *pyxidata* is Latin for 'box' or 'cubical,' not 'pixie.' The cups are thought to assist in dispersing the spores and other propagules through rain splash.

BLACK-FOOT CLADONIA • *Cladonia gracilis* ssp. *turbinata*

GENERAL: Medium-sized, **upright club lichen**, to 3–4.5 cm tall, arising from clusters of tiny, greenish basal scales; clubs **brownish green** to greenish grey with **blackish bases**, hollow, **smooth**, unbranched or sparsely branched, **flaring upward to a broad cup.**

REPRODUCTIVE: Brown apothecia often present on rims of cups; **soredia lacking.**

HABITAT: Forming extensive colonies over soil, humus, decaying wood and mossy rocks in open forests at low and mid elevations, especially abundant in young forests that develop after fire; common.

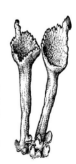

SIMILAR SPECIES: Orange-foot cladonia (*C. ecmocyna*) has narrower cups, is greyish green and usually grades to orange, never black, at the base. It is more common at upper elevations. • *C. phyllophora* is also similar, but the upper portions of its clubs are very finely woolly.

NOTES: The species name *gracilis* is Latin for 'slender,' and probably refers to a non-cupped subspecies.

HORN CLADONIA • *Cladonia cornuta*

GENERAL: Medium-sized, **upright club lichen**, to **4–8 cm tall**, arising from inconspicuous clusters of tiny, greenish basal scales; clubs pale greyish green or brownish green, hollow, generally unbranched and tapering to a pointed tip.

REPRODUCTIVE: Soredia on upper half of clubs; apothecia brown, but usually absent.

HABITAT: Over well-drained humus in open forests; also over decaying wood; best represented at low and mid elevations; common.

SIMILAR SPECIES: Horn cladonia specimens with narrow cups may be confused with *C. ochrochlora*. That species, however, is usually somewhat smaller and typically colonizes decaying logs and stumps, as well as tree bases.

NOTES: Horn cladonia can be distinguished from other *Cladonia* species by its tall, unbranched, soredia-bearing clubs that usually taper upward to a point. • Horn cladonia is usually an early invader after fire (it is also called pioneer cladonia), and it becomes scarce in older forest types. • The genus name *Cladonia* is Greek for 'club like'; the species name *cornuta* is Latin for 'horned.'

SULPHUR CLADONIA • *Cladonia sulphurina*

GENERAL: Medium-sized, **upright club lichen**, to 2.5–5 cm tall, arising from conspicuous clusters of greenish basal scales; scales white below, but **grading to orangish toward base**; clubs **pale yellowish green**, hollow, generally unbranched and flaring gradually upward to a shallow, often **somewhat tattered** cup.

REPRODUCTIVE: Powdery soredia covering clubs; apothecia red, but usually absent.

HABITAT: Over decaying wood and mossy soil in somewhat open forested sites, especially at high elevations; common.

SIMILAR SPECIES: *C. deformis* has smaller squamules, more regular cups and typically colonizes soil at low elevations.

NOTES: The tattered, non-flaring cups, yellowish-green colour, large basal scales and finely powdery soredia are diagnostic of sulphur cladonia. • Though present in cool forests throughout southern B.C., sulphur cladonia is especially characteristic of snowy, high-elevation forests.

433

SHRUB LICHENS

GREY REINDEER LICHEN • *Cladina rangiferina*

GENERAL: Medium-sized to large, **upright shrub lichen**, 5–8 cm tall (rarely to 10 cm); **intricately branched** from distinct main stem, with branch tips typically all pointing in 1 direction; branches **greyish white** and hollow with dull, **cottony surface** (visible with a hand lens).

REPRODUCTIVE: Apothecia occasionally present, brown, located on branch tips.

HABITAT: Forming extensive carpets over the ground in open coniferous forests and in open sites at all elevations; common, except sparse in areas having a heavy snowpack.

SIMILAR SPECIES: The green reindeer lichens (*C. arbuscula* and *C. mitis*) are a pale yellowish green, not grey. • Also similar are the prickle cladonias (*Cladonia uncialis* and *Cladonia amaurocraea*), although in those species the surface of the branches is hard and shiny, not soft and felt-like.

NOTES: As a group, the reindeer lichens are easily recognized by their pale colour, shrubby branching pattern and dull, felt-like surface. Grey reindeer lichen can be distinguished from related species by its grey 'woollen sock' appearance. • In northern B.C., reindeer lichens provide a critical winter staple for caribou. In southern B.C., however, winter snowpacks are deeper, and the caribou are forced to rely on tree-dwelling hair lichens instead. • The genus name *Cladina* is Latin for 'small branches,' and the species name *rangiferina* means 'pertaining to reindeer.'

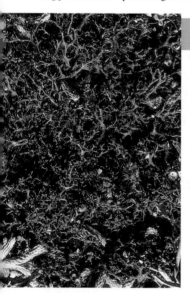

SPINY HEATH • *Coelocaulon aculeatum*
Cetraria aculeata, *Cornicularia aculeata*

GENERAL: Medium-sized, **upright shrub lichen**, to 2–3 cm tall (sometimes to 5 cm), dark **brown**; branches many, **solid**, **shiny**, stiff, **with pointed tips.**

REPRODUCTIVE: Apothecia usually absent.

HABITAT: Forming mats over open, well-drained ground in exposed sites at all elevations; most frequent in semi-arid grasslands and above treeline; scattered.

NOTES: Spiny heath is unlikely to be confused with any other lichen. • This is an asexual species, rarely forming fruiting bodies. Throughout most of its range, spiny heath probably depends for its dispersal on passing animals, to whose fur and feathers its spiny branches would tend to cling. In more exposed sites, however, it is dispersed at least in part by the wind. • The species name *aculeatum* is Greek for 'furnished with spines,' which in this case is quite to the point.

SHRUB LICHENS

COTTONTAIL CORAL • *Stereocaulon paschale*

GENERAL: Medium-sized to large, **upright shrub lichen**, to 3–5 cm tall, **pale greyish white** and much-branched; **branches solid** with dense, **coral-like 'foliage'**; lower surface bears **sparse tiny, black 'pompoms'** (use a hand lens).

REPRODUCTIVE: Brown apothecia usually present at branch ends.

HABITAT: Forming loose colonies over boulders and on the ground in open to somewhat shady sites at all forested elevations; common.

SIMILAR SPECIES: Cottontail coral might easily be confused with woolly coral (*S. tomentosum*), but the latter's branches have a thick 'woollen' covering (use a hand lens), and the secondary colonies of cyanobacteria appear as greyish lumps among the branches, instead of the tiny, black 'pompoms,' of cottontail coral.

NOTES: *Stereocaulon* species are also sometimes called froth lichens. The genus name *Stereocaulon* is Greek for 'solid stem.' The species name *paschale* is Latin for 'belonging to Easter,' in reference to the tradition (still prevalent in some parts of Scandinavia) of using this lichen as an Easter decoration.

WOLF LICHEN • *Letharia vulpina*

GENERAL: Medium-sized to large, upright or somewhat pendent **shrub lichen**, to 4–8 cm long, **bright greenish sulphur yellow** (chartreuse), with many angular, pitted, branches.

REPRODUCTIVE: Abundant **soredia and isidia** (use a hand lens) on branches; **apothecia usually absent**.

HABITAT: Forming tufts on conifers in open to somewhat exposed sites at all forested elevations; common.

SIMILAR SPECIES: Wolf lichen is a dominant species of open Douglas-fir forests, where it occasionally occurs with brown-eyed wolf lichen (*L. columbiana*), a closely related species that differs in having abundant apothecia and in lacking soredia and isidia.

NOTES: Interior native people used wolf lichen as a yellowish-green dye to colour fur, moccasins, feathers, wood and other articles. The Nlaka'pmx also used it as face and body paint. • The genus name *Letharia* (think 'lethal') is from the Latin for 'deadly,' and it refers to the presence of a **poisonous** substance, vulpinic acid. In northern Europe, wolf lichen was formerly mixed with ground glass and sprinkled over wolf bait or mixed with animal fat and nails.

SUGARED BEARD • *Usnea hirta*

GENERAL: Medium-sized, somewhat pendent **shrub lichen**, to 3–5.5 cm long; **pale yellowish green throughout** (including base) and highly branched; branches lax and smooth, bearing many short side branches, reinforced by a **tough, white, central cord**.

REPRODUCTIVE: Copious isidia throughout; apothecia absent.

HABITAT: Over conifers, especially Douglas-fir, in open forests at low and mid elevations; most well developed in less humid regions; common.

NOTES: Sugared beard's smooth, uniformly greenish branches and copious isidia distinguish it from all other *Usnea* species. Though most *Usnea* species are not easy to tell apart, the genus itself is readily recognized by its characteristic tough, thread-like central cord. The cord is present in all *Usnea* species, and provides elasticity, anatomical support and, possibly, a storage area for energy-rich polysaccharides. Check for it by slowly pulling the lichen lengthwise like a party

cracker. • The genus name *Usnea* appears to derive from the Arabic for 'moss.' The species name *hirta* is Latin for 'rough' or 'bristly,' and it clearly refers to the isidia.

POWDERED BEARD • *Usnea lapponica*
U. fulvoreagens

GENERAL: Medium-sized, tufted to somewhat pendent **shrub lichen**, to 3–8 cm long, **pale yellowish green, blackening at base** and highly branched; branches tufted to lax, **minutely bumpy**, bearing many short side branches, reinforced by a **tough, white, central cord**.

REPRODUCTIVE: Many **patches of soredia** on branches, at first round in outline but at maturity **encircling branches**; apothecia absent.

HABITAT: Over trees and shrubs, especially conifers, in open to somewhat shady forests at low elevations; abundant.

NOTES: The above description applies to several different *Usnea* species. Collectively, these lichens may be termed the *U. lapponica* group, an example of how lichenologists handle a species complex they have been unable to tease apart. In some forms the bumps (papillae) are raised and knob-like, whereas in others they are low and poorly developed. • The species name *lapponica* is Latin for 'pertaining to Lapland,' an indication that the *U. lapponica* group is wide ranging.

ANTLERED PERFUME • *Evernia prunastri*

GENERAL: Medium-sized, **semi-erect or some-what pendent leaf lichen**, to 3–8 cm long; lobes **elongate and divergently branched, with loose and cottony inner portions**, 1–4 mm wide; upper surface **soft, dull** and **pale greenish**; lower surface whitish green, lacking holdfasts.

REPRODUCTIVE: Tiny, powdery, ball-like **soredia** on lobe edges; apothecia rare.

HABITAT: Over deciduous and coniferous trees and shrubs in open sites at low elevations.

SIMILAR SPECIES: Antlered perfume is apt to be confused with rimmed gristle (*Ramalina farinacea*). That species, however, is much more compact and shiny and has a distinctly tough, not soft, upper surface.

NOTES: Antlered perfume also occurs in Europe, where it has been used since the 16th century in the manufacture of perfumes. Extracts of this lichen act as a fixative to keep the desired fragrance lingering in the desired spot for hours. • The genus name *Evernia* comes from the Greek for 'sprouting well,' but with a recorded growth rate of only 2 mm per year in this species, this name seems a trifle overstated. Stone and McCune (1990) give a method for determining age in antlered perfume based on branching patterns.

COMMON WITCH'S HAIR • *Alectoria sarmentosa*

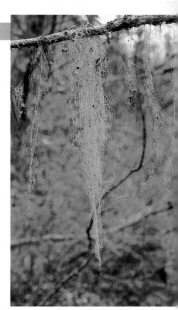

GENERAL: Large, **pendent hair lichen**, to 1.5–3 cm long (sometimes to 5 cm), **pale green** and intricately branched; branches dull, pliant, **lacking a central cord**, terminating in minute **black tips** (use a hand lens).

REPRODUCTIVE: Apothecia occasionally present; soredia absent.

HABITAT: Over conifers in humid forest types, especially at mid and high forested elevations; common.

SIMILAR SPECIES: Common witch's hair is superficially similar to various *Usnea* species, but it lacks a central cord. • Angel hair (*Ramalina thrausta*) is also similar, but its branches are more delicate and terminate in minute, green hooks (use a hand lens).

NOTES: The genus name *Alectoria* means 'unmarried' and presumably refers to the relative absence of fruiting bodies in these lichens. Common witch's-hair itself, however, is often fertile—look for tiny, brown 'saucers' (apothecia) scattered among the branches. The species name *sarmentosa* is Latin for 'twiggy.'

GREATER ROCKWOOL • *Pseudophebe pubescens*

GENERAL: Small, appressed **hair lichen**, to 2 cm long, **blackish, richly branching and resembling Velcro.**

REPRODUCTIVE: Apothecia rare.

HABITAT: Forming patch-like colonies to 7 cm across, attached to boulders, both above treeline over exposed outcrops and in similar (but always north-facing) areas in semi-arid grasslands.

SIMILAR SPECIES: Lesser rockwool (*P. minuscula*) has shorter, more flattened branches, the tips of which often become attached to the substrate.

NOTES: Greater rockwool (also called Velcro lichen) is restricted to windblown outcrops from which the snow is blown clear during winter months. There, the dark branches readily absorb the sun's heat—a feature that allows this lichen to be physiologically active even when air temperatures are far below freezing. • The rockwools are among the only hair lichens in which much of the thallus, rather than just the base, is attached to the substrate.

ABBREVIATED HORSEHAIR • *Nodobryoria abbreviata* *Bryoria abbreviata*

GENERAL: Small to medium-sized, **tufted hair lichen**, to 2–2.5 cm long, **dark reddish brown** and intricately branched; branches **dull**, somewhat **angular** and **brittle**.

REPRODUCTIVE: Many apothecia, bearing short spines along edges; soredia lacking.

HABITAT: Over conifers in open, usually rather dry forests at all forested elevations; scattered.

SIMILAR SPECIES: Olive thornbush (*Cetraria merrillii*) has branches that are dark olive brown to blackish (greenish when wet), but never reddish. • The related species *N. oregana* (also known as *Bryoria oregana*) lacks fruiting bodies and has longer, more pendent branches.

NOTES: In B.C., abbreviated horsehair is restricted to the southern Interior, north to approximately 53°N. • Abbreviated horsehair and *N. oregana* appear to be only distantly related to the *Bryoria* species, with which they have been classified until recently.

SPECKLED HORSEHAIR • *Bryoria fuscescens*

GENERAL: Medium-sized to large, **pendent hair lichen**, to 5–15 cm long, **dark, medium brown** or blackish, intricately branched; branches shiny, even and rather pliant.

REPRODUCTIVE: White, dot-like soredia on branches; apothecia absent.

HABITAT: Over conifers in open to somewhat shady forests at all elevations; occasionally over birch; common.

SIMILAR SPECIES: Speckled horsehair is easily confused with other sorediate horsehair lichens. *B. glabra*, however, has rather stiff and wiry basal branches, and the basal branches of *B. lanestris* are less than 0.25 mm wide, and its upper branches are brittle.

NOTES: The horsehair lichens disperse mostly, if not entirely, by asexual means, whether by fragmentation or by the soredia being borne away by birds and other animals. • The genus name *Bryoria* is a portmanteau name derived from *Bryopogon* (an earlier, but now invalid name, for the group) and *Alectoria* (the name of a related genus). The species name *fuscescens* is Latin for 'becoming dark.'

EDIBLE HORSEHAIR • *Bryoria fremontii*

GENERAL: Large, **pendent hair lichen**, to 30–45 cm long (sometimes to 1 m), **yellowish brown or somewhat reddish brown**, intricately branched; branches shiny, pliant, **irregularly grooved** (check thickest branches) and often becoming twisted.

REPRODUCTIVE: Apothecia occasionally present along branches; bright yellow soredia occasionally present.

HABITAT: Over conifers, especially Douglas-fir and ponderosa pine, in open forests at all forested elevations; common.

SIMILAR SPECIES: Only one other local hair lichen, *B. tortuosa*, resembles edible horsehair in having long, variably thickened, twisted, shiny, yellowish-brown branches. In that species, however, the main branches are thinly (and sparsely) lined with yellow. Both of these lichens also occasionally produce yellow soredia, another characteristic not shared with other *Bryoria* species.

NOTES: Southern Interior native people used edible horsehair as a staple and an emergency food. They washed it thoroughly, pit-cooked it with wild onions, roots and bulbs, and dried it in cakes for storage. They boiled the cakes with berries, roots or meat before eating them (Turner). This and other hair lichens also provide an important winter food for deer, elk, moose and especially flying squirrels and caribou.

Glossary

achene: a small, dry, 1-seeded fruit (fig. 5; pp. 106, 339)

alternate: borne singly, 1 at a time; usually refers to staggered leaf or branch arrangements (fig. 6); cf. *opposite*

annual: a plant that completes its life cycle in 1 growing season; cf. *perennial, biennial*

anther: the pollen bearing portion of a stamen (figs. 1, 11)

apothecium: [apothecia] the fruiting body of a lichen; disk- or button-shaped

appressed: lying close or flat against a surface; appressed hairs on a branch or leaf

aquatic: living in water

aril: the fleshy fruit of a yew (*Taxus* sp.) (fig. 5)

aromatic: having a distinctive odour

auricle: a projecting, ear-shaped lobe or appendage at the base of a leaf; especially in grasses (p. 308)

awn: a bristle-shaped appendage (p. 308)

axil: the upper angle between a leaf or branch and the stem (fig. 6)

banner: the upper, usually enlarged petal of flowers in the pea family (fig. 3); cf. *keel, wing*

basal: at or near the base of a structure (fig. 6)

berry: a fleshy fruit that usually contains several or many seeds (fig. 5)

biennial: a plant that lives for 2 years, usually flowering and producing fruit in its 2nd year; cf. *annual, perennial*

bipinnate: twice pinnate; a pinnately divided leaf with its main segments again pinnately divided (fig. 8); cf. *tripinnate*

blade: the broad part of a leaf or petal (fig. 6)

bract: a modified or specialized leaf associated with a flower, inflorescence or cone (figs. 6, 11; pp. 106, 339)

bulb: a short, vertical, underground stem with thickened leaves or leaf bases, used as a food storage organ (fig. 9); cf. *corm*

bulbil: a small, bulb-like reproductive structure often found in a leaf axil or replacing a flower in an inflorescence

calyptra: a thin covering or hood fitted over the upper part of the spore capsule of a moss

calyx: all of the sepals of a flower, collectively (fig. 1)

cambium: the tissue that produces the conducting tubes (xylem and phloem) in plants

capsule: a dry fruit, containing several chambers (carpels), that splits open at maturity (figs. 5, 11); cf. *follicle*; the spore-containing structure in bryophytes (p. 379)

catkin: a dense inflorescence bearing many small, usually unisexual flowers generally without petals; found in plants of the birch and willow families (fig. 11)

ciliate: fringed with hairs

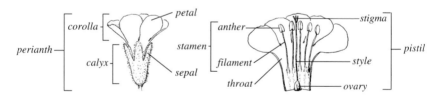

perianth — *corolla* — *petal*
calyx — *sepal*
stamen — *anther* / *filament* / *throat*
pistil — *stigma* / *style* / *ovary*

Figure 1. *Floral anatomy*

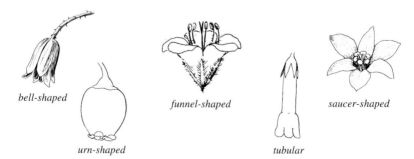

bell-shaped

urn-shaped

funnel-shaped

tubular

saucer-shaped

Figure 2. *Corolla shapes*

clasping: surrounding or holding tightly, as in the base of a leaf clasping the stem (fig. 6)

claw: a narrowed, stalk-like base found on some petals or sepals

cleft: deeply lobed

composite inflorescence: a flower-like inflorescence of the sunflower family, composed of ray and/or disk flowers (p. 106)

compound: divided into smaller parts, as in compound leaves or inflorescences (fig 8); cf. *simple*

cone: the dry fruit of conifers, consisting of woody, overlapping scales (fig. 5); the spore-bearing structure in horsetails, spike mosses and most clubmosses (fig. 10)

corm: a short, vertical, thickened underground stem without thickened leaves, used as a food storage organ (fig. 9); cf. *bulb*

corolla: all of the petals of a flower, collectively (fig. 1; p. 106)

crisped: with irregularly curled, wavy edges (fig. 6)

cultivar: a cultivated variety

deciduous: a plant part that falls away at the completion of its normal function; especially leaves or flower parts; cf. *persistent*

disk flower: a flower in the sunflower family (Asteraceae) with a tubular corolla; part of a composite inflorescence (p. 106); cf. *ray flower*

drupe: a fleshy or pulpy, 1-seeded fruit in which the seed has a stony covering, e.g., cherry (fig. 5)

elliptic: ellipse-shaped, widest in the middle (fig. 7)

elongate: having a slender form, long in relation to width

entire: without lobes, teeth or divisions (fig. 6)

filament: the stalk of a stamen (figs. 1, 11)

flexuous: bent in a zig-zag manner

floret: a tiny flower, usually part of a cluster; the specialized flower of a grass

follicle: a dry fruit, composed of a single chamber (carpel), that splits open at maturity (fig. 5); cf. *capsule*

fornix: [fornices] a small appendage (in rows) in the tube or throat of the corolla in some species of the borage family

fruit: a ripe ovary and any other structures that enclose it, at maturity (fig. 5)

gametophyte: the sexual life history stage in the alternating generations of plants, especially ferns and mosses (p. 379); the gametophyte bears the sperm and eggs, which combine to produce the sporophyte (cf.)

gemma: [gemmae] a small body, composed of a few cells, which serves as a means of vegetative reproduction, especially in mosses and liverworts

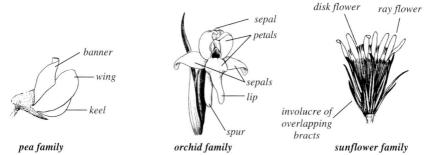

pea family   *orchid family*   *sunflower family*

Figure 3. *Irregular flowers*

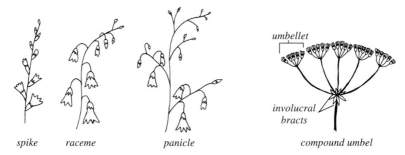

spike   *raceme*   *panicle*   *compound umbel*

Figure 4. *Inflorescence types*

gland: a small organ that secretes a sticky substance, borne on hairs or at the surface of various plant parts

glandular: bearing glands

glume: one of 2 bracts found at the base of a spikelet in a grass inflorescence (p. 308); cf. *lemma, palea*

hairpoint: a thin, hair-like extension to a leaf

herb: a plant without woody above-ground parts, the stems often dying back to the ground each year

herbaceous: herb-like

indusium: [indusia] a scale-like outgrowth of a fern leaf, which covers and protects the spore clusters (sori) (fig. 10)

inflorescence: a flower cluster (fig. 4; pp. 308, 339)

internode: the portion of a stem between 2 nodes (p. 308)

involucre: a set of bracts beneath an inflorescence, especialliy in the sunflower and carrot families (p. 106)

irregular flower: a flower with petals or sepals that are dissimilar in form or orientation (fig. 3)

isidium: [isidia] a wart-like outgrowth of the thallus in certain lichens, serving as a vegetative propagule

keel: a sharp ridge, shaped like the keel of a boat; also the 2 partly united lower petals of many species of the pea family (fig. 3); cf. *banner, wing*

lamella: [lamellae] a green ridge or plate on the midrib of some moss leaves or on the undersurfaces of lichens

lance-shaped: much longer than wide, widest below the middle, and tapering towards the tip (fig. 7)

lateral: at the side

layering: a form of vegetative reproduction in which branches droop to the ground and take root

leader: the upper shoot of a tree

leaflet: one of the divisions of a compound leaf (fig. 8)

legume: the distinctive fruit of the pea family (fig. 5)

lemma: the lower of the 2 bracts that enclose a grass flower (p. 308); cf. *glume, palea*

lenticel: a slightly raised area on root or stem bark, formed of loose corky cells

ligule: the flat, usually membranous projection from the top of the leaf sheath in the grasses (p. 308); the flat or strap-shaped part of a ray flower in the sunflower family (p. 106)

linear: long and narrow, with essentially parallel sides (fig. 7)

achene   aril   berry   capsule

conifer cone   drupe   follicle   legume

samara   schizocarp   silicle   silique

Figure 5. *Fruit types*

lip: one of the major divisions of some irregular flowers, often formed by the fusion of 2 or more petals, especially in the mint and figwort families; the expanded or projecting lower petal in an orchid flower (fig. 3)

lobe: a division of a leaf (fig. 6), or of the body (thallus) of a lichen

mazaedium: [mazaedia] a fruiting body of the fungal partner of certain lichens, in which the spores are formed in club-shaped asci

midrib: the main rib of a leaf (fig. 6)

midvein: the main vein of a leaf

nectary: a structure that produces nectar, often found on petals

nerve: a prominent vein of a leaf

node: the point on a stem where leaves or branches are attached, often swollen (figs. 6, 11; p. 308)

nutlet: a small, nut-like fruit

oblong: somewhat rectangular, with rounded ends (fig. 7)

operculum: the lid of a moss capsule (p. 379)

opposite: borne in pairs on the opposite sides of an axis; usually refers to paired leaf or branch arrangement (fig. 6); cf. *alternate*

oval: broadly elliptic (fig. 7)

ovary: the structure that encloses the young, undeveloped seeds (fig. 1)

ovate: egg-shaped (2 dimensional), with the larger end towards the base (fig. 7)

palea: the upper of the 2 bracts that enclose a grass flower; cf. *glume, lemma*

palmate: divided into lobes or leaflets that diverge from a common point, like fingers spreading on a hand (fig. 8); cf. *pinnate*

panicle: a branched inflorescence that blooms from the bottom up (fig. 4); cf. *raceme, spike*

papilla: a minute, wart-like protuberance

pappus: the cluster of hairs, bristles, or scales at the top of an achene in the sunflower family (p. 106)

parasite: an organism that gets its food and water from an attachment to another living organism; cf. *saprophyte*

pencilled: marked with coloured lines

perennial: a plant that lives for more than 2 years, usually flowering each year; cf. *annual, biennial*

perianth: the petals and sepals of a flower, collectively (fig. 1); the sheath surrounding a developing liverwort capsule (p. 379)

perigynium: [perigynia] an inflated sac that encloses an achene in sedges (p. 339)

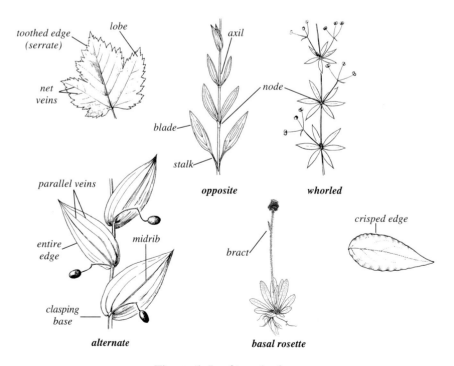

toothed edge (serrate)   *lobe*   *axil*

net veins   *node*

blade   *stalk*

parallel veins

entire edge   *midrib*

clasping base

alternate   **opposite**   **whorled**

bract   *crisped edge*

basal rosette

Figure 6. *Leaf terminology*

peristome: the fringe of teeth surrounding the mouth of a moss capsule

petal: one of the inner ring of modified leaves of a flower (figs. 1, 3)

pinnate: a compound leaf with the leaflets in 2 rows on opposite sides of a common midrib, in a feather-like arrangement (fig. 8); cf. *palmate*

pinnatifid: deeply cleft halfway to the middle into lobes that somewhat resemble pinnate leaflets (fig. 8)

pistil: the female organ of a flower, usually consisting of an ovary, style, and stigma (fig. 1)

pollinium: [pollinia] a mass of waxy pollen, as in the orchids

pome: a fruit with a core, e.g., an apple

pycnidium: [pycnidia] a flask-shaped fruiting body found in the fungal partner of certain lichens

raceme: an unbranched inflorescence with stalked flowers that bloom from the bottom up (fig. 4); cf. *panicle, spike*

ray flower: a flower in the sunflower family with a strap-like corolla; part of a composite inflorescence (p. 106); cf. *disk flower*

receptacle: the enlarged end of a stem to which the flower parts (or the ray and disk flowers in the sunflower family) are attached; an umbrella-like structure to which the sporophytes are attached in some liverworts (p. 379)

reflexed: bent backward

regular flower: a flower with its petals and sepals alike in form and orientation

rhizoid: a thread-like growth in mosses and liverworts that anchors the plant (p. 379)

rhizomatous: bearing rhizomes

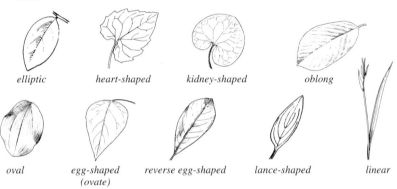

elliptic   heart-shaped   kidney-shaped   oblong

oval   egg-shaped (ovate)   reverse egg-shaped   lance-shaped   linear

Figure 7. *Leaf shapes*

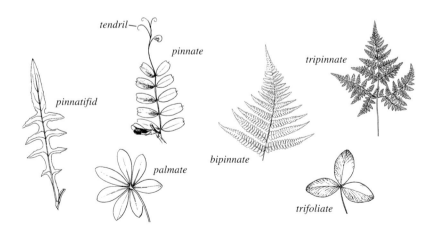

tendril

pinnatifid

pinnate

palmate

tripinnate

bipinnate

trifoliate

Figure 8. *Compound leaves*

rhizome: creeping underground stem, often elongate and with rooted nodes; distinguished from a root by the presence of buds or aerial shoots (fig. 9; p. 339)

rootstock: a short, erect underground stem from which new leaves and shoots are produced annually

rosette: a usually circular cluster of leaves at ground level or at the base of a stem (fig. 6)

runner: a horizontally spreading, aboveground stem, usually rooting at the nodes or tip and producing aerial shoots; a stolon

samara: a dry, usually winged fruit, as in the maples (fig. 5)

saprophyte: an organism that gets its nutrients from dead organic matter; cf. *parasite*

scale: a small, thin or flat structure (p. 339)

schizocarp: a dry fruit that splits into several parts at maturity (fig. 5)

sepal: one of the outer ring of modified leaves of a flower, usually green (figs. 1, 3)

serrate: sharply toothed (fig. 6)

seta: the stalk bearing the spore capsule in mosses and some liverworts (p. 379)

sheath: an organ that surrounds another organ, especially the sheath of a grass leaf, which surrounds the stem (p. 308)

silicle: a short, pod-like fruit of the mustard family, not much longer than wide (fig. 5); cf. *silique*

silique: a pod-like fruit of the mustard family, much longer than wide (fig. 5); cf. *silicle*

soredia: in a lichen, a clump of algal cells surrounded by fungal cells, which erupts as a powder at the lichen surface and serves as a vegetative propagule

sorus: [sori] a cluster of small spore cases borne on the underside of a fern leaf (fig. 10)

spike: an inflorescence with unstalked flowers (fig. 4; p. 339); cf. *panicle*, *raceme*

spikelet: a small secondary spike; the cluster of flowers that is the main unit of a grass inflorescence (p. 308)

sporangium: [sporangia] a spore case

spore: a single-celled, asexual reproductive structure

sporophyll: a spore-bearing leaf (fig. 10)

sporophyte: the asexual life stage in plants with visible alternating generations, especially ferns and mosses (p. 379); the sporophyte produces spores, which grow into the gametophyte (cf.)

spreading: diverging at nearly right angles, as from a stem

spur: a hollow, sac-like or tubular appendage on a petal or sepal (fig. 3)

spurred: with a spur

stamen: the male organ of a flower, usually consisting of an anther and a filament (figs. 1, 11)

stigma: the portion of a pistil that is receptive to pollen, usually at the tip of the style (figs. 1, 11; pp. 106, 339)

stipe: a stalk-like support for a plant part

stipule: an appendage (usually found in pairs) at the base of a leaf or leaf stalk

stolon: a horizontally spreading, aboveground stem (runner), usually rooting at the nodes or tip and producing aerial shoots (fig. 9); cf. *rhizome*

stoloniferous: with stolons

style: the stalk of a pistil, which bears the stigma (fig. 1)

substrate: the surface on which a plant grows

succulent: fleshy and juicy

taproot: a primary root, oriented and usually tapering downward (fig. 9)

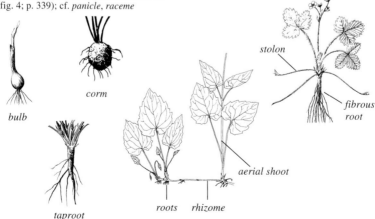

corm

bulb

stolon

fibrous root

aerial shoot

taproot

roots   rhizome

Figure 9. *Roots, stems and storage organs*

tendril: a slender, coiling organ used for support by a climbing plant, an extension of the midrib of the leaves of vetches (*Lathyrus* and *Vicia* spp.) (fig. 8)

tepal: a term for sepals and petals when the 2 are indistinguishable, as in many species of the lily family

terminal: at the end or top of, usually a stem

thallus: [thalli] the main, undifferentiated body of a lichen or liverwort (p. 379)

throat: the opening of a fused corolla (fig. 1)

trailing: lying flat on the ground but not rooting

trifoliate: a compound leaf with 3 leaflets (fig. 8)

tripinnate: thrice pinnate; a pinnately divided leaf with its main leaflets twice pinnately divided (fig. 8); cf. *bipinnate*

tubular: hollow or cylindrical, especially an elongate, fused corolla (fig. 2; p. 106)

umbel: an umbrella-shaped, often flat-topped inflorescence, with flower stalks arising from a common point (fig. 4)

urn-shaped: hollow and cylindrical or globose, contracted at the mouth; as in the corollas of many members of the heath family (fig. 2)

valve: 1 of the pieces into which a pod or capsule splits when ripe

vein: a bundle of conducting tubes, especially of a leaf (fig. 6)

whorled: structures (leaves, flowers, branches) arranged in a ring of 3 or more about an axis (fig. 6)

wing: a thin, flat extension from the side or tip of a structure (seed, stem); one of the 2 side petals in a flower of the pea family (fig. 3); cf. *banner*, *keel*

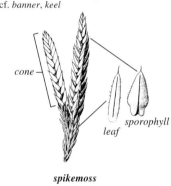

fern   *horsetail*   *spikemoss*

Figure 10. *Reproductive organs of ferns and fern allies*

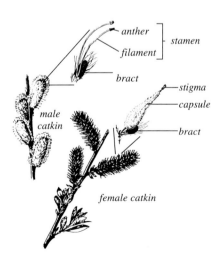

Figure 11. *Willow catkins*

References

Anderson, R.J. 1925. *Trees and Shrubs: Food, Medicinal and Poisonous Plants of British Columbia.* Dept. of Education, Government of British Columbia, Victoria.

Angove, K., and B. Bancroft, comp. 1983. *A Guide to Some Common Plants of the Southern Interior of British Columbia.* British Columbia Ministry of Forests, Victoria.

Arno, S.F. 1977. *Northwest Trees.* The Mountaineers, Seattle.

Bandoni, R.J. and A.F. Szczawinski. 1976. *Guide to Common Mushrooms of British Columbia.* Rev. ed. British Columbia Provincial Museum Handbook No. 24. Victoria.

Baumgartner, D.M., R.G. Krebill, J.T. Arnott and G.F. Weetman, eds. 1985. *Lodgepole Pine: The Species and Its Management.* Symposium Proceedings, Washington State University, Pullman.

Baumgartner, D.M., and J.E. Lotan, eds. 1988. *Ponderosa Pine: The Species and Its Management.* Symposium Proceedings, Washington State University, Pullman.

———. 1991. *Interior Douglas-fir: The Species and Its Management.* Symposium Proceedings, Washington State University, Pullman.

Brayshaw, T.C. 1976. *Catkin Bearing Plants of British Columbia.* Occasional Papers of the Royal British Columbia Museum, no. 18. Victoria.

———. 1985. *Pondweeds and Bur-reeds, and their Relatives, of British Columbia.* Occasional Papers of the Royal British Columbia Museum, No. 26. Victoria.

———. 1989. *Buttercups, Waterlilies and their Relatives in British Columbia.* Royal British Columbia Museum Memoir No. 1. Victoria.

Brough, S.G. 1990. *Wild Trees of British Columbia.* Pacific Educational Press, Vancouver.

Burbridge, J. 1989. *Wildflowers of the Southern Interior of British Columbia and Adjacent Parts of Washington, Idaho and Montana.* University of British Columbia Press, Vancouver.

Burns, R.M., and B.H. Honkala, tech. coord. 1990. *Silvics of North America. Vol. 1: Conifers.* U.S.D.A. Forest Service Agri. Handbook No. 654. Washington, D.C.

———. 1990. *Silvics of North America. Vol. 2: Hardwoods.* U.S.D.A. Forest Service Agri. Handbook No. 654. Washington, D.C.

Clark, L.J. 1973. *Wildflowers of British Columbia.* Gray's Publishing, Sidney, B.C.

———. 1974a. *Wild Flowers of Field and Slope in the Pacific Northwest.* Gray's Publishing, Sidney, B.C.

———. 1974b. *Wild Flowers of Marsh and Waterway in the Pacific Northwest.* Gray's Publishing, Sidney, B.C.

———. 1974c. *Wild Flowers of Forest and Woodland in the Pacific Northwest.* Gray's Publishing, Sidney, B.C.

———. 1974d. *Wild Flowers of the Sea Coast in the Pacific Northwest.* Gray's Publishing, Sidney, B.C.

———. 1975a. *Wild Flowers of the Mountains in the Pacific Northwest.* Gray's Publishing, Sidney, B.C.

———. 1975b. *Wild Flowers of the Arid Flatlands.* Gray's Publishing, Sidney, B.C.

Cody, W.J., and D.M. Britton. 1989. *Ferns and Fern Allies of Canada.* Research Branch, Agriculture Canada, Ottawa.

Comeau, P.G., M.A. Comeau and G.F. Utzig. 1982. *A Guide to Plant Indicators of Moisture for Southeastern British Columbia, with Engineering Interpretations.* British Columbia Ministry of Forests, Victoria.

Coombes, A.J. 1985. *Dictionary of Plant Names.* Timber Press, Portland, Ore.

Cormack, R.G.H. 1967. *Wild Flowers of Alberta.* Dept. of Industry and Development, Edmonton, Alta.

Coupé, R., C.A. Ray, A. Comeau, M.V. Ketcheson and R.M. Annas, comp. 1982. *A Guide to Some Common Plants of the Skeena Area, British Columbia.* Land Management Handbook No. 4, British Columbia Ministry of Forests, Victoria.

Craighead, J.J., F.C. Craighead and R.J. Davis. 1963. *A Field Guide to Rocky Mountain Wildflowers.* Houghton Mifflin Co., Boston.

Dirr, M.A. 1977. *Manual of Woody Landscape Plants: Their Identification, Ornamental Characteristics, Culture, Propagation and Uses.* Stipes Publishing Co., Champaign, Ill.

Douglas, G.W. 1982. *The Sunflower Family (Asteraceae) of British Columbia. Vol. 1: Senecioneae.* Occasional Papers of the Royal British Columbia Museum, No. 23. Victoria.

———. 1995. *The Sunflower Family (Asteraceae) of British Columbia. Vol. 2: Asterae, Anthemideae, Eupatorieae and Inuleae.* Royal British Columbia Museum, Victoria.

Douglas, G.W., G.B. Straley and D. Meidinger. 1989, 1990, 1991, 1994. *The Vascular Plants of British Columbia.* 4 vols. British Columbia Ministry of Forests, Victoria.

Dunn, D.B., and J.M. Gillett. 1966. *The Lupines of Canada and Alaska.* Monograph No. 2. Research Branch, Canada Dept. of Agriculture, Ottawa.

Elliott, C.R., and J.L. Bolton. 1970. *Licensed Varieties of Cultivated Grasses and Legumes.* Publication 1405, Canada Dept. of Agriculture, Ottawa.

Erichsen-Brown, C. 1989. *Medicinal and Other Uses of North American Plants: A Historical Survey with Special Reference to Eastern Indian Tribes.* Dover Publications, New York.

Flower, S. 1973. *Mosses: Utah and the West.* Brigham Young University Press, Provo, Utah.

Forest Service, U.S.D.A. 1937. *Range Plant Handbook.* National Technical Information Service, U.S. Dept. of Commerce, Springfield, Va.

Frankton, C., and G.A. Mulligan. [1955] 1987. *Weeds of Canada.* Publication 948, NC Press, Toronto.

Frye, T.C., and L. Clark. 1937. *Hepaticae of North America.* University of Washington Publications in Biology, vol. 6, nos. 1–5. University of Washington Press, Seattle.

Garman, E.H. n.d. *The Trees and Shrubs of British Columbia.* British Columbia Provincial Museum Handbook No. 31. Victoria.

Goward, T., B. McCune and D. Meidinger. 1994. *The Lichens of British Columbia: Illustrated Keys. Part 1: Foliose and Squamulose Species.* British Columbia Ministry of Forests Special Report Series, No. 8. Victoria.

Haeussler, S., and D. Coates. 1986. *Autecological Characteristics of Selected Species that Compete with Conifers in British Columbia: A Literature Review.* British Columbia Ministry of Forests & Lands and Canadian Forestry Service, Victoria.

Hedrick, U.P., ed. 1919. *Sturtevant's Edible Plants of the World.* J.B. Lyon Co., Albany, N.Y.

Henry, J.K. 1915. *Flora of Southern British Columbia.* W.J. Gage & Co., Toronto.

Hitchcock, A.S. 1971. *Manual of the Grasses of the United States.* Dover Publications, New York.

Hitchcock, C.L., A. Cronquist, M. Ownbey and J.W. Thompson. 1955, 1959, 1961, 1964, 1969. *Vascular Plants of the Pacific Northwest.* 5 vols. University of Washington Press, Seattle.

Hitchcock, C.L., and A. Cronquist. 1981. *Flora of the Pacific Northwest.* University of Washington Press, Seattle.

Hosie, R.C. 1990. *Native Trees of Canada.* 8th ed. Fitzhenry & Whiteside, Markham, Ont.

Hubbard, W.A. 1969. *The Grasses of British Columbia.* British Columbia Provincial Museum Handbook No. 9. Victoria.

Hultén, E. 1968. *Flora of Alaska and Neighboring Territories: A Manual of the Vascular Plants.* Stanford University Press, Stanford.

Jason, D., N. Jason, D. Manning, R. Inwood, T. Perry and Rohander. 1971. *Some Useful Wild Plants.* Talon Books, Vancouver.

Johnson, A.T. 1971. *Plant Names Simplified: Their Meanings and Pronunciation.* 2nd ed. Grand River Books, Detroit.

Kingsbury, J.M. 1964. *Poisonous Plants of the Unites States and Canada.* Prentice-Hall, Engelwood Cliffs, N.J.

Kruckeberg, A.R. 1982. *Gardening with Native Plants of the Pacific Northwest.* University of Washington Press, Seattle.

Kuhnlein, H., and N. Turner. 1991. *Traditional Plant Foods of Canadian Indigenous Peoples: Nutrition, Botany and Use.* Gordon & Breach, Philadelphia.

Lackschewitz, K. 1986. *Plants of West-Central Montana-Identification and Ecology: Annotated Checklist.* General Technical Report. U.S.D.A. Forest Service, Intermountain Research Station.

———. 1991. *Vascular Plants of West-Central Montana-Identification Guidebook.* General Technical Report, INT-277. U.S.D.A. Forest Service, Intermountain Research Station.

Lauriault, J. 1989. *Identification Guide to the Trees of Canada.* Fitzhenry & Whiteside, Richmond Hill, Ont.

Lawton, E. 1971. *Moss Flora of the Pacific Northwest.* Hattori Botanical Laboratory, Nichinan, Miyazaki, Japan.

Little, E.L. 1980. *The Audubon Society Field Guide to North American Trees: Western Region.* Alfred A. Knopf, New York.

Looman, J. [1971] 1982. *Prairie Grasses: Identified and Described by Vegetative Characters.* Publication 1413. Agriculture Canada, Ottawa.

Lyons, C.P. 1952. *Trees, Shrubs and Flowers to Know in British Columbia.* J.M. Dent & Sons, Toronto.

MacKinnon, A., J. Pojar and R. Coupé, eds. 1992. *Plants of Northern British Columbia.* Lone Pine Publishing, Edmonton, Alta.

Morice, Father A.G. 1892–93. *Notes Archaeological, Industrial and Sociological on the Western Denes with an Ethnographical Sketch of the Same.* Transactions of the Canadian Institute, Session 1892–93.

Moss, E.H. 1959. *Flora of Alberta.* University of Toronto Press, Toronto.

Palmer, G. 1975. Shuswap Ethnobotany. *Syesis* 9(2).

Parish, R., and S. Thomson. 1995. *Tree Book: Learning to Recognize Trees of British Columbia.* British Columbia Ministry of Forests and Canadian Forest Service, Victoria.

Peattie, D.C. 1980. *A Natural History of Western Trees.* University of Nebraska Press, Lincoln.

Petrides, G.A. 1992. *A Field Guide to Western Trees.* The Peterson Field Guide Series. Houghton Mifflin Co., New York.

Pielou, E.C. 1988. *The World of Northern Evergreens*. Comstock Publishing Associates, Ithaca, N.Y.

Pojar, J., and A. MacKinnon, eds. 1994. *Plants of Coastal British Columbia, including Washington, Oregon and Alaska*. Lone Pine Publishing, Edmonton, Alta.

Porsild, A.E. 1974. *Rocky Mountain Wild Flowers*. National Museums of Canada and Parks Canada, Ottawa.

Preston, R.J., Jr. 1989. *North American Trees*. 4th ed. Iowa State University Press, Ames.

Prior, R.C.A. [1879]. *On Popular Names of British Plants: Being an Explanation of the Origin and Meaning of the Names of Our Indigenous and Most Commonly Cultivated Species*. Fredrick Norgate, London.

Roberts, A., 1983. *A Field Guide to the Sedges of the Cariboo Forest Region*. Land Management Report No. 14. British Columbia Ministry of Forests, Victoria.

Ross, R.A., and H.L. Chambers. 1988. *Wildflowers of the Western Cascades*. Timber Press, Portland, Ore.

Sargent, C.S. 1965. *Manual of the Trees of North America*. Dover Publications, New York.

Schofield, J.J. 1989. *Discovering Wild Plants: Alaska, Western Canada, the Northwest*. Alaska Northwest Books, Seattle.

Schofield, W.B. 1992. *Some Common Mosses of British Columbia*. Royal British Columbia Museum Handbook. Victoria.

Scoggan, H.J. 1978. *The Flora of Canada*. 4 vols. National Museums of Canada, Ottawa.

Stone, D.F., and B. McCune. 1990. Annual branching in the lichen *Evernia prunastri* in Oregon. *The Bryologist* 93:32–36.

Straley, G.B. 1992. *Trees of Vancouver*. University of British Columbia Press, Vancouver.

Sudworth, G.B. 1967. *Forest Trees of the Pacific Slope*. Dover Publications, New York.

Szczawinski, A.F. [1962] 1975. *The Heather Family (Ericaceae) of British Columbia*. British Columbia Provincial Museum Handbook No. 19. Victoria.

Taylor, R.L., and B. MacBryde. 1977. *Vascular Plants of British Columbia: A Descriptive Resource Inventory*. University of British Columbia Press, Vancouver.

Taylor, T.M.C. 1973a. *The Ferns and Fern-allies of British Columbia*. British Columbia Provincial Museum Handbook No. 12. Victoria.

———. 1973b. *The Rose Family (Rosaceae) of British Columbia*. British Columbia Provincial Museum Handbook No. 30. Victoria.

———. 1974a. *The Lily Family (Liliaceae) of British Columbia*. 2nd ed. British Columbia Provincial Museum Handbook No. 25. Victoria.

———. 1974b. *The Figwort Family (Scrophulariaceae) of British Columbia*. British Columbia Provincial Museum Handbook No. 33. Victoria.

———. 1974c. *The Pea Family (Leguminosae) of British Columbia*. British Columbia Provincial Museum Handbook No. 32. Victoria.

Turner, N.J. 1975. *Food Plants of British Columbia Indians. Part 1: Coastal Peoples*. British Columbia Provincial Museum Handbook No. 34. Victoria.

———. 1978. *Food Plants of British Columbia Indians. Part 2: Interior Peoples*. British Columbia Provincial Museum Handbook No. 36. Victoria.

———. 1979. *Plants in British Columbia Indian Technology*. British Columbia Provincial Museum Handbook No. 38. Victoria.

Turner, N.J., R. Bouchard and D. Kennedy. 1980. *Ethnobotany of the Okanagan-Colville Indians of British Columbia and Washington*. Occasional Papers of the British Columbia Provincial Museum, No. 21. Victoria.

Turner, N.J., and M. Ignace. 1990-94. *Secwepemc Ethnobotany Fieldnotes and Manuscripts*. Secwepemc Cultural Education Society, Kamloops, B.C.

Turner, N.J., L.C. Thompson, M.T. Thompson and A.Z. York. 1991. *Thompson Ethnobotany*. Royal British Columbia Museum Memoir No. 3. Victoria.

Underhill, J.E. 1974. *Wild Berries of the Pacific Northwest*. Superior Publishing Co., Seattle.

Vidakovic, M. 1991. *Conifers: Morphology and Variation*. Graficki Zavod Hrvatske.

Vitt, D.H., J.E. Marsh, and R. Bovey. 1988. *Mosses, Lichens and Ferns of Northwest North America*. Lone Pine Publishing, Edmonton, Alta.

Viereck, L.A., and E.L. Little. 1972. *Alaska Trees and Shrubs*. Agriculture Handbook No. 410. U.S.D.A. Forest Service.

Whitney, S. 1985. *Western Forests*. National Audubon Society Nature Guides. Alfred A. Knopf, New York.

Whitson, T.D., ed. 1992. *Weeds of the West*. Rev. ed. Western Society of Weed Science, in cooperation with the Western United States Land Grant Universities Cooperative Extension Services, Newark, Calif.

Index to Common and Scientific Names

Primary entries are in boldface type.

INDEX

INDEX

INDEX

INDEX

INDEX